AF352523

A HISTORY OF JEWS IN GERMANY SINCE 1945

A HISTORY OF JEWS IN GERMANY SINCE 1945

POLITICS, CULTURE, AND SOCIETY

EDITED BY **MICHAEL BRENNER**

TRANSLATED BY **KENNETH KRONENBERG**

INDIANA UNIVERSITY PRESS

The translation of this work was funded by Geisteswissenschaften International–
Translation Funding for Humanities and Social Sciences from Germany, a
joint initiative of the Fritz Thyssen Foundation, the German Federal Foreign
Office, the collecting society VG WORT, and the Börsenverein des Deutschen
Buchhandels (German Publishers & Booksellers Association). This book is a
project of the Leo Baeck Institute for the History and Culture of German Jewry.

This book is a publication of
Indiana University Press
Office of Scholarly Publishing
Herman B Wells Library 350
1320 East 10th Street
Bloomington, Indiana 47405 USA

iupress.indiana.edu

Originally published as *Geschichte der Juden in Deutschland
von 1945 bis zur Gegenwart: Politik, Kultur und Gesellschaft*
© Verlag C. H. Beck oHG, München 2012
English translation © 2018 by Indiana University Press

Manufactured in the United States of America

Library of Congress Cataloging-in-Publication Data

Names: Brenner, Michael, author, editor.
Title: A history of Jews in Germany since 1945 : politics, culture, and society /
    edited by Michael Brenner ; translated by Kenneth Kronenberg.
Other titles: Geschichte der Juden in Deutschland von 1945 bis zur Gegenwart. English
Description: Bloomington : Indiana University Press, [2018] | Includes bibliographical
    references and index.
Identifiers: LCCN 2017037422 (print) | LCCN 2017038319 (ebook) | ISBN
    9780253029294 (e-book) | ISBN 9780253025678 (cloth : alk. paper)
Subjects: LCSH: Jews—Germany—History—1945-1990. | Jews—Germany—
    History—1990- | Judaism—Germany—History—20th century. | Judaism—
    Germany—History—21st century.
Classification: LCC DS134.26 (ebook) | LCC DS134.26 .B73513 2012 (print) |
    DDC 305.892/4043—dc23
LC record available at https://lccn.loc.gov/2017037422

1 2 3 4 5 23 22 21 20 19 18

CONTENTS

A HISTORY OF
JEWS IN GERMANY
SINCE 1945

INTRODUCTION

MICHAEL BRENNER

No one would have ventured to contradict Rabbi Leo Baeck when, after World War II, he stated that the age of German Jewry had come to a definitive end. Modern German-Jewish history, which began with the Enlightenment and continued to unfold through the Weimar Republic, could simply not continue seamlessly as if nothing had happened.[1] As a result, after 1945 the leading figures in the Jewish community came to reject the notion of "German citizens of Jewish faith," which was how German Jews had viewed themselves prior to 1933, and instead chose to call their organization the Central Council of Jews in Germany. This name signaled a break with the understanding that German Jews of previous generations had developed about their relationship to German society as a whole. It also acknowledged the fact that the majority of Jews now living in Germany came from Eastern Europe.

In the years immediately following the war, approximately 250,000 persons who had survived the Holocaust in Eastern Europe (the so-called displaced persons, or DPs) joined the 15,000 or so German-Jewish survivors and returnees from exile in camps mostly in the American sector in Germany. A distinctive topography developed in the Jewish community in Germany during the decades following the war. The German Jews began to coalesce around the Central Council and later the *Allgemeine Jüdische Wochenzeitung* (Jewish weekly newspaper), headquartered in Düsseldorf, while Eastern European DPs tended to gather in Munich, where most of the American facilities were to be found. The actual center of Jewish life during those years, however, the vibrant center of intellectual and economic life, was located in Frankfurt am Main, the "functional capital" of the Federal Republic. Although Berlin had lost its position as the dominant metropolis in Jewish life—before 1933 fully a third of Jewish citizens had lived there—the western part of the city continued to harbor the largest postwar German-Jewish community. At the same time, East Berlin was home to the only Jewish community of any significant size in the German Democratic Republic. And although organized Jewish life remained fairly modest in East Germany, the number of well-known persons with a Jewish family background who were active in politics and culture was larger than in the Federal Republic.

As Dan Diner emphasizes in the introduction to this volume, Jewish life in Germany first existed "in the shadow of a *herem* [ban]." In 1948 the World Jewish Congress proclaimed "the determination of the Jewish people never again to settle on the bloodstained soil of Germany." For many years, even decades, Germany remained for Jews a proscribed country. Nonetheless, small Jewish communities began to sprout up in both partitioned German states. But even more important than their small size was their symbolic significance, as then military governor and later U.S. high commissioner John J. McCloy made clear: "What this community will be, how it forms itself, how it becomes a part and how it merges with the new Germany, will, I believe be watched very closely and very carefully by the entire world. It will, in my judgement, be one of the real touchstones and the test of Germany's progress towards the light."[2]

Several times during the early 1950s, representatives of Jewish organizations made headlines with their public protests. These ensued, for example, when Veit Harlan, the director of the notorious film *Jud Süß* (Jew Süss), was exonerated in 1950 of aiding and abetting the Nazis and after the suicide of Philipp Auerbach, who had been a dominant figure in Jewish life, after the announcement of a guilty verdict on charges of embezzlement and fraud. Subsequently, Jews in the Federal Republic retreated into the private sphere or, as Dan Diner formulates it in this volume, into an "absent presence." The Central Council of Jews in Germany acted primarily behind the scenes, and as a result its leaders were virtually unknown to the public at large. For example, the council's general secretary, Hendrik George van Dam, who over a period of two decades played a crucial role in the political fortunes of Germany's Jews, used mainly back channels to advance the cause of financial compensation for the Jewish community so that it might flourish in the future.

The Jewish communities, which initially consisted of not more than twenty thousand members, lived in almost complete isolation from German society, which in any case showed little interest in what constituted Jewish life. Synagogues were often found in the courtyards of apartment buildings or in recently erected simple structures. Religious life was on a rather small scale; at times, fewer than a dozen rabbis ministered to the needs of the approximately eighty communities.

While the Jews who were born and raised in Germany tended to be elderly, most of the children of Eastern European families lived in the hope of establishing lives outside of Germany. Their parents had—in contravention of the ban pronounced by international Jewish organizations and the State of Israel—built lives for themselves, often meager but sometimes quite successful. They had stayed because they could not imagine uprooting themselves yet again and starting anew in war-torn Israel or distant America—despite what they had just lived through and the bitter memories of the family members whom they had lost. They had stayed because after years in concentration camps or flight to the Soviet Union they could not undertake yet another migration, or because they had to take care of sick relatives who were unable to travel, or because they had begun to rebuild their lives, or because their Yiddish mother tongue facilitated communication in Germany, or because they had found non-Jewish German spouses. Many of them, however, suffered a guilty conscience for remaining in the "land of the murderers."

The DPs contributed their part to the German economic miracle. With few exceptions, such as the film producer Artur Brauner, their names have not left much of an imprint on the political and cultural life of the country. Several prominent names, however, are to be found among the German-Jewish returnees. North Rhine–Westphalia, for example, had a Jewish minister of justice, Hamburg a Jewish mayor. The soccer teams FC Bayern München and Werder Bremen got their Jewish chairmen back, and Fritz Kortner, Therese Giehse, and several other prominent actors returned to the stage from exile. Several professors who had emigrated returned to German universities. In the GDR, where the organized Jewish community had shriveled to fewer than two thousand members as a result of antisemitic excesses in the Soviet Union and Czechoslovakia in the early 1950s, individuals of Jewish heritage became significant members of the cultural and political elite. These included writers such as Anna Seghers and Arnold Zweig, the literary scholars Hans Mayer and Alfred Kantorowicz, and even members of the politburo of the Socialist Unity Party of Germany (SED) Albert Norden and Hermann Axen.

Eventually, talk of the "bloodstained soil" abated as a second generation of Jews came of age in Germany, and it became clear that at least some of them would remain. At the same time, Germany saw a slow but steady increase in the immigration of Jews from countries where they now felt unsafe, including Hungary, Poland, and Czechoslovakia, but also Iran and even Israel. Even so, the Jews living in Germany continued to feel that they might have to leave at a moment's notice—"keep their bags packed," as the saying went. As late as the 1980s, Jewish life in Germany was viewed as something of an anomaly. Tellingly, books titled *Fremd im eigenen Land* (Alien in my own country, 1987) by Henryk M. Broder and *Dies ist nicht mein Land* (This is not my country, 1994) by Lea Fleischmann were especially popular among Jews who grew up in Germany after 1945. Even in the twenty-first century, several historians describe the history of Jews in postwar Germany as a paradox. Ruth Gay, for example, titled her 2002 work *Safe among the Germans: Liberated Jews after World War II*. Similarly dissonant titles include Susann Jael Heenen-Wolff's *Im Land der Täter* (In the land of the perpetrators, 1994), Anthony D. Kauders's *Unmögliche Heimat* (Impossible homeland, 2007), and Olivier Guez's *Heimkehr der Unerwünschten* (Return of the unwanted, 2011).

But a new discourse began to establish itself in the mid-1980s. The retreat into private life, which had begun in the 1950s with the Auerbach scandal, came to an end thirty years later with another scandal, this one involving Werner Nachmann, the chairman of the Central Council, who had defrauded the government of millions of marks that had been earmarked to compensate Jewish victims of Nazism. His successor, Heinz Galinski, did not shrink from pursuing the Jewish community's aims in public, and his successors, Ignatz Bubis and Paul Spiegel, were even more forthright in defending the community's interests. In 1985, for example, when US president Ronald Reagan with German chancellor Helmut Kohl visited the military cemetery in Bitburg, where members of the Waffen-SS were buried, this new spirit of open resistance was on full display. Vocal protests also erupted in Frankfurt later that same year against the opening of a play by film director Rainer Werner Fassbinder titled *Der Müll, die Stadt und der Tod* (published in English as *Garbage, the City, and Death*, 1985). But other voices were stirring within the Jewish community as well. In addition to the dominant orthodoxy, liberal communities developed, and groups of young Jews who were openly critical of Israeli politics—especially the 1982 Lebanon War—began to be heard in opposition to those of the Jewish establishment, whose support for Israel was total. In the process, a new generation of German-Jewish writers began to come into its own.

Synagogues and community centers started to look to and plan for the future. On the occasion of the opening of a Jewish community center in Frankfurt, the later chairman of that community, Salomon Korn, made popular a phrase originally uttered in 1960 by Max Brauer, the mayor of Hamburg, that captured the new spirit: "Who builds a house intends to stay." This desire to stay in Germany was strengthened by the increasing interest in Jewishness among the German public. Whereas Jewish life had had a very narrow public profile in the 1950s and 1960s, non-Jewish Germans now began to view the presence of Jews among them as an opportunity to engage with Jewish history and culture. Klezmer bands, Jewish museums, and scholarly institutions began to spring up everywhere, and the media presence of Jewish topics increased drastically during the 1980s. The subject of the "Holocaust" was a case in point, as German media competed to produce programs after the success of the American television series of the same title.

However, the biggest change in German-Jewish life came completely unexpectedly in 1989, of all things on November 9, the fifty-first anniversary of Kristallnacht, when synagogues throughout Germany were set on fire. That was the day that the Berlin Wall fell, and with it the Iron Curtain, an event that enabled Jews in the former Soviet Union to emigrate freely. While most of them chose to emigrate to Israel, between about 1990 and 2010 more than two hundred thousand people with a Jewish family background or with a Jewish spouse made their way to Germany. As a result, the Central Council and its member communities experienced an almost fourfold growth in membership from barely 30,000 to approximately 110,000.

But the situation in Germany in the twenty-first century should not be idealized. Although the number of Jews has grown considerably, Jews are still a vanishingly small minority in Germany, comprising under 0.3 percent of the population. And once again, the communities are aging and elderly. In addition, most of the Jews from the former Soviet Union are secular and have little ability to identify with a Jewish community that defines itself in religious terms. Synagogue attendance is as low as that of Christian churches.

Nonetheless, it cannot be denied that Jews have now lived for more years in the Federal Republic of Germany (and for a time in the GDR) than during all the years of the Kaiserreich and the Weimar Republic combined. They have created a pluralistic religious life and even founded their own rabbinical seminaries. They are more integrated into German life than ever before, and the Central Council of Jews in Germany is now perceived as an important partner by Israel and all international Jewish organizations.

German Jews have traveled a long way from ostracism "on bloodstained soil" via "packed bags" to the firm intention to stay where one "builds a house." On the occasion of the consecration of the new synagogue in Munich in 2006, then president of the Central Council Charlotte Knobloch reflected on this development when she declared that their bags are unpacked and that Jews are in Germany to stay. At the same time, the rise of a new extremism among both fundamentalist Muslims and radical nationalists poses new challenges to Jewish life in Germany and in the rest of Europe in the twenty-first century.

MICHAEL BRENNER is Professor of Jewish history and culture at the University of Munich and Seymour and Lillian Abensohn Chair in Israel Studies at American University in Washington, DC. He is a member of the Bavarian Academy of Sciences and international president of the Leo Baeck Institute. Brenner's publications include *A Short History of the Jews*, *Prophets of the Past: Interpreters of Jewish History*, *Zionism: A Short History*, and as coauthor, the four-volume *German-Jewish History in Modern Times*.

NOTES

1. Conversation with Leo Baeck, *Aufbau*, December 21, 1945, pp. 1–2.
2. Conference in Heidelberg on July 31, 1949, "The Future of the Jews in Germany." Minutes by Harry Greenstein, advisor on Jewish affairs, September 1, 1949, p. 21, in LBI, MS 168.

BANISHED

Jews in Germany after the Holocaust:
An Interpretation

DAN DINER

IN THE SUMMER of 1949, after a four-and-a-half-year stay in occupied Germany, Chaim Yahil wrote a detailed report upon his return to Israel about his work as head of the so-called Eretz-Israeli delegation, which had been active in Germany up to that point.[1] The emissaries from the *yishuv*, the pre-state Jewish community in Palestine, who were tasked with caring for the Jewish Displaced Persons (DPs) in the recently established Western zones of Allied occupation, had just moved to Munich. In significant measure, the delegation regarded itself as the vanguard of a Zionist "second front" to be opened up in Europe in the struggle for Jewish statehood in the Middle East.[2] Their intention was to direct the waves of Jewish refugees who were pouring in from an Eastern Europe that was increasingly closing itself off from the West and who were now on German soil under Western Allied protection to put political pressure on the British to open the gates to Palestine so that a Hebrew state could be established.[3]

Yahil had been elected to this task.[4] He was born Heinrich Hoffmann in 1905 in Moravia to a German-speaking Jewish family in the Habsburg Monarchy in the newly established Czechoslovakia, and although he came from a German-speaking Social Democratic background, he increasingly identified politically as a Zionist. Shortly after he settled in Palestine in 1929, at the behest of *yishuv* institutions he returned to Europe, where—in addition to his studies in political science in Vienna—he was entrusted with Jewish national affairs, especially welfare matters.[5] From 1933 to 1939 Yahil was stationed in Prague, where, among other matters, he was tasked with steering Jews fleeing from Nazi Germany toward Palestine.[6] He returned to the *yishuv* immediately after Nazi Germany invaded so-called rump Czechoslovakia. Later, after the founding of the Jewish state and Yahil's return from Germany in the summer of 1949, he held a variety of important diplomatic posts until his death in 1974. He became deputy head of the

"Israel mission" based in Cologne, which was in charge of regulating the material enactments of the 1952 reparations accord between Israel and West Germany, the so-called Luxembourg Agreement. His main ambassadorial postings were in Scandinavia, and, significantly, he was appointed director-general of the Israeli Foreign Ministry. His first official function after the founding of the state, however, was as the Israeli consul in Munich, accredited by the Allies.[7]

Yahil's background and experience had equipped him with a talent for trenchant political observation and judgment. The report that he wrote as head of the Eretz-Israeli delegation in Munich from 1945 up to the summer of 1949 not only serves as impressive documentation of activities on the "second front" opened up in Europe to create a Jewish state in Palestine but also provides striking evidence of the sheer breadth of his historical perspective.

The report, or, more precisely, its summary, is divided into two sections. The first section examines the overall political constellation that was taking shape in Europe in the immediate postwar period and the consequences of this new order for the Jews who still remained in Eastern Europe. The second section deals with the emptying from the DP camps in 1949–1950 of Jews remaining in Germany or of those endeavoring to settle in the recently established Federal Republic—a circumstance that, in the wake of the catastrophe that had befallen the Jews of Europe and the resultant upending of their sense of self, was viewed as downright scandalous.[8] And in fact, both the spatial-political constellation of the immediate postwar period and the eminently negative attitude toward any further Jewish life in Germany after the catastrophe were constitutive of the Jewish community that was attempting to establish itself despite stiff resistance.

It was striking that Yahil, who had arrived as a Zionist functionary immediately after the catastrophe in Europe, appeared less concerned with the immediate consequences of what came to be called the Holocaust than with the upheavals that were currently roiling Eastern Europe. It was not that Yahil was in any way indifferent to the tragedy that had recently befallen European Jewry. Yet on the eve of the founding of the Jewish state, he was primarily concerned with urgent unfolding events: the migration and flight from countries in Central Europe and eastern Central Europe that were transforming into ethnic "people's" democracies and increasingly closing themselves off from the West. Yahil was mindful of the situation that had characterized the interwar years, marked by festering minority questions, and he was familiar with a multiethnic Czechoslovakia that was still dominated by Czechs. He also foresaw the double homogenization—both ethnic and social—of the countries of Central Europe and eastern Central Europe that came under Soviet domination or influence after 1945. Yahil realized that this constellation held out little promise for the remaining Jews. In his view, there was no future for the Jews under the emerging circumstances, because the Jews did not conform either ethnically or socially to the new definitions of state and society that were evolving in the people's democracies. Moreover, the dictatorial nature of the regimes crystallizing in those countries precluded freedom of movement. This meant that the Jews remaining there would lose contact with world Jewry. In his view, these and other circumstances, especially the totalitarian encroachment that the new rulers made on all imaginable spheres of life, held out but one prospect for Jews, namely, total assimilation.[9] In the face of such dismal expectations, the only solution, the sole avenue promising Jews a Jewish life, was emigration. Furthermore, an obvious conclusion was that this migration would have to proceed via Allied-occupied Germany and from there to the shores of the Promised Land—to Palestine.

Yahil's analysis was far-sighted in every respect. He viewed as "revolutionary" the enormous upheavals taking place in eastern Central Europe, which was caught up in the process of ethnic and social homogenization. These changes, he believed, promised the remaining Jews, many of whom had escaped the Holocaust, few if any prospects for a Jewish life. They would be as scant as those open to the Jews who between 1939 and 1941 had fled, been deported or evacuated from the Baltic region and eastern Poland into the interior of the Soviet Union, only to be repatriated to their countries of origin as the war neared an end.[10]

Yahil also grasped the full import of the circumstances that loomed: occupied Germany offered the only conceivable passage for the Jews thronging westward, away from an Eastern Europe that was increasingly encapsulating itself. And he understood that the international Jewish aid organizations that were being set up to operate in the best interests of their clientele could effectively work only in the American zone of a Germany that had been completely stripped of its sovereignty. In his report, the Zionist emissary spoke explicitly of an extraterritorial "Jewish autonomy" being established within Germany.[11]

And in fact, Germany had indeed become an interim haven for Jews seeking to escape Eastern Europe, from where their overseas transfer, mainly to Palestine, could be managed with relative ease. This all the more so as the Bricha, the primarily Zionist refugee movement operating farther east, found itself increasingly up against official state controls and bureaucratic barriers in the countries of origin and transit that were rapidly transforming into closed people's democracies.[12] Furthermore, the welfare assistance provided by the Jewish international aid organizations to the Jews whose stay on German soil was temporary prevented any unwanted integration into a social and economic system that in any case was only barely functioning. According to Yahil, the transitory nature of their stay could be guaranteed only within occupied Germany, above all in the American zone.[13] Over and beyond that, the Jews arriving in Germany against the backdrop of the catastrophe and an emerging Jewish solidarity in the camps on German soil were developing a growing sense of commonality—this despite differences in origin, language, and way of life. They were referred to as She'erit Hapletah (Surviving Remnant, or the Remainder of Israel), a biblical phrase with great collective resonance, and it came to apply beyond just those who had survived the Nazi persecution and internment.[14] The term expanded to encompass the Jews of the Old World who, as a result of war, destruction, and the pogrom-like violence that erupted immediately after the war, desired to leave the Continent behind—preferably for Palestine, a migration that its organizers called the "1947 exodus from Europe."[15]

Much of Yahil's report was written in the dry, restrained language of the bureaucrat. However, his tone sharpened considerably when he came to speak about Jews who, after 1948–1949 (the year in which both the State of Israel was founded and the Federal Republic of Germany was constituted), endeavored to settle in that accursed place, on German soil, in the "land of the murderers." When speaking of them, Yahil could barely contain his condemnation, bordering on malediction. His contempt, echoed by Jews throughout the world and by the State of Israel, would long follow the Jewish community in Germany, which was hesitantly attempting to gain a foothold there.

In actuality, Yahil's report devoted only a few lines to the Jews who had remained in Germany or had chosen to settle there, but his attitude was all the more stinging and implacable for its brevity. His few lines reveal an attitude deeply engrained in Jewish consciousness, a collective avowal, conditioned by the catastrophe, to ostracize Germany and all that is German in perpetuity. At first glance, Yahil's words, written after he had returned to the recently established Jewish state, appeared to be aimed solely at those few who had failed to respond to the call of the Jewish homeland and remained in the "land of the murderers." In any case, Yahil viewed them as blemishes upon Israel's dignity—"parasitic" characters who, as Yahil put it, referring to a familiar biblical image, were evidently unwilling to renounce the corrupting fleshpots of Germany.[16]

Chaim Yahil's philippics are symptomatic of the collective post-catastrophe Jewish sensibility. What is striking is that this report, written by a person who now acted as an Israeli official, contains formulations in which the historical constellation of the venerable and time-honored German Jewry becomes intertwined with the Jewish presence becoming increasingly visible in Germany after 1949–1950. Yahil proceeded from a condemnation of Jewish existence in the Diaspora, emphatically denounced throughout the text, and from an implicit disparagement of the German-Jewish path to emancipation, which had been largely discredited and deemed a failure by Jews in light of the catastrophe. In his judgmentalism, he even resorted to images familiar from antisemitic discourse when speaking of those segments of the Jewish people whose behavior he considered especially loathsome. He most despised three groups: those Jewish DPs who openly declared their intention to remain in Germany; those German Jews who, frequently by virtue of living in so-called mixed marriages, had survived the Nazi period more or less unscathed; and those who were then considering a return from exile to Germany. The Zionist emissary was so contemptuous of such Jews that he even insinuated that the former Jewish presence in Germany had itself encouraged the rise of Nazism. And today, he suggested, the Jews who were settling in Germany were rekindling antisemitism anew by their "provocative" behavior. As a result, their stay in Germany would undoubtedly conjure up similar trends in the future. In addition, Yahil suspected that the Jews who remained in Germany would exert an undesirable and indeed dangerous magnetic attraction on other Jews of a similar mindset elsewhere—especially on Jews living in the newly established Israel.[17]

Thus it was that in Chaim Yahil's thinking (and by no means his alone), the DPs stemming from Eastern Europe, who were in the majority among Jews who chose to remain in Germany, came to stand for the reviled emancipatory path taken by German Jews—ironically so, because it was neither part of their own history nor one with which they sought to be seen as identifying. After 1949–1950, the minuscule Jewish community in Germany was therefore accorded far greater importance in the eyes of Jews around the world, especially in Israel, than its negligible numbers alone would have justified. But numbers were not the issue; their significance as a symbol was what drew the ire of Jews. As the internal Other of world Jewry, the Jews in Germany came to symbolize the disgusting counter-image of a Jewish community forced to reconstitute itself after 1945 as a Jewish collective after the Holocaust and primarily because of it.[18]

FORBIDDEN LAND

A ban, a *herem*, was placed on Germany after the catastrophe.[19] Although this ban was never officially pronounced, it was nonetheless ubiquitous. Neither a real ban nor a ritual exclusion based on religious law, it took the form of a rigorously maintained, categorical boycott of everything German. In usage of the time, the semantic meanings of "ban" and "boycott" tended to merge—especially because the Hebrew language does not distinguish between the two. Both "ban" and "boycott" are contained in the word *herem*. The fact that the Hebrew word contains both meanings meant, among other things, that the liturgical force emanating from the ancient damnation of biblical enemy peoples tended to become associated during the later era of exile with the rabbinical proscription of Jewish wrongdoers, which placed them outside the protection of the community. And this happenstance facilitated a merging of *herem* with the rhetoric of the modern boycott. In any case, the meanings of the word overlapped with the holy rage of the Jews after the catastrophe to suggest that the "land of the murderers" was to be avoided in perpetuity.

This conviction appears to have been dominant, especially in the newly established State of Israel. A striking constellation emerged simultaneously: the creation of a Jewish state and the ban on Germany. And this simultaneity brought with it an exorcism of everything that had once been German within the larger community of Jews—especially of the German language and culture. Above all, this exorcism was directed against any Jewish presence on German soil. It was to be proscribed forever.

No forgiveness, no atonement.[20] The spirit of a Jewish ban descended like a shroud upon Germany and everything German. Its weave was interlaced with the threads of Jewish memories—especially with the traces, traditionally deemed still ever-present, of the alleged Jewish ban issued in reaction to the Jewish expulsion from Spain decreed by Ferdinand and Isabella in 1492. The story of that expulsion and the religious rhetoric that it engendered experienced a visible revival after 1945. Accordingly, contemporary Germany was to be banned in analogy to early modern Spain.[21]

Initial attempts to pronounce a ban on Germany had already been undertaken during the war, such as the initiative by the then president of the Board of Deputies of British Jews. Another occurred immediately after the war, when the Jewish Brigade, which was under British command, set off from Tarvisio, in the Italian-Yugoslavian border region, toward Germany in July 1945. Upon departure, the troops were read the order of the day written in the style of a biblical ban: they were not to share accommodations with the Germans; all contact with their children and even belongings was to be avoided; and all that belonged to them was considered alien and Other. The ban, the censure, was eternal.[22]

The ban on Germany and everything German was primarily directed at Jewish communities throughout the world, that is, internally. That was the tenor of the resolution passed in Montreux by the World Jewish Congress (WJC) in the summer of 1948. The "determination of the Jewish people never again to settle on the bloodstained soil of Germany," as the resolution stated, had certain consequences.[23] In July 1949, for example, Harry Greenstein, an advisor to the American military administration in Germany, attempted to convoke in Heidelberg a conference of international Jewish organizations and representatives of Jews remaining in Germany. The purpose was to discuss questions relating to a Jewish future in Germany. During the conference, however, Greenstein's plan elicited vehement protest from representatives of the DPs, who saw themselves as living only temporarily in the "country of the murderers."[24] In 1950, the year that the Central Council of Jews in Germany was founded, the WJC took an even harder

Representatives from Bergen-Belsen in Montreux at the first meeting of the World Jewish Congress after World War II, July 1948. Yad Vashem / Hadassah Rosensaft.

line. Analogous to the rhetoric of the ban, one could note discourse that sought unambiguously to exclude forever any further Jewish existence in Germany. Of course, as it stated, the WJC was not in any position to prevent Jews from settling in Germany or in any other country that had committed similar crimes. However, the WJC stated that it was within its powers to decree that those Jews—who were addressed with an admonishment tantamount to a curse—henceforth fell outside the protective circle of the world Jewish community and were no longer their concern. Should a Jew choose to remain in Germany, he or she would no longer be a member of the community of world Jewry. Given the modes of secular speech customary among Jews, this decree amounted to a *herem*, a ban of "excommunication."[25] As if to underscore this position, both the British Jewish Relief Unit (JRU), which had been active in Germany, and the Zionist Jewish Agency closed their local offices. The latter followed up its decision in August 1950 with a dramatic call directed to the Jewish public in which it announced a deadline of six weeks for the Jews still remaining in Germany to leave this "cursed soil." If they refused, they would no longer be considered Jews. In October, Leon Kubowitzky, then secretary-general of the WJC, used even sharper language when he denounced Jews settling in Germany and encouraged all Jewish organizations to break off contact with any Jewish communities (*Gemeinden*, i.e., congregations under statutory law) seeking to establish themselves there. Such pronouncements were received by spokespeople for the Jews determined to remain in Germany with "melancholic regret." Philipp Auerbach, undoubtedly the most prominent and tragic German-Jewish personality of the transition between the immediate postwar period and the Federal Republic, appeared to be both crestfallen and annoyed by the tone of the statement, which was so reminiscent of traditional banning. He angrily rejected the notion that Jews should view their coreligionists living in Germany as "inferior" or "second-class" people and treat them as pariahs.[26]

The permanent presence of Jews in Germany after 1950 was the cause of much displeasure for representatives of international and Jewish institutions and facilities, and not only for those persons of a Zionist persuasion. For one thing, there was the unsettling spectacle of an increasing trickle of Jews from Israel to Germany after the founding of the Jewish state. This mainly involved a return by emigrants of Eastern Jewish origin, principally to the DP camps near Munich, which had not yet been dissolved, and this remigration was evidently viewed as tantamount to sacrilege. It was reported that in their despair, the Israeli authorities even encouraged the Bavarian police to arrest such persons. Israeli officials claimed that such individuals were guilty of a passport violation by crossing the German border; after all, they averred, passports issued by the Israeli state contained a specific official stamp that made them invalid for use traveling to Germany: "Prat le-Germania" (with the exception of Germany).[27]

In 1950 Gershom Schocken, the secular-minded publisher of the liberal Israeli daily *Ha'aretz*, called for reviving the tradition of the ritual ban. Schocken viewed the ban, which he supported, as a tried-and-true means for countering, as he put it, the repulsive and humiliating spectacle of Jews settling in Germany, in his view an intolerable situation that challenged the newly sovereign State of Israel to issue sharp sanctions.[28]

More severe sanctions in terms of public opinion were also directed at prominent Jewish-Israeli intellectuals who had shown themselves susceptible to the lure of German temptations. For example, Martin Buber had been awarded the Hanseatic Goethe Prize in 1951, yet it took him two years to make the trip to Hamburg to receive the honor.[29] Despite postponing his trip to the land of the Germans to assuage Israeli public opinion, the philosopher and educator was forced to run a moral gauntlet in the land of the Jews. Even the opinion of his supporters, that Goethe was less a German writer and much more a cosmopolitan poet writing in the German language, had met with little support. In 1944 the translator Yaacov Cohen had been found worthy of the Tchernichovsky Prize for his rendition of Goethe's Faust, which had been published by Schocken Publishing in 1943. This decision, however, met with massive protest by the Hebrew Writers Association.[30] Even works translated from the German language were deemed contaminated by the crimes that the Germans had committed against the Jews. By the time that Buber received his Hanseatic Goethe Prize in 1953, the storm of indignation had abated somewhat. In the meantime, the 1952 Reparations Agreement between Israel and West Germany had been signed in Luxembourg, but not without massive public protest erupting in Israel. Many in Israel viewed the acceptance of German reparations and the direct negotiations that they necessitated as an intolerable violation of the ban.[31] Once again, calls were heard to ban Germany and everything German as once had sounded against medieval and early modern Spain.

In Jewish awareness, present-day Germany and medieval Spain became increasingly conflated, forming a single negative reference point of Jewish self-understanding and belonging. Such an affinity had already made itself felt soon after the Nazis assumed state power in 1933. At the time, rabbinical authorities were inundated with questions from observant German Jews who intended to emigrate from Nazi Germany to Spain, if such a move were permissible under the *halakhah* (the foundation of Jewish religious law). The legal scholars who had been entrusted with examining such petitions largely arrived at the conclusion that no ban against the presence of Jews in Spain was discernible either historically or in accordance with religious law.[32] And even later, after the catastrophe that had befallen the Jews in Europe, Yitzhak Baer, the renowned historian of Spanish Jewry during the Middle Ages and early modern era, and Yitzhak Nissim, a former Sephardic chief rabbi of Israel whose command of the Sephardic *responsa* literature was unequaled, came to the same conclusion.[33] This information came about as a result of inquiries by the eminent British Jewish historian Cecil Roth, an authority on Spanish Jewish history who began during the war to research the iconic medieval Spanish ban allegedly invoked by the Jews.[34] He did so with Jewish cultural restitution in Germany in mind. Even after further investigation, the scholar was unable to uncover any signs of a ritual ban against Spain. What Roth's research did find, however, was a stance that came close to a ban under religious law, the so-called *haskamah*.[35] This was a sort of agreement primarily within the communities founded in northwestern Europe by former *conversos* (Jews who had been forced to convert), to the effect that the Iberian Peninsula and the territories of the Spanish Netherlands were to be avoided. This interdiction was more motivated by the ban on Jewish religious practices in those regions. Jews who nonetheless lived in those lands and had to masquerade as Christians had obviously contravened Jewish religious law and were subject to sanctions accordingly.[36] Roth demonstrated that this harsh sanction had not necessarily been the consequence of a ban on Spain by citing the example of Jacob Sasportas, the great Jewish legal scholar and *chacham* (rabbi) of the Sephardic congregations of London and Amsterdam who earlier, in the mid-1600s, had spent a lengthy stretch of time at the court in Madrid as a representative of the sultan of Morocco without having been aware of any *herem* against Spain.[37]

The stance taken by Jews toward Germany and all things German as a consequence of the catastrophe was much more in the spirit of *haskamah*—a widespread collective distancing, the result of principled revulsion. As such, the *haskamah* in customary law may certainly be interpreted as an implied ban—a common practice of the Jewish community as a whole (Klal Yisrael) and considered to have legal force based on everyday behavior and habitus and sanctioned by long tradition. Although it lacks the formality of religious law, it nonetheless radiates binding validity—the profane expression of a universally palpable Jewish collective self-understanding after the catastrophe. From this collective Jewish resonating board, intensified after the catastrophe, all talk of Germany and the Germans became increasingly more uniform, ritualistic, and canonical. It appeared in keeping with the long-practiced liturgy of a pervasive, omnipresent ban, albeit one pronounced by no religious authority.

The general sentiment for a Jewish ban hovering over Germany that came alive through the liturgical resonating board of memory was one source of the overall Jewish rejection of Jewish life on German soil, especially rejection of the establishment of Jewish representation in the "land of the murderers." The other source was of a more material sort and arose from Jewish property that had been rendered heirless by the genocide or was viewed as such—restituted property, primarily in the American zone of occupation, especially community property and real estate. According to the American military administration's Law 59 of November 10, 1947, and its Article 8, which was shaped by ideas from international Jewish organizations, any new Jewish communities that established themselves against all expectations were barred from laying claim to restituted property.[38] While they were to be temporarily tolerated as "liquidation communities," as at best provisional Jewish institutions in the process of dissolution, they were to have no future. This legal stance was justified on the grounds that the legal existence of the prewar Jewish communities as official bodies under public German law had been terminated by the Nazi authorities; in addition, the confiscation of those communities' assets and their forced incorporation in July 1939 into the Reich Association of Jews in Germany had brought about their liquidation as legal entities.[39] In this reading, there was no legally binding link between the former Jewish communities in Germany and those that after 1945 sought to establish themselves as their successors.[40] Added to this was an extralegal consideration that could not simply be dismissed: because of their negligible numbers, the few

Jewish survivors and immigrants to Germany did not exist in any appreciable proportion to the German-Jewish community that had been destroyed.[41]

Consequently, claims to financial assets would have to be made by the collectivity of Jews in the form of the Jewish people—represented by successor organizations established for that purpose, primarily the Jewish Restitution Commission, provisionally incorporated in May 1947 in New York under that name. It soon began work in the American zone of occupation as the Jewish Restitution Successor Organization (JRSO, or IRSO).[42] At issue was nothing less than the transformation of restituted German-Jewish communal property into Jewish collective property, while at the same time the Jewish communities that attempted to reestablish themselves in Germany were prevented by military law from claiming the assets of the former German-Jewish communities. This categorical denial led to numerous heated internal quarrels among Jews, as did the larger questions regarding the circumstances and conditions of Jewish existence in Germany after 1945. In other words, the transformation of former German-Jewish communal property into Jewish collective property, along with the tensions and disagreements between the Jewish successor organizations, on the one hand, and the Jewish communities attempting to reestablish themselves in Germany, on the other, which played out mainly in the American zone, were more than just a battle of a profane and material type. In fact, the contours of the larger, fundamental questions of Jewish existence after 1945 are discernible behind the façade of competing legal claims, primarily over financial assets.[43]

It was no accident that the argument regarding Jewish belonging after the Holocaust took place on German soil—starting from the question of the legitimacy of the Jewish community dwelling in Germany, whose legal status and small numbers rendered it a negligible entity. In fact, this Jewish community was of great importance to world Jewry as a whole in terms of the formation of its Jewish self-understanding after 1945. It was perceived as fundamentally contradicting the newly emerging collective awareness of the Jewish people after the Holocaust. At the latest by 1945, the various Jewries in the world had come to understand themselves more than ever before as part of a Jewish collective in the process of nationalization, as part of a quasi-political Jewish nation.[44] This had been a consequence of Nazi genocide.

The genocide perpetrated against the Jews of Europe had been absolute, that is, directed against *all* Jews and implemented *everywhere* within the reach of the German Wehrmacht. Jews were killed solely because of their origin as Jews—men, women, children, the elderly. But people only slowly became conscious of the categorical significance of this ultimate genocide, which later came to be known as the Holocaust. The radical consequences of this understanding appear to have dawned primarily in the minds of the representatives of Jewish institutions that had been engaged for some significant time with questions of postwar planning, more precisely, with the spiritual and material demands of the Jews that arose. In any case, the genocide had far-reaching consequences, especially in terms of Jewish property that had become heirless as a result of the destruction. Jewish organizations, both Zionist and non-Zionist, were enjoined to demand these heirless assets. The notion that merely because of legal technicalities the property and assets of the murdered heirs who would rightfully have inherited them would accrue to the state in whose territory these assets had been found—either to Germany or to another country involved in the plunder and murder of European Jews—was anathema. Such a consequence would have been simply too monstrous.[45] In other words, one did not have to entertain Zionist notions about the Jews as a collective political entity, which did not become widespread until after 1945, to conclude that Jewish property made heirless as a result of genocide was owed to the Jews collectively and thus as a nation.[46]

The collective claim of Jews to this heirless property derived compellingly as a natural right from the genocide itself. Because Jews were subject to destruction as Jews, that is, collectively, Jews as Jews should be able to claim restitution as a collective as well. Consequently, Jewish individual and community property made heirless by genocide necessarily entails the construction of a collective Jewish claim. This entitlement gives birth, as if out of itself, to a public-legal authority embodying it, something approaching an authority under international law: the Jewish people, represented by the Jewish successor organizations and by the State of Israel.[47]

The discourse about a Jewish people was nothing new. The notion of *am Yisrael* (the Jewish people), in its diverse variants and constellations, had been used throughout the centuries. However, its meaning was largely liturgical and in any case had no political or even legal implications. The phenomenon of heirless property, however, injected political content into the liturgical form—an act of transubstantiation, so to speak.[48] And the transubstantiation was also real inasmuch as the Jewish property viewed as heirless, especially in the American zone of occupation, had been disposed of at the best possible price by the responsible Jewish successor organizations and then transferred, mostly to the newly established State of Israel, in the form of either money or goods, to the extent to which the Allies restricted hard-currency transactions. Seen from this perspective, the Jewish state incorporated the lion's share of both material and immaterial goods belonging to murdered Jews and their communities, along with a large number of survivors. This also applied to Jewish cultural assets located in Germany. Jewish Cultural Reconstruction, Inc. (JCR), had been established in New York in 1944 for precisely this purpose.[49] It was headed by such outstanding personages as the historian Salo W. Baron, Gershom Scholem, and later Hannah Arendt, who held a leading administrative position. The JCR made every possible effort to get Jewish cultural assets out of Germany. For Jewish communities throughout the world, these books, Torah scrolls, and other ritual objects became relics, devotional articles of the Holocaust, and thus sacred signs of Jewish collective affiliation after the catastrophe.[50]

The consequences of this transformation or national collectivization of material and nonmaterial assets have been far-reaching, especially for the Jewish communities that sought to establish themselves in Germany after the war. The upheavals that followed resulted from an immediate contradiction that was fraught from the outset. On the one hand, there was the contradiction between the Jewish people and the State of Israel seeking to occupy its core of meaning as heir to individual and communal Jewish property remaining after the genocide. On the other, some Jewish authorities and individuals looked toward a continuity of Jewish communities in Germany beyond the rupture of the catastrophe, laying legal claim to restituted property.[51] As a result, two opposing types of Jewish affinity and membership emerged out of the controversies relating to restituted community property in Germany, the Jewish people as a whole and the Jewish communities in that country. This raised the question of who owned the former communal assets, principally real estate, along with the seemingly purely material question of overall Jewish communal property in Germany that was deemed to be heirless. And this combined with the larger, overarching question of Jewish belonging and self-awareness after the Holocaust—over which hovered the rhetoric of a ban on Germany and all that was German. The controversy surrounding assets and their ownership was loaded with liturgical energy. The restoration of institutional Jewish life in Germany after 1945, like the question of restitution itself, touched the very core of Jewish self-awareness after the genocide.

That constellation was probably not fully understood by the major actors at the time, even though in conflicts that erupted over restituted communal property between the "Jewish people" and its successor organizations and the representatives of German-Jewish communities that attempted to reclaim continuity one could sense the vibrations of an intense existential excitation. Of course, nothing could have been further from the intentions of the representatives of the communities than to sin against the Jewish collective created by the Holocaust by claiming their property and other Jewish communal assets. They had no more fervent desire than to be full constituents of that collective.

The Jewish ban imposed on Germany had been formative of the Jewish community beginning to gather there. And the aura surrounding this ban would haunt them permanently in the "land of the murderers"—the negative leitmotif of Jewish life in Germany after 1945. From the outset, the Jewish community that sought to become established in Germany attempted to rid itself of its bad reputation.

Its urgent search for legitimacy was met with constant objections, and not only from Jews around the world. Even internally, a considerable proportion of the Jewish community in Germany, especially those Jews who had come to Germany from Eastern Europe after 1945, were burdened by a multitude of self-imposed reservations, notably that they were not native to the country and would never become so. In effect, they participated in the mood and ambience of the ban in that they sought to extend the provisional status to which they had become accustomed in the immediate aftermath of the war into the era of the Federal Republic. From the outset, the Jewish community in Germany was subject to significant internal conflict. This conflict also mirrored the various origins of the Jews assembled there—German Jews and Jews of Eastern European origin—and was soon internalized by individuals as a kind of collective mentality, a kind of *absent presence* crystallized, a habitus that became characteristic of Jews in post-war Germany.[52]

THE SCHISM OF BELONGING

From the very beginning, a visible and increasingly structural difference could be discerned in the Jewish community in Germany—a tense fault line between Jews of German-Jewish origin, who tended more or less to favor a restoration of the destroyed historical Jewish community in the country, and Jews of primarily Eastern European origin, who mainly saw their stay in Germany as temporary but tried to prolong the self-imposed provisional circumstances of their lives for as long as possible. This latent, but sometimes also open, internal Jewish fault line between East and West was seen in diverse, overlapping, and charged constellations, such as in the demographic (mainly generational) tension between the largely elderly representatives of the German-Jewish community and the mainly younger members, primarily of Eastern European origin. This constellation was repeated and intensified by a sort of spatial schism that can be traced back to the composition of the communities—going back to their different origins—and to the regional associations of northwestern Germany, on the one hand, and southeastern Germany, on the other. Thus, the German-Jewish community in the north tended to be elderly, while in the south the majority of Eastern European Jews were considerably younger.[53]

These crucial differences among the Jews beginning to settle again in Germany had their origin in the policies of the British and American occupation authorities. During the period between the end of the war and the founding of the State of Israel, the British denied the Jews residing in their zone recognition as a separate ethnic collectivity; because of the salience of the Palestine Question, the British placed restrictions on Jewish immigration to Palestine, and as a result, they restrained international Jewish organizations operating in northern occupied Germany. By contrast, these organizations had a much freer hand in the American zone in the south—a circumstance that drew Jews, especially those seeking to leave Eastern Europe.[54] The consequence was that in the British zone, something of a balance developed between the few German Jews who had remained or returned and the DPs of Eastern European origin.[55] Another equalizing factor in the British zone was that the German Jews representing the Jewish community there tended in the early phase to be survivors of the concentration and extermination camps, who not least for this reason felt bound together as Jews in a nation-like collectivity. Even if they had not previously conceived of their Jewishness in national terms, this new self-concept made their thinking more similar to that of the Eastern European Jews. This is evidenced in different forms in the biographies of three of the leading representatives of the Jewish community in Germany, Norbert Wollheim, Philipp Auerbach, and Heinz Galinski.[56] Other important representatives of the Jews in Germany in the British zone and soon beyond its perimeters had returned from the catastrophe relatively unscathed, primarily from exile in England. These included Hendrik George van Dam, the general secretary of the Central Council of Jews, and Karl Marx, the publisher of the *Allgemeine Wochenzeitung der Juden in Deutschland* (General weekly of the Jews in Germany).[57] This attitude was manifested early on in their policy of integration into the new, unfolding German realities.

Circumstances in the American zone of occupation differed considerably from those in the British zone, especially in terms of demographic composition of the Jews residing there.[58] The DPs overwhelmingly outnumbered the German Jews who had remained or returned. As a result, the majority of Jews in Bavaria, largely former DPs, adhered far longer than those elsewhere to the notion that the presence of Jews in Germany was only temporary. This basic stance, in turn, created the impression that the southern communities were collectively "more Jewish" in thought and action than the communities and associations farther north. The melding of origin and existential experience together with the very different policies in effect in the British and American zones led to a situation in which the Jewish institutions established in the northwest increasingly began to bring their claims to the attention of the German authorities, while in the southeast, the Jews continued to call their concerns to the attention of the Americans.[59] By their behavior, the former made clear that they saw their future in Germany, while the latter signaled their desire to continue tarrying in the temporary abeyance of indecision.

The tragic figure of Philipp Auerbach is emblematic of the tension between the Jews in the north and those in the south, between the readiness to settle permanently in Germany and the notion of a provisional status that could be

From left to right: David Treger, the president of the Central Committee of Liberated Jews in the American zone; Willi Ankermüller, the Bavarian minister of the interior; and Philipp Auerbach, the Bavarian state commissioner for racial, religious, and political persecutees during the Third Congress of Jewish Displaced Persons in Bad Reichenhall, March–April 1948. Picture-alliance/DENA/dpa.

prolonged indefinitely.[60] All of the cumulative questions of Jewish life in Germany during the transitional phase between the immediate postwar and the occupation period were encapsulated in Auerbach's work and suicide in 1952. During this period, Jewish life was in many respects only barely regulated, and the conditions emerging with the establishment of the Federal Republic rapidly normalized into a well-ordered polity. Moreover, all of this occurred against the backdrop of scheduled negotiations aimed at regularizing the German-Jewish-Israeli relationship, concluded in the Reparations Agreement between Israel and West Germany in September 1952. Auerbach's arrest on suspicion of fraud and forgery in March 1951, when he was hauled out of his car on the autobahn during a police operation while traveling from Bonn to Munich, reflects in its dramatic staging precisely that key temporal juncture.[61]

Auerbach powerfully exemplifies the accumulated antagonisms within the Jewish community and those between the Jews and their non-Jewish surroundings. The way in which these contrasts and contradictions became concentrated and then broke apart in his person is emblematic. Philipp Auerbach came from a German-Jewish family in Hamburg, and during the war he had been an inmate in Auschwitz and other locations.[62] After his liberation from Buchenwald, he arrived in the British zone and took a prominent role in founding new Jewish communities. It was his intention to restore in Germany the "proud tradition of German Jewry in defiance of all powers."[63] The Landesverband Nordrhein (North Rhine State Association), which he founded, was the first regional Jewish association in postwar Germany. Auerbach's plans were vehemently opposed by, among others, Norbert Wollheim, the second chair of the Committee of Liberated Jews in the British zone—an association with little sympathy for notions of a Jewish future in Germany.[64] Auerbach, who had become a thorn in the side of the British primarily because of his independent work in uncovering Nazi crimes but also because of his impetuousness, soon offered his services to the Bavarian state government, which was under American auspices, and in the fall of 1946 he managed to become a Bavarian state commissioner, responsible for matters relating to racial, religious, and political persecutees.[65] This position, along with other functions that he assumed, primarily in Jewish institutions, gave him wide-ranging powers. These powers in the relatively unregulated interim period, which was marked by a profusion of official positions, were subject to little oversight or supervision.[66] Thus, in addition to his position as president of the Landesverband Israelitischer Kultusgemeinden in Bayern (State Association of Jewish Religious Communities in Bavaria), which he founded in 1947, he was also the chair of the Arbeitsgemeinschaft der jüdischen Gemeinden in Deutschland (Working Committee of Jewish Communities in Germany) in the American zone and later, after its founding in 1950, a member of the Executive Board of the Central Council of Jews in Germany—just to name a few of his more important involvements. Perhaps his most important contribution was in the area of restitution law. Under his guiding influence, Bavaria took the lead in Germany in legislating how property and assets were to be restituted. Nonetheless, in November 1949 Auerbach did not become president of the Bayerisches Landesentschädigungsamt (Bavarian State Restitution Office), as had been expected, because of concerns that had been voiced about him personally. However, he was appointed its acting head. Broad sections of the German public viewed Auerbach as a spokesman for concentration camp survivors—and as a purported profiteer from restitution. He came to be referred to by the public and in government offices as the "uncrowned king of Bavaria," a disparagement and back-handed compliment that was in many respects hypocritical.[67] In any event, the Bavarian state government understood very well how to make use of his services, as when he accepted the largely thankless task of implementing the government's fervently desired departure of Eastern European DPs, whose presence was generally viewed as an annoyance. He was their man for jobs rough or dirty. But Auerbach, who prided himself on his good relations with the American military authorities, also came into increasing conflict with them. In the end, they provided the impetus for a dramatic turn of events that eventuated in more than his dismissal.

Dissension was the last thing that the Americans wanted during the waning of the denazification process just as the Cold War was beginning to ramp up. In addition, Auerbach found himself increasingly isolated by the international Jewish organizations active in the American zone—a circumstance that the Bavarian legal authorities made use of and that in the end allowed them to risk their scandalous police raid on the autobahn. The organizations involved in increasingly open conflict with Auerbach included the successor organization JRSO, which was primarily responsible for heirless assets in the American zone, and the JCR, which was subsumed under the JRSO and had responsibility for the restitution of cultural assets.[68] The latter was at the time headed by Hannah Arendt.[69]

Auerbach's conception of the Jewish future in Germany, with German-Jewish communities continuing in their age-old traditions and with their assets fully restituted, was incompatible with the mission of the successor organizations, which was to claim these assets for the Jewish people as a collective and to spirit the assets out of the country.[70] Auerbach, in keeping with his intent to restore German Jewry, also emphatically refused to cooperate with the efforts of the JCR to uncover Jewish cultural assets and expedite their transfer out of Germany. Arendt, who took part in a meeting of the Bayerischer Landesverband in January 1950, which Auerbach chaired, was hard-pressed to conceal her distaste for him and the Jews in Germany whom he represented. Even before that meeting, she had written a letter to her husband, Heinrich Blücher, in which she referred dismissively to the developing Jewish communities in Germany as "theft communities," "barbarous and of extreme vulgarity and nastiness."[71] And in her letters and memoranda to Salo W. Baron in New York, she complained about Auerbach's maneuvers, which she claimed were hindering her work, accusing him of a devious personality.[72] But it was not to end there. In January 1951 a representative of the American Jewish Committee described Auerbach to the American state commissioner in Bavaria, George N. Schuster, as "a painful problem for the Jewish organizations." It was the latter who gave the impetus for the investigations against "Unknown" that eventually caused Auerbach's political fall and eventuated in his suicide.[73] Viewed in this light, Auerbach had been caught between the anvil of widespread anti-Jewish sentiment in the German population and officialdom and the hammer of the "Jews in their collectivity," represented by the international Jewish successor organizations. Their complaints intensified, culminating in action by the Bavarian judiciary.

Philipp Auerbach died on August 16, 1952, from an overdose of sleeping pills.[74] In his suicide note, he called down his "blood upon the heads of the perjurers."[75] His funeral was to be the last great public outpouring of the Jewish population of Munich, which consisted mainly of DPs. In effect, their demonstration represented the end of Munich's role as the functional capital of the Jews in Germany and as the site of the transition from the immediate postwar period to the nascent era of the Federal Republic. Thousands of people filed past Auerbach's coffin, which was draped with the flag of the Jewish state. Those who took part in the funeral services, in speeches and on placards, cursed the judges and Auerbach's principal constant adversary, the former Bavarian justice minister Josef "Ochsensepp" Müller. Quarrels between the DPs and the Munich police escalated during his funeral into riots that were put down with truncheons and water cannons.[76] This was the last public Jewish demonstration for many decades as Jews withdrew for the long term into their private affairs and avoided the public sphere.[77] If need be, they appeared as individuals. When they did finally reemerge as a community in public discourse, in 1985, it was in Frankfurt, not Munich.

Auerbach's tragic departure, which occurred at the same time as the restoration of responsible and independent German governance, acted to strengthen the communities and organizations in the northwestern part of the country in relation to those in the southeast. This trend favored the Jews of German origin to the disadvantage of the Eastern European immigrants, most of whom had little familiarity with the language or the country in which they now resided. Moreover, it became even more necessary to make use of German political structures and governmental authorities in dealing with matters of Jewish concern. The new circumstances, combined with the increasingly deteriorating position of Jewish Munich, manifested in the form of a major dispute that erupted in 1952–1953 between the Central Council, whose leadership role was then ascendant, and the State Association of Jewish Religious Communities in Bavaria, whose power was on the wane.

The dispute had begun with resistance in the south to the Central Council's policy of integrating Jews into the Federal Republic of Germany, the contours of which were rapidly consolidating. This resistance, a kind of trial revolt, was initiated by the newly elected representatives of the State Association of Jewish Religious Communities in Bavaria, which consisted largely of representatives of the councils of the DPs in the American zone. The conflict ended under humiliating circumstances for the State Association, which lost out to the policies promulgated by the Central Council in Düsseldorf.

In 1951 Maurice Weinberger, who had chaired the council of DPs in the American zone, was elected chairperson of the State Association of Jewish Religious Communities in Bavaria. His election presaged strife, which began almost immediately when Weinberger proved to be an uncompromising defender of the "policy of liquidation" and accused the Central Council, along with its policy of remaining in the land of the Germans, of illegitimacy, since it did not represent the majority of the Jews in the country. Instead, Weinberger came out squarely in favor of the 1946 resolution of the DP council in the British zone, which called for the expeditious dissolution of all Jewish communities on German soil.[78] But Weinberger's rearguard revolt had little staying power, and his resolve soon buckled. At a meeting of the Central Council, he confirmed the correctness of *its* policy of integration while at the same time declaring the ban advanced by the international Jewish organizations, especially by the World Congress, to be completely misguided. Weinberger's surrender had been preceded by a mobilization by the chairpersons of German-Jewish communities in Bavaria and by a measure taken by the Central Council, which left the State Association in Munich with little room to maneuver: the cancellation of subsidies for the Jewish welfare office in Munich struck the Bavarian opponents of integration in their Achilles' heel.[79] In the final analysis, their policy of provisional life in the land of the Germans was not least dependent upon international Jewish funding, which was now being disbursed from the central office in Düsseldorf.

Munich, which from 1945 to the dissolution of the DP camps had served as the functional capital of the Jewish presence in Germany, lost its leading position as the Allied occupying powers increasingly relinquished their authority in favor of the growing sovereignty of the Federal Republic and of the international Jewish aid organizations that had operated through those authorities. This development strengthened the policies of the Central Council in Düsseldorf, which were directed at the government in nearby Bonn, at the expense of the state associations, especially the one in Bavaria.[80] In addition, the Auerbach scandal and his suicide had contributed to both a personal and an institutional weakening of Jewish institutions in the south, from which the local state association would never really recover. From now on, the internal Jewish constellation privileged the northwestern part of the country in the Rhine and Ruhr regions, which became the economic and political powerhouse of the preunification Federal Republic.

The relationships that developed among the state associations and between them and the Central Council, together with the tensions between the British northwest and the American southeast—parts of the country that were largely congruent with the relative populations of German Jews and Jews of Eastern European origin—engendered a shift in weight within the overall Jewish population of the Federal Republic of Germany. And this constellation solidified into a sort of basic structure that was not, however, always readily discernible. Hendrik George van Dam, who had returned from exile in England and since 1950 had functioned as the influential general secretary of the Central Council, quite accurately characterized this structure using a topographical metaphor: speaking of the internal Jewish controversies raging in Bavaria, he called them a "dialectical battleground south of the Main [River] line."[81] The increasing tendency of this dividing line to dissolve as the boards of the newly constituted old communities, which had consisted largely of German Jews, slowly opened up to former Eastern European DPs after much initial resistance was not least the result of the large overriding question, that of heirless Jewish property. After all, the former DPs represented the future, if only because of their numbers and relative youth. The communities of the German Jews were ageing, and they needed the energy and drive of the former DPs in their negotiations with the Jewish successor organizations regarding "their" real estate in order to successfully secure buildings and other property assets. The topographical symbolism of the "dialectic of the Main line" functioned as a geographical-spatial dividing line between north and south whose salience could be sensed over time in fluctuating intensity throughout all of (West) Germany. But it was also the symbolic dividing line between German Jews and Jewish immigrants from Eastern Europe, a boundary marker of difference that over the later history of the Jews in Germany would prove increasingly porous. The eventual dissolution of that line was the result of a complex process of negotiation and settling differences. And the bargaining chip in this process of equalizing differences was the status of restituted community property; and it was this status that functioned as the outward manifestation, underscoring the difference between notions of continuity and those of new beginning in the evolution of German Jewry.

The quest for the legitimacy of Jews in Germany after 1945–1950—continuity or new beginning—thus solidified around the contested status of community property. The often contentious allocation of this property extended into the most minute institutional branches of communal life—for example, into the liturgical mode of *minhag*, the customary local rites of prayer. Such a link between property and ritual had been raised by Isaak Emil Lichtigfeld, the state rabbi of Hesse, who, as a result of his background, incorporated different chronological layers of Jewish belonging. Lichtigfeld originally stemmed from Galicia and had fought in World War I as a German soldier. During the Nazi period, he lived in exile in England, returning to Germany in 1954 but retaining his British citizenship. In Germany, he assumed spiritual leadership of the Hessian State Association of Jewish Communities, and in 1967 he was buried in Jerusalem in accordance with his wishes. In 1956 Lichtigfeld, in his capacity as rabbi of Frankfurt, changed the age-old local *minhag* in the Westend Synagogue to reflect the rituals of the Eastern European immigrants. This change elicited protests from Joseph Klibansky, who had in 1948 returned from exile and represented Jewish interests in Frankfurt. Klibansky, an attorney, had previously served as acting community chairperson; he was also a former judge in the higher regional court. Significantly, he was born in Frankfurt.[82] In an emotional letter, he told Lichtigfeld in no uncertain terms that the direct restitution of a few buildings, which the community of Frankfurt am Main had negotiated by itself, was justified on the basis of continuity and that this continuity was embodied in the local Frankfurt prayer ritual. As a result, according to Klibansky, the change in *minhag* would significantly compromise the claim of the Frankfurt community to restituted real estate—and this at an especially sensitive time. Thus, for example, the Frankfurt city council had approved restitution to the present community of five important pieces of property belonging to the prewar community along with the payment of more than 3 million DM. The negotiations had been especially tricky because the retransfer required approval by the JRSO, which as successor organization and in the name of the Jewish people had carved out for itself a prerogative in questions of restitution and, to put it mildly, was not exactly sympathetic to the present community's claimed continuity with earlier times.[83]

The new Jewish community in Germany was the result of a complex interplay between three rival components of Jewish self-understanding: the Jewish people, represented by the successor organizations; the relatively small and ageing German-Jewish representatives in the communities, who largely viewed themselves as heirs to prewar German Jewry; and the former Eastern European DPs, who were predominantly Jewish-national in outlook and who because of their relative youth and their offspring (largely born on German soil after 1945) comprised the actual demographic potential for a Jewish future in Germany.[84] The Eastern European DPs, who found themselves increasingly settled in the country, were the hinge between the two other, generally contentious components of Jewish self-understanding—that of the Jewish people in the form of the successor trustee organizations and the community boards of German-Jewish origin, which insisted on their continuity. As a result, the mediating position of the Eastern European DPs had two effects: on the one hand, the emphatic profession of belonging to the Jewish people as a collective with national overtones; and on the other, a local, less emphatically articulated option of a new German-Jewish future in Germany. Paradoxically, it was principally due to the entry of the Eastern European DPs with their ethnic Jewish self-understanding into the largely German-Jewish communities that had effectively positioned those communities to press for restituted portions of the old community's assets in negotiations with the successor organizations because they were able to prove their demographic viability.

Although the lawsuit was fought out in German courts, the cause of the Augsburg Jewish community was paradigmatic of the conflicted constellation of negotiated Jewish belonging and Jewish legitimacy in Germany based on the question of restituted assets.[85] The suit concluded in 1955 with the affirmation of the JRSO's prerogatives. It began with the insistence by the small Augsburg community that it was the legal successor to the old Jewish religious community there, which had numbered more than a thousand members. Based on this legal position, the community had negotiated with the Bavarian finance minister for restitution of community property in hopes of avoiding the provisions of Law 59, Article 8 of the military administration while also bypassing the JRSO, which claimed collective jurisdiction. The action by the Augsburgers was preceded by Philipp Auerbach's statement that the JRSO had agreed to such a procedure—an insinuation that was shown to be baseless during the proceedings. The postwar community of Augsburg, consisting of only thirty-two elderly members along with another thirty-eight from the surrounding area, claimed real estate that had been owned by the former community (among others, the synagogue building and the cemetery) to which the JRSO, as trustee of the Jewish collective, had already laid claim. The postwar community also based its argument on the expectation that a large number of former members would return to Augsburg from exile. During the dispute, the community pursued the matter through German courts—a move that Jewish organizations considered a sacrilege. And the German courts promptly sided with the community.[86] The dispute eventually came before the Court of Restitution Appeals (CORA) in Nuremberg in the American zone and led in 1955 to a landmark decision that required Act 59, Article 8 of the military administration to recognize the well-being of the majority of the survivors of Nazi persecution (based on principles of justice and equity) rather than the claims of the few surviving members in a given community.[87]

The Augsburg suit between a German-Jewish community board and a successor organization claiming to represent the "Jewish people as a whole" was also important in connection with the American Jewish Joint Distribution Committee's (JDC) favoring of the DPs in the allocation of support, viewed by German-Jewish community boards as deeply unjust.[88] And in fact, between 1945 and 1952, 85 percent of the support provided by the JDC to Jews in Germany went to the DPs, who were concentrated in camps or housing complexes (which meant that they could be supplied through "assembly centers"), while the remaining 15 percent of German Jews, scattered in the cities, had to make do with what was left.[89] Bitterness was a foregone conclusion, because the monies distributed by the JDC for the welfare of the Jews in communities consisted principally of the proceeds from the sale of real estate that had belonged to precisely those German-Jewish communities—which the JRSO had sold. As far as Benno Ostertag, chairperson of the Stuttgart community, was concerned, the members of his community, elderly and broken after the Nazi terrors, were once again being bullied and terrorized, but this time by Jewish organizations like the JDC, and therefore indirectly by the JRSO, to which these elderly people were forced, as anxious supplicants, to apply for their daily sustenance. In the opinion of the elderly and their representatives, they should be allowed to reclaim the community property owed them without having to go through foreign-based Jewish organizations. The process should be direct, and they should not have to stand in line as humiliated charity seekers. After all, the German Jews should have the right to demand what had been taken from them by Nazi Germany. However, this could be achieved only through financial independence from foreign Jewish organizations.[90]

The JRSO had in its capacity as collective trustee of the Jewish people been given control over former communal property considered heirless under occupation law. In December 1957 the JRSO came to an agreement with the state associations and the Central Council whereby compensation payments from the restituted communal assets were to be divided up more or less equally.[91] This agreement symbolized a compromise between the claims of the Jewish people as a successor of the murdered Jews and their destroyed communities and the new communities in the Federal Republic. This was the first visible step in legitimizing the new-old Jewish communities in Germany. Earlier, in June of the same year, the successor organizations had come to an agreement with the communities and with the federal government regarding the care and maintenance of Jewish cemeteries.[92] The large number of no longer "functioning" Jewish cemeteries was probably the most constant symbol of the old German Jewry in the postwar period. By taking them under their protection, the state associations inherited them.

ABSENT PRESENCE

Jewish history in postwar Germany may thus be interpreted in the light of the topographies that underlay it. The metaphor of the "dialectic of the Main River line" dividing Germany between north and south expresses this relationship. Accordingly, the history of the Jews in Germany after 1945 can suitably be told along the lines of such a demarcation in accordance with the interpretive schema of the "small-scale" topography, a concept to be developed further on.[93]

The constellation of a longer-term conflictual situation between Jewries in Germany that differed in terms of emancipatory and experiential history was, however, overlain by a far more fundamental sort of "large-scale" topography, the result of the unique geopolitical position of Western Germany, that is, the old, pre-unification Federal Republic, as the outcome of the world war, but determined even more by the emerging Cold War.[94] The historical constellation of Jewish migration from east to west, which had been largely canceled out by the catastrophe but had been a revealing lens through which to examine the history of modern European Jewry, was not crucial in this context. Rather, what became increasingly important was the new position of the Federal Republic, which had a paramount impact on the history of the Jews in Germany after 1945. This was because it was the easternmost of the Western European polities during the great political constellation of what soon became the all-pervading Cold War. And it was not simply that the political upheavals and civil revolts in Eastern Europe led to flight across the Iron Curtain directly into the Federal Republic and from there to other countries if possible.[95] The attraction exerted by the Federal Republic exhibited two main characteristics during the Cold War. First, it was geographically the most eastward-leaning Western country in the historical expanse of a Central European cultural realm in which the German language had been a lingua franca, even and perhaps particularly among the Jews. Its second attraction was the concentrated American presence there in the immediate postwar period—a "Little America" in Europe—combined with a well-functioning economic and social order in an increasingly stable democratic regime. And finally, Western Germany, while assuming the role of legal successor to the previous order, was prepared to accept responsibility in the present for claims arising from the Nazi past.[96]

Germany, or, more precisely, the old pre-unification Federal Republic, took on critical strategic importance for the international issues confronting Jews at the time. Most importantly, this involved making good on damages that resulted from Nazi crimes, as embodied in the September 1952 Luxembourg Reparations Agreement between the Jewish people, represented by the State of Israel and the Claims Conference, and West Germany, which was visible for all the world to see, both symbolically and in terms of pecuniary compensation.[97] Elements less visible but nonetheless of considerable importance to the Jews in West Germany followed from the impact of the political topography of the Federal Republic in the context of the Cold War. Its ultimately successful claim to represent Germany as a whole triggered a chain of consequences that greatly affected the Jews as well. Among these was a recognition, radiating eastward and based on ethnic and cultural affiliation, of belonging to the German people.[98] Another related aspect was the obligation placed on the West German state to accept and integrate refugees and displaced persons, supported in the early 1950s by a consistently implemented policy of redistribution in the form of collective burden sharing between those Germans who had been bombed out or were expelled from the eastern provinces and lost everything and those who had survived the war and immediate postwar relatively unscathed.[99] According to Paragraph 1, Section 2, Number 3 of the Federal Law on Refugees and Exiles, as members of the German linguistic and cultural community, Jews were also eligible to press claims under the Lastenausgleichsgesetz (Equalization of Burdens Act).[100] The Heimatloser Ausländer-Gesetz (Homeless Foreigner Law),[101] enacted in the Bundestag in April 1951, decreed equal treatment in terms of work and trade for those who had lived in the Federal Republic on or before June 30, 1950—a provision that covered the DPs and promised something approaching social integration but without the duties of citizenship.[102]

Questions of restitution and compensation were to intensify Jewish travel to West Germany soon after the war, especially after associated legislation went into effect. The visitors were largely persons pursuing individual restitution or commercial interests of one sort or another. But unregulated business transactions by Israeli companies and by cooperatives such as the *kibbutzim*, primarily for the purpose of buying German-made machinery, were viewed as highly problematic by Israeli authorities, and they were eventually regulated under the 1952 Reparations Agreement between the two countries. This agreement brought with it the involvement of Israeli institutions, or, more precisely, of Jewish international institutions whose operations were oriented toward Israel. Furthermore, persons and their families, primarily of German-Jewish origin who in the meantime had become acculturated in the Hebrew culture flocked from Israel into the Federal Republic. Their arrival blurred the more binary distinctions between German Jews and Eastern European Jews that had predominated up to then in postwar Germany. This influx of Israelis of German-Jewish origin during the second half of the 1950s was facilitated by a monetary incentive passed by German legislators in June 1956. This provision, for which the Central Council of the Jews in Germany had lobbied, provided that all German citizens who had emigrated or been deported or expelled between 1933 and 1945 and had resettled after May 8, 1945, in the territory of what soon became the Federal Republic would receive emergency assistance in the amount of 6,000 DM.[103]

Circumstances appear to have been especially favorable in Frankfurt for the integration of Jews of various origins gathering in the Federal Republic. There, directly on the "Main River line," the dissonances between German and Eastern European Jews had been smoothed over by the relatively early fusion in 1949 of two communities, which occurred primarily because German Jews from Breslau came to predominate in the mainly Eastern European Committee of Liberated Jews in Frankfurt am Main.[104] The addition of those German-Jewish returnees from Israel, which starting in the mid-1950s strengthened this trend toward internal Jewish integration,[105] was implemented mainly through social measures of child and youth care and not least by the overarching educational goals, whether explicitly Zionist (as from the late 1950s) or largely Jewish-national in overall orientation.[106] Furthermore, this Israelization of education was mainly carried out by persons who by virtue of their biographies and life experiences found themselves in an increasingly porous intermediate position,[107] strung between their original mission as formal and informal emissaries of the State of Israel or of the international Jewish organizations and the ever more pressing daily realities of life in the Federal Republic, which was transforming them into returnees.[108] Their prominence in Jewish institutions from the mid-1950s on, primarily in the areas of social work and youth services, was to have long-term effects.

Jewish organizations located in Frankfurt were mainly concerned with restitution and welfare. The JRSO, for example, transferred its central office from Nuremberg to Frankfurt in 1951. There it was run as a sort of personal union with Benjamin B. Ferencz's Claims Conference. In 1947 Ferencz had, at the age of twenty-seven, served as chief American prosecutor at the Nuremberg Einsatzgruppen trial; later, he participated in the negotiations leading to the 1952 Restitution Agreement and in the Claims Conference. In 1955 the Central Welfare Office for Jews in Germany (Zentralwohlfahrtsstelle der Juden in Deutschland, ZWST), which was to take on strategic importance in Jewish life in Germany at exactly that time and was led by the jurist, social pedagogue, and later university lecturer Berthold Simonsohn, was transferred from Hamburg to Frankfurt.[109] In his youth, Simonsohn had been a member of the Socialist Workers Party of Germany (Sozialistische Arbeiterpartei Deutschlands, SAP), as had Berthold Scheller, a returnee from Israel who was for many years in charge of social work activities in the Federal Republic. Max Willner, who was born during the late Wilhelmine period, the descendant of Eastern European immigrants, assumed leadership of the ZWST in the late 1950s after Simonsohn. Willner had survived a number of Nazi concentration camps, among them Auschwitz, and as long-time chair of the Hessian State Association of Jewish Communities, he became in some respects the éminence grise of Jewish politics in Germany during the 1960s and 1970s.[110] He was followed as head of the ZWST by Alfred Weichselbaum, who had for many years been chair of the *hevra kadisha*, the sacred Jewish burial society. Weichselbaum was a child of Eastern European immigrants to Frankfurt and as a youth had survived Auschwitz.[111] During the mid-1950s, these and other persons laid the institutional groundwork in Frankfurt for the absent presence that came to characterize the life of the Jewish community in the Federal Republic.

Frankfurt came to be known for the interlocking links between various milieus and for a number of outstanding personages. These included Erich Cohn-Bendit, the legal advisor to the Jewish community (and father of the later student leader and politician Daniel Cohn-Bendit); Robert W. Kempner, a former acting American chief prosecutor at Nuremberg, primarily in the Ministries Trial;[112] Henry Ormond, who took part in a number of trials of Nazis in his capacity as attorney and coplaintiff, especially in Norbert Wollheim's suit against IG Farben and the first Auschwitz trial;[113] and, of course, the prosecutor-general Fritz Bauer.[114] Jakob Moneta, who during the Weimar period had belonged to the youth organization of the SAP, became editor-in-chief of the metalworker union's newspaper *Metall* and was politically visible in Frankfurt along with Heinz Brandt, a trade unionist kidnapped by the East German State Security Service. An early returnee from Palestine, in the 1950s Moneta served as social attaché in the Federal

Republic's delegation in Paris.[115] Max Pulvermann returned to Frankfurt from Israel in 1954. He had served as an undersecretary in later Weimar cabinets and had been city treasurer under the aegis of Ernst Reuter, then mayor of Magdeburg.[116] The impact of Fritz Naphtali, who was the originator during the interwar years of the idea of economic democracy (*Wirtschaftsdemokratie*) and who held several ministerial portfolios in Israel during the 1950s under the name Peretz Naftali, continued to inspire from afar German trade unionists and other labor institutions concentrated in Frankfurt.[117]

A number of significant personal connections resulted from the shared experience of persecution and concentration camp imprisonment in the Nazi period, which continued across political boundaries and had a lasting effect on Jewish institutions despite the Cold War atmosphere of distrust and enmity between the Federal Republic and the German Democratic Republic (GDR). Emil Carlebach, a cofounder of the Association of Persecutees of the Nazi Regime / Federation of Antifascists and a Communist, remained in contact with anti-Communist Jewish representatives who shared his experience of concentration camp imprisonment.[118] Over time, these and other Jews or persons of Jewish origin provided a sort of cultural leavening in Frankfurt.[119]

The increasing Jewish integration into Frankfurt coincided with the city's development and especially with its increasing importance for the developing Federal Republic as a whole. In fact, Frankfurt became West Germany's functional capital. As a result of the partition of the country into two states, East and West, the city on the Main, which had previously been thought of as topographically situated in the west of historical Germany, found itself shifted to the very center of the Federal Republic. This shift was facilitated by the transport network, as Frankfurt was located at a crossroad of the autobahn system, and its airport became a hub that was used by both Allied military and civilian air traffic.[120] In addition, the relocation to Frankfurt of the great fairs in the Leipzig tradition, in particular the Leipzig Book Fair, also served to open up the city to a wave of foreign visitors and their impact. The founding of the later legendary financial center in Frankfurt was facilitated by the establishment of the Bank deutscher Länder (Bank of the German States), the future Bundesbank.[121]

But the overarching presence was that of the Americans. It was expressed architecturally in the U.S. Army's choice of the IG Farben building as its European headquarters, where many important decisions concerning Germany were made during the founding phase of the Federal Republic.[122] The importance of Frankfurt in the earliest history of West Germany extended to nearby Königstein, where the country's constitution (Basic Law) was framed at the conference of state prime ministers at the quickly restored Villa Rothschild in March 1949. For decades, administrative offices, service facilities, and utilities that served the

American forces and others were arrayed around the IG Farben building and other locations as well. Piled high in the PX were all manner of American-style consumer goods—but only accessible to American military personnel and their families. This fabulous emporium was located directly on the ring road surrounding the center of the city.

The intensifying American presence permeated the contexts of urban life and those of Frankfurt's surrounding localities. During the Cold War, the military ambience of the city actually extended from the Rhine River Valley all the way to the border with the GDR—the strategic region that later came to be called the Fulda Gap, which in the military doctrine of the time was viewed as the probable gateway for Warsaw Pact tanks in a potential invasion. The majority of the Jews settling in Frankfurt found themselves, even if indirectly, in the social slipstream of the U.S. Fifth Army Corps.

The extraordinary constellation that was Frankfurt may be understood as the topographical concentration of the overall conditions developing in the Federal Republic. "Frankfurt" stands for both the city itself and for the particular situation in which the Federal Republic found itself between the 1950s and the 1970s—the core sociopolitical decades of the West German experience. What is significant about the constellation of the Federal Republic tied up with the Frankfurt brand was the neutralization of national belonging that resulted from the partition of the country during the Cold War. In fact, in this sense the Federal Republic, in contrast to Germany, was actually a society, not a nation-state. As a result, the semantics of this society asserted itself in the interpretation of the realities of everyday life. Academically, this led to an evolving hegemony of the social sciences. This was manifest in the importance and symbolism of the return of the Frankfurt School of social theory and research to its city of origin after having relocated to New York in 1935.[123] Its founder and former director, Max Horkheimer, had been named rector of the University of Frankfurt in 1951 after his return from the United States in 1949, becoming no less than a public spokesperson for Jewish concerns. Significantly, Horkheimer was also a committed member of the city's B'nai B'rith chapter.[124]

The neutralization of national belonging driven by the ideological and territorial partition of the country in the wake of the Cold War and by the so-called Korea boom, the economic upturn resulting from the Korean War, as well as by the overall German economic miracle, permitted the Jews in the Federal Republic, especially in Frankfurt, to create a sphere for themselves in which their provisional sense of habitual discomfort in the land of the Germans could be expressed within a dynamic sphere of private life, in particular, in business. Avoiding the German public sphere, they understood themselves solely as part of a collective within the Jewish community and much less as individuals in their own right. Presenting themselves as Jews in the public sphere would have touched on a taboo, evoking the ambivalence of the prevailing Jewish stance toward life, the stance of absent presence that increasingly came to characterize Jewish community life in postwar Germany. It manifested in a palpable omnipresent inhibition about being visible, an expression, protracted and increasingly attenuated, that became associated with the ban over Germany and its Jews.

The drama of the Jews in postwar Germany, particularly of those who had settled in Frankfurt, was that they were most active and successful in the business sectors. During the transitional period between the 1960s and 1970s, this led to their unwanted but increasing visibility. The constant withdrawal and reserve that characterized their way of life was no longer manageable once they achieved a certain economic success—and that occurred at a time of urban conflict in the country. They were forced to step out of the shadows of their self-imposed seclusion and into the glaring light of the public stage. The fact that this occurred both in reality and symbolically in the mid-1980s, when members of the Jewish community prevented the performance of Rainer Werner Fassbinder's play *Der Müll, die Stadt und der Tod* (*Garbage, the City, and Death*), which they perceived as antisemitic, lent this act even greater visibility than it otherwise might have had.

A crucial element of postwar Jewish existence in Germany was compensation in the form of restitution and reparations, of charity and welfare, of prosperity and success. In the pursuit of this goal, two disparate domains of social participation came together from the very beginning: on the one hand, Jewish welfare and charity toward the impoverished that would ensure an economic minimum; on the other, the energetic economic bustle that aimed at private profit.

International Jewish aid organizations such as the JDC sought to meet the needs of impoverished Jews during the early phase of the Federal Republic; in Berlin, for example, more than 50 percent of community members qualified as impoverished.[125] These institutions continued their activities, which had begun during the period between the end of the war and the founding of the Federal Republic and the dissolution of the DP camps, but now followed the Jewish tradition of *tzedakah*, a precept of Judaism that is only partially covered by the English word "charity." This is why the ZWST, which had originally been founded in 1917 to minister to the needs of fleeing Jewish victims of pogroms in Eastern Europe, was reestablished in Hamburg in 1951 with funding made available first by the JDC and then by the Claims Conference.[126] The organization relocated to Frankfurt in 1955. Its importance for Jewish life in Germany may be gauged by the outstanding people who led its various committees, which were tasked with providing social and refugee aid, working with young people and the elderly, and hammering out social legislation, among many other things. One tendency is clearly discernible over the years: the more the federal government became involved in restitution and compensation, the less the ZWST spent on its core missions. However, since the mid-1950s, the organization had come to focus increasingly on youth work under the direction of Harry Maor.[127] In addition, the ZWST continued to support and integrate Jewish refugees, who flowed into the Federal Republic in keeping with the constant rhythm of ongoing crises enveloping the Eastern Bloc countries: in 1952–1953 from the German Democratic Republic in the wake of the Slánský show trial in Prague; in 1956 on the occasion of the Hungarian revolt; in 1968 because of the suppression of the Czech reform movement and the antisemitic campaign fomented in Poland that same year.[128]

The Jewish loan societies, which were set up by the JDC and the ZWST, took on a mediating function between the precept of *tzedakah*, with its emphasis on fighting poverty, integration, and social work, and the hustle and bustle of daily life aimed at propelling the economic success of the individual. This credit institution, which opened branches in Frankfurt, Munich, Hamburg, Berlin, and Hannover, attempted to give Jews the means in the form of small loans to establish themselves in trade, business, or the free professions. The goal was to spare people as much as possible the humiliation of dependency on public support or to prevent them from becoming reliant on social aid in the first place.[129] Traditional banking was not well suited for this type of assistance, which aimed at self-sufficiency. The banks would not have advanced credit to Jews who, after the catastrophe, generally had few or no relatives who were able to vouch for their credit-worthiness and reputation or willing to act as guarantors. In addition, the impoverished Jews lacked any roots at all in the places in which they had settled, and often they had no fixed address. Moreover, their status in the country was merely provisional, and all of these factors together scuttled from the outset almost all applications for credit. This was the situation to which the Jewish loan societies responded. Of course, like all banking institutions they attempted to assess the reliability of their borrowers. But in order to ensure that as many people as possible qualified, investigations of credit-worthiness tended toward the perfunctory, and in any case the loans, which could not exceed 3,000 DM, were made at an exceedingly low rate of interest. Even so, the risks involved would never have been accepted by a commercial institution. In effect, the Jewish loan societies were hybrid institutions tailored to the current situation facing Jews in Western Germany. Their mission was to follow the traditional precepts of *tzedakah* while functioning in accordance with conventional banking principles.[130] Occasionally, this led to situations that generated curious and even macabre comments. For example, the loan society in Frankfurt reported on the repayment of a loan "for reconstruction that had been deemed 'dead certain' which was rendered dubious by the death of our debtor."[131] But overall, the losses and forfeitures experienced by the five loan societies were minuscule, and thus they may be judged as having been very successful in terms of their stated mission.[132] The Frankfurt branch began work in 1954, with its funding coming from the JDC and especially from the Claims Conference. From the late 1950s on, it operated as a cooperative fund based on member deposits. It ceased operation in 1976, a signal that by all appearances the Jews in the Federal Republic had "arrived," at least in terms of economic status.[133]

There are, unfortunately, no reliable figures on the economic activities or professions practiced by Jews in Germany.[134] Nonetheless, it is quite probable that significant spatial patterns in working life developed for German Jews and Eastern European Jews. For example, the decision of German Jews to return to Germany was undoubtedly facilitated by their knowledge of the language, acquired prior to the catastrophe. That knowledge would again serve them well in their economic endeavors, primarily in professions relating to the law, as well as in spheres of culture and entertainment.[135] Jews of Eastern European origin, on the other hand, were dependent on employment that did not require a high level of proficiency in the language. Not that they completely lacked the proficiency in German needed for daily communications. Some of them had remained in or come to the Federal Republic because, as the easternmost country of the West in Continental Europe, it had certain cultural and other affinities with the countries of old eastern Central Europe, which were now under Communist rule. But this echo of a bygone Central European cultural geography based on the German language was hardly to be expected among the primarily younger former Eastern European DPs. For them, the German language was one of the hallmarks of their persecution, the language of command, so that memories of the catastrophe continually stymied its organic adoption in the postwar period. In addition, the Eastern European DPs harbored the notion that Yiddish would continue to serve them as a sufficient medium in the land of the Germans, a supposition that rendered their niche-based integration into Germany both more difficult and easier. Nonetheless, they did everything in their power to give their children the best possible education.[136]

Most of the economic activities engaged in by Jews of Eastern European origin, primarily in trade, had at least two things in common: they were aimed at short-term gain, and they required a minimum of social interaction. The business practices associated with these trades, which developed out of the absent presence conditioned by their provisional status, was focused on sectors with rapid turnover in order to compensate for the low level of social trust created by the transactions involved. In addition, in negotiating their business deals, which generally required intense communication and proximity, they tended to favor those in an intermediate zone between wholesale and retail trade. This permitted

First successful business: the Strumpfhaus Zentrum (hosiery shop) in Frankfurt am Main, with its proprietor, Simon Unger, about 1953. From Georg Heuberger ed., *Zedaka: Jüdische Sozialarbeit im Wandel der Zeit; 75 Jahre Zentralwohlfahrtsstelle der Juden in Deutschland 1917–1992*, catalogue for the exhibition at the Jewish Museum, Frankfurt am Main, from December 3, 1992 to February 28, 1993, p. 404 / photograph by Simon Unger.

them to occupy spaces if possible in the upper stories of buildings out of public view, and certainly not in street-level shops.

The beginnings of Jewish economic activity in postwar Germany are to be found primarily in the hotel, restaurant, and entertainment businesses. These sectors, in which the Jewish presence was especially prominent, particularly in Frankfurt and environs, developed out of the interaction between the needs of American military service and support personnel and those who had emerged mainly from the milieu of the former Jewish DPs. The habitual social behaviors that developed in this milieu became established between the end of the war and the German currency reform of 1948 against a backdrop of war, persecution, and concentration camps.[137] They emerged out of the confusing reality of the occupation and the modes of behavior that were facilitated by it, which were often only quasi legal. These behaviors, much modified, tended to intrude into the new realities of daily life becoming normalized in the new Germany.

The hotels, restaurants, and entertainment enterprises were ideal first businesses for accumulating capital quickly, although they were not always successful.

For the majority involved in these activities, the daily reality was a laborious slog. For example, the Jewish restaurant owners were often reduced to operating covertly as virtual franchisees or leaseholders, especially when the large breweries that supplied these restaurants demanded that they buy the breweries' products exclusively because they had provided the decorations and equipment. Over time, this decreased the number of owners of taverns and other establishments and reduced them to the status of what had in Eastern Europe been a largely Jewish profession, that of innkeeper.[138]

Jews were also conspicuously active in the textile industry in the 1950s and 1960s,[139] mostly in the clothing trade sector but also in the various stages of production of ready-to-wear products. Here and there, the Jews from Eastern Europe could exploit their traditional familiarity with tailoring; however, because of the clothing boom at the time, the profession was often plied by persons without such a background. Initially at least, Jews in this industry seem to have found success selling products that either were from the United States or were in the American style, such as blue jeans or knock-offs of these much-sought-after high-status items, often imported from Belgium. This was also true of nylon stockings, which early in the immediate postwar period had become a kind of currency. After the currency reform and the normalization of trade that it enabled, nylons continued to be a significant consumer item, signaling early West German modernity. Not only were nylons sold, but associated secondary services also developed, such as repair shops. In some instances, Jews in the Frankfurt area had set up businesses to manufacture nylon stockings and later stockings made of other materials as well, although large-scale production was more the exception. These small Jewish-owned businesses were able to make use of skills acquired before the war, for example in Łódź, once renowned for its textile industry.[140] Significantly, in most cases one company handled both the manufacture and the sale of these items. As in the early history of industrialization, actual production was outsourced to small shops located in the countryside. The catchment area of this form of production and sales extended from Frankfurt all the way to the region of the upper Main River.

Jews were also to be found in extremely undercapitalized industries run by owners who demanded a consistently high level of personal commitment bordering on self-exploitation. Examples included laundries and textile dry cleaning—occupations, interestingly, that lay somewhere between the hotel and restaurant business and the textile trade. A high level of self-exploitation was also a feature of the import-export business. Businesses run by Jews often dealt in staples and occasional items that were sold at bargain prices and quickly passed through to consumers. But there was also an active market in higher quality goods as well, such as porcelain and electrical devices. Customers came to trust some of these enterprises, which as a result stayed in business for many years. The jewelry and precious stone businesses also required a special level of client trust.[141] Such Jewish businesses were conspicuous in the urban landscape.

Coffeehouses served as informal information exchanges everywhere. In coffeehouses, people learned of opportunities or the risks involved in more or less profitable businesses. A cultural anthropologist observing the day-to-day topography of Jews in Frankfurt coffeehouses would, as in coffeehouses in other places, discern a spontaneously regulated order sorted by country of origin, profession, industry, and individual rank. The particular vernacular used in conversation would reveal a great deal about occupation, origins, and experience. The same could be said of the various cultures manifested in the synagogues and the particular rituals practiced in each. And a great deal would be revealed about both the topographical and day-to-day, life-world-oriented connections between synagogue and coffeehouse—in Frankfurt, for example, between the Westend Synagogue and the Café am Opernplatz. From this axis of Jewish interaction passing through the urban space of Frankfurt's Westend one could observe the transition, especially during the Jewish High Holy Days, from one place to the other, the passage from one sphere of daily life-world activity to the other—from the sacred to the profane. Also worth mentioning was the Club Voltaire, located in the immediate vicinity of Opernplatz, which since about the mid-1960s had been increasingly frequented by Jewish young people wishing to engage in intellectual debate. After attending synagogue, more than a few were busily involved there in discussion inspired by Enlightenment ideals. Jazz and the rock music popular at the time were presented live at a dance club with the evocative name Storyville, which was located on the upper floor of a downtown office building. The American Forces Network (AFN) dispensed contemporary American music, which could be heard on radios at home or on the hot mobile devices of the time: transistor radios.[142] In some instances, these youthful pleasures were transformed into serious enterprises, such as the most important concert agency for popular music in Germany.[143]

Public Jewish space in Frankfurt was divided into different milieus in different coffeehouses.[144] Because these were places of social communication, it was easy to read the position and status of the regulars. From the 1950s through the 1970s, status was measured exclusively by the symbols of economic success. Over time, people sought respect and social recognition based on their charitable contributions, although this was a later development. Earlier on, economic social ranking was measured differently, primarily in terms of more or less voluntary contributions to Israeli causes.

This sort of philanthropy as a measure of worth was not a new phenomenon, and in the Jewish world it has been and remains ubiquitous. A confluence of long-established Jewish traditions favored well-organized giving to Israel. The most important of these was the custom called *halukah*—a kind of collective Jewish charity based on contributions from communities or individuals, since early modern times earmarked primarily for Jews settling in the Promised Land for the purpose of studying scripture, especially in places like Safed, Tiberias, and Jerusalem. The tradition of *halukah* became increasingly secularized as Zionism took hold. The donations then came to be used for land acquisition and settlement and later for security purposes. In some respects they represented an informal Jewish national tax made available to the Jewish state by Diaspora Jews.

The liturgical importance of this charitable giving—it was not uncommon for money to be pledged openly at synagogue services—was especially salient to the Jews in Germany. Given the weight of the ban upon them because of their continued presence in Germany, the obligation to raise funds was morally freighted. If they were going to live in Germany in contravention of the worldwide Jewish consensus, they had a duty to be all the more generous with the money that they had earned there. The recognition of generosity and the sanctions against stinginess were felt in all areas of daily life, especially in the synagogue, with its hierarchical seating arrangement, and in such secular spaces as the coffeehouses, where information (and gossip) were exchanged. These were the places where hierarchies of respect and recognition were worked out—not least on the basis of charitable giving to the State of Israel. Closefistedness was not an option for community members of means.[145]

This was an area of life where the last remaining distance between the German Jews and the Jews of Eastern European origin tended to disappear, as was evident, for example, in the responses to a speech made by Paul Arnsberg, at the time a board member of the Jewish community of Frankfurt and its executive, during a meeting of solidarity with the State of Israel on the eve of the Six-Day War in 1967. Arnsberg, who had returned from Israel in the late 1950s, had as a youth been active in the revisionist current of the Zionist movement in Weimar Germany—a rarity among German Jews at the time. The speech, in which he spontaneously pledged the Jewish community's willingness to provide Israel with 1 million DM for the purposes of defense, was met with thunderous applause. Arnsberg, a jurist and later historian of Jewish life in Frankfurt and Hesse who had dedicated himself to serving the traditions of the old established Frankfurt community, was generally disliked by the Eastern European Jews of the city. However, his championing of the Israeli cause (with a pledge of real money), like a holy founding act, contributed to transforming the relationship.

And in fact, Israel's military victory in the Six-Day War led to an increasing acceptance on the part of world Jewry of the Jews who had settled in Germany. For example, the Bundesverband jüdischer Studenten in Deutschland (Federal

Association of Jewish Students in Germany, BJSD), founded in 1968, was immediately accepted into the World Union of Jewish Students (WUJS).[146] With justification, the leaders of the German-Jewish community viewed this success as a sign of their suddenly growing acceptance as Jews in Germany. After all, Jewish students around the world, particularly in Israel, had been especially fierce in their dislike of Germany generally and of Jews living in Germany in particular.

This dawning of a new era became visible with some delay with the establishment in 1979 of the Hochschule für Jüdische Studien (College of Jewish Studies) in Heidelberg and the dedication of a new building for the Jewish community in Frankfurt in 1986, publicly ratified by Salomon Korn's apothegm "Who builds a house intends to stay."[147] The so-called Börneplatz conflict in 1987 around the excavations in the old Judengasse symbolized the rootedness of the recently settled Frankfurt Jews in the history of the former Jewish community. The following year saw the founding of the Jewish Museum under Frankfurt community auspices. The evolution of a new German Jewry developed largely in parallel with the increasing historicization of the Jewish presence, a trend that culminated in the founding of the Jewish Museum in Berlin in 2001, an event with national and international resonance.[148] In parallel, the growing public interest in the Jewish presence was given an important boost and added rationale when Rachel Salamander founded the Literaturhandlung in Munich in 1982, a bookstore specializing in Jewish literature and scholarship. This was a private initiative devoted to the dissemination of Jewish knowledge across Germany and beyond.[149] German universities began to sponsor academic work in the area of Jewish studies, especially in the 1980s and 1990s, and although this was not a direct consequence of Jewish institutional initiative, it was another indication that this new German-Jewish community had taken root.

This development, however, took the span of an entire generation. It may well be that the dawning of a new era for Jews in Germany, especially their acceptance as Jews living legitimately in Germany, was aided by the Six-Day War. However, the more lasting transformation undoubtedly resulted from commercial enterprises, which from the very beginning had been constitutive of the Jewish presence in Germany. Business led to a qualitative and fundamental transformation of the Jewish presence in Germany from voluntary retreat into private life into the glaring limelight of the public stage. This transformation was first discernible in Frankfurt, a city that was itself experiencing an extraordinary acceleration in the pace of daily life, and the slipstream of this acceleration pulled the Jews into the public space that they had so long sought to avoid. In large part, this was facilitated by a significant shift in their economic activities from professions and commercial endeavors that were well matched to the Jewish habitus of withdrawal, of absent presence, into endeavors such as real estate that were both more visible and required a high degree of public trust and acceptance. The transformation was not merely a transition from one mode of endeavor to another; instead, at a deep level it entailed precisely the sort of visibility that the Jews in Germany had avoided out of their sense of reticence and transience. The result of these circumstances was a complicated interplay, a push-pull between the habitus of withdrawal and new economic roles that forced them to lay down roots in the city and to engage with middle-class society.

The real estate business, which is closely connected with construction, is a complex endeavor.[150] On the one hand, real estate is a commodity like any other. On the other, because it is an immovable commodity of great visibility, it becomes the object of constant attention, which brings with it a number of social consequences. This is especially true because apartment or commercial construction necessitates the intertwining of production and commerce. The phrase "Who builds a house intends to stay" then takes on a whole new meaning: whoever develops commercial real estate can no longer claim transient status.

The transformation that took place in Frankfurt between the 1960s and the 1970s, from trade in a variety of consumer goods to the development, construction, and sale of commercial real estate, was in effect paradoxically tantamount to laying down roots in the land of the Germans by virtue of this commerce in property. Because the Frankfurt area experienced a building boom at this time, and banks were willing to lend under conditions that attracted investors to construction and real estate, distortions were inevitable. This was especially the case when persons of Jewish faith and origin who still valued their provisionality and transience in Germany became active in a sector of the economy that is based on long-term social interaction. Such distortions were the consequence of the lax approval policies required to modernize the city and the almost trivial barriers to bank loans. These factors created unprecedented pressures that heated up the market, pressures to which Jewish developers, who were new to the sector, also succumbed. But they desired neither new visibility nor the social conflict that this situation brought with it, nor were they really prepared to deal with it.

The increasing acceptance that the German-Jewish community experienced among world Jewry as a result of the Six-Day War and the accelerating shift from trade into real estate led to a conflation of the conflict in the Middle East with the social protest against real estate "speculators" that took on antisemitic overtones. In retrospect, this mix came to be of iconic importance for the Federal Republic. The apparently odd timing of these factors points to two sets of events that have at different times left lasting marks. The first was the large-scale populist housing protests of the early 1970s in Frankfurt, which became linked in the public mind to the anti-Jewish Fettmilch revolt of 1614 in that city. And then, after an incubation period of a decade and a half, there came the heated public debate

Occupied house in the Bockenheimer Landstrasse in Frankfurt,
March 1973. bpk / photograph by Abisag Tüllmann.

over Fassbinder's play *Garbage, the City, and Death*, whose antagonist is a vengeful and rich Jewish real estate speculator who moves in corrupt social circles in Frankfurt. The protests by members of the Jewish community, which were successful in halting production of the play in 1985, engendered a great deal of ill feeling. Although it seemed at the time that the collective stand taken by the Jewish community had been perceived as reprehensible, paradoxically, in the long run it proved salutary. By protesting against something of immediate concern to them, the members of the Jewish community let it be known that they were a legitimate part of German society. In effect, the act of protest against Fassbinder's play finally broke the decades-long ban under which Jews had lived in Germany and therefore proved emancipatory.

And in fact, the career of Ignatz Bubis, who was reputedly the inspiration for Fassbinder's "rich Jew," may be seen in this light. A real estate investor, Bubis came to represent the Jewish community in Frankfurt. By origin and generation, he embodied the Eastern European Jews in the Federal Republic. His biography reads like a blueprint of the story of integration and social advancement of the Jews in Germany who arrived from Eastern Europe after 1945. Even the transition in his professional life from dealing with jewelry and precious metals into real estate is emblematic. His election to the board of the Jewish community in the early 1970s came about because of an unexpected switch in the communal council, the result of a successful electoral list put forward by Jewish students. Bubis also differed from most of the Frankfurt Jews of Eastern European origin. Even during the 1950s and early 1960s, he had no inhibitions about moving in non-Jewish German circles, which were not generally deemed especially hospitable to Jews. It is to his everlasting credit that he became politically active in larger German politics, specifically with the Free Democratic Party (FDP), an involvement that went well beyond representing Jewish interests in Germany. His political profile became all the more pronounced as Germany underwent reunification in 1989–1990. In fact, Bubis became so publicly prominent that his name was even bruited in the press as a possible candidate for Germany's presidential elections.

Because of his energy and assertive style, he became something of a prototype of Jews in Germany.[151] In his origins, profession, and way of life, he perhaps represented the Jews in Germany more authentically than did either his predecessors or his successors as presidents of the Central Council. At the same time, Bubis stood out in his community, and in his impetuousness he may also have acted independently of its collective interests. Always a Jew who understood himself in Jewish national terms, he attempted in his speeches and writings to bridge a historical distance that most of the Jews in Germany had a difficult time following—even fifty years after the catastrophe. Bubis seems to have intended by the power of his personality to transform the Jews in Germany into German Jews. We will never know whether he was conscious of the full import of his actions or whether he just felt it important in the tumultuous 1990s to strengthen German democracy after reunification as the path to German citizenship became more inclusive. When toward the end of his life he declared publicly, and enigmatically, that he might possibly have been mistaken in his endeavors, he may have recognized that the collective "we" of the Germans had not become sufficiently inclusive to accept him and the community whose history was embodied by his biography. Bubis reacted with visible and courageous outrage to the writer Martin Walser and his public call against using Auschwitz as a moral stick to beat the German people. The vehemence of Bubis's response may well provide evidence of his increasing skepticism about the project that had been the focus of his life's work: the idea that he was able to transform himself from a Jew in Germany into a German Jew. This probably does not, however, really explain his decision to be buried in Tel Aviv and not in Frankfurt, where he expended his vast energies.

Bubis's grave in Tel Aviv signaled to contemporaries and posterity that the path he had trodden, while perhaps not incorrect, may have been premature.[152] In any case, he and those like him, the generation of Jews in Germany of Eastern European origin, provided the anchor for the Jewish community after 1945 in the former "land of the murderers." Their collective biography reflects a great, perhaps even the most significant, part of a history of the Jews in Germany that began in 1949–1950 and concluded in 1989–1990 with German reunification and the major migration into Germany from the countries of the former Soviet Union. That the decades-long ban on Germany and the Jews who lived there had in fact been broken was paradoxically evoked at the Tel Aviv graveside of Ignatz Bubis. An Israeli artist walked up to Bubis's freshly filled grave after the conclusion of the burial ceremony and poured a dark liquid on it, an act of desecration spelling out his contempt for the deceased. However, no one really took notice of this caricature of ritual banning. The ban imposed on Jews living in Germany had long since run dry.

DAN DINER is Professor of modern history at the Hebrew University in Jerusalem, where he presently serves as the principal investigator of the European Research Council (ERC) project Judging Histories: Experience, Representation, and Judgment of WWII in an Age of Globalization. From 1999 to 2014 he directed the Simon Dubnow Institute for Jewish History and Culture at Leipzig University. He is a member of the Academy of the Sciences and the Humanities of Saxony, where he leads the long-term research and encyclopedic editing project on Jewish history and culture. Diner's English-language publications include *Beyond the Conceivable: Germany, Nazism, and the Holocaust, Cataclysm: A History of the Twentieth Century from Europe's Edge,* and *Lost in the Sacred: Why the Muslim World Stood Still.*

NOTES

I am grateful to Felix Pankonin and Ann-Kathrin Pollmann for their assistance in searching for material relevant to this chapter.
   1. C. Yahil (1980), C. Yahil (1981).

2. C. Yahil (1981), p. 169.

3. D. Diner (1997), pp. 240–244.

4. Chaim Yahil's biographical data have been summarized from his literary estate, in CZA, A 328/74 and A 328/84.

5. In Vienna Yahil wrote his dissertation in political economy and sociology. It was published in Prague in 1937 under the title Träger der Verwirklichung: Die Zionistische Arbeiterschaft im Aufbau.

6. Autobiographical fragment in CZA, A 382/84, p. 2.

7. Y. Jelinek (1988), p. 81.

8. C. Yahil (1981), pp. 169–170.

9. C. Yahil (1981), pp. 170–171.

10. C. Yahil (1981), pp. 170–171.

11. C. Yahil (1981), pp. 171–172.

12. C. Yahil (1981), p. 154; Y. Bauer (1990); Y. Bauer (1970a).

13. C. Yahil (1981), p. 171.

14. She'erit Hapletah is of biblical origin and comes from Chronicles (2 Chronicles 30:6; Ezra 9:14 and 15; Nehemia 1:2). It refers to the Judeans who evaded exile during the Babylonian Captivity and remained in the land of Israel. I. Gutman and A. Saf (1990).

15. C. Yahil (1981), p. 164; see also D. Bankier (ed.) (2005), and especially the article by P. Lagrou (2005).

16. C. Yahil (1981), p. 174.

17. C. Yahil (1981), p. 174.

18. For a bibliographical overview of the history of the Jews after 1945, see M. Brenner, "Bibliographical Essay," in M. Brenner (1997); E.-M. Timme (1992).

19. A. Gotzmann (1994). For more on the transformation in Deuteronomy of the frame of reference of cherem from the identification of external enemies to an internal instrument for the protection of religious dogma, see M. Greenberg and H. H. Cohn (2007); C. Schäfer-Lichtenberger (1994); F. Stern (1991), pp. 99–125; S. Mandl (1898).

20. N. Barzel (1996).

21. M. Brenner (1997), p. 66.

22. Y. Gelber (1983), p. 335 (Hebrew).

23. S. Shafir (1999), pp. 109, 114; Resolutions of the World Jewish Congress Second Plenary Assembly, Montreux of June 27 to July 6, 1948, pp. 7–8, in AJA, A46 5; see also M. Brenner (2010).

24. A. Grossmann (2007), pp. 253–254; M. Brenner (1997), pp. 66, 75–77.

25. A. Grossmann (2007), pp. 263–264.

26. A. Quast (2001), p. 94.

27. A. Grossmann (2007), p. 262, with references to G. Vida (1967), pp. 85–87. For more on limitations placed on the Israeli passport, see M. Mendel (2004).

28. Gershom Schocken, "We and the Germans," in Ha'aretz, September 2, 1949 (Hebrew).

29. N. Barzel (1994), pp. 290–291.

30. N. Barzel (1994), pp. 290–291.

31. N. Barzel (1994), p. 291.

32. M. Shapiro (1989), p. 389.

33. C. Roth (1957), p. 676.

34. Cecil Roth, Opening Address, Conference on Restoration of Continental Jewish Museums, Libraries and Archives, London, April 11, 1943, in C. Roth (1944).

35. C. Roth (1957), p. 677; J. D. Bleich (1983), pp. 208–209.

36. Y. Kaplan (2008), pp. 34–38; J. D. Bleich (1983), p. 208.

37. C. Roth (1957), p. 676.

38. A. Takei (2004), p. 114.

39. For more on the history of the Reich Association, see B. Meyer (2011), pp. 32, 44; O. Kulka (1986), p. 353; O. Kulka (1998), p. 383.

40. For more on legal succession, see H. Maor (1961), pp. 164–165. See also R. Schreiber (1997); J. Lillteicher (2007); C. Goschler (1992), esp. pp. 172–174; U. Büttner (1986).

41. J. Lillteicher (2007), p. 79.

42. A. Takei (2004), on the founding of the JRC, pp. 77–80, and on the formation of the IRSO, pp. 80–86.

43. A. Takei (2002), pp. 266–288.

44. O. Karbach (1962), p. 43.

45. For early literature on the question of restitution, see N. Sagi (1981); N. Balabkins (1971); F. Shinnar (1966); N. Robinson (1964); G. Landauer (1951); N. Robinson (1944); S. Moses (1944); F. Gillis and H. Knopf (1944).

46. C. Goschler (1992), p. 46.

47. On collective claims, see C. Goschler (1992), pp. 41–44; G. Landauer (1957), pp. 277–279; S. Moses (1944); F. Gillis and H. Knopf (1944).

48. D. Diner (2008b).

49. For literature on the JCR, see E. Gallas (2012); D. Heredia (2010); D. Herman (2008); K. Rauschenberger (2008).

50. E. Gallas (2010), p. 26.

51. A. Takei (2002), p. 272.

52. H. Maor (1961), p. 49. Maor speaks of a "semi-permanent presence."

53. For more on the demography of Jews in the occupation zones, see H. Maor (1961), pp. 3, 19, 57–68; J. H. Geller (2005), pp. 31–34.

54. W. Jacobmeyer (1983), pp. 432–436.

55. U. Büttner (1986), p. 375; J. H. Geller (2005), p. 31.

56. On Norbert Wollheim, cf. M. Brenner (1997), pp. 95–99; J. R. Rumpf (2010). On Philipp Auerbach, see H. Ludyga (2006); E. Fröhlich (1988). On the Philipp Auerbach affair, see E. Presser (1992). On Heinz Galinski, see A. Nachama and J. H. Schoeps (eds.) (1992); A. Nachama (1999).

57. On Hendrik George van Dam, see Michael Brenner, "Botschafter der Juden: Hendrik van Dam," *Jüdische Allgemeine*, November 9, 2006, p. 2. On Karl Marx, see B. Haunfelder (2006), pp. 304–305; "Marx, Karl," in J. Walk (1988), p. 257; A. Sinn (2010a), A. Sinn (2011).

58. U. Büttner (1986), p. 375.

59. J. H. Geller (2005), pp. 51–52.

60. H. Ludyga (2007); H. Ludyga (2005).

61. H. Ludyga (2007), p. 419.

62. H. Ludyga (2007), p. 412.

63. Philipp Auerbach, "Ein noch 'offeneres' Wort." *Jüdische Rundschau* 4/5 (1946), pp. 49–50.

64. H. Ludyga (2005), p. 38.

65. H. Ludyga (2007), p. 414.

66. J. Wetzel (1987), p. 54.

67. H. Ludyga (2007), p. 424.

68. C. Goschler (1989), p. 94.

69. N. Sznaider (2009), p. 61.

70. H. Ludyga (2005), p. 71; W. Bergmann (1999), p. 63.

71. Hannah Arendt to Heinrich Blücher, December 26, 1949, in H. Arendt and H. Blücher (1999), p. 185.

72. D. Herman (2008), pp. 210–211.

73. C. Goschler (1992), pp. 172–180.

74. H. Ludyga (2005), p. 129.

75. H. Ludyga (2005), p. 129.

76. H. Ludyga (2005), p. 130.

77. T. Lewinsky (2010), p. 24. With the founding of the Ner-Tamid Verlag in 1957 by Hans Lamm, the public production and sale of books on Jewish topics receded in Munich. For more on this, see A. Sinn (2008), pp. 121–122.

78. P. L. Münch (1997), pp. 98–99.

79. P. L. Münch (1997), p. 101.

80. A. Sinn (2010b).

81. Hendrik George van Dam, cited in P. L. Münch (1997), p. 101.

82. E. Carlebach and A. Brämer (1997), pp. 293–294.

83. E. Carlebach and A. Brämer (1997), p. 294; M. Kingreen (2008), p. 138.

84. H. Maor (1961), p. 67.

85. A. Takei (2002), pp. 277–279; A. Takei (2004), pp. 129–138.

86. R. Schreiber (1997), pp. 179–180; A. Takei (2002), pp. 277–278.

87. A. Takei (2002), p. 279. See also Y. Bauer (1989), p. 45.

88. Y. Bauer (1989), p. 45.

89. A. Takei (2002), p. 275, A. Takei (2004), p. 116.

90. A. Takei (2004), pp. 115–116.

91. R. Schreiber (1997), p. 181.

92. A. Wirsching (2002), pp. 38–40.

93. For works that are fundamental to the history of the German Jews after 1945, see M. Wolffsohn and T. Brechenmacher (eds.) (2008), pp. 183–280; A. Grossmann (2007); A. Kauders (2007); M. Richarz (2007); S. Tauchert (2007); S. Schönborn (ed.) (2006); J. Peck (2006); J. H. Geller (2005); E. Kolinsky (2004); Y. M. Bodemann (ed.) (1996b); Y. M. Bodemann (2002a); J. Geis (1999); M. Brenner (1997); E. Burgauer (1993); M. Brumlik et al. (eds.) (1986).

94. D. Diner (2010).

95. For the growing numbers of refugees from Communist Czechoslovakia after August 21, 1968, and their care by Jewish institutions, see the minutes of the ZWST board meeting on October 20, 1968, in ZA, B1/11, Zg. 96/10, no. 11.

96. For more on restitution, see N. Frei et al. (eds.) (2009); J. Lillteicher (2007), pp. 144–156, 236, 513; T. Winstel (2006), p. 385; C. Goschler and J. Lillteicher (eds.) (2002), especially the article by C. Goschler (2002); R. Zweig (2001), p. 18; C. Goschler (1992), pp. 91–98, 225–234, here p. 227; L. Herbst and C. Goschler (eds.) (1989), especially the article by N. Sagi (1989), p. 116; C. Kapralik (1962).

97. For more on the history of the 1952 Reparations Agreement between Israel and West Germany (Luxembourg Agreement), see N. Hansen (2002), pp. 155–366; Y. A. Jelinek (1997); C. Goschler (1992), pp. 257–285; M. Lemke (1990); G. Könke (1988); M. Wolffsohn (1988); R. Vogel (ed.) (1969).

98. According to the Law on the Affairs of the Expellees and Refugees (Gesetz über die Angelegenheiten der Vertriebenen und Flüchtlinge, Bundesvertriebenengesetz, BVFG) of 1953, section 6, paragraph 1, "Belonging to the German People," an individual is a "member of the German people [deutscher Volkszugehöriger] in the sense of this law . . . who in his homeland professed his allegiance to German national values and culture, insofar as this avowal is confirmed by specific characteristics such as descent, language, education, culture." Federal Expellee Law (BVFG), version promulgated August 10, 2007 (Bundesgesetzblatt 1, p. 1902), last altered by article 1 of the law of December 4, 2011 (Bundesgesetzblatt 1, p. 2426). On this, see Brunner and Nachum (2009).

99. On burden sharing, see W. Abelshauser (2011), pp. 333–336; P. Erker (ed.) (2004); M. L. Hughes (1999); L. Wiegand (1992).

100. ZA, B1/12, Z9 2/07, no. 97.

101. R. Smolorz (2009), p. 18; W. Jacobmeyer (1985), pp. 226–231; "Gesetz über die Rechtsstellung heimatloser Ausländer im Bundesgebiet," Bundesgesetzblatt 1/19 (April 27, 1951), pp. 269–271.

102. R. Webster (1993), p. 311.

103. M. Mendel (2004), p. 134. For more on the level of emergency aid, see H. Maor (1961), p. 31.

104. A. Tauber (2008), pp. 105–106.

105. H. Maor (1961), pp. 31–50.

106. R. Heuberger (1999).

107. Harry Maor, "Erster Gruß!," Jüdische Jugend, no. 1 (January 1956), p. 1. Complete text printed in W. Aden-Grossmann (2007), pp. 220–221.

108. These included to varying degrees people like Harry Maor; Ernst Noam as administrative director of the Frankfurt Jewish Community; and Jakob W. Oppenheimer, an educator who, among other things, published a book about Jewish youth in Germany.

109. On Berthold Simonsohn, see T. Käpernick (2008); W. Aden-Grossmann (2007). On Benjamin Berell Ferencz, see B. B. Ferencz (1979).

110. On Max Willner, see M. Neumann (1994); M. Neumann (ed.) (1991).

111. On Alfred Weichselbaum, see the entry in J. H. Schoeps (ed.) (1992), p. 474.

112. On Robert Max Wasili Kempner, see I. Müller (1997); R. M. W. Kempner (1983).

113. On Henry Ormond, see W. Röder and H. s. Strauss (1980), vol. 1, p. 544.

114. On Fritz Bauer, see I. Wojak (2009).

115. On Jakob Moneta's membership in the SJV, the youth organization of the SAP, see J. Moneta (1991), p. 113. On Heinz Brandt, see K. Andresen (2007).

116. I am grateful to Maimon Maor for the information about Max Pulvermann.

117. On Fritz Naphtali, see J. Riemer (1992).

118. On Emil Carlebach, see S. Niemann (1995), pp. 136–137; E. Carlebach (1988); E. Carlebach (1995); P. Arnsberg (1983), pp. 74–75. On the VVN, see U. Schneider (1997).

119. Between 1966 and 1972 Josef Neuberger, who returned from Israel in 1950, was justice minister and a member of the Social Democratic–led cabinet under Heinz Kühn, not in Frankfurt am Main but in North Rhine-Westphalia. B. Schmalhausen (2002).

120. On the general development of infrastructure in the FRG after 1945, see T. Südbeck (1994), pp. 86–102; on the development in Frankfurt am Main specifically, see W. Bendix (2002), pp. 255–281.

121. W. Abelshauser (2011), pp. 122–125.

122. On the IG Farben building, see H. Drummer and J. Zwilling (2007); H. Loewy (2001); W. Meißner et al. (eds.) (1999).

123. R. Wiggershaus (1987); D. Claussen (2005).

124. T. Freimüller (2009).

125. B. Scheller (1992), p. 146. In addition, the majority of the returnees drew pensions. See H. Maor (1961), p. 86.

126. B. Scheller (1992), p. 146.

127. J. Levinson (2004), p. 214.

128. ZA, B1/11, Zg. 96/10, no. 11.

129. ZA, B1/11, Zg. 92/19, no. 1.

130. H. Maor (1961), p. 190, fn. 19, states that the loan societies in Frankfurt had 203 members, according to a 1958 business report. The average loan in Frankfurt was 3,709 DM. From 1955 to the end of 1958, the five loan societies approved 1,775 loans totaling approximately 5 million DM. Ludwig Joseph, who was director of the Jewish loan society in Frankfurt for many years, stated that the credits went primarily to small business people and craftsmen ("Probleme der jüdischen Darlehenskasse Frankfurt," Frankfurter Jüdisches Gemeindeblatt, July 1958).

131. "Probleme der jüdischen Darlehenskasse Frankfurt," Frankfurter Jüdisches Gemeindeblatt, July 1958.

132. B. Scheller (1992), p. 150.

133. "Darlehenskasse, jüdische," in J. H. Schoeps (1992), p. 100.

134. For more on the topic in the 1950s, see H. Maor (1961), pp. 76–87.

135. On the subject of Jewish attorneys, see T. Winstel (2010), pp. 543–547; H. G. Hockerts (1989), esp. pp. 251–261; E. Douma (1994).

136. On the social history of the Federal Republic, see A. Schildt (2007). On developments in the political culture, see N. Frei (2003); Y. M. Bodemann (2002a).

137. On the social significance of the currency reform, see A. Schildt (2007), pp. 10, 12, 23, 76, 81.

138. On Jewish tavern keepers, see J. Goldberg (2008), pp. 1849–1852; M. Opalski (1986).

139. H. Maor (1961), pp. 81–82, speaks of approximately 30 percent Jews active in the textile trade and approximately 40 percent in the overall textile industry, including manufacture. The textile industry thus employed the greatest concentration of Jews in any industrial sector.

140. On the textile industry in Łódź, see J. Roesler (2006); W. Strobel (2006); L. Mroczka (1999); J. Tomaszewski (1991).

141. It appears that in 1958 there were about thirty-five Jews among the approximately five hundred fur dealers active in the Federal Republic, primarily in the wholesale and commission trade. See H. Maor (1961), p. 190, fn. 18.

142. On the social history of radio, see A. Schildt (2007), pp. 26–27, 47–48, 50–63.

143. On the social history of music, see A. Schildt (2007), pp. 27, 29, 50–51.

144. For an overview of the modern social, historical, and anthropological significance of communication in coffeehouses, see M. Rössner (ed.) (1999), especially the article by A. Rath, "Berliner Caféhäuser 1890–1933," pp. 108–125, esp. p. 116; H. B. Segel (1993), esp. p. 34.

145. A. Kauders (2008), p. 93; A. Kauders (2007), pp. 100–103.

146. On the Bundesverband jüdischer Studenten (BJSD), see U. Kashi (2005); R. Baruch (1994).

147. Salomon Korn's speech on the occasion of the opening of the Community Center on September 14, 1986, is in S. Korn (2001), p. 73.

148. On the Börneplatz-Konflikt, see K. Kufeke (2002), pp. 289–293; G. Heuberger (1992b); M. Best (1998).

149. B. Picht (ed.) (1997).

150. On the development of the real estate industry, see J. O. Hesse and L. Kühne-Büning (2005); V. Eichener (2000), pp. 63–77. On the character of real estate as commodity, see L. Kühne-Büning (ed.) (2005), pp. 8–12.

151. On Ignatz Bubis as a person, see F. Backhaus et al. (ed.) (2007); I. Bubis and P. Sichrovsky (1996).

152. Dan Diner, "Das Grab: Ignatz Bubis findet seine letzte Ruhestätte in Tel Aviv," *Frankfurter Allgemeine Zeitung*, August 17, 1999.

WAY STATION

ATINA GROSSMANN AND
TAMAR LEWINSKY

| DISPLACED PERSONS

Against all expectations, defeated and occupied Germany became the unlikely and unloved, to many abhorrent, safe haven for about a quarter of a million Holocaust survivors, of whom the majority moved on after 1948–1949. During this time, they created a remarkable transitional society, especially around the larger DP camps located in and around Munich, Frankfurt, and West Berlin. These camps provided a space for a last revival of an Eastern European culture that had been forever destroyed while at the same time preparing its inhabitants for a future in a new homeland far from Europe, especially in Palestine. In effect, in this waiting room Jewish survivors created new, though transient, social arrangements. They came into contact with Germans, among whom they lived, and with the Americans and British who policed, protected, and supported them.

The great majority of the Jews stranded in Germany were of Eastern European, mainly Polish, origin, stateless "displaced persons," or DPs, as they were referred to by the Allies. They named themselves the She'erit Hapletah (the Surviving Remnant). Concentration camp and death march survivors who had been liberated in the territory controlled by the Nazis were joined by Jews who had survived as partisans or in hiding. Many had hoped to find family members and reclaim property "at home," in villages and towns throughout Eastern Europe. Mostly, they found a "vast graveyard"; they were the sole survivors and were not welcomed by non-Jewish neighbors who had appropriated their possessions.[1]

The bitter truth was that almost all Jews who had been unable to evade capture during the German occupation had been murdered. The largest—and least researched—group of survivors living in the DP camps in Germany after 1945 were Jews who had found refuge in the Soviet Union under difficult, though often life-saving, circumstances and who had then been repatriated to Poland. But starting in late 1945, especially after the pogrom in the Polish city of Kielce on July 4, 1946, where at least forty-two Jews were murdered, and after about twice as many had been killed on trains and in neighboring towns, most of the surviving Polish Jews fled westward, as so-called infiltrees, to the American zone of occupation.[2]

"MIR ZENEN DO"

Far from creating a purely "Aryanized" Reich, the genocidal war conducted by the Nazis, based on the enslavement and destruction of "racial inferiors," had left behind a remarkably multiethnic territory in postwar Germany. World War II had brought about historically unprecedented levels of expulsion and migration. The available statistical data on migration and displacement during the years between 1945 and 1949 vary considerably, regardless of whether they were gathered at the time or are the result of later historical research. The sheer numbers—and their unreliability—are clear signs of the chaos that accompanied the cessation of war, of the rapidly changing circumstances in which people found themselves, and of the urgent need on the part of the victors and aid organizations to control and direct the ensuing flood of DPs. Estimates immediately after the war speak of fifty-five million Europeans who were forced to leave their homes against their will between 1939 and 1945.[3] As the Allies advanced into German territory, they found more than eight million people who qualified as displaced persons according to the guidelines laid down by the Supreme Headquarters Allied Expeditionary Forces (SHAEF). Most of the approximately six million forced laborers, two million prisoners of war, and seven hundred thousand former concentration camp inmates were repatriated astonishingly quickly. At the end of September 1945, only about 1.2 million DPs remained, especially in the American and British zones. These UN DPs had been placed under the "care and control" of the American and British military government and of the United Nations Relief and Rehabilitation Administration (UNRRA), which had been founded in 1943 primarily for the purpose of repatriating persons uprooted by Nazi violence and occupation.[4] The Soviets, however, were not willing either to cooperate with UNRRA or to recognize the existence of DPs; the later French occupation established only a few receiving centers.[5]

Nevertheless, the repatriation programs of the Western Allies and UNRRA proceeded with exceptional efficiency. The majority of Soviet citizens, a third of all DPs, were repatriated in accordance with the provisions adopted at Yalta by the United States, Great Britain, and the Soviet Union. By the end of 1945, approximately three million Soviet citizens, including prisoners of war, had returned home, some of them against their will. Those who remained sometimes tried to pass as citizens of other countries in order to evade forced repatriation. About a fifth of the DPs in the Western occupation zones were children, many of them "unaccompanied," in the euphemistic language of the aid organizations; that is, they were orphaned or alone.[6] Almost half (400,000–500,000) were non-Jewish Poles, and about a quarter (175,000–200,000) were Balts who did not want to return to their homelands, which had been swallowed by the Soviet Union. There were also Hungarians and Yugoslavs, as well as smaller groups of Greeks, Bulgarians, Czechs, Slovaks, and even Iranians and Turks.[7]

Originally, the Jews were a tiny minority in this sea of humanity forced from their homelands by the war and the population displacements triggered by the Nazi regime. Only about seventy thousand to ninety thousand Jews were liberated on German soil. Liberation came too late for many, and they died within a few weeks, leaving only between fifty thousand and seventy thousand Jewish survivors.[8] The estimates of the proportion of Jews in the total number of DPs vary depending upon when the counts were done. Initially, people spoke of only about 2 percent.[9] But as the repatriations progressed, the percentage of Jews soon reached between 10 and 20 percent, and after late 1945—intensifying after the Kielce pogrom—the flood of Jews from Poland changed the national and ethnic profile of the DPs considerably. Immediately after the war, many of the Jewish survivors were gathered in the British zone; however, the willingness of the Americans to take in Eastern European "infiltrees" led to a reversal, making the U.S. zone the most important destination for Jewish survivors.

Given the situation that Jewish survivors found in Eastern Europe, their "return to the home country had been a pseudo-repatriation. It had lacked the necessary ingredients of a bona-fide homecoming. It was rather the final visit of a mourner to his family burial plot—the refugee's last look at his native land to which his forefathers had been attached for generations, but which he had to leave forever. His homage paid to dear ones, his last glimpse taken, he then set out on a new exodus in the hope of eventually reaching more hospitable soil."[10] As a result of this migratory wave, by the fall of 1947 about 91 percent of all Jewish DPs were in the American zone, and they comprised at least a quarter of all DPs registered by UNRRA.[11] The precise figures are unknown and will probably remain so, but in any case, current estimates exceed the official figures at the time. Malcolm Proudfoot, one of the many officials in UNRRA and other aid organizations who wrote about Allied efforts to manage this mass of the "uprooted," counted 157,000 for the summer of 1947 alone, and current historical research suggests a total of about 250,000 Jewish DPs. These survivors of the Final Solution and forced Soviet exile unexpectedly became an irritating presence both for the Allies and for the Germans.[12] It was no accident that the Jewish survivors, no matter how varied their origins and wartime experience, defiantly adopted as their motto the refrain from Hirsch Glick's partisan song "Mir zenen do" (We are here), as if to demonstrate to all their collective presence in the territory of the Reich that had attempted to destroy them.

UNDER BRITISH CONTROL

Immediately after the end of the war, a large majority of the She'erit Hapletah in Germany was located in the British zone of occupation. Bergen-Belsen in particular had during the last year of the war become the final destination of numerous death marches: as the Eastern front moved inexorably westward, tens of thousands of inmates were evacuated from the concentration and death camps in the East. During the winter of 1944–1945, other transports from all over Germany began to reach the catastrophically overcrowded camp. The final weeks before the liberation was announced (in five languages) were especially dramatic. As many as five hundred inmates died each day. More than forty-three thousand people were wedged into a space that a year earlier had accommodated no more than two thousand.

The horror that confronted the British soldiers was indescribable. Epidemics had spread, and the stench of rotting corpses and fecal matter took the soldiers' breath away. It is estimated that sixty thousand persons, of whom half were Jews, were still alive—precisely how many will never be known, because the camp commanders had long since stopped keeping records. People continued to die as a consequence of the inhuman conditions that had prevailed at Bergen-Belsen, even after the British liberated the camp on April 15, partly as a result of rapid but misguided attempts to feed the survivors.[13] By the beginning of the summer, the situation had slowly begun to stabilize, and it is estimated that perhaps twenty thousand Jews were still in the camp, among them an unusually large number of women and almost five hundred children. Many of the liberated had only recently arrived at Bergen-Belsen with transports and death marches from Buchenwald and Theresienstadt.[14]

In order to contain the raging epidemics, the liberated inmates were evacuated from the infected barracks and taken to nearby Wehrmacht quarters. In fact, the British set Camp I of the Bergen-Belsen camp complex on fire. They had given the former Wehrmacht facility, consisting of barracks and officers' housing, the neutral-sounding name DP Hohne Camp, but in memory of the suffering endured in the concentration camp, the survivors insisted on renaming it DP Camp Bergen-Belsen.[15]

Despite efforts at repatriation, the new housing was totally unable to accommodate all of the concentration camp survivors, and so an attempt was made to find a solution in the nearby town of Celle, located north of Bergen-Belsen. In 1933 only seventy Jews had lived there; former barracks were repurposed, and a total of ten thousand DPs of various nationalities were distributed among four sites around the city. It is unclear exactly how many Jews were among them, but in all probability they constituted 25 percent.[16]

On May 6, 1,135 Polish Jews, along with non-Jewish Poles, were assigned to the Heidekaserne DP camp in Celle. The conditions there were catastrophic, and the food was completely inadequate. The majority of the DPs still had to wear their shabby, filthy inmates' garb, but the fact that their barracks were protected by British soldiers, that no barbed wire hindered their movements, and that the

The first religious service of survivors of the Bergen-Belsen concentration camp
after the liberation in 1945. Rabbi Zvi Asaria is at the center of the photo bearing
the Torah scroll. Yad Vashem / Hadassah Rosensaft.

streets of the city were populated by a mix of refugees from multiple countries
gave them at least a sense that freedom was at hand.

The number of Jews in Celle fluctuated widely. While some of the DPs returned to Belsen, others settled in private accommodations in the British occupation zone. As the situation in Celle slowly stabilized during the summer of
1945, Jewish survivors built a new community that was closely connected with
the Bergen-Belsen DP camp but completely different from the small prewar German-Jewish community.[17]

In the immediate postwar period, both the Americans and the British adhered strictly to the assembly and repatriation plans along national lines that had
been hammered out at Yalta and Potsdam. This segregation of refugees by national origin or citizenship meant that Jews and non-Jews from Eastern Europe
were housed according to their countries of origin—which in turn meant that
Jews from Poland, Russia, or the Ukraine might live in close quarters with former
Nazi collaborators. Moreover, they were often subjected to virulent antisemitism
by non-Jewish DPs.

While the Americans recognized the Jewish DPs as a separate national group
in the fall of 1945 and settled them in special DP camps, the British government

resisted such distinctions until the end of the occupation. The British, whose intensive efforts to save the survivors of Bergen-Belsen had garnered international attention, were, for multiple reasons, nonetheless unwilling to recognize the Jews as a separate group. Great Britain was preoccupied with its own postwar reconstruction, and the costs of occupying the most industrialized (and therefore least agrarian) part of Germany were a great burden. Ideologically, the British insisted that recognizing the identity of a certain ethnic or religious group would revive and give credence to precisely those racial categories that they had entered the war to oppose. But above all, they feared that recognizing Jewish DPs as a national group would facilitate immigration to Palestine and exacerbate the conflict between Arabs and Jews in the territory under British mandate.[18]

Despite British occupation policies, the Committee of Liberated Jews in the British zone, encouraged by decisions made in the American zone, succeeded in establishing separate Jewish housing units, at least in Bergen-Belsen. After a number of incidents and violent protests, the British finally decreed in May 1946 that non-Jewish DPs had to leave the camp, assuring that Bergen-Belsen developed into a de facto all Jewish DP camp. In fact, with a population of nine thousand it was until its dissolution in 1951 the heart of the She'erit Hapletah in the British zone and, indeed, the largest Jewish DP camp in occupied Germany.[19]

In addition to Bergen-Belsen, Jewish DPs in the British zone were housed in a total of forty-five DP camps, many of them very small. A few DPs settled in the cities.[20] In other regions in the British zone, by contrast, Jewish refugees continued to be housed together with Polish forced laborers and prisoners of war, and sometimes even with Lithuanian collaborators.

In early 1946, after border controls were tightened, the Jewish population in the British zone stabilized at approximately sixteen thousand persons. The vast majority were of Polish origin; Hungarian Jews comprised about a quarter, along with a fairly sizable group of Romanian Jews.[21]

THE AMERICAN ZONE AS SAFE HAVEN

The Jewish DPs in the American zone lived primarily in Bavaria, especially in the area controlled by Gen. George S. Patton's Third Army, XX Corps. At the end of 1945, about two-thirds of all Jewish DPs in the American zone lived in this region, located in and around Munich and bordering on Austria and the French occupation zone. Here, not far from the liberated Dachau concentration camp and its numerous subcamps, Jewish DP camps at Feldafing, Landsberg, and Föhrenwald, as well as the Jewish DP hospital in St. Ottilien Monastery, were established. Zalman Grinberg, the later chair of the Central Committee of Liberated Jews in the American zone, managed to commandeer the Benedictine mon-

Entrance and barracks at the Feldafing DP camp. United States Holocaust Memorial Museum / YIVO Institute for Jewish Research.

astery, which had previously served as an SS field hospital, and make it available to Jewish DPs. After the arrival of the Allies, Grinberg, then a young physician, was appointed head of the hospital, which soon cared for four hundred patients, all of them survivors of the death marches.[22]

The first inhabitants of Feldafing DP camp, which was located on the shore of picturesque Lake Starnberg, were also survivors from Dachau and its Kaufering subcamp. In August 1945 more than six thousand persons lived at the former elite Nazi boarding school (Napola), where only a few months earlier a new generation of Nazis had completed their training. Supported by the Jewish Brigade, a unit of the British army recruited in Palestine, and the American Jewish chaplain Abraham Klausner, the Feldafing DPs began to organize themselves. Feldafing therefore became the first purely Jewish DP camp in Germany, even before the Jewish DPs had been recognized as a national group.

In response to reports by ordinary Jewish GIs and Jewish chaplains serving in the American military about the terrible conditions in the camps, as well as pressure exerted by American Jewish organizations, President Truman sent Earl G. Harrison, the newly appointed dean of the Law School at the University of Pennsylvania and a former commissioner for immigration and naturalization under President Roosevelt, to investigate the "conditions and needs" of the displaced persons "particularly those who may be stateless or non-repatriable." The report that Harrison sent to Truman at the end of August 1945 proved to be a political bombshell and had wide-ranging consequences for the immediate and long-term future of the Jewish survivors.

Harrison, who had also served as the U.S. representative to the Inter-Governmental Committee on Refugees, now unexpectedly found himself the champion of the Jewish cause, giving voice to the bitterness and frustration of the survivors three months after liberation. In his report, he clearly endorsed resettlement in Palestine: "The civilized world owes it to this handful of survivors to provide them with a home where they can again settle down and begin to live as human beings." Most dramatically, he added, "As matters now stand, we appear to be treating the Jews as the Nazis treated them except that we do not exterminate them. They are in concentration camps in large numbers under our military guard instead of S.S. troops. One is led to wonder whether the German people, seeing this, are not supposing that we are following or at least condoning Nazi policy."

The outrage evident in this widely publicized report was in some ways overblown, given the substantial relief efforts on the part of the American military, and the comparison between concentration camps and DP camps was certainly unfair. But the report did lead to the official establishment of separate, entirely Jewish DP camps in the American zone, with improved conditions and rations, as well as a certain internal autonomy. U.S. occupation authorities thereby acknowledged and reinforced efforts that had already been undertaken by Jewish relief workers and the DPs themselves. Moreover, a special advisor for Jewish affairs was assigned to assist Gen. Dwight D. Eisenhower, replacing the national liaison officers whom military officials had already appointed for all DPs.

Contrary to the preferences of the State Department (but probably consistent with the desire of the government to limit Jewish immigration into the United States), the Harrison Report explicitly supported the DPs' urgent demand for permission to immigrate to Palestine. But in order to prevent massive Jewish emigration from Europe to their mandate, the British vehemently opposed this demand and continued to claim, rather disingenuously, that giving in to Jewish demands for separate treatment would be tantamount to reintroducing Nazi racial policies. Harrison dismissed this argument without mincing words: "While admittedly it is not normally desirable to set aside particular racial or religious groups from their nationality categories, the plain truth is that this was done for so long by the Nazis that a group has been created which has special needs." In contrast to most Germans and many occupiers, Harrison grasped the historical situation of the surviving European Jews: "Jews as Jews (not as members of their nationality groups) have been more severely victimized than the non-Jewish members of the same or other nationalities." He added, "Refusal to recognize the

Gen. Dwight D. Eisenhower and Gen. George Patton (*right*) at the Feldafing DP camp in the fall of 1945. United States Holocaust Memorial Museum / courtesy of Marc Block.

Jews as such has the effect, in this situation, of closing one's eyes to their former and more barbaric persecution, which has already made them a separate group with greater needs."[23]

The Harrison Report advocated forcefully for separate Jewish DP camps in the American zone and for special status for the Jews as persecutees who were entitled to improved food and accommodations. As a result, starting in late 1945, the American zones in Austria, Italy, and especially Germany drew those Jewish Holocaust survivors who were now facing renewed persecution in the countries of origin to which they had just recently returned. They also attracted Zionist organizations trying to prepare DPs for *aliyah* (immigration) to Palestine.

The Harrison Report helped bring about rapid improvements in the living conditions of Jewish survivors in both material and political terms. Inevitably, however, new decrees mandating increased rations for the victims of Nazism along with the confiscation of German property and German housing to benefit the DPs created tensions and rivalries among Jewish DPs, local Germans, and ethnic German refugees and expellees—all residing in the same territory and struggling to cope with the chaos and shortages of the immediate postwar period. The Jewish DPs were supported not only by UNRRA but also by the American Jewish

Joint Distribution Committee (JDC), which after initial difficulties gaining entry to Germany became, as of the fall of 1945, the main source of aid in the American zone. In the British zone, this role was assumed by the Jewish Relief Unit (JRU), which employed British Jews and numerous German Jews who had managed to flee to Great Britain before the war.[24] In both zones, chaplains attached to the occupation armies along with (for a brief period) soldiers from the Jewish Brigade, which had been formed in Palestine in September 1944 and arrived in Bavaria by way of Italy, gave the liberated Jews immediate aid, comfort, and hope. By the end of 1945, emissaries from Palestine, especially those associated with the Jewish Agency, were playing important roles as political activists and teachers in the Jewish DP camps.

In October 1946 President Truman issued a "Yom Kippur" statement, calling for a compromise on the question of Jewish immigration to Palestine, which was perhaps misinterpreted as favoring the Zionist plan for the partition of Palestine over the British recommendation of autonomy.[25] Already on December 22, 1945, an order from Truman had given DPs only limited preferential status when it came to immigration, but Jewish DPs nonetheless began to apply for U.S. visas. Some contemporary observers noted that if the gates to the United States had swung open earlier, the pressure for mass immigration to Palestine might have been considerably weaker.[26] Given the limited alternatives and the appeal of an actual Jewish homeland, especially for young survivors, virtually all Jewish DPs would come to support the creation of a national Jewish homeland in Palestine, regardless of their own personal preferred destination.

In the spring of 1946, an Anglo-American Committee of Inquiry, which had been formed after publication of the Harrison Report, recommended the immediate granting of one hundred thousand immigration certificates for Palestine. This awakened hopes among the Jews that a Zionist solution might actually be a realistic possibility. Moreover, a 1946 UNRRA "repatriation survey" (conducted among non-Jewish DPs as well) revealed that of the 19,311 adult Jews (persons above the age of fourteen) who responded, 18,072 gave Palestine as their first preference; 95 named other European countries, 393 the United States, and 13 Germany. Dramatically, 1,000 of those surveyed declared their sole second choice to be "the crematorium."[27] The number of those wishing to resettle in Palestine may have been inflated, but the obvious willingness of many DPs to declare their commitment shows the extent to which Jews believed that their collective future depended on the creation of a Jewish state—even though many of them might rather have settled in the United States or elsewhere in the Diaspora, where they could be reunited with their families or simply start a new life under more stable conditions. What some critics today characterize as an unrepresentative or fraudulent result or one given under duress was more probably the sincere response to a personally and politically complex situation.

The British, however, rejected the recommendations of the Anglo-American Committee of Inquiry, and over time, as immigration to Palestine came to be viewed as less realistic, given British intransigence, the enthusiasm reflected in the survey results may also have diminished. Jews sought out other destinations, especially in the United States, where many had family members. Until the United States began to open its doors with the DP Acts of 1948 and especially 1950, there were so many obstacles that only relatively few Jewish survivors were able to immigrate to the United States. As a result of these restrictive immigration policies—and because of the increasing number of Polish and other Eastern European DPs flooding the camps in the American zone—the number of Jews wishing to immigrate to Palestine continued to grow. In fact, the Zionist project of immigration to Palestine and the interests of the Americans in limiting entry to the United States were actually complementary. As Harrison had stated, brushing aside British concerns, "The evacuation of the Jews of Germany and Austria to Palestine will solve the problem of the individuals involved and will also remove a problem from the military authorities who have had to deal with it."[28]

In September 1946, in a step that further reinforced the special status of Jewish DPs, Gen. Joseph T. McNarney, military governor of the American zone and Eisenhower's successor as commander-in-chief of U.S. Occupation Forces in Germany, recognized the Central Committee of Liberated Jews as the official representative of all Jewish DPs with regard to both social welfare and internal self-government. The American army radio station sympathetically spoke of recognizing a "small democracy of 160,000 liberated persons in the heart of Germany."[29] Only a day earlier, however, in a conciliatory speech before Germans in Stuttgart, Secretary of State James Byrnes had underscored the American resolve to support Germany's reconstruction while announcing a retreat from denazification. This speech signaled that the relatively brief "golden age" during which Jewish DPs received privileged American protection and access to rations as a consequence of the Harrison report was about to come to an end.[30] The escalating Cold War, along with the acceleration in reconstruction efforts and the increasing economic and political autonomy of West Germany, brought about a general shift in direction. In 1947 responsibility for the DPs was shifted from UNRRA to the newly founded International Refugee Organization (IRO). In practical terms, this meant that responsibility for the Jewish DPs, especially the organization of immigration and social and material aid (particularly "supplementary" allotments of cigarettes, coffee, and chocolate, which were so valuable on the black market), was transferred to the Jewish aid organizations, especially to the JDC.

THE DEVELOPMENT OF JEWISH DP COMMUNITIES

The largest of the early Jewish DP camps in southern Germany was in Landsberg. A few weeks after the end of the war, historian Israel Kaplan, who survived Kaufering, one of the subcamps of Dachau, wrote: "About five thousand 'Israelites' have been crammed into the Landsberg camp. One of the largest groups among the little heap of Jews, these shards of thousands of decimated communities managed to survive. No complete and unscathed families live here, no people from the same cities or even from the same countries. It is a confusion of lonely individuals. Not a few of them are the last survivors of families counting in the hundreds of members, of a city, or even of an entire district."[31] The former workers' settlement of Föhrenwald near Wolfratshausen was among the first international assembly centers set up by the American army. Initially, it housed about three thousand Soviet, later Polish, Yugoslavian, Hungarian, and Baltic DPs along with about two hundred concentration camp survivors, primarily Lithuanian Jews. In September 1945, after the Harrison Report was published, a decision was made to set up a third large Jewish camp in the row houses of Föhrenwald south of Munich. This was all the more urgent, as new groups of refugees from Eastern Europe were arriving daily, and the two existing camps in Landsberg and Feldafing were already hopelessly overcrowded. But the capacity of Föhrenwald was soon exceeded as well. As early as January 1946 it contained 5,300 inhabitants, and food shortages and accommodations worsened significantly.[32]

As the number of refugees continued to swell, provisional tent cities were built close to the border of the American zone in which refugees could stay for at least a few days or weeks. In the long run, however, more stable DP camps had to be established, and as a consequence of the "illegal" movement of immigrants—tolerated by the Americans—by 1946 the topography of the Jewish DP camps had shifted increasingly toward northern and eastern Bavaria and Hesse and Württemberg.

At the end of 1945, a refugee camp had been erected virtually overnight at a military airport in Leipheim, where infiltrees were transferred.[33] In 1946 a camp for DPs arriving from Poland was erected in Vilseck in the Upper Palatinate that housed up to 1,700 persons.[34] Another facility was made available in Hessisch Lichtenau, near Kassel, in the middle of 1946 for refugees from Poland who had reached the American zone by way of Berlin. Hessisch Lichtenau consisted of four, later of five, individual camps, which by February 1947 were filled to capacity with four thousand inhabitants. As of October 1946, the eight hundred Jews in Bad Salzschlirf, near Fulda, continued to share a camp with Ukrainian DPs.[35] The four DP camps in Ulm, originally inhabited by Polish DPs and then set up for Jewish DPs in 1946, were settled primarily by those who had crossed into the

American zone illegally. The Boelcke barracks in Ulm, which had been cleared of Ukrainian DPs, took in Polish Jews who arrived directly from their harsh refuge in the Soviet Union; their clothing was in tatters, their children were barefoot—and they spoke Russian.[36]

As early as 1945, survivors from Kirchham, one of the subcamps of Flossenbürg, had founded a Jewish community in the small, undamaged town of Pocking in the district of Passau. Because it lay so close to the Austrian border, Pocking soon became a destination for both Jewish and non-Jewish refugees, as well as for Sudeten Germans. The Pocking-Waldstadt DP camp for Jewish refugees was opened in 1946. Remote from the organizational centers of the She'erit Hapletah, the dilapidated barracks of what became the largest Jewish DP camp in the entire American zone housed at times well over seven thousand people.[37] Conditions were so abysmal that Hungarian and Romanian Jews actually began crossing the border back into the Eastern European countries that they had sought to escape. At the same time, the Jewish communities in the surrounding villages and towns grew as more independent residents began to leave the camp.[38]

As these descriptions suggest, DP camps varied widely. At the former Ulan barracks in Bamberg, DPs were housed in the horse stalls of repurposed military barracks. The living quarters were partitioned with thick paper.[39] In the DP sanatorium at Schloss Elmau near Munich, on the other hand, Jews could convalesce in relative luxury.[40] In Markt Indersdorf, where the old monastery was remodeled into an orphanage, the children felt lost among the high, cold walls and ceilings, making it almost impossible for their caregivers to create a warm, homey atmosphere.[41] The Landsberg DP camp, another former military barracks, was surrounded by a high, barbed-wire fence. People slept in bunk beds with straw-filled mattresses and covered themselves with old Wehrmacht blankets. Communal latrines and enormous collective kitchens allowed for no private space.[42]

In Deggendorf, Lower Bavaria, the situation was completely different, yet again. In July 1945 approximately seven hundred German Jews from Theresienstadt were housed there, although it had first been inhabited by Yugoslavian prisoners of war and civilians, as well as by ethnic Germans from Hungary. The non-Jewish inhabitants were resettled under international pressure, and the food situation began to improve.[43] In sharp contrast to the mostly young Eastern European Jewish population in other DP camps, three hundred of the German-Jewish survivors were above the age of sixty, some of them even older than eighty.[44] Later, when a kibbutz with three hundred members was accommodated in the Deggendorf DP camp, the German Jews initially resisted a proposed further influx of Polish Jews. The food in the DP kibbutz was above average in quality, and with a park and a swimming pool, the DP camp generally had the feel of a sanatorium.[45]

Hotel Karwendel in Mittenwald, which had been transformed into a recreation center, with scenes from the concentration camps painted on the front, May 1946. United States Holocaust Memorial Museum / courtesy of Aviva Kempner.

Jewish refugees lived in villages and cities, as well as in DP camps. The number of Jewish "free livers" who resided outside the camps increased over time. Small temporary communities were created, primarily in the vicinity of the liberated concentration camps in southern Germany. DPs also began to settle in the Upper Palatinate in small towns that had largely escaped the ravages of war. Many of them were survivors from the death marches, which in April 1945 had led from Buchenwald to Flossenbürg and from Flossenbürg to Dachau.[46] The "free livers" who moved to towns and villages were attempting to escape the strictures of camp life and to live independently. By the end of January 1946, more than seventeen thousand Jewish DPs in the American zone were registered as living outside the camps. At the end of that year, more than 36,400 were living in 143 communities.[47] In the spring of 1948, there were still 110 primarily DP Jewish communities with a population of 26,316.[48]

In Bavaria and Lower Saxony in particular, this development sometimes led to the creation of DP committees in places where no Jews had previously lived or where no Jewish communities had existed after 1933. While most of these committees were relatively unstable as a result of a constant flux in membership and dissolved after 1948, a few, such as those in Weiden, Amberg, and Regensburg, formed the basis for today's Jewish communities. Of the eighty-three Jews living in Amberg prior to the war, only one woman returned from Theresienstadt. However, the DPs—initially death march survivors and later refugees from Eastern Europe—reestablished Jewish life in the destroyed community by re-consecrating the synagogue and burying their dead in the Jewish cemetery.[49] Immediately after the war, a total of three German Jews lived in Weiden, in the Upper Palatinate region, but the community grew rapidly. Located along the eastern border of Germany, the town was first settled by survivors of the death marches from Flossenbürg and soon became a destination for Eastern European Jews who crossed the border into Germany from Czechoslovakia. By the end of 1946, the Jewish community counted 643 members.[50]

At the end of April 1945, about forty male survivors of the Flossenbürg death marches reached the city of Regensburg. Their primary concern was the provision of food, clothing, and shelter and not the establishment of a permanent Jewish community. Nevertheless, a Jewish committee was formed in May 1945, and an official Jewish community (*Gemeinde*) followed in early October.[51] The number of Jewish inhabitants in this midsized city (population about 100,000) soon increased; 275 Jews lived there by the end of July, and the committee established a synagogue, a tracing bureau, a warehouse, and an office of cultural affairs. Eventually, the Jewish community offered language courses, opened a kindergarten and a school, and even published a local Yiddish newspaper. At the beginning of November 1945, the Jewish population had grown to 450, and in March 1947 about 1,400 Jews lived in Regensburg.[52]

The city had largely escaped destruction, and the availability of adequate housing attracted refugees. At the same time, Regensburg was the seat of UNRRA's district office and later that of the IRO. Jewish aid organizations had also opened offices in the city. In September 1947 the relief organizations headquartered in Regensburg supervised and supported the inhabitants of eighteen Jewish DP camps and thirteen Jewish communities—including those in Weiden, Straubing, Schwandorf, Schwarzenfeld, Cham, Stamsried, Falkenstein, Vilseck, Windischeschenbach, and Wörth an der Donau, with a total population of about twenty thousand.[53] In Lower Bavaria and the Upper Palatinate, the majority of the Jewish DPs lived in urban areas, in contrast to those in Upper Bavaria, with its large camps in Feldafing, Föhrenwald, and Landsberg.[54]

Overall, Jewish life was most likely to develop wherever aid organizations, UNRRA, and the Allies could offer assistance and security. Stuttgart became a center in Württemberg-Baden because in addition to UNRRA, the Jewish Agency and the Hebrew Immigrant Aid Society (HIAS) both maintained offices there.[55]

In addition, a Regional Committee, which had been founded there in 1946, represented the interests of the thirteen Jewish DP camps and the five communities in Württemberg-Baden.[56] The Stuttgart assembly center for Jewish displaced persons, opened in early August 1945, consisted of thirty-four confiscated apartment houses on Reinsburgstrasse. Its first inhabitants were about 250 Polish Jews who had been liberated from one of the subcamps of the Natzweiler concentration camp.[57] In an indication of survivors' urgent desire to seek some link to their destroyed former homes, Stuttgart quickly became a mecca for Jews from the Polish city of Radom.[58] Once the Stuttgart-West camp exceeded capacity, the American army began to house newly arrived "infiltrees" in private dwellings.[59]

However, Munich, the former "capital of the Nazi movement," became the real center of DP society. At the end of 1947, 7,200 DPs were registered with the city's Jewish committee, and by April of the following year, their number had increased to 7,648. Moreover, every day hundreds of DPs from the surrounding camps and communities came to Munich,[60] because each visit to an official agency could be combined with some business transactions. The once elegant Bogenhausen neighborhood, especially the Möhlstrasse and Siebertstrasse, served as the lively hub of the Jewish retail trade.[61]

TRANSIT STATION BERLIN

Berlin also became an important transit point for the "infiltrees" who streamed into the American zone from Poland. A considerable number of them stayed for several years, some even for the rest of their lives, thereby creating a community of DPs whose children and grandchildren became the pillars of West Berlin's postwar Jewish community—until a new wave of post-Soviet immigrants arrived from the East after 1990. By the end of 1945, about fourteen thousand Polish Jews had passed through the transit camps in Berlin—and many more arrived after the shock of the July 1946 pogrom in Kielce.[62] In the hope of stemming the tide, the American military government at first refused to set up anything more than transit centers on the grounds that "the Jewish population resident in Berlin in the main did not desire to have a camp created for them, stating that they had seen enough of camps."[63] However, the number of refugees steadily increased, and it was a more or less open secret that most of them were "infiltrees" who had been smuggled into West Berlin.

The Zionist underground network Bricha (flight) planned to use the DP camps in Berlin as a stopover on the way from Poland to the American zone and from there for the illegal immigration routes to Palestine.[64] From 1946 to 1947, between six thousand and ten thousand Jewish DPs, including many infants and children, resided in the camps run by UNRRA. The best known was a former camp for Soviet prisoners of war in the suburb of Zehlendorf, which the Americans named Düppel Center and the DPs, referring to the nearby S-Bahn train station, called Schlachtensee.[65] In the fall of 1946, the Soviets forced the Bricha to curtail its flight and rescue operations; nonetheless, tens of thousands of Polish Jews moved through the city between November 1945 and January 1947. Several thousand of the approximately ninety thousand to one hundred thousand people who took this route remained in Berlin, at least for a time.[66] The Berlin DP camps were not completely isolated from the Jewish community, but they developed a distinct life of their own. Three schools and two summer camps were opened, and in the fall of 1946, four hundred of a total of one thousand students attended the Hebrew-language Herzl School. Many young people joined Zionist youth organizations of all political persuasions, from the right-wing Betar to the socialist Hashomer Hatzair.

The official partition of Berlin into Eastern and Western sectors in the spring of 1949 changed the character of Jewish life in Berlin and put an end to the DP "problem": many of the DPs in West Berlin—the Americans had left them there as a further sign of U.S. commitment to its "outpost of freedom" within the Soviet zone—were flown out of Berlin in the same airplanes that supplied the city during the Soviet blockade.[67] This "reverse airlift" brought DPs to military bases in the Rhine-Main region, from where they were dispersed throughout the American zone. The departure of most Jewish DPs also represented a further step in the ongoing normalization of Berlin's status as a divided city.

INFLUX FROM THE EAST

By 1946 the few survivors of the Nazi concentration camps no longer constituted the largest group of Jewish DPs. The clear majority was comprised of Polish Jews who had been repatriated from their harsh but ultimately life-saving sojourn in the Soviet Union and then fled westward from hardships and antisemitism in postwar Poland. Some of them had been able to flee ahead of the advancing Wehrmacht to those portions of Poland that had come under Soviet control after the Hitler-Stalin Pact of August 1939. As suspect Polish aliens, they were then deported to forced labor camps and "special settlements" in Siberia and other remote regions in the Soviet interior—together with local Jews who had only recently come under Soviet dominion and had been denounced as "capitalists," Zionists, or other "undesirable" elements. There are no accurate statistics: perhaps between 350,000 and 400,000 Poles, Jews, and non-Jews. By February 1940 about 220,000 Jewish and non-Jewish Poles had been deported from eastern Poland to the interior of the Soviet Union, often having been arrested in the middle of the night or early morning. They were transported to collective farms (*kolkhozes*) and forced labor camps, where they worked under extremely difficult conditions. In sharp contrast, however, to the Jews left behind in German-occupied territories, they were not subject to systematic extermination. Their status changed after the German invasion of June 1941. In July 1941 the London-based Polish government-in-exile negotiated an "amnesty" with Stalin that provided for the formation of a Polish army under Gen. Władysław Anders, along with the release of Jewish and non-Jewish Polish citizens from the labor camps.

This precipitated a surge southward into the Central Asian republics, where the newly freed Poles hoped for better conditions based on "[false] rumors of a warmer climate and the abundance of fruit and other foods."[68] What they found instead was starvation and poverty, typhus and malaria, and severe overcrowding caused by the massive wartime evacuation of Soviet citizens, as well as deportations. At the same time, life on the "Tashkent Front" presented an extraordinary profusion of shared wartime opportunities and dangers, including evacuated universities, Red Army recruiters, threatening NKVD (People's Commissariat for Internal Affairs) agents, and local Uzbeks, who responded to this sudden influx of persons from the West with a complex mixture of incomprehension, suspicion, and generosity. After the final collapse of political relations between the Soviet Union and the Polish government-in-exile in spring 1943, Polish-Jewish refugees in Central Asia were cut off from their political representatives and the limited support they had provided. Refugee Jews struggled to survive, partially aided by relief packages that were organized by international Jewish organizations such as the JDC and the Jewish Agency and that arrived by way of Iran.[69]

Of the approximately 3.3 million prewar Polish Jews, only about 350,000 survived the war. Those Jews who had been forced into Soviet exile, in some cases from Warsaw to Białystok or Lviv, then to the Siberian steppes, and finally southward to Uzbekistan and Kazakhstan, comprised the majority of the survivors in Poland after liberation. At least 230,000 Polish Jews survived in the Soviet Union, of whom 180,000 returned to Poland immediately after the end of the war. By the end of 1946, the number of repatriates had risen to about 200,000.[70]

There was a brief revival of Jewish culture in places like Łódź and the so-called "recovered territories" assigned to Poland after the German defeat such as Breslau (Wrocław), where surviving Polish Jews were resettled in areas from which ethnic Germans had fled or been expelled. Nonetheless, many of the tragically few Jews who had survived in hiding or in partisan groups or had been able to return from concentration camps or labor camps, as well as those repatriated from the Soviet Union, sought to escape the "vast graveyard" of postwar Poland. Those who returned to what had been their homes were often met with incredulous stares, bitterness, and even outright violence. They were "cursed in the streets as Yids, pushed out of public transportation; at night, attempts were

Arrival of the first refugees from Eastern Europe at the Zeilsheim DP camp in 1945.
United States Holocaust Memorial Museum / photograph by E. M. Robinson /
courtesy of Alice Lev.

made to break into their dwellings." Some refugees who reached the DP camps
in American-occupied Germany carried with them the typewritten notifica-
tions according to which Jews who wished to reclaim their former possessions
and property were given ten days to pay "damages" of 10,000 or 20,000 zloty to
the local social welfare office under penalty of death "for the harassment of the
Polish population and for their enrichment by [Polish] property."[71] About twelve
hundred Jews were murdered in Poland between 1945 and 1947.[72] Just as the Allies were repatriating most of the (non-Jewish) DPs gathered in Germany, a new
wave of Jewish refugees, escaping privation and antisemitism, poured into the
American zone in the spring of 1947, especially from Poland but from Hungary,
Romania, and Czechoslovakia as well.

DESTINATION PALESTINE

In the late summer and early fall of 1945, the Bricha, a loose network of Zionist
activists from Palestine—former partisans, veterans of the Jewish Brigade, Jewish soldiers from the United States, and military chaplains—began to smuggle

Jewish survivors through the Soviet zone of occupation into the American zone. From there, they hoped to facilitate immigration to Palestine, whether legal or illegal.[73] Originally, the activists thought that they could bring Jews to Palestine directly by way of Romania and then Italy, but the British responded by blockading access to Italy. The United States, on the other hand, quietly left open the gates to the territory that it occupied, and as a result the destination shifted rapidly. After the Kielce pogrom of July 1946, about seventeen thousand Jewish refugees left Poland each month, among them many who had been repatriated from the Soviet Union.[74] American Jewish soldiers and military chaplains were intensely involved with these Zionist efforts. American cigarettes, coffee, and chocolate, which had been "liberated" from military warehouses or sent to Jewish GIs by parents or wives back home, facilitated border crossings in territories controlled by the Soviets, who, at least officially, did not even recognize the existence of displaced persons. Adamant about the return of Soviet forced laborers and prisoners of war, the Soviets also demanded the repatriation of all refugees but were willing to tolerate this semiclandestine flight.[75]

In a 1992 interview, former chaplain Herbert Friedman recalled, with evident pride, how supplies of three hundred cartons of cigarettes per truckload helped to placate border guards. The cartons had been donated by Friedman's father's Jewish congregation in New Haven and by Jewish GIs, who could otherwise have used the cigarettes, which cost them only seven dollars at the PX, to acquire all manner of "occupation bargains." Eventually, the cigarettes would be supplied directly by the JDC, which transported them from Antwerp to Berlin via Bremerhaven. As Friedman described the route, six army trucks using "liberated" gasoline made their way at dusk from Berlin to Stettin (Szczecin), each manned by two "Palestinians" (as the Jews from Palestine were called at the time), one of them as driver, the other riding shotgun. Upon arrival at about midnight, they found that agents from the Bricha had already assembled Jewish refugees on the Polish side of the border; some three hundred persons, fifty to a truck, were quickly loaded. By dawn, the convoy with its human cargo was back in West Berlin. It was a daunting operation—an adventure for the Americans and "Palestinians," and an uncertain and frightening risk for the determined refugees. But it was this massive influx of Polish Jewish infiltrees into the American zone that made possible a DP world in occupied Germany, two-thirds of whose population had survived beyond the front as a result of Stalin's deportations.[76]

However, the DP camps, which were already vastly overcrowded, could hardly hold the "infiltrees" now flooding in from Eastern Europe. In this situation, the agricultural *kibbutzim* and *hakhsharot* settlements, which were designed to prepare people for immigration to Palestine, served to take in much of the overflow. UNRRA, the JDC, and the Jewish Agency were in agreement—

though for different reasons—that the establishment of these communal agricultural training centers could take the pressure off the DP camps while also giving young adults employment and training for their future lives in a Jewish state.[77]

The earliest *hakhsharot* were created as soon as Jews began to organize in the American zone of occupation. They developed as a result of Zionist activities that had already started in the concentration camps: sixteen Buchenwald survivors comprised the very first class of pioneers, so-called *halutzim*, in postwar Germany in Kibbutz Buchenwald near Weimar. Shortly before the final borders of the zones were established, Kibbutz Buchenwald moved to Gehringshof near Fulda, where young German Jews had prepared themselves for immigration to Palestine prior to the war.[78] The *kibbutz* was constantly flooded with applications for membership because it promised communal life and work in a purely Jewish setting. Neither adherence to Zionism nor any other political party was a prerequisite for membership, and the founders of Kibbutz Buchenwald did not ask questions: for them, the catastrophe of the Holocaust provided the sole unifying force necessary for a national Jewish community.

Former concentration camp inmates also founded Kibbutz Nili near Nuremberg on farmland that had previously been owned by Julius Streicher, the publisher of the notorious antisemitic journal, *Der Stürmer*. This startling transformation made the site a destination for visits by reporters and witnesses at the Nuremberg trials. The Yiddish poet Avrom Sutskever, for example, who testified before the tribunal on the destruction of the Jewish community of Vilnius, gave his meeting with the young *halutzim* on the farm literary form while its former proprietor, "with his green, frog-like face," was facing the court. In his poem, "In Streicher's Palace," Sutskever is received by a young woman on Streicher's former farm, over which a blue and white flag now fluttered. Dehumanized under Nazi rule and given the number "ninety thousand and one," she relates the traumatic experience of the sixty inhabitants and speaks with pride about what has now been achieved. Finally, the poet is offered a fresh glass of milk: "Someone brings me milk from Streicher's cow / And he swears that one may drink it."[79]

Other *kibbutzim*, comparable in structure to the ones at Buchenwald and Nili but ideologically aligned with specific Zionist parties, were founded over time. Numerous such *kibbutz* groups had organized in Poland before the Bricha brought them to Germany.[80] Nonetheless, the emotional connection between group members was far more powerful than any ideological positions they might have held. Because the *kibbutzim* functioned as homeland and family for the orphaned survivors, efforts were made not to break up the arriving groups.[81] At the Hindenburg barracks in Ulm, the newly arrived members of Kibbutz Dror wrote in blue paint on the wall of their block, "We were 65 *haverim* in Kłodzko, and 65 we remain."[82]

Many of the *kibbutzim* were integrated into larger DP camps or set up in their immediate vicinity. For example, the *kibbutz* in Greifenberg—a former SS sanatorium—was attached to the Landsberg DP camp.[83] The training programs of the individual *kibbutzim* were supposed to take into account the various needs of a future Jewish state and offer alternatives to the supposed "demoralization" produced by transitory life in the DP camps. Kibbutz Khovshe Hayam (Conquerors of the sea) even trained sailors on the Danube at Deggendorf for service in a future Israeli navy.[84] By the end of May 1947, there were 278 *kibbutzim* with a total membership of 16,342 in the American zone alone.

The She'erit Hapletah initially comprised a society in which the youngest and the oldest generations were nearly entirely absent. They had almost always been immediately dispatched to the gas chambers. Thus, at the end of 1945 there were children under the age of three, only a few younger than seventeen, and hardly any persons over sixty-five.[85] In early 1946, Brajndl Kalka, age seventy-two, was considered something of a miracle. She served as grandmother for almost one hundred children in the Landsberg camp—of her own eight children, only two sons survived, and her eighteen grandchildren and ten great-grandchildren had all been murdered as well.[86]

The influx from Eastern Europe increasingly transformed the demography of DP society. During the first winter after the war, the voices of children could be heard who had lived with Polish families using false identities, who had been hidden away in monasteries and convents, or who had survived in the forests among the partisans. However, it was above all the arrival of repatriated Polish Jews from the Soviet Union that led to far-reaching changes in terms of age and family structures. Despite poverty, hunger, and disease, entire families or at least several family members sometimes managed to survive in Siberia and the Central Asian Soviet republics. A report published by the JDC in 1946 described the arrival of trains filled with Jews who had been repatriated: "In Lodz, Radom, Krakow and Warsaw, the resident Jews turned out to welcome the repatriates and to gape. They came not to stare at rags and hunger-ridden faces—any Jew who survived the Nazis inside Poland was familiar enough with these things. They came, instead, to gaze on walking miracles—*entire Jewish families*, complete with fathers, mothers and children!"[87] Many of these repatriates then made their way out of Poland into American-occupied Germany. For example, in 1946 a widow with four children arrived as a DP in postwar Kassel. The family, from the outskirts of Warsaw, had tried to escape the German bombardment at the beginning of the war. Both of her older sons had been arrested while trying to flee to the Soviet-occupied part of eastern Poland, and her husband died in the Soviet Union. Nonetheless, she and four children were able to return to Poland in 1946 from where they fled to the West.[88]

Young families at the Neu-Freimann DP camp in Munich. United States
Holocaust Memorial Museum / courtesy of Saul Sorrin.

By November 1946 the community of survivors, initially with almost no
children, had become a society in which, due to the influx from Eastern Europe
and the high birth rate, 20 percent of the Jewish DPs in the American zone were
below the age of seventeen. Moreover, of the more than twenty-three thousand
children and adolescents, almost 40 percent were below the age of five.[89] The Jewish DPs in the Western zones of occupation experienced a veritable baby boom
that testified to their vitality and resilience. Their birth rate was in fact considerably higher than that of the surrounding German population.[90]

The DP population reached its high-water mark in 1947. The stream of refugees from Eastern Europe far exceeded the small number able to emigrate from
the DP camps in Germany. In addition to Polish and Lithuanian Jews, the Western zones of occupation were also home to smaller groups of Jewish refugees
from other countries. Their numbers continued to increase even after the official closure of the borders: at the end of 1947, eight thousand Romanian Jews
lived in Germany.[91] After the government of Edvard Beneš collapsed in February
1948, approximately eleven hundred Czechoslovakian Jews sought refuge in the
American zone.[92] At the same time, Hungarian Jews attempted to reach the West
through Czechoslovakia. Despite countermeasures taken by the Hungarian and
Czechoslovakian governments, between four thousand and five thousand Hungarian Jews arrived in the American occupation zones in Germany and Austria.[93] The total number of non-Polish or Lithuanian Jews increased to about

ten thousand persons.[94] The British refusal to follow the recommendations of the Anglo-American Committee of Inquiry, which called for one hundred thousand entry permits to Palestine, and U.S. insistence on maintaining a restrictive immigration policy led to the development of an almost exclusively Eastern European Jewish transit society under Allied protection in the American zone. Despite very differing wartime experiences, the She'erit Hapletah began to build a new Jewish society on occupied German soil.

ATINA GROSSMANN is Professor of history at Cooper Union in New York. She has been a fellow at the Institute for Advanced Study in Princeton, the American Academy in Berlin, the United States Holocaust Memorial Museum, and the Davis Center at Princeton University. Her publications include *Jews, Germans, and Allies: Close Encounters in Occupied Germany* (on which parts of this section are based) and *Wege in der Fremde: Deutsch-jüdische Begegnungsgeschichte zwischen Feldafing, New York und Teheran;* and as a coeditor, *After the Nazi Racial State: Difference and Democracy in Germany and Europe and Crimes of War: Guilt and Denial in the Twentieth Century,* as well as *Shelter from the Holocaust: Rethinking Jewish Survival in the Soviet Union* (with M. Edele and S. Fitzpatrick) and *The Joint Distribution Committee: 100 Years of Jewish History* (with A. Patt, L. Levi, and M. Maud), both forthcoming from Wayne State University Press in 2018.

TAMAR LEWINSKY is curator of contemporary history at the Jewish Museum Berlin. Her publications include *Unterbrochenes Gedicht: Jiddische Literatur im Nachkriegsdeutschland, 1944–1950* and *Displaced Poets: Jiddische Schriftsteller im Nachkriegsdeutschland, 1945–1951.*

NOTES

1. A voluminous literature has developed over the past twenty years on the history of Jewish survivors who arrived in occupied Germany as DPs. See, for example, M. Brenner (1997); A. Grossmann (2012), which contain greater detail on various aspects of this and of the following chapter; W. Jacobmeyer (1985); A. A. Königseder and J. Wetzel (1994); and Z. W. Mankowitz (2002). For a good general overview of the DPs, see M. Wyman (1998) and M. Marrus (1985).

2. Based on the first American Displaced Persons Act, infiltrees were defined as those survivors who for one reason or another arrived in occupied Germany after December 22, 1945. The Displaced Persons Act of 1950 established January 1, 1949, as the "cutoff date" for entry into the zone, a date that tended to recognize the realities of Jewish DP migration.

3. See A. Holian (2011), p. 3, with reference to E. Kulischer (1948), p. 305.

4. A. Holian (2011), p. 3; W. Jacobmeyer (1985), pp. 82–84.

5. See, for example, M. Proudfoot (1956) for more on Allied DP policies.

6. See, among others, Arnold-Forster (1946). See also T. Zahra (2011).

7. J. A. Berger (1947), pp. 46, 51. As always, the statistics are inexact. The broad range of figures is the result of the time the target group count was taken and by whom and according to what definition.

8. Here, too, the figures vary according to source. Some speak of fifty thousand to seventy thousand having been liberated from the concentration camps. A description of the deaths after liberation is contained in B. Shepherd's (2005) study of British efforts in Bergen-Belsen.

9. On p. 334, M. Proudfoot (1956) speaks of only about twenty thousand Jews liberated in the Western zones. Historians give higher figures: on p. 28, H. Lavsky (2002), for example, speaks of sixty thousand to eighty thousand Jewish concentration camp survivors in Germany and Austria.

10. Z. Wahrhaftig (1946), p. 75.

11. M. Proudfoot (1956), pp. 259, 340. The statistics are unreliable here as well. For example, Donald Niewyk states that in 1945 Jews were "less than one percent of the 14 million refugees from Hitler's war, although by 1947, they made up a far larger proportion—perhaps as much as one third—of the approximately 700,000 unrepatriated, displaced persons in Europe" (in D. Niewyk [1998], p. 21).

12. In the introduction to his pioneering book *Between Memory and Hope: The Survivors of the Holocaust in Occupied Germany* (2002), Zeev W. Mankowitz, like many historians, refers to the generally accepted total number of Jewish survivors constituting the She'erit Hapletah as "the collective identity of some 300,000 displaced persons in Occupied Germany, Austria and Italy."

13. H. Lavsky (2002), p. 59; P. Kemp, (1997). See also J. Reilly et al. (1997), p. 25; A. Königseder and J. Wetzel (1994), pp. 173–174. Regarding the "handover" rather than, strictly speaking, the "liberation," of the camp by the Germans, who feared the spread of diseases, see B. Shepherd (2005).

14. H. Lavsky (2002), p. 60.

15. H. Lavsky (2010), p. 227.

16. T. Rahe, "Die jüdische DP-Gemeinde," in Gesellschaft für Christlich-jüdische Zusammenarbeit Celle e. V. (ed.) (2005).

17. T. Rahe (2005), pp. 16–17.

18. A. Kochavi (2001), pp. 32–56.

19. A. Königseder and J. Wetzel (1994), p. 184; Lavsky (2002).

20. H. Lavsky (2002), p. 61.

21. H. Lavsky (2002), p. 60; "Displaced Persons in UNRRA-Controlled Assembly Centers," report dated November 16, 1946, in ARMS, UNRRA, S-400, box 3, file 20.

22. On the St. Ottilien Monastery, see T. Kleinjung (1998).

23. The quotations above come from "The Harrison-Report," in appendix B, L. Dinnerstein (1982), pp. 305, 300–301, 295. The text is also available at http://www.ushmm.org /exhibition/displaced-persons/resourc1.htm.

24. Hagit Lavsky found that the joint was given immediate access to Buchenwald and Belsen; see Lavsky (2010), p. 233. For more on the British zone, see H. Lavsky (2002).

25. The British attributed the American position to the Democrats, who were trying to win Jewish voters, and the "Zionist lobby" because of the impending midterm elections. See A. Kochavi (1990), esp. p. 540; J. Reilly et al. (eds.) (1997).

26. See, for example, A. Hyman (1993), p. 373.

27. A. Hyman (1993), p. 370. See also Z. W. Mankowitz (2002), pp. 124–125; and Wyman (1998), p. 139.

28. L. Dinnerstein (1982), p. 305.

29. A. Hyman (1993), pp. 153–160.

30. Samuel Gringauz found "in retrospect" that the time between the fall of 1945 and the summer of 1947 was "a kind of golden age"; see S. Gringauz (1948), p. 509.

31. I. Kaplan (1948), pp. 45–51.

32. A. Königseder and J. Wetzel (1994), pp. 99, 102.

33. UNRRA—US-Zone Germany—History Report No. 30, History of Individual Camps, Jewish Camp Leipheim Airport (District No. 5), June 1947 (no exact date), in ARMS, UNRRA, S-425, box 6, file 17; letter from the headquarters of the Third U.S. Army and Eastern Military District to the UNRRA director for Bavaria regarding "Movement of Infiltrees," December 24, 1945, in ARMS, UNRRA S-425, box 10, file 12; see also Fassl et al. (eds.) (2011).

34. D. Dörner (2009), p. 133.

35. Newspaper editors, "Undzer onhoyb," *Zaltsshlirfer lebn*, October 1946.

36. Mordkhe Libhaber, "In di naye yidishe lagern," *Undzer veg*, September 6, 1946, p. 4.

37. A. Königseder and J. Wetzel (1994), pp. 259–260; "Lager Poking," *Der nayer moment*, November 22, 1946.

38. "Yoman ha-mishlahat shel ha-sokhnut ha-yehudit le-Eretz Yisrael be-Germani-yah ha-kvushah," no. 3, Munich, February 9, 1947, p. 11, in CZA, S 25/5231.

39. H. Jablokoff (1969), pp. 510–511.

40. E. Landau, "PURIM AUF ELMAU," 1946, in YIVO, RG 294.1, folder 535, reel 46, Bl. 1060–1066.

41. "Chana Levita to Sochnut, Indersdorf," January 16, 1948, in CZA, S 86/343.

42. I. Heymont (1982), p. 8.

43. "The Jewish Community of Bavaria," report by Eli Rock, senior field representative, Third Army, October 25, 1945, in YIVO 294.1, folder 164, reel 17, Bl. 34–49.

44. "Fun di yidishe lagern in Daytshland," *Undzer veg*, April 15, 1946, p. 10.

45. "Camp Deggendorf," report by Mr. Holger, undated, in YIVO, RG 294.1, folder 164, reel 17, Bl. 31.

46. Skriebeleit (2009), pp. 223–224. As of the end of August 1944, Jewish inmates were transferred to do forced labor in arms factories. Since the end of the year, transports had also arrived from Groß-Rosen and Auschwitz. At the time of liberation, the number of people in the Flossenbürg camp complex came to more than twenty-two thousand.

47. Z. W. Mankowitz (2002), pp. 21–22.

48. H. Maor (1961), p. 18.

49. D. Dörner (2009), pp. 133–134.

50. S. Schott (2009), p. 117; M. Brenner and R. Höpfinger (eds.) (2009).

51. A. Angersdorfer (2009), p. 93.

52. UNRRA—US-Zone Germany—History Report No. 30, History of Individual Camps, Jewish Community, Regensburg (District 3), March 1947, in ARMS, UNRRA, S-425, box 6, file 17.

53. A. Angersdorfer (2009), pp. 91–92.

54. Rock, "The Jewish Community of Bavaria."

55. S. Dietrich and J. Schulze-Wessel (1998), p. 53.

56. S. Dietrich and J. Schulze-Wessel (1998), p. 57.

57. S. Dietrich and J. Schulze-Wessel (1998), pp. 46, 48–49.

58. L. Schwarz (1953), p. 40; S. Dietrich and J. Schulze-Wessel (1998), p. 50.

59. S. Dietrich and J. Schulze-Wessel (1998), p. 50.

60. Letter from the Jewish Committee to the Zentralkomitee regarding statistical information from Munich, November 30, 1947, in ITS, F18–151.

61. A. Kauders and T. Lewinsky (2006), p. 190. See also K. Crago-Schneider (2010), pp. 167–194.

62. A. Grossmann (2012), p. 118. See also J. Maginnis (1971), pp. 323–329.

63. Letter from Lt. Col. Harold Mercer, chief of Displaced Persons and Welfare Section (OMGUS), February 5, 1946, in LAB, OMGUS, 4/20–1/10.

64. See A. Nachama (1995), p. 272; A. Königseder (1997). On the organization of illegal immigration in general, see I. Zertal (1999).

65. According to UNRRA statistics, there were exactly 6,644 Jewish DPs in Berlin in May, including more than a thousand small children. See "Berlin Reports," in ARMS, UNRRA, A/399, box 1, file 2. See also A. Königseder (1998); R. Gay (2002).

66. A. Nachama (1995), p. 272.

67. See, for example, A. Grossmann (2007), pp. 238–247.

68. See S. Pettiss and L. Taylor (2004), pp. 145–149. The quotation is from A. Pettiss and L. Taylor (2004), p. 149. For more on the Soviet evacuations to Central Asia, see R. Manley's (2009) study. See also N. Belsky (2015).

69. On the JDC operation, see A. Grossmann (2015). This crucial story of Jewish death and survival in the Soviet Union during World War II has only recently received sustained attention in Holocaust studies. Considerable research is in progress (which could not be adequately reflected in this volume, published in German in 2012), and much more further research is required. See D. Engel (2008); J. T. Gross (1991), p. 73. Other estimates speak of up to a half-million; see J. Litvak (1997), p. 147; J. Litvak (1983); K. Sword (1991), p. 145. Despite the scant attention paid by researchers to these survivors—according to Z. W. Mankowitz (2002), p. 19, "fully two-thirds of the *She'erith Hapletah*"—their existence was fully noted by contemporary observers. See, for example, the discussion in K. Pinson (1947) or in K. Grossmann (1951), pp. 14–15. Among the more recent publications, see L. Jockusch and T. Lewinsky (2010); J. Goldlust (2012); A. Grossmann (2012); E. Adler (2014). For an overview of the current research on both deportation and evacuation of Jews in the wartime Soviet Union, see Mark Edele, Sheila Fitzpatrick, Atina Grossmann, eds. *Shelter from the Holocaust: Rethinking Jewish Survival in the Soviet Union* (Detroit: Wayne State University Press, 2017).

70. From the perspective of Soviet sources, see A. Kaganovitch (2010); A. Kaganovitch (2012).

71. "Report on Conditions in Poland," July 1, 1946, PDP 1–3, contains such reports, in CJA, 5A1/39. These experience were also described in, among other places, Skorneck, "Report on Berlin," February 21, 1946, in YIVO, RG 294.1, folder 516, reel 45.

72. J. T. Gross (2006).

73. See Y. Bauer (1970a).

74. Details in Z. W. Mankowitz (2002), pp. 17–19; in accordance with two Polish-Soviet agreements (September 1944 and July 1945), at least 195,000 Polish Jews were repatriated between the end of 1944 and mid-1946.

75. Notwithstanding, according to the census of October 29, 1946, 4,500 Jews were still registered in the Soviet zone, primarily in Berlin and Leipzig. Presumably there were more, however, because in contrast to the Western zones, many were not registered as Jews. But most of them moved on, and by the end of 1946 only 250 remained, for example, in Leipzig (in comparison to 2,700 "racially persecuted"), a minute figure in comparison to the approximately 250,000 Eastern European DPs who landed in the British zone and especially in the American zone. For more on the situation in the Soviet zone, see L. Mertens (2001); R. Willingham (2004); H. Niether (2015).

76. It was precisely the Jews living in the border region created by the Molotov-Ribbentrop Pact of 1939 who either were not deported or were unable to flee eastward who fell prey to the murderous German onslaught and made up a good proportion of the victims of the Final Solution; see, for example, T. Snyder (2011).

77. A. Patt (2009), pp. 55–57.

78. Y. T. Baumel (1997), pp. 26, 30–31; Patt (2009), pp. 23–25, 31–35.

79. A. Sutskever (1963), vol. 1, pp. 562–563.

80. Patt (2009), p. 68.

81. UNRRA—US-Zone Germany—History Report No. 21, History of Individual Camps, in ARMS, UNRRA, S-425, box 6, file 11.

82. Mordkhe Libhaber, "In di naye yidishe lagern," *Undzer veg*, September 25, 1946, p. 13.

83. A. Patt (2009), p. 63.

84. S. Katsherginski (1955), pp. 432–433; H. Jablokoff (1969), p. 527.

85. A. Patt (2009), p. 210.

86. B. Ben-Neryja, "Brajndl Kalka: Di elteste jidisze froj fun der szejris-haplejto," *Landsberger Lager-Cajtung*, February 15, 1946, p. 10.

87. Report by two Polish rabbis who survived in the Soviet Union, in *J.D.C. Digest* 5/5 (July 1946), p. 1.

88. Letter from Alta Kruk in Kassel to the aid community in California, January 28, 1948, in YIVO, RG 1169, box 1.

89. A. Patt (2009), pp. 210–211.

90. A. Patt (2009), p. 211. For more on the baby boom, see A. Grossmann (2007), chap. 5.

91. Cited in Y. Gar (1957), vol. 3, p. 106.

92. K. Grossmann (1951), pp. 15–16.

93. K. Grossmann (1951), p. 16.

94. Letter from Samuel Haber, Federation of Hungarian Jews, to AJDC Paris, October 3, 1947, in USHMM, RG-68.066M GI 5B3 C-45.020.

2 AN AUTONOMOUS SOCIETY

The Jewish survivors in the liberated Bergen-Belsen concentration camp began to organize themselves even as the misery and dying continued. A provisional Jewish committee was elected on April 18, 1945, whose most urgent demand was that, contrary to stated British policy, Jews be given their own housing, separate from the rest of the multinational DP population within the camps. Under the chairmanship of its charismatic leader, Josef Rosensaft, the committee quickly expanded its sphere of activities. As the political representative of the Jews in meetings and negotiations with the British occupation, it also organized the rehabilitation of survivors and the search for surviving family members.[1]

When the provisional committee announced its first conference in the British zone of occupation at the end of September 1945, just as the Belsen trials were beginning in Lüneburg, more than two hundred delegates representing forty-two DP camps and communities, including German Jews from the Rhineland and displaced persons from Lübeck and Neustadt on the Baltic Sea, came to Bergen-Belsen from all over Germany. From then until the committee's dissolution in 1950, Rosensaft was the acknowledged chair of the Central Committee and the leader of Jewish efforts at self-administration in the British zone. Norbert Wollheim, a German Jew who had survived Auschwitz, became deputy chair, and he represented the concerns of the newly founded Jewish communities. Wollheim, who was born in Berlin in 1913 and grew up there, had helped to organize the children's transports to England in 1938 and had been responsible for the professional and trade schools run by the Reich Representation of German Jews (Reichsvertretung der Juden in Deutschland) until 1941. On March 12, 1943, he and his family were deported to Auschwitz; he was the sole survivor.[2]

As early as July 25, 1945, representatives from the British zone had traveled to St. Ottilien in Bavaria in order to work with the Jews in the Western occupation zones in Germany and Austria to facilitate immigration to Palestine and to improve the living conditions in the DP camps. This conference was the only one in which displaced persons from the American and the British zones of occupation met together, and it was the high point of a series of gatherings and proceedings in the American zone since the end of the war in May. The confer-ence began with the almost one hundred participants singing a partisan hymn whose refrain, "Mir zenen do!" (We are here!), was picked up in the opening speech by Zalman Grinberg, later the chair of the Central Committee of Liber-ated Jews in the American zone. That refrain was declared the motto of the DP organization.[3] The conclusion of the conference was celebrated in a highly sym-bolic ceremony in the Bürgerbräu cellar in Munich. Here, amid desecrated Torah scrolls, in the same place from where in 1923 Adolf Hitler had begun his Putsch, a declaration was read aloud demanding a Jewish state and the recognition of national rights for the Jewish people.[4]

As in the British zone, the survivors in southern Germany had begun to organize immediately after liberation. More precisely, they simply transformed the organizational structures that had been created in the underground into legal ones. The roots of the Central Committee of the Liberated Jews in the American zone, which since October 1945 had represented the interests of the DPs in in-teractions with the American army and aid organizations, lay in the subcamps of the Dachau concentration camp. Members of Zionist organizations who had been transported from the Kovno (Kaunas) ghetto in Lithuania to Dachau-Kaufering took leading roles immediately after their liberation.[5] Among them was Zalman Grinberg, a young physician from Kovno who directed the Jewish DP hospital that had been established at the Benedictine monastery of St. Ottil-ien. The monastery attracted public interest at the end of May, when hundreds of DPs, representatives of the military government, and the United Nations Relief and Rehabilitation Administration (UNRRA) attended a concert given by sur-viving members of the former Kovno ghetto orchestra.[6]

A year later, the Central Committee, which was now officially recognized by the U.S. military government as representing the Jews in the American zone, began to organize the rapidly growing She'erit Hapletah from its base in Munich. The July 1945 conference at St. Ottilien and the first conference of liberated Jews in the American occupation zone, which took place in Munich city hall on Janu-ary 27–28, 1946, were milestones on the path to official status and to international recognition for the Central Committee.[7] In the Western zones of occupation, overarching structures at the zonal level and the relative autonomy of the local committees, which soon formed in all of the DP camps and cities where DPs lived, led to a high degree of self-organization. Externally, the local DP commit-tees formulated their material and political concerns and demands in relation to the Allies, UNRRA and its successor organization, the International Refugee Organization (IRO), and the other aid organizations; internally, they facilitated a fundamental shift in DP society, which, though it remained financially depen-dent, nonetheless developed certain autonomous structures.

Whereas centralized policies directed from Bergen-Belsen fostered a certain continuity in the British zone, the Central Committee in the American zone soon gave up its representational status and transformed itself into an administrative and organizational apparatus with responsibility for a growing number of Jewish refugees. In 1947 Salomon Adler-Rudel, who at the time served as director of international relations for the Jewish Agency, characterized the Central Committee as probably the most important Jewish organization on the European continent.[8]

NEW OPPORTUNITIES

The most urgent challenges of the self-administered DP committees and the aid organizations involved employing and educating the survivors and refugees. Years of persecution had robbed Jewish displaced persons of formal education, and even those who had gone to school during the interwar years needed the kind of training that would enable them to pursue job opportunities after emigration.

In the British zone, survivors with an academic background or teaching experience had since June 1945 taught in the first elementary school in Bergen-Belsen.[9] In southern Germany, schools were opened in Landsberg, Föhrenwald, and Feldafing in early September. The smaller DP camps lacked such facilities, but Jews did not want to send the few surviving children to German schools. When children of all ages began to arrive in Germany with the Bricha a more broad-based educational system had to be established. In the American zone, where the number of children and adolescents rose most precipitously, a total of sixty-six schools, including a Hebrew high school in Munich, served a student population of 11,240 in 1946. There were also sixty-two nursery schools for pre-school population of about two thousand.[10]

The case of Bad Salzschlirf, a small town in Hesse, illustrates the multiple educational challenges confronting the changing DP society. Seventy-six children attended the Jewish elementary school that had opened in July 1946 shortly after the founding of the camp. Some of the children had survived the Holocaust in their countries of origin, but many had been repatriated to Poland from Central Asia. Finding a manageable and educationally appropriate solution was well-nigh hopeless, given the extreme variety of educational levels and life experiences among these children. Age differences of as much as six years in a single class were not unusual, and a common language was almost impossible to find. The students spoke a mixture of "Russian, Polish, Kazakh, and Tatar," but according to one teacher, their mother tongue was just as foreign to them as Jewish culture.[11] Teachers, Zionist groups, and local committees also vehemently disagreed about whether classes should be given in Yiddish or Hebrew, that is, whether Jewish history should be taught based on an Eastern European Jewish narrative or from a Zionist perspective. A unitary curriculum was developed only in 1947, when the Central Committee, the American Jewish Joint Distribution Committee (JDC), and the Jewish Agency created a department of education. Despite protests from non-Zionists, the students were increasingly taught based on the school system of the Yishuv—not least with the help and support of teachers from Palestine.[12]

The influence of the Yishuv was less pronounced in secondary education, especially because the educational model that had become standard in Eastern and Central Europe since the turn of the century prevailed. In October 1945, when Jakob Oleisky dedicated the first vocational school in Landsberg, he was continuing with the work he did for the Organization for Rehabilitation through Training (ORT), the Jewish association for the promotion of skilled trades, whose Lithuanian section he had led from 1927 until the liquidation of the Kovno ghetto and his deportation to Dachau.[13] Oleisky's experience served him well when he adapted tried-and-tested educational structures to the needs of the She'erit Hapletah.[14]

The close collaboration between UNRRA and the World ORT Union since November 1945 helped the Landsberg model to prevail in the Western zones of occupation. By the end of 1947, the DPs in the American zone could choose from among fifty-five vocational schools and be trained in almost as many trades. Tailoring and similar traditional trades, however, continued to attract the greatest number of trainees, and they were especially popular with women. The school principals were convinced that the practical orientation also had a psychological aspect. They were a form of therapy.[15] Because the goals of the training programs did not necessarily correlate with the needs in the Yishuv, the approach taken by the ORT was not always consistent with the dominant Zionist ideology in the DP camps.[16] Indeed, the ORT schools differed in many respects from regular trade schools. In the district of Bamberg, for example, the average age of the students was about forty, and several family members—father and daughter or grandmother and grandchild—might sit together at improvised workbenches.[17]

Academic training could be pursued at the (temporary) UNRRA University located in the German Museum in Munich or at German universities. In both instances, higher education required dealing with non-Jews. UNRRA University, which trained displaced persons from many countries, sought to promote transnational alliances among the students independent of nationality and religion.[18] Although Jewish DPs formed one of the largest student groups, they were skeptical of this form of internationalism. On the one hand, most of them were committed Zionists, and on the other, they avoided working together with non-Jewish DPs, some of whom they suspected of having been collaborators and even war criminals.[19] At the same time, study at a German university required at least partial and temporary integration into German society and a confrontation with the personnel and ideological continuities that characterized postwar German academia.[20]

CULTURAL ACTIVITIES

Newspapers were founded at the same time as DP self-government was established at the local and supraregional levels. This led to a wide-ranging and active press that in subsequent years would provide the DPs with news and educational and ideological material, as well as entertainment. Before and immediately after liberation of the concentration camps, the publications founded in Dachau-Kaufering and Buchenwald were closely connected to emerging political forces. Members of the Zionist organization Irgun Brit Zion who had been deported from Kovno smuggled their Hebrew newspaper, *Nitzotz* (Spark), into Germany and distributed seven issues in the camps even before liberation. By November 1945, *Nitzotz*, now based in Munich, supported the work of the left-leaning Zionist unity party, Achida. In Buchenwald, the underground Zionist and Communist groups had begun discussing the future of European Jewry in their one issue, published in Yiddish on May 4, 1945, and titled *Tkhies Hameysim* (Resurrection of the dead). The editors of *Undzer Shtime* (Our voice), which started on July 12, 1945, had published the first regular Yiddish newspaper in the British zone, consisted of the small elite that was also active in other parts of DP society: three Polish Jews, Rafael Olewski, Paul Trepman, and David Rosenthal, were members of the Central Committee in the British zone, as well as editors and heads of the cultural office.

The press in the American zone developed in both Munich, the capital city of the She'erit Hapletah, and in the individual DP camps. Places like Bad Salzschlirf, Stuttgart, Landsberg, and Regensburg are prominent on the mastheads. Initially, the publications lacked not only journalists but also printing presses and Hebrew typeface. While the smaller newspapers copied their first editions by hand, in other places, Yiddish newspapers were printed using Latin typefaces; Hebrew type became available only in the fall of 1947.[21]

At the same time, the politicization of the She'erit Hapletah under the influence of the various Zionist parties led to the almost total replacement of the local press by the party-affiliated newspapers. In terms of content, however, the party press generally continued the educational efforts of the local papers, featuring fiction as well as social, political, and scientific reports in laymen's language. In so doing, the press supplemented the educational system and, in the absence of well-stocked libraries, provided urgently needed reading material.

Most of the editors were also intent on familiarizing their readers with the history and culture of Eastern European Jewry. The consensus seems to have been that no national Jewish consciousness could form in the absence of an understanding of the history of Ashkenazi Jewish culture in Europe. This was also the reason why the Zionist parties supported Yiddish-speaking writers in Germany, whether by including generous dabs of classical and contemporary literature in their culture sections (feuilletons) or by publishing literary works in the party-political press.

Eastern European Jewish traditions also continued to thrive on the stage. Almost every larger camp had a nonprofessional theater group, and professional ensembles, such as the Kazet Theater in Bergen-Belsen and the Munich Yiddish Theater, put on guest performances in the British and American zones. Their repertoires included Yiddish classics by Avrom Goldfaden and Sholem Aleichem along with cabaret skits and vocal numbers. But they also presented programs that dealt directly with the Holocaust. Theater thereby fulfilled a dual educational task, providing, on the one hand, a taste of the achievements of prewar Yiddish theater and, on the other, a sharpened historical consciousness of what had transpired under Nazi occupation for precisely those DPs who, as a result of flight or deportation, had been only indirect witnesses to persecution and extermination.[22]

Notwithstanding their highly varied wartime experiences, DPs also considered it an obligation to document the recent history that lay "on the tips of their tongues."[23] The first historical commission began work at the Bergen-Belsen DP camp on October 10, 1945, the initiative of journalists Paul Trepman, David Rosenthal, and Rafael Olewski and the actor Sami Feder. A month later, the journalist and history teacher Israel Kaplan and the Polish bookkeeper Yosef Feigenbaum founded what became the Central Historical Commission in Munich, which was connected to the cultural department of the Central Committee and, until its dissolution in 1948, oversaw the activities of more than fifty local commissions.[24] The commission gathered together everything that might provide useful documentation, such as pictures, photographs, and ritual objects. They archived museum objects along with documents, clothing, songs, poems, and anecdotes from the ghettos and camps. Scores of contemporary testimonies documented in questionnaires and interviews were collected. In 1948 thousands of documents of the most varied provenance were shipped to Israel and in 1953 given to the newly opened Yad Vashem Holocaust Memorial in Jerusalem.[25]

The commissions were staffed by laypeople who had not been trained in the methodological tools used by professional historians. As a result, they primarily saw their task as collecting, while systematic appraisal and historical analysis would be left to future generations. Nonetheless, a number of historical studies

Citizens of Neunburg vorm Wald in Bavaria bearing the victims of the death march from Flossenbürg concentration camp to be buried at the local cemetery, April 1945. United States Holocaust Memorial Museum / National Archives and Records Administration, College Park, Maryland.

were published, and the Central Historical Commission in Munich published a journal, *Fun letstn khurbn* (From the latest destruction). The journal aimed to present a broad spectrum of historical sources and especially to recruit DPs as participants in the historical projects—whether as members of the commission or as contemporary witnesses.[26] This documentation, however, served much more than the purposes of historiography; it was understood to represent a symbolic gravestone for the murdered Jews of Europe, and as such it served as an integral part of national memorialization.[27]

The historical commissions were not alone in their attempts to keep alive the memory of the victims of National Socialism. Local and supraregional committees and *landsmanshaftn* (associations of emigrants or refugees from the same region) held memorial events for destroyed Jewish communities and their persecuted inhabitants. In May 1947 several hundred Jews from Kielce gathered in the town center of Passau, forming a procession in memory of their children who had been murdered only five years earlier. Traffic was stopped, and the police ordered passersby to view the procession in silence: "Uniformed Jewish policemen marched in the front rows with magnificent national flags; they were followed by children with floral wreaths with inscriptions dedicated to our murdered Jewish children, and behind them—rows upon rows upon rows."[28]

Observant DPs used communal prayer to commemorate those who had been murdered. Daily worship replaced in symbolic terms all that was no longer possible: the mourner's prayer at the grave of the deceased, the week of mourning, and the placing of a gravestone.[29] The survivors celebrated the exhumations and reburials of victims of the death marches as not only religious but also political acts.[30]

The efforts of the legal department of the Central Committee in the American zone went beyond the symbolism of memorialization. Although the committee had no direct judicial powers, it collected incriminating evidence against war criminals and was in contact with the military tribunals in Nuremberg and Dachau, with German denazification authorities, and with other institutions in Germany, Austria, and Poland. With the help and support of the DP population, it was able to uncover more than a hundred cases and pass along the evidence to the appropriate authorities.[31] In addition, the Central Committee's legal department oversaw the activities of the so-called honor courts, which adjudicated cases initiated internally by DPs against former collaborators, Jewish council members, ghetto and concentration camp police, and *kapos* (inmate functionaries). Despite genuine efforts to follow legal procedures, the judicial precedents for convicting the accused were weak, and so the trials had a primarily psychological and moral significance.[32]

RELIGIOUS LIFE

The Orthodox religious minority began to reassert itself in the DP camps. In October 1945 a Jewish observer was struck by a procession of Hasidic men dancing and singing in the Föhrenwald DP camp in honor of their rabbi, the Klausenburg rebbe Yekusiel Halberstam, who was attired in the traditional fur hat and caftan.[33] Pocking DP camp briefly became another center of Hasidic life when several hundred Lubavitch Hasidim stopped there after fleeing their Russian homeland before continuing on to Paris.[34] Religious schools were established in both the British and the American zones of occupation, among them two Talmud Torah schools and a Bais Yaakov school for girls in Bergen-Belsen.[35] There, as in numerous other DP camps, religious men studied the Talmud in yeshivas.

Supported by the Orthodox religious aid organization Vaad Hatzalah and by the JDC, observant Jews attempted to create all the structures in the provisional DP camps that were crucial to the religious life of a traditional community, including kosher kitchens that provided refugees with ritually permitted food. *Mikvot* (ritual baths) were consecrated, and trained *mohelim* performed circumcisions. Prayer books, *tefillin* (small leather boxes containing verses from the Torah), and *mezuzot* (capsules containing Torah verses affixed to a door post) were distributed, as was *matzah* (unleavened bread) for Passover and kosher dishes. Newlyweds received a set of bed sheets from Vaad Hatzalah.[36]

The Rabbinical Council (Vaad Harabanim) for the American zone was founded in Munich in the summer of 1945 and led by the former Lithuanian army chaplain Samuel A. Snieg. Snieg had been chief rabbi of the Orthodox Jewish communities in Bavaria since 1946, and among his accomplishments was the complete reprinting of the Babylonian Talmud in postwar Germany.[37] Hermann Helfgott (later Hebraicized to Zvi Asaria) became the chief rabbi in the British zone in 1947 and, together with the other rabbis in Belsen, Celle, and the rest of the occupation zone, served under the supervision of the Rabbinical Council.[38] A former Yugoslavian officer, Helfgott had been a prisoner of war, and after the end of the war he refused Tito's repatriation order so that he could dedicate himself to the survivors in Bergen-Belsen. He had arrived there shortly after his liberation, and despite his weakened condition after years of internment, he helped to bury the dead.[39]

Among the most urgent problems that confronted the rabbis was the question of *agunot* and *agunim*, that is, married persons whose partners had disappeared. After the Holocaust this matter of religious law had acquired completely new relevance. How was one to decide whether a person could remarry if the death of a husband or wife was probable but not proved? Concerned about maintaining religious law, the rabbinate in Bergen-Belsen consulted with a rabbinical committee that was headquartered in Jerusalem and helped in the adjudication of individual cases of *agunot*. By the end of 1946, the rabbinate in Bergen-Belsen had already pronounced the necessary permission to remarry 770 times.[40]

In the British zone, the Rabbinical Council also debated the question of the halakhic status of persons who had been persecuted by the Nazis as so-called half-Jews or quarter-Jews. In 1947 the Rabbinical Council decided to accept, in accordance with Jewish law, only those persons as Jewish whose lineage was matrilineal. The rabbis rejected conversions to Judaism and scrutinized conversions undergone prior to the war. Jews with non-Jewish partners could not assume leading functions in the DP communities. If the marriages were entered into after the war, the couple could expect exclusion from the community. In addition, the Rabbinical Council decided that no marriages could be entered into without the prior consent of the rabbinate. The DP communities were ordered to submit lists of all mixed marriages and all uncircumcised boys. They were also encouraged to observe Jewish religious law.[41]

BUILDING NETWORKS

For the displaced persons, the Holocaust meant not only the loss of their family members and homelands but also the collapse of all professional and private points of reference. In an attempt to renew disrupted lives, various networks began to form within the She'erit Hapletah that built on older, disrupted connections.

The effort to bring together fellow professionals such as physicians, writers, engineers, and actors reflected the desire to reconnect with familiar prewar structures and aimed to establish contacts with colleagues abroad that might provide the basis for a professional future after emigration. *Landsmanshaftn* served to connect the past and the future; emotional, moral, and practical considerations frequently overlapped. These associations of people from the same region supported newly arrived refugees financially and helped them search for relatives and old acquaintances; supported historical commissions and honor courts in searching for collaborators and *kapos*; collected material for Yizkor books, commemorative books in which the fate of the individual communities during the war was documented; and helped the local committees in the task of education.[42] As a result, by stressing local affiliations, the associations of Polish, Lithuanian, Hungarian, and Romanian Jews to some extent countered the nationalist policies being pursued by the central and regional committees.[43]

At the same time, the *landsmanshaftn* contacted sister organizations in the United States and Palestine that they hoped would provide them with financial support and aid during the long-drawn-out emigration process.[44] The *landsmanshaftn* in the United States were inundated with personal letters in which the survivors described their relatives, neighbors, and acquaintances in the locales where they had lived in hopes of reconnecting to their lost world and gaining material and moral support.[45] And in fact, these calls for help were often answered. For example, compatriots in North America from the former Polish city of Grodno formed an aid committee. The president of this committee, the Yiddish actor Herman Jablokoff, made personal contact with Jews from Grodno during a tour of the European DP camps that lasted several months in 1947. Appalled, he telegraphed the committee from occupied Europe, "I cannot find the words to describe the horrible fate of our Grodner *pleytim* [refugees] whom I visited in the concentration camps [*sic*] in Germany, Austria, and Italy. In the name of humanity and in remembrance of those who perished, I urgently request your support, my Grodner *landsleit* [compatriots]."[46]

Jewish *landsmanshaftn* in the United States also protested against the refugee policies in the zones of occupation. In September 1945 the American Federation of Polish Jews accused the Allies of standing idly by in the face of anti-Jewish rioting in Europe.[47] The transnationally organized *landsmanshaftn* remained important to the former DPs even after they emigrated from Europe, supporting them in their social and economic integration while keeping alive the memory of their lost homes and communities.

The considerable success of the survivors, weakened as they were by all that they had recently endured, in organizing themselves as a unified group would not have been possible without the support of Jewish individuals and organizations from abroad. The DPs found their first advocates among the Allied forces. In the American zone, Chaplain Abraham Klausner dedicated himself to serving the She'erit Hapletah until the end of 1946. The information office that he improvised in Dachau published five lists of names of Jewish survivors in Bavaria.[48] In the British zone as well, army chaplains were among the first to provide humanitarian aid. The Orthodox chief rabbi's Religious Emergency Council was admitted to Bergen-Belsen earlier than other Jewish institutions because as a religious aid organization the British recognized that it met the needs of a specific group of survivors.[49] The lion's share of the humanitarian aid to the Jews in Europe, however, was provided by the JDC. By 1950 this American Jewish organization, founded in 1914 and known as "the Joint" to the survivors, had provided $200 million to the DPs in Europe. The JDC not only brought food, clothing, and medications to Germany but also promoted social activities in the DP camps and Jewish communities.

Nonetheless, relations between the JDC and the DPs were not without conflict: because the aid organization was unable to send official representatives to Germany earlier than July 1945, it stood accused of leaving the survivors in the lurch for far too long. Indeed, the relationship between the autonomous Jewish administrative bodies and the JDC remained ambivalent for years, the main bone of contention being who was responsible for what.[50] A number of other American and international Jewish organizations, including the World Jewish Congress, the American Jewish Committee, the Hebrew Immigrant Aid Society, religious organizations like Vaad Hatzalah, and the non-Zionist Jewish Labor Committee, also advocated for the DPs—either by providing concrete aid to the camps, like charitable activities internationally, or by lobbying the American government and the United Nations.

Unlike the JDC and other American Jewish organizations, the Jewish Relief Unit (JRU), which had been active in the British zone since June 1945, was a completely new organization. In the summer of 1946, more than ninety of its representatives began to provide aid in the British zone and even in Berlin and the American zone. Its work was financed primarily by the JDC.[51] The JRU, which included numerous German-Jewish refugees who had fled to England, took on important functions, especially in the new (non-DP) communities. It facilitated contacts with German and British authorities and the clarification of restitution questions. Hendrik George van Dam, who would later become general secretary of the Central Council of Jews in Germany, played an important role in this respect. The JRU was instrumental in persuading the former Berlin rabbi Leo Baeck, who had survived Theresienstadt and immigrated to England after liberation, to visit Germany in 1948 to celebrate the High Holy Days despite having rejected all calls for a permanent return to Germany.[52]

Other organizations, such as the Women's International Zionist Organization (WIZO), also provided assistance to help people help themselves. Even before its workers arrived in Germany, female DPs in the American zone who had been involved with WIZO before the war or knew of its work through their mothers or grandmothers had built up an organization without outside help; by 1947 it counted more than four thousand members and coordinated the work of thirty-eight local groups from its headquarters in Munich.[53] Such self-help initiatives seemed all the more important because the professional UNRRA and JDC social workers, often single women who were not fluent in Yiddish, shunned specifically Eastern European Jewish family and childraising customs in favor of rationalized "modern" notions of hygiene, which the DPs distrusted.[54] Having started its relief work in the Belsen DP camp, WIZO looked after the needs of infants and schoolchildren, the sick, pregnant women, and nursing mothers at sites throughout the British and American zones.[55] In addition to child care, WIZO's main field of activity was in training women in the skills needed to maintain a household. It founded nursery schools and children's homes, including one, in February 1948, for the children who had been on board the *Exodus 1947* and were stranded in Pöppendorf DP Camp near Lübeck after the ship returned to Hamburg following its unsuccessful landing attempt in Palestine.[56]

ZIONISM AND THE CONNECTION TO PALESTINE

Unlike American Jewry, the 650,000 Jews in the Yishuv, the Jewish community in Palestine, were unable to offer the survivors material support. Nonetheless, their existence had both ideological and moral significance for the She'erit Hapletah. The process of nationalization among the Jewish DPs that had been triggered by the events of World War II and by critical turning points in the immediate postwar era—the Harrison Report, the pogrom in Kielce, and the Anglo-American Committee of Inquiry—developed to the point where most of the DPs had come to view the Zionist leadership in the Yishuv as their political representatives.[57] When David Ben-Gurion traveled through Germany in October 1945 and visited the DP camps in the American zone, he was treated like a heroic redeemer. Maj. Irving Heymont, the American Jewish officer who was in charge of the Landsberg DP camp, described the rapturous reception for the future prime minister of Israel in a letter to his wife: "To the people of the camp, he is God. It seems that he represents all of their hopes of getting to Palestine. . . . I don't think that a visit by President Truman could cause as much excitement."[58] And the DPs made a deep impression on Ben-Gurion as well. Among the survivors was a large number of heroic individuals: "They were ready for anything: they could endure physical, moral and psychological torture for the sake of Zionism," and nowhere, not even in Palestine, could one find more convinced Zionists.[59]

In contrast to the aid organizations, the interest of the Yishuv in the DPs was not primarily humanitarian. The Jewish community in Palestine was dependent on the She'erit Hapletah, which after the destruction of European Jewry formed a reservoir of urgently needed future citizens. The first momentous encounters between the survivors and the Yishuv occurred when soldiers from the Jewish Brigade in Palestine reached southern Germany by way of Tarvisio, Italy, in June 1945 and the British zone a month later.[60] For the DPs, the sight of military uniforms with Star of David insignias not only symbolized the possibility of active Jewish resistance but also rehabilitated a symbol that had been officially denigrated by the antisemitic laws of the National Socialists. The Star of David became a symbol of national Jewish identity and self-defense. Although the soldiers of the Jewish Brigade were unable to provide anything but very limited relief from the material and humanitarian catastrophe, their presence provided an immense psychological boost to the survivors—especially since the arrival of Jewish aid organizations during the first postwar summer had been blocked by bureaucratic hurdles.

The members of the Jewish Brigade, along with the Jewish soldiers in the Allied forces, were the first foreign Jews to witness the utterly desperate situation in the DP camps in southern Germany after the end of the war. Many of the soldiers in this unit had left Poland, Germany, and other European countries in the 1930s and were only now encountering their compatriots again or setting foot on the soil of their former homeland for the first time. Their informal assistance for the survivors was inextricably linked to their search for lost family members.[61]

The first representatives (*shlichim*) of the Jewish Agency (Sochnut), wearing UNRRA uniforms, finally began to work in the DP camps in the American zone in December 1945.[62] Kurt Lewin, an emissary from the Jewish Brigade, was permitted to travel to Bergen-Belsen in the British zone only in March 1946.[63] The work of the representatives concentrated mainly on education and job training along with immigration to Palestine and Zionist political organization.[64] Since 1946 the Jewish Agency had coordinated its efforts from a central Palestine office in Munich (Misrad Ha-Eretz-Yisraeli). This office, which was also active in the local DP camps in Bavaria, was involved in political education and in promoting *ha'apalah*, the illegal immigration into Palestine. It worked closely with the Central Committee of Liberated Jews with regard to the Palestine question.[65]

When the emissaries arrived in Germany, they found the structures of political organization already in place, organized by the survivors themselves and committed to an ideology of Zionist unity. In the American zone, this included the founding in September 1945 of the nonpartisan Achida (United Zionist Organization) and its youth wing, Nocham.[66] For the survivors of the concentration camps, Zionism was no longer a theoretical or an ideological matter but had become a concrete national demand—the "civil religion" of the She'erit Hapletah.

The new Zionist organization in Germany therefore also viewed the arrival of the emissaries of the Jewish Agency (shlichim) with some concern. Out of fear that the emissaries might destabilize political unity, the Achida contacted Jerusalem in early September 1945—more than three months before the arrival of the first official emissaries—asking the authorities to forbid their political agitation. According to the Achida, it was the task of the She'erit Hapletah to fight for its nationalist demands on a unified basis rather than in splintered individual parties.[67]

However, the policies of the Achida had already been threatened at its founding not only from outside but also internally. Even before the first emissaries from Palestine began their work in Germany, the Bricha had transferred, along with the waves of refugees, a wide variety of Zionist ideologies into Germany, which initially provided cohesion for the various newly formed kibbutz groups. Before the Sovietization of Poland, the postwar government permitted the rebuilding of most Jewish parties.[68] At first, the Achida, which represented dreams of unity forged in the concentration and labor camps, was hopeful that it could gain sufficient influence over the Polish refugees once they had reached Germany: "In the future as well, we will succeed in influencing Polish Zionism—the classic factionalized Zionism."[69] The Achida activists hoped that their unified Zionist organization in Germany could avoid the divisions that characterized the movement in both Palestine and Poland. This dream of unity among the survivors of the Holocaust would, however, remain unfulfilled.[70]

The consequences of this splintering into different parties, and the controversies associated with it, for the internal cohesion of the She'erit Hapletah were visible at the latest by the second conference of liberated Jews in the American zone. The delegates arriving in Bad Reichenhall to discuss education, employment, and assistance for the DPs quickly became bogged down in ideological bickering. Representatives of the various parties in the camps advanced motions to vote for the foundation of the state as well as for and against the partition of Palestine. The right-wing revisionist Zionists did all they could to disrupt the event.[71] In February 1947 the decision was made to completely dissolve the Achida, which had served as the unifying nonpartisan organization during the early phase of the She'erit Hapletah.[72]

Electioneering at the Zeilsheim DP camp in 1945. United States
Holocaust Memorial Museum / courtesy of Alice Lev.

When the United Nations voted for the partition of Palestine in November
1947, the founding of Israel moved one step closer to realization—and, as a result, the possibility of legal immigration of displaced persons to a new Jewish
state. The first DPs to whom emigration was to be offered were young men and
women of military age. From the perspective of the Haganah, the prestate Israeli
army, they represented the future soldiers of a country they had never seen. The
kibbutz organizations, which had demonstrated their Zionist commitment by
their support for *ha'apalah*, the illegal immigration to Palestine (especially the
events surrounding *Exodus 1947*), and with assurances from the Central Committee about the general enthusiasm for Zionism among Jewish DPs, encouraged
the representatives of the Haganah and local organizations to call for a military
draft. In accordance with the resolutions of the third conference of liberated Jews
in the American zone in Bad Reichenhall, mobilization became an official policy
of the Central Committee in February 1948, on the eve of the founding of the
State of Israel.

All men and all women between the ages of seventeen and thirty-five were
called upon to present themselves for military service. The slogans employed by
the *giyus* (draft) implied that this was a national duty for each individual DP.
While the press addressed itself to the general population, the youth organizations

kept an exact accounting of whether all members had voluntarily registered. However, despite their unwavering ideological support for Zionism, numerous eligible young people refused active military service. They failed to register for the draft, and many of them took off for German cities. In retaliation, the Central Committee and the Jewish Agency published the names of resisters, barred them from leadership functions in the committee, and in some cases even reduced their rations and hampered their future immigration to Israel.[73]

JEWISH DPS AND GERMANS

Ideologically, the She'erit Hapletah turned its back on a Germany and a Europe that had betrayed the trust that modern Jews had placed in them. However, the realities of the immediate postwar years meant that Germans and Jews came into daily contact with each other. As a British officer of German-Jewish extraction wrote to a friend in Palestine in 1946, "'I hate the Germans,' is a common expression. 'I can't stand to look at them, I could kill them all in cold blood.' But if the conversation continues, it becomes evident that soon one is talking about 'my friend Schmidt' and 'our dear neighbors the Müllers,' because after all, even the greatest hater cannot live in total isolation if he is forced to continue living at the site of his torture."[74] "How can I stay, Kurt?" Gerda Weismann asked the German-Jewish GI fiancé she was desperate to join in the United States after she discovered that her presence was protecting her kind landlord, a former Nazi, from denazification penalties. "What am I to say to people who treated me civilly, no matter what their motives might be?" she agonized, acknowledging, "I can hate Germany, all things German with a passion, but I can't hate individuals."[75]

The Möhlstrasse in Munich became the most visible trading and meeting place for Jews and Germans. David Wohl described this encounter in the Munich Yiddish newspaper *Undzer veg* (Our way):

> The walls here are plastered with placards, in faulty Yiddish, in Latinized Yiddish, with the faces of Jewish actors and artists, announcing balls for Hannukah and Purim and Passover and all the other Holy Days . . . and there is a stand with Yiddish newspapers. It's alive; it lives and breathes Jewishness. As if a strange thoroughfare had wrapped itself in a mortally sinful Jewish skin. And its pulse is Jewish. It is presumably no lie, gentlemen, to say that more Yiddish is spoken here than in all of New York. There are Jewish restaurants with blaring international names: Trocadero, Bristol, Astoria, Amor, and the like in which one can get *cholent* and *kishke* [traditional Jewish dishes] and meet Jews. People wheel and deal. Are we supposed to cry over the bitter fate that has tied Jews to this country for a time? But Jews, too, must live, move about, and earn money.[76]

Newspaper stand in the Neu-Freimann DP camp in Munich. United States Holocaust Memorial Museum / photograph by Jack Sutin.

The quarter itself consisted of about a half-dozen blocks in which were housed numerous Jewish and international organizations, among them the JDC, HIAS, the Jewish Agency, the Central Committee, the JRSO, and the World ORT Union. The area's shops offered better-quality merchandise at lower prices than were to be had elsewhere, partially because the illegal trade evaded sales taxes and import duties.[77] In fact, the black market had thrived during the Nazi period as well, a recent history that many Germans preferred to forget whenever they connected this trade with "foreigners" and especially with Eastern European Jews. The majority of the customers shopping in the Möhlstrasse were Germans, eager to purchase better and cheaper merchandise, not to mention luxury goods that could not be found elsewhere. American occupation soldiers and officers were also frequent customers.[78]

Many encounters, both harmonious and hostile, between Jews and Germans revolved around food. The apparent disparity in caloric intake and rations

Mounted police carrying out a raid against black marketeering in the Möhlstrasse in Munich, May 1949. United States Holocaust Memorial Museum / photograph by Alex Hochhauser.

for Germans and Jewish DPs masked the fact that most Germans in the cities and villages close to the DP camps did not rely on rations alone but on their connections with local farmers. DPs who maneuvered to supplement their (somewhat more ample) food rations were, however, condemned and often arrested for black marketeering. In the most notorious and tragic incident, in March 1946 some two hundred German police officers with bullhorns and barking dogs, along with a handful of American military police, conducted a raid in a DP camp in Stuttgart. The inhabitants of the camp resisted searches, and in the ensuing upheaval, German police shot and killed Schmul Dancyger, a survivor of Auschwitz and Mauthausen who had just the evening before been reunited with his wife and children. The raid succeeded in recovering several illegally kept chickens.

Jewish military government and aid organization officials were constantly at pains to point out to their disapproving colleagues that the Jews involved in the black market were merely participating in a virtually universal and necessary practice—as pervasive and impossible to ban as fraternization—and that, in any case, they were only "small fish" among the mainly German "sharks" in the black market trade.[79]

Trade in food and, more generally, the informal black and gray markets that constituted the postwar economy in occupied Germany marked one, but certainly not the only, key site of interaction between Jews and Germans (as well as with the American occupiers). Notwithstanding claims from both sides that despite inhabiting the same territory they existed in strictly separate worlds, German nannies, cleaning personnel, drivers, plumbers, mechanics, and other skilled workers, as well as teachers, office employees, and physicians, entered the Jewish DP camps every day—just as the Jews themselves ventured out beyond their guarded but porous gates. Jews could leave to search for supplies and work or attend school or job training programs, while the local Germans, albeit officially only those with work permits, also moved in and out daily. Indeed, the constant pressure on DPs to demonstrate their moral and physical rehabilitation to both the internal camp authorities and the aid organizations ironically served as an impetus for many "close encounters" between Jews and Germans. German workers were recruited to help satisfy the rather unrealistic demands for orderliness and cleanliness that the camp administration set forth as part of a pervasive rhetoric of duty and obligation to the community and, in purely practical terms, as a necessity for would-be immigrants who had to prove their health, fitness, and capacity for labor as a condition of entry to either Palestine or some other country.[80]

Jewish DPs, however, for whom survival during the war—whether they had been under Nazi occupation or in the Soviet Union—had so often depended on their ability to work, now used their very lack of ability to meet standards set unreasonably high for a refugee population housed in overcrowded and temporary quarters as a lever for gaining German assistance and labor power. If you want us to be so tidy, the message often seemed to be, send us some Germans—the generally acknowledged cleanliness mavens—to clean up after us. The head of the Feldafing tailor shop coolly informed the DP camp sanitation department that since his workshop had been deemed too messy, he had engaged an elderly German woman so "she should keep it clean."[81] As annoyed JDC officials noted, Jewish survivors were often of the opinion that "we have worked so much for the Germans, it is about time the Germans now worked for us."[82]

Local German women, hired, paid, and regulated by camp welfare authorities, often cared for the precious new offspring of the Jewish DP baby boom. Jewish marriages and births were registered in the local German registry offices. German doctors wrote the medical affidavits (*Atteste*) certifying that Jewish women needed help with babies and housework.

The dependence on German physicians and nurses did lead to controversy and tension. On the one hand, relief officials were often frustrated by Jewish mistrust of German personnel hired by the aid organizations. But on the other hand, determined to keep their babies alive, DPs had few compunctions about hiring the most competent help or insisting that a sick baby be treated by the best professors at the universities in Munich or Frankfurt, notwithstanding their own "deep-rooted antipathy" or the Germans' actions during the war.[83] JDC and UNRRA workers often complained that while the DPs insisted on qualified German personnel, they grumbled in the same breath about mistreatment by German doctors. Initially, UNRRA repeatedly rejected as "not feasible" efforts to create a central Jewish facility within the Bogenhausen Hospital in Munich, where Jews from the entire American zone could be trained in medicine as well as treated. There were hardly enough qualified German physicians, let alone Jewish ones.[84] Eventually the Bogenhausen hospital, which in April 1946 had six Jewish and five German physicians and one German chief surgeon—who was known to have been an active Nazi—was handed over to the Central Committee of Liberated Jews.

DP life, therefore, provided, and frequently necessitated, numerous opportunities for encounters between Jews and Germans. Jewish DPs resided in two types of camps: those that were situated outside of the cities, and those located right in the middle of cities like Stuttgart, Frankfurt-Zeilsheim, and Dieburg, in Hesse. In accordance with Allied regulations, which differed by zone and region, the survivors could be assigned living quarters that belonged to former Nazis (and in which they often still lived), a policy that precipitated confrontation. Moreover, German Jews were, at least theoretically, able to demand the return of their "Aryanized" property. Over time, however, as more and more Jews left the overcrowded camps and moved into German towns and cities, Germans resisted ever more vehemently the allocation of their living space to Jewish DPs.[85] The complaints from the population were often met with open sympathy by local authorities, and as a result DPs searching for housing were increasingly confronted with resistance from both the population and the bureaucracy. Occasionally violent confrontations between DPs and local Germans ensued.[86] In some cases, American occupation authorities had to step in to restore order and an uneasy peace. For example, at the end of May 1946 a riot broke out in the small Bavarian village of Oberrammingen, where 120 Jewish survivors, many more than had ever lived there before the war, were quartered among only 500 locals. The American military police intervened and arrested the purported ringleaders from both groups. Tried in an American military courtroom, both the Jews and the Germans were "advised" by the occupiers that "they must get along together until better conditions prevail for both," a clear reference to the shared conviction among Jews, Germans, and Allies that the generally prevailing coexistence depended on the "temporary" nature of the Jewish DP sojourn in Germany.[87]

Boxing match at the Zeilsheim DP camp. United States Holocaust Memorial Museum / photograph by E. M. Robinson / courtesy of Alice Lev.

But despite these and similar clashes, Germans and Jews developed a mostly pragmatic coexistence in varying registers, from sober business relationships, to the care of children and sick people, and even to sexual and romantic relationships and, in a relatively small number of cases, marriages. Despite official disapproval of fraternization by the political and the religious leaders of the DPs, almost every aspect of Jewish life in occupied postwar Germany required a certain degree of contact and cooperation with the German population. In the film *Lang ist der Weg* (Long is the road), a 1948 German-Jewish coproduction, some of the actors were German, some were Jewish, and Jews from the Neu-Freimann camp in Munich served as extras. The director and male lead of the film was a former Polish Jewish partisan named Israel Beker who was also deeply involved in Yiddish theater in Munich. Starting in 1946, the Bavarian State Radio broadcast programs in Yiddish. Both Germans and Jews attended sporting events organized by the DPs, such as a boxing match held in the Circus Krone building, and German musicians also played in camp orchestras, if only to get additional rations.[88]

Over a thousand young Jewish DPs studied at German universities, especially in medicine, dentistry, and mechanical engineering. German state restitution funds paid their tuition, their food rations were provided by the DP camps in which they remained registered, and their student IDs enabled them to attend cultural events at reduced prices in cities like Munich, Frankfurt, and Berlin. The Association of Jewish Students in Munich had 405 members in February 1947; by the fall of that year there were more than 460.[89] Jewish student associations were formed in other cities in the American zone as well, in particular in Frankfurt, Stuttgart, Heidelberg, Marburg, and Erlangen.[90] During the 1947–1948 winter semester, their membership increased to 729, a high point, with an additional 68 Jewish students in Berlin.[91] With the help of the JDC and the German-Jewish camp survivor Philipp Auerbach, who was the head of the Bavarian State Commission for Racial, Religious, and Political Persecutees, the student association in Munich was able to provide members with substantial social and financial assistance. The Student Association also took on another important function, setting up its own committee to test the academic competence of Jewish students, who were often unable to provide written proof of prior education or training. Instead of attending the improvised UNRRA University with its temporary status and doubtful academic credentials, young Jews, eager for the education they had been denied during the war, often preferred to attend venerable, traditional German institutions, which remained highly respected despite their recent Nazi past. Some students in Munich lived in the UNRRA headquarters in the German Museum or in the DP camps, but with the support of the military government, UNRRA, and the Bavarian state commission, most were able to live more independently, assigned to rooms in apartments occupied by Germans.

Although the Jewish students generally tended to keep to themselves—in Munich many gathered at their own "kosher mess hall" at the Café am Isartor—they still (usually) managed to have friendly relationships with their German counterparts in the lecture halls, seminars, and beer gardens, even though they knew that some of them had served in the Wehrmacht or had even been members of the SS. As one Jewish mechanical engineering student recalled, "I couldn't care less. I wanted to get an education, even if I was going to get it from the devil."[92] The larger group of students and pupils who lived in the DP camps were taught Hebrew and the geography and history of an imagined new homeland that they had never seen, often by teachers who had come from Palestine. By these means, they attempted to finish or further the educations that had been interrupted by war, flight, and captivity. Organizations like ORT also offered them the opportunity to apprentice in such trades as automotive mechanics either in the camps or in local German businesses. Some young Jews managed to enter standard German apprenticeship training, taking all of the examinations required for official certification. ORT vocational schools were opened in many DP camps, such as those in Dieburg, Gabersee, Leipheim, and Weilheim. In Weilheim, DPs were housed in two former hotels attached to an agricultural school that prepared participants for life on a kibbutz.

In 1947–1948 a Jewish vocational school with the resonant name Masada was founded in the abandoned and damaged train station in central Darmstadt, a building that had served as the National Socialist People's Welfare office for the Hesse-Nassau district. The school was led by a Zionist activist from the militant nationalist Betar movement who had survived the war in the Soviet Union. About forty-five adolescents from the DP camps in the vicinity—such as Zeilsheim near Frankfurt, which had once provided company housing for a pharmaceutical company's employees and where Soviet prisoners of war were later quartered, or Babenhausen, which consisted of old artillery barracks—attended the school. With the support of the local head of government and the superintendent of schools, as well as the local military government and Betar, a total of about sixty students between the ages of thirteen and thirty-one learned trades such as electrical engineering, lathe operation, carpentry, and machine or building fitting, as well as Hebrew and Jewish history. Both Germans and Jews served as instructors. The women, mostly the wives of teachers, worked in the kitchens and offices; the JDC supplied the food, including chocolate, sugar, cheese, eggs, and even meat, which was sometimes shared with the German personnel. The students' wartime experiences mirrored those of Jewish DPs generally, in that many had survived in the Soviet Union and were now among the very few survivors of what had been large extended families. After 1948 many of them immigrated to Israel; however, some remained in Germany, earning their livelihoods in such businesses as real estate or as owners or managers of bars frequented by American GIs, some of which sported names like Hawaii or California, symbols of their owners' dreams of immigrating to the United States.[93]

In this transitional period from 1945 to 1949, the occupying powers suppressed the open antisemitism of the Nazi era, which, however, continued after the war as a generally silent and latent force. Explicit racism was displaced onto nonwhites, especially onto African-American soldiers.[94] Occasionally, it was vented in openly expressed resentment against "homeless foreigners." Rehearsing traditional antisemitic prejudices as well as persistent Nazi racial stereotypes, these "alien" elements were often associated with the black market and business and real estate speculation, with sexual threats to German women, or with privileged access to Allied merchandise such as cigarettes and coffee, which were well suited to black market sale or exchange. Even the specter of the new enemy, Communism, was invoked, especially with reference to Polish-Jewish "infiltrees" who had survived in the Soviet Union.[95] Notwithstanding the putative "disappearance" of Nazis in postwar Germany and the protective presence of the Allies, Jewish DPs and their official representatives were well aware of an entrenched "neo"-antisemitism.

ATINA GROSSMANN is Professor of history at Cooper Union in New York. She has been a fellow at the Institute for Advanced Study in Princeton, the American Academy in Berlin, the United States Holocaust Memorial Museum, and the Davis Center at Princeton University. Her publications include *Jews, Germans, and Allies: Close Encounters in Occupied Germany* (on which parts of this section are based) and *Wege in der Fremde: Deutsch-jüdische Begegnungsgeschichte zwischen Feldafing, New York und Teheran;* and as a coeditor, *After the Nazi Racial State: Difference and Democracy in Germany and Europe and Crimes of War: Guilt and Denial in the Twentieth Century,* as well as *Shelter from the Holocaust: Rethinking Jewish Survival in the Soviet Union* (with M. Edele and S. Fitzpatrick) and *The Joint Distribution Committee: 100 Years of Jewish History* (with A. Patt, L. Levi, and M. Maud), both forthcoming from Wayne State University Press in 2018.

TAMAR LEWINSKY is curator of contemporary history at the Jewish Museum Berlin. Her publications include *Unterbrochenes Gedicht: Jiddische Literatur im Nachkriegsdeutschland, 1944–1950* and *Displaced Poets: Jiddische Schriftsteller im Nachkriegsdeutschland, 1945–1951.*

NOTES

1. J. Rosensaft (1957), p. 27.

2. M. Brenner (1997), pp. 32 (interview), 95–99; S. Jochims-Bozic (2004), pp. 58–68; H. Lavsky (2002), pp. 66–67, 75–77.

3. Inaugural speech by Dr. Zalman Grinberg (Dachau) at the conference of Jews liberated from slave labor camps in Germany, July 25, 1945, in CZA, S 25/5231. See also Z. Mankowitz (2002), pp. 49–51.

4. Z. Mankowitz (2002), pp. 49–50; A. Grossmann (2012), pp. 137–138.

5. Y. Bauer (1970b); Z. Mankowitz (1990).

6. Z. Mankowitz (2002), pp. 30–31.

7. Z. Mankowitz (2002), p. 51.

8. Letter from S. Adler-Rudel to executives of the Jewish Agency for Palestine, April 17, 1947, in CZA, S86/283.

9. H. Lavsky (2002), p. 171.

10. "2-ter kongres fun sheyres-hapleyte in der amerikaner zone in Daytshland. Bad Raykhnhal 25–27 febr. 1947. General-barikht," Munich 1947, p. 14.

11. [A teacher], "Di shul in Bad Zaltsshlirf," *Zaltsshlirfer lebn*, October 1946.

12. T. Lewinsky (2008), p. 68; Z. Mankowitz (2002), pp. 137–138.

13. S. Kavanaugh (2008), pp. 44–53, 77–80. For more on the history of ORT (Obchestvo Remeslenogo Truda, Association for the Promotion of Skilled Trades), see L. Shapiro (1980).

14. S. Kavanaugh (2008), p. 74.

15. V. Mishelski, "Di 'ORT'-tetigkayt in der amerikaner zone," *ORT: Distrikt Bamberg-Regensburg. Ilustrirte oysgabe,* December 1947, p. 10; Jakob Oleisky, "'ORT'-problematik in der amerik. Zone," *ORT:Distrikt Bamberg-Regensburg. Ilustrirte oysgabe,* December 1947, pp. 6–7.

16. "Taasukah le-plitim be-machanot be-Germaniyah 1946–1947," (Employment of refugees in the DP camps in Germany 1946–1947), March 6, 1947, in CZA, S 25/5226; "Yoman ha-mishlachat shel ha-sokhnut ha-yehudit le-Eretz Yisrael be-Germaniyah ha-kvushah," no. 4, Munich, April 8, 1947, in CZA, S 25/5231.

17. "The Pedagog Looks at ORT To Day," *ORT: Distrikt Bamberg-Regensburg. Ilustrirte oysgabe*, December 1947, p. 11.

18. A. Holian (2008), pp. 168, 172.

19. A. Holian (2008), pp. 190–192.

20. J. Varon (2014).

21. T. Lewinsky (2008), p. 36.

22. T. Lewinsky (2008), pp. 165–170.

23. I. Kaplan (1947), p. 24.

24. L. Jockusch (2007), pp. 445–446; see also L. Jockusch (2006).

25. L. Jockusch (2007), pp. 445, 449.

26. L. Jockusch (2007), p. 467.

27. See L. Jockusch (2012); L. Jockusch (2007), p. 451.

28. "Biuletyn nr. 4. Arojsgegebn dorch dem ferband fyn kielcer jidn, Gauting," August 19, 1947, p. 2.

29. "Shma Jisrael! Rabbinat Hannover," in YIVO, RG 294.2, folder 1575, reel 114.

30. M. Myers Feinstein (2010), for example, in Tirschenreuth, Bavaria, pp. 89–90.

31. "2-ter kongres," p. 18.

32. A. Hyman (1993), p. 162; M. Myers Feinstein (2010), pp. 238–248. For recent research, see also G. Finder and L. Jockusch (eds.) (2015).

33. Föhrenwald report by M. Warburg, October 6, 1945, in CZA, S 75/4780.

34. S. Kaczerginski (1955), p. 425; A. Grobman (2004), pp. 135–136, 138–140.

35. H. Lavsky (2010), p. 243.

36. A. Grobman (2004), pp. 115, 121, 157, 163, 166; E. London (1957).

37. T. Weger (1999), pp. 204–205; P. Honigmann (1997), pp. 258–263; G. Korman (1983).

38. Z. Asaria (1975), p. 168.

39. Z. Asaria (1975), pp. 102, 109.

40. "Tetikayts-barikht fun rabinat in Bergn-Belzn," *Undzer shtime*, December 15, 1946, p. 32; Z. Asaria (1975), pp. 154–155.

41. E. London (1957), p. 184; "Resolution des Zentralrabbinats zum 2. Kongress der 'Scherith-Hapletah' in der britischen Zone Deutschlands," July 22, 1947, in CZA, S 6/3659.

42. "Groyse oyfgabn," *Ibergang*, November 17, 1946; Mordkhe Libhaber, "Dos pojlisze Jidntum konferirt," *Ibergang*, November 16, 1947; "Di Rezolucjes fun der II. Landeskonferenc fun pojliszn Jidntum in U.S. Zone Dajczland," in YIVO, RG 294.2, box 1280, folder 91.

43. AJDC Munich, Landsmannschaften contributions, November 27, 1947, in USHMM, WJC, RG-68.066M GI 6A1 C-45.050.

44. Y. Gar (1957) p. 147.

45. See, for example, Abraham Ain Collection, correspondence with survivors from Swislocz, in YIVO, RG 336.

46. Telegram from Jablokoff to the Grodno Relief Society, October 18, 1947, in AJA, MS286 1/2.

47. Address at the Protest Meeting by Joseph Tenenbaum, President, American Federation for Polish Jews and World Federation for Polish Jews, New York, September 10, 1945, in YIVO, RG 1015, box 1.

48. Z. Mankowitz (2002), p. 39. See also his memoirs (written many years afterward). A. Klausner (2002). For more on Klausner's dramatic and controversial career in occupied Germany, see also A. Grossmann (2012), pp. 136–138, 145–146, 168.

49. H. Lavsky (2002), pp. 93–94.

50. Z. Mankowitz (2002), pp. 113–116.

51. On the JRU and the JDC in the British zone, see A. Königseder and J. Wetzel (2001), pp. 172–176; H. Lavsky (2002), pp. 94–98; H. Lavsky (1995).

52. H. Lavsky (2002), p. 97.

53. Fay Grove-Pollak, however, speaks of only three thousand members and thirty branches; see F. Grove-Pollak (ed.) (1970), p. 69.

54. See, for example, the complaints against young social workers by Zippi Tichauer in A. Grossmann (2009b).

55. Minutes of the special meeting held on Monday, August 18, 1947, Mrs. Kissman's report, in CZA, F 49/434.

56. "Report about the Work of WIZO Groups in Europe in the Areas of Child Care, Education, Training, Social Work, the Restructuring of Work from 1949," in CZA, F 49/431; Dr. Chajim Hofman, "Ha-sokhnut ha-jehudit Le-Erets Yisrael, Hahashlacha harashit le-Germaniyah," October 1, 1947, in CZA, F 49/436.

57. See also D. Diner (1997).

58. I. Heymont (1982), pp. 65–66 (letter 19, October 22, 1945). See also A. Patt (2009), pp. 57–60.

59. Report by Mr. Ben-Gurion on his visit to the camps given at a meeting in London on November 6, 1945, in CZA, S 25/5231.

60. Y. Gelber (2005).

61. I. Keynan (1996), pp. 86–87.

62. Regarding the negotiations and difficulties during the preliminary stages, see I. Keynan (1996), pp. 103–105.

63. H. Lavsky (2002), p. 104.

64. I. Keynan (1996), p. 112.

65. Y. Gar (1957), pp. 245–247.

66. Hatzharah, "Have'ida ha-tzionit ha-I shel she'erit ha-pletah be-Germaniyah," circular letter, Landsberg, September 11–12, 1945, in CZA, S 25/1988.

67. "Ha-merkaz ha-tzioni la-eksekutivah ha-tzionit birushalayim," circular letter, Munich, September 3, 1945, in YIVO DPG 294.2/402/MK/R33, 435.

68. A. Patt (2009), pp. 72–73.

69. "Ha-merkaz ha-tzioni."

70. See also I. Keynan (1996), p. 122.

71. II. Congress of the Sherith Haplejta in the U.S. Zone of Germany, letter from S. Adler-Rudel to executives at the Jewish Agency, London, April 2, 1947, in CZA, S 86/283.

72. I. Keynan (1996), pp. 121–122.

73. A. Patt (2009), pp. 243, 246, 252–253.

74. J. Posener (2001), p. 144.

75. G. W. Klein and K. Klein (2000), p. 191.

76. David Wohl, in *Undzer veg*, March 31, 1950.

77. K. Crago-Schneider (2010), p. 178.

78. See also A. Holian (2012).

79. Comment about fishes and sharks from a conversation between Atina Grossmann and Shlomo Leser, Haifa, Israel, November 2006. On the arguments between the Jews and the Germans about nutrition and food rations, see A. Grossmann (2012).

80. On the rhetoric and expectation of the "duty," see A. Patt (2009), pp. 1–12, 235–268. See also A. Grossmann (2012), pp. 200–208.

81. To Sanitätsamt (Feldafing), May 7, 1947, YIVO DPG 294.2/402/MK483/R33, 435.

82. Letter from Joseph Schwartz, JDC Paris, to Moe[ses] Leavitt, November 9, 1946, in JDCA, 390.

83. See A. Grossmann (2012), pp. 214, 208–217.

84. Memo from C. H. Martini, "Segregation of Jewish DPs in Hospitals without German Staff," to the UNRRA headquarters in Arolsen (Acting Director Relief Services), May 4, 1946, in ARMS, UNRRA, A/401, box 7, file 4. See also YIVO, DPG 294.2, folder 46, MK483, reel 4. There were very few physicians among the Jewish survivors in the DP camps.

85. See, for example, letter from the Jewish community in Hamburg to the housing management office, Ortsamt Fuhlsbüttel, June 14, 1945, in StAHH, 522–2, no. 74.

86. See, for example, letter from the head of the Höchst administrative office to the mayor, August 16, 1946, in ISG Frankfurt, Magistratsakten 8841.

87. On Oberrammingen, see Case no. 227 of the Intermediate Court, May 27, 1946, in YIVO, RG 294.1, folder 461, reel 38.

88. For more on sports, see, for example, P. Grammes (2006); J. Tobias (2006); G. Finder (2008). On the entire question of German-Jewish encounters, see A. Grossmann (2012).

89. JSU, statistics regarding Jewish students in Munich from October 15, 1946; "Tätigkeitsbericht der Vorstandschaft zur Generalversammlung, vom 3. Oktober 46 bis 31. Januar 47." The memberships in the association's documents indicate no discrepancies, cited from J. Varon (2014).

90. See J. Varon (2014).

91. AJDC, Educ. Dept. Students' Branch; Re: Statistics of university students from January 26, 1949, cited from J. Varon (2014).

92. Telephone conversation between Atina Grossmann and Arnold Kerr on August 5, 2004. In January 1947 Ruth Klüger was an exception in that she studied humanities like philosophy, history, and literature as a teenager at a Catholic theological seminary, the only institution of higher learning in Regensburg where her mother, with whom she had survived Auschwitz, worked for UNRRA. See her memoir: R. Klüger (2001), pp. 163–169. The Association of Jewish Students in Munich had about four hundred members in the early 1950s. Five hundred and seventy Jewish students were registered at a German university, more than a third of them women. See M. Syrkin (1980), p. 31. Of the 449 Jewish students in Munich, 408 belonged to the student association. In 1947 there were seventy-two Jewish students in Frankfurt and seventy in Berlin. Most of the German Jews attended Humboldt University; the DPs were primarily registered at the Technical University. See A. Königseder (1998), p. 155; also YIVO, RG 294.1, folder 529, reel 46; and J. Varon (2014).

93. R. Dreesen and L. Dror-Batalion (eds.) (2011). The role of former DPs in postwar German real estate and so-called red-light districts will be addressed in part 2 of this volume.

94. M. Höhn (2002). See also R. Chin et al. (2009).

95. M. Berkowitz and S. Brown-Fleming (2010), p. 172. See also A. Grossmann (2009a), pp. 55–79.

3 GERMAN JEWS

After the artillery had gone silent and Russian tanks had begun to roll through the streets of Berlin, Hans Rosenthal dared to leave the hiding place where he had spent almost two years in the Dreieinigkeit (Trinity) garden colony and venture out into the bombed-out streets of the former capital of the German Reich.[1] Almost a fifth of the few Jews in Berlin in 1945 had, like Rosenthal, gone underground as "illegals" or "submarines," thereby evading the deportations that since 1941 had led to the ghettos, concentration camps, and extermination camps in the so-called Ostmark and the Reich protectorate.

In fact, the National Socialists never succeeded in making Germany completely *judenrein* (purified of Jews): as early as May 9, 1945, the journalist Margret Boveri, evidently astonished and not a little irritated, wrote in her diary that "everywhere top posts are now crawling with Jews; they simply emerged from hiding. But reinforcements are also supposedly coming from Eastern Europe, especially from Poland—those who are smuggling themselves in with the refugee trains."[2] Others, returning refugees and émigrés, soon joined them. German Jews in the uniforms of the occupiers, especially of the Americans, served as interpreters, interrogators, cultural officers, and ordinary GIs. Several thousand—some historians now estimate as many as nine thousand—exiles with a Jewish background returned to the Soviet occupation zone, mostly for political and ideological reasons. Some came from the Soviet Union, where they had found a precarious but life-saving refuge while others fell victim to Stalinist persecution—or, as was more often the case with the Jewish Communists, they returned from exile in the West, emigration destinations that would quickly become suspect in the Soviet zone. They traveled to the Soviet zone from the United States, Mexico, or England in hopes of building a new anti-Fascist democratic Germany in which socialism would finally vanquish antisemitism. But most of them did not identify as Jews, at least not publicly.[3]

The majority of German Jews in Germany at the end of the war had avoided or delayed deportation because they were married to "Aryans" or because they were Christians of "mixed race" (*Mischlinge*).[4] The pernicious categories of the Nuremberg Laws, which divided people according to religious or "racial" identity, marriage partners, children, and gender, had determined the kinds of persecution persons in mixed marriages or of "mixed race" were likely to face. They determined whether one was subject to forced labor, obligated to wear a Star of David, dependent on reduced rations, or deported to Hitler's "model" camp at Theresienstadt or, in some cases, even to an extermination camp.[5]

Overall, approximately fifteen thousand Germans who had been persecuted as Jews survived the war in their homeland.[6] Another nine thousand survivors returned from the liberated concentration camps in Poland and Czechoslovakia during the first weeks and months after the end of the war. A significant number of this minuscule set of survivors had only been declared Jewish by the Nuremberg Laws.

After the liberation of Munich on April 30, 1945, 398 Jews were officially found to be living in the city, almost all of them married to non-Jewish partners, a circumstance that had spared them deportation.[7] Another 160 Munich Jews returned from Theresienstadt—almost ten times that number had been deported there between June 1942 and February 1945.[8]

These devastating statistics reflected the situation in all large German cities. When American forces marched into Frankfurt on March 29, 1945, for example, between 150 and 200 Jews remained in the city; more than 11,000 Frankfurters had been murdered because of their Jewish origins. Almost none of the survivors, however, had belonged to the two flourishing Jewish communities in Frankfurt that had numbered more than 26,000 members prior to the Nazi seizure of power.[9] The city administration brought back another 336 persons from Theresienstadt, and a few other scattered survivors returned from other concentration camps or emerged from hiding places. Of the 650 persons persecuted as Jews who were living in Frankfurt in the summer of 1945, only about half had two Jewish parents.[10]

The members of the postwar Jewish communities that were reconstituted with a tiny fraction of their original numbers were generally elderly. The great majority of the younger generation of German Jews had been able to escape the country after 1933. Those who remained were generally older people who had not wanted to believe that their citizenship rights would be abrogated, found it too daunting to start afresh in a new country with a new language, or had simply been unable to leave before the outbreak of war in September 1939, despite their desperate efforts, as well as family members and others who had already emigrated. Initially, there were almost no children in postwar German-Jewish communities. In March 1946, of the 7,768 members of the Berlin community, only 70 were children below the age of six; the majority were over sixty.[11] Of the barely 1,400 German Jews in Hamburg, more than half were at least fifty years old.[12]

Mixed marriages and an aging population remained features of postwar German-Jewish communities throughout the entire occupation period, although the demographic details varied from community to community based on geographical location, the policies of the occupation, and the communal context. Returnees who decided to remain in Germany either temporarily or permanently for economic, cultural, or political reasons settled mainly in the cities. During the early postwar years, there were more than twice as many Jewish communities in the British zone as in the American. Three years after the end of the war, twenty-three Jewish communities were registered in the American zone. There were fifty communities, often very small, in the areas in northwestern Germany occupied by the British.[13] The new presence of Eastern European DPs would have a long-term effect on the development of these Jewish communities, especially in the American zone.

FOUR OCCUPATIONS

In the American occupation zone, the first stable community structures began to emerge in those places where Jews lived immediately after the end of the war even before concentration camp survivors returned. In Frankfurt, the American army installed an advisor for Jewish affairs a few days after the army's arrival in the city on April 1, 1945. This advisor not only looked after the interests of the Jews in Frankfurt but also was responsible for those who had been discriminated against and persecuted because they had been categorized as "mixed race," as well as their non-Jewish partners.[14] At the same time, the first religious service symbolized the establishment of new community structures, which soon began to consolidate. Rabbi Leopold Neuhaus, who had been deported in 1942, was among the survivors of Theresienstadt who returned to Frankfurt in early July. He led the new congregation and, if only for a short time, served as a bridge to the old prewar community. Neuhaus, who was born in Rotenburg an der Fulda in 1879, was the only German rabbi to resume his post in his old community immediately after the Holocaust.[15]

An American chaplain helped to rebuild the community in Stuttgart shortly after the end of the war, and by June 2, 1945, services were being held in an improvised synagogue in the Reinsburgstrasse. Here, too, the provisional leaders of the Jewish community (*Israelitische Kultusvereinigung*) made every effort to have 105 Jews from Württemberg returned from Theresienstadt and to feed and supply them and the 75 other survivors who arrived from Stutthof, Buchenwald, and other concentration camps.[16] Among them was Josef Warscher, who after five and a half years in Buchenwald was let off a bus in eastern Stuttgart, "and there I was. It's funny, you get out in some part of the city, stand there in the middle of the street, and ask yourself, What now? I came home, and there was no more home. I didn't know anyone anymore when I came back to Stuttgart."[17]

As of July 19, 1945, there was also once again a Jewish community in Munich under the leadership of Julius Spanier and Siegfried Neuland. In October Aaron Ohrenstein was named the first postwar rabbi of Munich. By March 1946 the new Jewish community in Munich numbered about twenty-eight hundred members, of whom barely eight hundred had lived in Munich before the war. The dedication of the synagogue in the spring of 1947 was a high point of the early postwar years.[18]

Jewish life began to reemerge in smaller cities as well. In Würzburg, for example, returnees from Theresienstadt set about reestablishing the community. They reopened the Jewish old-age home and repaired the cemetery; by November 1945 they had dedicated a memorial in the cemetery for Jews from Würzburg and Lower Franconia who had been killed in the concentration camps.[19] Only very few German Jews returned to the more rural areas. However, numerous so-called Jewish committees were founded, mostly organized by displaced persons; most of these committees had dissolved by the end of the 1940s, when the mass immigration of Jewish DPs to new homes outside of Germany made them obsolete. A few of these early DP communities have, however, lasted to the present day.

The communities in the British zone were founded almost exclusively by German Jews who had belonged to them in the prewar era.[20] The Jews of Essen who had evaded deportation, for example, gathered together to pray in May 1945. Initially, services had to be improvised in a hospital and guesthouse because the synagogue in the heart of Essen, which had been dedicated in 1913, had been left in ruins after Kristallnacht on November 9, 1938. The celebrated Art Nouveau design of the synagogue interior was destroyed, as was the plaque that memorialized the Jewish soldiers who had died fighting for Germany in World War I.[21]

The founding assembly of the Jewish community in Hamburg was held on September 18, 1945, with the support of the JDC, the American Jewish aid organization.[22] Most of the founding members were married to non-Jews. In March 1947 only three-quarters of the 1,268 registered members of the community identified as practicing Jews, while the rest of the members viewed the Jewish community as an organization representing the interests of those who had been racially persecuted.[23]

Of the twenty thousand Jews who had lived in Cologne, eleven thousand had been murdered; thousands had been able to flee Germany in time. When a few older people returned from Theresienstadt, they found provisional shelter in the ruins of the former Jewish homeless shelter and were integrated into a community that had been newly constituted even before the war had officially ended. Over the next several years, membership increased from eighty persons at the end of March 1945 to several hundred. The community consisted of Jewish

DPs in addition to returnees from Western countries; in 1949 the Jewish community of Cologne had 687 members, of whom a quarter had come from Eastern Europe.[24]

Jews who had fled the Nazis returned to other parts of Germany as well during the first months and years after the Holocaust. Displaced persons who had settled in the cities increasingly joined the existing communities. In September 1947 the Jewish community of Dortmund, which had been decimated by the Holocaust, numbered two hundred members, most of whom had not been born in Germany. Moreover, Jewish communities also developed outside the larger cities like Cologne, Düsseldorf, Hamburg, and Dortmund as some Jews settled in rural areas. In the Westphalian town of Warendorf near Münster, Hugo Spiegel, who had survived the Buchenwald, Auschwitz, and Dachau concentration camps, set up a small prayer room in a side room of the former synagogue. Services were held in early September 1945 with a Torah scroll that had been salvaged from the desecrated synagogue in November 1938 by a leather dealer in Warendorf who hoped to return it to the Jewish community after the war.[25] After his return, Spiegel, the father of Paul Spiegel, who would serve as chair of the Central Committee of Jews in Germany from 2000 to 2006, helped to organize the Jews who lived in the vicinity of Münster. He also helped to found the Jewish community, which at first numbered only twenty-eight members. By 1948 a total of forty-five Jews lived in Münster and environs.[26]

In July 1946 a community was founded in Detmold to represent the interests of Jews, "half-Jews," and the wives and children of those who had been murdered in the camps.[27] Many of the people cared for by the Detmold community had only recently arrived. In June 1946 forty-three refugees from the city of Breslau joined the survivors of concentration camps and their family members. These refugees had lost their homes more than once in the previous years. As Germans living in so-called mixed marriages they had endured persecution and exclusion due to the Nazi racial laws. Ironically, however, after the war that same status meant that life in Breslau, now Wrocław, which had become part of postwar Poland, became intolerable. Although the official policy of the Polish government was to rebuild Jewish communities in its newly "recovered" territories in the western part of the country, all those defined as German citizens were expelled. When the refugees finally arrived in the British occupation zone, where Detmold was located, however, they were denied DP status because the borders had been officially closed to infiltrees from the East at the end of 1945, and they therefore became dependent on the support of the local Jewish community.[28]

The number of Jews living in the French zone remained extremely low. Very few German Jews had survived in southwestern Germany or had returned there, and there were also very few Jewish DPs. The region was far removed from the routes used by the Bricha to funnel Jews from Eastern Europe to the DP camps; furthermore, the opportunities for emigration were limited because the zone had no American consulate, and French immigration laws were highly restrictive. The Jewish communities in Freiburg and Baden-Baden, as well as in Speyer, Niederlahnstein, Mainz, Koblenz, Saarbrücken, Trier, Neuwied, and Landau, in the northern part of the French zone, were therefore founded almost exclusively by German Jews.[29] The southern part, by contrast, became a temporary home for Eastern European DPs, the majority of whom found shelter in *kibbutzim* or in the cities, where they were supported by UNRRA and the JDC.[30] The only exception was the Jewish community of Freiburg, which had about a hundred German members.[31] The center of Jewish life in the French zone was Constance, with over 180 persons, of whom only a handful were, or had been, city residents. Most of them were DPs supported by the Central Committee of Jews in the French occupation zone and the aid organizations that had established their offices there.[32]

Developments in the Saarland differed from those in the French zone as a result of specific historical circumstances: after two years of American and then French military administration, the Saarland had in 1947 been granted semiautonomous status, which ended only in 1957, when the region was integrated into the Federal Republic of Germany. Encouraged by a vigorously pursued process of denazification, refugees had begun to stream back into the Saarland, primarily from exile in France, and they played leading roles in rebuilding the region. Over time, returnees, including Jews, began to arrive, and in June 1946 they reestablished the Jewish community of Saarbrücken.[33] The community leadership consisted almost entirely of Jews from the Saarland, and the majority of members were also returnees.[34] In March 1947 the communities in Saarbrücken, Saarlouis, Völklingen, and Neunkirchen had a total of 153 members.[35] In contrast to the other West German occupation zones, 60 percent of the Jews in the Saarland had survived the Nazi period in France, and relatively few of them had experienced a concentration camp.[36]

Persecution and deportations had also taken a disastrous toll in the Soviet-occupied portions of Germany. Approximately thirty-five hundred Jews lived there in 1945—barely 3 percent of the pre-1933 Jewish population.[37] Only fifteen survivors returned to the Erfurt community, which had previously numbered eleven hundred members. In Dresden, a city almost completely destroyed by Allied bombing, the former six-thousand-member community had dwindled to about a dozen survivors.[38] And when American troops entered Leipzig in April 1945, only about two dozen Jews remained of the twelve thousand who had constituted the community before the war.[39]

Nonetheless, Jewish life began to reemerge in eastern Germany almost immediately after the end of the war. In May 1945, even before the Soviets officially occupied the city at the beginning of July, about fifteen Leipzig Jews met to reestablish the Jewish community.[40] In June 1945 an estimated nine hundred to twelve hundred persons lived in Leipzig who, according to National Socialist racial teachings, had been classified as Jews or had reason to fear persecution because of Jewish family members. At the end of January 1946, the Jewish community's former status as a public corporation was reaffirmed.[41] In the meantime, the number of survivors there had increased: the first returnees were Jewish forced laborers from the armaments factories in Germany and concentration camp survivors from Buchenwald and its subcamps. In the early summer of 1945, about two hundred Leipzig Jews were brought back from Theresienstadt, and they were later joined by about sixty survivors of the last transports to the Eastern European concentration and extermination camps.[42] However, the number of official community members in Leipzig remained modest—only about 280 persons in the spring of 1947.[43]

Jewish communities were also reestablished between 1947 and 1949 in Magdeburg, Dresden, Chemnitz, Erfurt, Halle, and Schwerin; they managed to sustain themselves throughout the existence of the German Democratic Republic.[44] Until 1948 tiny, short-lived communities had also been established in Aschersleben, Bitterfeld, Dessau, Eisenach, Gera, Görlitz, Jena, Mühlhausen, Plauen, and Prenzlau, but some of them simply had too few members to constitute the required *minyan* (prayer group) of ten adult males.[45] These small communities were primarily comprised of former members and Jews who had settled there for ideological reasons. Since there were no DP camps in the Soviet occupation zone, the few Eastern European Jews who joined the communities were concentration camp survivors or refugees from Poland who had been part of the stream of refugees that had flowed toward the Western occupation zones starting in the summer of 1945 and had for various reasons been stranded in the Soviet zone.[46] Overall, the number of members in communities in the Soviet zone continued to decline. As in the communities in the Western zones, the population losses were driven by emigration and old age. A census in October 1946 showed that there were about 4,500 Jews in the entire Soviet zone, more than half of them living in East Berlin.[47] At the time of the founding of the GDR in October 1949, the eight largest communities that had united in a national association counted 1,250 members. The 2,500 Jews registered in East Berlin belonged to the separate Gesamt-Berliner Gemeinde (United Berlin Community), which encompassed both West and East Berlin.[48]

These figures, however, reveal little about how many Jews and persons of Jewish origin actually lived in the Soviet zone during the second half of the 1940s. German Jews who returned for political reasons, for example, such as the writers

Stefan Heym and Anna Seghers, the literary scholar Hans Meyer, and the philosopher Ernst Bloch, only rarely joined the newly reconstituted communities.

"Berlin represents a special category all for itself," wrote the JDC representative Koppel Pinson in January 1947 in his report "Jewish Life in Liberated Germany."[49] What he meant—and critically at that—was the peculiar combination of a relatively large number of surviving German Jews, of whom he estimated that more than half were "half-Jews," "quarter-Jews," and Jews married to "Aryans," who had been joined by an ever larger group of DPs, the "infiltrees" who had arrived in the former Reich capital from Poland.

In July 1945 the former Reich capital, captured by the Red Army in late April and early May, counted 6,000 to 7,000 Jews, the truncated remnant of a vibrant community that had once totaled 160,000 to 200,000. They included, according to official sources, 2,444 in the Soviet sector, where the (Soviet) Military Administration had ordered the immediate reestablishment of the Berlin Jewish community, centered in the war-damaged Oranienburger Strasse synagogue. Some of them had survived disguised as "Aryans" or as "submarines" (U-boats) or "illegals," hidden in factory lofts, in apartments, or in one of the small shacks that dotted the garden colonies of Berlin workers. Others survived on the grounds of the Weissensee Jewish cemetery or both officially and secretly in the strange, ambiguous world of the Jewish Hospital—right under the eyes of the Gestapo. A very few returned from the death camps and concentration camps, among them Heinz Galinski and Julius Meyer, who had survived Auschwitz and later led the Jewish community in Berlin, one in the West (after 1949) and the other in the East (1946–1953). Some elderly persons returned from Theresienstadt as well. Others had survived in precarious situations, in so-called privileged mixed marriages or because they themselves were classified as being "mixed race." Of the presumably five thousand to seven thousand "full Jews" who went underground, only between fourteen hundred and seventeen hundred lived to see liberation.[50] The fact that any of these German Jews, all of whom had been the targets of Nazi racial terror, had, against all odds, survived bordered on the miraculous. Berliners in general had endured massive air strikes and anti-aircraft flak, as well as the final battle for the city. But the Jews remaining in Berlin also were forced to contend with a lack of food ration cards, no regular shelter, the constant danger of denunciation, and the nerve-racking specter of arrest and deportation.[51]

Under the National Socialists, categories such as "full Jew," "half-Jew," and "quarter-Jew" or having an "Aryan" partner delineated the possibilities of survival. After the war, the question of who was Jewish and why took on an entirely new meaning. In a time of tumult and extreme scarcity, in which minimal goods and services were doled out according to calibrations of victimhood or guilt, such assigned identities were of great material importance. They determined access to

Employees of the Jewish Hospital in Berlin during a march commemorating the victims of Fascism, 1946. bpk / photograph by Abraham Pisarek.

support and protection by the Jewish community, to jobs with the occupying powers, to food rations, to housing, and to property claims. Sometimes they were simply a means of clarifying identity after personal loss (of family and property) or negotiating bitter and conflicted memories.

Jewish members of the Allied armed forces, Berlin Jews, and DPs gathered together for religious services at the Harnack House, the American officers club in the suburb of Dahlem, which had gotten through the war unscathed. In the fall of 1945, many celebrated the High Holy Days there for the first time after the war. The American Chaplains Center, a comfortable Dahlem villa that had been confiscated from a Nazi family and was still filled with "an abundance of Nazi literature, pins, emblems, and paraphernalia," became a meeting place for Jewish soldiers from all four armies and the British army's Jewish Brigade.[52] In April 1946 an enormous Seder was held at Passover in the Rathaus Schöneberg for more than two thousand soldiers from all of the occupying powers, as well as local Jews. The Seder was led by Herbert Friedman, who, like many Jewish chaplains in the American army, attempted to reconcile the duties of his office with his role in helping the Bricha spirit Polish Jews into the American zone.[53]

HOME AS AN ALIEN PLACE

In its inaugural issue on March 1, 1946, *Der Weg* (The road), the semiofficial organ of the Berlin Jewish community, raised a number of key questions about the future of Jews in Germany. The editors adopted a wait-and-see attitude toward the alternatives for "Jewish fellow citizens," either emigration or participation in the reconstruction of Europe and Germany. Germans, the editors seemed to insist, would have to prove themselves worthy of a Jewish presence in their midst. At the same time, it was obvious that the editors fervently hoped that a newly reconstructed postwar Germany would be welcoming—a hope that soon proved illusory. In a rather astonishing expression of undaunted German-Jewish Enlightenment tenets, the lead article stated that "in this manner" the journal "wished to contribute to totally eliminating the chasm that had opened up between Jews and non-Jews as a result of twelve years of uninhibited hate campaigns against Jews." And as if readers in 1946 still required reminding, the article continued that "despite all efforts, the antisemitic poison that Hitler had administered to the German people, and not only since his coup d'état, has not yet been everywhere and completely neutralized."[54] Each subsequent issue expressed increased anger and anxiety in the face of continuing antisemitism and the absence of remorse among the Germans. If, as the former Berliner and then British occupation officer Julius Posener reported back to Palestine, "in the summer of '45 it was considered good form to think that something had to be done for the Jews," that initial sentiment quickly faded, turning to German resentment over perceived privileges and the all-too-familiar-sounding conviction that "since they were Jews, they would probably do well (after all, Jews always know how to get along)."[55]

Views on the proper future for Jews in Germany depended on each person's experiences during the war. For the DPs, the perpetual question was when and how they could leave "the cursed, bloodstained" soil of Germany behind them; for the German Jews, it was usually more a question of "whether." Jews who had survived underground tended to have the most positive, but also the narrowest, view of the future. They were often the most optimistic about the potential for reconciliation and cooperation in building a new democratic Germany. In general, they owed their survival not just to a single person but to entire, mostly informal, networks of people who were willing to help or at least tolerate others who did.[56] Hans Rosenthal, who became a spokesman for the "reconciliationist" faction in the community even as he developed his career as one of Germany's most prominent and popular radio talk show (and later television) hosts, perhaps summed up this position most explicitly in his memoirs. The memory of three older women who had protected and looked after him in a Berlin *Schrebergarten* (garden colony) had sustained his identification with the new Germany. They had made it possible for him, "after this for us Jews so terrible time, to live freely (without reservation) in Germany, for me to feel as a German, to be without hatred, a citizen of this country."[57] Others urged a differentiated attitude, arguing that while "the population was indifferent" and "a large majority just didn't care about the fate of the Jews, another (smaller) group helped the Jews and supported them." "In part, however, this help was provided only in exchange for significant compensation. Still, it cannot be denied that a part of the population did provide selfless help."[58]

Reflecting the shell-shocked mood of its readers, *Der Weg* often seemed burdened by a split personality. At some points, its invocation of the Jewish contribution to German *Kultur* read, as if in a surreal time warp, like a revived if reduced version of a pre-Nazi perspective represented by the Central Association of Germans of Jewish Faith (Central Verein deutscher Staatsbürger jüdischen Glaubens, the mainstream self-defense organization). Articles about the early nineteenth-century Jewish *salonnières* Henriette Herz and Dorothea Schlegel and other German-Jewish luminaries offered homage to the destroyed German-Jewish "symbiosis," as if stubbornly insisting on that history could somehow lead to its resurrection. At the same time, people were more or less in agreement that "the few exceptions only confirm that as a rule the crimes committed against the Jews were tolerated and approved." Moreover, the courageous solidarity of the few could not outweigh the guilt and responsibility that the Jews ascribed to (and that were steadfastly rejected by) the great majority: "The courageous people who supported us will not be forgotten when collective guilt is assessed, and they will testify for the German people, but they cannot erase that collective guilt."[59]

The "illegals" who had survived in Berlin found themselves on the defensive and pressured into protesting that they, too, had suffered, albeit in ways different from those who had gone through the concentration camps. But a bittersweet sense of homecoming to a place that, despite everything, felt familiar often welled up even in the Jews who straggled back from the death camps. This was especially true for someone like nineteen-year-old Hans Winterfeldt, who had lived underground and was deported relatively late. Despite himself and fully aware that "a year and two months ago, on June 15, 1944, I was deported to Auschwitz-Birkenau in a cattle car," he wrote, "I felt somehow at home again." The Berlin dialect sounded so familiar, and "despite the devastation wreaked by bombs and street fighting," he still knew exactly "how to get from one place to another."[60]

RETURN WITH MIXED FEELINGS

In response to the anti-Jewish boycott on April 1, 1933, the philosopher Hans Jonas wrote, "No matter how long this ordeal lasted, no self-respecting Jew could stay in this country." He further "vowed never to return except as a soldier in a conquering army," which he did as a British soldier and member of the Jewish Brigade in July 1945.[61] As his unit with its Star of David insignias approached a camp for displaced persons in Landsberg am Lech, their encounter with surviving Jews was memorable. "People streamed out of the camp, took up positions along the highway, and cheered us as we passed. We stopped, and they embraced us and kissed the Star of David on our uniforms. They'd been liberated by the Americans, but here they were encountering armed Jews—coming as victors, not as martyrs or victims!"[62]

The German journalist Ursula von Kardoff, who had fled from Berlin to Bavaria to escape the Soviet takeover, described the rapid power reversal from a very different perspective. Seeing a military convoy that included vehicles bearing the "Stars of Zion," apparently belonging to a "Jewish division" on the autobahn, it seemed to her "a demonstration of divine justice," as "these soldiers in the uniform of the victors rode on one side [of the road]," while "on the other, open trucks carrying German prisoners of war sped by." Although she had never been a member of the party, Kardoff had unwaveringly pursued her career as a journalist under the Third Reich. Now she flashed back to scenes only a few years earlier when young German officers bedecked with medals had strutted along Berlin's Kurfürstendamm past Jews who were forced to wear as a sign of humiliation the same star now proudly displayed by the victors.[63] The local inhabitants, suddenly confronted with former concentration camp inmates emaciated and in rags and then with a further influx of refugees from Eastern Europe, approached their new neighbors with "a mixture of fear, contempt, and bewilderment."[64] As Jonas recalled, after the soldiers of the Jewish Brigade had distributed their rations of corned beef, peas, coffee, and chocolate among the survivors, duty forced them to move on: "That was our first mass encounter with survivors."[65] The survivors were from Poland and spoke Yiddish, and many of the brigade members from Palestine spoke Yiddish as well. For the first time they heard about Treblinka and Auschwitz, names that during their mission in Italy had been little more than rumors. As they continued through destroyed cities like Karlsruhe, Pforzheim, and Kassel, Germany "resembled a moonscape, full of bomb craters, ruined buildings silhouetted against the sky. This sight inspired an emotion that I hope never to experience again but don't wish to deny: a sense of rejoicing, of satisfied, or at least half-satisfied, revenge."[66] For a long time, Jonas recalled, the sight of these devastated German cities were among the happiest moments of his life. The brigade continued on toward Frankfurt by way of Saarbrücken into northeastern France, finally reaching Venlo in southeastern Holland, twelve miles from Jonas's home city of Mönchengladbach. The British insisted that the brigade be stationed outside of Germany, fearing that the men from Palestine

Deputy Mayor Ferdinand Friedensberg welcoming Jewish returnees from Shanghai in Reinickendorf, Berlin, August 1947. Bildarchiv Abraham Pisarek / akg-images.

might engage in acts of revenge. Jonas, however, did cross the border, and like so many others who returned, if only briefly, to what had once been home, he reported the cynicism and shock he felt when confronted with his former neighbors' apparent disbelief and their unwillingness to admit what had happened. They even asked after his mother, who had been deported to Auschwitz and murdered: "'And how's your mother? Have you heard from her?' I replied, 'She was killed.' 'Killed? Who would have killed her? People don't do that to an old lady.'" Standing in front of his father's desk in his former home, both of which had been appropriated, he had to listen as the current inhabitants labeled as mere "atrocity stories" reports of the murder of Jews in Auschwitz.[67]

Jonas, who remained in Europe until November 1945, wanted nothing to do with denazification or the rebuilding effort: "The German people could go to the devil, for all I cared. . . . [T]he majority of Germans you ran into either refused to acknowledge what had happened or repeated ad nauseam that they hadn't been involved."[68] Repulsed by the same denial and servility that Hannah Arendt would later describe in her now classic "The Aftermath of Nazi Rule: Report from Germany," he returned to Palestine in late 1945.[69] However, he was unable to "get a firm footing in Jerusalem." Sensing the beginning of a new "endless war" and bereft of the lively intellectual life and social solidarity he remembered experiencing in prewar Jerusalem, he and his family immigrated to the United States in 1948. "I have two small children now," he wrote, "and they should have a chance to grow up in peace, and not be subjected to mortal danger and deprivation."[70] Only many years later did he reestablish contact with friends and colleagues in Israel. The parents of his wife, Lore, on the other hand, returned to Germany. As a lawyer, Jonas's father-in-law reestablished a practice that developed as a result of the restitution laws, a specialization that for obvious reasons offered opportunities to the few Jewish lawyers who had returned.[71]

But in reality only a tiny minority of surviving German Jews returned to Germany, and when they did it was often with foreign passport in hand and only for a short time. In the immediate postwar period between 1945 and 1947, the Jewish presence was, however, clearly visible and was widely commented on, usually in a manner way out of proportion to the actual number of survivors. Jews were especially visible when they appeared in the uniform of the occupiers. Berliners were surprised by the flawless German spoken by some of the occupiers or, as the actress Hildegard Knef recalled, a German that got better with each sentence.[72] One of the young Polish officer Marcel Reich-Ranicki's first forays into the Berlin of his youth took him to the apartment of his beloved high school teacher Reinhold Knick: "Casually he remarked that many of his visitors now wore American or British uniforms. These were his former Jewish pupils."[73] For these Jews wearing the uniform of the victor, it was a strange "homecoming to the foreign," an especially haunting and poignant position between two worlds. They could no longer see themselves as Germans but were not yet completely at home in the United States (and even less so in Great Britain). To some extent, they were distrusted by both their old and their new compatriots.

Jewish actors and writers had an especially difficult time finding a foothold—the audience and applause associated with success, so essential to artists—outside of the German-speaking world. In 1948 Fritz Kortner, who had returned from the United States, stirred genuine gratitude and spontaneous thunderous applause when he attended a performance (as an audience member) at the Kurfürstendamm Theater in his (chosen) home (*Wahlheimat*), Berlin. It was this applause that enabled him to endure to the end the "unimaginably abominable" performance with, in his view, its intolerable stage language.[74] That a return to Germany was associated with real problems and psychological pitfalls, even for someone like Kortner, was made clear in his semiautobiographical film *Der Ruf* (*The Last Illusion*, 1949), which not only recounts the return of a Jewish professor to a German university but also describes the continued unvarnished antisemitism that he faces. In a 1947 letter, the actress Steffi Spira articulated the mixed feelings of many Jewish returnees: "I must confess that the life I lead in Germany, from which I had been separated for many years, is not easy for me. Hitler fascism has left deep wounds. Not only did it turn to rubble the old cities, it also destroyed the sensibilities of people, their moral and intellectual values, to a degree that is difficult to imagine from the outside, even in one's fantasies."[75]

Kortner returned to Germany as an American citizen, convinced that National Socialism had been a totalitarian system imposed upon the Germans, something that, under certain circumstances, could have happened in any other nation. His return made him many enemies among émigrés in the United States.[76] His own doubts about his decision never disappeared. He had "returned completely without bitterness," he said later in an interview on the occasion of his sixty-fifth birthday. But in his memoirs, he described the reaction of those who had remained behind and who viewed the refugees as tourists on vacation ("pleasure travelers") during the war, while they had suffered in Germany: "Most of them were obstinately convinced that no suffering could approach theirs. In all probability, they needed to believe that they had suffered the most injustice in order to assuage their subconscious [guilt]."[77]

Some returnees elected to settle in the Soviet zone, either temporarily or permanently, because they were committed socialists or Communists. Louis Fürnberg arrived in Berlin in 1949 as a cultural attaché with the Czechoslovakian embassy. Several years earlier he had been reluctant to return to Germany. In November 1945 he wrote to Arnold Zweig, "We can't decide whether to return to Germany. Not for reasons of caution. But because it is good to let a little grass grow over one's feelings."[78] Zweig himself could not be dissuaded from returning to East Berlin from Haifa, although numerous friends and acquaintances advised him against it. In a letter to his friend Lion Feuchtwanger, Zweig explained the task facing writers in the reconstruction of Germany:

> The zone-zebra called Germany will perhaps be transformed into a unitary horse if we German writers reinforce and support the efforts being made that are supposed to lead to German reconstitution. Whether we can do that by staying away is contested by some. Of course, I would give such voices credence only if I had bestirred myself in Germany. On the other hand, I have absolutely no desire to give people material for idle chatter about my "return to Germany" after having deflected it with such scorn last year. And finally, I value my productivity greatly, so that I cannot put up with difficult living conditions that are made even more difficult by my impaired vision. Another consideration is that housing and living expenses here are high and that I no longer wish to spend my time as a big fish in shallow Palestinian waters.[79]

This return was a decision that he seems never to have regretted: "But, dear Feuchtwanger, do not believe that I have regretted for even a second what we resolved to do and did last year. I do not think that one can live anywhere else with the same sense of a clean decision. Of course this is not a criticism of you—everyone remains for as long as possible in the place that he has created for himself."[80]

ATINA GROSSMANN is Professor of history at Cooper Union in New York. She has been a fellow at the Institute for Advanced Study in Princeton, the American Academy in Berlin, the United States Holocaust Memorial Museum, and the Davis Center at Princeton University. Her publications include Jews, Germans, and Allies: Close Encounters in Occupied Germany (on which parts of this section are based) and Wege in der Fremde: Deutsch-jüdische Begegnungsgeschichte zwischen Feldafing, New York und Teheran; and as a coeditor, After the Nazi Racial State: Difference and Democracy in Germany and Europe and Crimes of War: Guilt and Denial in the Twentieth Century, as well as Shelter from the Holocaust: Rethinking Jewish Survival in the Soviet Union (with M. Edele and S. Fitzpatrick) and The Joint Distribution Committee: 100 Years of Jewish History (with A. Patt, L. Levi, and M. Maud), both forthcoming from Wayne State University Press in 2018.

TAMAR LEWINSKY is curator of contemporary history at the Jewish Museum Berlin. Her publications include Unterbrochenes Gedicht: Jiddische Literatur im Nachkriegsdeutschland, 1944–1950 and Displaced Poets: Jiddische Schriftsteller im Nachkriegsdeutschland, 1945–1951.

NOTES

1. H. Rosenthal (1987), p. 88.
2. M. Boveri (2004), pp. 127–128. For further detail and analysis of the Jewish presence in immediate postwar Berlin, some of which is included here, see the original English-language version in A. Grossmann (2007).
3. See, for example, U. Breitsprecher (2010); K. Hartewig (2000).
4. H. Maor (1961), p. 2.
5. There, too, they were "privileged and were not sent automatically to Auschwitz. When Theresienstadt was liberated in April 1945, almost 37 percent of the inmates were 'non-Mosaic Jews.'" A. Barkai (1997), p. 362.
6. K. R. Grossmann (1951), p. 10.
7. M. Strnad (2010), pp. 147–148, especially "Einwohnerstatistik der jüdischen Münchner 1933–1945," pp. 178–180.
8. Stadtarchiv München (ed.) (2000), p. 15; A. Heusler (ed.) (2007), vol. 2 (M–Z), p. 894.
9. A. Tauber (2008), pp. 22–24.
10. A. Tauber (2008), p. 29.
11. A. Grossmann (2007), p. 95.
12. H. Lavsky (2002), p. 81.
13. J. Zieher (2005), p. 14, fn. 17.
14. A. Tauber (2008), pp. 24–25.

15. A. Tauber (2008), pp. 33–34.

16. Statement of the first board of the Jewish community (*Israelitische Kultusvereinigung*) Württemberg for the time between June 10, 1945 and May 24, 1946, May 25, 1946, in StadtAS, IRGW 1026/492.

17. J. Warscher (1997), cited in M. Brenner (1997), p. 112.

18. A. Kauders and T. Lewinsky (2006), pp. 185–186.

19. "Mahnmal der Juden: Würzburg ehrt die gemordeten jüdischen Mitbürger," *Main Post: Würzburger Stadtblatt,* November 24, 1945; T. Sauer (1988), pp. 70–71.

20. For example, for Dortmund, Düsseldorf, and Cologne. J. Zieher (2005), p. 45.

21. H. Elkan (1959), pp. 13–17.

22. "Minutes of the Meeting for the Purpose of Founding the 'Jewish Community in Hamburg' on Tuesday, September 18, 1945, 5 PM at the House at 38 Rothenbaumchaussee," in StAHH, 522–2, no. 605.

23. U. Büttner (1997), pp. 78–79.

24. Z. Asaria (1959a), p. 28; J. Zieher (2005), pp. 39–40, 45–46 cite the following figures: April 1945: 80 persons; October 1946: 437; May 1947: 635; 1948: 655; 1949: 687.

25. P. Spiegel (2003), pp. 85–86.

26. P. Spiegel (1961), pp. 33, 35.

27. W. Müller (1994), p. 170.

28. W. Müller (1994), p. 169; K. Friedla (2010).

29. "Report on the Situation of the Jews in the French Zone, November 19, 1946," and "Report on the Situation of the Jews in the French Zone, April 28, 1947," both in YIVO, RG 294.1, folder 514, reel 45.

30. Report no. 1, issued by the Comité Israélite Central pour la zone d'occupation française en Allemagne, October 1948, in MVO, DPG, 1635/116.

31. "Report on the Situation of the Jews in the French Zone, April 28, 1947."

32. "Report on the Situation of the Jews in the French Zone, November 19, 1946," and Report on the Situation of the Jews in the French Zone, April 28, 1947." See also Leyb Kurland, "A bazukh bay di yidn in Konstants," *Undzer veg,* August 30, 1946.

33. W. Kasel (1960), p. 229.

34. A. Gemeinhardt (2010), p. 36.

35. A. Gemeinhardt (2008), p. 61.

36. A. Gemeinhardt (2008), p. 65.

37. A. Timm (2002), p. 18.

38. L. Mertens (1997), p. 27.

39. S. Held (1995), p. 11.

40. S. Held (1995), p. 9.

41. S. Held (1995), p. 11.

42. S. Held (1995), pp. 13–15.

43. S. Held (1995), p. 8. More on this in H. Niether (2015).

44. E. Burgauer (1993), p. 138.

45. L. Mertens (1997), pp. 29–31.

46. S. Held (1995), p. 37.

47. L. Mertens (1997), p. 28.

48. A. Timm (2002), p. 18.

49. K. S. Pinson (1947), p. 106. The other quotations in the paragraph are from the same source.

50. F. Stern (1992a), p. 23. A. Nachama (1995), pp. 268–269, assumes that there were approximately seven thousand Jews in Berlin immediately after the end of the war. See also A. Seligmann (1992). All of these statistics have to be considered approximate.

51. A. Grossmann (2005); M. Kaplan (1998), esp. pp. 145–228; W. Benz (ed.) (2003). See also the recollections of L. Brandt (1984); L. Gross (1982); E. Fischer (1995); P. Wyden (1992).

52. Introduction to photo album, Collection of Saul M Loeb, pp. 2, 3, in JMB Archiv 2001/197/4.

53. For more on Friedman, see the oral history interview with Herbert Friedman, June 12, 1992, in United States Holocaust Memorial Museum, Washington, D.C.

54. *Der Weg*, March 1, 1946, p. 1.

55. J. Posener (2001), p. 139.

56. Regarding such networks of rescuers, see R. Andreas-Friedrich (1947); G. Beck (1999); also W. Benz (ed.) (2003); E. Boehm (1985); L. Gross (1982); C. Kahane (1999).

57. H. Rosenthal (1987), p. 80.

58. Report on conditions in the Gemeinde (o.D.), pp. 60–63, in CJA, 5A1/3 (Stiftung Neue Synagoge Berlin—Centrum Judaicum, Archiv).

59. Wilhelm Meier, "Kollektivschuld," *Der Weg*, July 5, 1946.

60. Hans Winterfeldt, "Deutschland: Ein Zeitbild 1926–1945. Leidensweg eines deutschen Juden in den ersten 19 Jahren seines Lebens," unpublished, in LBI Archive NY, ME 690 (online), p. 440.

61. H. Jonas (2008), pp. 74–75.

62. H. Jonas (2008), pp. 131–132, 135.

63. U. von Kardorff (1962), p. 291. Clearly, the units involved belonged to the Jewish Brigade.

64. S. Schochet (1983), p. 131.

65. H. Jonas (2008), p. 131.

66. H. Jonas (2008), pp. 131–132.

67. H. Jonas (2008), p. 135.

68. H. Jonas (2008), p. 139.

69. See H. Arendt (1950), pp. 342–353.

70. H. Jonas (2008), pp. 150–151, 163.

71. H. Jonas (2008), pp. 161, 163.

72. H. Knef (1971), pp. 133–150.

73. Knick had taught at the Werner-Siemens-Realgymnasium. M. Reich-Ranicki (2001), p. 33.

74. F. Kortner (1986), p. 560.

75. Letter from Steffi Spira to Nico Rost, October 9, 1947, in AdK, Steffi-Spira-Archiv IIc (preliminary call number).

76. F. Kortner (1986), p. 431.

77. F. Kortner (1986), p. 358.

78. Letter from Louis Fürnberg to Arnold Zweig, November 11, 1945, in AdK, Louis-Fürnberg-Archiv 991.

79. Letter from Arnold Zweig to Lion Feuchtwanger, December 17, 1947, in AdK, Arnold-Zweig-Archiv 6745/6748.

80. Letter from Arnold Zweig to Lion Feuchtwanger, May 25, 1948, in AdK, Arnold-Zweig-Archiv 6760/6763.

4 DISSOLUTION AND ESTABLISHMENT

THE SITUATION IN the immediate postwar period was chaotic and volatile, and Germany's future was uncertain. By 1947, however, the political situation and everyday life had changed: for the defeated Germans, for the victorious powers, and for the Jewish survivors. In the face of efforts aimed at denazification, justice and restitution took a backseat. Given the ever-heightening Cold War tensions, the American military government in particular elected to cooperate with its former enemy, rebuild the German economy, and grant the country greater political autonomy. In April 1947 Gen. Lucius D. Clay ordered the dismissal of all those who had become naturalized Americans after 1933, clearly signaling the declining influence of anti-Nazis who had gone into exile—whether Jewish, left-wing, or both. The era that Samuel Gringauz, one of the leading spokesmen of the DPs, later characterized as the "golden age" of the DPs, from the fall of 1945 until the summer of 1947, was coming to an end.[1] The Germans demanded in no uncertain terms that they be given more control over their own affairs. Both the Allies and the Germans became increasingly impatient with a Jewish refugee population requiring economic assistance, especially given the social and economic burden of integrating almost twelve million ethnic German refugees and expellees from the parts of Europe that were now dominated by the Soviet Union.[2]

The Jewish DPs themselves were becoming increasingly frustrated and impatient with lives that consisted largely of waiting. Their mood sank to a new low in the summer of 1947 when passengers aboard the SS *President Warfield*, renamed *Exodus 1947* by the Haganah, were denied entry into Palestine. This episode dramatically demonstrated how the fate of the Jewish DPs in Germany was inextricably linked to British policies regarding Palestine and the international efforts to create a Jewish state. In 1946 the British government had rejected the recommendations of its own Anglo-American committee to release one hundred thousand emigration certificates for Palestine. A year later, the run-down former American steamer set sail from a port near Marseille with forty-five hundred Jewish survivors, while at the same time members of the United Nations Special Committee on Palestine (UNSCOP) were in Palestine on a fact-finding mission.

Demonstration at the Bergen-Belsen DP camp against British policies in Palestine after the *Exodus 1947* affair, September 1947. Yad Vashem / Hadassah Rosensaft.

The *Exodus 1947* aimed to run the British blockade of Palestine and ferry a large number of Jewish survivors to the nascent Jewish state, which required avoiding the internment of passengers on Cyprus, a fate that had befallen most potential immigrants before them.

A confrontation in the port of Haifa led to the death of two DPs and one American crew member, as well as numerous wounded passengers. Although the organizers of *Exodus 1947* failed in their purpose—the ship was forced to return to Europe—the battle to reach Palestine demonstrated the determination of the Zionists. When the French government refused to use force to bring the passengers on land in Toulon, the British decided to send them back to their point of origin—Germany. On September 8, 1947, the survivors of the Holocaust who had embarked for Palestine were returned to the British zone, where they were interned. These dramatic events, which were reported worldwide, elicited precisely the sympathies that the Zionist organizers had hoped for. They led to massive demonstrations of solidarity among the Jewish DPs and intensified the political pressure to create a Jewish state that could take in the survivors. Shortly thereafter, on September 20, the British government decided to give up its mandate in Palestine, and two months later, on November 29, the General Assembly of the United Nations voted to partition Palestine along the lines of the UNSCOP report.[3] The DPs in Germany were jubilant. People danced with joy in the camps, and on the streets of German cities they hoisted the flag of a state whose independence had not yet been achieved. The State of Israel was declared a half-year later, on May 14, 1948. In the meantime, however, the DPs were generally still not permitted to leave their temporary refuge in occupied Germany.[4] At the same time, the Yishuv, foreseeing an escalating conflict with the Arabs once the British had withdrawn and the state was declared, pushed ever more insistently for open entry to young Jews who would be able to settle and defend the land, soon to be a Jewish state. Most of the Jewish DPs, in turn, became increasingly anxious to leave an ever more assertive Germany. The events of 1948 were to prove a turning point. Major milestones included preparations for the founding of the Federal Republic of Germany in 1949 and the transition from the military government to civilian "supervision" by the High Commissioner for Occupied Germany (HICOG); the loosening of American immigration laws; the escalation of the Cold War, especially in Berlin; and the declaration of independence of the State of Israel.

In fact, 1948 also marked the beginning of a mass exodus from Germany not only by DPs but also by a significant number of remaining German Jews. In April 1948 there were still about 165,000 Jewish DPs; by September only 30,000 remained. In 1950 the total number of both DPs and German Jews had shrunk to 30,000. By the time Jews celebrated their third Passover after the end of the war, the exodus from the German Diaspora seemed to have finally become a reality.[5]

CLOSURE OF THE CAMPS AND ITS CONSEQUENCES

The DP camps began to empty out with the beginning of mass emigration in 1948. The IRO, which had taken control of the camps, began to decrease their number and to concentrate the remaining population in better facilities. Of the sixty-five larger camps set aside for Jewish DPs at the end of 1946, only fifty-three remained at the end of June 1948. A year later, the number had dwindled to seventeen, to which were added eight Jewish DP hospitals and sanatoriums.[6]

This consolidation enabled the IRO and the aid organizations to substantially decrease their administrative costs.[7] Not coincidentally, the relief agencies also hoped that repeated resettlement would motivate the refugees to emigrate.[8] But the closure of camps did not always run smoothly, because their "liquidation"—the DP jargon—led to fears that Jews might lose their temporary home. Protests against the planned closures, including property damage, by the camp population, which the DP police refused to control, and even marches to the DP "capital," Munich, became part of everyday life.[9] Jewish refugees without official DP status were especially hard hit. For example, at the end of 1948 a group of 250 Romanian Jews were transferred to Bindlach in the vicinity of Bayreuth

First official immigration of Jewish displaced persons to Israel departing from the Funkkaserne freight depot in Munich, July 13, 1948. Haus der Bayerischen Geschichte Augsburg (Bayerisches Pressebild).

in Bavaria, where they were forced to share their barracks with 300 Sudeten Germans.[10]

To facilitate the emigration of the last DPs, they were divided into four categories and transferred to special transit camps according to their final destination. In addition to potential immigrants to Israel and the United States, there were the so-called hard-core, who for personal or health reasons were unwilling or unable to leave Germany, and those classified as "undecided" because they were unable to immigrate to the country of their choice. Immigrants to Israel were housed in transit camps by the Zionist Organization, where they were prepared for what lay ahead, including in the *aliyah* (immigration) camp "Negev" in Geretsried, near the town of Wolfratshausen, some thirty-five kilometers from Munich.[11] However, the conditions were so problematic that even the Zionist press voiced criticism.[12]

Many of the remaining Jewish DPs chose to settle outside the camps to avoid further resettlement. The character of the small German-Jewish communities changed as a result of this migration to the cities. Thus, for example, the Frankfurt community experienced an increase in membership of about a thousand persons after the closure of the DP camp in Zeilsheim, and even smaller

Table 4.1

COMMUNITIES (STATE ASSOCIATIONS)	MEMBERS	NUMBER OF GERMAN JEWS	PERCENT	NUMBER OF DPS	PERCENT
Baden	600	300	50.0	300	50.0
Bavaria	4,800	300	6.3	4,500	93.7
Berlin	7,000	5,000	71.4	2,000	28.6
Hamburg	1,300	910	70.0	390	30.0
Hessen	2,005	526	26.2	1,479	73.8
Lower Saxony	775	594	76.6	181	23.4
North Rhine-Westphalia	1,907	1,454	86.2	453	23.8
Palatinate	373	323	87.0	50	13.0
Schleswig-Holstein	295	173	58.0	122	42.0
Württemberg	1,441	265	18.4	1,176	81.6
Soviet Zone	1,149	1,149	100.0	—	—
Total	21,645	10,994	50.7	10,651	49.3

Note: German Jewish MP3s in the communities (March 1949) quoted from Maor: *Über den Wiederaufbau,* p. 19, Table II.

communities were affected by the dismantling of DP infrastructure.[13] When the IRO ceased operations in the Bavarian town of Cham at the end of 1948, the Jewish community there increased by about two hundred DPs. At the beginning of 1949, the number of members rose to 250, who lived dispersed in and around Cham. But these figures soon decreased again: at the end of September 1949, only about one hundred persons still belonged to the Jewish community of Cham; by the beginning of 1950, only sixty-two.[14]

The Jewish DP population declined continuously until the end of 1949. Those who remained until ratification of the new American immigration laws in 1950 were primarily those who had entered Germany after the initial cutoff date for immigration eligibility of December 22, 1945. Well into the 1950s, Germany remained a temporary unloved home for thousands of invalids and people with chronic illnesses.

The differing DP policies promulgated by the Western occupying powers had long-term effects on the character of the Jewish communities in the Federal Republic. In the northwestern part of Germany, the proportion of former DPs in the communities was not more than 30 percent. In Berlin, a good 70 percent of community members were German Jews. In Bavaria, on the other hand, which had the most DPs, "German-Jewish" communities hardly existed at all, because more than 90 percent of their members came from Poland and other countries in

Central and Eastern Europe. Overall, about half of the people registered in a Jewish community in Germany were not German citizens.[15] Almost 100 percent of the Jews born in Germany at the time were children of DPs, because the German-Jewish survivors and returnees, a small group, were mainly elderly.[16]

Although most of the Jews in Germany insisted on the necessity of a Jewish state, and Zionism seemed the most feasible political solution for European Jews in a postwar world of consolidated national states, many individual DPs continued to dream of crossing the Atlantic. This other "Promised Land" was especially attractive to those who already had family in the United States.

However, the long-awaited Displaced Persons Act of June 1948, with its 30 percent quota for agricultural workers, favored ethnic Germans, especially those from the Baltic region, rather than Jewish DPs. Even the original precondition, that DPs wishing to immigrate to the United States had to have entered the American zone of occupation in Germany between September 1, 1939, and December 22, 1945, de facto excluded the overwhelming majority of Jewish DPs, who had entered the American zone as "infiltrees" from Eastern Europe after 1945. However, the law did provide loopholes that enabled thousands of Jews to immigrate between 1948 and 1950. Many more entered the United States after the amended Displaced Persons Act of June 1950 extended the crucial cutoff date to January 1, 1949. Many DPs quickly grasped at the opportunity to obtain an American visa, sought out sponsors, and weighed the alternatives, especially the economic advantage of staying in Germany in hopes of obtaining restitution, which had initially been tied to residence, versus the pressure to book the Atlantic passage from Bremerhaven.

On July 31, 1949, Harry Greenstein, the last advisor on Jewish affairs to the American military government in Germany, convened a remarkable conference in Heidelberg to discuss, as its title announced, "The Future of the Jews in Germany." Representatives of all the relevant interest groups were invited, including the American Jewish Committee and the American Jewish Joint Distribution Committee (JDC), the Israeli consulate (represented by the newly appointed Eliahu Livneh), the Jewish Agency for Palestine, the International Refugee Organization (IRO), the U.S. Army, the Jewish Restitution Successor Organization (JRSO), the soon to be disbanded central committees of liberated Jews in the American and British zones, and the newly founded communities. This meeting, which had been preceded by preliminary discussions in March, was meant to clarify the situation of Jews in Germany and their relationship to German society. Unsurprisingly, the representatives of the DPs held firm to the position that there was "no place for Jews in Germany," while the German Jews in particular maintained that "the extinction of the Jewish community in Germany would be tragic, and constitute a very dangerous precedent."[17]

Ironically, the most passionate plea for a Jewish future in Germany came from John J. McCloy, high commissioner for the U.S. zone, who succeeded Lucius D. Clay, the military governor, after the installation of a civilian administration in the now independent Federal Republic. McCloy urged the Jews to assume a moral duty toward the country of their murderers. The continuing presence of Jews, he argued, would serve as a sort of barometer and guarantor of the moral rehabilitation of the Germans. "To end Jewish life in Germany would be almost an acknowledgment of failure," McCloy argued. Like so many who hoped for reconciliation, he placed the burden of the first steps on the victims. Employing well-intentioned stereotypes and referring rather clearly to the reputation of the Jews for shady business dealings, McCloy suggested that, "with the tenacity, persistence, courage and vigor of the race [*sic*] and with the habit of honest and fair dealing, the Jew in Germany will be restored to a position which he occupied in the past in this community and will reach even higher levels." However, he acknowledged, "I do not know how long that will take." McCloy summarized the significance of the Jewish presence as a test of the political maturity of West Germany as follows: "What this community will be, how it forms itself, how it becomes a part and how it merges with the new Germany, will, I believe, be watched very closely and very carefully by the entire world. It will, in my judgment, be one of the real touchstones and the test of Germany's progress." Moreover, it was the task of the Jews themselves to accomplish the work of assimilation and integration—a view that ran completely counter to the understanding and intentions of the remaining DPs. "The success of those who remain," the high commissioner insisted, "will to a large extent depend upon the extent to which that community becomes less of a community in itself and merges with the general community."[18]

Using different but perhaps more credible arguments, Eugen Kogon, the non-Jewish representative of a liberal and anti-Fascist "other Germany" who had survived Buchenwald and now published the journal *Frankfurter Hefte*, also concluded that the Jews should not leave Germany. He expressed his deep disappointment that the Germans had become preoccupied with their own victimhood. There had been no "horrified outcry" over the crimes that had been committed; to the contrary, the presence of the survivors had triggered further "insufferable antisemitism." In effect, the resentment toward the Jews was a symptom of the visible and unwelcome memory of the crimes of the Germans, which in one way or another demanded restitution. Nonetheless, Kogon, too, pleaded for a certain degree of reconciliation.[19] His stance was vigorously countered by Philipp Auerbach, a Hamburg-born German Jew who had survived the concentration camps and, in an unusual step, had been named Bavarian state commissioner for racial, religious, and political persecutees in 1946. This position enabled him to promote compensation for the Jewish victims of Nazism, especially for those few who remained in Germany. Among other things, he demanded payment of tuition and room and board for Jewish students at German universities. The campaign for financial compensation Auerbach contended was not, as so many even apparently friendly critics suggested, "an undue fixation on restitution" or an incitement to antisemitism.[20] It was, rather, the only means still available to force responsibility upon a "German people" that "had no sense of guilt and are not held culpable by others." Whereas the Germans saw corruption, favoritism, and a confirmation of the old stereotypes about money grubbing, Jews pressed the demand for a minimum of justice.[21]

This debate was open and nuanced and characterized by a broad spectrum of opinions. But representatives of German Jews who had immigrated to other countries kept pointing out that it would be a travesty if "whatever has been built up by and for 550,000 people in the course of many hundreds of years of history and designed for the needs of a great number of people, can be claimed by 20,000 to 25,000 people," of whom only a few had even a loose connection to Judaism. In any case, more than two hundred thousand German-Jewish survivors lived in other parts of the world, and their demands were represented by the newly founded organizations the JRSO (1948) in the American zone and the Jewish Trust Corporation in the British (1949) and French (1950) zones.[22]

DISCONTENT AMONG THOSE WHO REMAINED

In August 1949, shortly after the Heidelberg conference, the *Süddeutsche Zeitung* ran a lead article supporting McCloy's statement, according to which the German attitude toward the Jews would be a "touchstone" for Germany's acceptance into the circle of democratic nations. In a characteristic expression of philosemitism, the Germans were urged to enter into dialogue with the Jews in Germany—especially since the latter embodied such positive characteristics as "a feel for quality in the material and intellectual sense."[23] Of the four responses that were published by the *Süddeutsche Zeitung* on August 9, 1949, two were positive and one was "slightly critical." The fourth letter to the editor came from a certain "Adolf Bleibtreu" (Stay True to Adolf) with the fictitious address "Palästrina-Straße." The anonymous author, who identified himself as "a 100 percent German" and among the "silent in the country," availed himself of openly antisemitic jargon: "I work for the Americans, and several of them have already said that they forgive us everything, except one thing and that is: that we didn't gas all of them, for now they [the Jews] are gracing America with their presence." The *New York Herald Tribune*, commenting on the publication of this letter, called it "unquestionably the most vitriolic assemblage of anti-Semitic feeling that any western-licensed newspaper has dared to print since the war ended."[24]

Demonstrations by Jewish survivors in the Möhlstrasse in Munich against an anti-Jewish letter to the editor published in the *Süddeutsche Zeitung*, August 10, 1949. bpk / Bayerische Staatsbibliothek / Archiv Heinrich Hoffmann.

When the *Süddeutsche Zeitung* appeared, DPs staged riotous demonstrations centered in the Möhlstrasse, the heart of Jewish Munich. Assuming that the letter represented the opinion of the editors, a crowd of several hundred or several thousand DPs—figures differ according to the source—began to march in the direction of the newspaper offices. Ironically, anger and frustration over the impending loss of American protection, as West Germany was becoming a "semisovereign" state, also targeted the offices of the JDC, the American Jewish aid organization that had taken on much of the responsibility for Jewish welfare, and thereby also generated so much frustration among the DPs during the U.S. occupation. In reaction, mounted German police attempted to break up the march but were met with sticks and cobblestones. One police bus was set on fire. Additional police dispatched to quell the riots swung their truncheons and allegedly shot into the air or, according to another description, shot and wounded three Jewish DPs. JDC workers and an American army chaplain managed to calm the crowd, but order was finally restored only when the American military police, who continued to exercise considerable authority among the Jewish DPs, intervened. The American security forces ordered the Munich police to leave the area, and the irate DPs dispersed after about two and a half hours.[25]

Interestingly, fewer demonstrators were involved in the Möhlstrasse protest than in a demonstration by anti-Communist, non-Jewish DPs a few months earlier. In both instances, participants carried banners written in English, suggesting that their protests were directed toward a broader audience than the immediate German public. In the Möhlstrasse incident, the demonstrators demanded that the *Süddeutsche Zeitung*'s Allied-issued license to publish be revoked, indicating the extent to which the DPs continued to view the Americans as the real authority in Germany. Furthermore, the Central Committee's response to the riots was exactly what both the Americans and the Germans wanted to hear: "Not a single one of us has any intention to remain in Germany. We do not wish to stay on this soil any longer. We have our own homeland, but as long as we are forced to remain here, we will fight with all our strength any attempts to mount anti-Jewish actions."[26]

Remarkably, another letter was published right next to the infamous Bleibtreu missive, this one by Hans Lamm, a German Jew who had returned to Germany from exile in the United States in 1945. After working as a translator at the Nuremberg Trials, Lamm later became the president of the Jewish community in Munich. Bitterly, he noted that the Germans viewed the putative criminality of Jewish traders in the Möhlstrasse district as a kind of punishment for their own crimes, as if the paltry profits generated by such shady practices somehow made up for Auschwitz.[27] As of 1949, the young, semisovereign, "occupied" Federal Republic took increasing responsibility for the problems associated with the DPs and refugees. At the same time, Jewish institutions began to focus on the sort of activity that came to characterize them in the postwar era. Instead of building a community or religious identity, they would devote much of their time and energy to caring for a fluctuating community and to documenting and protesting antisemitic incidents.

THE "HARD-CORE" CASES

At the end of 1948 there were about thirty thousand Jewish DPs in Germany. Between 1949 and 1953, some twenty-five hundred to three thousand former DPs who had been unable to integrate into the beleaguered and war-torn young state of Israel returned to Germany. These returnees were especially stigmatized because they had turned their backs on the Promised Land and come back to the land of the murderers. The members of this "hard core" created problems for both the German and Jewish authorities because they stubbornly resisted all attempts at resettlement or integration. Some of them were successful businesspeople who had made money first on the black or—to use a more appropriate term—gray market. Many others were simply too sick or exhausted to leave the protection of the DP camps. In June 1950 nine thousand people were still living in four camps. Landsberg was closed on October 15, 1950, Feldafing on May 31, 1951. Many of the remaining 1,585 DPs in the Feldafing camp were relocated to the Föhrenwald camp in Wolfratshausen near Munich, which provided the last refuge for the hard-core DPs. Föhrenwald finally closed in February 1957. In 1951 formal responsibility for the DPs in Germany, including those in Föhrenwald, was transferred to the Federal Republic of Germany. The Jewish DPs were now "homeless foreigners" for whom the Germans and not the international community were responsible.[28]

The resentment felt by the Germans and the frustration of the aid organizations and Jewish institutions, especially the JDC, which were obligated to support the dwindling number of former DPs who remained in Germany, hardened over time. The remaining Jews, supposedly privileged as a result of their "supplements" from the JDC, were an unwelcome reminder to the Germans of Nazi crimes and of the occupation era. Complaints about the "antisocial" behavior and criminality of the remaining hard-core cases became ever more strident and uninhibited. The defeated Germans seemed to have regained their former arrogance, all the while insisting that they themselves had been the victims. Now armed with an expanding array of powers and facing the burden of millions of German expellees and returning prisoners of war, federal and communal authorities attempted to divest themselves of additional responsibility for the Jewish refugees. At the same time, members of the JDC who had become increasingly sympathetic to the Zionism of their charges made no effort to conceal their frustration at the endless demands and apparent lack of self-discipline of DPs who were unable to decide to leave the country. The representatives of the Jews in Germany wanted more control and autonomy in internal matters without, however, having to relinquish the financial support provided by the JDC. The JDC, for its part, was of the opinion that although autonomy was a worthy and necessary goal, the Jews who continued to live in Germany could not be trusted to properly handle their financial affairs and the distribution of aid. These problems were exacerbated by the contempt that most of the Jews living abroad held for those who remained in Germany and by the resentment on the part of Germans at the supposed material advantages and political protection afforded this group of putative outsiders. Ironically, this aversion was often packaged in the less than flattering differentiation between the "good" German Jews, who had apparently mysteriously disappeared, and the "bad" Eastern European Jews who replaced them.[29]

Although a hollow philosemitism was not uncommon, open antisemitism was by no means taboo in Germany in the late 1940s—especially when it was directed at Eastern European Jewish "homeless foreigners." The latter became associated with corruption and speculative business transactions, especially in connection with claims for restitution and the eventual transition from black market dealings to formal enterprises after the currency reform of 1948. But these businesses were often just as suspect, especially the bars and other establishments of "ill repute" that, as was the case in many German cities, were patronized by American GIs. Indeed, the sex trade that accompanied the occupation was another source of antisemitic resentment.[30]

By 1949–1950 the establishment of the State of Israel had loosened the immigration policies of the United States, and the founding of the semisovereign Federal Republic led to the end of the DP era. Of the approximately 250,000 Jewish DPs, between 100,000 and 142,000 settled in Palestine and then Israel. Between 72,000 and 77,000 found homes in the United States. Canada took in another 16,000 to 20,000, Belgium 8,000, France 2,000, Australia 5,000, and various other countries like South Africa and Latin American states another 5,000.[31]

The Central Committee of Liberated Jews, which had been the primary representative of the DPs, dissolved itself in a final meeting held at the German Museum in Munich on December 17, 1950. Administration of the remaining two camps was transferred to the West German authorities in 1951, and other DPs joined German-Jewish communities. This brought the Jewish DP era in Germany to an official end.

ATINA GROSSMANN is Professor of history at Cooper Union in New York. She has been a fellow at the Institute for Advanced Study in Princeton, the American Academy in Berlin, the United States Holocaust Memorial Museum, and the Davis Center at Princeton University. Her publications include *Jews, Germans, and Allies: Close Encounters in Occupied Germany* (on which parts of this section are based) and *Wege in der Fremde: Deutsch-jüdische Begegnungsgeschichte zwischen Feldafing, New York und Teheran*; and as a coeditor, *After the Nazi Racial State: Difference and Democracy in Germany and Europe* and *Crimes of War: Guilt and Denial in the Twentieth Century*, as well as *Shelter from the Holocaust: Rethinking Jewish Survival in the Soviet Union* (with M. Edele and S. Fitzpatrick) and *The Joint Distribution Committee: 100 Years of Jewish History* (with A. Patt, L. Levi, and M. Maud), both forthcoming from Wayne State University Press in 2018.

TAMAR LEWINSKY is curator of contemporary history at the Jewish Museum Berlin. Her publications include *Unterbrochenes Gedicht: Jiddische Literatur im Nachkriegsdeutschland, 1944–1950* and *Displaced Poets: Jiddische Schriftsteller im Nachkriegsdeutschland, 1945–1951*.

NOTES

1. S. Gringauz (1948), p. 509.

2. As with the DPs, there are no firm figures for those expelled from their home-land. The literature, which is extraordinarily large, includes, among others, P. Ahonen (2003); A. Kossert (2008); W. Benz (ed.) (1995).

3. For the complex details about the *Exodus 1947* affair, see A. Halamish (1998); A. Kochavi (2001), pp. 79–86, 266–284; H. Lavsky (2002), pp. 193–196. For an eyewitness report, see R. Gruber (2007).

4. See, for example, S. Gringauz (1948), pp. 508–509.

5. M. Brenner (2001a), p. 154.

6. A. Hyman (1950), p. 317.

7. "IRO U.S. Zone: Plan for the Consolidation of DP/R Installations," October 25, 1948, in USHMM, GI 6A2 C-45.068.1.

8. A. Hyman (1950), p. 318.

9. "Alts naye tsores fun lagern-'likvidatsye,'" *Faktn un meynungen*, July 1949, pp. 6–7; "Naye faktn vegn der 'likvidatsye' fun di yidishe di-pi-lagern in Daytshland," in YIVO, 1400 ME 18, box 1270, folder 173; "Vi azoy me hot likvidirt dem lager Nay-Frayman?," in YIVO, 1400 ME 18, box 1270, folder 175; letter from William Haber to Kurt Grossmann, November 23, 1948, in USHMM, GI 6A2 C-45.068.1.

10. "Ot vi es lebn yidishe di-pis in di lagern," *Faktn un meynungen*, January 1949, pp. 2–3.

11. "Regulamin fun durkhgangs-lager 'negev,'" in CZA, S 6/6763.

12. Ovadya Feld, "Hokhland un Geretsrid," *Tsienistishe shtime*, December 9, 1948.

13. Theodore D. Feder to M. Beckelman, "Plan for Consolidation of DP Installations U.S. Zone of Germany of November 18, 1948," in USHMM, GI 6A2 C-45.068.1.

14. "Die Jüdische Gemeinde Cham im Jahre 1949 vom 14. Februar 1950," and letter to the Landesverband der Israelitischen Kultusgemeinde in Bayern (Auerbach), September 29, 1949, both in LVB archive, file "Cham I 1."

15. H. Maor (1961), p. 19.

16. H. Maor (1961), p. 20.

17. "Conference on 'The Future of the Jews in Germany' in Heidelberg on July 31, 1949," report from Harry Greenstein, advisor on Jewish affairs, September 1, 1949, p. 5, in LBI, MS 168. Among many other sources, see A. Grossmann (2007), pp. 253–257; J. Geller (2005), pp. 72–77; M. Brenner (1997), pp. 75–76.

18. "Conference on 'The Future of the Jews in Germany,'" pp. 20–22. In contrast to McCloy's comments about the Jews as touchstone of German progress, Heide Fehren-bach in her book *Race after Hitler* determined that many "liberal" Germans looked at the treatment of "mixed-race" children, mostly the children of German women and black military personnel, as a test of "social maturity ([2005], p. 94). Her book also raises questions about the comparison between West German reactions toward Jews in the postwar period and those toward new "Others," especially African Americans. In addition, Geller found that McCloy had placed a particular "burden of proof" on the Jews ([2005], p. 75).

19. Kogon, "Conference on 'The Future of the Jews in Germany,'" pp. 23–26.

20. See R. Webster (1993), p. 304. The quote refers to the JDC.

21. Auerbach, "Conference on 'The Future of the Jews in Germany,'" p. 27.

22. This according to the JRSO representative Max Kreutzberger; see "Conference on 'The Future of the Jews in Germany,'" p. 52. For more on this conflict, see R. Zweig (2001), pp. 55–58.

23. W. E. Süskind, "Judenfrage als Prüfstein," *Süddeutsche Zeitung,* August 2, 1949.

24. Marguerite Higgins, "Munich Police Battle a Rally of 1000 Jews," *New York Herald Tribune,* August 11, 1949, cited in A. Holian (2011), p. 199. See also W. Bergmann (1994).

25. Report from Mr. Harry Greenstein, advisor on Jewish affairs, to U.S. Commander in Germany on the riot of August 10, 1949, August 31, 1949, in AJDC A, 499. Here, too, there are many different descriptions of the events. See, for example, N. Mühlen (1993), pp. 163–165; A. Kauders (2004), p. 139; A. Holian (2011). A year earlier, on April 17, 1948, the *Süddeutsche Zeitung* had printed an article titled "Antisemitismus 1948," which in the "debate" section made the "antisocial behavior" of the DPs responsible for antisemitism and contrasted it to the "unobtrusive" profile of the remaining German Jews. See also W. Bergmann (2001), p. 195; J. Wetzel (1995), pp. 433–444, 454, fn. 30.

26. "Der Tumult in der Möhlstraße," *Münchner Merkur,* August 12, 1949, p. 1.

27. Recorded and cited in K. Crago-Schneider (2010), p. 172. For more on the biography of Hans Lamm, see A. Sinn (2008).

28. See, for example, A. Grossmann (2009a).

29. See, among others, M. Brenner (1997), pp. 48–49.

30. See M. Höhn (2008); H. Fehrenbach (2005).

31. See A. Hyman (1993), p. 376; M. Wyman (1998), pp. 155, 178–204; K. Grossman (1951), pp. 28–29; R. Sander (1988), pp. 586–587; and D. Ofer (1995), p. 82, fn. 11. Y. Grodzinsky (2004), p. 223, has somewhat different figures.

PART TWO: 1950–1967
CONSOLIDATION

MICHAEL BRENNER
AND NORBERT FREI

5 INSTITUTIONAL NEW BEGINNING

THE FOUNDING OF THE CENTRAL COUNCIL OF JEWS IN GERMANY

July 19, 1950, was the date on which a new Jewish community in Germany was officially constituted. On this day, twenty-five leading representatives of the reestablished Jewish communities met in Frankfurt am Main to found an umbrella group that would represent all Jews living in Germany. They decided to call it the Central Council of Jews in Germany.[1] This choice of name was a clear repudiation of the identity of the German Jews prior to 1933, who viewed themselves as German citizens of the Jewish faith.

Many years of preparation had preceded the founding of the Central Council. In June 1947 a loose working group of Jewish communities in Germany was established, and two years later sixty-three representatives met in Heidelberg to discuss fundamental questions and to plan for the future. This meeting had laid the groundwork for the founding of a German-Jewish representative body.

But what exactly was the reason for the formation of the Central Council in 1950? The Federal Republic of Germany, a new democratic German state, was founded only one year earlier, and it created the framework within which Jewish life could be reorganized. In addition, it had become clear that not all Jews would choose to leave Germany. The federal government also preferred to deal with a central representative body. Therefore, Chancellor Konrad Adenauer proposed the naming of a representative for Jewish affairs in the federal government. The establishment of the Central Council was the final step in setting up a democratically elected body that would represent the Jewish community to the authorities of West Germany and at the same time look after the most important matters facing the community internally.

The last organizations representing Jewish displaced persons were being phased out at about the same time, and in addition the Jewish Agency, whose main concern had been the immigration of Jews to Israel, withdrew from Germany. Its withdrawal was associated with considerable threats against those who

Nachdem die jüdischen Organisationen Deutschlands sich bereits im Juli 1950 zusammengefunden hatten, um — über die Zonengrenzen hinweg — die Grundlage für eine jüdische Gesamtvertretung in Deutschland zu schaffen, trafen sich Anfang Januar in Hamburg die Vertreter der jüdischen Landes- und Zonenverbände zur Konstituierung des Zentralrates der Juden in Deutschland. Das bisherige provisorische Direktorium wurde auf dieser Tagung endgültig gewählt (von links): Heinz Galinski (Berlin), Dr. Philipp Auerbach (amerikanische Zone), Norbert Wollheim (britische Zone), Leonhard Baer (französische Zone) und Julius Meyer (Ostzone). Weiteres Direktoriumsmitglied ist Josef Rosensaft.

Gemeinsame Arbeit

Der Zentralrat der Juden in Deutschland konstituierte sich

Der bisherige Vertreter des Jüdischen Weltkongresses in Deutschland, Dr. Gerhard Jacoby, berichtete vor seiner Rückkehr nach den USA umfassend über seine in den letzten 10 Monaten in Deutschland gesammelten Erfahrungen. Heute hat Dr. Jacoby als Vertreter des Jüdischen Weltkongresses einen Sitz im Wirtschafts- und Sozialrat der UNO.

Rabbiner Dr. Freier (Berlin) umriß in einer bemerkenswerten Ansprache die kulturellen und Kultusaufgaben der jüdischen Gemeinden.

Auf der Hamburger Konferenz wurde der bis dahin nur provisorisch bestellte Generalsekretär Dr. van Dam endgültig gewählt. Er hat seinen Sitz in Hamburg.

Der Ehrenvorsitzende der Hamburger Tagung, der israelische Konsul in Deutschland, Dr. E. Livneh, gab in seinem hervorragenden Referat einen Ueberblick über die jüdische Situation in Israel und der Welt sowie über die jüdische Arbeit in Deutschland seit 1945.

Eine ausführliche Tagesordnung ließ den Delegierten und Rabbinern nur wenige Minuten zum Verschnaufen. Zu vielfältig waren die Probleme, mit denen sich die Tagungsteilnehmer zu befassen hatten. — Im Vordergrund von links nach rechts: Rabbiner Dr. Levinson (Berlin), Professor d'Avidor und Rabbiner Dr. Weinberg (Frankfurt). (Fotos: dpa)

2

Report in the *Jüdische Illustrierte* on the establishment of the Central Council of Jews in Germany, February 1951. *Jüdische Illustrierte* 1/6 (February 1951), p. 2.

remained in Germany. Thus, in early August 1950 the Jewish Agency announced that anyone who remained in Germany beyond the next six weeks would no longer be viewed as Jewish and could no longer count on support for future immigration to Israel.[2] After several such announcements, the Israeli consulate in Munich, which had been heavily involved in organizing immigration, closed its doors on July 1, 1953.[3]

The three central figures of the founding period were all German Jews who had survived Auschwitz: Philipp Auerbach, Bavarian state commissioner for racial, religious, and political victims of Nazi persecution; Heinz Galinski, president of the Berlin community, which until 1953 was still united; and Norbert Wollheim, spokesperson for the Jews in the British zone.[4] These three men belonged to the first directorate of the Central Council. Their evolution over the following years could not have been more different: Wollheim emigrated to the United States in 1951, greatly disappointed in political developments in Germany; Auerbach committed suicide a year later in reaction to his conviction before a court in Munich; and Galinski remained the president of the Berlin Jewish community until his death more than four decades later.

Immediately after his liberation, Wollheim attempted to reorganize Jewish life in northern Germany from his base in Lübeck. His main concern was the most urgent needs of the survivors. Once the British relinquished control, Wollheim viewed his mission as finished: "I never considered remaining and living in Germany. I lost my first wife and my child in Auschwitz. I left Germany when I considered that the work was done."[5] In press releases before and after his emigration, he expressed how little hope he placed in a truly democratic Germany that could serve as a home country for Jews. In his public farewell address, he gave voice to his fear that Germany stood on the cusp of a return to National Socialist policies.[6]

Auerbach was surely the most visible and undoubtedly the most combative Jewish functionary during the postwar years. In numerous newspaper articles and radio interviews, he expressed his doubts about democratic reconstruction and his worries about continued virulent antisemitism. His passing from the political stage began just a few months after the founding of the Central Council, in which he had played a leading role. Auerbach came under considerable pressure in the fall of 1950 as a result of the collapse of the Jewish Industrial and Trade Bank in Frankfurt. A number of his colleagues on the directorate had fled Germany after the illegal transfer of several million marks. No investigations were initiated against Auerbach at this time. But in January 1951, investigating officials targeted the "Caesar of Restitution," as the news magazine Der Spiegel called him, for alleged irregularities in handling matters relating to restitution.

On February 25, 1951, the directorate of the Central Council published a statement in which it came out against these inflammatory attacks, which were supposedly aimed at Jews as a whole. The Central Council asked for a thorough and objective investigation while at the same time demanding that it would not be used as a pretext to cripple the work of the restitution authorities.[7] But their worst fears were realized when the Bavarian State Restitution Office was shuttered until further notice, which brought restitution claims to a complete standstill in the German state with the most people eligible for restitution. There were considerable differences within the Central Council directorate about whether or how to support its beleaguered member. On February 11 Auerbach submitted to the majority vote and agreed to stop performing his functions in Jewish community organizations until the investigation was completed.[8]

On March 10, 1951, Auerbach was arrested on the autobahn in his official car and taken into custody. The best-known representative of the Jews in Germany was charged with forgery of documents, obtaining the title of Ph.D. under false pretenses, contact with the Communist Party of Germany, and embezzlement. German Jews themselves were of divided opinion. While some viewed him as the "Robin Hood of Restitution," someone who got justice for Jewish concentration camp survivors by unbureaucratic means, even if sometimes by bending the rules, others were appalled that one of their own was now forced to answer before a German court. But all agreed on one thing: the shadow of the Auerbach affair must not fall over the entire newly reconstituted German-Jewish community.

It would be difficult to imagine a worse situation for the Central Council to find itself in. Its most prominent representative had been accused of very serious crimes, the success of restitution negotiations was now in question, and anti-semitism was given fresh impetus.

The Auerbach affair ended as dramatically as it began. On August 14, 1952, Auerbach was sentenced by five judges (three of whom had been members of the National Socialist German Workers Party [Nationalsozialistische Deutsche Arbeiterpartei, NSDAP] or one of its official associations) to two and a half years in prison and a fine of 2,700 DM. Auerbach did not serve his sentence. Two days after the verdict was handed down, Philipp Auerbach, who maintained his innocence to the end, took his own life. But for the representatives of the Jewish communities, Auerbach's tragic passing posed the question whether they could or should serve the public in an official capacity at all. One consequence of the Auerbach trial was that many Jews retreated into private life. For example, during a meeting of the Central Council in 1952, Julius Dreifuss, the chair of the Düsseldorf community, let it be known that "we Jews should consider whether a Jew can or should be a high functionary within the Jewish community while at the same time occupying a high state or political office." In addition, given the fact that most German judges were former members of the NSDAP, Dreifuss questioned the competence of German courts in matters relating to Jews: "In our future deliberations, we must examine how we might prevent a judge or a court that is occupied by persons who belonged to the NSDAP to pass judgment in important suits against Jews. Regardless of how impartial a judge or associate judge might seem, he will never be able to adjudicate in that manner."[9]

Several years after Auerbach's suicide, his widow, Margit, converted to Catholicism, a decision that was sanctioned by Auerbach's brother Walter, himself a high-ranking Social Democratic government official in Lower Saxony (and later in the Federal Ministry of Labor). Walter Auerbach had already parted ways with the Jewish religion, and he assured his sister-in-law, "I write to tell you that I respect the step you are taking."[10]

The exit of Wollheim and Auerbach meant that the two most charismatic representatives of Jewish life in the immediate postwar years had disappeared. Galinski had mainly been active at the local level in Berlin, and in 1963 he was forced out of his leading role after the Central Council, which by now was recognized as a corporation under public law, was restructured. According to its new bylaws, the Central Council now had three organs: the council assembly to which delegates of all the Jewish communities belonged; an eighteen-member directorate; and an administrative council consisting of six members, including the general secretary.

Although the majority of the Jews living in Germany had come from Eastern Europe, the leading committees of the Central Council consisted exclusively of German Jews. This was true not only of the chairpersons of the directorate but also of its members. As late as 1969, the eighteen members of the directorate included fifteen German Jews. The Eastern European representatives were mainly sent from the Bavarian Jewish communities.[11] But even in Bavaria, where 90 percent of the Jewish population came from Eastern Europe, the community chairmen were often German Jews.

In 1963 Galinski was replaced as chair of the Central Council by Herbert Lewin, who was also an Auschwitz survivor.[12] Lewin was chief physician of the gynecology service at Offenbach Hospital and a professor at the University of Frankfurt. Born in 1899 in the then Prussian province of Posen, he had fought in World War I and had lived in Berlin in the 1930s. In other words, like his colleagues, he also represented German-Jewish traditions.[13] Lewin had known Konrad Adenauer, who later became chancellor, since the immediate aftermath of the war, when the latter was mayor of Cologne and had tasked Lewin with returning the surviving Cologne Jews from Theresienstadt.[14]

By electing Lewin, the delegates hoped to ensure a lesser concentration of power at the top and a more muted public voice. Whereas Galinski had used his

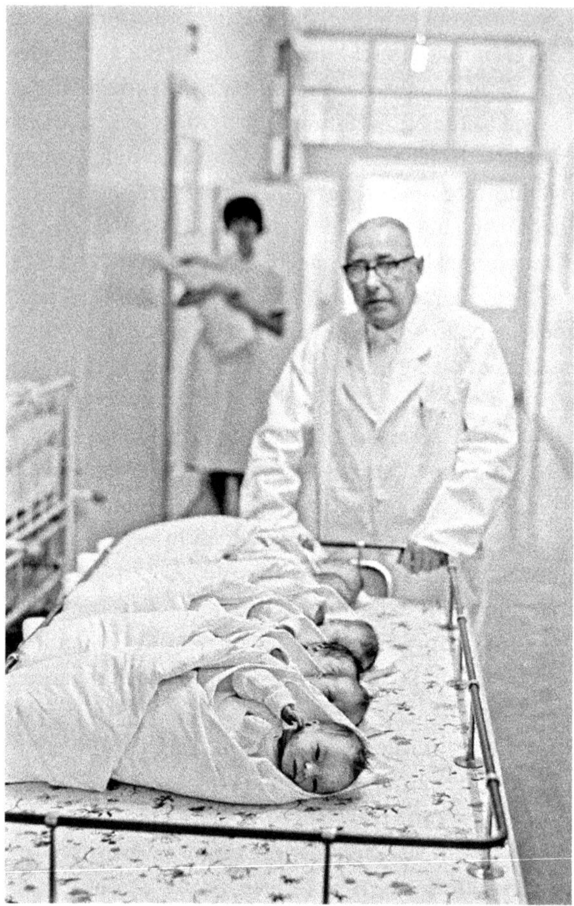

Professor Herbert Lewin, gynecologist at the women's clinic in Offenbach am Main and chair of the Central Council of Jews, 1961. Leonard Freed / Magnum Photos.

position to direct the policies of the Central Council, Lewin viewed his function as merely representational. In 1964, at a meeting of the council, he promised greater reticence in his dealings with the public: "But what irritates me the most is the fact that we are constantly bombarded with requests for interviews and that we actually yield to them. I have frequently rejected, and I will as a rule of thumb continue to reject, taking part in interviews, because all interviews for a newspaper, especially for a German, non-Jewish newspaper, necessarily pose a real danger for us Jews because of a mixture of ignorance, pure fantasy, or lack of empathy on the part of the journalists."[15]

During the first two decades of the Central Council's existence, its most important figure was not an elected chairperson but the general secretary, whom the chair had named. Hendrik George van Dam was born into a Jewish upper-middle-class family in Berlin. His family had immigrated to the Reich from Holland in the nineteenth century, and his father was the last court antiquary to Kaiser Wilhelm II; his grandfather on the maternal side had been a city counselor in Bremen. Van Dam left Germany in 1933 and fled to England after stopovers in Switzerland and Holland. His fiancée did not survive Bergen-Belsen. In 1946 he returned to the British zone in Germany as a member of the Jewish Relief Unit. As a lawyer, his main focus was on restitution for Jewish survivors. In 1947 he had organized the first conference of Jewish lawyers. A memorandum that he wrote in 1950 served as the basis for the Restitution Agreement between Israel and West Germany, which was signed two years later.

At first, some members of the directorate resisted van Dam's attempts to act independently. In 1953 Carl Katz, the president of the Bremen community and its representative in the directorate, attempted to rein in van Dam's almost unlimited powers and place control over financial and cultural functions under the directorate. Conflicts were resolved by giving responsibility for individual departments to directorate members; however, van Dam's power remained largely untouched, especially with regard to the all-important question of restitution.[16]

He was fully aware that the Jews living in Germany were a litmus test for German democracy—and he understood the dangers and risks associated with such a position in society. Thus, in December 1951 he warned the leading representatives of Jewish communities against misconstruing where they stood:

> It should, however, not go unrecognized that the mere fact of the existence of any Jewish community in Germany, regardless of how small, provides a certain alibi for German democracy and one of the reasons for the controversies around the right of German Jewry to exist, but also a reason for the interest in this Jewish group, which stands in no relation to its numerical and cultural significance. It follows that the Jews in Germany and their representation cannot be ignored, but they are also in danger to the extent that they falsely construe reality.[17]

By stating the matter this way, van Dam was alluding to the symbolic function of the Jews living in Germany, a function that leading politicians never ceased to emphasize and that U.S. High Commissioner John McCloy had first broached in 1949 at the conference on the future of Jews in Germany.[18]

However, the Central Council did not view itself as a short-term symbolic presence in Germany. In contrast to the much-cited "packed bags" upon which the Jews had supposedly been sitting, ready to go, van Dam spoke in 1954 at a meeting of the Central Council of the end of the "liquidation phase": "I believe that we may say today that the Jews have a history after 1945. Behind us lies an era that has already concluded, the period of the liquidation of the Jewish people in

Germany. The idea that Jews have nothing further to seek in Germany and must leave Germany immediately and that their presence is an emergency solution has become obsolete."[19]

The American journalist and screenwriter Leo Katcher described van Dam in his 1968 book Post Mortem as "a modern corporation executive. He is not a man of warmth. Of all the Jews with whom I talked in Germany, he was among the least emotional. Or, perhaps better, he displayed least emotion. He was direct, a stick-to-the-facts pragmatist, who considered each word, each phrase, he used as if he were in a courtroom. He is the unofficial ambassador of the Jews in Germany both to the German government and the world." The Jews in Germany, on the other hand, should view themselves as German citizens whose interests were congruent with Germany's interests: "His was the attitude of those Jews who had lived in an earlier era, in the time of [Walther] Rathenau. The years in between had added to van Dam's knowledge but not to his perspective."[20]

Van Dam led the Central Council in the 1950s and 1960s, a time when a lawyer was called for. Restitution, that is, the restoration of assets and compensation for the crimes committed by Nazi Germany, was top on the agenda. The Central Council viewed itself both as the advocate of the members registered in its communities and as a mediator in negotiations with international Jewish organizations and the State of Israel. In this respect, van Dam was the most competent of spokesmen and the most serious of negotiators.

Just how quickly the Central Council consolidated its position in government circles as the most important and reliable voice of the German Jews is made clear by a conversation between its representative and Chancellor Adenauer on April 1, 1952, when the chancellor expressed his satisfaction that the establishment of the council meant that German Jews were now speaking with a single voice.[21]

Karl Marx, founder and publisher of the *Allgemeine Wochenzeitung der Juden in Deutschland* (General weekly of the Jews in Germany), was the second most important representative of German Jews in the Federal Republic. Marx had been a confidant of West Germany's first president, Theodor Heuss, and, like van Dam, had returned from exile in England.[22] Like van Dam, he gave the German Jews confidence and was optimistic in his assessment of German democracy. The sociologist Y. Michal Bodemann accurately described the roles played by both of these men: "While van Dam represented the welfare apparatus of organized German Jewry, Karl Marx attempted to explain the raison d'être of the community in Germany to Jews and other countries. In short, van Dam represented the institutional structure, Marx the ideological superstructure of this new community."[23]

Only a few functionaries of the Jewish community were known outside of their communities. The justice minister of North Rhine–Westphalia, Josef Neuberger, was a member of the directorate of the Central Council. Jakob Altmaier,

Hans Rosenthal (*right*), chair of Tennis Borussia Berlin from 1965 to 1973, with the cabarettist Wolfgang Neuss. Archiv Tennis Borussia Berlin.

Peter Blachstein, and Jeanette Wolff were all members of the Bundestag in the 1950s and 1960s. All of them belonged to the Social Democratic Party of Germany (Sozialdemokratische Partei Deutschlands, SPD). An initiative in the mid-1960s to elect van Dam to the Bundestag as a Social Democrat failed because he would have had to renounce his office as general secretary of the Central Council, as later Chancellor Willy Brandt made clear.[24]

Probably the best-known German Jew in this period was popular radio and TV quizmaster Hans Rosenthal, who also served in high-ranking positions in the Berlin Jewish community and in the Central Council. Additionally, Rosenthal harked back to a tradition from the time before 1933, when numerous Jews took leading positions in German sports clubs. From 1965 to 1973 Rosenthal was president of Tennis Borussia Berlin. Kurt Landauer, under whose leadership Bayern München had become German soccer champion in 1932, returned to his home city from Swiss exile and served as president of that team once again between 1947 and 1951. In the same year (and again from 1963 to 1967), Alfred Ries was president of the Werder Bremen soccer club. He, too, had led the club in the 1920s. It was said that at his behest the colors used to decorate the new synagogue in Bremen—green and white—were selected to match the colors of his team. Ries, who was heavily involved in Jewish affairs, was also vice president of the German Sports Federation and one of the Federal Republic's few Jewish professional diplomats, his final posting having been ambassador to Liberia.[25]

Before assuming offices within the Jewish community, the German-Jewish representatives were often subjected to critical internal discussions. For one thing, the question arose whether they might have collaborated with Nazi officials during the Third Reich. Two decades after the end of the war, such debates still roiled the Jewish community of Bremen. Former functionaries of the Reich Association of Jews in Germany who now held important positions in the community accused each other of having worked with the Nazis.[26] In Frankfurt, Paul Arnsberg, who only a few years earlier had returned to Frankfurt from Israel, allegedly claimed that the German-Jewish community had for years allowed itself to be led by Gestapo informers. However, none of the accusations were ever proved.[27]

A second factor affecting qualifications was marriage to a non-Jewish spouse. Here, different standards were applied to German Jews, who often survived only because they had lived in mixed marriages, and to Eastern European Jews, whose official representatives denounced "fraternization" with the Germans. While some Jewish communities allowed their representatives to be married to non-Jewish spouses, others dismissed them. Thus, the bylaws of the Munich community contained a provision that no member married to a Christian spouse could be elected to the board.

THE JEWISH COMMUNITIES IN THE FEDERAL REPUBLIC

Despite such controversies, the Central Council tried to project unity to outsiders. Internally, however, this unity was not always so easy to achieve. The Jews who remained in Germany were an extremely heterogeneous group. In the 1950s the surviving German Jews and the Eastern European DPs were increasingly joined by returnees from exile and other immigrants from Eastern Europe, especially from Poland, Romania, and Hungary. The German-Jewish community was geographically split. In 1949 Eastern European Jews made up 93.7 percent of the Jewish population in the area. In Württemberg, too, they formed a clear majority with 81.6 percent. But they were only 29.6 percent of the Jewish population in Berlin, 24.4 percent in Lower Saxony, and 13.8 percent in North Rhine–Westphalia. Even in the former French zone of occupation, the Rhineland Palatinate, Eastern

European Jews were a small minority in 1949 as well at only 13 percent.[28] The size of the Jewish communities in relation to their prewar membership varied greatly. In Berlin, for example, postwar membership was only 3 percent of what it had been in 1933, while in Munich that figure was over 30 percent. The Jewish population in some small Bavarian towns such as Straubing and Amberg was virtually the same in the 1950s as in 1933.

Eastern European Jewish traditions held their own for many years in Bavaria. Up until the early 1970s, the only Yiddish weekly newspaper in Germany was published in Munich, and small communities such as those in Fürth, Regensburg, and Amberg continued to be led by rabbis completely steeped in Eastern European traditions. As late as the 1960s, the Munich community printed official invitations in both German and Yiddish.[29]

Hans Erich Fabian, the first chair of the postwar Berlin community, called the conflicts between the few German Jews who had returned and the majority Eastern European Jews in southern German communities the "southern German problems."[30] Fabian feared that German-Jewish traditions would not survive in those communities. To protect their dominant position—even as a minority group—within the communities, the German Jews in numerous locales supported the notion that suffrage or even community membership be reserved solely for German citizens. In Stuttgart, noncitizens were to be given the right to vote after three years, and in Frankfurt, resistance to granting voting rights to displaced persons was stiff. In Munich, Julius Spanier, the chair of the community, endeavored to grant the right to vote only to those who had been community members in 1938. However, he was unsuccessful.[31]

The controversy was especially heated in Augsburg and Hannover. In Augsburg, the thirty-two German Jews denied community membership to the approximately sixty Jews who were not German citizens. The State Association of Israelite Religious Communities in Bavaria disapproved of this position and sought to prevent the foundation of a second community in the city.[32] In a statement, the Central Council came out forthrightly against the exclusion of Eastern European Jewish members:

> The directorate is of the unanimous opinion that membership in a Jewish community is independent of citizenship and place of birth. This also means that any community member who by personality has been shown to have the qualities necessary for such a function may be elected to the board or become a representative. The directorate also considers it important that, if possible, community members who were born in Germany be represented in the representative committees, even in communities in which the German-born element is not the majority. Discrimination in the right to vote in community elections is thus inadmissible.[33]

The concession granted by the leaders of the Augsburg community—to give Eastern European Jews two of the nine seats on the board and voting rights to half(!) of them—was rejected. In the end, the matter was settled in court, and the German-Jewish leadership was forced to grant full membership and equal rights to non-German citizens.[34]

In Hannover, the mostly Eastern European survivors of the Bergen-Belsen concentration camp had for a decade been members of the Jewish Committee, which had existed in parallel to the German-Jewish community. Efforts to unite the two groups were stymied by Norbert Prager, the chair of the Jewish community, who was himself born in Poland but had lived in Hannover already before the war. In February 1954 the community adopted a bylaw according to which a board member had to have belonged to a Jewish community in Germany prior to 1945. The same was to apply to three-quarters of all elected representatives. The Eastern European Jewish Committee dissolved only in 1955. Its members joined the Jewish community, which as a result grew from 250 to 363 members. In addition, the average age decreased from fifty-four to forty-six, and for the first time there were enough children for religious instruction.[35] Despite these positive developments, the Hannover community retained its discriminatory bylaw until 1957.[36]

The cultural differences between the German and Eastern European Jews also formed the backdrop for personal and structural conflicts between the Central Council and the state associations with large numbers of Eastern Jews. For example, in 1952 the State Association of Jewish Communities in Bavaria, which had been founded in 1947, threatened to leave the Central Council over differences regarding Philipp Auerbach's successor on the directorate. Furthermore, a "Council of Jews," which had been founded after the Central Committee of Liberated Jews in Bavaria dissolved, represented a potential competitor to the Central Council. The chair of this council, Maurice Weinberger, succeeded Auerbach as president of the State Association of Jewish Communities in Bavaria.[37]

A visit by the two most influential German-Jewish leaders, Hendrik George van Dam and Karl Marx, to Munich in October 1951 gives some indication of how emotional the tensions were between the German-Jewish establishment and the Jewish DPs centered around the Möhlstrasse in Munich-Bogenhausen. As Marx later described it to German president Heuss, neither he nor van Dam felt physically safe during their visit to Munich. Apparently, van Dam left Munich earlier than planned "because he feared being done in by people in the Möhlstrasse."[38] To calm the waters, the Central Council was forced to deny that they represented only the interests of German Jews.[39] The conflict was finally resolved in 1953, when the Bavarian State Association was given a larger role in the committees of the Central Council.

New controversies erupted in Bavaria just a few years later when the Central Council refused to recognize the election of Max Bachmann, a former official in the Bavarian Ministry of the Interior, as president of the Munich Jewish community.[40] Many Munich Jews had also protested because the election site had been moved on short notice, and only 198 of the 1,850 people eligible to vote actually did so. The lawsuit that ensued in Munich courts stretched out over two years. This conflict over representation ended with new elections held in March 1960, with the attorney Siegfried Neuland being reelected chair of the Munich community.[41]

The situation in Bavaria was further complicated by the existence of the Föhrenwald DP camp at Wolfratshausen, which was not closed until 1957. The Eastern European Jews who lived there—in 1954 there were still fourteen hundred—either were not able to emigrate or did not want to, but they were unwilling to live among Germans either. The result was an anomalous situation in which a sort of extraterritorial Jewish zone existed in the Federal Republic for almost a decade, with its own school and hospital, its own rules and laws, which the German authorities found difficult to break through: "Föhrenwald was a world all its own, a closed society, a spaceship that had landed on an alien planet. People spoke Yiddish, there was a Jewish police force, a Jewish administration. It was a throwback to Poland. The parents tried to keep alive a piece of the culture that they had lost, to salvage it in the present." That was how Leibl Rosenberg, who grew up in Föhrenwald, remembered his childhood in the early 1950s.[42] Abraham Ben, who was born in Bamberg in 1947 and came to Föhrenwald with his family in 1950, recalled an idyllic childhood:

> A place surrounded by forests that were wonderful to play in. We had a Jewish school, a Jewish nursery school, and our parents had a lot of time for us. The street belonged to us, and there were only a few cars. I think that life back then was a little like in the old shtetl. For example, there was the blechatsh. He made simple kitchen utensils out of tin, and at Passover he put up an enormous cauldron with water. A big fire brought the water to a boil. The utensils were made kosher in this boiling hot water. We children stood in a circle around the bubbling cauldron and observed the procedure with great interest.[43]

Ben also told stories about "Berele the shnorrer," about "Shlomole," who dealt in tobacco, and about the bus that shuttled between Föhrenwald and Möhlstrasse in Munich.

When the German authorities began to oversee the camp in December 1951, they had to ensure that German laws were followed in the camp while acting with restraint, because "even the smallest infringement by the police will be interpreted as an antisemitic measure and fought accordingly." A police memorandum further stated that "the mentality of the camp occupants, their religious rites, and the other conditions in the camp must be taken into account."[44] And in fact, on May 28, 1952, there was a violent clash between the German authorities, who had entered the camp unannounced to investigate some business dealings, and the inhabitants of the camp, who pelted the cars of the police and tax officials with stones. Beno Salamander described the incident from the perspective of a boy growing up in the camp:

> The news of the impending police raid spread like wildfire, and many, we children as well, of course, rushed to the camp entrance. We heard "Nazis out" and "This time we're not letting you in" and even "You've killed enough already." One young man by the name of Gidale Bines bared his chest, ran forward, threw himself onto the ground, and screamed, "Only over my dead body." At this point, the first stones began to fly at the well-armed police squad. It didn't take long before the police retreated from the camp amid cheering from the crowd.[45]

After that, the police tended to refrain from such actions, but they continued to report irregularities. For example, police reports complained that shop closure times were not obeyed. Because Saturday was a day of rest, the shops were open on Sunday. Reports made repeated mention of the black market. In addition, the camp movie theater did not meet legal requirements and did not comply with the laws protecting youth. Finally, the reports indicated, poultry was slaughtered "in the open." They also mentioned the alarming porousness of the camp gates. Of particular concern to the police was the fact that the Bavarian population went freely into the camp to purchase goods after normal closing hours and that young people went to the movies there. The Bavarian police in Föhrenwald were well aware that "if we intervene in these matters, previous experience has shown that we can count on numerous complaints being lodged with all possible authorities."[46]

The most difficult problem at Föhrenwald was the so-called illegals. Most of them were DPs who had returned from Israel and were now unable to show papers in Germany but would rather live there than in Israel. There were about eight hundred such illegals in Germany at the end of 1951; it is said that as many as thirty-five hundred returnees from Israel passed through Föhrenwald between 1949 and 1953.[47] This situation, too, posed a dilemma for the German authorities. On the one hand, the law had to be obeyed; on the other, historical circumstances often led them to act with a certain grudging forbearance. Then again, there was the position taken by Israel that Germany should not make it easy for people who ran away from the Jewish state to find a home in Germany. And in any case, Israeli passports could not legally be recognized because they bore the qualifier

"Valid for all countries with the exception of Germany." When the Föhrenwald camp was finally dissolved in February 1957, many of its inhabitants continued to live segregated in closed settlements. But most of them were relocated to Munich and Frankfurt, where they were housed in apartments that were in close proximity to each other.

Leibl Rosenberg recalled that social differences continued even among the Eastern European Jews in Munich in the 1950s. The DPs who had arrived in Munich immediately after the end of the war and were already economically successful tended to lord it over the newcomers from Föhrenwald, who had continued to live in the camp for a decade and were now living in a few residential areas in the city: "Those of us who came from Föhrenwald were the outsiders. The Jewish children whom we got to know at the Maon Hanoar youth club let us know that we had arrived too late. They looked down on us."[48] In other words, there were differences within the Eastern European Jews of Munich and those in other German cities that had nothing to do with the presence of German Jews.

That there could also be significant differences between entire communities that were geographically close is exemplified by the communities in Fürth and Nuremberg, which are only a few miles apart in Franconia. Fürth had a reputation for the richness of its traditions; for centuries it had been known for the Talmud study in its yeshiva, its long line of rabbis, and its internationally acclaimed Hebrew print shop. By coincidence, Fürth would once again become an important place of Jewish learning and scholarship in Germany after 1945. According to a census taken in September 1948, Fürth had by far the largest Jewish community in Franconia. The majority (218) of its 349 members had come from Poland, fewer than a third were from Germany. Only 45 of its members reported wanting to stay in Germany. In Nuremberg, on the other hand, 135 of the 154 community members were German Jews. The number of children in the two communities demonstrates the difference as well. Whereas Fürth with its predominantly Eastern European population had a total of sixty-six children below the age of sixteen, there were only eight Jewish children in Nuremberg. In Fürth, twenty Jews lived in mixed marriages, while almost half of all Nuremberg community members (sixty-two) were married to non-Jews.[49]

The differences between these two communities may also be gauged by how they handled their members' non-Jewish spouses. Whereas in Nuremberg, most of the community members had survived the Nazi era only because of their marriage to a Christian, and the first three postwar chairpersons had been married to non-Jewish women, Rabbi David Kahane Spiro of Fürth decreed that in his city, Jews living in mixed marriages would be excluded from the community. This decree reflected the discomfort felt by a significant proportion of Eastern European Jews about mixing with Germans.[50]

The postwar Jewish community in Fürth consisted largely of displaced persons from Poland who had been housed in the Finkenschlag DP camp near Fürth.[51] In 1947 Jean Mandel, the son of a family that had moved to Fürth from Galicia before the war and who had grown up in that city, became chair of the community. He had returned to his home city in 1945 and served as its chair until his death in 1974. Mandel represented the melding of Eastern Jewish and German-Jewish destinies. In 1949 he founded the *Nachrichten für den jüdischen Bürger Fürths* (News bulletin for the Jewish citizens of Fürth), which developed into the most intellectually interesting local Jewish newspaper in postwar Germany and created a link between the former Fürth Jews who had emigrated and the postwar community. Like many Jews of his generation, Mandel remained skeptical that a permanent Jewish life was possible in Germany, although he did for a time represent the Jews in the Bavarian senate. Nonetheless, he had his children educated in boarding schools abroad, and they would not return to Germany.

The fact that the Fürth community consisted primarily of Eastern European Jews was also a factor in long-term planning. In December 1949 a meeting convened by Rabbi Spiro resolved that "the remaining assets of the Jewish community be liquidated for the purpose of building the religious, cultural, and economic institutions in the Holy City of Jerusalem, and that they be transferred there."[52] Not long thereafter, the plans were fleshed out in greater detail. The former assets of the Fürth community were to be used to found a settlement near Jerusalem that would serve as a new home for the Jews living temporarily in Fürth. This plan would have meant the dissolution of the postwar Jewish community and was opposed by the few German Jews of the city. And although they were in the minority, the plans did not move forward, because neither Rabbi Spiro nor the other Eastern European Jews of Fürth would take the final step and leave. Of the thirty-three signatories who declared their intention to emigrate and found a settlement in Israel, only three actually did, while almost all of the rest eventually ended up in the United States.

The community in neighboring Nuremberg developed completely differently.[53] It had been founded and led immediately after the end of the war by former members who saw their future in Nuremberg. The number of Jews living in Nuremberg increased during the 1950s and 1960s, when a few Nuremberg Jews returned, and there was also an increase in Eastern European Jews, most of them from the DP camps in Fürth but also from the Föhrenwald DP camp after its closure. In 1954 the community had about 200 members, and by 1970 the number had grown to about 270, some of whom had fled Czechoslovakia during the Prague Spring. This influx made Nuremberg the largest Jewish community in Franconia.

Nuremberg was also the home of the Bar Kochba Jewish sports association, the local Zionist branch, a Jewish women's association, and the *Jüdische Gemeindeblatt* (Jewish community bulletin). The Jewish community in Nuremberg was one of the few German communities after the war to publish a newly edited prayer book, which was largely based on the prewar Nuremberg prayer book of Reform Jews. However, it also included several traditional prayers along with a prayer for the State of Israel. In essence, the Nuremberg community was attempting to bridge the differences between the German Jews who had grown up with Reform traditions and the Eastern European Jewish members steeped in the Orthodox rites.

The Nuremberg-Fürth case exemplifies the cultural differences within the Jewish society in Germany at the microlevel. Whereas Eastern European Jews were concentrated in southern Germany, organized Jewish life in the Federal Republic was controlled from the British zone, where most of the German-Jewish survivors and returnees were living. Karl Marx founded the *Jüdische Gemeindeblatt für die britische Zone* (Jewish community bulletin for the British zone) in Düsseldorf; it was later renamed the *Allgemeine Wochenzeitung der Juden in Deutschland* (General weekly for the Jews in Germany), thereby proclaiming its intention to speak for all Jews living in the country.[54] In June 1952 the Central Council, which had been founded in Frankfurt, moved its headquarters from Hamburg, where van Dam, its general secretary, had briefly conducted business, to Düsseldorf as well, which reflected the council's closeness to the federal government in Bonn and tightened its relationship with the most important Jewish newspaper.

The 1950s saw another wave of German-Jewish returnees, many of them from Israel and South America. Approximately six thousand Jews returned to Germany between 1955 in 1959, 60 percent from Israel, and many others from South America.[55] They were joined by a number of immigrants, mostly from Hungary and Romania. The reasons for this migration were many. For one thing, the refugees often had a hard time integrating culturally into South America or Africa. The hot climate on those continents also played a considerable role. The beginning of restitution payment was undoubtedly another reason for returning. Finally, for those who had lived in Eastern European countries, political repression was no small factor.

Statistics from that time indicate that the increase in population largely resulted from immigration, as the birth-to-death ratio was hardly favorable. In Frankfurt, for example, there were only 21 births during that period but 126 deaths; in Berlin the ratio was even more stark: 40 births and 522 deaths.[56] Nonetheless, the 1950s and 1960s were growth years for many of the larger communities. This was especially the case in Frankfurt, where the community increased from 1,082 in 1952 to more than 5,000 members during the mid-1970s.

As Dan Diner describes in detail in his essay at the beginning of this volume, Frankfurt played a special role in the history of the Jews in the Federal Republic. Although the Central Council soon migrated from the city of its founding on the Main to the Rhine, where it was closer to the seat of government, Frankfurt became the intellectual and economic hub of Jewish life. For one thing, it was possible there to hook into prewar traditions. For example, part of the Institute for Social Research returned to the city that, before 1933, had had the largest proportion of Jews of any major city in Germany and whose mayor called upon the Jews to return to Frankfurt after 1945. In the 1950s the university had three Jewish rectors. The once almost exclusively Jewish domain of psychoanalysis found a new home in Frankfurt at the Sigmund Freud Institute. Frankfurt also became the headquarters of the Bank deutscher Länder and later the Bundesbank, making it the financial center of the young republic. The Holocaust survivors who came to Germany without any ties to specific places and nothing to lose were often inclined to take high financial risks. They found outstanding conditions for starting anew in the capital of the German economic miracle. Of all Jewish communities in Germany, Frankfurt experienced the widest fluctuations in population. In the three years between 1956 and 1959, its Jewish population virtually doubled, even though 14 percent of community members moved away during the same period. Like the city itself, the Jewish community of Frankfurt was more international and cosmopolitan than the rest of the Federal Republic. The combination of economic freedom and a traditionally run social democratic state enabled Jewish life to flourish. The intellectual, economic, and political representatives from Frankfurt played a critical role in the larger Jewish life of the Federal Republic.

The Jewish community in Hamburg developed quite differently from that in Frankfurt and exerted relatively little influence in the Federal Republic. Before the Nazi era, the community had numbered twenty thousand members; by the early 1950s it had barely a thousand. By the end of the 1950s, this figure had increased to about fourteen hundred members as a result of German-Jewish returnees, the influx of Jews from central Eastern Europe, and later—and this was specific to Hamburg—the immigration from Iran of several hundred Jews. Nonetheless, what had once been the largest Jewish community in Germany was now merely a shadow of its former self. While Altona, Hamburg, and Wandsbek were once famous for their important rabbinical authorities, the Hamburg community was now largely served by guest rabbis or by rabbis whose main duties lay elsewhere. Until the end of the 1950s, the community had no established home, and its activities were divided among the many buildings improvised for specific purposes. It took until 1958 for a Jewish old-age home to be dedicated, and it was joined two years later by a new synagogue and a Jewish hospital. In contrast to the communities in Berlin, Frankfurt, and Düsseldorf, the one in Hamburg tended to be more withdrawn and kept a low public profile. But in Hamburg as well, a single person for decades shaped the way in which the community was perceived by outsiders. Unlike Heinz Galinski in Berlin, who was constantly in the news, the Breslau-born Günter Singer, who between 1953 and 1989 served the Hamburg community in various capacities, including as cantor and business manager, avoided the public eye whenever possible.

While Jewish life in Hamburg languished relative to pre-1933 times, the smaller northern German communities constantly risked dissolution. For example, the Jewish community in Schleswig-Holstein, which consisted of two small communities in Kiel and Lübeck, dissolved in 1968 and merged with the Hamburg community.[57] In Braunschweig, the community continued to be housed in a completely unsuitable building. In the early 1960s, its board appealed to the State Association for funding for a new facility, "or must we remain for yet another year to celebrate the High Holy Days in this shabby and worm-eaten synagogue?" In another letter the board wrote, "Our Torah shrine consists of an old discarded clothes cabinet with a curtain, and the Torah scroll is not ornamented in any way."[58] The community soon shriveled to fewer than fifty members. The few German Jews who returned suspected the few former Eastern European DPs of wanting to "seize power in the community."[59] Here, too, the existence of the community was dependent on a single person, in this case Carl Mosberg, who had been community chair since 1945. There was no successor when he stepped down in 1958 at the age of eighty-three. As a result, in 1966 the community turned over the reins of leadership to the chair of the State Association of Jewish Communities in Lower Saxony "to simplify management and facilitate financing."[60] The Braunschweig community continued to be centrally administered from Hannover until the fall of 1978.

Communities faced other structural problems in southwestern Germany. Here, partitioning into zones left traces that outlived the departure of the French and Americans. The state associations of the communities of southern and northern Baden merged in July 1953 and formed the Supreme Council of the Israelites of Baden. The council harked back to prewar days in both name and personnel. Many of the leading representatives in the Supreme Council had been active in the religious life of the region before the war. And the fact that these Jewish communities were geographically close to those in Switzerland and France, where the infrastructure had remained considerably more intact, was an important factor in their recovery.

For the Saar region, which was autonomous until 1956, the links to France were even more important. Almost all of the Jews in this region had returned from France after the war and maintained their tight relationships with the Jewish communities there. What emerged was, by German standards, an unusually homogeneous Jewish community. Most of the Saar Jews kept their French citizenship and sent their children to the single Francophone school in Saarbrücken. They also used French in their invitations to community celebrations. In addition, these returnees played a palpable role in the reconstruction of the region as lawyers and in some cases as political officials. Another important factor was that the governor and later high commissioner Gilbert Granval, one of the leading figures during the French occupation, was also of Jewish origin.

It was certainly not by chance that the synagogue in Saarbrücken was dedicated already in January 1951, earlier than any new synagogue in the Federal Republic. The continuities in that community were simply greater than elsewhere in Germany. For example, Shlomo Rülf, the prewar rabbi, was able to help restore the community during his one-year visit, and aside from the Pestalozzistrasse synagogue in Berlin, it was the only one in Germany to again use its organ in the tradition of prewar Reform congregations.[61]

Some small communities had more graves to tend than members. The Jewish community in Stuttgart was now the only one in Württemberg. Würzburg inherited all of the communities in Lower Franconia, which had once numbered over a hundred, and the two cities of Kaiserslautern and Neustadt an der Weinstrasse, which together formed the Jewish Community of Rhineland-Palatinate, were the successors to seventy-two prewar communities. However, the greatest losses were felt in Berlin. Although the community was still the largest in postwar Germany, it never attained more than 5 percent of its prewar membership of 170,000.

IN THE GERMAN DEMOCRATIC REPUBLIC

The special status of postwar Berlin also affected the Jewish community there. In Berlin, more than anywhere else, Jews had been able to survive the war hiding. They were joined by survivors from mixed marriages, returnees from exile, and displaced persons, especially from the Schlachtensee DP camp. Although the Berlin community had lost considerably more members than other communities, in the mid-1950s, as in 1933, about a third of all Jews in Germany lived in the former Reich capital.

As with the Protestant and Catholic churches, the Jewish community remained, at least nominally, under a single unified administration after the founding of the two German states. The Jewish Community of Greater Berlin had its headquarters in the Oranienburger Strasse in the eastern sector of the city. Heinz Galinski, chair of the community in West Berlin, and Julius Meyer, his counterpart in East Berlin, cooperated across sector borders, and the cantor Estrongo Nachama, who lived in the western sector, was a regular presence in the eastern sector as well. The State Association of Jewish Communities in the GDR (originally the Soviet zone of occupation), which was founded in 1947, continued to be represented in the Central Council.

Julius Meyer also served as the president of the State Association of Jewish Communities in the GDR and was the most important actor in the East German–Jewish community. Like Galinski, he was born in West Prussia and had survived Auschwitz. He had joined the Communist Party of Germany (Kommunistische Partei Deutschland, KPD) in 1930 and become a member of the East German Socialist Unity Party (Sozialistische Einheitspartei Deutschlands, SED) after the war. He also belonged to the Association of Persecutees of the Nazi Regime (Vereinigung der Verfolgten des Naziregimes, VVN), which was allied with the SED, and in 1949 and 1950 he was a delegate to the People's Chamber. Like other association functionaries and committed Communists, he defended the policies of the GDR. However, there were also areas where he deviated from the official party line. In June 1952, for example, he suggested that the meetings of the State Association begin with an expression of solidarity with the people in the State of Israel.[62] If the Jewish community in the West served as a guarantor of German democracy vis-à-vis the Western nations, the small Jewish community in the East would serve to justify the GDR vis-à-vis the Federal Republic. Jewish citizens in the GDR were constantly urged to sign declarations that counterposed its image as an anti-Fascist state to the intended image of the Federal Republic as a place where former Nazis were often given prominent roles.

Of course, in reality the notion that anti-Fascism was incompatible with antisemitism proved to be considerably more complicated than Meyer and other Jewish citizens of the GDR at first realized, as the small Jewish community was soon drawn into the conflicts of the Cold War. As early as the 1950s, the leadership of the SED had adopted a critical stance toward all contacts between Jewish functionaries and Israeli or American Jewish organizations. This position hardened as Moscow forced its satellite states to purge their Soviet-aligned parties of "counterrevolutionaries" and unreliable elements. When the arrest of the former general secretary of the Communist Party of Czechoslovakia, Rudolf Slánský, led to a show trial in 1952, the underlying antisemitism would have been hard to miss. In addition to Slánský, another ten of the fourteen persons accused were of Jewish origin. Among the eleven who were executed on December 3, 1952, eight, including Slánský, were Jews. Even if they were not directly defamed as Jews, the constant drumbeat of "Zionists and cosmopolitans" would have made clear to an impartial observer of the trial what was intended.

The Slánský show trial in Czechoslovakia had profound effects on Jewish life in the GDR as well. Party functionaries who advocated the payment of restitution to Jews or negotiations with Israel were watched closely. The most prominent victim of the resultant purges was not Jewish. Paul Merker, a former secretary of state and member of the central committee of the SED, had advocated for reparation payments to Jews by any successor German state even during his exile in Mexico. In addition, he had voted for negotiations with Israel and recognition of the Jews by the GDR as a national minority, comparable to the status enjoyed by the Sorbs. These positions soon became untenable within the SED, and in 1950 Merker was relieved of all political functions. Here, too, one may discern a purge conducted by returnees from Moscow, who dominated the central committee of the SED, against the Communists who had returned from Mexico. Along with Merker, Jewish returnees from Mexico came under increasing pressure. Leo Zuckermann, for example, one of the coauthors of the constitution of the GDR, was forced to resign as head of the chancellery of GDR president Wilhelm Pieck, and in December 1958 the Central Commission for Control of the Party (Zentrale Parteikontrollkommission, ZPKK) resolved to strip Alexander Abusch of any important party functions in the future because of statements he had made about the "Jewish question."[63] Abusch was the former editor-in-chief of the newspaper Freies Deutschland (Free Germany), published in Mexico.

Events came to a head a week after the death sentences announced in Prague on November 27, 1952, and the executions a week later. On November 30 Paul Merker was arrested and accused of having been "an agent of imperialist secret services." A self-justifying memorandum published by the SED on December 20, 1952, with the title "Lessons from the Trial against the Slánský Conspiracy Center" was marked by antisemitic diatribes against the "traitor" Paul Merker. Later interrogations demonstrated that his relations with Jewish comrades, especially during his Mexican exile, loomed large. He was asked whether he had connections with Jewish organizations in the GDR and whether he knew Julius Meyer. As is evident from a letter sent to the SED's Central Committee for the Control of the Party, he did not let himself be pushed around: "I am neither a Jew nor a Zionist—in any case, neither would constitute a crime." In addition, he restated his opinion that it was the duty of any postwar German successor state to work actively to return to Germany Jews who had been forced into exile.[64] Merker, who was sentenced to eight years in prison in 1955, was released in January 1956 during the de-Stalinization push. In December 1956 he was again allowed to join the SED but was denied the right to hold political office.[65]

But after the wave of interrogations and arrests of supposed Zionists and cosmopolitans, there would be no way back into the party or the state for Leo Zuckermann, Julius Meyer, and other Jewish citizens of the GDR, despite their having dedicated most of their postwar lives to its ideals. The situation became even more grave when, in early 1953, a number of prominent Russian-Jewish physicians were arrested under the pretext of being part of what was called a "doctors' plot." On January 6 Meyer was interrogated about his links to Prague and

Employees of the Jewish community of Greater Berlin at a demonstration on May 1, 1953. From Ulrike Offenberg, *"Seid vorsichtig gegen die Machthaber": Die jüdischen Gemeinden in der SBZ und der DDR 1945–1990* (Berlin: Aufbau-Verlag, 1998).

the West. He was pressured to proclaim publicly his support for the show trials in Prague, accuse the American Jewish Joint Distribution Committee of being a Western spy organization, and condemn Israel as a Fascist state. Meyer and other leaders of the Jewish communities were unanimous in not signing such a declaration. On January 13 and 14, just as the "doctors' plot" was going to trial, Meyer and the chairs of the Jewish communities of Leipzig, Dresden, Halle, and Erfurt fled to the West. Between the end of 1952 and the beginning of 1953, more than five hundred members of Jewish communities in the GDR arrived in the Federal Republic. The Jewish children's home in Niederschönhausen in the East was dissolved and transferred to the Jewish Hospital in Berlin-Wedding in the West. In addition, most of the administrative files of the community were brought to West Berlin.[66]

Developments in the GDR were a major challenge to the Jewish communities in West Berlin and the Federal Republic. How should the West Berlin community react? While the Berlin rabbi Nathan Peter Levinson took the unambiguously political position at a press conference that the Jews in the GDR should flee to the West, the community's chair, Heinz Galinski, was more circumspect, not wishing to risk the unity of the Berlin community as a whole. Internally, Galinski and the Central Council condemned outright Levinson's statement to the press, but they decided to express their condemnation publicly with "deliberate blandness" in order to preserve the veneer of unity.[67] The same pattern was repeated during the distribution of the refugees. Here, too, they signaled solidarity to the public, while in private the controversy grew heated. The Berlin community took in the majority of the refugees, and Galinski accused the Frankfurt community of not accepting its fair share. Berlin agreed to welcome 300 of the 570 refugees while a quota was being worked out for housing the rest in the various federal states.[68]

Even Jews who were not functionaries in Jewish communities in the GDR fell victim to the purges when they were accused of links to the State of Israel or to Western Jewish organizations. Leo Zuckermann, who in a letter dated December 7, 1952, had denounced Julius Meyer as an "agent of Israeli governing circles," had already fled to the West before Meyer.[69] As committed Communists, Meyer, Zuckermann, and others had settled in the eastern part of Germany to help build a new, democratic state. A few years later they had to admit that their experiment had failed. Even Hanns Eisler, the author of the national anthem of the GDR, was accused on May 16, 1953, of "rootless cosmopolitanism" in the daily *Neues Deutschland*.[70]

Residual Jewish communities remained in the GDR, but most of their functionaries had left the country, and the committees that existed were viewed with suspicion. The party leadership now wanted to leave nothing to chance and placed the leaders of new communities under special scrutiny. The Association of Jews in the GDR was forced to reconstitute. The once-united Berlin community was for all intents and purposes now split. In 1955 the West Berlin community consecrated its own cemetery so that its members no longer had to be buried in Weissensee in the eastern part of the city. When board elections were held in East Berlin in 1957, a list of measures published by the Ministry of the Interior stated, "For the election in the Jewish community, instructions for the comrades must come from the district leadership, because attempts have been made to recommend reactionary forces for the board."[71] Throughout the 1950s, the board of the East Berlin community, which had been installed after Julius Meyer's flight in 1953, was able to prevent new elections.[72]

In East Berlin the SED engineered the election of party members to leadership positions. Even the spiritual leader of the community, Martin Riesenburger, dubbed the "red rabbi," became a willing tool of the party bosses.[73] On the other hand, Hermann Baden from Halle, the new president of the State Association of Jewish Communities, who belonged to no party, was not as pliable. He continued to insist on a certain independence, for which he was constantly criticized in

Hanukkah with Rabbi Martin Riesenberger in Berlin, 1957. Stiftung Neue Synagoge Berlin–Centrum Judaicum.

Stasi reports. Some of the chairmen of smaller communities behaved similarly. In order to retain some semblance of independence from the East Berlin community, the State Association refused to recognize Riesenburger's rabbinate and rejected the membership of the East Berlin community in the association. Riesenburger, who had been a student at the Hochschule für die Wissenschaft des Judentums (Reform Rabbinical Seminary, dissolved in 1941) but had not been ordained a rabbi there, was described by the association as a "rabbi" (quotation marks in original) in a letter dated 1957 "who in the area under the Association of Jewish Communities in the German Democratic Republic holds no position and has no mandate for such."[74] The association continued its membership in the (West German) Central Council, and its chair participated in its meetings. These contacts, however, came to an end when the Berlin Wall was erected in 1961.[75]

The East Berlin community was finally accepted into the association in February 1960, and Riesenburger was named rabbi for the entire GDR a year later. In 1961 the State Association began to publish the quarterly Nachrichtenblatt

(*Bulletin*), which hewed closely to the party line; in addition to historical articles and book reviews, it became known for its birthday congratulations to party functionaries. After Baden's death, Helmut Aris from Dresden, a compliant SED member, became head of the association. In the early 1960s the official committees of the Jewish communities in the GDR were forced to hew to the party line. After Stalin's death in 1953, the GDR had begun to distance itself from his policies. Among other things, the leadership of the country took it upon itself to preserve the tiny Jewish community by renovating synagogues, maintaining an old-age home, subsidizing kosher meat, and hiring a rabbi from Budapest after Riesenburger's death in 1965. Rabbi Ödön Singer, however, returned to Hungary in 1969, and the rabbinate remained vacant thereafter in all of East Germany.

After the exodus of Jews from the GDR in 1952–1953, membership in the Jewish communities dropped precipitously. In 1955 they had a total of 1,715 members; by 1976 that figure had dwindled to 728. Outside of Berlin, no community had more than a hundred members.

MICHAEL BRENNER is Professor of Jewish history and culture at the University of Munich and Seymour and Lillian Abensohn Chair in Israel Studies at American University in Washington, DC. He is a member of the Bavarian Academy of Sciences and international president of the Leo Baeck Institute. Brenner's publications include *A Short History of the Jews, Prophets of the Past: Interpreters of Jewish History, Zionism: A Short History,* and as coauthor, the four-volume *German-Jewish History in Modern Times.*

NORBERT FREI is Professor of modern and contemporary history at the University of Jena and is director of the Jena Center 20th Century History. During the 2008–2009 academic year, he was a member of the Institute for Advanced Study in Princeton, and in 2010–2011 he was Theodor Heuss Professor at the New School for Social Research in New York. Frei's publications include *1968: Jugendrevolte und globaler Protest, 1945 und wir: Das Dritte Reich im Bewußtsein der Deutschen,* and *Adenauer's Germany and the Nazi Past: The Politics of Amnesty and Integration;* he is also coauthor of *Das Amt und die Vergangenheit: Deutsche Diplomaten im Dritten Reich und in der Bundesrepublik.*

NOTES

1. Minutes of the meeting held on July 19, 1950, with the purpose of creating an organization representing all the Jews in Germany, in ZA, B1/7.221.1.

2. For more on this, see P. Münch (1997), p. 85.

3. Y. Jelinek (1988), p. 88.

4. For greater detail on the board members of the Central Council, see M. Brenner (2007), pp. 124–133.

5. H. Galinski (1995), p. 147.

6. "Undemokratische Behandlung in Deutschland," *AWJD*, July 20, 1951, p. 7.

7. On the declaration of February 25, 1951, by the directorate of the Central Council, see "Unsere Meinung," in *AWJD*, March 16, 1951.

8. A. Sinn (2011), p. 242.

9. Minutes of the meeting of the Central Council on August 31 and September 1, 1952, in Düsseldorf, in ZA, B.1/7.221.25/26.

10. Letter from Walter Auerbach to his sister-in-law Margit Auerbach on the occasion of "Christmas 1954," in AdsD, 1/WAABII 31. As noted in the margin, Auerbach did not post this letter.

11. "Das Direktorium des Zentralrats der Juden in Deutschland," *Jüdischer Pressedienst* 1–2 (1969), pp. 3–4.

12. Minutes of the meeting of the Central Council on January 13–14, 1963, in Cologne, in ZA, B.1/7.860.

13. See the birthday appreciations and obituary for Alexander Ginsburg in *Jüdischer Pressedienst* 3 (1969), p. 6; Alexander Ginsburg, "Professor Dr. Lewin zum Geburtstag," *AJW*, April 6, 1979, p. 2; Ginsburg, "Abschied von Professor Dr. Herbert Lewin," *AJW*, December 3, 1982. Also the article by Moritz Neumann, "Symbol helfender Menschlichkeit," *AJW*, March 26, 1969, p. 3.

14. See J. Geller (2005), p. 19.

15. Minutes of the meeting of the Central Council on March 22–23, 1964, in ZA, B.1/7.815. See also his own description of himself after his reelection in 1967, "Begrüßung durch Prof. Lewin auf der Ratsversammlung vom 26. November 1967," pp. 1–5, in ZA, B.1/7.891.

16. J. Geller (2005), pp. 281–285. Weinberger complained about disunity in the directorate, which made it possible for the general secretary to pursue official business however he wished (minutes of the meeting of the state committee of the LVB on December 20, 1953, in Munich, in Archiv LVB, file "Protokolle vom Oktober 1947 bis 10. Juli 1955").

17. Letter from H. G. van Dam to the members of the directorate and council, all state associations, and the communities of Berlin, Bremen, Hamburg, and Cologne with regard to Jews in Germany and the organizations of world Jewry (foreign organizations), November 15, 1951, in ZA, B.1/7.121.

18. Cited in T. Anthony (2004), p. 61.

19. Contribution by H. G. van Dam at the meeting of the Central Council on July 7–8, 1954, in Düsseldorf, in ZA, B.1/7.221.55.

20. L. Katcher (1968), pp. 19–23.

21. J. Geller (2005), p. 214.

22. For more on Karl Marx's contacts with Theodor Heuss, see J. Geller (2005), pp. 263–367; J. Geller (2006).

23. Y. Bodemann (1996a), pp. 33–35.

24. Letter from Willy Brandt to Annemarie Renger, December 9, 1964, and the response, December 18, 1964, in AdsD, Willy Brandt A6 48 (old signature).

25. H. Klingebiel (2009), pp. 60–62.

26. Minutes of the meeting of the directorate of the Central Council on March 22, 1964, in Hannover, in ZA, B.1/7.856; minutes of the meeting of the directorate of the Central Council on December 5, 1965, in Cologne, in ZA, B.1/7.828. At issue here are the mutual accusations leveled by community functionaries Carl Katz and Max Plaut of Bremen.

27. Minutes of the meeting of the Central Council on June 16, in Cologne, in ZA, B.1/7.860.

28. H. Maor (1961), p. 19.

29. For example, the invitation to the 1963 Hannukah ball at the Hotel Bayerischer Hof with Abi and Esther Ofarim, see in LBI, AR 1921.

30. Hans-Erich Fabian, "Süddeutsche Probleme," *Der Weg*, July 26, 1946, p. 3.

31. A. Kauders (2004), p. 42.

32. Minutes of a meeting of the state committee of the LVB on December 20, 1953, in Munich, in Archiv LVB, file "Protokolle vom Oktober 1947 bis 10. Juli 1955."

33. Position on community membership and citizenship at the meeting of the directorate of the Central Council on December 13, 1953, in Munich, in ZA, B.1/7.221.44.

34. Letters of the Aktionskomitee zur Vorbereitung demokratischer Wahlen in der Israelitischen Kultusgemeinde Augsburg, January 1954, in LBI, AR 5890/3.

35. A. Quast (1996), p. 119.

36. A. Quast (1997), p. 73.

37. See also A. Sinn (2011), pp. 249–258.

38. Record of the meeting between federal president Theodor Heuss and Karl Marx, the publisher of the *AJW*, on October 25, 1951, in Bonn, in BArch, B 122/2080.

39. Minutes of the meeting of the directorate of the Central Council on April 29–30, 1951, in ZA, B.1/7.221.13.

40. Decision by the Central Council at the council meeting on June 3, 1958, in Düsseldorf, in ZA, B.1/7.852.

41. A. Kauders (2004), pp. 48–51.

42. L. Rosenberg (2004), p. 92.

43. A. Ben (2004), pp. 138–139.

44. Letter from the state police office of Bavaria to the head office for Upper Bavaria, December 6, 1951, in StAM, Pol. Präs. Obb. 298.

45. B. Salamander (2011), pp. 42–43.

46. Letter from the Bavarian State police, Föhrenwald police headquarters, to the office of the state police inspector at Wolfratshausen, September 4, 1953, in StAM, Pol. Präs. Obb. 298.

47. A. Königseder and J. Wetzel (1994), p. 167.

48. L. Rosenberg (2004), p. 101.

49. Membership figures for the Israelite religious community (Israelitische Kultusgemeinde, IKG) of Nuremberg as of April 10, 1949, and of the Israelite religious community (IKG) of Fürth as of April 15, 1949, in Archiv LVB, file "Protokolle vom Oktober 1947 bis 10. Juli 1955."

50. M. Berthold-Hilpert (1998), p. 374.

51. The following remarks are based on M. Berthold-Hilpert (2002), pp. 197–212, as well as M. Berthold-Hilpert (1998), pp. 361–380.

52. M. Berthold-Hilpert (1998), p. 371.

53. The following remarks about Nuremberg are based especially on the master's thesis of K. Heilmann (1989). They also draw on contemporary reports by Bernhard Kolb, *Die Juden in Nürnberg 1839–1945*, a 1946 typescript preserved at the Nuremberg Stadtarchiv and available at http://www.rijo.homepage.t-online.de/pdf/DE_NU_JU _kolb_text.pdf, and the articles by Paul Baruch in the *Gemeindeblatt der israelitischen Kultusgemeinde Nürnberg*, vols. 1 and 2 (1967–1968). See also the relevant chapters in

A. Müller (1968), and Stadt Nürnberg (1993). See also the webpage of the Jewish community of Nuremberg, www.ikg-nuernberg.de.

54. The Jewish newspaper changed its name several times: *Jüdisches Gemeindeblatt für die Nord-Rheinprovinz und Westfalen* (1.1946,1–15); *Jüdisches Gemeindeblatt für die britische Zone* (1.1946,16–3.1948/49,8); *Jüdisches Gemeindeblatt* (3.1948/49,9–41); *Allgemeine Wochenzeitung der Juden in Deutschland* (4.1949/50,1–20.1965/66,52); *Allgemeine unabhängige jüdische Wochenzeitung* (21.1966/67,1–28.1973,5); *Allgemeine Jüdische Wochenzeitung* (28.1973,6–56.2001,26); *Jüdische Allgemeine* (57.2002,1–today).

55. H. Maor (1961), pp. 43, 45.

56. E. Burgauer (1993), app.

57. S. Jochims (1998), p. 100.

58. R. Bein (2005), p. 41.

59. R. Bein (2005), p. 29.

60. R. Bein (2005), p. 34.

61. For more on the history of the Jews in Saarland, see A. Gemeinhardt (2008).

62. U. Offenberg (2001), p. 152.

63. J. Illichmann (1997), pp. 86–91.

64. J. Illichmann (1997), pp. 108–109.

65. J. Herf (1994), pp. 151–190.

66. U. Offenberg (2001), p. 152.

67. Minutes of the meeting of the directorate of the Central Council on January 27, 1953, in Düsseldorf, p. 2, in ZA, B.1/7.221.33.

68. Minutes of the meeting of the directorate of the Central Council on May 3, 1953, pp. 6–12, in ZA, B.1/7.221.37.

69. J. Illichmann (1997), p. 92.

70. For a microstudy of the consequences of the Slànsky trial, see E. Ludwig (1994), pp. 228–244.

71. J. Illichmann (1997), p. 186.

72. U. Offenberg (1998), pp. 102–104.

73. U. Offenberg (1998), p. 97.

74. J. Illichmann (1997), p. 187. A more positive description of Riesenburger as a person is in H. Simon (2003), pp. 7–33. See also L. Mertens (1997), pp. 160–164.

75. U. Offenberg (1998), pp. 109, 127; L. Mertens (1997), pp. 80–85.

6 RELIGION AND CULTURE

"Who builds a house intends to stay." Ever since Salomon Korn spoke these words on September 14, 1986, at the dedication of the Frankfurt community center that he had designed, they have been used over and over again to characterize the evolving fortunes of the Jews in Germany.[1] But even during the first postwar decades, German Jews were not without a roof over their heads. If we take Korn's phrasing seriously, then the 1950s and 1960s were decades during which the Jewish communities in Germany took root with the building of more than forty new synagogues and prayer rooms and the reconstruction of two prewar synagogues. And in fact, the sentiment behind Korn's words was already evident in 1960, when the synagogue in Hamburg was opened. At the dedication, Hamburg mayor Max Brauer stated: "No one erects a house for a temporary stay. A building dedicated to service to the Highest is built only by those with a firm intention to stay."[2]

The first two postwar German synagogues were built outside the territory of the Federal Republic. The new synagogue in Dresden, which was converted from the former mourning chapel at the Jewish cemetery, was dedicated in 1950. The first newly constructed synagogue was opened a year later in Saarbrücken, which belonged to the Saar region, at the time a semi-independent French protectorate. The shadows of the past hovered over both buildings. The newly opened Dresden synagogue, a modest affair, replaced the magnificent synagogue built by Gottfried Semper, which had been destroyed during Kristallnacht in 1938. And although the Saarbrücken synagogue was typical of new construction at the time, according to Korn it nonetheless availed itself of the vernacular forms of the Third Reich, with its pseudosacred hall architecture, "presumably the sole example of the merging of Jewish sacred building with formal elements of the architecture of National Socialism."[3]

The first newly constructed synagogue in the Federal Republic proper was dedicated in 1952 in Stuttgart and drew on the democratic traditions of the Bauhaus school. Representing a clear break with the synagogue architecture of the nineteenth and early twentieth centuries, it became a template for later buildings in its functionality and modesty of means. Two Jewish and one non-Jewish architects

The Saarbrücken synagogue, dedicated on January 14, 1951.
Stadtarchiv Saarbrücken / photograph by Fritz Mittelstaedt.

Dedication of the Dresden synagogue after conversion of the former mourning hall at the cemetery, 1950. Archiv der Jüdischen Gemeinde zu Dresden.

designed about half of all the new synagogues during the 1950s and 1960s.[4] In line with contemporary synagogue architecture in the United States, the new German constructions tended to combine a synagogue with a community center. The new buildings not only were for prayer but increasingly provided other functions, including a meeting place for the elderly and activities for children and young people.

Thus, for example, the Cologne synagogue was rededicated in 1959 but with a considerably smaller prayer room, the remaining space being used as a community center. In the words of its architect, "The new community center fits in with the times. That means the creation of a total living space: a place of worship, a community hall, administration, youth center, nursery school, and old-age home all in one. In other words, a living, organic whole."[5] The dedication of new synagogues in postwar Germany was not always met with approval from the new Jewish state. For example, when the head of the Israeli mission delivered his greetings in Cologne, he expressed the hope that this new synagogue would be "a preliminary stage for future generations living together in Israel." The community rabbi, undoubtedly countering such a challenge at the dedication, responded: "To the objection of our brothers and sisters abroad: 'Will not this new building also go up in flames tomorrow?' we respond: Your fears are ours as well.

Synagogue in Düsseldorf, 1961. Leonard Freed / Magnum Photos.

Nonetheless, our Jewish duty demands of us—ever since our wanderings in the wilderness—that we strike a tent to the Eternal, wherever we may be."[6]

The building of a new synagogue was not only a moral wager but also a financial one. Although building costs were at least partially subsidized by the city and state, the small communities had to ask themselves whether they could carry the ongoing costs of such a building over time. These considerations moved Hendrik George van Dam, the general secretary of the Central Council, to caution the communities: it was necessary that they "be clear that not every community undertaking, especially every building, is advantageous, but that there are also gifts that are actually very costly."[7] When a new synagogue was built in Hannover in 1961, van Dam wondered whether a community room and a prayer room would not have sufficed.[8] Three years earlier, when the new synagogue in Düsseldorf was dedicated, van Dam had warned that a "building constitutes only

The Jewish community center in the Fasanenstrasse in Berlin-Charlottenburg, 1960. Bundesarchiv / photograph by Gerd Schütz.

an external form, and it is our hope that the Jewish community in Düsseldorf will be able to fill it with spiritual life."[9]

And in fact it was easier to build synagogues than to fill them with life. In the words of a teacher of Jewish religion, "the communities in the old style, with their own rabbi, cantor, religious teachers, etc., have almost completely disappeared. Although state authorities support the construction of synagogues in many places," these "frequently serve more to gather the scant number of remaining Jews for cultural events than for actual religious devotion."[10] While a few of the larger communities had their own old-age homes, ensured the availability of kosher food, and offered social events, others were too small to hold weekly religious services and limited themselves to prayers during the High Holy Days. During the 1950s daily religious services took place in only four cities: Berlin, Frankfurt, Munich, and Fürth. Many communities found it difficult to find suitable religion teachers and prayer leaders. Rabbis were a scarce commodity. Even in Berlin, communities looked to institutions abroad to at least "lend" them a rabbi for certain rabbinical functions.[11] The Liberal Jewish rabbinical seminary in London expressed its desire to help but made it clear that the German-Jewish community would have to train its own rabbis in the future.[12]

Kosher butcher shop in Frankfurt am Main, 1961. Leonard Freed / Magnum Photos.

Of course, there were quite a few German-speaking rabbis, but few of them would consider returning from exile. And some who did soon left Germany disappointed. The first postwar rabbi in Frankfurt, Dr. Leopold Neuhaus, emigrated to the United States in 1946; his successor Dr. Wilhelm Weinberg left Germany in November 1951. On the occasion of his farewell sermon, he declared: "Even those who are politically blind will eventually realize that those figures who worked for the seamless implementation of the Nazi campaign of world conquest once again haunt the new Germany, today disguising their martial visage with a look of offended innocence, but tomorrow once again baring their true face."[13]

There were only seven official community rabbis in Germany in 1960, plus a handful of rabbis in the Bavarian communities trained in Eastern Europe. Despite the small number, they were soon able to organize. The state rabbi for Hessen, Isaak Emil Lichtigfeld, assumed a leading role, and he was made chair of the Federal Republic's Rabbinical Conference, which was founded in March 1957. The purpose of this organization was to coordinate all of the rabbis' religious and social duties. A rabbinical court association was to meet regularly to rule on questions of religious law. While the Rabbinical Conference succeeded in bringing together Orthodox and Liberal rabbis, the traditional rabbis of the primarily Eastern European communities in Bavaria refused to join. They had founded in 1954 their own short-lived Association for Torah-Observant Jewry, to which a few

German-Jewish rabbis had initially belonged as well.[14] The Munich rabbi Samuel A. Snieg justified his opposition to the Rabbinical Conference, saying that "this organization was created prematurely" and that it had members who had no competence to decide on important questions such as Jewish divorce laws.[15] While the Eastern European members accused their German-Jewish colleagues of not being sufficiently well versed in rabbinical law, the latter feared that the Eastern European rabbis would be unable to represent their communities to the outside world.

The most important rabbinical authority among the Eastern European rabbis was David Kahane Spiro, who was born in Poland in 1901 and who during the war had been the youngest member of the Warsaw rabbinate. He had belonged to the Judenrat (Jewish Council) until the liquidation of the ghetto and survived numerous concentration camps. He was liberated from Dachau in the spring of 1945. Spiro settled in Fürth and remained a central figure in Jewish religious life in Bavaria until his death in 1970. He provided daily religious instruction, set up a kosher kitchen, and oversaw the ritual slaughter of cattle. The Association for Torah-Observant Jewry was founded in his honor by several Orthodox rabbis in Fürth. Like his colleagues in Munich, Regensburg, and Amberg he had received no formal training at a Western rabbinical seminary but rather at a traditional yeshiva, and he was viewed as a preeminent authority, especially by the Eastern European Jews.

Liberal Judaism had a more difficult status in postwar Germany. Although it had been founded in Germany in the nineteenth century, the Eastern European—and therefore the Orthodox—tradition remained dominant after the war. This was why all attempts by the World Union for Progressive Judaism in the 1950s to gain greater influence in Germany failed.[16]

The rabbinate was not spared its own scandals. For example, the Bavarian state rabbi Dr. Aaron Ohrenstein, who originally came from Poland but had been trained in Germany before the war, was sentenced to a year in prison in connection with the accusations against Philipp Auerbach. While Auerbach was arrested on the autobahn, Ohrenstein was picked up at the Munich airport, where he had booked a one-way ticket to Switzerland. The Federal Constitutional Court voided the decision handed down by the Munich state court after he had already served a portion of his sentence. The prison term meted out by the state court in Augsburg after a new trial was then suspended. Despite protests by several hundred community members, Ohrenstein was dismissed from his position in Munich in 1955. His protest against the leadership of the Munich community culminated in a hunger strike that he announced while in prison in Stadelheim, although it lasted for only twenty-four hours.[17] Years later, some of the German Jews in Munich accused him of unethical machinations. Karl Marx went so far

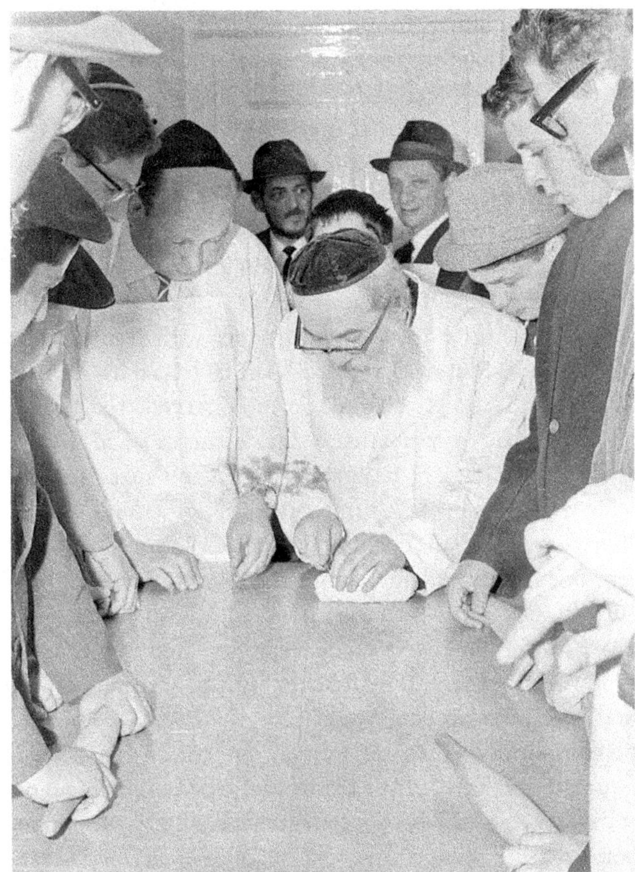

Baking matzoh, with Rabbi David Spiro, 1960s. Jüdisches Museum Franken.

as to tell German federal president Theodor Heuss that he was "convinced that Ohrenstein was not a rabbi, nor did he have a Ph.D."[18]

An even more spectacular "rabbinical scandal" took place in Berlin. The Jewish community of Berlin, which more than a decade after the end of the war still had not managed to acquire a permanent rabbi, in January 1957 invited a certain Dr. Isaak Goldstein, who originally came from Hungary and later lived in Romania and Paris, to serve as rabbi of the largest Jewish community in Germany. But soon after his arrival, Goldstein made demands that surprised the board. He laid claim to the title chief rabbi of Berlin, wanted to rebuild the Hochschule für die Wissenschaft des Judentums (the prewar Liberal Rabbinical Seminary), and convert the Liberal synagogue in the Pestalozzistrasse into an Orthodox one while building a new Liberal synagogue in the Fasanenstrasse. When the community sought to verify Goldstein's credentials, it turned out that he had served for only a short time as rabbi of a small Romanian community but had never been chief rabbi of Bucharest, as he claimed. And in Bucharest he was known under the name Pater (Father) Erwin (or Dr. Erwin Pater). In addition, he had already come to the attention of authorities in Romania, Israel, and France for a variety of offenses. By some accounts he had even converted to Christianity. Goldstein was dismissed without notice in September 1957.[19]

Goldstein subsequently conducted a vendetta against representatives of the community and the Central Council, which culminated in an interview in the *Deutsche Soldaten-Zeitung* (German soldiers' newspaper) in January 1960. In the interview, he credited that radical right-wing newspaper with "remarkable clarity and courage" while ferociously attacking Heinz Galinski, Karl Marx, and Hendrik George van Dam. In addition, he claimed in the interview that thousands of Jews deported by the Nazis to Transnistria during the war had in fact died "as a result of poisoned vegetables."[20] It should come as no surprise that this interview, which made headlines in the German media, would have loosed a storm of outraged indignation in the Jewish communities. In Berlin, Goldstein was physically assaulted by one community member and publicly insulted by another. Goldstein subsequently sued both—and then pursued suits against Marx, Galinski, and even van Dam's wife.[21] Goldstein's wife, Georgette, went so far as to publish a book on the affair. In the entire colorful history of the Jews in postwar Germany, this episode was surely one of the most lurid.[22]

As employees of the community, all rabbis were dependent on the elected community boards, a circumstance that did little to forestall jurisdictional squabbles. These tended to escalate when a rabbi made statements about political matters or the community board gave an opinion on questions of religious law. When Nathan Peter Levinson, the rabbi of the Berlin community, reacted to the interrogation and the arrest of Jewish functionaries in the German Democratic Republic (GDR) by advising the Jews living there to leave, he was fired by Heinz Galinski, the chair of the community.[23] On another level, the rabbis viewed it as their province to decide who could become a community member, while the lay leadership of many community boards believed it to be their right to regulate. In Bremen, the community chair even took it upon himself to convert to Judaism a woman married to a member of the community. In 1957 in a letter to the chair of the Rabbinical Conference, Rabbi Robert Raphael Geis of Baden wrote that the leaders of the community had "often in complete ignorance arrogated to themselves the right of religious decision making and representation."[24]

The Central Council made it abundantly clear to the Rabbinical Conference that it was not to involve itself in public matters and that only the Central Council could negotiate with the German authorities. The rabbinical meeting had originally planned to call itself the Rabbinical Council, which elicited protests from van Dam that this name could easily be confused with the Central Council. This in turn caused indignation within the Rabbinical Conference, whose chair, Isaak Lichtigfeld, reported to a colleague: "The gentlemen who are at the top want to remain in the spotlight and don't want anyone else sharing the glory with them, except in such matters where the presence of a rabbi is absolutely necessary, even in the eyes of non-Jews. In other words, for whom we are necessarily and accordingly required as decoration."[25] And in an inflammatory speech at a meeting of the Central Council, Lichtigfeld complained that the rabbis had come to view themselves as mere employees of the community, were denied adequate support, and had been degraded to a "mere shadow existence": "Rabbis in Germany are like children in England. They may be seen but not heard."[26]

And in fact, the rabbis were seldom heard. On formal occasions, the chair or the general secretary of the Central Council—not the chair of the Rabbinical Conference—served as the official representative of the Jews living in West Germany.

In the GDR, organized religious life became increasingly difficult after the Berlin community was split and most of the active members fled from the East to the West. As a result, in most communities, religious and social life were reduced to religious services on the High Holy Days and to the annual Hanukkah ball. There was a Jewish old-age home in East Berlin until 1990, and kosher meat continued to be available at a butcher shop in Prenzlauer Berg. *Matzah* was imported from Hungary. Because of the exodus of so many adult males, many communities, contrary to tradition, decreased the *minyan* (prayer quorum) from ten to three.[27]

THE HISTORICAL LEGACY

Like many prewar German rabbis, their successors often viewed themselves as local historians. In 1959 Rabbi Zvi Asaria-Helfgott of Cologne published a five-hundred-page history of the Jews of that city. Later, as rabbi of Lower Saxony, he wrote a similar history of the Jews there.[28] A few scholars who were ordained as rabbis concentrated on their scholarship after their return to Germany. These included the historians Bernhard Brilling and Heinz Mosche Graupe, men with very similar pasts. Both were born in 1906, Brilling in the province of Posen, Graupe in Berlin. Both were ordained in 1932, Brilling at the Jewish Theological Seminary in Breslau (Wrocław), Graupe at the Hochschule für die Wissenschaft des Judentums. Both emigrated to Palestine but returned to Germany to pursue their scholarly interests. Brilling, the former archivist of the Breslau Jewish community and later archivist of the city of Tel Aviv, was hired in 1957 by the Institutum Judaicum Delitzschianum in Münster and published numerous histories of the Jews in Silesia. He was awarded the symbolic title of professor only after his retirement in 1971.[29] Graupe, who wrote his doctorate in philosophy, returned to Hamburg in 1964 as director of the newly founded Institut für die Geschichte der deutschen Juden (Institute for the History of the German Jews).[30]

The return of these two scholars should be viewed in the larger context of the recording and researching of the intellectual and cultural legacy of German Jewry, whose centers of activity had relocated abroad. The Leo Baeck Institute was founded in 1955 and dedicated itself to that legacy in Jerusalem, London, and New York. The émigrés who founded the research institute made a point of not establishing a branch in Germany. The plan advanced by the anti-Nazi Christian pacifist Gertrud Luckner in 1954 to found an institute for German-Jewish studies in Germany made little headway in governmental circles. Luckner herself feared that the Jewish community outside of Germany would reject such an institute.[31]

And in fact, Israeli archivists had little interest in creating a new research center in Germany; rather, they were intent on transferring the archival material (or at least copies thereof) that had survived in Germany relating to the prewar Jewish communities to their own archives. However, German authorities resisted such a transfer, especially of original documents. In addition, they feared that politically explosive material from the Nazi period might be uncovered. At a conference of archivists in 1955, objections were raised about giving copies of other archival material from the recent past "to the Jews." A senior governmental official in North Rhine–Westphalia expressed concern that the transfer of copied files from the period after 1933 was problematic "because the Jews would be handed material about the persecution of the Jews from 1933 to 1939." And his colleague from Lower Saxony doubted that "it is in the general interest of Germany if, for example, material from the secret state police and so on were released for filming."[32]

The Central Council actively opposed the plans advanced by Alex Bein, the director of the Zionist Central Archives in Jerusalem, to obligate the Jews who remained in Germany to aid in the transfer of Jewish archival material to Israel.[33] In response, van Dam suggested that "a special archival department for the history of the Jews be set up in Germany."[34] Although the initial plans were abandoned, by the early 1960s people had begun to consider creating such a Jewish archive. What brought this idea to the fore again was the question of what to do with the considerable archival holdings of the Hamburg Jewish community. After lengthy hearings before the restitution office in a Hamburg court, it was finally decided that a large proportion of the material would be left in Hamburg and not transferred to Israel. The department for the history of the Jews in Germany founded by Brilling at the Institutum Judaicum in Münster would now be moved to Hamburg at the suggestion of the director of the Instititum Judaicum Karl Heinrich Rengstorf, and the sponsors from Hamburg, Hans W. Hertz and Eric M. Warburg. The intention of the institute in Hamburg was "in a practical sense to grow into the role of a German Leo Baeck Institute."[35] Rengstorf's certificate of appointment had already been prepared when, in early 1964, objections were raised to a director of an institute for German-Jewish history who was also chair of a Lutheran organization of missionaries among the Jews and professor of New Testament studies. Rengstorf was forced to step down on February 29, 1964, never having really assumed the post.[36]

The first actual director of the Institute for the History of the German Jews was Heinz Mosche Graupe, who took up the reins in November 1964. Once installed, he rapidly began to build the institute, setting up a library, sponsoring lectures at the university, and publishing a series of scholarly works. The first book to be published was his own volume on the intellectual history of German Jewry from 1652 to 1942. Plans to create a historical archive were dropped, however, and realized only decades later in 1987, when the Central Archive for Research on the History of the Jews in Germany was opened in Heidelberg.

While the Central Council decided to leave its archival holdings in Germany, the State Association of Jewish Communities of Bavaria transferred the holdings of the prewar communities to Israel. The very different ways in which German and Eastern European Jews dealt with the past make clear just how differently they viewed their role in Germany. For the Central Council, which mainly represented the German Jews, it was a foregone conclusion that the documents relating to their own history in Germany would remain in Germany. By contrast, the Jewish communities of Bavaria, which consisted primarily of Eastern European displaced persons, had no emotional connection with local Jewish history and wanted the primary sources documenting their past to be housed where, in their opinion, the future of the Jewish people lay, namely, in Israel.

The officials of the Bavarian State Association were convinced that no one in Germany would subject these sources to scholarly analysis. Under no circumstances would these officials hand over these documents to historians who, before 1945, had been active in the Nazi institutes and libraries that engaged in "research on the Jewish question," thereby all too often providing intellectual cover for Nazi crimes. After the war, some of these same historians felt no shame publishing the research that they had conducted at these antisemitic institutes.[37]

Other non-Jewish historians dared not touch the history of the Jews during the first several decades after the war. As the Berlin historian Wilhelm Treue wrote in his 1952 review of Selma Stern's *The Court Jew* in the *Historische Zeitschrift*:

Questions relating to Jewry, whether of a political or historical nature, are to-day taboo in Germany, and with good reason. Any engagement with it conjures up the suffering that millions of Jews experienced at the hands of National Socialist Germany. And anyone who, with the utmost of caution and fervent striving to discern the truth, engages critically with any problems of Jewish history faces not only the obvious accusation that new antisemitism is being added to the old but also the risk of judging where restraint and acceptance would seem more appropriate.[38]

As a result, works of Jewish history published in the first two decades after 1945 were written mainly by Jewish authors who worked outside of the networks of professional historians. For example, Stefan Schwarz, who came originally from Poland and was liberated from the Flossenbürg concentration camp in 1945, was associated with the Historical Commission of Liberated Jews in the immediate postwar years and cofounded the small Bavarian Jewish community of Straubing, which he led for many years. His *Die Juden in Bayern im Wandel der Zeiten* (The Jews in Bavaria over the course of time), published in 1963, was one of the first books of Jewish history to appear in the Federal Republic.[39] Schwarz was an academic outsider with no university affiliation, nor did he receive research grants from any German scholarly organization. His work was financed by the Jewish Claims Conference in New York. As an academic outsider and a Holocaust survivor (i.e., in the eyes of many German historians as someone emotionally affected), Schwarz was doubly suspect for his supposed lack of professionalism and doubtful objectivity, accusations that ended up making life impossible for another Polish Jewish historian in postwar Germany.

Joseph Wulf, who was born in Chemnitz in 1912 and grew up in Cracow, had survived Auschwitz and made it his life's work to document the crimes of the Third Reich. Beginning with *Das Dritte Reich und die Juden* (The Third Reich and the Jews), published in 1955, Wulf, who had lived in Berlin since 1952, published numerous volumes of documents relating to Nazi policies. Although he was awarded the Leo Baeck Medal by the Central Council and received an honorary doctorate from the Free University of Berlin, he remained an outsider in academic circles. He was either ignored by conventional historians or rejected outright. Among other things, he was accused of being obsessed with detail and with polemicism. But even more irritating was his interpretation of National Socialism, which placed the Holocaust at the center. In addition, Wulf was not shy about naming perpetrators and identifying their deeds. This did not win him many friends among German historians. His relationship with the Munich-based Institute for Contemporary History was especially conflictual. Early on, he had suggested setting up a documentation center at the Wannsee villa, where the "final solution to the Jewish question" was laid out in January 1942. His ideas were not received positively. Deeply scarred by his experiences during the Holocaust and disappointed by what he saw in the new Germany, he jumped out of a window of his Berlin apartment on October 10, 1974. In a suicide note to his son, he wrote, among other things: "I have published 18 books about the Third Reich here, and none of it has had any effect. You can document yourself to death with the Germans; there may be a democratic government in Bonn—but the mass murderers are walking around free, have their little houses, and cultivate flowers."[40]

If anything, Jewish historians who studied the persecution of the Jews under National Socialism had an even harder time getting their work published in the GDR. Here, Jews were not supposed to appear as a group of victims of their own but rather as Russian, Polish, or German victims of Nazi murder. This depiction of events was consistent with the Soviet narrative. In the Soviet Union, Jews were subsumed under Soviet victims. This was true not only at the sites of mass murder themselves but also on memorials and at former concentration camps located on the territory of the GDR. The persecution of European Jews was discussed as a side issue.

When the historian Helmut Eschwege, who lived in Dresden, attempted to publish his documentation of the disenfranchisement and destruction of the Jews, he encountered considerable resistance. As a committed Communist, Eschwege had returned to East Germany from Palestine at the end of the war in order to help build a new society; however, he got caught in the maelstrom of anti-Jewish measures that characterized the late Stalinist era. He was excluded from membership in the Socialist Unity Party (Sozialistische Einheitspartei Deutschlands, SED) several times but then rehabilitated. Shadowed by state security, he was accused of "Zionism" and for a time was demoted to a janitor from his position as librarian. Eschwege was a solitary fighter who since the 1950s consistently attempted to document the history of the Jews in Germany and their persecution, frequently against considerable official resistance. Most of his books could not be published in the GDR at all or only many years after they were written. It is one of the paradoxes of the GDR that, under considerable pressure, Eschwege later cooperated with the Stasi and passed along information about the Jewish communities.[41]

The scholars of Jewish studies who had gone into exile could not imagine a revival of Jewish culture in Germany. The best known of them, the Berlin-born Gershom Scholem, who taught at Hebrew University in Jerusalem, expressed this in a letter dated November 6, 1949, to the historian of religion Hans-Joachim Schoeps, who had recently returned from exile in Sweden: "My impressions from Germany are such that I feel constrained to reject numerous offers from there to publish a German edition of my English book in Germany. I am astounded that you can breathe this air."[42] Scholem was not the only German Jew who was flabbergasted by Schoeps's decision to return. The writer Max Brod, who collaborated with Schoeps in publishing Franz Kafka's writings, wrote to him on June 4, 1946: "I cannot understand why you would want to live and teach among this despicable people." Schoeps, true to his convictions, responded on June 18, 1946, with the firm belief that the area of Old Prussia between the Vistula and the Elbe was his home, "the country that I cannot renounce, in which I wish to live and be buried. Even the evil deeds of its inhabitants cannot change a thing."[43]

Hans-Joachim Schoeps, who began his academic career in 1946 at the University of Marburg and who since 1950 had been a full professor of religious and intellectual history at the University of Erlangen, remained what he had been before 1933: a conservative monarchist and diehard Prussian.[44] In 1929, as a student, he had founded a youth movement called Freideutsche Kameradschaft (Free German Comradeship). When Hitler was named Reich chancellor on Schoeps's twenty-fourth birthday, he responded immediately by founding the conservative German-Jewish association the German Vanguard.[45] In his magazine *Wir deutsche Juden* (We German Jews) he wrote in 1934: "Even if our Fatherland repudiates us, we will remain: Prepared for Germany."[46] But soon enough, even Schoeps was forced to realize that National Socialism was leading his own family to destruction along with all of the Jews in Germany. In late December 1938 he fled to Sweden. His father was murdered in Theresienstadt, his mother in Auschwitz. Almost his entire family was eradicated. Nonetheless, he returned to Germany immediately after the end of the war.

In many respects Schoeps was an exotic figure. He was a Jew teaching history at a university that had practically no Jews; he was a committed Prussian at a time when it had been expunged from the map; he was a conservative in an academic landscape in the process of revolutionary change; and he was gay at a time when such behavior was still criminalized.[47] He founded the *Zeitschrift für Religions- und Geistesgeschichte* (Journal of religious and intellectual history), and he was one of the few returnees to engage in the study of Jewish intellectual history. Nonetheless, Schoeps became popular in Germany as a "Prussian author." He delivered a provocative lecture at the University of Erlangen on January 18, 1951, at the only public event in the Federal Republic to commemorate the founding of the Prussian state 250 years earlier. That same year, his speech was published in an edition of ten thousand copies, which sold out within weeks.[48] His *Preußen— Geschichte eines Staates* (Prussia: History of a state) went through nine editions totaling about fifty thousand copies in one decade. This was followed by other publications on Prussia and contemporary German history.

It is hard to tell whether Schoeps spent relatively little time on Jewish subjects after his return merely because there would have been so few interested readers. "The few big-city communities that reconstituted themselves," he wrote, "were elderly, and their people had become tired and dulled; there was no movement in terms of religion either."[49] Schoeps took part in several interconfessional debates as a representative of the Jews, although he never considered himself a representative of the official Jewish communities. He believed that there was little future for Jewish intellectual life in Germany because there were almost no young people. "The fact that we once again have a well-written Jewish newspaper and that Jewish 'business' is being conducted by a few enterprising men should not lead us to misconstrue things as they really are." He himself was very skeptical of a German-Jewish future.[50]

Schoeps was one of the favorite targets of the student movement in the late 1960s. Small wonder: since the 1950s he had been championing a "conservative renewal" in opposition to the "moral vulgarity and coarsening of Germany," which he found abhorrent.[51] In a movement that he cofounded, he advocated the right of "qualitative voting" (i.e., granting additional votes depending on age, profession, and public engagement), an upper chamber consisting of the "elites of society," and the restoration of the monarchy.[52] In December 1967 he demanded that the state use its police powers to protect democracy from student extremists. For this, of course, he was pilloried in student leaflets as, among other things, a "Nazi Jew" and a "Jewish *Obersturmbannführer*." He became increasingly isolated when his own faculty refused to back him in solidarity. The final break with his faculty occurred after his retirement, when his chair was eliminated.[53]

Among Schoeps's doctoral students was Hans Lamm, who had served as a translator at the Nuremberg trials and returned to Munich. In 1951 he submitted his dissertation, "On the Internal and External Development of German Jewry in the Third Reich."[54] It is indicative of how little public interest there was at the time that no publisher could be found to print his dissertation. The same, incidentally, happened a few years later when Lamm's colleague Harry Maor tried to publish his dissertation on the reconstruction of the Jewish communities in Germany, which to this day is the most elaborate depiction of this early phase.[55]

Given the lack of interest in his own research, Lamm undoubtedly understood the utility of promoting contemporary literature. After a brief return to the United States and a stint as cultural advisor to the Central Council of the Jews, Lamm founded the Ner-Tamid publishing house in the late 1950s, specializing in literature on Jews and Judaism. In 1960 Ner-Tamid published a volume titled *Erziehungswesen und Judentum* (Education and the Jews), which examined the depiction of Jews in Germany in schools and universities. It contained summaries of the teaching materials available in the 1950s, or, more precisely, it documented the significant lack of a discussion of Jewish subjects in German middle and high schools. It also contained a full listing of courses on Jewish history and culture at German universities—a list that fit onto a single page.

The first lecturers in Jewish studies were generally Jews who had returned from exile or arrived in Germany as DPs. However, there were no paid positions in this field at German universities during the 1950s or early 1960s. Thus, Baruch Graubard, an educator from formerly Polish Lemberg (Lviv) who after the war served as director of the DP's Hebrew high school in Munich, was offered only an unpaid teaching position at the University of Marburg in the 1950s. He fulfilled his mission "in the name of the people to whom I belong according to my origins, upbringing, intellectual disposition, and education." It was important, he believed, "to talk with young people who know nothing about Jews and to show them a Jew."[56] Graubard was one of the very few Eastern European Jewish scholars to settle in Germany permanently after the war. He published numerous essays and books, among them a collection of his lectures on the weekly Torah portion, which he read on Bavarian radio every Friday afternoon. Like his brother-in-law Stefan Schwarz, Graubard was active in Jewish institutions during the 1950s and 1960s. Among other things, he was vice president of the Jewish community of Munich and a board member of the State Association of Jewish Communities of Bavaria and the Central Council.

It would take another few years to establish a professorship in Jewish studies in Munich. Leo Prijs was born in 1920 in Breslau and grew up in Munich, where he became an adjunct professor at the University of Munich in 1962 after his postdoctoral qualification. Only later was he elevated to a permanent position and then in 1980, shortly before his retirement, to full professor of Jewish studies. Prijs was following in a family tradition. His father had taught Jewish studies at the same university before 1933.[57]

In 1952 Adolf Leschnitzer lectured in German-Jewish history at the Free University of Berlin for the first time. After three guest professorships, the Free University made him an honorary professor of the "History of the German Jews" in 1955. This made Leschnitzer, who until 1933 had taught at a high school in Berlin and later took a permanent position at City College in New York, the first university lecturer in Jewish history in postwar Germany. Like many other scholars, he was only partly a returnee, as he received most of his income in the United States, even though he regularly lectured at the Free University over the following two decades.[58]

The Free University was also the site of the first Jewish studies institute in the Federal Republic. In the mid-1950s Leschnitzer was joined by guest lecturers Ernst Ludwig Ehrlich, Hermann Levin Goldschmidt, and Johann Maier, and in 1963 Jacob Taubes, who had been teaching at Columbia University, was appointed the first professor of Jewish studies in Germany.

Taubes was a descendant of renowned rabbis, and his father had been a rabbi in Vienna and Zürich. He himself had been ordained at the yeshiva in Montreux during the war. His expertise was undisputed, since after the war he had dedicated himself to further studies at Hebrew University, where he took up contact with Gershom Scholem (with whom he soon had a falling out, however), Martin Buber, and Ernst Simon. In the 1950s he taught religious studies at Columbia University, where he frequently met with other German-Jewish immigrants like Hannah Arendt, Leo Strauss, and Hans Jonas. Several of the founders of the American Jewish magazine *Commentary* were among his students in New York.

By the time Taubes returned to Germany in 1961, he had already established himself as an academic light in Israel and North America and had contacts with the leading intellectuals of his time. His horizons were thus broader than Schoeps's or Leschnitzer's. The fact that he did not publish another book after his dissertation on Occidental eschatology and that he trained few students in his capacity as professor of Jewish studies in Berlin did not hurt his academic reputation. He was one of the most brilliant intellectuals of the 1960s and 1970s, and he advised people as disparate as Siegfried Unseld on matters of publishing at Suhrkamp Verlag and Rudi "Red" Dutschke on student protests in the streets. And while Schoeps was one of the professors most detested by the student radicals, Taubes was one of the most idolized. Together with his friend Herbert Marcuse, whom he brought to the Free University as an honorary professor, he engaged fully with the radicals' concerns. At the request of the then left-wing radical (and later right-wing radical) attorney Horst Mahler, Taubes wrote an expert opinion for the communards of Kommune 1, and he was actively involved in founding the so-called Department 11 for Philosophy and the Social Sciences.

Taubes increasingly withdrew from the Institute for Jewish Studies, dedicating himself to his second professorship, that in philosophical hermeneutics. He spent a great deal of time in Jerusalem and Paris, and in the years preceding his death in 1987, he came to be viewed as an eccentric scholar who engaged with the teachings of the apostle Paul and oscillated between Orthodox Judaism and Christianity. He disengaged increasingly from institutional academic life.[59] It would be hard to imagine a greater contradiction than that between Schoeps and Taubes, both of them early teachers of Jewish intellectual history in postwar Germany.[60]

Fearing their reproaches and the possible loss of their positions, German professors were often not favorably disposed to the return of their Jewish erstwhile colleagues during the first postwar years. In addition, the prospective Jewish returnees had to contend with a flood of German professors from universities in the East such as Königsberg, Danzig, and Breslau and from Strasbourg in the West who had continued with their careers during the Nazi years and were now looking for positions in what was left of Germany.

The practice of awarding appointments to returnees varied greatly. Of the 112 mathematicians who emigrated, only 8 returned, because most of them—like many natural scientists—found ready offers and outstanding working conditions in exile and in addition were not dependent on the German language. Thus, only 3 biologists returned (all from Turkey) and only a few professors of medicine. Of the 134 historians who emigrated, 21 returned, as did approximately half of those in the field of education who had gone into exile.[61] Among the returnees, many had been baptized or were strongly assimilated, and only very few joined the Jewish community. Conditions also differed from university to university. At the University of Hamburg, for instance, only 3 of the 56 scholars who had been forced out were given full positions, and not a single scholar of the humanities was among them.[62] In Göttingen that figure was 4, the same as in Heidelberg, from where a total of 34 professors had been forced to emigrate.[63]

The great exceptions were the Free University of Berlin, which had been founded by the Americans, and the University of Frankfurt, which had been established a generation earlier by Jewish patrons. Not only did the Free University establish the first Jewish studies institute, it was also the first to call back a number of German-Jewish émigrés, often at first as guest professors, including Franz Neumann, Ernst Fraenkel, and Ossip Flechtheim. The university made a series of other appointments, including with the philosopher Michael Landmann and the political scientist Richard Löwenthal. In Frankfurt three returnees (the sociologist Max Horkheimer, the economist Fritz Neumark, and the physician Oscar Gans) became presidents of the university. Most of the returnees were in the social sciences and economics. It should not, however, be forgotten that, compared with the situation in the Weimar Republic, only a minuscule number of Jewish scholars and creative artists found work in the two postwar German states.

The relocation of the Institute for Social Research and the "Frankfurt School" from the Hudson to the Main changed little in this respect. Theodor Adorno and Max Horkheimer were among the best-known academic returnees. Horkheimer's hesitation and doubts were undoubtedly shared by other returnees. In May 1948 he wrote to his wife about his first visit to Germany: "The president, the two deans, and others greeted me with honors, sweetly, slick as eels, and full of mendacity. They don't yet know what to make of me, whether I'm a relatively influential American traveler or the brother of their victims who has their memory in mind."[64] Nonetheless, three years later Horkheimer was made president of the University of Frankfurt.

Adorno wrote much the same to Thomas Mann in 1949: "Except for a couple of movingly marionette-like scoundrels of the old type, I haven't seen a single Nazi yet, and I say that not in the ironic sense that no one wants to admit to

Max Horkheimer (*left*) and Theodor Adorno (*right*) during the Max Weber sociologists' conference in April 1964. Jeremy J. Shapiro.

having been one, but rather in the far more uncanny sense that they believe that they never were; that they completely repress it."[65] But as both of them began to work with students, their impressions changed dramatically. Horkheimer called his work with students "extremely positive," and Adorno went so far as to write: "The sort of passionate engagement that I find there is impossible to describe. A comparison with a Talmudic school is not inappropriate; sometimes it feels to me almost as if the spirits of the murdered Jews had migrated into the German intellectuals."[66]

However, no Talmudic school would be founded in postwar Germany; in its place, Jewish studies institutes were established, where Christian scholars taught mostly Christian students. The Martin Buber Institute for Judaic Studies, which was established in 1966 in Cologne, reflected a new understanding within the churches that they would do well to examine their own relationship to Judaism. Many of the students and professors at the Martin Buber Institute, including its first director, Johann Maier, had been trained as theologians. Analogous to the changed attitudes toward Jews evident in the Catholic Church under Pope

John XXIII, reframing the Christian-Jewish relationship went well beyond the approaches of the associations that pursued Christian-Jewish cooperation. The large exhibition about the Jewish religion called *Synagoga,* mounted first in Recklinghausen and then in Frankfurt (1960–1961), was part of this transformation.

Public interest in recent German-Jewish history was also awakened at that time. Reporting on the Eichmann trial in Jerusalem and the Auschwitz trial in Frankfurt led to a number of theatrical events. As early as the mid-1950s, a play had been written about Anne Frank, and a film about her made in the United States became extraordinarily popular in Germany. In 1963 thirty-two-year-old Rolf Hochhuth caused a veritable scandal with his docudrama *Der Stellvertreter* (published in English as *The Deputy*), which accused Pope Pius XII and the Catholic Church generally of complicity in the murder of the Jews. October 19, 1965, saw the premiere—on fourteen stages simultaneously and in both parts of Germany—of Peter Weiss's *Die Ermittlung* (published in English as *The Investigation*), which was based on the Auschwitz trial. Weiss had become a Swedish citizen in 1946. And almost at the same time another docudrama titled *Joel Brandt* by Heiner Kipphardt began playing. Its subject was the ransoming of Jewish prisoners from concentration camps.

The drama *Andorra* by the Swiss playwright Max Frisch, which premiered in 1961, was especially successful. A year later, it was performed in more than forty different stagings in West and East Germany. Andri, the protagonist of the play, is claimed by his foster father to be Jewish and is subjected to numerous acts of prejudice in the town as a result. The portrayal of antisemitism in the absence of actual Jews was criticized in some quarters. The Austrian Jewish cabaret artist Georg Kreisler reacted with a biting satire, a radio play that he titled *Sodom and Andorra*. In it, Kreisler noted the dangers of philosemitism, which distorted the reality of Jews in much the same way as antisemitism.[67]

In 1959 Heinrich Böll cofounded the German-Jewish library Germania Judaica in response to a new outbreak of antisemitic incidents in Cologne. Böll often commented on the opportunism all too frequently evident in Christian-Jewish rapprochement, occasionally sarcastically, as in his 1963 novel *Ansichten eines Clowns* (published in English as *The Clown*). In this work, the mother of the protagonist transformed within a few years from a committed National Socialist into a member of the "Executive Committee of the Societies for the Reconciliation of Racial Differences."[68]

The year 1963 also saw the opening in Cologne of *Monumenta Judaica*, the largest exhibition about German-Jewish history in postwar Germany. At the exhibition, the German public was for the first time shown a large number of impressive exhibits on the subject of "2000 years of the history and culture of the Jews along the Rhine." The idea of reconciliation was at the center of both the exhibition's conception and its reception. A glance at the list of authors in the accompanying nine-hundred-page book, the first larger work of postwar German-Jewish historiography, is instructive. It included historians who had once worked in the service of National Socialism, members of a new generation of Germans intent on reconciliation, and Jewish Holocaust survivors. They all coexisted in this one volume: Hermann Kellenbenz, now a full professor but who once did research for the antisemitic Reich Institute for the History of the New Germany and who at the end of the war had personally burned the papers of its Research Department on the Jewish Question;[69] Bernhard Brilling, who had recently returned from Israel and was now a lower-ranking university instructor; Father Willehad Paul Eckert, one of the cofounders of the Jewish-Christian dialogue; Rabbi Emanuel Schereschewski from Cologne; Ernst Ludwig Ehrlich, who had studied under Leo Baeck; and Theodor Schieder, who had done research on the East for the Nazis and who now, as president of the University of Cologne, oversaw the scholarly accuracy of the exhibition.

Germania Judaica and *Monumenta Judaica*, the Jewish studies institutes in Berlin and Cologne, plays about Anne Frank and the Auschwitz trial, and increasing interest in the media produced ambivalent responses in the Central Council. General Secretary van Dam had warned as early as 1964 against too much exposure in the media: "The Jewish topic has in recent years increasingly come to the fore in the mass media. The response was partly advantageous, partly disadvantageous and has stimulated much discussion. On the one hand, the choice of these topics was a remarkable attempt to fight indifference, to elicit empathy, and to come to terms with unpleasant manifestations. On the other hand, there was also the sense of a certain oversaturation and fatigue in public opinion."[70]

ON THE PUBLIC STAGE

A few years after the end of the war, a certain Professor Mauthner accepted an offer to return to his old university in Germany. His émigré colleagues had strongly advised against it, and, having barely returned, he was confronted with uninterrupted antisemitism, which in the end he was unable to withstand. Mauthner was the name of the protagonist in the film *Der Ruf* (The last illusion), which was made in 1948–1949. The part of Mauthner was played by Fritz Kortner, who also wrote the screenplay. Kortner, who had been one of the most renowned actors in prewar Germany, returned to Germany in 1947. Neither he nor his wife, the actress Johanna Hofer, ever really shook off their doubts, which they expressed at the time, about returning to Germany. In 1952, for example, Hofer wrote her husband, "Fritz, if you aren't by my side, life in Germany is simply intolerable. It is alien and diabolical." And a year later she complained: "Consciously or unconsciously, I think constantly about our American citizenship. I so dislike everything here that I really have to consider whether we shouldn't return there and perhaps remain for years. Here or there—both are bad alternatives."[71] Even a decade later, Kortner had no illusions about the disappearance of antisemitism: "Clerical fascism and antisemitism stop when faced with celebrity. However, in clandestine ways it ensures that no Jewish tree will grow to the heavens."[72] He wrote this in 1962 upon being asked whether he saw signs of antisemitism toward young Jewish actors by American(!) movie studios. His laconic response: "To my knowledge there are no young Jewish actors in this country. If there were, their existence would surely be known to me. In fact, there are hardly any young Jews here."[73]

Kortner, who after the war directed many plays at the Münchner Kammerspiele, one of the most important theaters in Munich, was not the only first-rate actor to be lured back to the German stage. In Munich, Kortner was joined by a number of Jewish returnees, including the actors Therese Giehse, Harry Buckwitz, and Kurt Hurwitz. And from 1960 to 1969 Ivan Nagel, who was originally from Hungary, was its artistic director. In Hamburg the actress Ida Ehre, who had survived the Fuhlsbüttel concentration camp, led the Hamburger Kammerspiele from 1945 to 1989. She transformed that theater into one of the most important in Germany. But these were all old hands; Kortner's observation that there were no young Jewish actors in Germany was undoubtedly entirely correct.

There were of course young Jews, and at least one of them made a name for himself as a writer after the war. Wolfgang Hildesheimer had emigrated to Palestine as an adolescent with his parents and returned a year after the end of the war at the age of twenty-seven as a translator at the Nuremberg trials. Afterward, he became a painter and then a writer, living both in Munich and at nearby Lake Starnberg. From his letters to his parents it is clear that after initial doubts he had found a home in the alpine uplands of Bavaria. It was not without a certain irony that he could write to his parents in Haifa in praise of the simple and comfortable life that he lived among his friends in the village of Ambach on Lake Starnberg, south of Munich—while just on the other side of the lake, thousands of Jewish DPs were cramped into camps awaiting their chance to emigrate to Palestine. Shortly before the Feldafing DP camp across the lake was dissolved at the end of 1951, he wrote, "In any case, I am happier here than I ever was before." And two years later, after his articles had been published in numerous German newspapers and literary journals and he was asked to join Group 47, the postwar German literary association, he gushed, "I'm slowly becoming famous." He completely masked out the Nazi past of his immediate surroundings. "Were my friends Nazis?" he asked himself, immediately providing the corrective, "It should read, Were Nazis my friends? The answer is a categorical and unambigu-

Premiere of the film *Der Ruf* in Berlin: Fritz Kortner with his wife, Johanna Hofer (*middle*), and Rosemary Murphy, 1949. Akademie der Künste, Berlin, Fritz-Kortner-Archiv, Sign. 181.

ous No." And without a tinge of irony, he continued, "As to who is a Nazi, I determine that."

Nonetheless, it slowly dawned on Hildesheimer that he could not escape the shadows of the past either in his group of friends or even in Group 47. Increasingly disappointed by the provinciality and hypocrisy of the West German cultural scene and by the political climate in the country, he decided to emigrate to Switzerland in 1957. Five years later, he enumerated the reasons for his emigration in an article for an anthology edited by Hermann Kesten titled *Ich lebe nicht in der Bundesrepublik* (I don't live in the Federal Republic), which he retracted before publication. As he put it, "I felt comfortable in Germany, because I gave credence to the belief that the guilty had been in the minority. Today I know that they were in the majority." Two-thirds of all Germans, he continued, continued to harbor antisemitic prejudices. In part, Hildesheimer's radical reversal may have been touched off by his correspondence with the German-language poet Paul Celan, who was living in Paris at the time. From the very beginning,

Celan had harbored no illusions about the distance between himself and the non-Jewish writers in Group 47. Thus, he expressed to Hildesheimer his feelings about being among the members of Group 47, where in his own words he had "a reputation as a 'hypersensitive person,' 'of suffering from paranoia' etc." In early 1960 he admitted Hildesheimer into his "club": "So you see, my dear Wolfgang Hildesheimer, we are simply the unhappy few, and perhaps we have nothing with which to counter the new and the old darknesses other than our friendship and solidarity." Hildesheimer's path from "happier here than I ever was before" to membership in Celan's club of the "unhappy few" was indeed long and tortuous.[74]

Péter Szondi might have felt comfortable in that club as well. Born in Budapest in 1929, he and his family were interned in Bergen-Belsen in 1944, and they had been among the 1,650 or so Hungarian Jews permitted to leave Germany for Switzerland in June 1944—in exchange for money, gold, and precious stones—as part of the controversial Kasztner agreement. In 1965 Szondi was made director of the newly founded Department for Comparative Literature at the Free University in Berlin. The first institute of its kind in the Federal Republic, it is now named after him. As a guest professor in Princeton and Jerusalem and host to numerous scholars from around the world, among them émigrés, he played a preeminent role in internationalizing literary studies.

Like many returnees, Szondi essentially became a person without a home. After a visit to Israel in 1968, he wrote to Gershom Scholem:

> In Jerusalem, you once asked me with a clarity that, though not surprising was nonetheless unforgettable, why I live in Germany and plan to remain here: because I have unlearned to be at home (I never was at home, neither during my childhood in Budapest nor in Zürich, and strictly speaking in another sense as well, never with my parents either). That is a disease that might perhaps be curable by the drastic means, for whatever reason, of emigration. But I would be just as unable to take such a step of my own free will as I was two years ago in Jerusalem, where I not only felt at home, but also realized that I would find it unbearable. I know that this could and should change, but this knowledge is not enough to break the resistance within me now—that is, as long as I can bear it in Germany.[75]

Szondi remained in Germany, but he never did find his way home. He committed suicide in 1971 at the age of forty-two.

While many of the (few) Jewish literary returnees to the Federal Republic remained outsiders—among them the lyrical poet Hilde Domin, who returned from the Dominican Republic in 1954, and Hellmuth Freund, the editor at the S. Fischer publishing house, who returned from Uruguay in 1960—those who returned to the German Democratic Republic often took prominent roles. Anna

Seghers, for example, who came back from exile in Mexico, served as president of the East German Writers' Association from 1952 to 1978. Arnold Zweig, who returned from Palestine, served as a delegate to the Volkskammer, the East German parliament, for almost twenty years and was president of the (East) German Academy of the Arts from 1950 to 1953. Stephan Hermlin, who had also lived in Palestine for a time, became a leading member of the Academy of the Arts. Jewish writers varied greatly in their attitudes toward both the party and the state. Seghers, for example, toed the party line her entire life and as president of her association remained silent even as the state passed numerous measures that disadvantaged association members. Zweig, too, let himself be used to lend prestige to culture in the GDR, but on the other hand, he refused to sign an anti-Israeli declaration during the 1967 Six-Day War. Hermlin, who had been a friend of Erich Honecker's during the 1950s, was relieved of his post in the academy after a reading by young poets in December 1962, and he distanced himself privately from the official party line after the suppression of the Prague Spring. In 1976 he, along with Stefan Heym, who had been banned from publication since 1965, signed a protest letter against the expatriation of songwriter and poet Wolf Biermann. Biermann, the son of a Jewish dockworker in Hamburg who was murdered in Auschwitz, had in 1953 at the age of seventeen resettled in East Germany to live out his Communist ideals. There he made a name for himself as a songwriter and poet. However, he got into serious trouble with the authorities in the early 1960s because of his play *Berliner Brautgang* (Berlin bride hunting), in which he examined the building of the Berlin Wall. His punishment was a six-month performance ban. Jurek Becker, who had survived several concentration camps as a child, also signed the protest letter against Biermann's expulsion from the GDR and followed him to the West a year later, in 1977. Becker was one of the few authors who wrote about Jewish topics. His 1968 screenplay *Jakob der Lügner* (published in English as *Jacob the Liar*) takes place in a fictional ghetto during the war years, and although Becker worked at DEFA (the state-owned film studio) as a screenwriter, his script of the same title was initially rejected. It was filmed only after the success of his novel in 1974.

The GDR also attracted a number of prominent Jewish scholars from exile. Most of them probably did not share Albert Einstein's conviction, as expressed in his response to birthday congratulations from Johannes Becher in the name of the Cultural Association for the Democratic Renewal of Germany: "When I hear the words 'renewal of Germany' I recall the appropriate phrase by that witty Frenchman, 'Plus ça change, plus ça reste la même chose.'"[76] However, some of the cultural and intellectual lights who returned to the GDR ended up leaving after a few years. Hans Mayer, who had returned to the American zone in 1945, where he was briefly director of Radio Frankfurt, went over to the Soviet zone in 1948 with his friend Stephan Hermlin. There he became a professor of literature at the University of Leipzig. Mayer remained in close contact with literary developments in West Germany and participated in some of the meetings of Group 47. He was one of the people who discovered the writer Uwe Johnson, and he became one of the most important Thomas Mann scholars. Frustrated by the official political line in the GDR, Mayer simply failed to return after a trip to the West. Instead, he accepted an appointment at the University of Hannover. Mayer was for many years a colleague of the philosopher Ernst Bloch in Leipzig. Bloch had long been an intellectual bulwark of state socialism, and during the first years of the GDR he had been awarded numerous prizes. As with Mayer before him, the suppression of the uprising in Hungary in 1956 became a turning point in Bloch's identification with the GDR. After the Berlin Wall was erected in 1961, Bloch, again like Mayer, decided not to return from a trip to the Federal Republic, where he accepted a guest professorship at the University of Tübingen.

The writer and German literary scholar Alfred Kantorowicz had a similar experience when in 1949, three years after his return from exile, he accepted a professorship in contemporary German literature at Humboldt University in Berlin. Kantorowicz made his name primarily by publishing the works of Heinrich Mann. He, too, increasingly distanced himself from the brutal suppression of the anti-Communist uprising of June 17, 1953, in the GDR and the response by his chosen homeland to the uprising in Hungary three years later. In 1957 he, too, fled to the Federal Republic, where, however, he was never able to find a permanent academic position.

Other Jewish scholars retained their academic positions in the GDR. Jürgen Kuczynski, who had returned from London, was not only the most prominent economist but also a member of parliament and of the Central Committee of the SED. Victor Klemperer, the scholar of Romance languages, also sat in parliament. His book *LTI* provides a sharp analysis of the language of the Third Reich, and the extensive diaries that he wrote obsessively between 1933 and 1945, which were published posthumously, offer a unique glimpse into the progressive constriction of daily life for Jews under the Nazis. Leo Stern, who survived the war in the Soviet Union, became one of the most influential historians in the GDR. He was cofounder of the *Zeitschrift für Geschichtswissenschaft* (Journal of historical scholarship), a professor of contemporary history at the University of Halle, and after 1953 the president of that university.[77] Hanns Eisler, a student of the composer Arnold Schoenberg and friend of Bertolt Brecht, returned from the United States and led the master class in composition at the German Academy of the Arts. The state conservatory where he taught later bore his name, and he composed the national anthem of the GDR. His brother Gerhart was chair of the

State Committee for Radio in the GDR and since 1967 a member of the central committee of the SED.

Most of the Jews who became active in the cultural and political life of the GDR chose to live there rather than in the Federal Republic for political reasons and would have readily identified as "non-Jewish Jews," as Isaac Deutscher had so aptly put it. They were never members of the official Jewish communities, did not in any way participate in religious life, and had few sympathies for the State of Israel. Nevertheless, because they were born as Jews, they were often viewed as such by the people around them. They tended as a result to be very conscious of this and were especially sensitive to anything that smacked of antisemitism. However, they played no role in ensuring the existence of a Jewish community in Germany.

MICHAEL BRENNER is Professor of Jewish history and culture at the University of Munich and Seymour and Lillian Abensohn Chair in Israel Studies at American University in Washington, DC. He is a member of the Bavarian Academy of Sciences and international president of the Leo Baeck Institute. Brenner's publications include *A Short History of the Jews*, *Prophets of the Past: Interpreters of Jewish History*, *Zionism: A Short History*, and as coauthor, the four-volume *German-Jewish History in Modern Times*.

NORBERT FREI is Professor of modern and contemporary history at the University of Jena and is director of the Jena Center 20th Century History. During the 2008–2009 academic year, he was a member of the Institute for Advanced Study in Princeton, and in 2010–2011 he was Theodor Heuss Professor at the New School for Social Research in New York. Frei's publications include *1968: Jugendrevolte und globaler Protest*, *1945 und wir: Das Dritte Reich im Bewußtsein der Deutschen*, and *Adenauer's Germany and the Nazi Past: The Politics of Amnesty and Integration*; he is also coauthor of *Das Amt und die Vergangenheit: Deutsche Diplomaten im Dritten Reich und in der Bundesrepublik*.

NOTES

1. For example, see the titles of books about the postwar communities in Frankfurt: G. Heuberger et al. (eds.) (1998); R. Bein and B. Schmidt-Czaia (eds.) (2005); J. Bertram (2008); and E. Presser (2005). See also E. Rees-Dessauer (2017).

2. R. Michalski (1991), p. 108.

3. S. Korn (1992), pp. 187–214.

4. Hermann Guttmann, who continued his architectural studies in Munich after the war, built the synagogues in Offenbach (1955–1956), Düsseldorf (1956–1958), Hannover (1961–1963), Osnabrück (1967–1969), and Würzburg (1966–1970). He also designed the renovations of existing synagogues in Augsburg (1963), Bayreuth (1965), and Fürth (1967).

His colleagues Helmut Goldschmidt and Karl Gerle were mainly active in West Germany. The former built the synagogues in Dortmund (1956), Bonn (1959), and Münster (1961), as well as the prayer rooms in Cologne-Ehrenfeld (1949), Koblenz (1950), Wuppertal (1962), and Mönchengladbach (1967). The latter was responsible for the synagogues in Minden (1958), Paderborn (1959), Hagen (1960), and Bremen (1961), as well as the prayer rooms in Recklinghausen (1955), Aachen (1957), and Mülheim an der Ruhr (1959).

5. H. Goldschmidt (1959), p. 30.

6. H. Goldschmidt (1959), pp. 5, 18.

7. Report on the extraordinary meeting of the Central Council on June 3, 1958, in Düsseldorf, pp. 1–5, in ZA, B1/7.852.

8. A. Quast (1996), p. 126.

9. "Die neue Synagoge in Düsseldorf: Zur Einweihung am 7. September 1958," Düsseldorf, 1958.

10. H. Nothmann (1953), p. 232.

11. See, for example, the letter from the head of cultural affairs, Dr. Glückstein, to Bruno Woyda of the World Union for Progressive Judaism in London, January 22, 1957, and Woyda's response, January 29, 1957, in AJA, MS16 D4.2. Three years later, no solution had yet been found. See the letter from Heinz Galinski to S. Smith of the World Union, May 13, 1959, and to Lily Montagu of the World Union, August 11, 1960, in AJA, MS16 D5.2. In a report dated December 5, 1962, Bruno Woyda promised to continue to help find a rabbi for Berlin, in AJA, MS16 D5.3.

12. Letter from Rabbi Lionel Blue to Heinz Galinski, April 21, 1965, in AJA, MS16 F2.1.

13. Y. M. Bodemann, "Ich verlasse dieses Land in Verbitterung," *Menora* 6 (1995), p. 352.

14. P. Honigmann (1994), pp. 38–41.

15. A. Brämer (2006), p. 81.

16. Letter from S. Smith, general secretary of the World Union, to Karl Marx, August 14, 1958, in AJA, MS16 D4.2. The World Union sent identical letters simultaneously to selected representatives of Liberal Jewry in various German cities.

17. The process is described in detail based on court files in A. Mohr (2011), pp. 71–77.

18. Notes about a meeting between the federal president, Theodor Heuss, and Karl Marx, the publisher of the *AWJD*, on October 25, 1951, in Bonn, in BArch, B 122/2080. Ohrenstein, who originally came from Tarnopol, was ordained a rabbi at the Breslau Jewish Theological Seminary in 1935 and graduated the same year from the University of Prague. See "Ohrenstein, Aaron," M. Brocke and J. Carlebach (eds.) (2009), p. 471. See also the report "Bedauerliche Vorfälle in München," *AWJD*, June 8, 1951, p. 3.

19. Report by H. G. van Dam on the investigations undertaken in the "Goldstein" case, March 3, 1960, in ZA, B.1/7.130.

20. G. Goldstein-Lackó (1961), p. 67.

21. Copy of the private action initiated by Isaak Goldstein against Irma Wilma van Dam on October 16, 1961, in ZA, B.1/7.132.

22. G. Goldstein-Lackó (1961).

23. N. P. Levinson (1995), p. 160.

24. A. Brämer (2006), p. 84.

25. A. Brämer (2006), p. 85.

26. Minutes of the council meeting of the Central Council of Jews in Germany on March 22–23, 1964, pp. 8–9, in ZA, B.1/7.864.

27. U. Offenberg (1998), pp. 98, 117.

28. Z. Asaria (1959a); Z. Asaria (1979). Asaria, who originally came from Yugoslavia and was chief rabbi in the British zone after the war, turned to a subject that non-Jewish scholars approached only later, and hesitantly even then: Jewish religious history. His small book about Samson Raphael Hirsch's work in Lower Saxony was published in 1970.

29. H. Richtering (1988), pp. 9–13.

30. M. Richarz (1998), p. 64. For more detail, see M. Brenner (2008b), pp. 207–223.

31. Letter from Ernst Ludwig Heuss to Oberregierungsrat Dr. von Heyden, March 2, 1954, in BArch, B 122/2084.

32. Minutes of the sixth meeting of archival experts on September 19, 1955, in Augsburg, in BArch, B 106/21559.

33. "Bedauerliche Vorfälle in München," *AWJD*, June 8, 1951, p. 3.

34. Letter from H. G. van Dam to Ministerialdirektor Prof. Dr. Hübinger, February 10, 1956, in BArch, B 106/21559.

35. For more on the history of the planned archive, see the highly informative article by P. Honigmann (2004).

36. Specifically on this matter, see P. Freimark (1989).

37. See, for example, H. Schnee (1953–1967); H. Kellenbenz (1958).

38. W. Treue, "Rezension zu *The Court Jew*," *Historische Zeitschrift* 171 (1951), p. 571.

39. A brief biography is included in M. Karger-Karin (1966), pp. 523–524.

40. N. Berg (2003), pp. 337–370.

41. H. Eschwege (1991); K. Hartewig (2000).

42. G. Scholem (1995), p. 14.

43. J. H. Schoeps (ed.) (1985), pp. 117, 120.

44. For more detail on Schoeps, see M. Brenner (2012).

45. For more, see C. Rheins (1981).

46. H.-J. Schoeps (1934), p. 52, previously published as H.-J. Schoeps, "Der Jude im neuen Deutschland," *Der deutsche Vortrupp: Blätter einer Gefolgschaft deutscher Juden*, no. 1 (October 1933), p. 2. The second issue of *Vortrupp* contained similar sentiments: "If Germany today reflects on blood and race, it will really fulfill the law of the hour that Adolf Hitler correctly recognized and interpreted," in *Der deutsche Vortrupp*, no. 2 (January 1934), p. 5.

47. For more on his sexual orientation see M. Keilson-Lauritz (2009), pp. 199–212.

48. F.-L. Kroll (2001), p. 235.

49. H.-J. Schoeps (1963), p. 142.

50. H.-J. Schoeps (1953), pp. 212–213.

51. H.-J. Schoeps (1963), p. 177.

52. In 1970 he attempted, unsuccessfully, to found a party (the Konservative Sammlung) to press for his political goals.

53. For more, see J. H. Schoeps, "Nil inultum remanebit," *Zeitschrift für Religions- und Geistesgeschichte* 52 (2002), pp. 266–278.

54. For more on Hans Lamm, see the biography by A. Sinn (2008).

55. The unpublished dissertation, "Über den Wiederaufbau der jüdischen Gemeinden in Deutschland" (1961), by Harry Maor is accessible on the Internet at www.harry maor.com/thesis.htm (last accessed November 30, 2015).

56. J. Geis (2010), p. 74.

57. I. Tamari (2009), pp. 107–118.

58. M. Richarz (2006).

59. J. Z. Muller (2013), pp. 40–61.

60. For more on their philosophical and theological contradictions, see R. Faber (2009), pp. 63–92.

61. M. Krauss (2001), p. 83.

62. U. Büttner (2008), p. 67.

63. M. Krauss (2001), p. 85.

64. M. Kingreen (2008), p. 133.

65. M. Kingreen (2008), p. 134.

66. M. Kingreen (2008), p. 135.

67. Cultural restitution was a mainstay of the German stage during the 1960s. For more on this, see A. Feinberg (1988).

68. H. Böll (1963), p. 29.

69. See H. Heiber (1966), pp. 456–457; S. Rohrbacher (2000), pp. 166–167.

70. Memorandum from H. G. van Dam for the meeting of the directorate of the Central Council "Tagung über kulturelle Fragen" on October 25, 1964, in Cologne, in ZA, B1/7.856.

71. Letter from Johanna Hofer to Fritz Kortner, May 27, 1952, in AdK, Johanna-Hofer-Kortner-Archiv 219; letter from Johanna Hofer to Fritz Kortner, May 29, 1953, in AdK, Johanna-Hofer-Kortner-Archiv 221.

72. Letter from Fritz Kortner to Dr. Eleonore Sterling, December 10, 1962, in AdK, Fritz-Kortner-Archiv 278.

73. Letter from Fritz Kortner to Dr. Eleonore Sterling, December 10, 1962, in AdK, Fritz-Kortner-Archiv 278.

74. All previous quotations are from S. Braese (2001), pp. 242–265.

75. S. Braese (2001), p. 303.

76. Cited in K. Hartewig (2000), p. 204.

77. K. Hartewig (2000), p. 135.

7 GERMAN JEWS OR JEWS IN GERMANY?

REJECTION AND ACCEPTANCE

Many Jews around the globe expressed their opposition to the reestablishment of Jewish life on the "bloodstained soil of Germany." That was how a resolution passed by the World Jewish Congress (WJC) in 1948 worded it. Decades later, Jewish organizations working in Germany were still forced to deal with this reproach.[1]

For the State of Israel, whose existence depended on creating a viable homeland for Jews from around the world, Jews who chose to live in Germany, of all places, were a provocation. The Israeli consulate in Munich, which had been accredited by the American authorities, did all it could to facilitate the emigration of Jewish DPs from Germany. However, in the early 1950s it became clear that not only did some of them choose to remain, but increasing numbers of returnees from Israel were joining them. Observing this, the Israeli consul, Chaim Yahil, issued an ultimatum in 1951. These people were, so he huffed, "a source of danger for the entire Jewish people. Those who are lured by the fleshpots of Germany should not expect Israel or the Jewish people to stand by their side with support for their convenience."[2] The Israeli consulate let it be known that it would no longer give preferential treatment to German Jews who did not immediately apply to emigrate to Israel.[3] And in 1950 the Jewish Agency announced that those who remained in Germany would no longer be viewed as Jews and could not count on assistance if they decided to immigrate to Israel in the future.[4]

This boycott included the German-Jewish community as a whole. When the Zionist World Congress met in 1951, the German Zionists were not invited. And when the World Maccabiah Games were held, athletes from Germany were not permitted to compete as an official German team. And yet, Israeli politicians were quite clear that there was a considerable gap between their official position and the situation on the ground in Germany. The second Israeli consul in Munich, Eliahu Livneh, continued the policies of his predecessor, rejecting the existence of a Jewish community in Germany in a letter to the Israeli foreign ministry in 1951: "The Jewish world therefore views this Jewry as a coincidental bunch of people, which it will under no circumstances recognize as the bearer of its own independent political will." The response from the Foreign Ministry was somewhat more realistic. The ministry told Livneh that although his position was correct, it was nonetheless illusory: "You continue with your policy of resistance [to official relations with the Jewish community], which you had practiced so far, with the inside knowledge, however, that in the long run this position is not tenable. Thus, it is not worth your putting too much energy into the matter."[5]

The German-Jewish community did, however, receive moral support from its leading intellectuals living abroad. Although Rabbi Leo Baeck, who had accompanied his community to Theresienstadt and emigrated to England after the war, asserted that the age of German Jewry had passed, he stressed that the Jews currently in Germany had a future. On the occasion of his visit to Germany in 1951, he stated, "The soil from which strength may be derived, from which roots may draw their strength, are small and narrow. But there will be Jews in Germany for a long time."[6] The second great authority to have emerged from German Jewry was Martin Buber, the philosopher of religion who was now living in Israel. He waited somewhat longer than Baeck before visiting Germany. When he was awarded the Goethe Prize in December 1951, the indignation in Israel about his acceptance was so intense that he decided not to attend the awards ceremony in Hamburg. Buber finally collected his prize in 1953, when he received the Peace Prize of the German Book Trade at the Paulskirche in Frankfurt. While German students were especially reverential toward him and attentive to what he had to say, his closest friends in Israel and America strongly advised him that it was much too early for a Jew to appear in public in Germany and to speak before audiences of potential murderers and their accomplices.[7]

The World Jewish Congress had since its founding in 1936 functioned as an umbrella organization of Jewish organizations worldwide. From the very beginning a contingent of the membership had categorically opposed the settlement of Jews in Germany, although more nuanced voices were also heard. And under the leadership of Nahum Goldmann, the organization's president of many years, the WJC steered a pragmatic course. In 1949, for example, it opened an office in Frankfurt to act as an intermediary between Jewish organizations in Germany and to monitor antisemitism.[8]

Despite this de facto recognition of Jewish life in Germany, the Central Council and the WJC continued to wrangle over who was competent to represent the Jewish community in dealings with German authorities. When Goldmann visited Germany for several days a year later, he did not consider it necessary to take up contact with the Central Council, a slap that was met with indignation: "The board has noted with profound dismay Dr. Goldmann's failure to use his presence of several days in Germany to engage in discussion with the Central Council and has instructed the secretary to write to Dr. Goldmann accordingly."[9] Of course, the Central Council knew all too well that Goldmann was unwilling to snub the Jewish organizations abroad because the slightest scandal would have undermined his own position.

The Central Council's general secretary, Hendrik George van Dam, was forced to tread a fine line. On the one hand, he had to appear self-possessed when dealing with international Jewish organizations; on the other, he needed to make clear to his own people that despite constant rejection no good could come from alienating those organizations. One especially galling point of contention for the international organizations and the State of Israel was the ongoing immigration of Israelis to Germany. Given this circumstance, the Central Council at first made concessions to Israeli and international Jewish demands. For example, in a resolution the board warned

> expressly against the immigration or remigration to, or even the migration through, Germany of persons who did not have their permanent place of residence in Germany prior to the onset of World War II. The influx of Jews from Israel to Germany gives rise to social, political, and not least moral problems of great consequence. The board of the Central Council expressly declares that it will no longer support financially, judicially, or politically emigrants or migrants from Israel belonging to the named group.[10]

Van Dam attempted to assuage the displeasure expressed by the representatives of Jewish communities as a result of their exclusion from international Jewish organizations and because of the financial demands made upon them with regard to German-Jewish property and assets:

> It is important to understand that any declaration or action that might be interpreted as a break with world Jewry weakens the position of Jews living in Germany for the above-cited reasons. Our chief strength and our characteristic trait is this bond, which is all the more important the smaller and the more inconsequential the Jewish community is in a country. One thing is certain, that the Jewish community in Germany can exist only if its connection with world Jewry is especially close. For this reason, and not because of "colonial dependence," the very self-confident founders of the Central Council wrote into the bylaws that the representatives of the large Jewish organizations must be present at its deliberations.[11]

If the Central Council were to become isolated from the Jewish world, he continued, the results would be anything but "splendid"; they would be catastrophic.[12]

The debates over the independence of the Central Council continued for a number of months.[13] Amazed at the new self-confidence of the German Jews, the representative of the WJC in Germany reported in May 1952 to the London office:

> Some German Jews are beginning to develop a new "ideology" according to which German Jewry is called by history to assume the role of a mediator between Germany and world Jewry. . . . The very small group of people who speak for the Jews would like to establish a standing for the Jewish community in Germany. The attitude of the postwar forties, even of 1950, has been reversed. They do not consider the existence of Jews here as transitory, nor do they pretend their stay as transitory. Just the opposite is now the prevalent philosophy. "The history of the Jews in Germany is not finished." This is the slogan. . . . Although they do not know what is the mission of the Jews in Germany, or what they would like it to be, they want it very emphatically.[14]

Relations between the WJC and the Central Council remained tense throughout the 1950s, among other things because the former accused the latter of downplaying antisemitic incidents in Germany.

The distance between the former DPs and the German Jews was on full display at the meetings of the WJC, even in terms of the languages they used. In addition to English and Hebrew, French and Spanish were not uncommon at the conference in 1953. Whereas some of the delegates who had left Germany gave their presentations in German, Maurice Weinberger, the president of the State Association of Jewish Communities in Bavaria, availed himself of his mother tongue, Yiddish. He stressed that most of the Jews in Germany were old and sick and that 90 percent wanted nothing more than to leave the country. It fell to the WJC to help them to emigrate.[15] But at home, Weinberger did whatever he could to induce the international Jewish organizations to recognize the communities that in fact existed in Germany. At a meeting of the Central Council in October 1953, for example, he stated that it is "the duty of the international organizations to give the Jews living in Germany a subsistence." In the same debate, the chair of the Jewish community of Hamburg went a step further and demanded that "the Jews abroad and in Israel strengthen our position. The newly elected board must demand that we be respected in every way by the international organizations."[16]

Progress in recognizing Jewish life in Germany and the activities of the Central Council by the international Jewish organizations was slow in coming, but by July 1954 van Dam was able to report at a meeting of the Central Council that "this opinion is now shared in certain circles, though not in all, and that they are trying to let us do this work."[17]

One of the first Jewish organizations to express itself positively about Germany and Jewish life in Germany was the American Jewish Committee, which had been founded at the turn of the century by German-Jewish immigrants. In the early 1950s, it began to reach out to the German public with its Operation

Candle program and to present Germans with a nuanced picture of Jews.[18] Looking back on this initiative, it was said that it "brought a storm of protest and some villification [*sic*] from other Jewish organizations, and the AJC was bitterly assailed. But in a few years this position was silently adopted by the other organizations."[19]

In 1954 a three-member delegation from the Anti-Defamation League (ADL) spent several weeks on a fact-finding mission in Germany. The ADL representatives visited a number of different communities, where they were continually confronted with the issue of whether Jewish life in Germany was justifiable. Their report painted an overwhelmingly bleak picture, detailing empty synagogues and elderly congregants, although they also reported on a lively Purim celebration in Düsseldorf.[20]

Two decades after the end of the war, Germany's position in the world had changed considerably, as had that of the Jews living there. The State of Israel and the Federal Republic of Germany established diplomatic relations in 1965, and in view of that the WJC held a special session on the relations between Jews and Germans at a meeting in Brussels the following year. The most important speakers were Gershom Scholem, the leading proponent of Jewish studies in Israel and a vehement critic of the notion of a "German-Jewish symbiosis"; the historian Golo Mann (a son of the writer Thomas Mann); and German federal president Eugen Gerstenmaier. When several delegates protested the appearance of a German politician, even though he was known to have been an opponent of the Nazis, WJC president Goldmann angrily defended the agenda as it stood.[21]

During the mid-1960s, German Jews began to experience growing recognition internationally, as an official report of the Central Council from 1964 makes clear: "The Central Council has since its founding advanced the position that the Jewish community in Germany has a right to exist. We have the right to our existence as an organized community in the face of much resistance, especially in the face of world opinion. Purely externally, our success is evident in that we are today represented in many international Jewish organizations."[22] But in fact this was very much a work in progress even in the mid-1960s. Representatives of the Central Council showed evident irritation when the WJC failed to consult with it on a meeting titled "Germany and the Jews of the World" or even invite them to speak. Werner Nachmann, who later became chair of the Central Council, labeled it disrespect of the highest order that van Dam had not been invited to consult on this topic of obvious relevance to Jews living in Germany. Twenty years after the end of the war, the German-Jewish community still felt constrained to point out that "the Jewish community in Germany has no cause to denigrate itself" (so said Heinz Galinski, the chair of the Berlin community) and even questioned "whether, because of the expected attacks against the Jewish community in Germany, it is even advisable to send a delegation" (this from later general secretary Alexander Ginsburg).[23]

Lilli Marx, who for many years chaired the Jewish Women's League in Germany, recalled similar marginalization at international conferences: "There were many who wouldn't speak to us at all. Or they said in English so that I wouldn't understand it, 'Did you hear that the Jewish women from Germany are going to be represented? How can we even talk to them.' So I turned around and said, 'But of course you can!'"[24] In the 1960s the World Union of Jewish Students (WUJS) considered whether to accept German-Jewish representatives, with motions to that effect being rejected by the majority as late as 1967. After sharply condemning the permanent settlement of Jews and particularly of Israelis in Germany and Austria at the previous WUJS meeting, a bare majority voted for a resolution to the effect that it was "unfair" to ignore the existence of Jewish students in Germany and that henceforth contact with these students should be permitted. However, the best way to integrate them into the World Union would be "to promote *aliyah* [immigration to Israel] among them, which will enable them to escape the growing Neonazism in Germany."[25]

While the German-Jewish community was forced to fight for recognition abroad, its existence was a gift to the official organs of the Federal Republic. A "Jew-free" Germany would only have fed the fears that no actual renewal had taken place after the defeat of National Socialism. The presence of a Jewish community, by contrast, was viewed as a guarantor of recognition for Germany within the community of democratic nations. In the words of Anthony Kauders, a sort of "exchange of gifts" took place.[26]

The federal government was only too happy to display Jewish representatives on the international stage to build Germany's image. In the late 1950s, for example, Karl Marx, the publisher of the *Allgemeine Wochenzeitung der Juden in Deutschland* (General weekly of the Jews in Germany), who had excellent personal relationships with high-ranking political officials, including with federal president Theodor Heuss, was sent on an international mission. In South America, where numerous Jewish émigrés lived alongside former Nazis, what the Jews living in Germany had to say was of special consequence. After attacks on one of Chancellor Konrad Adenauer's closest advisors, Hans Globke, who had played a role in drafting the antisemitic Nuremberg Laws, was forced to withdraw from a planned trip to South America in the summer of 1957 on the occasion of Lufthansa's maiden flight to Montevideo. The Federal Press Office selected Marx for a three-week trip to South America in Globke's stead. The trip was not to be viewed as a propaganda tour, and it was not supposed to leak to the public that it had been paid for by the German government.[27]

West German president Theodor Heuss receives representatives of the Jewish religious community during a visit to Berlin at the Schöneberg city hall on April 15, 1953. *From left to right:* governing mayor Ernst Reuter; Karl Marx, publisher of the *Allgemeine Wochenzeitung der Juden in Deutschland*; Heuss; and Heinz Galinski, chair of the Jewish community in Berlin. ullstein bild / dpa.

Shortly before, Marx had turned to Globke, of all people, for help in preventing the appointment of the former Nazi Josef Röder as prime minister of the Saarland.[28] In his report to the Federal Press Office, Marx wrote that the goal of his trip had been to defuse the resentment against Germany felt by many Jewish émigrés in South America "but also to give them a clear picture of the positive democratic developments in the Federal Republic." He reported that he not only painted a more positive picture of Germany for the Jewish press in South America but also received permission from the Israeli embassy to strengthen its private connections with the German embassy. The German diplomats in the countries that he visited all reported to Bonn on the success of the mission. The press office of the German embassy in Buenos Aires noted that the critics that Marx had talked to "have largely dropped their grudges." However, the office also admitted that some of those present had recognized Marx's mission as a "marketing campaign for Adenauer" and referred to him as the "Bundesredner" ("Federaloquist").[29]

The Central Council was thoroughly aware of the role played by the Jews in postwar Germany and early on tried to point out the risks, as noted earlier.

The Association of Jewish Communities in the German Democratic Republic (GDR) did not serve the same function as the Central Council in the Federal Republic. After people fled the eastern half of Germany in 1952 and 1953, it consisted of a much more elderly community that was also much smaller. In addition, after the late Stalinist waves of repression, it was also hesitant to express opinions. Nonetheless, an "exchange of gifts" took place in the GDR as well. As soon as the communities had been brought in line, they were, like other institutions, monitored to the *n*th degree by a system of informers both within and without the community. Once this system was in place, the political leadership had little trouble using the community for its purposes. As in the Federal Republic, the leadership of the GDR did not want to be accused of creating a "Jew-free" state. As a result, the state made sure that the community's religious needs were taken care of, among other things by making kosher meat available. On the other hand, the Jewish communities now toed the official political line, distanced themselves from Israel, and accused the Federal Republic of protecting and furthering the careers of former Nazis.

After 1953 the official representatives of the Jewish communities played hardly any role in public life in the GDR. But in contrast to the Federal Republic, a much larger contingent of returnees of Jewish origin represented the state internationally, both politically and economically. For instance, Hans-Paul Ganter-Gilmans, who died at the age of thirty-seven in 1955, came from a Jewish family and served as deputy minister for international trade. Gottfried Lessing had a high position in the foreign ministry; among other things, he had cofounded the Communist Party in Southern Rhodesia, where he had spent the war years. In the GDR he was for a time chair of the Committee to Promote World Trade and the Chamber for Export Trade; department head for African countries in the foreign ministry; and ambassador to Uganda, where he was killed during riots against Idi Amin's rule 1979. Stefan Heymann and Friedrich Wolf served as ambassadors to Poland and Hungary in the immediate postwar years; in 1963 Horst Brie became the chargé d'affaires at the GDR's embassy in China.[30] People like this were undoubtedly chosen for their roles not because they were Jews but because they tended to be more educated, were more likely to have mastered a foreign language, and had often had experience living abroad due to being forced to live in exile during the Nazi years.

LIVING IN ENEMY TERRITORY?

Jews once again lived in Germany, but only a few continued to identify as "German citizens of the Jewish faith," in the terminology of a bygone era. As Eastern

European Holocaust survivors, most of them had ended up in the American or British zones without having consciously chosen to live in Germany. They stayed because they had become economically successful, received monetary compensation, or had found a partner with whom to share a life.

Although the Eastern European Jews maintained business relationships with Germans, they kept their private contacts to a minimum. Their relationships with Germans were marked by distrust and a bad conscience, accusations, and feelings of guilt. The Central Welfare Office for Jews in Germany, which was reestablished in 1951, played an important role in the integration of the Jews into Germany. Called the Central Welfare Office of the German Jews between 1917 and 1933, it was an umbrella organization that after the war became the place to go to resolve the social problems faced by Jews living in Germany. This included the care of the aged and infirm along with emotionally at-risk young people. It also provided economic start-up help for Holocaust survivors and returnees, who generally had no assets. Capital from the Central Welfare Office and the American Jewish Joint Distribution Committee (JDC) was used to create five Jewish loan institutions or banks that provided loans to start small businesses or acquire necessary equipment. The loans were made at low interest, and these banks were not designed to turn a profit. They provided the capital for countless postwar economic successes. The Central Welfare Office had its own children's recreation homes, supported the construction of local youth centers, and in 1956 began publishing the journal *Jüdische Sozialarbeit* (Jewish social work).

A few figures make clear just how urgent social work really was. Of the forty-six hundred members of the West Berlin community in 1956, about eight hundred, that is, just under 20 percent, were cared for by the welfare department.[31] The resettlement of the last inhabitants of the Föhrenwald DP camp in 1957 into their own apartments, mostly in Munich, Frankfurt, and Düsseldorf posed an enormous challenge. The Central Welfare Office provided advice on how to set up homes and how to run a household. A report in *Jüdische Sozialarbeit* explains why this assistance was often necessary:

> These people have not been integrated into any normal social order for more than twenty years. Most of them grew up in a foreign country. In addition, they speak a non-German mother tongue. During their developmental years, they mostly existed outside the bounds of law and order. They were never able to learn a proper profession. They are frequently sick, often so much so that no foreign country is prepared to take them in, even if they have the means. They have become accustomed to viewing every person as an enemy or exploiter.[32]

This report is one of the few published sources we possess that openly criticizes the consequences of the economic ascent of a portion of the displaced persons and accuses them of glorifying money and having come to view love solely as a consumer good. The woman who wrote it made no attempt to hide her displeasure at the obvious fact that some Eastern European Jews were profiting from the pleasure industry, especially in military enclaves, where they maintained the illusion of living and working in a domain somehow outside of Germany. The Central Council was also concerned with this problem, and General Secretary van Dam suggested that "persons who are the proprietors of dubious premises should not be given community functions, and that Jewish institutions should accept no contributions from them."[33]

As late as 1978, the chair of the Jewish community in Würzburg and member of the Bavarian senate, David Schuster, felt constrained to mention this problem in an overview of Jewish life in Bavaria: "Openly stated, we are not pleased to see Jews operating bars and nightclubs, but there is nothing that we can do about it." Schuster explained this phenomenon as resulting from the fact that many young Holocaust survivors who lacked schooling found work only with the American army after the war. They saw the nightclubs for GIs, and so "they hit upon the idea of running something like that themselves. I don't think that many such Jewish businesses still exist, particularly because the Jewish communities have let it be known that they do not gladly see them."[34]

Most of the former DPs were not in the pleasure trade but were involved in building textile businesses or restaurants. Real estate was another preferred occupation. A relatively large percentage of survivors was dependent on disability pensions and social welfare because of physical injuries sustained under the Nazis.

Leading a normal life was especially difficult for children and adolescents. As *Jüdische Sozialarbeit*, for example, reported, "Life for a Jewish child in Germany is very confusing. If parents live in Germany and raise their children here, they must also be clear that efforts must be made to smooth the child's path into the non-Jewish community and give him or her the opportunity to make contacts. The child must not get the feeling that he or she is living in enemy territory."[35] The Eastern European Holocaust survivors who were forced to leave the safety of the DP camps and now found themselves on the German street were particularly apt to feel beleaguered in enemy territory. Thus, David Stopnitzer, who was born in a DP camp near Munich in 1946, remembered how his mother would send him to the baker with the words, "Go to the murderer and get four rolls." As Stopnitzer added laconically, "All I knew was that among the 'murderers' there were some very nice ones and some who were less nice."[36]

The Jewish children who grew up in Munich in the 1950s and 1960s experienced the tail end of an Eastern European Jewish way of life that was often tightly connected with the American presence. Stopnitzer, for example, described his parents' grocery store, which dealt almost exclusively in American products from the PX. After leaving the Föhrenwald DP camp, Abraham Ben's family moved to a residential block in Munich-Giesing that was called "Little Jerusalem" because about sixty or seventy Jewish families lived there, not infrequently next door to the families of the local police.[37] Leibl Rosenberg, who also resettled in Munich after leaving Föhrenwald and who later became a journalist, was one of those who, though speaking Yiddish at home, soon mastered Bavarian dialect as his second language: "I was the one in high school who read [the antisemitic Bavarian poet] Ludwig Thoma's Christmas story out loud in Bavarian, and later I was asked by Bavarian Radio to read certain things or to speak. My Bavarian was more authentic than that of some of the radio announcers or actors."[38]

Many parents expected their children to do something that the parents had been unable to do, that is, leave Germany. In 1960 the chairperson of the Women's International Zionist Organization (WIZO), Helen Israel from Düsseldorf, admitted to a group of visiting American Jews that she and her husband—both Auschwitz survivors—had built a life in Germany and did not feel capable of starting all over again somewhere else. But their son's future would not be Germany.[39] And from Frankfurt, Cilly Kugelmann, who was also the daughter of DPs, reported, "My parents lived here but had no contact with Germans. My parents had no German friends whatsoever. It was a problem for me to invite German school friends to our home."[40]

The only empirical study of the emotional state of Jewish young people in Germany in the 1960s was conducted by Walter Oppenheimer, who was active in Jewish youth work. He came to the conclusion that for most of the respondents there was an unbridgeable gap between their "Jewish identity" and their "German identity." In his view, these young Jews were dealing with a suppressed guilt complex over the fact that they stayed in Germany or had come to Germany.[41] Oppenheimer found that the young people were an extremely heterogeneous group. Only a third of the 274 children between the ages of nine and fifteen who were questioned had been born in Germany; a third came from Israel and spoke Hebrew; while a quarter spoke Yiddish along with German. Approximately 18 percent of the parents were still stateless. Although most of the adolescents attended Jewish religious instruction, a vanishingly small number went to services regularly or followed the religious commandments. While 73 percent of the respondents stated that they would prefer to live in Israel if they could, only 8 percent chose Germany as their most preferred country.[42]

In the absence of Jewish schools, it was also impossible to pass along Jewish knowledge to the next generation. During the 1950s and 1960s, large numbers of Jews living in Germany sent their children to Jewish private schools in England or France, from where only a few returned to Germany. In the early 1960s, the State Association of Jewish Communities in Bavaria and the Central Council

Opening of the Jewish elementary school in Frankfurt am Main, with
Rabbi Lichtigfeld, 1966. Jüdisches Museum Frankfurt am Main.

began to discuss plans to build a Jewish boarding school in Germany. A commission was set up within the Central Council, and in 1962 a council meeting voted overwhelmingly to build such a school.[43] Over the following years, discussions largely settled on Bavaria. After lengthy negotiations among the Jewish communities involved, the Augsburg community announced that it would provide the necessary building. The plan was to provide schooling for forty to fifty students between the ages of twelve and sixteen, mostly from Bavaria. The school was to open in September 1965. The board of the State Association wrote a resolution to that effect, but the idea ran aground for financial reasons and because of a dawning realization that within a few years there might no longer be enough Jewish children in Germany to justify such an undertaking.[44]

Instead, the communities decided to found Jewish elementary schools, first in Frankfurt (1966) and a little later in Munich. The schools formed the cornerstone of the education of Jewish young people in Germany. No longer would students be raised to leave the country as soon as possible; instead, they would be encouraged to build a future in Germany. By the 1960s, even the few Eastern European Jewish representatives on the Central Council began to express the opinion that perhaps they should integrate into German society as citizens, with all that that entailed. Baruch Graubard, who held leadership positions in many Jewish organizations, stated that "whoever is of the opinion that Germany is not or cannot become his fatherland, whoever is of the opinion that Jews have no future here in Germany, has no business being in the leadership of the Jews." Graubard was attempting to alleviate their guilty consciences about living in Germany. He stressed the need for dialogue with non-Jewish youth, although it was important to maintain a critical stance and to remain anchored in Judaism: "Even they, the German young people of today, do not want to see us assimilated; they especially wish to view us as bearers of our own culture."[45]

In 1964 Jeanette Wolff, the Social Democratic delegate to the Bundestag and member of the Berlin Jewish community's representative assembly, expressed what many adult Jews were thinking: "We sin against our young people when we bring our packed suitcases into our children's childhoods. Let us first become good Jews at home and good human beings outside the home."[46] Wolff received support from Hans Rosenthal, who was then still working in radio and held leadership positions in the Berlin community and the Central Council:

> We must give our children a perspective. Should I tell my child, who is going to school with non-Jews, that you don't belong there? What I have to do is tell my child, you are a German, or I have to tell him, we're going to emigrate later. But one way or another, the children must have something to hold onto. Everyone has a point of view. However, we need to consider the following, namely, that we have built up communities, and now look at this house, the synagogue. We are German-Jewish communities. The leadership committees must work to ensure that these communities in Germany become permanent communities. They are communities that were created for the future.[47]

For German Jews like Wolff and Rosenthal, a future in Germany seemed far more plausible than it did to Jews from Eastern Europe who had been left stranded in Germany after the war. The cattle dealer Hugo Spiegel returned to his home in Warendorf in Westphalia to take control of his business again. He was just as active in the local shooting club as in the Münster Jewish community, where his son was the first to have a bar mitzvah after the end of the war.[48] An elderly Julius Schuster, whose family had a history in Lower Franconia going back more than 450 years, returned to Würzburg from Israel in 1956 with his wife and son David in order to administer family property in nearby Bad Brückenau. As chair of the community, David Schuster attempted to revitalize Franconian Jewish traditions, especially the Orthodox ones.[49] Ernst Loewy, who originally came from Krefeld, returned to Germany in 1956 as well. "It was the yearning for a different, certainly not a 'whole' world, but one that was somewhat more promising," he wrote later.[50] For Loewy, as for many other returnees, it also meant a return to his own language and culture. He, too, traveled in both spheres, the Jewish and the German. After a stint as head of the Judaica department in the Frankfurt city and university libraries, he became an advisor to the German radio archive and published important works on exile literature. The lives of these families and individuals are emblematic of a very different path than that taken by the Eastern European DPs. The children of German Jews grew up in a German milieu that was far more "normal" than that experienced by DP children. The study conducted by Oppenheimer showed that children from German-Jewish families simply had far more contact with non-Jews than did their DP counterparts.[51]

But integration was not always a simple matter for the children of German-Jewish returnees, especially if they had already attended school in Israel. While their parents remembered Germany as it had been and brought the German language with them, their children had been torn out of the only environment they had ever known and were forced to come to terms with a foreign country. At the same time, they would have sensed that their parents did not necessarily feel better integrated than the Eastern European refugees. For example, in a letter to the editor of *Der Spiegel*, a lawyer who had returned to Wuppertal wrote:

> As a former attorney, I returned five years ago and have since then been employed in the same profession in the same place. They have been five years of disappointment. My acceptance by the Wuppertal judiciary was not marked by excessive enthusiasm about my return. To date, not a single person has expressed curiosity about where I might have lived during those many years of emigration since 1933 or what I did. In fact, I think they would rather that I had remained where I was. I often wonder whether they may not be right.

In another letter to the editor, an Austrian Jew living in Wiesbaden wrote, "For the next ten to twenty years it will be impossible to live normally as a Jew in the Federal Republic."[52]

A third much smaller but growing group joined the immigrants and the German Jews over the following decades: Christian Germans who had converted to Judaism. As Rabbi Nathan Peter Levinson of Berlin reported, during his tenure more prospective converts applied to be accepted into the Jewish community than there were total members.[53] The first systematic examination of the records on conversions during the 1950s and 1960s from the estates of Orthodox rabbis shows that about two-thirds involved young women between the ages of twenty and thirty-five who intended to marry a Jewish man or had already married one. Their applications usually contained supportive letters from the husband or community members such as this one: "My wife is actually the prototype of what one calls a 'good Jewish mother.' She reads my mother's Jewish cookbooks and

Hugo Spiegel, father of Paul Spiegel, who later became president of the Central Council, with his shooting medals, in Warendorf, 1961. Leonard Freed / Magnum Photos.

on Friday evening lays out fresh tablecloths and prepares schnitzel with potato salad and *challah*!" Others wanted to convert for religious reasons, and some said that they would rather be counted among the victims than the perpetrators. One of them wrote, "I know why I wish to commit completely to Judaism: as penance for the million-fold victims that my Jewish fellow human beings were forced to sacrifice."[54] It is one of the ironies of history that some of the applicants submitted to the rabbis documents from the personnel departments of the NSDAP or family trees from Nazi genealogical research that classified them as *Mischlinge* of the first degree (i.e., children of mixed marriages). To deal with the large number of complicated conversion applications, the Rabbinical Conference founded a conversion commission in 1961. But during the 1960s, rabbis tended to be hesitant about accepting new members. This was especially the case when applicants expressed political motives. Of the 345 applications for conversion that were examined, only 73 were shown to have been successful. But given the generally high barriers to conversion, the rates of rejection by the Orthodox rabbis were not that unusual.

Knowledge of Judaism, however, was increasingly imparted to a larger circle of persons who were not interested in conversion. In the 1960s the groundwork was laid for establishing Jewish cultural institutions. In Berlin, where the first Jewish elementary school was opened in 1986, the Jewish adult education center (*Volkshochschule*), which was founded in 1962, enabled anyone with an interest to find out about Jewish culture and history. At first, the lectures concentrated on topics of more general interest like "Israel—the Country and Its People," "Jewish Artists and Jewish Art," and "The Essence of the Talmud." Among the lecturers were well-known experts in the areas of Jewish culture and religion, including Hans Lamm, the head of cultural affairs at the Central Council; Adolf Leschnitzer, a permanent visiting professor at the Free University of Berlin; and Isaak Emil Lichtigfeld, the state rabbi of Hessen. During the adult education center's inaugural year, the philosopher of religion Hermann Levin Goldschmidt, who lived in Basel, gave a lecture about Franz Rosenzweig, who had founded an innovative Jewish adult education system in Frankfurt after World War I called the Freie Jüdisches Lehrhaus (Free Jewish house of learning). In contrast to the *Lehrhaus* in Frankfurt, the *Volkshochschule* in Berlin catered primarily to a non-Jewish public that sought to learn about the German-Jewish culture that had only recently been stamped out.

The Central Council, too, became increasingly involved in activities beyond restitution and political representation. As early as 1957, the Central Council began bestowing the Leo Baeck Prize for outstanding cultural achievements on people who had supported the Jewish community. It probably says something about the meagerness of the German-Jewish culture of the time that most of the laureates of the 1960s have fallen into oblivion.

TIES TO ISRAEL

Most of the Jews who originated primarily from Eastern Europe did not come to Frankfurt or pass through the city in order to make a contribution, of whatever sort, to Judaism in Germany or even to German culture, but rather primarily for material reasons. . . . From the perspective of Jewish community policies, material support for community institutions is the precondition for social, charitable, and cultural achievements. However, for the individual this perspective meant investing in a country, in a city, in a community that many still viewed as a way station—perhaps compensating for their guilty conscience. Far more durable, according to this mentality, are investments for a Jewish future outside the country, e.g., in Israel; and thus they send donations of money—as proxies for their own persons—to that place where they themselves prefer not to go.[55]

What Salomon Korn, the later president of the Frankfurt community, said of that city applied to the rest of Germany in equal measure. For most of the Jews living in Germany, Israel was the keystone of their identity. The Central Council made this clear again and again in its resolutions. For instance, in 1955 it made the following appeal: "The Central Council of Jews in Germany assures the State of Israel, which is fighting for its existence, of its indissoluble ties and its support in this hard battle. It urges all Jews in Germany to support by their personal sacrifice Israel's just cause and the salvation of hundreds of thousands of Jews who are at risk."[56] The communities were urged to pledge a portion of their income to Israel as a sort of tax:

> On the occasion of the rebirth of Keren haYesod (United Israel Appeal) in Germany, the Central Council of Jews in Germany calls upon the Jewish communities in Germany that in addition to contributions from individual persons for the United Israel Appeal, the Jewish communities as a collective renew their earlier tradition of an annual subsidy for Keren haYesod. Today this is all the more important because the Jewish communities in Germany in the aggregate have a large number of committee members who are not in a position to tax themselves for Keren haYesod. The annual contribution from the communities will then be a symbolic overall payment in the name of those people who are not in a position to contribute to the work of Israel through Keren haYesod. The Jewish communities in the entire Jewish world tax themselves as community institutions for the Magbit [collection campaign for Israel]. It is the duty of honor of each Jewish community in Germany to join in this effort.[57]

Not everyone could afford to travel to Israel, but they could demonstrate their solidarity with the threatened state by contributing money. Although these contributions were, strictly speaking, voluntary, the Jewish communities did not always view them as such. The words of Juan Rosengold, the president of the Regensburg Jewish community (and a native of Regensburg), surely expressed the feelings of many about the necessity of contributing to Israel: "Not donations, not alms, a tax. One more tax! We are used to paying taxes, mostly for others, so why not for once a tax for ourselves, for our children and their future, for our people?"[58] This was not simply one tax more, but the only tax to be levied for their own people. Rosengold's remark says much about the problem of identity for many Jews living in Germany. It was customary to contribute money to Israel to commemorate births, bar mitzvahs, and marriages. In the 1960s Keren haYesod published yearbooks with lists of donors and the amounts of their donations. The yearbooks also contained photographs of children who donated their entire savings or bar mitzvah presents to Israel.[59]

Jewish education, especially in the communities dominated by Eastern Europeans, was geared toward emigration to Israel. For example, in Augsburg, the young people of the community took part in annual celebrations of Israel's independence. In 1962 they recited such poems as *"Ein Gruß dem Volk"* (*A greeting to the people*), *"Juble mein Volk"* (*Rejoice my people*), *and "Ein Land voller Fahnen"* (*A land full of flags*), along with quotes from Theodor Herzl. They also read the Balfour Declaration, the United Nations Palestine Partition Resolution, and the State of Israel's Declaration of Independence. At the end they sang the Israeli national anthem.[60] In some communities, those who failed to contribute to Israel were excluded from religious services or socially shunned. Community institutions often reflected this attitude, sometimes taking on the trappings of Israel travel agencies. Photographs of the Negev Desert and Mount Carmel decorated the rooms along with portraits of Israeli politicians from David Ben-Gurion to Golda Meir.

There were certainly critics of this orientation toward Israel, but they remained in the minority. From the conservative camp, for example, Hans-Joachim Schoeps challenged the Jews in Germany to answer the question "whether they wish to be viewed and treated as a foreign organization of the State of Israel or as German citizens with all the political rights and responsibilities that a commitment to Germany entails." In his view, they would do well to define themselves as a religious community, as before 1933.[61] Similar criticisms came from the radical Left as well. Jakob Goldberg, who was active in the Communist Party of Germany, disagreed vehemently with "the Zionist thesis of an 'extraterritorial world nation' of the Jews, where class divisions did not apply. Jewish citizens simply do not comprise a unity, except in the sense of a religious community." The solution to antisemitism was not the formation of a Jewish state but the destruction of the capitalist class system.[62]

The establishment of diplomatic relations between Israel and the Federal Republic of Germany in 1965 further legitimized the presence of Jews in Germany. There had, of course, already been contacts between the two nations, and these were not limited merely to reparations negotiations. They included economic and scientific exchanges such as the visit by representatives of the Max Planck Society to the Weizman Institute in Rehovot in 1959 and an official agreement between the Minerva German Science Foundation and the Weizman Institute five years later.[63] Visits to Israel by German student and youth groups were rare during the 1950s but increased steadily thereafter. In 1960 about forty German groups visited Israel; by 1961 that figure had increased to more than sixty and in 1963 to more than two hundred. In 1963, for example, the Offenbach Gesellschaft für Christlich-Jüdische Zusammenarbeit (Society for Christian-Jewish Cooperation) sent thirty-one young people "as goodwill messengers and ambassadors."[64] But only the exchange of official ambassadors between the two states gave the Jews living in Germany the sense that they were no longer viewed as despised relations living in a pariah state.

MICHAEL BRENNER is Professor of Jewish history and culture at the University of Munich and Seymour and Lillian Abensohn Chair in Israel Studies at American University in Washington, DC. He is a member of the Bavarian Academy of Sciences and international president of the Leo Baeck Institute. Brenner's publications include *A Short History of the Jews*, *Prophets of the Past: Interpreters of Jewish History*, *Zionism: A Short History*, and as coauthor, the four-volume *German-Jewish History in Modern Times*.

NORBERT FREI is Professor of modern and contemporary history at the University of Jena and is director of the Jena Center 20th Century History. During the 2008–2009 academic year, he was a member of the Institute for Advanced Study in Princeton, and in 2010–2011 he was Theodor Heuss Professor at the New School for Social Research in New York. Frei's publications include *1968: Jugendrevolte und globaler Protest*, *1945 und wir: Das Dritte Reich im Bewußtsein der Deutschen*, and *Adenauer's Germany and the Nazi Past: The Politics of Amnesty and Integration*; he is also coauthor of *Das Amt und die Vergangenheit: Deutsche Diplomaten im Dritten Reich und in der Bundesrepublik*.

NOTES

1. Resolutions Adopted by the Second Plenary Assembly of the World Jewish Congress, Montreux from June 27 to July 6, 1948, London, 1948, p. 7. For more details, see the introductory chapter in this volume by Dan Diner.

2. *Jewish Frontier*, May 1951, pp. 18–21.

3. Y. Jelinek (2004), p. 133.

4. See also P. Münch (1997), p. 85. See also A. Gottwald (1997); and T. Anthony (2004). Regarding the United States, see S. Shafir (1999).

5. Letter from Elijahu Livneh to the Western European Division of the State Department, February 12, 1951, cited in T. Anthony (2004), p. 173; letter from Gershon Avner to Elijahu Livneh, May 16, 1951, cited in T. Anthony (2004), p. 174.

6. Baeck said this in an interview with the journalist Gerhard Löwenthal, "Die Zukunft der Juden in Deutschland," *AJW* (supplement titled "Der Weg"), August 31, 1951, p. 1.

7. M. Friedman (1988), pp. 109–123.

8. European Executive Meeting of February 13–14, 1949, in Montreux, in USHMM, WJC RG-68.045M, reel 178.

9. Report by Julius Dreifuss on a visit by Nahum Goldmann to Cologne at a meeting of the board of the Central Council on October 9, 1952, in ZA, B1/7.221.28.

10. Position on migration at the board meeting of the Central Council on December 13, 1953, in Munich, in ZA, B1/7.221.44.

11. Letter from Hendrik G. van Dam to the members of the board and of the council, all state associations, and the communities of Berlin, Bremen, Hamburg, and Cologne, November 15, 1951, "Betreff Juden in Deutschland und die Organisationen des Weltjudentums (Ausländische Organisationen)," in ZA, B1/7.121.

12. Letter from Hendrik G. van Dam to the members of the board.

13. For more detail, see M. Brenner (2010).

14. Memorandum from S. Sokal to A. L. Easterman, May 27, 1952, in USHMM, WJC RG-68.059M, reel 164.

15. Proceedings of WJC Plenary Session 1953, in USHMM, WJC RG-68.059M, reel 130.

16. Minutes of the meeting of the Central Council of Jews in Germany on October 12, 1953, in Bremen, in ZA, B1/7.221.39.

17. Paper presented by H. G. van Dam at the meeting of the Central Council on July 7–8, 1954, in Düsseldorf, in ZA, B1/7.221.55.

18. S. Shafir (1999), p. 98.

19. Report from the Solomon Andhill Fineberg Archives Germany on February 8, 1973, in AJA, MS149 2.2.

20. "Germany Nine Years Later (a Report of the Anti-Defamation League of B'nai B'rith of a Study Tour Undertaken at the Invitation of the Federal Republic of West Germany by Jacob Alson, Benjamin R. Epstein, Nathan C. Belth)," July 1954, p. 8. The library of the USHMM contains a copy of this report.

21. Proceedings of the WJC conference in Brussels on August 5, 1966, p. 24, in USHMM, WJC RG-68.059M, reel 132.

22. Report by the administrative council of the board of the Central Council, reported by General Secretary H. G. van Dam on March 22, 1964, in USHMM, WJC RG-68.045, reel 127.

23. Minutes of the administrative council of the board of the Central Council on April 30, 1966, in Munich, in ZA, B1/7.818.

24. L. Marx (1995), p. 182.

25. M. Kalman (1997), pp. 35–37.

26. A. Kauders (2007), pp. 129–131.

27. Notes by Dr. Unverfehrt (BPA) on a meeting on August 12, 1957, with Karl Marx, August 14, 1957, in BArch, B 136/24654.

28. Letter from Marcel Gärtner (on behalf of Karl Marx) to State Secretary Globke, March 13, 1957, in BArch, B 136/24654.

29. Report by Karl Marx to head of section Dr. Janz, November 14, 1957, in BArch, B 136/24654, including excerpts from a letter from Hans Koster, press officer of the German embassy in Buenos Aires, to Karl Marx, November 7, 1957.

30. K. Hartewig (2000), pp. 224–229.

31. Heinz Galinski, "Praktische Sozialarbeit in Umrissen," *Jüdische Sozialarbeit*, February 21, 1956, pp. 5–6, here p. 5.

32. Marianne Pulvermann, "Die ZWST in Bayern," *Jüdische Sozialarbeit*, March 1, 1957, p. 12.

33. Minutes of the meeting of the board of the Central Council on March 31, 1963, in Cologne, in ZA, B1/7.856.

34. D. Schuster (1978), p. 36.

35. Thea Baer, "Klarer Weg statt Chaos!," *Jüdische Sozialarbeit*, December 23, 1960, p. 55.

36. D. Stopnitzer (2004), p. 159.

37. A. Ben (2004), p. 141.

38. L. Rosenberg (2004), p. 99.

39. The report of a mission to Germany in the summer of 1960 by ten B'nai Brith representatives, p. 28, in LBI, AR 1445.

40. R. Fabian, "Ein Erbe als Herausforderung," *Tribüne* 38/149 (1999), p. 194.

41. W. Oppenheimer (1967), p. 169.

42. W. Oppenheimer (1967), p. 148.

43. Minutes of the meeting of the Central Council on May 20–21, 1962, in Düsseldorf, p. 3, in ZA, B1/7.859.

44. Minutes of the meetings of the presidium of the LVB on October 1, 1964, and January 17, 1965, in Archiv LVB, file "Präsidiumsprotokolle vom 18. Juli 1947 bis 11. Oktober 1967."

45. Minutes of the meeting of the Central Council on March 22–23, 1964, in Hannover, in ZA, B1/7.864.

46. Minutes of the meeting of the Central Council on March 22–23, 1964.

47. Minutes of the meeting of the Central Council on March 22–23, 1964.

48. P. Spiegel (2006), p. 11.

49. R. Ries (2010), p. 29.

50. I. Wiltmann (ed.) (1999), p. 98.

51. W. Oppenheimer (1967), pp. 125–127.

52. *Der Spiegel*, August 14, 1963, pp. 5–6.

53. N. P. Levinson (1995), p. 159.

54. StadtAS, IRGW 1026/268. This and the following comment are from the unpublished master's thesis by L. Barner (2008).

55. S. Korn (1991), p. 415.

56. Resolution of the Central Council at its meeting on November 27–28, 1955, in Düsseldorf, in ZA, B1/7.221.62.

57. Resolution of the board of the Central Council at its meeting on March 14, 1955, in Frankfurt, in ZA, B1/7.221.56.

58. J. Rosengold (1966), p. 111.

59. "Unsere jungen Magbit-Spender," in M. Karger-Karin (1966), p. 112.

60. Program of the celebrations of the national holiday on May 12, 1962, in Archiv LVB, loose-leaf.

61. H.-J. Schoeps (1953), p. 212.

62. J. Goldberg (1979), p. 195.

63. L. G. Feldman (2003), pp. 316–317.

64. E. Schlee (1964), p. 8. The figures are on p. 66. See also the anonymously published travel report by a Frankfurt school (1965) titled "Schalom Israel: Ein Bericht."

8 AFTER THE DEED

Little in the way of pathos was discernible when Chancellor Konrad Adenauer, in office for barely five days, took to the podium on September 20, 1949, and in his first policy statement laid out before the German Bundestag the tasks facing his newly installed government and the goals it would pursue. The head of the Christian-Conservative coalition spoke for almost an hour and a half, but what he had to say about Germany's future was limited to a dry listing of the constitutive acts that since the elections on August 14 had been implemented by the still makeshift parliament in Bonn.[1] The routine manner with which he addressed the business of this body gave little hint as to whether it was consciously staged or merely the result of the time pressures of the preceding days, but in any case he continued in this vein when he came to speak about the social and political problems of the present. The sequence in which he addressed these problems was surely not random. Starting from the overall economic situation, he then addressed the expellees, then the middle class, followed by officials, "former military personnel," the war disabled and widows and orphans, youth, and finally all those who felt disadvantaged by the process of "denazification." Because the latter had caused "much unhappiness and much damage," the chancellor held out hope for discussions with the high commissioners—and an amnesty. "The Federal Government," Adenauer stated, "is determined wherever possible to let bygones be bygones." However, he continued, "It is nonetheless firmly determined to learn the necessary lessons from the past as regards all those who endeavor to upset the foundation of our State, whether they be of a rightist or leftist radical nature."[2]

Only in this context, more than halfway through his first policy statement, did the chancellor touch fleetingly on the Jews, but not as a group needing and deserving the same political and social help as (in the very next breath) the "prisoners of war and German deportees," whose "question" could now be "take[n] up more strongly than before." Nor did it occur to Adenauer to address directly all of the Jews still or again living in Germany, and those who had been persecuted into exile, concerning what had occurred in their former homeland. Instead, he described the Jews as a kind of political problem, as the objects of attitudes and incidents that should be overcome in a post-Nazi society: "In this connection permit me to say a word or two about antisemitic trends that seem to have arisen in a few cases. After everything that took place in the National Socialist period we consider it unworthy and incredible *per se* that there should still be individuals in Germany who persecute and despise Jews because they are Jews."[3]

It would be difficult to imagine a more convoluted and hedged way of describing the antisemitism still endemic in the country. Apparently, Adenauer, who had been elected by a razor-thin majority, did not wish to alienate non-Jewish popular opinion. Rather than put off the (West) German public in his first appearance as federal chancellor by recalling the conscious forms of perpetration and complicity, of which he was well aware, he accepted and strengthened Germans' self-perception as victims of the "recent past," as the Nazi era would all too often come to be called.[4]

That Adenauer's calculus came at the expense of the victims of the Third Reich was made clear the next day, when Kurt Schumacher was the first to respond in the name of the Social Democratic opposition: "One cannot be against Nazism without remembering the victims of fascism. One cannot feel enthusiasm for helping certain classes of the underprivileged—however necessary aid for them may be—if the victims of fascism are arbitrarily relegated to the position giving precedence to the rights of others."[5] Schumacher, who had spent about ten years in concentration camps, where he had been severely abused, also recognized the necessity of a broad policy of social and political integration. But in contrast to Adenauer, he demanded much more forceful words than the chancellor seemed capable of: "What the Government Statement of Policy had to say yesterday about the Jews and the terrible Jewish tragedy in the Third Reich was too insipid and weak. Spiritless statements and a rueful accent are of no help in this connection. It is not only the duty of international socialism, but of every German patriot to train the spotlight on the fate of German and European Jewry, and to offer all the help that may be necessary."

Of course, Schumacher was also intent on speaking the truth in a manner that he hoped that postwar Germans could accept: "Hitler's barbarism brought dishonor on the German people through its extermination of six million Jews. We have to bear the consequences of this dishonor for an unforeseeable long time to come." And as if intent on placing in perspective the figures and statistics that Adenauer had used to describe the fate of prisoners of war and deportees, the SPD chair thundered: "Only thirty thousand out of six hundred thousand German Jews live in the entire territory of the four Zones today. The majority of them are elderly people or invalids. Even they experience, again and again, shameful and degrading incidents. No political movement in Germany should forget that any nationalism bears within itself the seeds of antisemitism, and that all forms of antisemitism bear in themselves the seeds of nationalism. Anything along these lines means in fact, the voluntary self-isolation of Germany in the world." And then Schumacher took up a line of argumentation from the Weimar period with which Socialists had attempted to persuade antisemites by appealing to their own self-interest: "Antisemitism indicates an ignorance of the great contributions German Jews have rendered to the German economy, to German intellectual life and German culture, and to the fight for German freedom and German democracy. Today the German people come to grips with the construction of a new Germany. It would be in a better position if it had in its ranks those forces of the Jewish intellect and of the Jewish economic potential."[6]

Such admonitions and appeals from the first days of the German parliament were a foretaste of how hard it would be for most Germans to admit forthrightly to their own responsibility as former "comrades" in the Third Reich. The immensity of the task facing the leading representatives of the new republic was made clear during the two days of debate following Adenauer's statement, when a certain Dr. Franz Richter, representing the German Right Party, began to speak: "In the past few years some fools have stooped to confronting the German people with elaborately dressed-up bills of particulars about misdemeanors committed by isolated individuals of our people, misdemeanors of the sort that might occur among any people. I repeat—committed by isolated individuals."[7] Two years later, Richter, who by then was a member of the openly right-wing radical Socialist Reich Party, was revealed to be Fritz Rößler, a former NSDAP *Gauhauptstellenleiter* (district main office leader). He was arrested in the plenary hall.[8] But the opinions of which he unburdened himself about the bombing raids and the "real victims" had long since entered the mainstream, and hardly anyone would have contradicted him. This included sentiments like the following from the same speech: "But as long as we are discussing crimes against humanity, then, ladies and gentlemen, I believe we might also present a counterclaim. Let us begin with, say, Hamburg, Cologne, Mannheim, Munich, Stuttgart, Hannover, and end with Dresden. That claim would hardly be an insubstantial one."[9]

Federal president Theodor Heuss perhaps countered such sentiments more clearly than the heads of parties who were competing for votes. On the occasion of his election on September 12, 1949, Heuss warned the Bundestag that the same applies to peoples as to individuals. It is "a blessing to forget. But I fear that some people in Germany will misuse this blessing and wish to forget too quickly."[10] This did not, however, prevent him from assisting convicted war criminals behind the scenes.[11] But by his own frankness, Heuss was treading where he knew he would encounter resistance. It had become, "in a manner of speaking, one of the passive professional functions of my office" "to receive letters, including anonymous and open ones," he declared on December 7, 1949, in a speech carried on radio. He went on to speak openly about the murder of the Jews: "We must not simply choose the way of least resistance and forget the things which people would like to forget. We must neither forget the Nuremberg Racial Laws nor the Star of David which Jews had to display on their person, neither the burning of the synagogues nor the deportation of the Jews into disaster and death."[12] Heuss had been invited to Wiesbaden by the Gesellschaft für Christlich-Jüdische Zusammenarbeit (Society for Christian-Jewish Cooperation), and one of the guests at the hotel was U.S. High Commissioner John J. McCloy, who during the summer of 1949 had met with representatives of the Jewish communities. Together, they had sketched out the sorts of policies they expected from the new government in Bonn.[13]

Against this backdrop, it should not be surprising that the federal president's speech would have met with widespread approval both in Germany and abroad. By 1951 the digest version published by the Koordinierungsrat der Christlich-Jüdischen Gesellschaften (Coordinating Council for Christian-Jewish Cooperation Organizations), which bore the title that Heuss had himself selected, "Mut zur Liebe" (Courage to love), was in its third printing, for a total of sixty-two thousand copies.[14] One of the reasons for the attention paid to this speech was undoubtedly that the highest representative of the young republic had said what needed to be said with utter clarity. As the director of the JDC, Rudolf Jorysz, wrote from Shanghai half a year later, it had given hope "to a few who had despaired here of 'risking' the return to our old homeland."[15]

But there was something else that lent weight to the speech: in Wiesbaden, Heuss had referred to the term "collective guilt," which "agitated people, here and abroad," as he put it. But Heuss now took up this concept in a nuanced fashion that was rare among politicians, linking it with the concept of "collective shame," a notion that many Germans found more acceptable:

> There is no point in beating about the bush. We must speak up about the fiendish injustice meted out to the Jewish people, asking ourselves: "Because we lived in Germany, are we also guilty of this fiendish injustice? Am I? Are you?" Four years ago this question agitated people, here and abroad. It prompted the talk of the German people's "collective guilt."
>
> The term "collective guilt" and its implications are an oversimplification, a distortion of the kind pounded home by the Nazis in talking about the Jews. In their eyes the mere fact that someone was a Jew automatically proved him guilty. But something like "collective shame" did grow up in that time and has remained with us. Hitler injured us in many ways, but that he drove us to the point of being ashamed of calling ourselves Germans in the same breath with him and his henchmen, that was the foulest blow of all.[16]

Heuss knew how to speak to the consciences of his compatriots: by combining an uncompromising recognition of the political and moral catastrophe brought about by the Third Reich—without at the same time implying that each individual bore equal guilt for that catastrophe. He accomplished this balancing act by applying the same rhetorical forms used by almost all politicians who spoke about the murder of the Jews during the early years of the Federal Republic. Although Heuss's comments were not nearly as abstract and oddly impersonal as Adenauer's, the crimes that he addressed remained the heinous deeds of a few. And like Schumacher, Heuss reminded his readers of all the things that Germany had lost as a result of the Nazis' murderous policies. Behind his words, one may discern the hope that self-interested anti-antisemitism might become the new norm for the citizens of this new republic: philosemitism as a return to reason.[17]

The tone was not much different when Heuss addressed the "Jews in Germany" (the officious locution "Jewish fellow citizens" became common currency a few years later). For example, on the occasion of the Jewish New Year on September 24, 1949, he described "a strong sense of the immense bitterness that still adheres in the soul when one recalls the desecration and destruction of houses of God, all of the human suffering from which no Jewish family remained spared during the years of Satanic destruction. That was the time during which we, too, suffered because the name of the German people, our people, our own name, was besmirched by a brutal ethos. The Jews will never, and honest Germans may never simply forget. But together they must transcend this terrible heritage."[18]

The fact that Heuss never missed the opportunity to send New Year's greetings during the ten years in which he was in office was more than a mere expression of obligation. It was a sign of his determination to reestablish connections and with them a new basis for trust—and to mark the progress made as a result. Just how much he accomplished in this relatively short time at the level of his office and in his dealings with the representatives of the Central Council may be gauged by a humorous groan in response to Karl Marx, the publisher of the *Allgemeine Wochenzeitung der Juden in Deutschland*, in the summer of 1956: "I understand very well that I cannot just ask the Jews to drop New Year's on my account."[19]

Although Heuss believed he observed "a certain inner and spiritual consolidation" in the German people at the time, his greetings the following year demonstrated how much the attitude of "collective shame" had already been displaced by a new confidence. On the occasion of Rosh Hashanah in 1957, Heuss thought, "to feel, and some evidence for this passes through my hand, that with the organization and more rapid processing of so-called 'restitution' much existential fear, especially among older Jewish people, has been alleviated, that a returning sense of safety has dampened some of the all too understandable bitterness." Of course, this did not change the circumstance, that "the brutality of cemetery desecrations are once again being reported, which in my opinion are less specifically antisemitic excesses than actions intended to inflict moral damage on the growing respect accorded the Federal Republic in the free world." This, he believed, was countered by "the reception of the *Diary of Anne Frank* on countless stages throughout the Federal Republic," which, according to Heuss, was characterized by "hushed emotion": "This is undoubtedly the most powerful spiritual process in this sphere full of suffering and pain. May this be interpreted as the lasting power of purification? I believe so."[20]

The federal president's growing optimism was undoubtedly based on the understanding that his attempts at enlightening his people had not been unsuccessful—although he did try, like many in Bonn, to claim that the cemetery desecrations were the result of machinations by the German Democratic Republic— and that his success had been recognized by the Jews. Accordingly, when he sent greetings to Marx on the occasion of his sixtieth birthday, he thanked him for always having informed him "with openness and tact about Jewish matters," to which Heuss appended a remark about the close friendships that he had had with Jews in his childhood. And he continued with a remarkable recollection of the situation (now seemingly overcome) in which, eight years earlier, he had spoken of "collective shame": "Our surviving friends abroad knew that for us loyalty and love had not been spoiled by Hitler, but after 1945 all of us encountered unfamiliar Jews with a feeling of uncertainty."[21]

For Heuss, the positive outlook was confirmed in September 1957, when the chancellor and his party, the CDU, running on a platform of "no experiments," won an absolute majority in the third Bundestag elections. His landslide victory also ratified Adenauer's strategy of strengthening ties to the West. At the same time, it allowed him to continue his policy of settling Germany's "war debts," so defined, which was surprisingly easy, given the country's booming reconstruction economy. An essential cornerstone of both strategies—with effects both internally and abroad—was the policy of restitution to the Jews. Both Heuss and Adenauer had come to understand its importance.

"RESTITUTION"

The idea of systematic restitution to the victims of National Socialist violence was older than the Federal Republic, but the policy was driven by the Western occupation forces after 1945, in part making use of concepts that had been formulated by exiles.[22] In the Soviet zone of occupation, by contrast, any restitution of Jewish property was viewed as potentially procapitalist, as a result of which the GDR simply refused to deal with the issue. Only Paul Merker, who for a brief

Johanna von Koczian and Friedrich Maurer in the premiere of *The Diary of Anne Frank* by Frances Goodrich at the Schlosspark Theater, Berlin, 1956. ullstein bild.

period was a member of the GDR leadership, advanced the principled position that the Jews should be compensated.[23] In the end, Merker was accused of "Zionist" tendencies and imprisoned for undermining the state. In the early 1950s, the West German government, on the other hand, felt compelled to develop a policy of restitution, primarily because of American pressure. From a distance of more than half a century, the actions that they took in this regard seem nothing short of revolutionary in terms of "transitional justice" and as an advance in the theory of international law. Previously, international law had been an instrument of reparation between states but did not take into account claims by groups or individuals against a state. No outward signs marked this change at the beginning of the new republic. Nonetheless, there are significant reasons to view the incipient development of German-Jewish-Israeli relations as a complex learning process that unfolded on a more or less ongoing basis, with the issue of restitution at its center, at least during the first several decades.[24]

"Mensch, ärgere Dich nicht" (Man, don't get excited), a parody from the June 1951 edition of the *Jüdische Illustrierte* about the long-drawn-out compensation process. From Georg Heuberger, ed., *Zedaka: Jüdische Sozialarbeit im Wandel der Zeit; 75 Jahre Zentralwohlfahrtsstelle der Juden in Deutschland 1917–1992*, catalogue for the exhibition at the Jewish Museum, Frankfurt am Main, from December 3, 1992 to February 28, 1993, p. 394 / Archiv Zentralwohlfahrtsstelle der Juden in Deutschland, Hamburg.

Adenauer took the first steps in late November 1949 in an interview with Karl Marx—undoubtedly responding to McCloy's admonitions, but probably also as a corrective to the opportunity he missed in his official policy statement of September of that year. Although this initial foray in Marx's *Allgemeine Wochenzeitung* brought the chancellor into indirect contact with Israel,[25] it did not represent a breakthrough. Not only did his offer of support for Israel in the form of goods valued at 10 million DM appear miserly, but the fact that it had been made in a public forum proved unwise. Just how unprepared were policymakers in Bonn—not to mention the Jewish communities (the Central Council did not yet exist)—in this new terrain was demonstrated by another announcement made by Adenauer in the same interview. He proposed a special "department" within the Ministry of the Interior that would be "transferred to a German Jew" and "give the Jews living in Germany the certainty that everything would be done by the federal government to protect the full scope of their civil rights."[26]

But in fact the plan was never carried out, and it would take almost two more years before the federal government would declare its intentions in matters relating to restitution. By now, however, the government had learned the lessons of public relations, having organized a series of behind-the-scenes discussions in which the Social Democrat Jakob Altmaier, one of the two Jewish delegates to the Bundestag, played an important role.[27]

Now well prepared, on September 27, 1951, four days before Rosh Hashanah, Adenauer spoke before a "solemn session" of the Bundestag and explained "the position of the Federal Republic of Germany with regard to the Jews."[28] Adenauer's comments were made in response to growing doubts internationally regarding "whether the new state would be guided in this important question by principles that did justice to the terrible crimes of a bygone epoch and would place the relationship between Jews and the German people on a new and healthy foundation." Although the "attitude of the Federal Republic toward its Jewish citizens" was firmly established in German Basic Law, all legal norms, according to the chancellor, could "come into full effect only when the attitude from which they were born becomes the common property of the entire people. This is a problem of education." It was important, according to Adenauer, that "the spirit of humane and religious tolerance be recognized by the entire German people, especially by German youth, not just in formal terms, but becomes reality by spiritual attitude and practical deed." In order that this process of education not be derailed, the federal government proposed to amend the penal code and fight antisemitic agitation by "rigorous prosecution." Adenauer felt forced to take this position because of the ongoing scandal involving right-wing radical Bundestag delegate Wolfgang Hedler, whose appeal of a verdict against him for insulting the victims of the Nazis was currently making its way through federal court.[29]

In the second part of his brief declaration, the chancellor laid out a minutely detailed exposition of the responsibility for the murder of the Jews—without mentioning the word "guilt" or naming those who were guilty. The federal government, according to Adenauer, and the "large majority" of Germans "were aware of the immeasurable suffering that the time of National Socialism had brought to the Jews in Germany and the occupied territories." The "overwhelming majority" of Germans had "abhorred" these crimes, and "many" had "demonstrated a willingness to help" their Jewish fellow citizens. This was followed by the passage for which the Israeli government had been waiting for months: "However, unspeakable crimes were committed in the name of the German people that demand moral and material restitution for both individual damage that Jews suffered as well as for Jewish property for which individual claimants are no longer present. Initial steps have been taken in this regard. However, much is left to be done."[30]

In an effort to demonstrate the unity of parliament in this matter, Adenauer's speech was not subject to follow-up discussion. Instead, there were numerous brief declarations from the parties, which Paul Löbe began in the name of the SPD with an avowal of the "moral obligation to work with all our might for a reconciliation with the State of Israel and the Jews throughout the world." The Social Democrats "would have welcomed it" if this step by the federal government, which they supported "with all their heart," "had been taken earlier and with greater determination." Löbe, chair by seniority of the Bundestag, was the only one who spoke directly about the murder of the Jews, although he, too, took pains to distinguish between a minority of perpetrators and the majority of Germans: "The criminal leadership of National Socialist tyranny inhumanly persecuted Jewish Germans and the Jews in Europe, and six million persons— men, women, children, and the elderly—were murdered merely because of their Jewish ancestry. We do not want to forget this immeasurable suffering. Every right-thinking person is ashamed of the outrages that were perpetrated in abuse of the German name to the horror of the overwhelming majority of the German people." Much as Kurt Schumacher had two years earlier, Löbe then took note of the German-Jewish Nobel laureates and alluded to the subtle distinctions between German Jews, who were entitled to restitution, and those from the rest of Europe, who were not: "We know that we are indissolubly linked with the Jews, who like us were born as Germans, and we cannot imagine our history without their contribution."[31]

The ceremony ended with closing words by Bundestag president Hermann Ehlers. The delegates then rose "in commemoration of the victims."[32] With that, the Federal Republic had given the signal that Jews throughout the world, though by no means all, had expected and hoped for.

McCloy sent the chancellor a congratulatory telegram in which he noted how very impressed he had been by the tone and contents of the declaration.[33] Leo Baeck wrote from London in the name of the Council for the Protection of the Rights and Interests of Jews from Germany that he had been "deeply moved."[34] The American Jewish Committee, like the Central Council of Jews, was more reserved, given the existence of groups that "today still preach racial theories, National Socialism, and militarism in Germany," and the World Jewish Congress underscored the importance of the reeducation of the German people.[35] Overall, however, matters were now on the right track, as the federal government's press and information office noted in a hastily put together statement. Two and a half months later Adenauer met in London with Nahum Goldmann, the president of the World Jewish Congress. Adenauer assured Goldmann of his intention, now in writing, to make a memorandum from the Israeli government of March of that year the "basis for discussions." In that memorandum, Israel had demanded

$1.5 billion for the costs of integrating about half a million immigrants.[36] That assurance led to official negotiations. This, in turn, led to the signing of the Restitution Agreement between Israel and West Germany (also known as the Luxembourg Agreement) and with Goldmann's Conference on Jewish Material Claims against Germany on September 10, 1952.

In his declaration at the end of September 1951, Adenauer noted the limits of Germany's "capabilities," given the "need to care for the numerous war victims and for refugees and expellees." During the ratification debate on March 4, 1953, he had to explain to the Bundestag (or, more precisely, to doubters in his own party) how and why the Federal Republic should bear the costs of the agreed-upon deliveries of goods to Israel having a value of 3 billion DM along with payments of 500 million DM to the Claims Conference. He carefully explained to them the various payment modalities and the differences between reparations, integration assistance, and global compensation for heirless restitution claims. But the chancellor did not stop at mere technical details. The German people, he noted, had "the earnest and sacred duty to help, even if sacrifices are demanded, perhaps serious sacrifices, even from those of us who do not feel personally guilty."[37]

It seemed as if Adenauer had learned a great deal in the course of discussions over the past months. More clearly than ever, he named the "horrible dimensions of the extermination measures against the Jews"; those measures had—"which tends to be forgotten by us"—included "almost all Jews of foreign nationality." The chancellor also made a point of the *singularity* of the murder of the Jews, a concept that hardly anyone had expressed before. At the same time, he demonstrated not only how awkwardly the proverbial "man on the street" talked about genocide but also how this clumsiness was still evident among the country's political representatives. During the first decade "after the deed," when Auschwitz could not yet be cited metaphorically and the concept of the Holocaust was still unknown, it testifies to that awkwardness that no one in the Bundestag, according to the minutes, objected to Adenauer's unfortunate use of the formerly innocuous word *Sonderbehandlung* (special treatment, a neutral term transformed by the Nazis into a euphemism for the mass murder of Jews) in a speech that was otherwise clear and to the point: "The Jews not only in Germany but wherever the arm of National Socialism extended—and for many years during the war that included most of Europe—were forced to endure the most brutal persecution. The extent of this persecution, the sacrifice of human beings and tangible assets in which it resulted, does not justify, rather it demands special treatment for restitution to Jewish persecutees."

According to Adenauer, the Luxembourg Agreement and the German Restitution Laws, which were being drafted at the time, provided "a solemnly promised conclusion for each German to one of the sorriest chapters in German history." He was well aware that the Germans, "after all that has happened, must demonstrate patience and trust in the consequences of our willingness to make reparations, and finally in the healing power of time." But he also expressed his "justified hope" that the agreement would "lead to a completely new relationship between the German and the Jewish people as well as to normalization of relations between the Federal Republic and the State of Israel."

This expression of hope for rapid normalization was echoed by most of the speakers during the second and third sessions of negotiations on the law on November 18, 1953. But there was now no doubt that the governing coalition would be dependent on votes from the opposition to move the agreements through the Bundestag. The right wing of the FDP and most of the delegates of the German Party refused, as did the young Franz Strauss of the CSU (who was not yet using his middle name, Josef), who sought to justify his nay vote and those of his colleagues, citing a purported lack of due diligence in the preparation of the agreement and the fear that fulfilling the terms of the speech would "make difficult and in any case delay individual restitution."[38]

The fact that his arguments were mere pretexts may be gauged from the explanation by Karl Count von Spreti, who in his capacity as rapporteur of the foreign affairs committee commented on the draft before the vote. Spreti was one of the few CSU delegates who voted for the measures. And Eugen Gerstenmaier (CDU) also made clear that he distrusted the reasoning of those who objected when he worked hard for passage of the agreement, recalling

> the outbreak of insanity to which it is estimated six million German, French, Belgian, Polish, Russian, Hungarian, Danish, and other European citizens fell victim. Systematically and with nearly perfect technique, they were, from the infant to the elderly, shot, gassed, exterminated for no other reason than that they were supposedly or actually people "of a different blood," people of the Jewish race. Orders went out to make Germany, "Greater Germany," and even Europe "Jew free." Those who did not escape fell victim to the executioner. Those who gave the orders and those who carried them out were unspeakable murderers.[39]

Given such statements, it can hardly be said that the murder of the Jews went unnoted during the first German Bundestag. But the Communists in particular ensured that the proceedings would have some rough edges; among other things, they rejected the agreement with Israel because its "beneficiaries" were primarily the "masters of the American armaments industry and high finance." While cries rang out from the Communist Party benches accusing the speakers from the ruling parties of being "hypocrites" and "Nazis," those speakers, in turn, availed themselves of a rhetoric that shielded their constituents. They spoke of "barbarism in the name of Germany," pointed to the limits of Germany's economic capabilities and the claims made by other groups of victims, and distanced themselves from any sense of a "collective guilt of all the Germans."[40] Only someone with the courage of an Eugen Gerstenmaier, a former member of the Kreisau Circle, a group of anti-Nazi dissidents, would add that the number of *non-Jewish* "martyrs to humanity," that is, German resisters, was by far not great enough to establish the idea of a "collective guiltlessness" of the Germans. Gerstenmaier talked about the "gas ovens" and the "enormous ghetto" into which the National Socialists had transformed all of Germany, only to massage the popular spirit in the next breath: "For us Germans, the walls of hatred, contempt, and rejection that had been drawn around us even before the war and that held us captive after the war were more insuperable than the walls of an Oriental ghetto." Even for the theologian Gerstenmaier the agreement with Israel was not merely a "document of a new attitude" but also an instrument "to lead Germany out of its ghetto."[41]

The fact that Adenauer was dependent on support from the German Social Democrats to pass the Luxembourg Agreement casts a harsh light on the reservations felt by Germans generally about the notion of restitution—including skepticism expressed in periodicals like *Der Spiegel* and *Die Zeit*. Elisabeth Noelle and Erich-Peter Neumann, who would soon become Adenauer's favorite pollsters, had already surveyed the citizens of the Federal Republic in August 1949 about whether they believed that "Germany has a duty of restitution to the surviving German Jews." A little over half agreed, about a third rejected the idea, and 15 percent were undecided.[42]

The responses to questions regarding the restoration of "Aryanized" assets, which in the Western zones had begun early and in 1957 led to the (controversial) Bundesrückerstattungsgesetz (Federal Restitution Law of 1957), were even more skeptical. In 1949 the Allensbach Institute for Public Opinion Research asked the following question: "If a non-Jew bought a Jewish business after 1933 and the former owner demands that it be returned under the same conditions, would you say that his claim is valid or invalid?" In this case, 39 percent felt that the claim was justified, 28 percent were of the opposite opinion, and 25 percent felt that "it depends." Two years later, in a survey conducted by the American High Commission, 96 percent of respondents were in favor of supporting war widows and orphans, but only 68 percent favored assistance to Jews.[43] Given such clear discrepancies, it should not be surprising that the agreements with Israel and the Claims Conference in August 1952 were favored by a mere 11 percent of West Germans.[44] Of course, the question never even came up in East Germany.

ANTISEMITISM AND PHILOSEMITISM

The strength and "quality" of antisemitism had an enormous impact on how Jews viewed the possibility of life in the two postwar German states. Outside of Germany, obviously, no one believed that the Germans had simply renounced their anti-Jewish attitudes after the end of the Nazi regime. Nonetheless, the sheer presence of the occupying powers had changed the situation dramatically, and the political and legal frameworks that they established ensured that public expressions of antisemitism or even antisemitic riots would be tamped down, if only because legal sanctions were now in place. A completely different question concerns not only the extent to which the new ethical norms had been recognized politically and anchored in law—in the West by the German Basic Law and the programs of the democratic political parties, in the East primarily by the overarching ideology of anti-Fascism—but also the extent to which these new norms had penetrated German society as a whole. After all, more than a decade of carefully inculcated and practiced racist principles and the habits of mind that went along with the racially conceived "people's community" had had a lasting effect that could not simply be wished away.

Certainly, the demographic data that the Americans began gathering in the West shortly after the end of the war, along with the material provided by the Allensbach pollsters after 1949, do not give us a comprehensive picture of the situation on the ground.[45] This is not only because questionnaires filled out by a majority in a society tell us little or nothing about the attitudes or perceptions of a minority, especially when that minority is as small as the tiny community of Jewish DPs, German-Jewish survivors, and Jewish returnees was at the time. It should also be noted that survey methodology was still relatively unsophisticated and that the questions were not generally asked with the necessary consistency. Rather, surveys were often conducted in response to current events and reflected current moods. This was especially true for the political class in the Federal Republic, which viewed antisemitism as an awkward subject best left untouched.

In a longitudinal analysis, Werner Bergmann correlated the data from the Allensbach surveys with those of the newly founded Deutsches Institut für Volksumfragen (German Institute for National Surveys) up to 1955, which had been commissioned by the reaction analysis staff of the American high commissioner for Germany. Bergmann believed that it was too simple to assume that antisemitism had receded more or less continuously since the end of the war.[46] Rather, he found that certain events or incidents, such as the debate over the agreement with Israel, consistently led to measurable increases in antisemitic attitudes. But even the attitudes of West Germans to more or less consistently posed questions,

Table 8.1

	1952	1956	1958	1963	1965
BETTER	37%	26%	22%	18%	19%
NOT BETTER	19%	24%	38%	40%	34%
UNDECIDED	44%	50%	40%	42%	47%

such as whether it would be "better if there were no Jews in the country," changed considerably.[47]

At first glance, the figures shown in table 8.1 would seem easy to interpret, such as the increase of seven percentage points in undecideds between 1958 and 1965. This change may have been attributable to the Auschwitz trial, which was just concluding in Frankfurt. But what exactly can we make of the presumed decrease in tolerance (37 percent to 19 percent between 1952 and 1965 of those saying that it would be better to have no Jews in the country) and so much additional undecidedness? Indifference? Rejection? Ignorance? Or perhaps the fear that the lenient sentences could trigger renewed animosity toward the Germans, who were now peaceable? Or the thought that all of the reports about the horrors of Auschwitz could harm the standing of the Federal Republic in world opinion? In fact, it is advisable to bear in mind that demographic data that yield seemingly unambiguous findings to not unambiguous questions should be taken with a grain of salt.

Nonetheless, it seems plausible overall to assume a self-stifling mechanism rather than a change in attitude with regard to antisemitism during the 1950s and 1960s,[48] not to mention people's growing cynicism about the transparent questions asked by opinion researchers. One thing that one may say with certainty is that the consistent political ostracism of and criminal penalties for antisemitism in the young Federal Republic—with the criminal penalties being somewhat less consistent given the all too frequent inertia in the legal system—had a pronounced effect on public discourse about the Jews.

A more detailed look at the individual stages whereby anti-antisemitism became normative during the Adenauer era yields an often very dynamic interplay between politics and media. And politics did not always take the lead. From the very beginning, several independent and critical journalists and people in public life played an important role. For example, the scandal that engulfed Bundestag delegate Wolfgang Hedler at the end of November 1949 resulted not from his behavior in parliament but from information that came to light in response to a speech he gave in Einfeld in Schleswig-Holstein. Although the SPD-led state government had appealed to the court to conduct an accelerated investigation, without reporting by the *Frankfurter Rundschau*, Hedler's slandering of the German resisters who tried to assassinate Hitler on July 20, 1944, would have remained a regional scandal, as would his remark, "Whether the means for gassing the Jews was the best way, about this one can be of different minds. Perhaps there would have been better ways of ridding ourselves of their kind."[49] Only after the *Rundschau* sounded the alarm did the Council of Elders of the Bundestag agree to lift Hedler's parliamentary immunity, and the German Party, which was in a ruling coalition with the CDU, ejected him from its caucus only after his trial had begun before a district court in Neumünster in Schleswig-Holstein in January 1950. Without the ceaseless attention of the media, which tended to be left leaning, and pressure from the Social Democrats, Hedler's acquittal in the court of first instance—to the jubilation of his supporters—might have been the end of the matter.

This was because of how the judges chose to deal with the question of whether the witnesses to his speech had had the "impression" that Hedler had approved of the "methods" of the National Socialists, namely, gassing. And the three judges (two of them former Nazi Party members) issued a judgment that was obviously preordained: not one of the thirty-seven witnesses who had heard the speech could say that the accused had approved of the methods of the National Socialists. In addition, the members of the German Party went so far as to declare that Hedler had "distanced himself sharply from the gassings." This created a space for the opinion of the court, namely, that it would have been "a gross insult to German Jews" if Hedler had expressed himself literally in the manner that the first witness (a Social Democrat) had claimed. This wrong impression had justifiably angered the press, especially the foreign press, "because it gives the impression as if something like incitement against the Jews is in the process of occurring in Germany once again. It is clear that such statements as the accused is charged with having made do extraordinary damage to our reputation, especially abroad. Therefore, anyone who is guilty of such irresponsible statements bears an enormous burden of guilt, and the court wishes there to be no doubt that it would have punished the accused exemplarily with imprisonment if his guilt had been proved. However, it was not."[50] And of course, given the testimony of so many witnesses, no insult to the Jews could be demonstrated.

However, the court did find the criterion of threats to the peace according to Paragraph 130 of the penal code to have been met. The statement by the expert witness Hendrik George van Dam from the Jewish legal protection office in Hamburg claimed that Hedler's remarks had had an "agitating effect on the class of Jewish citizens." However, the accused, it was found, had intentionally incited neither physical violence nor "class warfare." For him to have done that, Hedler would have had to have been conscious that his statements were apt "one day to give impetus to the class of non-Jewish citizens to proceed with violence against the class of Jewish citizens. He would furthermore have had to approve inwardly of the potential eventuation of such an outcome, and if such had actually occurred, would have had to have wanted it (*dolus eventualis*). However, in the opinion of the court the preponderance of the evidence gathered in no way suffices for such a finding." Consequently, the accused was acquitted for lack of evidence "on the count of Jews." And the judges in Kiel even found ways to dismiss all of the other counts against Hedler.

Among the representatives of the approximately thirty Jewish religious communities who protested to President Heuss against the "shameful verdict" and the "collective insult" was Moritz Goldschmidt, the chair of the religious community in Cologne. In his telegram, he warned: "All efforts by the Jews in Germany who are committed to understanding and reconciliation, and who advocate abroad for giving the Federal Republic the opportunity to demonstrate goodwill and to come into contact with all the democratically thinking peoples, are condemned to failure by such verdicts." Unimpressed by the way the large majority of the West German press chastised the verdict—as observers from the American High Commission noted with relief—Goldschmidt interpreted the acquittal as a warning sign for the young democracy: "We must consider whether or not to draw the ultimate conclusion from this. We cannot permit our small body of survivors of persecution by the Nazi regime to be subjected to new dangers."[51]

Given the immensity of such fears, which were undoubtedly shared by other Jewish communities as well, the corrective to that verdict was not exactly swift in coming. The higher regional court in Kiel, to which the public prosecutor's office had appealed, sent the matter back to the district court for another hearing. It took until July 20, 1951, for Hedler to be sentenced to nine months in prison for "public defamation in coincidence with public slandering of the memory of the deceased and with public defamation." Hedler served about two-thirds of the sentence; his appeal to the Federal Supreme Court was rejected, as was his complaint to the Federal Constitutional Court.

Noteworthy in the Hedler affair was how critical was the determination of those who had been persecuted to ensure that this scandal would not only be forgotten but become a vital element in the critical examination of National Socialism and antisemitism. The Social Democrats and their chairperson, Kurt Schumacher, whom Hedler had smeared as traitors to their country, had felt especially challenged ever since the initial press reports. That was probably also why Rudolf Katz, who had returned from exile in the United States in 1946 and had since 1947 served as justice minister of Schleswig-Holstein, gratefully accepted the suggestion from his fellow party member Jakob Altmaier that "you as a member of the Jewish race bring suit yourself against your Bundestag colleague Hedler for the statements that he made about the Jews in his speech. The public prosecutor's office sees it as urgently advisable that such a suit be brought by a German Jew."[52] Hynek Lewitt from the town of Eutin served as coplaintiff, so that in the end it was left to two Jews to raise their voices against the insult to the "members of the Jewish community."

The intensity of the debate probably led McCloy to conclude that if Hedler "did in fact say the things which are attributed to him, I doubt that he can or will ever be acquitted morally by public opinion of the world, or indeed, of Germany."[53] With this statement, the high commissioner introduced an idea into public discourse the full import of which few contemporaries probably recognized, although some had undoubtedly concluded, namely, that the Germans could not hope to escape their "recent past" anytime soon.

In the early 1950s such an idea was foreign, even to the most determined and vocal opponents of antisemitism, who advanced the cause of social enlightenment often by unearthing scandals. This was true of Erich Lüth, who played a prominent role early on.[54] In September 1950 Lüth, head of the state press office in Hamburg, called for a boycott of the screen adaptation of a story by Theodor Storm ("Aquis submersus") titled *Unsterbliche Liebe* (Undying love), which was to be director Veit Harlan's postwar debut. This had been preceded by a series of sensational trials in which Harlan, the director of the 1940 film *Jud Süss* (Süss the Jew), had, by means of absurd, self-serving assertions, been exonerated of having aided and abetted in the persecution of Jews. A jury court in Hamburg found that although "the fact of the crime against humanity had been demonstrated in objective and subjective respects," Harlan had not acted under orders from Goebbels.[55]

Lüth's public attacks on "Nazi film director No. 1," "who is the least suitable of all" to restore the moral reputation of German film, were echoed by the Social Democrats and the unions. But in the spring of 1949, after Harlan's initial exoneration, the conservative Catholic monthly *Neues Abendland* (New Occident) asked how it was possible to deny that, "given the atmosphere in the Third Reich, the film *Jud Süss* had abetted in the acts of mass murder, that it had simply served to create a moral alibi for these acts, with its help priming 'healthy public sentiment' so that it approved of the horrible misdeeds of tyranny or at the very least, doubting, accepted them silently." The journal seems to have sensed what lay ahead: "What is shocking about our times is that today every revealed truth can be argued away, crushed underfoot, and falsified. One merely needs to be brazen enough to try it."[56]

And this was precisely how Harlan's production company proceeded—with a petition for a temporary injunction against Lüth. At the same time, his distributor in Frankfurt, where the magistrate of the city had spoken out against the performance of the Storm adaptation, organized a "referendum." Allegedly, 88.6 percent of those surveyed agreed with the Association for the Protection of

Democratic Rights, which then used this figure in its advertising for *Unsterbliche Liebe*—neglecting to mention that two-thirds of the one hundred thousand ballots that had supposedly been distributed were never filled out. And as if that was not enough, the director sought President Heuss's assistance, claiming to be an innocent and persecuted artist. But the debate had by now come to such a boil that Heuss felt it necessary to take a position, in answer to Harlan, on the legal rights of the individual. "Moral justification," so the president claimed in both vague and soothing words, could "not be enforced by the powers of the state." Nonetheless, he was persuaded that "public opinion develops a correct elementary feeling of guilt and responsibility."[57] Whatever Heuss was attempting to indicate, the legal system proved intransigent. In November 1951 Erich Lüth was legally banned from making statements against Harlan or influencing the film distributor or the theater owner and by so doing attempting to hinder the denazified director from making a new professional start.

Outraged by such rulings and supported by Adolf Arndt, the legal expert of the SPD faction in the Bundestag,[58] the director of the senate appealed to the Federal Constitutional Court. Lüth, who had initiated the "Peace with Israel" campaign and was a cofounder of the Society for Christian-Jewish Cooperation in Hamburg, understood full well that his freedom of expression had been compromised. The judge in Karlsruhe did not hand down his ruling until early 1958, but in it he confirmed that freedom of expression is "one of the primary human rights." Because it is "quite simply constitutive" of a free democratic society, this fundamental right takes precedence over the right to unimpeded economic activity of the sort that Harlan's attorneys attempted to claim.

The high court's decision in the Lüth case has gone down in the history of German constitutional jurisprudence as a milestone that continues to be cited today. Hardly less important than the privilege given to freedom of expression, however, was what the court in its opinion had to say—and expressly recognized—about Lüth's motives:

He was moved by the concern that Harlan's reappearance could—especially abroad—be interpreted to mean that nothing had changed in German cultural life since National Socialist times; as he had been then, Harlan was now once again the representative German film director. These fears concerned a very important question for the German people, namely that of its moral posture and the respect in the world upon which it hinges. Nothing has so damaged Germany's reputation as the brutal persecution of the Jews by National Socialism. There therefore exists a decisive interest that the world may be assured that the German people has rejected this mentality and condemns it not for reasons of political opportunism but rather as a result of insight into its reprehensibility gained through its own inner conversion.[59]

With this passage, the Federal Constitutional Court in Karlsruhe firmly established the rhetoric of anti-antisemitism that has become standard in Bonn. It has always served as a statement of principle to the world at large and has been referenced even more frequently whenever exculpatory statements have been made in Germany concerning the Nazi past or antisemitic incidents have made the headlines. But the court went out of its way to recognize and praise voices in society that it viewed as exemplary, such as the position taken by forty-eight professors at the University of Göttingen who in early 1952 had spoken out against the director in the *Deutsche Universitätszeitung* (German university newspaper).[60] Carlo Schmid was also quoted in the opinion. A Social Democrat, Schmid had been shocked into action when student protesters in Freiburg were beaten by police.[61] He protested in the Bundestag that "in of all places at the seat of the German parliament, which in this country to an extraordinary extent must be the protector and herald of true tolerance, films are screened by a man who at least indirectly contributed to creating the mass-psychological preconditions for the gassings in Auschwitz."[62] Schmid was applauded by almost all factions of the Bundestag when he called it "a disgrace that the concoctions of this man can even be shown and attended in Germany." This response was undoubtedly just as much a judgment on the director's unworthiness as it was a reaction to the impertinence with which Harlan and his wife, the actress Kristina Söderbaum, played on the emotions of their fans—a fatal mixture of defiance and loyalty that was rooted in Nazi times. But there was probably another intention as well behind Schmid's efforts to make people forget these favorites of Goebbels, along with their works. As much as he was appalled by Harlan's movie, he was also uncomfortable with the idea of a renewed discussion of *Jud Süss*, a film that was intended to be understood as an open call to deport the Jews.[63] After all, the production company's advertisements read: "*Jud Süss* tears the mask from the face of the Jews and shows our people the path to liberating action."[64]

Ambiguous motives characterized many, if not all, gestures of early philosemitism. The goodwill that motivated activists like Erich Lüth often went hand in hand with their impatience with the protracted process of reconciliation. In their fight against Harlan, as in their enthusiasm for Israel, they spoke from the very beginning of "reconciliation" and even "normalization." But their efforts were often met with skepticism; with its customary cynicism, *Der Spiegel*, for example, mocked Lüth's unannounced exploratory trip to the Near East in the spring of 1953: "What 'Israel-Lüth'—that's what his friends call him with a mixture of mischief and respect—dictated to reporters upon landing at Hamburg-Fuhlsbüttel [Airport] with the 'Flying Dutchman' was the observation that, as before, the German-Israeli relationship continues to require the greatest circumspection. The Israelis who had emigrated from former German-occupied

Veit Harlan after his acquittal, April 1949. bpk / Bayerische Staatsbibliothek / Archiv Heinrich Hoffmann.

countries are still suffering from what they experienced. Unlike a large part of the German people, they cannot so quickly forget the millions of liquidated Jews."[65]

INSTITUTIONALIZED RECONCILIATION

The overwhelming need to forget was also the basis for the work of the societies for Christian-Jewish cooperation that had been founded since 1948. Neither the idea nor the initiative for them originated with Germans in the postwar era; instead, they came from the United States, to be precise, from the National Conference of Christians and Jews, which had been founded in the 1920s. Carl F. Zietlow, a Methodist pastor from Minnesota and now working for the U.S. military government, laid out a framework for such associations that was closely patterned on an American model. He envisioned an "educational program to overcome intolerance and antisemitism" that would be overseen by a coordinating council and implemented in small groups. Financed by American funders, the first local societies were limited to the American zone; after Munich, where in November 1947 the Committee to Fight Antisemitism was founded, they were followed by similar groups in Wiesbaden, Stuttgart, Frankfurt, and Berlin.[66]

These Christian-Jewish societies typically had three chairmen, Catholic, Protestant, and Jewish. The number of members was less important to the founders than their reputation and influence. As in the United States, the societies were to function as "a kind of Rotary Club of the well-intentioned and well-meaning."[67] For Pastor Zietlow, the future and the long history of German-Jewish cultural accomplishment were more important than the immediate past.[68] As a result, the coordinating council in Bad Nauheim tended to publish and organize conferences on the foundations of Western culture, evidence of fraternal and humane thinking in the eighteenth century, and German classicism. Additionally, the council published practical works for educators ("Overcome Your Prejudices") and books for young people. In terms of the Nazi past, although the council's program dealt with the persecution of the Christian churches and their resistance, it had nothing to say about the persecution of the Jews or the extermination camps.[69]

During the first few years of Christian-Jewish cooperation, very little attention was paid to German crimes generally, nor was there any attempt to deal with the antisemitism that was still endemic in German society. Every once in a while, criticisms were heard about applying American methods too directly to the German landscape.[70] But they tended to hew to a model that seemed to underscore the society's desire for discretion. "Our fight advances steadily; however, it does not enter the public arena," as the business manager of the Stuttgart society wrote in his annual report for 1952–1953. "We are not interested in publicizing all of the negative things, but intend rather to draw the attention of our fellow citizens to the most difficult problems, but in a positive light."[71] Significantly, the Stuttgart board members—three Jews, one Catholic, and one Protestant—did not wish to be photographed together because, they thought, it would give the public "an unfavorable impression."[72]

Although such calculations were probably not the rule among the local societies, they were not the exception either.[73] It is difficult to know at this remove what sorts of considerations motivated the individuals or, for example, how many of the non-Jewish Germans were trying to deal with—or gloss over—their own past by their involvement in such groups. In any case, in the summer of 1949, when the Munich society protested to the coordinating council about the "immense exaggeration" of McCloy's characterization of antisemitism in Germany, Franz Böhm, the Protestant chair of the Frankfurt society, had a clear response. It cannot be the task of the societies, he noted, to absolve the majority of the Germans of their guilt and responsibility for the murder of the Jews or to use their Jewish members to shield the German people from criticism from abroad. "We have not come together," Böhm declared, "to document to the world that there are Germans who reject antisemitism, who turned away 'in horror and revulsion' from the persecution of the Jews even during the Third Reich. Rather, we have come together to oppose antisemitism, and to form a determined, active, influential, and effective countermovement to that inhuman prejudice."[74]

Böhm knew what he was talking about. A lawyer and economist, he had, like Max Horkheimer, Theodor W. Adorno, and Friedrich Pollock, returned to Frankfurt and the Institute for Social Research from exile in the United States. Böhm wrote a pessimistic foreword to the institute's famous "group experiment," a large-scale study, funded by the American High Commission, of the authoritarian mentality and prejudices of the postwar Germans. In it, he contrasted the "purified views of proper public opinion" with the "poorly washed and often distinctly malodorous opinions of non-public opinion," and, shocked, he noted the extent to which "the most malicious and callous arrogance" still holds sway in the minds of the "Müllers and Schulzes" of Germany.[75] Two years later, Adenauer asked Böhm to lead the German delegation in restitution negotiations with Israel.

When the Americans stopped financing Christian-Jewish cooperation in 1952, the federal government and the states took up the slack. The title of the budgetary fund that financed this work makes clear what policymakers hoped to gain from the coordinating council and the societies: "Promotion of Efforts to Fight Racial Hatred and Demagoguery."[76] In line with this, there would now be a Week of Brotherhood throughout the country, the model for which was the World Brotherhood, which had been founded in Paris in the summer of 1950 under American auspices and sought to bring together Christian-Jewish associations from various nations. And in fact, twelve European countries (along with the United States and Canada) responded to the proposal for regular spring meetings.[77]

The first such weeklong event in West Germany took place on March 7–16, 1952. Theodor Heuss gave the opening address, which was broadcast throughout the Federal Republic. German postal authorities designed a special postmark, and the cultural ministry ensured that brotherhood would be the topic of discussion in schools that week. Parties and politicians, high church dignitaries and representatives of the Jewish communities, representatives from the trade unions and industry, scientists and journalists, the Association of German Cities and Towns, the *Börsenblatt für den Deutschen Buchhandel* (German book trade gazette), and radio stations all lent their support to these events, which took place in nineteen cities, often in close cooperation with local "America Houses." Events included performances of Verdi's *La forza del destino* and Mozart's *Die Zauberflöte* in Munich, a celebration in the ceremonial room of Landshut city hall, a slide show about German war graves in Augsburg, an afternoon social for the elderly and poor and a visit with American military families in Stuttgart, a celebration for white and black orphans in Wiesbaden—all accompanied by lectures about brotherhood. Religious topics were presented along with issues relating to minorities, human rights, and the problem of social justice. But only in Augsburg did two young historians talk about the history of the local Jewish community, including that of the years after 1933.[78]

The Central Council of Jews in Germany had been restrained in its response to the brotherhood weeks. The *Allgemeine Wochenzeitung* made clear that it was not looking for "bombastic declarations" but "simple acts of human friendship that spread peace, a peace in this world."[79]

Initiated by the Americans and non-Jewish Germans, the Week of Brotherhood would remain for decades the same elite project as at its outset. Nonetheless, the early criticism that was leveled at it missed the mark in that it was limited to its critique of the events either as "philosemitic rituals" or as an institutionalization of religious dialogue, which had undoubtedly been the emphasis at the beginning.[80] Because aside from the potential for real social encounters between Jews and non-Jews, which were otherwise very rare, the events always provided an opportunity for Germans to examine what for most was a very uncomfortable topic: the existence of National Socialist ideology in the present. For this reason, particularly during the early years, these events provided a regular focus for the minority of Germans unwilling to accept the "repression" of the past that had become such a feature of contemporary German reality. As such, these events should not be underestimated.

Two speeches at the Week of Brotherhood in 1955, which the coordinating council published in pamphlet form and distributed as far abroad as the United States, make this function clear. For example, although expressing himself in the rhetorically awkward antitotalitarian mode of the times, Bundestag president Eugen Gerstenmaier used the opportunity to define the country's political task ten years after the end of the war: "I believe that, for example, in Germany neither Communism nor National Socialism will have a real chance with the next generation. Nonetheless, the state will always stand before the task of combating the stubborn remnants of National Socialism and of militant Communism and of eradicating all attempts at violating the state by intolerance."[81] Adolf Freudenberg, the pastor of a refugee community in Bad Vilbel and since 1952 active in a "Protestant working circle in Hessen and Nassau in service to Israel," seconded this sentiment in graphic terms: "We should not let ourselves be fooled; these journeymen of evil are still in our midst, many of them. And it will be quite a job for each of us to deal with these subterranean and hidden forces. The nightmarish figures of the final act of the National Socialist regime have not yet completely disappeared, sunk and dissolved into smoke and dust and nothingness."[82]

When acknowledged opponents of Nazism like Gerstenmaier and Freudenberg—the former a member of the Kreisau Circle, the latter a returnee—supported the work of the coordinating council, it was out of more than noncommittal philosemitism. And when, in its annual report, titled "5 Years of Work against Prejudice," the Christian-Jewish Society of Berlin declared it "foolish to expect so-called concrete successes," it could point with pride to the cooperation that it had enabled with schools, adult education centers, and institutions of higher learning, which had had an "awakening effect."[83] Among other things, it could point to the "Erlebnisbericht aus der Zeit der Verfolgung" (Experiences from the time of persecution), a report that Jewish cochair Siegmund Weltlinger had presented to the public at the America House on January 30, 1954, fifty thousand copies of which were eventually printed. The former stock trader vividly recalled Kristallnacht and the terrors of deportation, which he as a member of the Jewish community knew all too well. And he described the circumstances under which he and his wife had been able to survive in hiding after 1943. "Have you really forgotten so soon?" he asked. "No, you may have repressed your consciousness of it, but you haven't forgotten. Human beings so easily tend to repress into the unconscious all that is uncomfortable. But this is not right." Weltlinger concluded, "Therefore, tell your children, your parents, tell it to your students, your teachers, over and over again! Then we may hope that with God's help never again will such a shadow fall over Germany, a shadow that must obscure for the world the great virtues of this people."[84]

In those years, it was hard to find people who could express matters as clearly as Weltlinger had. Nonetheless, this basically conservative man—a member of the CDU in Berlin since 1946 and a CDU delegate to the Berlin State Parliament in 1959—got the tone right that the coordinating council was striving for even in the late 1950s: "Help us, and you help Germany, whose reputation in the future will be determined by how it responds to the Jewish question posed to it."[85]

MICHAEL BRENNER is Professor of Jewish history and culture at the University of Munich and Seymour and Lillian Abensohn Chair in Israel Studies at American University in Washington, DC. He is a member of the Bavarian Academy of Sciences and international president of the Leo Baeck Institute. Brenner's publications include *A Short History of the Jews*, *Prophets of the Past: Interpreters of Jewish History*, *Zionism: A Short History*, and as coauthor, the four-volume *German-Jewish History in Modern Times*.

NORBERT FREI is Professor of modern and contemporary history at the University of Jena and is director of the Jena Center 20th Century History. During the 2008–2009 academic year, he was a member of the Institute for Advanced Study in Princeton, and in 2010–2011 he was Theodor Heuss Professor at the New School for Social Research in New York. Frei's publications include *1968: Jugen-*

drevolte und globaler Protest, 1945 und wir: Das Dritte Reich im Bewußtsein der Deutschen, and *Adenauer's Germany and the Nazi Past: The Politics of Amnesty and Integration;* he is also coauthor of *Das Amt und die Vergangenheit: Deutsche Diplomaten im Dritten Reich und in der Bundesrepublik.*

NOTES

1. BT, 1. WP, stenographic reports, meeting on September 20, 1949, pp. 22–30.

2. http://images.library.wisc.edu/History/EFacs/GerRecon/Gparliament/reference /history.gparliament.adenauerk1.pdf, p. 25 (last accessed February 25, 2016); for more details, see N. Frei (1996), pp. 27–28.

3. http://images.library.wisc.edu/History/EFacs/GerRecon/Gparliament/reference /history.gparliament.adenauerk1.pdf, p. 25.

4. See also J. Zieher (2005), p. 168.

5. http://images.library.wisc.edu/History/EFacs/GerRecon/Gparliament/reference /history.gparliament.schumacherk.pdf, p. 33; subsequent quotations are from this same source.

6. http://images.library.wisc.edu/History/EFacs/GerRecon/Gparliament/reference /history.gparliament.schumacherk.pdf, p. 33.

7. http://images.library.wisc.edu/History/EFacs/GerRecon/Gparliament/reference /history.gparliament.richterf.pdf, p. 87.

8. See Richter-Roessler, "Gesinnung behalten," *Der Spiegel,* February 27, 1952, p. 28.

9. http://images.library.wisc.edu/History/EFacs/GerRecon/Gparliament/reference /history.gparliament.richterf.pdf, p. 87.

10. BT, 1. WP, stenographic reports, meeting on September 12, 1949, p. 10.

11. For example, several weeks after taking office, he assisted Ernst von Weizsäcker, the former secretary of state of the Foreign Office who had been sentenced to seven years' imprisonment at the Nuremberg Wilhelmstrasse trial; see E. Conze et al. (2010), p. 433; N. Frei (1996), p. 180.

12. T. Heuss (1964b); for English, see also http://images.library.wisc.edu/History/EFacs /GerRecon/omg1950Jan/reference/history.omg1950jan.heusscourage.pdf, p. 5 (last accessed February 25, 2015).

13. Remarks by John J. McCloy, High Commissioner US Zone in Germany, in Office of Adviser on Jewish Affairs (ed.), Conference on "The Future of the Jews in Germany," Heidelberg, July 31, 1949, pp. 20–22. See also K. Marx, "Realistische Arbeit: Gründung der Dachorganisation der Juden in Deutschland," *AWJD,* August 5, 1949, p. 1.

14. Copy in LBI, AR 491.

15. Letter from Rudolf Jorysz to Theodor Heuss, May 5, 1950, in BArch, B 122/2083.

16. T. Heuss (1964b); for English, see also http://images.library.wisc.edu/History/EFacs /GerRecon/omg1950Jan/reference/history.omg1950jan.heusscourage.pdf, p. 5 (last accessed February 25, 2015); see also F. Stern (1991), p. 298.

17. See also F. Stern (1990), pp. 180–196.

18. T. Heuss (1964a), p. 113.

19. Letter from Theodor Heuss to Karl Marx, August 2, 1956, in BArch, B 122/2086.

20. T. Heuss (1964a), pp. 118–119.

21. T. Heuss (1964c), esp. p. 162.

22. For more, and summarizing the following, see C. Goschler (2007); H. G. Hockerts, "Wiedergutmachung in Deutschland," *Vierteljahrshefte für Zeitgeschichte* 49 (2001).

23. See J. P. Spannuth (2007); J. Herf, "Antisemitismus in der SED," *Vierteljahrshefte für Zeitgeschichte* 42 (1994).

24. Along these lines, see N. Frei et al. (eds.) (2009), introduction, esp. p. 15.

25. See A. Sinn (2011), p. 180.

26. K. Marx and K. Adenauer (1996), p. 295.

27. For these discussions, see BArch, B 122/2080, B 145/4123. For Altmaier's role, see C. Moß (2006).

28. BT, 1. WP, stenographic reports, meeting on September 27, 1951, pp. 6697–6698; the following quotations are from the same source.

29. For details on the Hedler case, see N. Frei (1996), pp. 309–325.

30. BT, 1. WP, stenographic reports, meeting on September 27, 1951, p. 6698; the following quotations are from the same source.

31. See N. Frei et al. (eds.) (2009), pp. 25–26.

32. BT, 1. WP, stenographic reports, meeting on September 27, 1951, p. 6700.

33. Quoted from BPA (ed.), *Deutschland und das Judentum* (Bonn, 1951), p. 9, in AJA, MS16, D4.7.

34. BPA (ed.), *Deutschland und das Judentum*, p. 11.

35. BPA (ed.), *Deutschland und das Judentum*, p. 10.

36. Letter from Konrad Adenauer to Nahum Goldmann, December 6, 1951, in Mensing (ed.) (1987), p. 150; see also J. Deligdisch (1974), p. 18.

37. BT, 1. WP, stenographic reports, meeting on March 4, 1953, p. 12092; the following quotations are from the same source.

38. BT, 1. WP, stenographic reports, meeting on March 4, 1953 p. 12362.

39. BT, 1. WP, stenographic reports, meeting on March 4, 1953, p. 12276.

40. See also N. Frei, "Von deutscher Erfindungskraft," in N. Frei (2009), pp. 228–233.

41. BT, 1. WP, stenographic reports, meeting on March 4, 1953, p. 12276.

42. Cited from C. Goschler (2007), p. 133.

43. C. Goschler (2007), p. 133.

44. C. Goschler (2007), p. 134. See also W. Bergmann (1990b), p. 108.

45. No data whatsoever exist for the GDR; however, one may assume relatively small differences during the early years.

46. W. Bergmann (1990b), p. 108.

47. W. Bergmann (1990b), p. 115.

48. W. Bergmann (1990b), pp. 112–113, speaks of increasing "communication latencies."

49. "From the Bonn office: 'Geteilte Meinung' eines Abgeordneten über Vergasung von Juden," *Frankfurter Rundschau*, December 12, 1949, p. 2; for more detail, see N. Frei (2003), chap. III.1; the following data and quotations are from the same source.

50. This and the following quotations are from the available printed written opinion (with annexes), March 9, 1950, in ADL, N1/1005.

51. For the American High Commission's response to the verdict, see "The Hedler Case," *HICOG Information Bulletin*, April 1950, pp. 43–45. Quote from letter from Moritz Goldschmidt to Theodor Heuss, February 17, 1950, cited in J. Zieher (2005), p. 251.

52. Letter from Jakob Altmaier to Rudolf Katz, January 3, 1950, in AdsD, 1/JAAA 4.

53. AP report, cited in *Frankfurter Allgemeine Zeitung*, February 16, 1950, p. 3; English wording in *HICOG Information Bulletin*, April 1950, p. 43, http://images.library.wisc.edu /History/EFacs/GerRecon/omg1950April/reference/history.omg1950april.i0020.pdf (last accessed February 25, 2016).

54. Greater detail in T. Henne and A. Riedlinger (eds.) (2005), especially the chapters by F. Liebert (2005) and A. Riedlinger (2005); see also P. Reichel (2001), pp. 129–138; P. Reichel and H. Schmid (2005), pp. 32–35.

55. Quoted from BVerfG Urteil, January 15, 1958 (1 BvR 400/51); the following quotation is from there as well.

56. Quoted from F. Liebert (2005), p. 111.

57. Quoted from A. Riedlinger (2005), pp. 166–167.

58. See D. Gosewinkel (1991), pp. 493–498.

59. BVerfG Urteil, January 15, 1958 (1 BvR 400/51).

60. See W. Kraushaar (1996), esp. vol. 1, pp. 542–544, 548, 551, and vol. 2, pp. 749, 942.

61. See A. Riedlinger (2005), pp. 170–173. The students were protesting the latest Harlan film titled *Hanna Amon*; see also Leo Wohlleb, *Der Spiegel*, January 23, 1952, p. 37. The demonstrations continued for years. On March 24, 1954, *Der Spiegel* (p. 34) reported on protests by "young troublemakers" against Harlan's film *Sterne über Colombo* in Berlin-Charlottenburg. The head of the SPD faction, Franz Neumann, who happened to be passing by, had encouraged the young people.

62. BT, 1. WP, stenographic reports, meeting on February 29, 1952, p. 8474; BVerfG Urteil, January 15, 1958 (1 BvR 400/51). After Schmid's speech, Harlan wrote a long letter to SPD Bundestag member Jakob Altmaier asking for support for his request, "in particular to be heard before a committee of the Bundestag"; letter from Veit Harlan to Jakob Altmaier, May 7, 1952, in AdsD, 1/JAAA 3.

63. See D. Kuhlbrodt (1997), p. 101.

64. Quoted from W. Kraushaar (1995), p. 8.

65. "Israel-Tour: Der Reisende aus Cypern," *Der Spiegel*, April 29, 1953, pp. 14–15.

66. Essential both here and in the following, J. Foschepoth and W. Jochmann (1993), pp. 61–74; see also J. Foschepoth (1991); J. Foschepoth (2001); F. Stern (1991), pp. 284–298; F. Stern (1992b), pp. 182–209.

67. J. Foschepoth and W. Jochmann (1993), p. 119.

68. J. Foschepoth and W. Jochmann (1993), p. 124.

69. J. Foschepoth and W. Jochmann (1993), pp. 125–126.

70. J. Foschepoth and W. Jochmann (1993), p. 124.

71. Quoted from J. Foschepoth (1991), p. 65.

72. J. Foschepoth (1991), p. 69.

73. See P. Kratz (2016).

74. Quoted from J. Foschepoth and W. Jochmann (1993), p. 67.

75. F. Pollock (ed.) (1955), pp. xvi–xvii.

76. J. Foschepoth and W. Jochmann (1993), p. 140.

77. J. Foschepoth and W. Jochmann (1993), pp. 141–142.

78. J. Foschepoth and W. Jochmann (1993), pp. 145–148; see also J. Foschepoth (2001), pp. 262–264.

79. "Eine Oase der Nachdenklichkeit," *AWJD*, March 7, 1952, p. 1, quoted from J. Foschepoth and W. Jochmann (1993), p. 148.

80. "Philosemitic rituals" is from F. Stern (1990), p. 186.

81. Eugen Gerstenmaier, "Aufgabe und Grenze der Toleranz, Rede zur Eröffnung der 'Woche der Brüderlichkeit,' Munich, March 6, 1955," reprinted in *Zwei Reden*, published by the Deutsche Koordinierungsrat der Gesellschaften für Christlich-Jüdische Zusammenarbeit, Frankfurt am Main, 1955, in LBI, AR 493.

82. Adolf Freudenberg, "Der verpflichtende Hintergrund unserer Arbeit," in *Zwei Reden*, published by the Deutscher Koordinierungsrat der Gesellschaften für Christlich-Jüdische Zusammenarbeit, Frankfurt am Main, 1955, p. 10, in LBI, AR 493.

83. "Gesellschaft für Christlich-Jüdische Zusammenarbeit Berlin 5 Jahre Arbeit gegen das Vorurteil," Berlin 1954, in LBI, AR 492.

84. Siegmund Weltlinger, "Hast Du es schon vergessen? Erlebnisbericht aus der Zeit der Verfolgung," pp. 2, 30, in LBI, AR 492.

85. J. Foschepoth (1991), pp. 69–70.

9 GERMANS AND JEWS DURING THE DECADE OF THE "ENLIGHTENMENT"

OLD AND NEW HATRED OF THE JEWS

Toward the end of the 1950s, the phrase "unmastered past" began to crop up in the political language of the Federal Republic. This locution originated in Protestant discussion circles and academies before becoming increasingly commonplace in Christian-Jewish dialogue. Once it entered the political lexicon, it came to signify the process of self-enlightenment that was taking hold in West Germany. This transformation in West German society had two major causes. The first, and only seemingly paradoxical, was the far-reaching exculpation of the Nazi past that took place during the initial two legislative terms, an exculpation that led to an almost endless chain of scandals involving personal and institutional continuities with that past. The second was the growing political presence of younger generations. Former members of the Hitler Youth and young people (sometimes children) who had been deployed in antiaircraft positions at the end of the war began to take part in public discourse and in effect supported the formerly persecuted intellectuals who had since the occupation years voiced support for enlightenment and democracy. Many of these young people had learned from their experiences and were now pragmatic members of what the German sociologist Helmut Schelsky called the "skeptical generation." They were soon joined by the rising generation of children born during the war and in the immediate postwar period, who would later be identified as the generation of 1968.

Measured solely by the number of people involved, support for "mastering the past" was comparatively modest in the mid- to late 1960s, and proponents were fairly cautious in their advocacy. But from the beginning, their cause had a moral valence that was fed by the wall of silence that surrounded the murder of the Jews and the guilt and complicity of the German people in that murder. One early and impressive example of the dynamic that resulted from this suppression of awareness was the protests—supported internationally—by professors and students at the University of Göttingen in the spring of 1955, which forced a right-wing radical to resign from the Culture Ministry of Lower Saxony.

After a dubious career during the first few years after the war and a variety of forays into ultranationalist party politics in 1951, Leonhard Schlüter became a delegate of the extremist German Reich Party in the state parliament of Lower Saxony, although he soon switched over to the Free Democratic Party (FDP). There, Schlüter rose in the right wing of the party to become deputy head of the party faction. He was nominated to run for culture minister in the Landtag elections of May 26, 1955, in a Bürgerblock alliance of conservative parties that opposed the SPD and consisted of the German Party (DP), the CDU, the League of Expellees and Deprived of Rights (Bund der Heimatvertriebenen und Entrechteten, BHE), and the FDP. On May 26, 1955, the day he was to have been sworn in, the rector, the members of the senate, and the deans of the university resigned in protest—whereupon the students joined the protest. They went on strike and held a torchlight procession.[1]

What was unusual about the Schlüter affair was that his numerous opponents did not level specific charges against him or accuse him of neo-Nazi statements but rather attacked him on principled grounds for his unsuitability for office—for reasons of political hygiene, so to speak. An article in the respected *Deutsche Universitätszeitung* (German university newspaper) dated June 8, 1955, put it as follows: "The Schlüter case has become a touchstone of the spirit of freedom in the Federal Republic. By it we may see who stands for democracy in form only and who in terms of fundamentals; who wishes to preserve the spirit of the authoritarian state within democratic forms and who intends to defend a liberal concept of the state, if need be against parliamentary abuse. The Schlüter case allows us to gauge the future of our state."[2]

A day later, the minister, a mere two weeks into his term and already on leave, resigned—so quickly that *Der Spiegel*, usually right on top of political developments, was forced to reconstruct the fiasco after the fact.[3] The news magazine's cover story detailed Schlüter's professional career over many pages. Among other things, in 1939 this son of a World War I officer and a Jewish mother had applied to join the Wehrmacht and was accepted, even though he was a "half-Jew" in accordance with the Nuremberg Laws. Schlüter was seriously wounded in combat, but when he applied for a position as an officer, his application was rejected, and he was discharged. Nonetheless, he was admitted to the University of Göttingen, where he studied law. Because he was barred from taking the state examinations for "racial reasons," he began to write his doctorate under Rudolf Smend, although he failed the oral examination (the aptly called *Rigorosum*) in 1944. After the war, he did a brief and undistinguished stint as head of the criminal police in Göttingen and then worked with the British Field Secret Service (BFSS) before becoming a publisher of more or less apologetic works on the "recent past." His publishing house, the Göttinger Verlagsanstalt für Wissenschaft und Politik, published short pieces by Hitler's vice chancellor, Franz von Papen; the former head of the Gestapo, Rudolf Diels; and a number of professors who had been forced from their positions during the denazification process. The latter included Herbert Grabert, who had previously been a lecturer in Würzburg in what under the Nazis was called *Weltanschauungskunde* ("worldviewology") and a consultant in the Reich Ministry for the Occupied Eastern Territories. Schlüter's screed titled "Hochschullehrer klagen an: Von der Demontage deutscher Wissenschaft" (University professors accuse: On the dismantling of German scholarship) met with considerable disapproval in the proud university city of Göttingen. Summarizing its research, *Der Spiegel* characterized him as follows: "Neither before 1945 nor afterward did Leonhard Schlüter wish to be a 'half-Jew' but rather a German patriot of equal standing. He attempted to balance his provenance, which he viewed as a stain, by outdoing his patriotic-minded countrymen in nationalist zeal." The report also made clear that Schlüter's mother had avoided deportation shortly before the end of the war only because a member of the SA and one from the Gestapo interceded on her behalf. As Schlüter told it, "The fact that they helped me back then was one of the reasons why I decided to help National Socialists after 1945."[4]

At the high point of the protests and public controversy, Schlüter's name was painted, replete with swastikas, on the pavement in front of the university. But his resignation was not the end of the matter; the political activities of Schlüter's opponents continued unabated. Rectors and professors throughout Lower Saxony expressed solidarity, as did faculty members in Marburg, Tübingen, Freiburg, and Bonn and at the Free University of Berlin. News of this movement spread rapidly through intellectual circles in the West. The International Committee for Science and Freedom mobilized Raymond Aron (Paris), Edward Shils (Chicago), Sidney Hook (New York), and a number of prominent German-Jewish émigrés. In a telegram sent to Prime Minister Heinrich Hellwege (DP) of Lower Saxony, the committee declared that the naming of a neo-Nazi minister of education posed an "immediate threat."[5] However, the Frankfurt student newspaper *Diskurs* was more direct in its assessment of Schlüter's danger: "He is a big talker of the young platoon-leader type whose career was frequently stymied by the war, formed in a thousand years [i.e., by the Thousand Year Reich], embittered by its collapse. These men embody many of the feelings of their voters and represent a force that is still hard to gauge."[6]

It should hardly be surprising that the political and legal process, given the complicated adversarial context from which it developed, dragged on until the spring of 1960. Schlüter responded to a parliamentary committee of inquiry and the suspension of his immunity—he was now a delegate to the Landtag without a party—by publishing a "factual report" in his own publishing house, which

Cover of the June 15, 1955, edition of *Der Spiegel* showing Leonhard Schlüter shortly after he was forced from office in Lower Saxony because of involvement in the right-wing radical movement. *Der Spiegel.*

kicked up more dust, at least in Göttingen. Finally, the Third Criminal Division of the Federal Supreme Court sentenced him to two months' imprisonment for "subversion" and "treason," while another of his authors, Herbert Grabert, who under the pseudonym Hugo C. Backhaus had published another book in 1955 titled *Volk ohne Führung* (A people without leadership), was sentenced to nine months.

The duration of the controversy undoubtedly heightened the importance of the Schlüter case for how the Nazi past would be dealt with in the Federal Republic. For half a decade, the publisher and his products provided reasons to argue about the limits of historical apologetics and the necessity of an enlightened understanding of history. For example, at the Frankfurt Book Fair in the fall of 1955, several political activists took matters into their own hands and emptied the booth occupied by the radical right-wing Plesse Verlag, for which Schlüter had worked before founding his own press.[7]

From this historical remove, the connection between the ongoing scandals around the past and the growing readiness of the society to deal with them is quite evident. Still, it is not clear whether the willingness of Germans to reflect

Students at the University of Göttingen take part in a torchlight demonstration against the naming of Leonhard Schlüter as minister of culture in Lower Saxony, May 27, 1955. SZ-Photo.

on their history came after the scandals or before. Likewise, the question arose at the end of the 1950s whether—after a relative "calm" that had set in, at least in public in the mid-1950s—an "upsurge" in antisemitism was again observable, or whether it was simply being scrutinized more intently in the media because of growing societal condemnation.[8] In other words, did more sophisticated notions of "mastering the past" encourage antisemites to show their faces, or did a more or less constant virulent antisemitism sharpen the need for discussion and corrective action?

ANTISEMITISM IN THE TAVERN

A scandal that unfolded at the end of 1957 in southwestern Germany makes the latter seem more probable. Shortly before Christmas, *Der Spiegel* reported on a secondary school teacher and a textile wholesaler who had gotten into a heated argument in a tavern in Offenburg about conditions in the Third Reich, Hitler's role, and the recent desecration of Jewish cemeteries. Ludwig Zind, the teacher, made the case that not everything that was "brown" had been bad and that the worst desecrations had been greatly exaggerated. When Kurt Lieser, the businessman, vehemently disagreed and questioned Zind's suitability as a teacher, the latter allegedly yelled, "Far too few Jews got gassed!"[9] *Der Spiegel* reported the continuing argument word for word:

LIESER: Herr Zind, I just want to let you know that as a half-Jew I spent time in a concentration camp in the Third Reich.

ZIND: What! So they forgot to gas you too?

LIESER: So if you had the opportunity today, you would have me taken to a concentration camp?

ZIND: Absolutely. And I'll tell you something else: I'm going to knock you off myself.

LIESER: And I suppose you would gas my wife as well?

ZIND: Absolutely. I would do that too.

LIESER: I have two children...

ZIND: As far as I'm concerned, they can live. And furthermore, I'm proud that me and my men broke the necks of hundreds of Jews with shovels during the war.[10]

A young reporter from the office of *Der Spiegel* in Stuttgart reconstructed the interaction, which had occurred in April, based on testimony from Lieser and two witnesses, although several differences in the last sentence developed over the following weeks.[11] Not only did Zind corroborate the exchange, but the former Wehrmacht officer refused to apologize. When Lieser, who had already informed the State Association of Jews in Baden, received an invitation six weeks later from the director of the high school where Zind taught to discuss the matter, he hoped for a few words of regret. However, the teacher stood firm, and in the presence of an official from the school department declared, "I would rather sweep streets than change my opinion!"

Initially at least, that seemed to be the end of the matter. The school director—his son was one of the two students who had witnessed the argument and helped prevent physical violence—tried to minimize the incident, saying, "That was beer talking," as Zind was known to be a heavy drinker. And the school authorities apparently thought that they might be able to avoid further trouble. However, several months later, when Lieser made a formal move, the school authorities disclosed that an investigation had been initiated against Ludwig Zind. Nothing had been decided three months later, and when *Der Spiegel* questioned the Ministry of Education, it responded that a teacher could be suspended only for moral offenses where "there was, in effect, a permanent danger to the children."

It is difficult to imagine that no one in Offenburg knew of the deficiencies of a teacher who was active in the social life of the city, but the report published by *Der Spiegel* was met with stony silence.[12] Nonetheless, matters began to move quickly elsewhere. The public prosecutor's office opened an investigation and questioned the two witnesses on Christmas Eve, and Zind was provisionally suspended from his duties on December 30. In mid-January 1958 the Arbeitsgemeinschaft deutscher Lehrerverbände (Working Group of German Teachers Associations) weighed in—in the name of its approximately one hundred thousand members. "Oppose the Beginnings," read the headline in a full-page spread that the working group had taken out in several daily newspapers. It went on to deplore that it had taken an article in *Der Spiegel* "for action to be taken against this stain on German pedagogy." It then continued in language that was unmistakable if not excessively nuanced: "The ineducability of the moral and intellectual inferiors who destroyed Germany yesterday threatens the Federal Republic today. Whoever remains silent is complicit in the calamities of tomorrow."[13]

This was when the "Zind affair" broke through the political surface. At the end of January, the Landtag of Baden-Württemberg began debates on the matter; two delegates, Walter Krause (SPD) and Otto Dullenkopf (CDU), had placed the issue before the state parliament, and neither side was sparing in its criticisms of the school authorities, the Ministry of Education, and Gebhard Müller, the president of an all-party coalition, who attempted to head off further damage by rebuking *Der Spiegel* and falsely accusing Lieser of having himself been convicted of a crime. But Dullenkopf complained that Zind had been suspended only as a result of the "pressure of public opinion," although his antisemitism "could not be denied": "I am prepared to name students who studied under him and on the day of that infamous Kristallnacht in 1938 reported that Herr Zind had asked who had participated in these riots, and then been praised by him."[14] Krause, Dullenkopf's ally in this matter, then asked a rhetorical question: What would have happened if *Der Spiegel* had not written a report and the Working Group of Teachers Associations had not protested? The fact that this was brought to the public's attention should be praised, not criticized, "because the Zind affair will also serve as a warning to the many who perhaps entertain similar ideas but do not dare to speak them. All of us who lived through the Third Reich know just how widespread antisemitism was, and we can hardly believe that it has now been completely eradicated."[15]

The question of how to deal with the scandal, not to mention antisemitism, was controversial both within the parties and in the press. This became evident a mere twenty-four hours later, when Wolfgang Haußmann, Baden-Württemberg's truly liberal minister of justice, summoned the Offenburg public prosecutor to Stuttgart. Haußmann would go on to play an important role in establishing the Central Office of the State Justice Administration for the Investigation of National Socialist Crimes that same year. Visibly dissatisfied with the actions of the ministry in a "pending case," *Die Zeit* newspaper commented:

The result: Ludwig Zind was immediately arrested on charges of having approved publicly of violent crimes and of having insulted the reputations of the deceased. And so he was taken to Hohenasperg prison, and his chances of becoming a "martyr" to the cause of the few Nazis who are still around are not at all bad. How much better it would have been had the Zind case been heard matter-of-factly and objectively eight months earlier. That Zind must be questioned before a judge and that his antisemitic statements be investigated from disciplinary and criminal perspectives—that is unquestionable. What is questionable, however, is how this case has been handled to date—first too slowly and then too noisily.[16]

In April 1958, one year after the argument in the tavern, Zind faced charges before the court in Offenburg, a trial that was now being observed and reported on in the world press.[17] However the reporters might have tried, they could not have outdone the judges in their opinion:

> At every opportunity that offered itself in which the Jews were mentioned, the accused began shouting loudly in a passionate denunciation of the Jews that exhibited all the signs of deep hatred. With rage-distorted face and excessively agitated gesticulations, he identified the Jews without exception as a national danger, sought to justify the methods of National Socialism against them, and protested the judgment against the regime for such mass crimes. All attempts to placate him failed due to the accused's intransigence, and he insisted on making his well-prepared statements, quoting copiously from documents and literature references that he had brought with him.[18]

After a three-day trial, Zind was sentenced to one year's imprisonment without probation for slander, in addition to continued denigration of the memory of the deceased. The reactions ranged from satisfaction, especially on the part of survivors like Heinz Galinski, who had acted as a coplaintiff, to outright solidarity with Zind. *Die Zeit* had a ready explanation for the latter:

> In Offenburg, Ludwig Zind, the bowler and chair of the gymnastics association, was a respected man. The citizens of Offenburg are assuredly not antisemites. However—the textile salesman who appeared as the primary witness against Zind is a "newcomer." That's what it amounts to. The people of Offenburg sharply condemned Zind's antisemitic provocations without qualification. But the fact that it was, of all things, a "newcomer" for whom in addition one harbors no sympathies for various other reasons, who took the old-established citizen to court, that was something that did not sit right with them one bit.[19]

Such attempts at drawing a clear line between the antisemitism of the accused, which was demonstrated in court, and the motives of his fellow citizens' solidarity were seen in other newspapers in the spring of 1958 as well. Less frequently, however, did one read that a high city official who had been called as a defense witness had declared that Zind's arrest triggered "a kind of crisis of confidence in the legal system."[20] And it took half a century for a former colleague of Zind's to admit that his fourth-year students had stood for a minute in silence after his guilty verdict became known.[21] Similarly astonishing was the state prosecutor's stated reason, after the fact, for the indictment: "Zind's antisemitic statements were so outrageous that they greatly damaged the reputation of the German people in the world, that had with such effort been regained."[22] Similar sentiments that related less to Zind's individual guilt than to the political consequences of his act were to be heard in the court's pronouncement of judgment, which was quoted in the American magazine *Time*: "'Zind's words rip open the old, barely healed wounds of the German people,' declared Presiding Judge Johannes Eckert. 'What thousands have tried to repair, one man with such words can destroy.'"[23]

Given the relatively harsh verdict—although *Die Tat*, the weekly published by the Vereinigung der Verfolgten des Naziregimes (Association of Persecutees of the Nazi Regime), criticized it as too lenient—it was no surprise that Zind's attorney lodged an appeal. The final passage of the *Time* article made clear that he was not acting solely on behalf of his client but on that of many citizens of Offenburg as well: "In the dock Zind denied nothing, and arrogantly announced that if Germany did not want him, a teaching job awaited him in Egypt. [As] Ludwig Zind walked out of the courtroom, where the audience had been plainly on his side, women wept at the verdict and men reached out to shake his hand."[24]

The appeal of Zind's verdict was to be heard before the Federal Supreme Court on the morning of November 28, 1958. However, Zind had absconded to Egypt on the 24th, something that he had intimated he might do in the Offenburg courtroom. His flight was not noticed until the judges in Karlsruhe had rejected his appeal; the original verdict was thus upheld, and Zind was scheduled for arrest that afternoon. The uproar in the press was all the greater because a mere half year earlier, Hans Eisele, a physician at the Buchenwald concentration camp, had followed the same escape route to evade prosecution. The *Stuttgarter Zeitung* commented sarcastically: "Strange how such slipups always seem to occur with people of Zind's or Eisele's ilk, whereas anyone only faintly suspected of Communist activities or attitudes may be certain of the most focused attention from our secret services and police organs."[25] In the West German media, long-suffering observers shook their heads over the disaster in southern Baden; in East Berlin, on the other hand, a campaign against "Hitler's blood judges in Adenauer's service" was in full swing, and the leadership there was all smiles. The East German newspaper *Neues Deutschland*, which had used the first report by

Der Spiegel to fire fresh salvos in the direction of Bonn, now confabulated a dramatic conflict between the leaders and people of the Federal Republic. Whereas the good German people—in Offenburg and elsewhere—supposedly demanded information and punishment, the "clerico-fascist Adenauer regime" was in bed with Zind and cohorts. Under the title *Scandal in Offenburg*, the central organ of the SED published an entire pamphlet with conspiracy stories. In their telling, the state secretary of the federal chancellery, Hans Globke, who had long been in the crosshairs of GDR propaganda, became an old friend of Ludwig Zind's, and Franz Burda, who owned the conservative *Ortenauer Heimatblatt*, had allegedly made a private airplane available for Zind's escape. The kernel of truth in this tale was that Burda had attended his former colleague and hunting companion's three-day trial.[26]

In 1959 the director Wolfgang Staudte based a film on the plausible suspicion that Zind had—like many before him—enjoyed help from the justice and police apparatus, which was full of "former members." In *Rosen für den Staatsanwalt* (Roses for the state prosecutor), the arrival of a bouquet at the home of the former court-martial judge Dr. Schramm signals that a teacher going by the code name "Zirngiebel" had safely crossed the border.[27] The film provided a satirical outlet for the outrage at continuing antisemitism, unpunished Nazi crimes, and the ongoing influence of National Socialist thinking at just the moment when a new instance of open antisemitism was beginning to roil policy-makers in Bonn—and upset world opinion.

"JEWS OUT"

In Cologne during the night of December 24, 1959, someone desecrated a memorial to the victims of National Socialism and then the façade of the Roonstrasse synagogue.[28] The two perpetrators, both members of the right-wing radical German Reich Party, were caught less than twenty-four hours later as a result of the tip from the local party chair. Arnold Strunk and Paul Josef Schönen, both in their mid-twenties and both from Cologne, had been school friends, and both had previously been sentenced for theft and fraud. Despite or perhaps because Christmas Day was otherwise a slow news day, news of what they did quickly spread around the globe. In retrospect, it can probably be said that no swastika painted in Germany after 1945 triggered as much media attention or had greater political consequences than the one that they smeared at the entry to that Cologne synagogue.

The directorate of the Central Council of Jews in Germany immediately sent a declaration to the press: "The synagogue community of Cologne and the secretariat of the Central Council have received numerous messages of sympathy and

Desecration of the restored Cologne synagogue, December 1959. ullstein bild.

protest from the public against this latest self-defilement of the German name, not only from statesmen but from a Nobel laureate as well."[29] It continued, stating that the "repugnant act" was apparently aimed "against all Jews, but to a much greater extent against Christian teachings, and especially against the reputation of the German people." Although the Jewish representatives were "disturbed that inadequate police measures had been taken after the desecration of the synagogue in Düsseldorf the previous year," they nonetheless suggested an interpretation that the Federal Republic would come to embrace after an initial phase of disarray: opposing antisemitism as a sign of commitment to the Federal Republic and as a battle for respect in the world.[30]

Josef Dufhues, the interior minister of North Rhine–Westphalia, had not yet understood this when he spoke before a television camera on December 25. The CDU politician declared that the desecration of the synagogue was not proof of antisemitism but had been committed by "outsiders." But over the following days, news and images—of painted swastikas and the slogan "Germans demand: Jews out"—flashed around the world, and the authorities realized that a chain reaction had been triggered: within a month, the Federal Office for the Protection of the Constitution reported a total of 685 "incidents." Of those, 215 were purportedly "mere children's scribbles," but given the sheer volume of incidents, there was no bright side to the picture. Politicians were forced to admit that the country had experienced a flood of "antisemitic and Nazi incidents" and that determined measures were required to counter them.

On January 7, 1960, two days after the beginning of Strunk and Schönen's trial, the wave of desecrations hit a high-water mark of fifty-eight. Many of these new incidents were not, however, just "copycat" crimes; they were also committed by people who wished to express their displeasure at the trial and their sympathy for the accused. Swastikas, SS runes, and slogans such as "Jews out," "Heil Hitler," and "Down with Adenauer" now adorned Christian churches, cemeteries, memorials, and advertising columns. Nor were state offices such as restitution agencies spared. Adenauer, Berlin mayor Willy Brandt, and Erich Ollenhauer, the leader of the Social Democratic opposition in the Bundestag, were all labeled "Jew helpers" and "Jew friends"; government officials and police officers were called "democratic swine" to their faces.

Under considerable pressure, the cabinet met in special session on Epiphany (January 6) at Adenauer's private residence. Foreign Minister Heinrich von Brentano reported that "the world's response to the antisemitic incidents is becoming increasingly threatening."[31] On January 15 the ministers reconvened in Rhöndorf, and the next day the chancellor addressed the nation on radio and television. Adenauer first reminded the public of the solemn rededication of the Cologne synagogue four months earlier, which he had attended. The desecration had produced "a wave of indignation against those responsible, and in some other countries a wave of hatred against all Germans and particularly against the Germany of today."[32] At this point, the chancellor attempted to connect with his listeners at home and abroad with a personal, even private, appeal that was most unusual for the time:

> My family and I were ourselves victims of National-Socialism. It will suffice for me to tell you that my name figured four times on a list of persons condemned to death by the National-Socialists, and it is almost a miracle that I was able to survive those years. And what is my attitude towards the Jews? Well, when my family and I were in great financial straits during the period of National-Socialism, it was two Jews who were the first to offer me financial assistance. They knew on what terms I had always stood with the Jews.

Adenauer recalled the Restitution Agreement with Israel ("In so doing, I wished to show the whole world that the Germany of today absolutely rejects antisemitism"), called the desecration of the memorial stone and synagogue "a disgrace and a crime," and expressed his hope that "it will meet with rigorous punishment by the Courts of Justice." In the end, however, his interpretation of the events met with criticism not only from the Social Democratic opposition in the Bundestag but from an increasingly critical press, which found it inadequate, even trivializing: most of the copycat crimes (of which, as he noted, there had also been several in other countries) were "cases of hooliganism that appear to have no political background." His "Jewish German fellow-citizens," according to the chancellor, should "have no reason to worry": "This State supports them with all its power; I vouch for this word." And Adenauer, now eighty-four years old, had an assignment for "all my German fellow-citizens": "If you come across one of the hooligans anywhere, inflict punishment on the spot and give him a good thrashing. That is the penalty he deserves."

About a third of his brief speech was aimed expressly at critics abroad who were "hostile" or "doubtful." Adenauer declared that the German people were united in opposition to antisemitism: the "majority of the German people served National-Socialism during the period of its sway only under the heavy yoke of dictatorship," and the "few incorrigibles who still exist will not achieve anything." At the conclusion, the chancellor showed himself to be both a bold and cool analyst: "The condemnation of antisemitism and National-Socialism now so spontaneously and unanimously revealed among the German people is the brighter side of these abominable occurrences."[33]

In fact, Adenauer was not wrong, because from this remove the response to the synagogue desecration was a turning point in the society's debate around the Nazi past that continued to feed on new events and gain momentum. This was not only because someone like Hans Globke could continue to serve in the chancellery but also, for example, because the demands that Theodor Oberländer be removed from his position as head of the Ministry for Displaced Persons, Refugees, and War Victims came to be seen in a completely different light. Oberländer was a former Nazi "eastern expert" and officer in the Abwehr, the military intelligence organization, who became the subject of a show trial in the GDR.[34] He finally resigned in early May 1960, just a few days before Adolf Eichmann's arrest in Argentina.

But as much as Adenauer's comments may have contributed, what was needed in January 1960 was deeds, not abstract reflections. Because of this, the chancellor, for whom the reputation of the Federal Republic was the focal point of all considerations, frowned upon the public talk about alleged behind-the-scenes instigators from East Berlin who were responsible for the wave of desecrations. Defense Minister Franz Josef Strauss and Interior Minister Gerhard Schröder delivered evidence of such instigation a few days after Adenauer's televised speech.[35] The ever-cautious Schröder had already decided to take the unusual step of having a white paper drafted for the federal government about antisemitic and Nazi incidents, which he presented to the Bundestag in mid-February 1960. This hastily compiled official publication detailed the incident in Cologne, of course, but in addition the type and scope of copycat acts, the motives of the perpetrators, the status of legal proceedings, and the "influence of anti-constitutional forces" from both the Right and Left.[36] Perhaps even more significant than Schröder's detailed account were the conclusions that he presented. Although he spoke of "connections to wire-pullers in the Soviet zone," his attention focused on self-criticism: "What has been lacking in the instruction of German youth concerning the guilt and disaster of the 'Third Reich'? What do our youngsters know of Hitler, and what of the Jews? What has been done in the way of enlightenment so far?"[37]

The interior minister pointed to the work done by the Federal Center for Home Service and the Institute for Contemporary History. A collaboration between the two institutions had, for example, led to the publication of a monograph on the fifteenth anniversary of Kristallnacht that, though thin, was based on original sources and was anything but an apologia. Over the years it was published in numerous editions.[38] Schröder reported on conferences that had been sponsored, films produced, and books distributed at no cost. Just a few months earlier, history teachers at all German secondary schools had been assigned Alan Bullock's *Hitler: A Study in Tyranny*. And he spoke out with astonishing clarity against the "desire of the older generation to forget and suppress." In the process, he identified with Hannah Arendt, who, when she was awarded the Lessing Prize in 1958, had spoken skeptically about attempting to "master" the past: "This probably cannot be done with any past, and certainly not with this one. The most that can be attained is to know and to face the fact that it has been so and not otherwise, and then to see what conclusions are to be drawn."[39]

Quoting Arendt was certainly remarkable for a conservative Protestant who, born in 1910, had become a member of the NSDAP in early 1933 and made a career as a lawyer in the Third Reich, although it should be noted that he resigned from the party in 1941.[40] It was a sign that the process of rethinking had begun within the bourgeois middle class, not across the board, but certainly among many.

Despite mounting criticism of the federal government, both from abroad and internally—*Der Spiegel* was especially vociferous.[41] The wave of desecrations did not lead to a lasting break in relations with Jewish organizations.[42] Adenauer feared that this recrudescence of antisemitism could weaken the Federal Republic's position in future East–West negotiations. Meanwhile, the Central Council of Jews was more concerned about the Anti-Defamation League's intention to encroach on its turf by opening an office in West Germany—and that the incidents in Cologne might make the Bonn government more supportive of the

ADL's plans. As Hendrik George van Dam tried to make clear to Schröder a month after the desecrations, "There is no reason and no need for foreign Jewish organizations to engage in such activities that would benefit only the employees of such organizations."[43]

However, a consensus had already formed among important Jewish and non-Jewish voices in the political sphere and the media in West Germany, as well as among important representatives of the Jews abroad. As Edwin Guggenheim, the European president of B'nai B'rith, wrote to Adenauer, he was more concerned about a German youth that, "in marked contrast to the gratifying young proponents of an utterly decent and humane ethos, seem to care little or nothing about the terrible misdeeds that occurred under the National Socialist regime, but are influenced by persons, parents, or educators who have drawn no lessons from the past but continue to be filled with the same spirit of faith and racial hate." The new educational spirit of the times was fully in line with Guggenheim's final recommendation, in which one might detect a veiled barb against Adenauer's call for self-administered justice ("a good thrashing"): "We therefore believe that in addition to thoroughgoing measures aimed at preventing such acute antisemitic occurrences, a fundamental examination of educational methods and teaching materials would be appropriate in this regard. We are more interested in prevention than punishment."[44]

"EDUCATION AFTER AUSCHWITZ"

The wave of desecrations also had a profound effect on school authorities, pedagogues, and social philosophers. Despite differences in terms of particularities—not to mention the convoluted path between educational theory and school practice—on balance, the new thinking brought about real historical and political enlightenment.

For example, on January 30, 1960 (the anniversary of the Nazis' assumption of power), the Deutscher Ausschuss für das Erziehungs- und Bildungswesen (German Committee for Education and Training) came out with a statement. This initially rather conservative committee, which had been formed by the government in 1953, was alarmed by inadequacies in the teaching of citizenship and social studies that had become evident over the past decade in many places. These classes had failed "to arm young people against the seductions of political inhumanity and to tell them and make clear what had happened to the German people over the past half century and what it must take responsibility for and master."[45]

The experts on the committee did not hold back in their tough assessment of the current situation: because of a "lack of courage and insight, or of surreptitious sympathy for a National Socialism whose indivisible reality is being glossed over by splitting it into a criminal and a praiseworthy part, for reasons of questionable 'objectivity,'" urgent educational tasks were being neglected in many schools. "Although the key events relating to National Socialism have been laid out clearly, contemporary history is frequently scanted out of a lack of necessary historical distance, or it is being discussed 'objectively,' that is, without judgment and without personal engagement on the part of the teacher." In the opinion of the committee, it was also true that many teachers were under pressure from parents "who did not want their children to learn the truth about National Socialism." The reason was, not least, a general "discomfort" with politics: "Many Germans only nominally believe in democracy."[46]

Although Theodor Adorno had not contributed to this text, the parallels to a lecture that he had given at an "educator conference" sponsored by Christian-Jewish associations nearly two months before the wave of antisemitism erupted are unmistakable. In Wiesbaden in early November 1959, Adorno asked about "the meaning of working through the past," and his response was to the point: it was not only that he perceived behind the thought of "working through" the desire "to close the books on the past" or even to "draw up a balance sheet"; in fact, to the former émigré the false consciousness that manifested in this "balance sheet" was even more dangerous than the existence of right-wing radical organizations: "I consider the survival of National Socialism *within* democracy to be potentially more menacing than the survival of fascist tendencies *against* democracy."[47] Thoughts and fears like these, in addition to a revolving door of revelations of Nazi scandals and political charges, played no small role in the New Left's belief in the 1960s that the Federal Republic, founded in 1949, was little more than a democracy "in form" that still needed transformation.

But in contrast to many of his academic interpreters and followers who all too often just cited only the title of Adorno's lecture, the author himself was very precise. In retrospect, quite a few passages read as if he had predicted the desecration of the Cologne synagogue. And he knew very well how to connect incisive descriptions of prejudicial social structures with the results of the "group experiments" conducted by the Institute for Social Research, which had returned to Frankfurt in the early 1950s: "All too often the presupposition is that anti-Semitism in some essential way involves the Jews and could be countered through concrete experiences with Jews, whereas the genuine anti-Semite is defined far more by his incapacity for any experience whatsoever, by his unresponsiveness."[48] This is why, according to Adorno, "one should not expect too much from the recourse to the facts." Instead, "they should be made aware of the mechanisms that cause racial prejudice within them. A working through of the past understood as enlightenment is essentially such a turn toward the subject, the reinforcement of a person's self-consciousness and hence also of his self."[49]

A few years later, during the incubation period of the extraparliamentary opposition, Adorno's desire for social change became a little clearer, despite the hermetic style of his cultural criticism. His reflections on "education after Auschwitz," which were broadcast on the radio station Hessische Rundfunk in April 1966—half a year after the verdict in the ("big") Frankfurt Auschwitz trial, during which a second, smaller trial ran concurrently—contained many concrete recommendations for a pedagogy of "debarbarization." At the end of his comments, perhaps recalling Walter Benjamin's Parisian exile, Adorno even allowed himself a bit of confidence: Benjamin had felt that "the people who *do* it, as opposed to the bureaucratic desktop murderers and ideologues, operate contrary to their own immediate interests, are murderers of themselves while they murder others." "But," he added, "there are people who do it down below, indeed as servants, through which they perpetuate their own servitude and degrade themselves, and that there are more Bogers and Kaduks: against this, however, education and enlightenment can still manage a little something."[50]

If in the 1950s public discourse between Jews and non-Jews was largely restricted to a few representatives from both sides speaking mainly about restitution, the 1960s saw a burgeoning interest in "mastering the past." Frankfurt am Main, the most Americanized city in postwar West Germany and the center of Jewish life in the Federal Republic, was and remained a city of special significance in this regard.[51] Mayor Walter Kolb (SPD) had asked Adorno and Max Horkheimer to return and in cooperation with the American High Commission had laid the groundwork for the Institute for Social Research, which soon became a politically and intellectually respected institution that was able to attract funding.[52] In addition, Hessen's Social Democratic prime minister, Georg August Zinn, had hired Fritz Bauer (also a returnee) as district attorney. He became a major factor in bringing Nazi criminals to trial. Otto Brenner, head of the powerful corporation IG Metall, supported the movement against the German Emergency Acts from his base in Frankfurt.[53] Critics, especially those on the Left and especially in Frankfurt, feared that this emergency legislation would open the door to something like the Nazi Enabling Act of 1933. Furthermore, *The Diary of Anne Frank* continued to resonate in the city of her birth. Originally published in German in 1950, this document of the Nazi era became a best seller when it was published in paperback in 1955 by S. Fischer Verlag, an important publishing house that had recently reopened in Frankfurt. Shortly thereafter, it became one of the most frequently staged plays in both parts of Germany.[54]

As the *Frankfurter Neue Presse* put it in June 1957, "The little Jewish girl about whom we do not even know how she died, has triumphed."[55] The occasion was what would have been the twenty-eighth birthday of the now-renowned diarist, which was officially celebrated by the city for the first time that year. The ceremony in the assembly hall of the Johann-Wolfgang-Goethe University was part of a wave of publicity about which Hans Lamm had commented in the *Allgemeine Wochenzeitung der Juden in Deutschland*. He wrote that this should not be viewed as mere sentimentalizing: "Viewers who later speak of an 'Anne Frank craze' or 'cult' confuse their own cynicism with the spirit of a generation that once caused Martin Buber to speak of 'Youth, humanity's eternal chance for happiness.'" Not everyone who is touched by Anne Frank's message could be dismissed as "emotional naïfs," although it cannot be said that "all of the readers of the *Diary* are companions with whom one might wish to join forces in the battle against prejudice, racial hate, or national pigheadedness. The Anne Frank phenomenon and its effect on German-speaking people is far too multilayered to allow simplifiers from one or the other political wing to fight over her to validate their pet theories."[56]

Even back then, it was argued, doubtlessly with justification, that Anne Frank, the individual witness, was not really representative of the murder of the European Jews. But whatever the interpretation, it can be argued that her diary came to symbolize the mass extermination by describing vividly what had preceded it. Furthermore, the concentration camp documentation that was released in the immediate postwar period during the Nuremberg trials lacked the personal immediacy of the diaries, which now touched younger Germans with an intensity that was unprecedented.

One example was a twenty-year-old trades trainee named Werner Lerch, who sent a letter dated July 20, 1957, to Werner Bockelmann, the new mayor of his city. Introducing himself as "a Frankfurt lad born and bred," he asked for assistance. Lerch had completed his training as a plumber a year earlier—having received the highest marks in the entire state of Rhineland-Palatinate, as he proudly noted—and he now wished "to give the Jews a gift." His wording may have been a bit clumsy, and the dates may have been wrong, but his motives were crystal clear: "Today we write the year 1957. Exactly 10 years ago in July, my mother still tells of it, was the terrible night of the Jews. She and my older siblings watched as men and our young people were incited and spurred on to destroy all of the property of these people, among them their synagogues." He now hoped to approach "the highest council of the Jewish community" and "make some restitution" with the "Sabbath candelabra" that he had forged in his free time; he would do so "in the name of the young people who back then unconsciously helped in this hard reality" and "as a sign that the young people of Frankfurt are not so bad and that good fellows still exist today."[57]

In fact, Lerch was given the opportunity to pass on his heartfelt gift in November 1957. During a small ceremony, Isaak Lichtigfeld, the state rabbi of Hessen, gratefully accepted the menorah, and representatives of the Frankfurt Jewish community promised that it would be given a place of honor. Given the formality of the words of thanks spoken by community executive director Adolf Olkowicz, as reported in the *Frankfurter Rundschau*, the well-intentioned young plumber may not have fully grasped the implications for the future of what was said: "As a result of such young people, a new life will begin in Germany, one in which we are prepared to participate." The next day, Mayor Bockelmann gave the young man a small sum of money in recognition of the "beautiful offering" and "the spirit from which it springs."[58]

The cautious and awkward gestures that were often evident on such occasions did not entirely disappear during the 1960s. But they lessened somewhat, and there were undoubtedly several reasons. One reason was the growing distance, both temporal and mental, from the traumatic experiences of the war years; more important, however, was the rapid economic transformation of the Federal Republic, the modernization that it facilitated in German society, and the rise of a new generation that was slowly supplanting the old. In addition, opportunities opened up for young Germans to interact with Jewish peers who had grown up in postwar Germany, the children of survivors. These encounters took place in schools and universities and since 1961 (the year of the Eichmann trial) in Israel as part of Aktion Sühnezeichen Friedensdienste (Action Reconciliation Service for Peace).[59]

The teaching of history began to reflect the general "working through the past" that was taking hold in Germany. Wolfgang Scheffler, a postwar German historian, published the first history of "the persecution of the Jews in the Third Reich" in 1960. This thin volume soon became a standard assignment in many high schools. The following year, Scheffler was asked by the federal government to observe the Eichmann trial in Jerusalem, and he subsequently played an important role as an expert in the trials of former Nazis.[60] The Frankfurt Auschwitz trial, which is said to have been observed by about twenty thousand people between 1963 and 1965, became a magnet for schoolteachers attempting to make real to students the political lessons of the past. An accompanying exhibition in the Paulskirche organized by the Bund für Volksbildung (League for National Education) and inaugurated by the Buchenwald survivor Eugen Kogon reinforced Fritz Bauer's notion that the trial be used as a form of self-confrontation with Nazi crimes, especially the murder of the Jews. In the words of the district attorney, Germans must "put ourselves on trial."[61]

However, during the mid-1960s, the first stirrings of a New Left critique of "mastering the past" began to be heard, parts of which echoed some of the arguments being advanced against Fascism in the GDR. "Our Auschwitz," Martin Walser's contribution in the spring of 1965 to Hans Magnus Enzensberger's newly founded journal *Kursbuch*, may serve as an example. Walser, a former Hitler youth, antiaircraft helper, and young soldier, was eighteen when the war ended.

The jury trial began in Frankfurt on December 20, 1963, against twenty-two former SS guards at the Auschwitz concentration camp. SZ-Photo / ddp images / AP.

In his article, he formulated principled objections: "Only the supporting cast sits on the bench at the Auschwitz trial. Accomplices, executioners, seducees. Products of a ferocious expenditure in German education. Perpetrators in the most outmoded sense of the word." To Walser, who was just beginning to make a name for himself, the trial and the media coverage seemed like bourgeois pseudoenlightenment. In particular, Walser criticized the tendency to remove the deed "from the conditions of the system, from our German history between 1918 and 1945. And the deed will be removed from our national context and viewed as a personal crime for as long as it takes until nothing other than pure brutality remains."[62]

Peter Weiss's "Frankfurter Auszüge" (Frankfurt excerpts), which reads like a log book and comprises the first part of the *Kursbuch* "dossier" on the Auschwitz trial, took a similar tack. Weiss attended only a few court sessions but based his article on a multitude of press articles, such as the minutely detailed reports by Bernd Naumann in the *Frankfurter Allgemeine Zeitung*. Nonetheless, his semi-documentary text served as a prelude to Weiss's play *Die Ermittlung* (published in English as *The Investigation*), which premiered in October 1965 on numerous stages in both West and East Germany. But in contrast to the "Frankfurter Auszüge," the playwright made some very sharp political points. According to literary scholar Christoph Weiss in his comprehensive history of its origins and reception, the play, subtitled *Oratorio in 11 Cantos*, sought "to expose the double connection between fascism and capitalism and National Socialist and Federal Republican society."[63]

This line of argumentation was certainly not lost on the ministerial bureaucracy in Bonn, which was not only carefully monitoring the effects of the Auschwitz trial on Germany's reputation in the world generally but also keeping an eye on Peter Weiss's work, which was increasingly critical of capitalism. And the alarm bells began to go off when it became clear that his play was destined for international success. A bureaucrat at the Federal Press and Information Office took nervous note of the impending English-language premiere in London: "It is to be expected that the reading and—especially—televised broadcast of the play will trigger renewed discussion of Auschwitz among the British public. The same should hold true for the Scandinavian countries." He recommended that an essay in the conservative *Die Welt* be distributed to all foreign missions "to enable them to inform the local media there regarding the Leninist-Marxist orientation of the author."[64]

THE YEARNING FOR NORMALCY AND THE
CRITICAL STANCE OF YOUNG PEOPLE

At this point, the establishment of diplomatic relations between Israel and the Federal Republic was little more than half a year in the past; the "criminal case against Mulka and others," that is, the Auschwitz trial, had come to a conclusion in August 1965 after having been heard for 183 days; and the problem of the statute of limitations for Nazi war crimes seemed to have been satisfactorily resolved. On May 8, 1965, the Bundestag had prolonged by a good four years the deadline for pursuing war criminals, an act that was criticized by the Allies in the West and by their opponents in the East.[65] In other words, although by middecade the past was still very much present, it seemed to many as if the much-hoped-for "clean break" was palpably near.

Ludwig Erhard, who had succeeded Adenauer two years earlier, touched on this theme in his government statement on November 10, 1965: "The postwar period is over!" As proof, Erhard, an economics professor, trotted out some facts and figures: "The 5th German Bundestag was elected in the 20th year after the end of World War II. 167 of its 518 delegates reached majority age only after 1945. Two-thirds of our population were children or had not yet been born in 1933. To almost half of all the people in our country, the years between 1933 and 1945 represent the historical past without personal memory." And although Germans—of all generations—bore the consequences of the "policies practiced" in those years, these should no longer be viewed as the "reference points."[66]

Apparently believing that he could decree the end of memory, the chancellor formulated expectations that could only lead to friction. In 1963 Adenauer delayed the long-overdue exchange of ambassadors with Israel because of the protests by Arab states—and because by threatening to establish diplomatic ties with East Germany if West Germany forged closer ties with Israel, these states would undermine Bonn's claim to being the sole legitimate representative of the German nation as a whole. A few years later, Erhard demanded that these countries have understanding for "how important it must be for us Germans to have *normal relations* with Israel."[67]

Erhard's goal, twenty years after the end of the war, was to make "normalcy" the basis for German Middle East policies; however, this was to prove unrealistic even before his resignation only twelve months later. Nonetheless, this attempt is illustrative of the moods and intentions in the Federal Republic, which are probably best understood against the backdrop of the aftermath of Adenauer's legendary first meeting with David Ben-Gurion at the Waldorf Astoria in New York in mid-March 1960.[68] During this conversation between the two aging founders of states—captured for the world to see in a highly symbolic photograph—the federal chancellor had promised the prime minister even more than economic assistance beyond the term of the restitution agreement. For a time thereafter, Bonn became, in diplomatic parlance, an important strategic military "business partner" of Israel. This wording was meant to conceal the extensive top-secret weapons deliveries that were about to begin.

However, despite all efforts to keep the transport of tanks under wraps, the fact that Israel was receiving weapons and equipment from Bundeswehr stockpiles leaked out in the fall of 1964. *Der Spiegel* took the opportunity presented by this diplomatic embarrassment to publish a lengthy report about Israel that began with a witty description of the frustrations of "thirty-two kibbutz volunteers [from North Rhine–Westphalia] who were prepared to atone."[69] From there, the author, Hermann Schreiber, quickly got down to the point of the article: alarmed about "German rocket researchers in Nasser's service" (since the 1950s, a number of Nazi experts had resettled in Egypt), the Knesset had posed the question

> whether Bonn is really on the up and up with Israel, since Konrad Adenauer no longer governs and Gerhard Schröder's "pragmatic" foreign policy enjoys broad support. Erhard—every German visitor to Israel these days hears this in almost every conversation at least once—may follow Adenauer's line in practice, but the almost religious zeal that "the old man" had brought to reconciliation with the Jewish people—this was what they missed, even though Konrad Adenauer had not achieved what he had set out to do. When Ad-

David Ben-Gurion and Konrad Adenauer during a conversation at the Waldorf Astoria Hotel in New York, March 14, 1960. ullstein bild / BPA.

enauer was still in office, it seemed to many of Israel's citizens that a sense of deep guilt that could not be erased by material payments alone had guided Bonn's policies. In Erhard, by contrast, they felt they were dealing with a man who made efforts to keep his policies free of such encumbrances, at least in the international sphere.[70]

On the other hand, Schreiber sensed that in Israel, too, a new generation of politicians had arisen that was prepared "to carve out, so to speak, the past and all of the doubts that it had left behind, and to go beyond them and engage in practical politics with Germany." This applied not only to the economic sphere, although that was where the new spirit manifested most clearly. "Even more clearly, though in secret," wrote *Der Spiegel* with, for it, unusual delicacy, "has this developed in the common arena of defense. The most convincing contributions from the Federal Republic to Israel are today in this area. Unfortunately, this cannot be stated loudly enough in Israel itself."[71]

As might be expected, opinion surveys now reflected the normalcy discourse that had since the mid-1960s become standard in political circles and parts of the media, such as the report in the tabloid *Bild* after the private visit to Israel by the elderly former chancellor in 1966, which, it should be noted, was not free of misunderstandings. The headline read, "Adenauer in Israel: A Clean Break with the Past!"[72] This was consistent with the fact that only 14 percent of West Germans thought that it would have been better had the Eichmann trial not taken place; the corresponding figure for the Auschwitz trial had been 39 percent. But between 1965 and 1969 the percentage of West Germans who opposed continuing prosecution of Nazi crimes continued to rise, from 52 to 67 percent.[73]

German attitudes toward Israel developed in rather peculiar contrast to such views. In this regard, the Six-Day War in June 1967 became a turning point. Whereas the media in the GDR intensified the "anti-Zionism" that they had been practicing for years, many West Germans evinced great enthusiasm for the power and efficiency of the Israeli army—not least because of reporting in conservative newspapers owned by Axel Springer. Like Kurt-Georg Kiesinger, the chancellor of the grand coalition, Foreign Minister Willy Brandt proclaimed political neutrality, on the one hand, while signaling that this was not tantamount to indifference, on the other. (It took until November 13, 1973—i.e., after the Yom Kippur War—for Brandt, speaking as chancellor of the SPD-FDP coalition, to state before the European Parliament in Strasbourg that for Germans there can be no "neutrality of the heart and conscience.")[74]

Below this official level, matters clarified rapidly. The associations for Christian-Jewish cooperation, the German-Israeli Society, and of course the Jewish communities called for greater solidarity with Israel. But so did the German Trade Union Federation, the individual unions, and even the Workers' Samaritan League.[75] And in taverns and elsewhere, Germans discussed the war, as Yohanan Meroz, the later Israeli ambassador to Bonn, wrote, "as if it were 'their' war."[76] Many Germans were more than willing to root for the Jewish David against the Arab Goliath. And after its complete victory over the Arab armies of Egypt, Jordan, and Syria, Israel could count on the sympathies of a large majority of West Germans.[77]

However, their attention was divided, given what was going on within Germany itself. On June 2, 1967, Benno Ohnesorg, a student attending a demonstration in West Berlin against a visit by the shah of Persia, was shot in cold blood by a policeman (who as we know today was an agent of East German state security). This incident sparked the increasing radicalization of the student movement. It also had the immediate effect of attracting young people while at the same time leaving their elders increasingly perplexed.[78] The student movement had developed from a critique of the "dominant order" and the "establishment" and—at least in the Federal Republic—in large part as a reaction to the society's refusal to deal self-critically and forthrightly with the past. Why, students asked, were so many Nazi judges still sitting on the bench? The so-called New Left came to identify increasingly with the Marxist theories of the Weimar era, not least with the Institute for Social Research. Herbert Marcuse, who, in contrast to Horkheimer and Adorno, had remained in exile in the United States, became an idol and mentor to the student movement worldwide during the protests against the Vietnam War. But he was perhaps most revered in West Berlin, where he was born.

While many of the intellectual father figures of the extraparliamentary opposition were Jewish, so were some of its younger proponents. The most prominent of these was Daniel Cohn-Bendit. Born in 1945 in Montauban, the son of German- and French-Jewish parents, he was unique in that in 1968 he caused a furor on both banks of the Rhine—thereby underscoring the transnational and even global character of the movement. The sudden ubiquity of antiauthoritarian ideas did not, of course, diminish the need for structures. On the contrary, new groupings and associations were constantly being formed, including the Bundesverband Jüdischer Studenten in Deutschland (BJSD, Federal Association of Jewish Students in Germany) in March 1968. Its demand, echoing the rhetoric of the times, was for "more democracy" in the Jewish communities and on the Central Council. However, the students also trained their sights on the rightward drift that had become evident in West German society during its first, if rather slight, economic recession in 1966, which led to some Landtag electoral advances by the National Democratic Party. Finally, they aimed their ire at Israel's occupation policies, from which some were now carefully beginning to distance themselves.[79]

Politically, the activists of the BJSD were largely in accord with the radical, democratic, and left-wing socialist positions taken by members of the Sozialistischer deutscher Studentenbund (SDS, Socialist German Student League) and other left-wing groups. However, they began to part ways during a downturn in the protest movement, when parts of the radical Left began to discuss the "violence question" with increasing vehemence, and anti-Zionism, driven by anticapitalism, began to make headway. This began to reverse what had been widespread pro-Jewish and pro-Israel attitudes among critical young Germans in particular. Though planted by an agent provocateur from the West German Office for the Protection of the Constitution, the bomb that luckily failed to detonate in the Jewish community center in Berlin on November 9, 1969, signaled an upswing in left-wing antisemitism that was not limited to the Tupamaros West-Berlin group but would eventuate in the terrorism of the 1970s.[80]

Of course, criticism of Israel by the extraparliamentary Left was only one aspect of the social realities in the Federal Republic during the late 1960s. There was also a remarkable Israeli—perhaps even more than Jewish—presence in popular culture. This included the satirist Ephraim Kishon, whose light novels such as *Drehn Sie sich um, Frau Lot* (published in English as *Look Back, Mrs. Lot*) became best sellers, and the actor Shmuel Rodensky, whose portrayal of Tevye the dairyman in the German version of the Broadway musical *Fiddler on the Roof* was a sensation. Others included the pop music duo Esther and Abi Ofarim, who along with Daliah Lavi in the 1970s introduced the Israeli "sound" to an appreciative German public.

However, the general German population seems to have been more or less unaware that a number of German-Jewish artists had been making their mark, some of them since the early postwar years. For example, not until 1980, when he published his autobiography, did it really sink in that Hans Rosenthal, one of the most successful and popular German radio and television personalities, was a Berlin Jew and, furthermore, one of only a few thousand to have survived underground in hiding during the Third Reich.[81] The fact that the popular quizmaster had been involved with the Central Council of Jews since the 1960s went largely unnoticed. This blindness is undoubtedly a sign of how limited was the German public's ability even to perceive the Jewish community and its organizations at that time.

MICHAEL BRENNER is Professor of Jewish history and culture at the University of Munich and Seymour and Lillian Abensohn Chair in Israel Studies at American University in Washington, D.C. He is a member of the Bavarian Academy of Sciences and international president of the Leo Baeck Institute. Brenner's publications include *A Short History of the Jews, Prophets of the Past: Interpreters of Jewish History, Zionism: A Short History,* and as coauthor the four-volume *German-Jewish History in Modern Times.*

NORBERT FREI is Professor of modern and contemporary history at the University of Jena and is director of the Jena Center 20th Century History. During the 2008–2009 academic year, he was a member of the Institute for Advanced Study in Princeton, and in 2010–2011 he was Theodor Heuss Professor at the New School for Social Research in New York. Frei's publications include *1968: Jugendrevolte und globaler Protest, 1945 und wir: Das Dritte Reich im Bewußtsein der Deutschen,* and *Adenauer's Germany and the Nazi Past: The Politics of Amnesty and Integration;* he is also coauthor of *Das Amt und die Vergangenheit: Deutsche Diplomaten im Dritten Reich und in der Bundesrepublik.*

NOTES

1. For more on that and on the following, see H.-G. Marten (1987); W. Kraushaar (1996b), vol. 2, pp. 1193–1195.

2. See "Der Fall Schlüter," *Deutsche Universitätszeitung,* June 8, 1955, quoted from H.-G. Marten (1987), p. 7.

3. "Ein Feuer soll lodern," *Der Spiegel*, June 15, 1955, pp. 12–24, quotation on p. 13; see also "Der Streit um den Minister Schlüter," *Die Zeit*, June 2, 1955.

4. "Ein Feuer soll lodern," *Der Spiegel*, June 15, 1955, p. 13.

5. Quoted from W. Kraushaar (1996b), vol. 2, p. 1194.

6. Werner Wilkening, "Schlüters Stammrolle," *Diskurs*, June 5, 1955, p. 2; quoted from W. Kraushaar (1996b), vol. 2, p. 1195, facsimile of the article, p. 1267.

7. W. Kraushaar (1996b), vol. 2, p. 1266.

8. "Upsurge" according to W. Bergmann (2001), p. 187.

9. "Lehrer: Israel wird ausradiert," *Der Spiegel*, December 18, 1957, p. 35; here quoted somewhat differently from Gerhard Ziegler, "Zind und seine Mitbürger," *Die Zeit*, April 17, 1958.

10. "Lehrer: Israel wird ausradiert," p. 35.

11. Here based on the interrogation records of the public prosecutor, A. Lörcher (2008), pp. 47–57.

12. See A. Lörcher (2008), pp. 138–149.

13. Quoted from W. Kraushaar (1996c), vol. 3, p. 1777.

14. Quoted from "In SPIEGEL veritas: Aus den Beratungen des Baden-Württembergischen Landtags über den Fall Zind," *Der Spiegel*, January 29, 1958, p. 22.

15. "In SPIEGEL veritas," p. 23.

16. G.Z., "Im Falle eines Falles," *Die Zeit*, February 6, 1958, p. 4.

17. See W. Kraushaar (1996c), vol. 3, p. 1843.

18. Verdict against Zind on June 8, 1958, p. 13, quoted from A. Lörcher (2008), p. 85.

19. G. Ziegler, "Zind und seine Mitbürger."

20. *Offenburger Tageblatt*, April 11, 1958, quoted from A. Lörcher (2008), p. 109.

21. See "Leiche im Keller der Stadtgeschichte," *Badische Zeitung*, October 15, 2008.

22. *Frankfurter Rundschau*, April 12, 1958, quoted from W. Kraushaar (1996c), vol. 3, p. 1843.

23. "The Ugly Scar," *Time Magazine*, April 21, 1958.

24. "The Ugly Scar."

25. Quoted from "Zind: Mit Flinte," *Der Spiegel*, December 10, 1958, pp. 32–34, here p. 34.

26. See A. Lörcher (2008), pp. 148–149, 176–181.

27. See "Kriegsrichter: Die Mörder sind über uns," *Der Spiegel*, September 2, 1959, pp. 72–73.

28. All statements of fact, to the extent not otherwise noted, according to Government of the Federal Republic of Germany (ed.) (1960); see also J. Zieher (2005), pp. 260–272; W. Bergmann (1990a).

29. Report from the German embassy in Madrid on January 11, 1960, containing a copy of the declaration of the Central Council on December 25, 1959, in BArch, B 145/1133; the following quotations as well.

30. The synagogue in Düsseldorf had been desecrated during the night of January 17, 1959, shortly after its reconsecration. No perpetrator was convicted. See J. Zieher (2005), pp. 257–259.

31. Special meeting on January 6, 1960, in "Kabinettsprotokolle der Bundesregierung," vol. 13, 1960, http://www.bundesarchiv.de/cocoon/barch/0001/k/k1960k/kap1_2/kap2_3/para3_1.html.

32. Quoted from Government of the Federal Republic of Germany (ed.) (1960), pp. 41–42. Subsequent quotes in the text are also from this source.

33. Government of the Federal Republic of Germany (ed.) (1960), pp. 41–42.

34. After the cabinet had met in special session to deliberate about Adenauer's planned television appearance and the procedure for implementing emergency legislation, it was decided, in Oberländer's presence, to defray the legal costs from budgetary funds, since the "smear campaign" that was aimed against the minister was an "attack by Communist propaganda against the federal government that had to be defended against"; special session on January 15, 1960, in "Kabinettsprotokolle der Bundesregierung," vol. 13, 1960, http://www.bundesarchiv.de/cocoon/barch/0001/k/k1960k/kap1_2/kap2_3/para3_1.html.

35. It should also be noted that Adenauer kept abreast of the international reaction in the press; see, for example, "Bericht des Presse- und Informationsamts, US-Presse zu den antisemitischen Vorfällen (III)" January 12, 1960, in BArch, B 145/1133. For more on the efforts of the representatives of the Federal Republic in the United States, see LBI, AR 1446.

36. Government of the Federal Republic of Germany (ed.) (1960), pp. 30–37.

37. Government of the Federal Republic of Germany (ed.) (1960), p. 50.

38. H. Graml (1953); for context, see vol. 2 (2010) of *Münchner Beiträge zur Jüdischen Geschichte und Kultur*: "Von der Kristallnacht zum Novemberpogrom: Der Wandel des Gedenkens an den 9. November 1938."

39. Government of the Federal Republic of Germany (ed.) (1960), p. 60.

40. See T. Oppelland (2002).

41. See, for example, Moritz Pfeil (i.e., Rudolf Augstein), "Säuberung," *Der Spiegel*, January 13, 1960, p. 16.

42. American Jewish Committee, "The German and American Reaction to Vandalisms, January 19, 1960," in AJA, MS149 2.2.

43. Letter from Hendrik G. van Dam to Gerhard Schröder, January 25, 1960, in BArch, B 106/193.

44. Letter from Edwin Guggenheim to Konrad Adenauer, January 18, 1960, and the notation BMI Referat III 6 (signed Geißler) about the visit of Messrs. Epstein and Belth from the American B'nai B'rith, January 26, 1960, both in BArch, B 106/21565.

45. See H.-E. Tenorth (2010), p. 282.

46. Copy of the declaration of the German committee on January 30, 1960, in BArch, B 106/21565.

47. T. Adorno (1998b), pp. 89–90, emphasis in the original.

48. T. Adorno (1998b), p. 90. For more detail on the institute, see M. Boll and R. Gross (eds.) (2009).

49. T. Adorno (1998b), pp. 101–102.

50. T. Adorno (1998a), p. 204, emphasis in the original. SS-Oberscharführer Wilhelm Boger and Rapportführer Oswald Kaduk were among the six accused in the Frankfurt Auschwitz trial who were sentenced to life imprisonment.

51. See T. Freimüller (2010a); T. Freimüller (2010b).

52. See R. Wiggershaus (1987), esp. pp. 449–486.

53. For more on the context, see N. Frei (2008), pp. 93–98.

54. See "Frank-Tagebuch: Im Hinterhaus," *Der Spiegel*, October 10, 1956, pp. 39–40; S. Kirschnick (2009), esp. pp. 59–61.

55. Quoted from P. Loewy (1998), p. 36.

56. *AWJD*, January 23, 1959, quoted from S. Kirschnick (2009), p. 14.

57. "Vorgang in ISG Frankfurt," Magistratsakten III/2–1979/972; my sincere thanks to Dr. Tobias Freimüller for making me aware of these holdings.

58. "Die Jugend ist nicht so schlecht," *Frankfurter Rundschau*, November 14, 1957.

59. See A. Skriver (1962); also A. Legerer (2011).

60. W. Scheffler (1960); see also H. Grabitz et al. (eds.) (1994).

61. See I. Wojak (ed.) (2001), p. 23; C. Brink (2000).

62. M. Walser (1965), p. 194.

63. C. Weiß (2000), vol. 1, p. 116.

64. At issue is presumably an essay by Hans-Dietrich Sander titled "Das Ende eines 'dritten Weges': Peter Weiss und seine politischen Metamorphosen," *Die Welt*, September 18, 1965, reprinted in C. Weiss (2000), vol. 2, pp. 256–260. Referring to his speech at the Internationalen Schriftstellertreffen in Weimar on May 19, 1965, at which Weiss had characterized his own work in the West as that of a "partisan" who was duty-bound to the truth, Sander called Weiss a "convert" who had "caustically embraced the party of the East." The text quote is from a note from Hübener to Diehl, October 18, 1965, in BArch, B 145/6624.

65. In 1969 the Bundestag decided on a further extension of ten years; in 1979 a law was passed abolishing the statute of limitations for murder and genocide.

66. L. Erhard (2002), p. 122.

67. L. Erhard (2002), p. 122, emphasis added.

68. For more on the following, see Y. Jelinek and R. Blasius (1997).

69. "Der Kurier kam zu spät: Spiegel-Reporter Hermann Schreiber über die deutsch-israelischen Beziehungen," *Der Spiegel*, October 21, 1964, pp. 126–131.

70. "Der Kurier kam zu spät."

71. "Der Kurier kam zu spät."

72. See Y. Jelinek and R. Blasius (1997), p. 321.

73. See W. Bergmann (1990b) pp. 122–123.

74. Quoted from http://www.cvce.eu/obj/Rede_von_Willy_Brandt_vor_dem_Euro paischen_Parlament_Straßburg_13_November_1973-de-27b2333f-7ea1-4fc0-b908-756 c562ccc6d.html; see also J. Deligdisch (1974), pp. 131–133.

75. See A. Kauders (2007), pp. 104–105.

76. Quoted from M. Weingardt, "Deutsche Israel-Politik," *Aus Politik und Zeitge-schichte* 15 (2005), p. 26.

77. As late as May 1970, 45 percent of those surveyed stated that they were "on the side of the Israelis"; 7 percent were on the side of the "Arabs"; 32 percent remained "neutral"; and 16 percent had no opinion; see E. Noelle and E.-P. Neumann (eds.) (1974), p. 593.

78. N. Frei (2008), pp. 113–130.

79. A. Kauders (2007), p. 178.

80. For more on the bomb, see W. Kraushaar (2005).

81. H. Rosenthal (1987); see also U. Heikaus (ed.) (2011).

PART THREE: 1968–1989

ALIGNMENTS

CONSTANTIN GOSCHLER
AND ANTHONY KAUDERS

10 THE JEWISH COMMUNITY

A JEWISH SOCIAL HISTORY?

In 1991 Avraham Barkai expressed the hope that the time had come "to write a comprehensive economic and social history of the Jews that lives up to the standards" set by Nachum Gross for a real economic history. It should be based on comprehensive information and be as quantitatively accurate as possible. And it should describe the history of ordinary people and society as a whole, not concern itself merely with the leading figures of Jewish life.[1] Unfortunately, this hope has not been borne out, especially not for the 1970s and 1980s. While we have impressive statistical studies dealing with the demographic, economic, and social realities of Jewish life in Germany—not least because Jewish institutions produce such material in order to refute antisemitic prejudices with empirical data—this has not been the case for the time since 1945, primarily because the experience of the Third Reich made both Jews and non-Jews understandably leery of gathering separate statistical data on Jews. At the same time, stable figures were virtually impossible to come by because of postwar migration. Even such a seemingly simple question as the number of Jews in Germany after 1945 quickly becomes mired in a definitional swamp. This is certainly true of the Federal Republic, but even more so of the German Democratic Republic. There, the differences between the small number of persons who claimed to belong to Jewish communities and the comparatively larger number who denied their Jewish origins or lived their Jewishness outside of the established Jewish communities were enormous.

The problems only get larger when dealing with the social and economic circumstances of the Jews in the 1970s and 1980s. Given the relative lack of reliable statistical source material, historians are often forced to rely on the more or less impressionistic descriptions of contemporaries. The available sources thus conceal a considerable source of distortion: since scholars have always been more apt to publish works about their lives and experiences than have, say, supermarket cashiers, we quickly run the risk of reproducing old stereotypes about the social and economic role of Jews. Nonetheless, no comprehensive history of the Jews in Germany during these decades can avoid these questions, and so we will attempt to sketch out the demographic, social, and economic lay of the land, but with the methodologically required restraint.

The data on the number of Jews in Germany during the decades discussed here depend primarily on the definition of membership used in collecting and analyzing those data. Membership in a Jewish community is in fact the only criterion from which precise figures can be drawn. On the other hand, this criterion excludes various groups that are of equal importance in terms of Jewish demographics. Among other things, Jews frequently include factors other than religion under the rubric of "Jewishness," including an element of ethnicity or membership in a "community of fate," which the individual cannot simply renounce.[2] This was why official figures on community membership were cited, while more or less valid "estimates" were published as well. With regard to West Germany in the 1970s and 1980s, such estimates applied to two groups in particular: first, Israeli citizens who lived in the Federal Republic and did not belong to a Jewish community;[3] and second, "ethnic" Jews from the Soviet Union, only some of whom joined Jewish communities in Germany. Then there is the even more pressing question of the number of "crypto-Jews" in the GDR, which is estimated to be a multiple of the vanishingly small membership in the existing Jewish communities there.[4] As a result, the following attempt to sketch out the number of Jews in Germany in the 1970s and 1980s must take into account the demographic and statistical discourses upon which such figures are always based.

If membership in Jewish communities is the sole criterion, it is clear that the trends of previous years continued largely uninterrupted during this time period. Whereas the number of Jewish communities in the Federal Republic decreased from sixty-eight to sixty-four between 1970 and 1990, membership increased slightly over the same period, from twenty-seven thousand to about twenty-eight thousand. This trend was primarily tied to immigration, while the ratio of births to deaths yielded an increasingly negative balance (1970: 18 to 141; 1980: 95 to 456; 1990: 109 to 431). Still, average age, which had peaked in 1970 at 50.6 years, began to decrease somewhat, and in 1985 it was 44.3.[5] In the GDR, where there was no immigration from outside, the Jewish population dropped off with increasing steepness because there were so many more deaths than births: while the eight Jewish communities in the GDR had 1,078 members in 1970, only 372 remained in 1990, most of them elderly. Additionally, the task of caring for approximately 160,000 graves fell to those few.[6] By extending these trends, it was generally expected that the Jewish community in the GDR would die out in the foreseeable future, while in the Federal Republic a tiny but still fairly stable minority would continue on. But at the time, no one could foresee the end of the Cold War and the reunification of Germany, which would permanently alter this picture after 1990.

These overall figures can be contextualized only if they are broken down at the local level. The vast majority of Jews lived in communities in large cities. Numerous smaller and even very small communities existed alongside relatively large Jewish communities in West Berlin, Frankfurt am Main, and Munich. But even in the larger communities, in certain age groups practically everyone knew everyone else—which limited considerably the choice of marriage partners. The *Nachrichtenblatt der Israelitischen Religionsgemeinschaft Württemberg* (Newsletter of the Israelite religious community in Württemberg)—a community that at the time had about 770 members—offered the following statistical overview for 1976: seven births, one bar mitzvah, and two marriages, signifying the renewal of Jewish life, but fourteen deaths. And one conversion to Judaism was more than outbalanced by five people who left the community.[7]

Stabilization of the smaller Jewish communities was a constant topic in the leadership committees. There were two main causes for the losses, leaving the fold and "mixed marriages," and both were tightly bound up with the question of Jewish identity. Thus, Heinz Galinski spoke about the reasons for leaving the fold at a meeting of the Central Council, the primary one, in his opinion, being the desire not to pay community taxes levied by the state. According to Galinski, "Leaving the Jewish community is not the same as when Catholics or Protestants leave their churches. Those who leave are simultaneously attempting to withdraw from the community of fate, and that is not possible."[8] From this perspective, it was reprehensible if not completely impossible to renounce Jewish identity. And so, as the general secretary of the Central Council, Alexander Ginsburg, declared in 1980, Judaism has two enemies: "Ignorance and assimilation along with the problem of mixed marriage."[9]

In 1977 the mass-market illustrated magazine *Stern* counterposed this position taken by Jewish officials with the perspectives of young Jewish women in the Federal Republic. Based on almost one hundred interviews, author Paula Almqvist presented portraits of eight of approximately two thousand Jewish women and girls between the ages of sixteen and thirty, most of them the daughters of Eastern European Jewish concentration camp survivors. The article delved in detail into the expectation of their parents, widespread at the time, that they married only Jewish men. The women who chose otherwise were often haunted by intense feelings of guilt. The article also discussed the limited choices available in small Jewish communities. "They live among Germans, but for love they yearn for a Jew—and they are rare," read the trivializing lead.[10] The article presented the young Jewish women visually as indistinguishable from their non-Jewish peers. The title, "Anything—Just Not a German Man," was completely divorced from reality, however, since between 1973 and 1981, approximately two-thirds of all Jews married non-Jews, which merely continued the previous trend.[11]

As a result, the boundaries between Jews and non-Jews in German society were becoming increasingly (and permanently) fluid, and even constant anguished outcries by top officials like Werner Nachmann could do nothing to stem this process.[12]

Because the German Democratic Republic sealed itself off from all migration that was not tightly controlled by the state, Jews there neither emigrated nor immigrated. Matters were quite different in the Federal Republic, where transnationality and transterritoriality, which had characterized Jewish existence since the beginnings of the modern nation-state,[13] played an important role during this period as well. Many of the Jews living either permanently or temporarily in the Federal Republic also carried an Israeli passport and belonged to no German-Jewish community. And for many of the Jews in the Federal Republic born after 1945, it was simply expected that they would have lived for a time in Israel. This was especially the case with young Jews, whom the State of Israel attempted to recruit for *aliyah* (immigration).[14] This meant a constant coming and going, a circulatory migration, especially between West Germany and Israel. Thus, although there had been a net inflow of immigrants in the previous decades (in 1970, 406 immigrants and 135 emigrants), by 1980 the ratio stood at 1,115 to 330; in 1985, 595 to 346; and in 1990, 1,070 to 202.[15] What the statistics cannot tell us, however, is how many of these people moved back and forth between Israel and the Federal Republic during this period.

The complexity of this migration pattern is made more so by the migration of Jews from the Eastern Bloc countries. Polish, Romanian, and Hungarian Jews had been emigrating to the Federal Republic since the 1950s. But after the end of the 1960s, further waves of Jews fled to Austria and then to the Federal Republic, where they often requested political asylum because of the political events taking place in Poland and Czechoslovakia.[16] And starting in the 1970s, larger numbers of Jews were able to leave the Soviet Union because of diplomatic pressure from the United States. The peak years were 1973 and 1979. At first, most of them were routed to Israel by way of Austria. But this changed in 1973, because many Soviet Jews came to prefer a destination other than Israel, especially the United States. But in 1978 the United States restricted its quotas for Jewish immigrants from the Soviet Union, whereupon the majority of these people went to Israel, at least initially. However, this did not stop many of them from pursuing emigration to another country. As a result, increasing numbers of Jews from the Soviet Union found their way to the Federal Republic in the 1970s.[17]

The following years were marked by repeated friction between representatives of the Central Council and the Israeli government or Jewish communities in other European countries. In contrast to the latter, West German-Jewish officials were vehement in their defense of the right of Soviet Jews to choose their own destination—including the Federal Republic. In effect, this stance was indirectly part of their own battle for legitimacy as Jews in Germany. Since 1973 increasing numbers of "Russian" Jews had arrived in the Federal Republic by way of Israel, and when their number grew to more than 650 at the beginning of 1975 in Berlin alone, the media began to take note, something that Jewish representatives would rather have avoided.[18] Offenbach was a second center for Soviet-Jewish newcomers, although the precise number is unclear: while the Offenbach city administration spoke of 1,200 Jewish immigrants, only 336 of them had registered with the local Jewish community. "The others," according to Galinski, "had preferred, apparently on the advice of some attorneys, not to identify themselves as Jews."[19] Nonetheless, because of their sheer numbers, this group placed a heavy strain on both public and Jewish welfare organizations.

After the "brief dream of perpetual prosperity" was shattered by the first oil crisis in 1973, a heated debate began in the Federal Republic about the limits of foreign immigration. Against this backdrop, the subject of "Russian" Jews became freighted with the potential for scandal, not least because some of them had entered the country illegally. Within the Central Council, Galinski spoke of "real human trafficking," in which "Russian" Jews with counterfeit passports were brought into the Federal Republic from other European countries. Jewish institutions anxiously observed how the initial generosity of German authorities toward this group was beginning to fray. In particular, this affected the practice of recognizing "Russian" Jews as political refugees, even though they had immigrated from a safe third country such as Israel.[20] Because of this, in 1974 Werner Nachmann protested to Werner Maihofer, the West German minister of the interior, regarding a presumed agreement between the Foreign Office and the Israeli government "whereby such immigrants were to be routed to Israel."[21] But even earlier, the government had begun to stop recognizing members of this group as "refugees belonging to the German people" and naturalizing them according to German law.[22] As a result, in 1977 the Federal Ministry of the Interior had asked the interior ministries of the federal states to preference Jews entering from Eastern European states, in particular, such persons "who without belonging to the German people grew up speaking German and are closely connected with the German cultural area."[23] This triggered public discontent about competition with migrants on the labor market, and federal policymakers and administrators were hard-pressed to reconcile this with Germany's special historical obligation toward Jewish immigrants.

Outside of places like Berlin and Offenbach, where "Russian" Jews had been a significant proportion of the Jewish population in the 1970s, these immigrants did not at first change the social and economic profile of this group, at least to the extent to which one can make general statements about this time period.

Although most Jews began their new lives after the war at a low economic level because of the total destruction of their social networks, their careers, and complete dispossession, which was only partially compensated for by German restitution, they, too, became beneficiaries of the West German economic miracle. Many became members of the middle class, the status that had mutated into the overarching social model during these decades.[24] Upward mobility also decreased the Jewish presence in several economic spheres that had been important during the immediate postwar period: the DPs who worked in the red-light districts, especially in the vicinity of American barracks, as well as the fairly large number of Jewish attorneys who represented restitution claimants. However, the relative overrepresentation of Jews in the film and textile industries also lessened due to economic restructuring, on the one hand, and upward social mobility, on the other.[25] Micha Brumlik has described Jewish real estate brokers in connection with the controversies surrounding the demolition and redevelopment that took place in Frankfurt's West End during the 1970s and the subsequent attacks on them. According to Brumlik, their social ascent during the postwar decades "from whorehouses and kebab stands by way of jewelry and textiles" to real estate deals had been "an open fact which nonetheless was treated as if it were a secret."[26] The widespread antisemitic tirades against Jewish black marketeers in the postwar period were replaced in the 1970s by attacks with a marked anticapitalist flavor against Jewish "real estate speculators." But perhaps the most important, though least conspicuous, aspect of the economic transformation among the Jews in the Federal Republic was that the number who were employable and required no government support for themselves or their families gradually increased.[27]

In any case, the number of Jews as a proportion of the total population, which had sunk to minuscule levels in comparison to the time before 1933, would have made it impossible for them to achieve a predominant position in any single economic sphere, except where local particularities were conducive. This was especially true in the German Democratic Republic, where the tiny Jewish community was statistically insignificant. The only striking social and professional fact was that statistically they were overrepresented as pensioners.[28] Therefore, the question of representativeness is not of interest here with regard to either the GDR or the Federal Republic. What is of interest is how they were represented: the attacks on both "black marketeers" after the war and "real estate speculators" later in the 1970s referred to them as "Jewish," though mostly only in encoded— but easily decoded—language. As a result, a line of continuity may be drawn from the antisemitic deflection of guilt of one era to that of another.

One final question in this context concerns the extent to which a special Jewish economic mindset may have existed in the Federal Republic in the postwar period and to what extent it may have changed in the 1970s and 1980s. The sociologist Y. Michal Bodemann discerned a "preference for professional qualifications that are relatively transportable, that is, not bound to a country or the language of that country."[29] But this finding, too, must remain tentative because of a paucity of data, especially as this pattern, if that is what it was, may have indicated increased adaptation to the non-Jewish environment. Biographies, interviews, and intergenerational studies generally seem to indicate that the readiness to pick up and leave that had developed during the postwar decades along with the economic mentality associated with it may have been replaced in the 1970s and 1980s by an increasing desire to remain permanently in the Federal Republic.[30] In other words, the more their own children became part of West German society, the more contradictory appeared the former attitude of a provisional existence in Germany. As a result, generational conflict between the "old" and the "young" increasingly came to characterize the intellectual climate in the communities during this time.

GENERATIONAL CONFLICT AND GENERATIONAL TRANSFORMATION

The year 1970 was a turning point for the small Jewish community in Germany. That, at least, was the assessment of the Central Council in its end-of-year review, which was written by its general secretary Hendrik George van Dam and distributed to all the communities in the Federal Republic. Van Dam summarized the work done by the Central Council during the two decades since its founding in 1950. Back then, according to him, the main issue had been the reestablishment of the West German-Jewish community's legal rights. Material and moral restitution was the first order of business, followed by the establishment of relations with the rest of the Jewish world. Although these goals remained of continuing importance twenty years later, van Dam felt that important new tasks had come to the fore—tasks that were central to the life and survival of the community.

The Jewish community circa 1970 no longer lived in isolation from the rest of society (which had, in fact, never been completely the case); rather, it had become part of the Federal Republic, and in many respects Jews were behaving much like their Christian neighbors. This was true in two senses. On the one hand, since the Jews no longer lived with their suitcases packed, it was simply not credible when "the inhabitant of a country speaks of a temporary stay, while having remained here for twenty years with regular employment." The other sense is quite concrete, in that young Jews were increasingly struggling to assert their "identity" and their "position in society."[31]

It may even be stated that young Jews, critical as young people are, put the transformation of Jewish life in West Germany to the test by their activities both within and outside their communities. The contemporary zeitgeist was on their side: the coalition formed under Willy Brandt between the Social Democratic Party and the Free Democratic Party attempted to make the political process more democratic while laying a new foundation for relations with Eastern Europe. In effect, a left-wing anti-imperialism coexisted with a general hope for an easing of tensions in the world, and, finally, increasing numbers of people were looking at alternative living arrangements. These changes meant considerably more for the Jewish community than for other groups in the country because it placed in question their own identity and their role within the Federal Republic.

In other words, young people were not acting in a vacuum when they began to examine the premises of Jewish life in West Germany. Since the late 1960s, more than a few young Jews had taken the "liberalization and pluralism of models, life plans, and worldviews" as an opportunity to reform the communities from within.[32] At the same time, many believed that the transition from the grand coalition to Brandt's SPD-FDP coalition would change society as a whole and not just reform the state and economy.[33] In this connection, Bernd Faulenbach has spoken of a fundamental politicization that was associated with "an increasing claim to participation on the part of society."[34] For young Jews, democracy, Israel, and "mixed marriage" were especially important.

The generational conflict in the communities is the subject of this section. The conflicts between the young and old remained moderate at first, at least in comparison to the controversies that were to come. There were three main reasons for this. The first was that "unpacking suitcases" had not advanced to the point where the power relationships within the communities were at risk. Debates could still be steered in certain directions, and no one was yet capable of taking on the status quo, that is, the positions taken by the older generation. Second, almost everyone still accepted that status quo, including the importance of Israel and thus the self-image of the community. And third, several of the officials sympathized with the concerns of the younger generation.

These officials included Hans Lamm. In 1968 the former head of cultural affairs of the Central Council and later president of the Munich community wrote an open letter to an unnamed Jewish professor in the United States who had rejected a teaching chair at a German university because the protesting students reminded him of the Hitler Youth. Lamm lamented the "students of today" but refused to compare them with "those filled with National Socialist hatred, those bellowing antisemitic and other songs during the 1920s and 1930s." It was a historical error to mention the Sozialistischer Deutscher Studentenbund (SDS) and the SA and SS in the same breath. The professor, so Lamm continued, might be confused because he was "separated from the scene of the action by four thousand kilometers [*sic*], and you are often dependent on unreliable sources of information."[35] Van Dam made similar points at a meeting of the Central Council in May 1968, just as the protests were reaching their high point in France. He discerned a connection between the earlier warnings by the Jewish community that National Socialism was alive in the Federal Republic and the actions of the extraparliamentary opposition. At one time, after all, young people were accused of a Jewish "witch hunt" and "vindictiveness," for example, when they tried to find out which former National Socialists had been given key positions in the West German government and economy.[36]

Lamm and van Dam were open to changes in West German society. Conversely, at this time Jewish young people had little interest in sparking a revolution; they were intent on bringing to the attention of community leaders the widespread problems that they observed. The founding conference of the Federal Association of Jewish Students in March 1968 fully demonstrated this intention. Benjamin Korn, a sociology student and brother of the later vice president of the Central Council, Salomon Korn, called upon the participants to seek a Jewish identity "in order to avoid the psychologically horrendous emigration or assimilation alternatives that merely simplified the problem." Given the "situation in the Federal Republic today," he called on them to put a brake on the "Teutonic ox that time and again charges toward the Right and regularly bangs its head there." Antitotalitarian and radical-democratic politics, Korn declared, could put a stop to this.[37] By contrast, Dan Diner, a law student, pleaded for a new, less emotional relationship with Israel.[38] Neither Korn's image of the Teutonic ox nor Diner's plea for greater distance from Israeli foreign and defense policy robbed the Jewish elites of much sleep. This was because the students aimed their criticism at "German" issues that did not necessarily have anything to do with the Jewish community: university reforms, the Nazi past of German officials, the power of the right-wing press, "imperialist" wars in Southeast Asia. And so the officials could continue to act as if the young people were not primarily interested in reforming the Jewish community. In addition, while young people questioned their upbringing, they did not question their inclusion in the West German-Jewish collectivity. Lamm essentially said the same in October 1969 when he averred that Jews who tended "toward individualism and nonconformism" had never turned their backs on the community.[39] In addition, a report written by Paul Spiegel about the first youth conference that took place in October 1969 in Berlin found much the same. Despite a number of splits, there was a common denominator, Spiegel noted. Even the opponents of "radical Zionist ideology" endorsed "the transmission of Zionist knowledge" as "an integral part of Jewish education." In addition, the same group stressed the "duty of Jewish young people to work together on community policies."[40]

Despite their openness to dialogue, Jewish officials perceived a fundamental "youth problem." Various leaders agreed that large numbers of young people had become alienated from community life. In other words, young Jews attended synagogue only rarely, were barely interested in community politics, and were increasingly more apt to socialize with non-Jews than with other Jews. This was one of the reasons why van Dam had encouraged the youth conference.[41] Officials like Heinz Galinski were worried as well. In the spring of 1970 he again stressed how important young people were to the community. At a meeting of the Jewish Women's League, he stated that those in responsible positions had made a mistake when they "had not considered twenty-five years ago" that children eventually grow up. Now the Jewish communities were faced with "this state of affairs," and they ran the risk "of losing the young Jews who still remain." At that meeting Galinski also criticized the "old patriarchal" way in which some rabbis neglected young people when practicing their calling.[42]

Galinski was talking about a problem that would not disappear overnight. It soon became apparent that van Dam's characterization was essentially correct: in 1970 young Jews were like their Christian counterparts more often than was comfortable. Unlike their parents, they had never experienced the terrors of persecution and were therefore more at ease with life in Germany. Furthermore, the second generation was now attending German schools and universities, which ineluctably led to greater integration into German society. Like other young people, they were more comfortable with pluralism and politicization, and they demanded to be heard in their communities.[43] While representatives of the Jewish community often paid lip service to greater involvement, pluralism and politicization usually signified something very different to them.

The situation in the 1970s might well be summed up as follows: while young people were bent on greater democracy, the older generation wanted more religion. Tensions arose frequently as a result. Matters became increasingly pointed in the Jewish community of Frankfurt, where a variety of factors converged that encouraged tensions to become conflicts and conflicts outright skirmishes. Three of these factors are noteworthy in this context: first, the efforts made to develop a Jewish liberalism, which had begun quite early; second, the upsurge in left-wing activity at the universities; and third, the role of eloquent spokespeople, including Arno Lustiger and Dan Diner.

In the summer of 1969 the Federal Association of Jewish Students sponsored the Week of Peace in the Middle East at the University of Frankfurt, an event that was vehemently criticized by the community leadership. The students were seeking neither to overturn the communities' support for Israel nor to prompt the resignation of their officials. Rather, in Diner's words, the students' goal was to make the communities more accessible to other voices and opinions, in short, to make them more pluralistic: "If a heterogeneous political engagement were possible within the Jewish sphere in Germany as had earlier been customary, each and every deviation from the traditionally conveyed line would no longer necessarily entail a sense of being expelled from the Jewish community."[44]

In the following years, Diner, who was at the time a member of the board of the Frankfurt Jewish community and a member of the directorate of the Central Council, made the case for the urgency of reforms to deal with the apathy of many Jews regarding political action in the Federal Republic. Much like van Dam, he distinguished between an early phase, during which the community had achieved the economic and social integration of its members, and the present, from which emerged an entirely new set of challenges. Outsiders needed to be integrated, and current projects had to be planned and carried out by those who had a stake in them. Democratization was viewed as "self-help by the individual in all spheres."[45] Diner then spoke about young people. In a draft for the Central Council—here again, the openness to internal Jewish dialogue was evident—he described the current situation as disastrous. The education available to date, with which Jews in Germany were forced to live in a self-chosen "permanent provisional state," verged on "ruthless educational exploitation." In addition, this "negative identification" with the Federal Republic had ended in "fiasco." In any case, the activities of the young German generation had demonstrated their "rejection of their contaminated childhood homes," and the student unrest had been the "real turning point for a large proportion of the Jewish young people in Germany." Diner did not, however, touch on the relationship with Israel or religion in his draft. His call for pluralism and thus for eventual "normalization" was meant to open the door for various positions, different perspectives, and different ways of thinking.[46]

While Diner and his cohorts demanded democracy within the Jewish community, others sought a solution in culture or religion as a way to salvage young people. But those who advanced the notion of a religious-cultural renewal had very clear ideas of the norms and values that were required. There was still something tentative about the way that Lustiger expressed this. Lustiger, who was born in prewar Poland and was now the chair of the Zionist Organization in Germany, claimed that of the more than one hundred employees of the community, not a single one was involved in organizing cultural or social events. He would much rather that young people felt at home at a coffeehouse for young Jews (not yet built) than at leftist spots like Club Voltaire and Libresso.[47] Marek Glezerman, who was in fact the head of the office for culture and the press in the Frankfurt Jewish community, seemed to contradict Lustiger. Glezerman began by agreeing with the analysis of the present situation put forward by van Dam and Diner.

The only source of cohesion among Jews in the past had been the socioeconomic sphere, Glezerman stated, "with shared and similar personal destinies, a similar past, shared geographic and cultural roots, similar economic circumstances, and the resultant cross-connections." But this was no longer the case in 1971. The leadership of the Jewish community in Frankfurt and the community members were on increasingly divergent tracks. Glezerman complained that instead of focusing on the Torah and Talmud, sources of knowledge and ethics that had brought civilization to the Jews at a time when "the frogs still croaked" in Paris and New York, everyone was now intent on his own personal well-being.[48] And complaints about the ignorance of young people, their lack of enthusiasm for religious services, and the "lack of a Jewish spirit" in cultural life were heard well beyond Frankfurt.[49] The general opinion was that something had to happen, either by making the communities more pluralistic or by reviving cultural and religious spirit generally.

Despite the spirit of optimism, a feeling of ambivalence was palpable, not least among those in positions of responsibility. Although they made plans, implemented initiatives, and organized conferences, these ventures were not to go too far. After all, there had to be limits, and no one should exceed his authority. The consequence of this ambivalence was that many officials felt misunderstood, and many young people distrusted the plans being worked out at the top.

At the end of 1970, the Central Council founded an initiative group for youth questions in the Central Council with the goal of discussing current topics and problems at regularly scheduled seminars.[50] The first meeting of this sort took place a year later in Sobernheim in the Rhineland-Palatinate, where the participants mainly discussed the "problem of mixed marriages." All participants agreed that it was the responsibility of Jewish parents to educate young people at home and in the community to be "fully integrated Jews." And one way of guaranteeing the Jewish education of young people, according to the summary report, involved integrating the children from those mixed marriages.[51] At the same time, according to later statements on the topic, they understood full well the scope of the "problems and risks" that potentially came with mixed marriages.[52]

The minutes from the following years yield an unclear picture. Although the initiative group continued to sponsor seminars, the results remained rather modest. No real answers were found to urgent questions, resolutions remained vague, and in general, communication with rabbis and officials was difficult.[53] Nor did the Central Council provide the support that was hoped for. The members of the initiative group complained about a general lack of interest in their activities, and they brought up the June 1974 meeting of the Central Council in Hannover, where they had not even been permitted to present their work. In addition, discussions during the event made it clear just how little most of the officials knew about what they were doing. Small wonder, then, that the item "Youth Work" at the last meetings of the Central Council had been placed at the end of the agenda and as a result was never discussed.[54] Similar seminars followed, sometimes even twice a year. But even looking back from the vantage point of 1976, when past topics were reviewed, the overall tone was not exactly effusive. Even the title of the retrospective—"Has Jewish youth awakened from its deep sleep?"—seemed innocuous if not downright placatory. And the fact that the question was never answered says more than a little about the entire enterprise. Overall, it appeared that topics had been consciously formulated so as to avoid uncomfortable controversies.[55]

It cannot be determined from the documents whether the Central Council organized the youth and cultural congresses between 1977 and 1985 because the seminars in Sobernheim and elsewhere had been fruitless. In any event, in this official attempt to discuss the future of the Jewish community, it became clear that the few engaged young people and the community officials were talking past each other. While the former openly debated whether mixed marriages between Jews and non-Jews should be rejected in principle—and, above all, whether children from such marriages or the children of a non-Jewish spouse should be allowed to take part in community life—some on the Central Council believed that banning mixed marriages once and for all was the only way to ensure the future of the Jewish community. This issue would become increasingly salient during the 1970s and 1980s.

Jewish institutions reacted in another arena as well. In the early 1970s the idea arose to establish a Jewish educational center in order to increase the number of religion teachers, cantors, and rabbis. The point was to encourage a younger generation of scholars so that West German communities would no longer be dependent on trained personnel from abroad. The biggest problem was that teachers from other European countries, Israel, and the United States could not generally be induced to remain in the Federal Republic, which meant constant fits and starts. The plan to found a Jewish theological seminary came primarily from the Central Council, although it soon received support from governmental circles. In September 1978 a conference of ministers of education "welcomed" the founding of "a Jewish theological institute" and "noted with approval that this institute would be established in Heidelberg under the auspices of the Central Council of Jews in Germany." In addition, it approved shared financing at both the federal and state levels "with a financial formula of 30:70."[56] This meant that 30 percent of the running costs would be covered by the Federal Ministry of the Interior as a subsidy to the Central Council and 70 percent by the states, of which Baden-Württemberg would be responsible for a quarter. And the Ministry of the Interior declared that it would provide startup funding in the amount of

120,000 DM.[57] At the end of January 1979, the directorate of the Central Council formally decided to establish just such a private institute, which would draw on "the great traditions of the time before the catastrophe."[58] In addition to rabbis, cantors, and teachers, the institute would also train social workers, administrative lawyers, and economists.[59] At the inaugural meeting of the founding committee of the institute in May 1979, Professor Leon Feldman from Rutgers University was elected founding rector.[60] He suggested that the institute be renamed the Hochschule für Jüdische Studien (College of Jewish Studies) so that "Jewish knowledge in its entirety might be [conveyed] to Jewish and non-Jewish students." This motion was approved by the members of the committee and sometime later by the education ministers of the states as well.[61]

Feldmann had introduced the future curriculum at a meeting in May, and it came into effect as of the winter semester of 1979. A total of sixteen students began their studies on October 17. The college offered five major subjects: Talmud, Jewish history, Tanach (Bible) with commentaries, the Hebrew language and literature, and the history of Jewish ideas and philosophy. The students could also choose from minor subjects such as Midrash and the sociology of the Jews.[62] Most of the teachers came from Israel and the United States: Shlomo Eidelberg from New York taught Bible and Jewish history; Abraham Wasserstein from Jerusalem, Jewish philosophy and intellectual history; Alexander Guttmann from Cincinnati, sociology of the Jews; and Chaim Rabin from Jerusalem, Hebrew literature.[63] During its few first years, the academic advisory board included members from Great Britain, France, Israel, and the United States, with none from the Federal Republic.[64]

The great promise of the founding phase fairly quickly gave way to some sobering realities, which could hardly have been avoided given the small size of the community. On the one hand, student interest remained low. Although the number of enrolled students increased from sixteen during the 1979–1980 winter semester to thirty-six during the 1981–1982 winter semester, the figure had dropped to thirty-three a year later. On the other hand, those auditing courses increased. During the 1982 summer semester, eighty-six auditors took part in various events.[65] Several months earlier, the new rector of the school, Shmaryahu Talmon, had called upon the board of trustees to "concentrate on the number of students," since a "comprehensive teaching program with renowned teaching staff" had been created. The college should reach out to a broad public by way of seminars and speaker series, especially with the help of the communities of the Central Council.[66] The rather modest response brought with it other problems as well. During the first years, Werner Nachmann's mother cooked the kosher meals, which were then frozen and transported from Karlsruhe to Heidelberg, where they were thawed out in the small dining room.[67]

In addition, the teaching staff was not as solid as Talmon had supposed. As early as November 1981, Werner Nachmann, the chair of the Central Council, described the situation as a "founding depression," not least because only one qualified lecturer was able to perform to the level required.[68] And during the following fall, Nachmann frankly admitted that the stability of the institution and "with it the possibility of making long-term appointments" depended on "how the future of the Jewish communities in the Federal Republic would be judged." In his opinion, it would be difficult to find suitable teachers under these circumstances.[69] And, in fact, holding on to teaching staff remained a real problem for many years. During the first few years of the institution's existence, most of them could be lured for only one or perhaps two semesters.[70] However, in 1989 Julius Carlebach was named rector, and he was able to lend the institution a certain stability, which markedly improved its reputation.

The influence of the Central Council and specifically Nachmann's omnipresence led to a certain amount of conflict. When the founding rector, Leon Feldman, resigned in October 1981, he blamed Nachmann for his resignation. According to Feldman, Nachmann had reneged on promised positions, arbitrarily canceled existing contracts, and vilified colleagues for their religious beliefs.[71] That these accusations cannot simply be dismissed is made clear from a letter from Wolfgang Schluchter, the dean of the faculty of social and behavioral sciences at the University of Heidelberg.[72] And not least, the mission of the college was at issue as well. Originally conceived to train rabbis, cantors, and religion teachers, it soon became clear that scholarship would take pride of place. Nathan Peter Levinson, the state rabbi of Baden, received no support when he complained about this trend during the institution's second year, especially about the "underrepresentation of Jewish scholars" and the lack of a "rabbinical diploma." Even his suggestion that a representative from the Rabbinical Conference be made a member of the board was rejected.[73] This is more evidence of the extent to which the Central Council—and not the Rabbinical Conference—was determinative of Jewish life in the Federal Republic.

POLITICS AND RELIGION

Despite general secretary van Dam's broad knowledge of the problems facing the small Jewish community, his end-of-year review for 1970 evinced a significant blind spot: the Central Council's own responsibility for those problems. It was obvious that the emphasis on restitution, reintegration, and the resumption of relations with the Jewish world had been the council's chief priorities. This is why it is appropriate to characterize the first decades of the Jewish presence in West Germany as dominated by political considerations. As a result, it is not surprising that the Rabbinical Conference, founded in 1957, had hardly any room to maneuver and consequently languished in the shadow of the Central Council. Nor is it surprising that individual community leaders repeatedly preempted the rabbis in questions of religion.[74] And this situation came to a head in the 1970s. Although the extant sources are modest, it is nonetheless possible to follow the concerns and interests of the various sides in the letters that exist.

Numerous members left from the communities during the 1970s, and although the numbers never really posed an existential threat, those in the leadership were troubled. The Central Council believed that the primary reason was financial. According to Galinski at a council meeting in April 1972, some members were simply no longer prepared to pay the required taxes. The following discussion was interesting not so much because members agreed with this reasoning but because of Ignatz Bubis's suggestion of forming a commission of representatives of the Central Council and the Rabbinical Conference to deal with this problem.[75] Bubis must have known that the success of such a commission (which was never formed) would have been doubtful from the outset because of the tense relationship between the two bodies. The subsequent tensions may be understood as part of an ongoing dynamic in which the politicians found fault and then expected remedies from the rabbis, while the latter were not prepared to accept the primacy of the Central Council or the separation of Jewish politics from Jewish religion.

It is astonishing how often the rabbis were accused of inaction, indifference, and even ignorance. This came up not only around the larger issues, since there were more than enough ongoing problems that required religious authority. In February 1972, for example, there was the behavior of Polish immigrants who were absolutely opposed to having their sons circumcised but had no intention of leaving the Jewish community in Mainz. The chair of the community complained that the Rabbinical Conference had yet to decree guidelines on circumcision.[76] Although this case was an entirely internal Jewish matter, the larger political realities peeked through in another instance. Here, Nachmann and Galinski expressed their dismay that the Rabbinical Conference had not taken a position on Section 218 of the German penal code, which outlawed abortion. Ever since Alice Schwarzer began her campaign against that law with an article in the mass-market magazine *Stern*, Jewish political leaders had complained that young people felt leery about seeking advice from rabbis, who were oblivious to these larger debates taking place in society. It appeared to them that no relationship of trust existed.[77]

The rabbis for their part constantly accused the officials of not consulting the rabbinate when making decisions. In February 1976 the Munich rabbi H. I. Grünewald wrote an urgent letter to Alexander Ginsburg, the general secretary, about this matter. In it, he accused Ginsburg of not having found it necessary to invite the Rabbinical Conference to the meetings of the Central Council. Furthermore, the rabbi had been waiting for a year for a tentative date for a meeting. The Central Council had not even dignified with a response the request by the rabbis to be represented on the editorial committee of the *Allgemeine Jüdische Wochenzeitung.* As a result, it should come as no surprise that the newspaper had recently published a misleading article about *kashrut* (the Jewish dietary laws). Grünewald concluded his letter with the following accusation to the members of the Central Council: "It pains us that in contrast to other central Jewish organizations in the countries of Europe, the rabbinate in the FRG [Federal Republic of Germany] is not dignified with the position owed to rabbis in the Jewish community and that the leading authorities are content to invite the rabbis [solely] for representational purposes (e.g., on the Yad Vashem committee) without requesting their collaboration. Consistent with what was written above and for the purpose of working out a plan of cooperation, we again request a conversation, which has for so long been discussed."[78] No response is known.[79]

Matters came to a head in 1978. In its draft budget for 1979, the directorate of the Central Council decided not to include a budget item for the Rabbinical Conference. According to Ginsburg, this was done because the rabbis had continuously canceled meetings, often on short notice. But he also noted an additional reason from which one may conclude that the Central Council did not approve of the new division of authority in the Rabbinical Conference: "The directorate has more than justified doubt as to whether the conditions that led to the founding of the Rabbinical Conference by the Central Council of Jews in Germany still pertain. One of the important conditions for the creation of this committee was the involvement of all rabbis living in Germany in this conference with equal rights and responsibilities, regardless of their religious orientation."[80] The chair of the Rabbinical Conference, Ernst Roth, the state rabbi of Hessen, twice responded to this letter. The initial response seemed unconcerned. In it, Roth explained to the Central Council that in the future the rabbis would make their own way even without financial support; furthermore, the Rabbinical Conference had never canceled a meeting on short notice. A month later, the language in a second letter was more hedged after Roth had been told of many cancellations that had occurred prior to his taking office. He now took full responsibility for the last cancellation but stressed that current differences should not be interpreted as a lack of interest on the part of the Rabbinical Conference in cooperating with the Central Council.[81] The sources contain no further information about the cutoff of finances, as some degree of cooperation, however cursory, seems to have been reestablished.[82] In fact, the preponderance of the evidence suggests that the squabbles between the Rabbinical Conference and the

Central Council had decreased in salience as the rabbis concentrated increasingly on their own problems, especially the religious orientation of the communities.

After 1945 the Liberal movement had to contend with a religious Orthodoxy that was determinative of religious life almost everywhere.[83] Although Berlin had the only Liberal community in the Federal Republic, the Liberal rabbis were often quite Orthodox.[84] The Frankfurt community allowed a small group of members to hold Liberal services only in 1967, albeit without organ music. This deviation from the status quo was the work of Irene Militscher, who was a member of the community board and herself belonged to the Liberal group.[85] But even in Frankfurt, the potential for building a Liberal community within the greater Jewish community was limited. In the beginning, many people took on religious functions, whether on the Sabbath or the High Holy Days. No regular religious services were held, and no fixed space or building was set aside for the purpose.[86] In later years, Liberal Jews in Frankfurt and elsewhere depended on the moral, financial, and organizational support of the World Union of Progressive Jews, which sent rabbis from all over Europe and Israel to Germany to hold occasional religious services.[87]

Over time, the conflict between the Liberal and Orthodox communities became a supraregional problem. In 1979–1980 the Rabbinical Conference tried to deal with this conflict, not least because of impending decisions about personnel. The Orthodox community had much to lose. In early November 1979 a decision was made at a meeting in Frankfurt that each member of the Rabbinical Conference could run as a candidate for the board. H. I. Grünewald, who wanted to retain the previous unwritten rule that only Orthodox colleagues could be entrusted with board membership, was especially upset. For him it was simply unimaginable, because Orthodox rabbis would find it impossible to recognize someone on the board "who questions, even if only in a limited way, the binding force of religious law." Grünewald refused to participate in the vote—and the Beth Din (Rabbinical Court) in London agreed with him.[88] To circumvent the problem of board membership, at least temporarily, he suggested founding various working groups. The *halakhah* (religious law) working group would be reserved solely for Orthodox rabbis, and they alone would adjudicate questions of religious law.[89] Grünewald stated that he had always viewed himself as a student of the Berlin rabbi Esriel Hildesheimer, who in contrast to the Frankfurt rabbi Samson Raphael Hirsch had no objections to working with those of different religious orientations—as long as Orthodoxy retained the upper hand in questions of religious law. He continued to support the idea of a Jewish unitary community.[90] But when the more Liberal Emil Davidovic, the state rabbi of Westphalia, became chair despite these objections, Grünewald and Roth in August 1980 announced their provisional resignation from the Rabbinical Conference.[91]

This confrontation provides a glimpse into several developments. First, it should be noted that religious orientation had nothing to do with an individual's attitude toward the outside world. Thus, although Grünewald insisted on a unitary community under Orthodox leadership, he was in favor of dialogue with the Christian churches. Davidovic, by contrast, rejected all such contact, although he was closer to a Liberal conception of Judaism. But the most important change that occurred during this time was undoubtedly that the monopoly exercised by Orthodoxy was slowly dissolving, although this did not lead to immediate power shifts at the local level. On the contrary, Orthodox community rabbis like Grünewald continued to hew to traditional laws. Nonetheless, the election of Davidovic was a turning point at the symbolic level. The debates around conversion and mixed marriages increased, and even the Central Council could not prevent these questions from being debated. In other words, the community was moving, even at the religious level.

The Rabbinical Conference was not the only institution embroiled in controversy at the time. Arguments became heated in the Central Council, in the communities, and at youth and cultural congresses whenever the topic of mixed marriage was on the agenda—and it was often on the agenda. Between 1973 and 1981 approximately two-thirds of all Jews in Germany married non-Jews. Even if this statistic is moderated somewhat when marriages entered into in Israel are included, the figures were still high.[92] And since ferment was everywhere, the issue could no longer be ignored.

According to one report about a youth and cultural event in Hannover in October 1979, the issue of mixed marriages was so explosive that "a completely spontaneous working group" was formed to discuss the question.[93] The working group on interconfessional marriage led by Pnina Navè Levinson and Janos Paal at a similar event in Stuttgart in 1983 was the most heavily attended of all. The report in the *Allgemeine Jüdische Wochenzeitung* showed that the matter was discussed openly by all sides. All of the participants stated that they had been confronted with this problem in the past, and a number of them said that they were living in "a—completely happy—mixed marriage or would be marrying a non-Jewish partner in the near future."[94]

The problem of mixed marriages also played a role in community politics, but unfortunately only the Frankfurt sources are robust. In 1986 a New Jewish list ran for office in the community elections. Micha Brumlik, Susann Jael Heenen-Wolff, Susanna Keval, and others demanded more "democracy and transparency" in the community and pushed for a Jewish life "*in* Germany." The most important plank in their list's platform, however, had to do with the question of mixed marriage. The young politicians criticized the old attitudes toward the children of non-Jewish mothers, who were not permitted to join the community. In addition, they complained that non-Jewish spouses could not be integrated. It was therefore past time to give all children with a Jewish parent the right to become members of the Jewish community. Courses in the religion, culture, and history of Judaism should be organized for non-Jewish family members, and they should be offered instruction in Yiddish and Hebrew. If that did not happen, they warned, the Jewish community would have no future in the Federal Republic: "Whoever views the children of 'mixed marriages' as *goyim* robs Jewish life in Germany of its foundations and carelessly gambles away its future. He is a fool who hides from the fact that there will be many marriages between Jews and non-Jews in the foreseeable future, since 28,000 Jews live in a pluralistic society among 60 million non-Jews."[95]

Where did the Central Council stand on this matter? Clearly, the organization had tackled a number of salient problems since the 1970s. In 1970 it started an action group on Jewish questions; in 1977 it organized the first youth and cultural congress; and in 1979 it founded the Hochschule für Jüdische Studien in Heidelberg. But in retrospect, it is clear that in whatever endeavor it was involved, the Central Council pursued it only reluctantly and hesitantly, frequently responding solely to pressure from outside. And it often allowed only those issues to be discussed that did not put its authority in question. No matter how much the work of the Rabbinical Conference was overshadowed by internal dissension, or the lack of interest in young people shown by individual rabbis, or how provocative some young people could be, or how much time the organization spent on the requirements of day-to-day policy setting, the fact is that during these years the Central Council neither sought new paths nor developed strategies that might have offered alternatives to a shrinking Jewish community.

This was certainly the case with mixed marriages. Nachmann believed that only outright rejection could save the Jewish community.[96] As early as a council meeting in 1982, thereafter at numerous board meetings, and finally in public, he took the position that no Jew married to a non-Jew was fit to assume a leadership position in a Jewish community, especially not in work with young people.[97] In this instance, the non-Orthodox Nachmann allied himself with a certain tradition. In June 1947, for example, the Central Rabbinate in the British zone had decided that a Jew who had married a non-Jewish woman could not become a board member or represent the community or DP committee.[98] In 1966 the board of the Frankfurt community wished to introduce new bylaws whereby a person whose marriage partner was not a member of the community could not run for election.[99]

Nachmann based his position on two arguments. First, children from mixed marriages generally received no Jewish education, and second, it should be possible for young Jews to find a Jewish partner.[100] The board of the Central Council approved this position at a meeting in October 1984 and sent the following resolution to the communities: "The Board of Directors recommends that the member associations of the Central Council send representatives to the Board with whom, to the extent that they are married, both parties to the marriage belong to the Jewish religious community."[101] Although there were certainly those who regretted this decision, there was no real resistance. The public protest by Franklin Oberländer, who later became a well-known psychologist, was something of an exception. In an article in the *Frankfurter Jüdisches Gemeindeblatt* he reminded community members of the people living in mixed marriages who after 1945 were honored for their contributions to the rebuilding efforts. The recommendation of the Central Council, Oberländer wrote, was a "sneer at their blessed memory."[102]

For many years, board meetings of the Central Council were dominated by conflict between Galinski and Nachmann, and it is not always easy to discern the reasons for the tension between them. In some non-Jewish circles, Nachmann was viewed as a "dove" on the Central Council, while Galinski was seen as a "hawk," although the available sources do not really bear out these characterizations. To the extent that there was any reality to them, it was always with regard to relations with the outside world.[103] That leaves personal animosity based on power and jurisdiction as the most likely cause. Unbridgeable ideological differences were probably less salient.

As noted, differences of opinion were palpable with regard to relations with the outside world. Here, Galinski raised objections whenever he feared that Nachmann was making too many concessions or prematurely assuming "normalcy" in relations between Jews and non-Jews. In September 1975, for example, Nachmann expressed the desire to understand the internal structure of the Bundeswehr, the German military. As he put it, the Bundeswehr was a necessary component of a democratic society, which meant that the Jewish community would do well to demonstrate interest in its role and the politics surrounding it. Josef Neuberger and Alfred Weichselbaum supported Nachmann's initiative. Galinski, on the other hand, believed that such a step might under certain circumstances lead to a split in the community and "possible consequences for the greater community of Berlin."[104] Although Galinski never detailed why Nachmann's plan would necessarily have such grave consequences, Jewish misgivings about the Bundeswehr were too widespread for a policy of rapprochement to go unchallenged. Rapprochement was also the cause of board member Herbert Dressel's complaint to Nachmann about Galinski. The issue here was the counterterrorism tactics of the government of Helmut Schmidt, which Galinski had criticized in a public statement. In Dressel's opinion, it was simply not Galinski's place to comment on the

The members of the board of the Central Council of Jews in Germany meeting on February 15, 1970, at the Jewish community house in Düsseldorf. *From left to right:* Jeanette Wolff, Herbert Lewin, Werner Nachmann, and Hendrik G. van Dam. picture-alliance / Roland Scheidemann.

freeing of hostages and similar matters.[105] We do not have Nachmann's response, but in all probability he would have viewed Galinski's statement as meddling in his policy of quiet diplomacy.

From these seemingly "ideological" differences, it becomes clear that the two men's power centers were the real issue. Nachmann led the community in Karlsruhe, while Galinski alone held the reins of power in the Berlin community. To whatever extent political differences between the two may have reflected actual differences, the distribution of power and authority was frequently at the root of the tensions between them. And this was no coincidence, because next to General Secretary van Dam, Galinski had been the most powerful member of the Central Council. However, in 1963 he was rejected as chair of the Central Council, and after Nachmann succeeded Herbert Lewin in the position in 1969, Galinski would have felt frozen out of any future leadership position within the organization. Galinski, in effect, created his own power center in Berlin, from where he hoped to influence the Jewish community as a whole.

In November 1975 Galinski and Nachmann met to patch up their differences in a meeting that had been urged upon them by Günter Singer, Max Willner, and Alfred Weichselbaum. Both were conciliatory at the next meeting of the Central Council. Nachmann gave assurances that he had nothing against potential initiatives from Berlin or elsewhere as long as he was informed in advance. For his part, Galinski stressed that any initiatives coming from Berlin would be discussed with the Central Council for the good of the Jewish community.[106] However, the detente between them was short-lived, as the conflict reescalated less than two years later.

In his report about a trip by the Central Council to Israel, Nachmann criticized Galinski for having set up a separate meeting with Deputy Prime Minister Simcha Ehrlich, during which Galinski had conveyed a message from German foreign minister Genscher, although Nachmann himself had intended to meet with Ehrlich. Galinski insisted that he would not allow himself to be pushed "to the wall." The problem, he insisted, was Nachmann, who because of his "unquenched ambition" could not stand that Galinski had been received by the deputy prime minister.[107] A mere two months later, Galinski complained in a letter to Singer about the work of the Central Council leadership, which had led to a boycott of Galinski. In any event, General Secretary Ginsburg was neither willing nor able to mediate between the two; furthermore, the members of the administrative council were seldom informed about the steps taken by the chair and the general secretary. Finally, Galinski's press releases had not been printed in the *Allgemeine Jüdische Wochenzeitung*, with the threadbare excuse that the newspaper never published statements that had already been reported on in the general press. Given such practices, Galinski declared, he would henceforth desist from participating in meetings of the board and the administrative council of the Central Council of Jews in Germany "unless a fundamental transformation in the working practices of these committees and the behavior of their two leading elected officials is instituted immediately."[108]

Galinski found allies in the meeting of representatives of the Jewish community in Berlin. They took the position that Galinski could not be ignored on the board because ever since the founding of the Central Council he had been at the forefront of serving the needs of the Jewish community. Furthermore, his "political power" had to be recognized. Hans Rosenthal, the Berlin representative on the Central Council, showed understanding for both sides and sympathized with Galinski while recognizing that Nachmann, as unanimously elected chair of the board, did not always deem it necessary to discuss his positions with Galinski.

But neither Nachmann nor Ginsburg was looking for conciliation. They insisted that the Central Council speak with a single voice—Nachmann's voice.

Because of the office that he held, Galinski was not in a position to represent "the Jews in Germany." Furthermore, Ginsburg criticized the Berlin Jewish community's frequent failure to communicate with the Central Council, communication that, when it occurred, revolved "almost exclusively" around claimed expenses. The board sided with Nachmann. In December 1977 the majority of members stated that they would welcome Galinski's return to the committee, but only if he recognized the chair of the board and its general secretary as the sole official representatives of the Jews in the Federal Republic. Galinski responded by staying away from both board and administrative meetings over the following months.[109]

The conflict between Nachmann and Galinski had broader implications as well. In 1978 the Jewish community in Berlin and the state association of North Rhine, which included the Düsseldorf community, considered leaving the Central Council. The situation was so precarious that the Central Council dedicated an entire board meeting to the crisis and shelved the agenda item "Reports," which had always been a welcome occasion for Nachmann to hold forth on his trips and his thoughts. Delegates from North Rhine held that the policies of the Central Council were primarily established by Nachmann and Ginsburg, with the opinions of other members largely ignored. Furthermore, the board meetings were now held solely for the purpose of information and not collaboration. While the Central Council should speak with a single voice, it was still unclear "whether this voice always had to be that of the chair of the board." One suggestion was to allow Nachmann to represent the council, Ginsburg to deal with administration, and Galinski to represent the council in political matters relating to the Federal Republic. Although a resolution was passed at the end of the discussion that called for collaboration among all those involved, it devolved upon Hans Lamm to recommend the only realistic scenario, namely, that "the Central Council makes political statements, as does Herr Galinski."[110] That Nachmann was able to retain power as long as he did despite all of the complaints and considerable opposition from Berlin largely had to do with his image. After his death, both his allies and his opponents were unanimous in their opinion that he had been "charming," "eloquent," and a "personality" who had acted "dynastically." He was, in short, a "doer." Galinski claimed that his colleagues had looked upon him "as upon a monument."[111] But there was one thing that Nachmann the doer and Galinski the cautioner could agree on: the Jewish community must continue to defend against all attacks.

ISRAEL AND ITS CRITICS

From the very beginning, Israel had been a focal point of Jewish life in the Federal Republic. The country would once again take on special significance at the end of the 1960s, before and after the Six-Day War. Community leaders urged their members to support Israel unconditionally not only out of fear that it might be destroyed by the Arab states but also in order to demonstrate the German community's resolve to Israel and to the rest of the Jewish world. In some communities, those who resisted these calls or lagged in their response were pilloried.[112]

While solidarity with Israel remained strong, this time period may be viewed as a turning point. Some young people not only questioned the religious and political goals of Jewish officials but also openly criticized the Zionism of their parents. In the late 1970s Micha Brumlik summarized the situation as follows: "But those things by which one could until now shape one's life in a Jewish manner become increasingly incomprehensible: the Jewish religion and the State of Israel. Who still believes in God? Who really still derives meaning from all the rituals? Who is still really proud of Israel?"[113] And not long thereafter, Hans Jakob Ginsburg declared on the occasion of a Jewish youth meeting in Hannover that the Israeli flags and the picture of President Yitzhak Navon on the walls of the community hall had been of little help and that in 1979 Zionism contributed little "to resolve the problem of Jewish identity in this Diaspora."[114]

How had that happened? For one thing, many young Jews who had studied in the late 1960s and 1970s were not unimpressed by the criticisms of Israel swirling around the universities, especially in Berlin and Frankfurt. Students and others who sought to advance the cause of anti-imperialism and support the various national liberation struggles in the Third World accused Israel of colonialism. At the same time, many were disappointed by the official "bloodless" Zionism of their parents and disillusioned by the realities of Israel.

In 1980 Dan Diner, Micha Brumlik, and Cilly Kugelmann established the Frankfurt Jewish Group, and that year also saw the inaugural issue of *Cheschbon* (Accounting), a journal published by the German Federal Association of Jewish Students in Munich. Both had as their goal the inclusion of voices critical of Israel as part of West German-Jewish identity. The Frankfurt Jewish Group consisted of forty to fifty persons.[115] It was originally founded as an encounter group, and the questions of mixed marriage, Jewish identity, and Jewish life in Germany were of fundamental importance to its members. Most of them were comfortable identifying with the Left, because rightist and conservative parties were largely unthinkable for younger (and many older) Jews. In addition, as Jews living in the Federal Republic, the antimilitarism and internationalism of left-wing parties and groups appealed to their sense of history.[116]

The editors of *Cheschbon* also demanded a reorientation of the West German-Jewish community. The need for transformation was perhaps formulated most poignantly by Micha Brumlik when he declared the "Torah, Talmud, Tanakh, and *Halakhah*" to be central to Jewish identity. Because, in his opinion, "the Zionist experiment has already failed in political and moral terms," it must be possible to imagine a Judaism "without the State of Israel."[117] Heschel Freudig, another member of the editorial board, held that it was high time to rethink Jewish identity in the Federal Republic. Israel still perceived the Diaspora "as a sort of apostasy," he wrote. But in fact, the Diaspora no longer represented the insecurity for which Israel was supposed to be the answer. The haven that Israel once represented had, "to a great extent, [transfigured] our judgment of the Jewish state at the cost of any necessary debate over Israeli politics in light of the history of Zionism." In addition, "blind support" of Israel glossed over the fact that control over another people—Freudig meant the occupation of Gaza and the land west of the Jordan River—had already almost completely destroyed Israeli democracy.[118] That *Cheschbon* had captured a certain zeitgeist may be gauged from Werner Nachmann's question at a board meeting of the Central Council in June 1981. He asked "whether it is right to identify always and everywhere 100 percent with Israel."[119]

The right-wing nationalistic policies of Israeli prime minister Menachem Begin and the skirmishes between Begin and Helmut Schmidt undoubtedly added to this change in mood.[120] But what really transformed the views of many Jews in the Federal Republic was the war in Lebanon in the summer of 1982. Groups formed in Berlin, Hamburg, Frankfurt, Düsseldorf, and Cologne to condemn Israeli policies, especially the behavior of the army during the massacres at Sabra and Shatila by allies of Israel. For many members of these groups, among them the historians Julius H. Schoeps and Mitchell Ash and the political scientist Ossip Flechtheim, the massacre recalled the earlier persecutions of the Jews. They demanded that Israel withdraw from Lebanon and negotiate with the Palestine Liberation Organization (PLO), and they expected Jewish officials in West Germany to enter into dialogue with Palestinians living in the Federal Republic.[121] Some, like Diner and Brumlik, responded even more sharply. On June 13, 1982, they, along with twenty-three other members of the Frankfurt Jewish Group, protested the killing of Palestinians in Lebanon and demanded recognition of the PLO just a few hundred meters from the Israeli embassy in Bonn.[122] But this demonstration also signaled the growing gap between young Jewish intellectuals and the German Left. To distance themselves from the anti-Israel forces on the Left, they made a conscious decision to demonstrate without them.

For their part, Jewish officials often failed to appreciate or even perceive this fine point and simply rejected all demands out of hand. For many political and religious Jews, any criticism of Israel whatsoever challenged the very idea of Zionism. As a result, the responses were often just as drastic as the supposed provocations of the younger generation. Rabbi H. I. Grünewald, for example, compared the anti-Zionism within the Jewish community "with the antisemitism of neo-Nazi circles in Federal German society," characterizing both as negligible. In any case, Brumlik's opinion was "damaging to the community" and "reprehensible," especially since it repeated the arguments "of our enemies" and strengthened them in "their intentions, which threatened Israel and endangered the Jewish people."[123] Arno Lustiger, chair of the Zionist Organization in Germany, even denied the Jewish "oppositionals" the "bonus of being useful idiots according to Lenin's understanding," because "in contrast to the alterno-, sponti- and anarcho-rank-and-file, they knew Israel well from long stays there." After Israel's victory over the PLO, Lustiger continued in the same vein: the whiners, he said, were probably crying because "their heroic, terrorist PLO brothers could no longer murder Jewish children in the north of Israel."[124] And even Nachmann, not known as an ardent Zionist, threatened to withdraw financial support to *Cheschbon* because the journal had "challenged the State of Israel and the fundamental values of Judaism."[125] Some of the vehemence of the reaction may at least in part have stemmed from the shocking radicality of the criticism of Israel felt by many. Along these lines, Georg Heuberger, the former chair of the Association of Jewish Students and future director of the Frankfurt Jewish Museum, expressed his astonishment in a report about a preparatory seminar for the fifth youth and cultural congress sponsored by the Central Council in Wiesbaden. According to Heuberger, one of the participants had complained about the lack of emotional attachment to Israel and missed the *ahavat Yisrael* (love of the Jewish people), whereupon one woman countered that love makes blind—an answer that most of those present seemed to have "felt as a liberation."[126]

In retrospect, this trend was probably unavoidable. First, their parents had so venerated Israel that the reality for these young people could only be disappointing. Second, the democratic rhetoric coming out of the Central Council had an effect on young Jews, and as a result some in this age group began to question the Israeli state, given its military and occupation policies after 1967. And third, identifying with the supposed universalism of the Left was a natural position for young people to take. Not only was it "in the air," it offered young Jews a political home that was not to be found in the conservative milieu in which they were raised.

Also in retrospect, it seems obvious why Diner, Brumlik, and other left-wing Jews would want to distance themselves even further from the criticisms of Israel advanced by their non-Jewish companions once their antisemitism had become clear. Something similar had happened in the early 1970s during the battles over housing in Frankfurt.[127] At that time, understanding had not yet reached the point where Jews could publicly protest left-wing antisemitism. That had already changed by the mid-1980s. This became evident during the Fassbinder scandal, when many felt secure enough (and sufficiently "at home") to demand their "Jewish" rights and to hold a mirror to the Left. This change can be conclusively documented based on the examples of Diner and Brumlik and the newspaper *links* (Left).

Not three years after the Lebanon War, there was a fundamental change in the tone and content of many articles. Economic analyses, references to colonialism, and support for the Palestinian cause increasingly faded into the background. These were supplanted by the politics of memory: Diner and Brumlik began to emphasize the differing ways in which Germans and Jews dealt with the past. In March 1985 Diner criticized the trip to Israel taken by a delegation of Green Party members for their lack of sensitivity toward the past. The Greens, as an "eminent German party," should have known that such a trip "is *also* always a trip into the past." And although the party proclaimed a higher morality for itself, it had not wanted to confront the explosiveness of its undertaking. Nor did it perceive a historical problem with using the hackneyed dictum "Never again Fascism, never again war" in relation to the Holocaust when party members visited Yad Vashem, the Holocaust museum in Israel. The Jews had been the victims of German National Socialism and not, according to Diner, of international Fascism in World War II.[128] Brumlik agreed. As a member of the Greens in Frankfurt, he noted that at the latest since Israel's invasion of Lebanon it had become customary to compare "Israeli activities" with those of the Nazis such that "in the end the images of Israel today and National Socialist Germany merge to the point of indistinguishability." This recurrent comparison, he said, demonstrated a loss of historical understanding, political judgment, and moral sensitivity.[129]

A public debate developed in April of the same year that, in addition to Diner and Brumlik, also involved Daniel Cohn-Bendit, Otto Schily, Ulrich Tilgner, and Jürgen Reents, all members of the Greens. Brumlik tried once more to make clear that in the end talk of the victims meant placing Auschwitz and the Israeli politicians on an equal footing. He also attempted to place the history of Zionism in historical perspective by blaming European antisemitism for the early influx of Jews into Palestine. Diner for his part noted historical continuities between Germans and the Arab world that were conditioned by an underlying anti-Western tradition. Diner was also intent on explaining to his interlocutors the Jewish relationship with Israel. He spoke of the reassurance that Israel represented for most Jews and how any criticism of Israel would be interpreted as an attack on them, "as a continuation of their persecution."[130] These few examples make it clear how historical and psychological arguments were increasingly being mustered as a way of examining German and Jewish sensitivities.

This trend manifested even more clearly in Brumlik's article "Warum ich mit Ignatz Bubis solidarisch bin" (Why I am in solidarity with Ignatz Bubis). In it, he distanced himself from his political home on the left. Its members had not been in the least upset by the *Historikerstreit* (Historians' Dispute), in which conservative West German historians and intellectuals had tried to question the uniqueness of the Holocaust, or even by the Bitburg meeting between Ronald Reagan and Helmut Kohl. For many years, people had "in the tens and even hundreds of thousands poured into the street for each and every dead tree, for each and every drained habitat, for each and every rocket too many," but the "reinterpretation of the Holocaust as a normal war" had had no effect on them. Brumlik went on to attack the antisemitic strands of left-wing anticapitalism. But he also took to task Fassbinder's supporters, who had gotten worked up about Jewish protests against the staging of *Der Müll, die Stadt und der Tod* (*Garbage, the City, and Death*). Brumlik came to believe that the argument, according to which preventing the performance concealed a taboo against addressing the supposed rapaciousness of Frankfurt's Jewish real estate developers, actually masked a very different taboo: the "deep-seated desire once again to speak out against the Jews, to express openly that perhaps they had not been completely blameless in their terrible fate under National Socialism." And this impulse signaled the desire of many young Germans "to make peace with their parents and grandparents—a desire unachievable at any price other than the reinterpretation of the crimes or inaction of these parents' and grandparents' generations under National Socialism."[131]

In many respects, Brumlik's article represented the endpoint of a development that transformed members of the Jewish Left into independent Jewish intellectuals in the Federal Republic. Brumlik continued to be active on the left, but no longer from the perspective of one among many well-known faces at the Socialist office in Offenbach; instead, he was a decidedly Jewish intellectual who repeatedly took up Jewish topics and defended Jewish interests. By defending Bubis, Brumlik at least for a time substituted Jewish concerns for class warfare. In 1986 he, Diner, and other young Frankfurt Jews founded the journal *Babylon* as a forum for debate.

Toward the end of the 1970s and the beginning of the 1980s, other Jews who had grown up in Germany began to break with the political Left as well. Lea Fleischmann, a teacher who had grown up in the Föhrenwald DP camp, created a sensation in 1980 with the publication of *Dies ist nicht mein Land* (This is not my country), in which she discussed her reasons for emigrating to Israel. A year later, the journalist Henryk M. Broder wrote an article in *Die Zeit* titled "Warum ich gehe" (Why I'm leaving): "I cannot fight against reaction and repression alongside a Left that accepts me only as long as my Jewishness—a very rudimentary one—does not disturb them. This Jewishness also includes the 'insight that a Jewish state is a historical and political necessity that may not be meddled with.'"[132] In an interview in *Der Spiegel*, he made it clear that the realization that there can be no normalcy after Auschwitz had become ever clearer over time and that it separates the Jews from their German surroundings: "Our parents came to Germany because of their history, and we are leaving because of our history."[133] Broder yearned for an "end to life as an exotic," or, as Fleischmann put it, "I want to be like everyone else. For once I want to be a majority."[134]

CONSTANTIN GOSCHLER is Professor of contemporary history at the University of Bochum. He has been a visiting scholar at, among other places, Harvard University and the University of Prague. Goschler's publications include "Keine neue Gestapo: Das Bundesamt für Verfassungsschutz und die NS-Vergangenheit" (co-author); *Die Entschädigung von NS-Zwangsarbeit am Anfang des 21. Jahrhunderts* (editor, four volumes); *Europäische Zeitgeschichte nach 1945* (with Rüdiger Graf); *Schuld und Schulden: Die Politik der Wiedergutmachung für NS-Verfolgte seit 1945*; and *Wiedergutmachung: Westdeutschland und die Verfolgten des Nationalsozialismus 1945–1954*.

ANTHONY KAUDERS is reader in modern European history at Keele University in England. He is currently researching the history of hypnosis in Germany in the twentieth century. His publications include *Der Freud-Komplex: Eine Geschichte der Psychoanalyse in Deutschland, Unmögliche Heimat: Eine deutsch-jüdische Geschichte der Bundesrepublik, Democratization and the Jews: Munich 1945–1965*, and *German Politics and the Jews: Düsseldorf and Nuremberg 1910–1933*.

NOTES

1. A. Barkai (1991), p. 214; N. Gross (ed.) (1975), p. x.
2. M. Brenner (2001b).
3. E. Burgauer (1993), p. 26. See there also the thorough discussion about the available figures for Jews in East and West Germany, pp. 26–31, 153, as well as the statistical appendix, pp. 356–359.
4. E. Burgauer (1993), p. 156; for a strict delimitation of the criteria for community membership, see L. Mertens (1997), pp. 17–19; by contrast, Karin Hartewig recommends adoption of the category "Jewish Communists" as a "third identity" for citizens of the GDR of Jewish origin. See K. Hartewig (1993), pp. 292–302.
5. Membership statistics for individual communities and state associations in the Federal Republic and West Berlin compiled by the Zentralwohlfahrtsstelle der Juden in Deutschland e. V., 1970–1990, in ZWST, Referat Öffentlichkeitsarbeit; *Statistisches Jahrbuch für die Bundesrepublik Deutschland 1971*, published by the Statistisches Bundesamt Wiesbaden, Stuttgart and Mainz, 1971, p. 97; *Statistisches Jahrbuch 1976*, Stuttgart and Mainz, 1976, p. 125; *Statistisches Jahrbuch 1981*, Stuttgart and Mainz, 1981, p. 92; *Statistisches Jahrbuch 1986*, Stuttgart and Mainz, 1986, p. 95; *Statistisches Jahrbuch 1991 für das vereinte Deutschland*, Wiesbaden, 1991, p. 110. The data for the *Statistisches Jahrbuch* are based on information from the Zentralwohlfahrtsstelle der Juden in Deutschland e. V., Frankfurt am Main, and from the Central Council of Jews

in Germany. Contrary to the desired statistical precision, a note is placed throughout this entire time period for these figures to the effect that the total number of Jews is estimated to have been approximately thirty thousand for the years for which data were available. For a detailed analysis based on the same sources, see E. Burgauer (1993), p. 356. According to this, the precise membership figures for 1974 were 26,799 and for 1980, 28,173.

6. E. Burgauer (1993), p. 359; J. Thompson (1978), p. 249.

7. IRGW, circular letter, December 29, 1976, in StadtAS, IRGW 1026/415.

8. Minutes of the council meeting of the Central Council on April 16, 1972, in Düsseldorf, in ZA, B.1/7.868.

9. Minutes of the council meeting of the Central Council on June 16–17, 1980, in Frankfurt, in ZA, B.1/7.907.

10. Paula Almqvist, "Alles—nur kein deutscher Mann," *Stern*, no. 28 (1977).

11. A. Kauders (2007), p. 193.

12. A. Kauders (2007), pp. 195–196.

13. S. Volkov (2006), p. 190; see also D. Diner (2008b).

14. M. Brumlik (2000), pp. 63–94; H. Broder and M. Lang (eds.) (1979a); R. Schneider (2000).

15. ZWST, Membership statistics for individual communities and state associations in the Federal Republic and West Berlin, each on January 1, 1971, 1981, 1986, and 1991, in ZWST, Referat Öffentlichkeitsarbeit.

16. Draft of a letter from the head of BK Horst Ehmke to Ulrich Dübber (NDR), February 24, 1970, in BArch, B 136/9439.

17. On this and the following, see K. Bade (2002), pp. 418–419.

18. Minutes of the meeting of the administrative council of the Central Council on November 23, 1974, in Düsseldorf; minutes of the meetings of the board of the Central Council of Jews on November 24, 1974, in Düsseldorf and on February 16, 1975, in Munich, all in ZA, B. 1/7.904.

19. Minutes of the meeting of the board of the Central Council on September 5, 1976, in Frankfurt, in ZA, B.1/7.904.

20. Minutes of the meeting of the board of the Central Council on June 8, 1975, in Munich, in ZA, B.1/7.904.

21. Memorandum dated November 5, 1974, regarding a conversation between Federal Minister of the Interior Werner Maihofer, Werner Nachmann, and Alexander Ginsburg on November 4, 1974, in BArch, B 106/70787.

22. Götz von Coburg, "Berlin stellt jüdische Emigranten anderen Ausländern gleich," *Die Welt*, December 4, 1974; Ernst L. Levy, "Berlin drosselt die Zuwanderung von Juden," *Frankfurter Allgemeine Zeitung*, December 10, 1974.

23. Letter from Dr. Hartkopf (BMI) to the interior ministers of the states, August 17, 1977, in BArch, B 106/70787. On the problem of the recognition of Eastern European Jews as "members of the German people," see J. Brunner and I. Nachum (2009).

24. A. Kauders (2007), p. 73; E. Burgauer (1993), pp. 29–31.

25. "Heimstätte auf verfluchter Erde?," *Der Spiegel*, July 31, 1963.

26. M. Brumlik (2000), p. 116.

27. "Heimstätte auf verfluchter Erde?; E. Burgauer (1993), p. 30.

28. E. Burgauer (1993), pp. 153–156.

29. Y. Bodemann (2002), p. 128. See also Y. Bodemann (2005), p. 8.

30. For more, see especially S. Tauchert (2007).

31. *Jahresbericht 1969–1970*, in ZA, B.1/7.250.

32. G. Metzler (2002), p. 103.

33. A. Döring-Manteuffel (2007), p. 567.

34. B. Faulenbach (2004), p. 17.

35. Hans Lamm, "Parallelität der Entwicklung?," *AJW*, February 23, 1968, p. 1.

36. Hermann Levy, "Wir bestehen darauf, zu bestehen," *AJW*, May 31, 1968, pp. 1–2.

37. The editors, "Die Verantwortung der ersten Generation: Bundesverband jüdischer Studenten in Deutschland gegründet," *AJW*, April 12, 1968, p. 3.

38. The editors, "Die Verantwortung."

39. Hans Lamm, "Das innerjüdische Gespräch: Vorschlag zur Aktivierung des Gemeindelebens," *AJW*, October 16, 1969, p. 1.

40. Report by Paul Spiegel on the conference of Jewish young people in Berlin on February 12, 1970, in ZA, B.1/7.13.

41. Hermann Levy, "Umwelt nicht unbedingt freundlich: Ratsversammlung des Zentralrats der Juden in Deutschland," *AJW*, February 14, 1969, p. 5.

42. Letter from Kantor Wolf Gerstel (Münster) to Paul Spiegel about the meeting of the Jüdischen Frauenbund in Deutschland in Münster on May 31, 1970, in ZA, B.1/7.417.

43. *Annual Report 1969–1970*, in ZA, B.1/7.250.

44. Dan Diner, "Die Diskussionswoche und ihre Folgen in unserer Gemeinde," *Frankfurter Jüdisches Gemeindeblatt*, no. 6, 7, 8 (June–August 1969), p. 6. See also Heschi Rotmensch, "Persönlichkeitserfahrungen des jüdischen Jugendlichen," in *Frankfurter Jüdisches Gemeindeblatt*, no. 6 and 7 (June–July 1971), p. 4.

45. Dan Diner, "Die Demokratisierung der Gemeinde," *Frankfurter Jüdisches Gemeindeblatt*, no. 2, 3, 4 (Passover edition, 1971), p. 8.

46. Dan Diner, "Ansätze für eine jüdische Jugendarbeit in Deutschland," received on May 10, 1971, in ZA, B.1/7.113.

47. Flyer "Die Jüdische Gemeinde Frankfurt," on the occasion of community elections of January 31, 1971, in ZA, B.1/13.364.

48. Dr. Marek Glezerman, "Judentum und Inhalt: Warum auch unter diesem Gemeinderat die Kulturarbeit versagen musste," *Frankfurter Jüdisches Gemeindeblatt*, no. 11, 12 (November–December 1971), pp. 1–3. Glezerman emigrated to Israel in 1972.

49. See, for example, the minutes of the community meeting in Düsseldorf on May 28, 1970, in ZA, B.1/5.158.

50. For initiatives at the local level, see A. Kauders (2007), pp. 188–191.

51. Summary report of the seminar in Sobernheim on December 23–26, 1971, in ZA, B.1/7.113.

52. Letter from Naomi Barlev, Daniela Thau, and David Wasserstein (initiative group for youth questions of the Central Council) to Mr. V. N. Lewy, January 23, 1972, in ZA, B.1/7.391.

53. See, for example, letter from Daniela Thau, Ruwen Isser, and Michael Bock (IGJZ) to the members of the board, February 13, 1974, as well as the summary report of the seminar in Sobernheim of December 21–27, 1973, both in ZA B.1/7.391.

54. Letter from Ben Klar, Ben Prinz, and Michael Bock to the Central Council, dated June 18, 1974, in ZA, B.1/7.391.

55. Michael Bock, Ruwen Isser, Ben Klar, Benno Reicher, and Ralf Spier, "Ist die jüdische Jugend aus dem Dornröschenschlaf erwacht? IGJZ—gestern—heute—morgen," undated, in ZA, B.1/7.391.

56. Resolution of the conference of ministers of education of September 29, 1978, appendix 1 to report VtK II2, Re.: "Errichtung einer jüdischen theologischen Hochschule," June 8, 1979, in BArch, B 106/70796.

57. Report VtK II2, Re.: "Hochschule für Jüdische Studien im Allgemeinen," December 4, 1979, in BArch, B 106/70786.

58. Resolution of the board of the Central Council of Jews in Germany of January 28, 1979, in BArch, B 106/70796.

59. Letter from the Central Council to the boards of the Jewish communities in the Federal Republic, undated, in BArch, B 106/70796.

60. Report VtK II2, Re.: "Errichtung einer jüdischen theologischen Hochschule," June 8, 1979, in BArch, B 106/70796.

61. Minutes of the constituting meeting of the founding committee of the Hochschule für Jüdische Studien in Heidelberg on Wednesday, May 30, 1979, p. 4, and minutes of the meeting of the founding committee of the Hochschule für Jüdische Studien on October 16, 1980, p. 4, in BArch, B 106/70796.

62. Minutes of the constituting meeting of the founding committee of the Hochschule für Jüdische Studien in Heidelberg on Wednesday, May 30, 1979, p. 5.

63. "Faculty during the academic year 1980–1981," in BArch, B 106/70796.

64. "Classes during the 1979–1980 winter semester," in BArch, B 106/70796.

65. "Overview of the student numbers for the 1979–1980 winter semester to the 1982–1983 winter semester, as of August 1982," in BArch, B 106/70796.

66. Minutes of the meeting of the board of trustees of the Hochschule für Jüdische Studien in Heidelberg on Wednesday, February 24, 1982, p. 3, in BArch, B 106/70786.

67. Minutes of the meeting of the board of trustees of the Hochschule für Jüdische Studien in Heidelberg on Wednesday, February 24, 1982, p. 4, in BArch, B 106/70786.

68. Minutes of the constituting meeting of the board of trustees of the Hochschule für Jüdische Studien in Heidelberg on Monday, November 23, 1981, pp. 5–6, in BArch, B 106/70796.

69. Minutes of the meeting of the board of trustees of the Hochschule für Jüdische Studien in Heidelberg on September 1, 1982, p. 5, in BArch, B 106/70786.

70. Minutes of the constituting meeting of the board of trustees of the Hochschule für Jüdische Studien in Heidelberg on Monday, November 23, 1981, p. 1, in BArch, B 106/70796.

71. Letter from Leon A. Feldmann to Werner Nachmann, October 19, 1981, and letter from Leon A. Feldmann to the scientific advisory board and the representatives of the University of Heidelberg, October 19, 1981, both in BArch, B 106/70796.

72. Letter from Wolfgang Schluchter to Werner Nachmann, November 25, 1981, in BArch, B 106/70796.

73. Minutes of the meeting of the founding committee of the Hochschule für Jüdische Studien on October 16, 1980, pp. 5–6, in BArch, B 106/70796.

74. A. Braemer (2006), pp. 84–89.

75. Council meeting of the Central Council on April 16, 1972, in Düsseldorf, in ZA, B.1/7.868. One response to withdrawal from the community was social ostracism. In March 1974 the members of the Central Council agreed to report all resignations by name to the individual state associations and communities. Minutes of the board meeting of the Central Council in Frankfurt on March 24, 1974, in ZA, B.1/7.904.

76. Letter from Alfred Epstein to the Central Council, February 8, 1972, in ZA, B.1/7.387. In the instances mentioned, both parents were Jewish.

77. Council meeting of the Central Council on June 16–17, 1974, in Hannover, in ZA, B.1/7.904.

78. Letter from the Rabbinical Conference to the Central Council, February 19, 1976. The request for a seat on the editorial committee of the *AJW* had been made in December 1975. Other complaints of this sort followed. See the letters from Ernst Roth to Werner Nachmann, July 5, 1978, and H. I. Grünewald to Hans Jakob Ginsburg, November 28, 1978. For more on the role of the German rabbinate in Europe, see also the letter from Fritz Bloch, H. I. Grünewald, and N. P. Levinson to Ernst Roth, February 17, 1977, all in ZA, B.1/7.387.

79. In a later letter Nachmann claimed that the Rabbinical Conference under the leadership of H. I. Grünewald had canceled numerous dates. Letter from Werner Nachmann, June 27, 1978, in ZA, B.1/7.387.

80. Letter from Alexander Ginsburg to Ernst Roth, December 13, 1978, in ZA, B.1/7.387.

81. Letter from Ernst Roth to the Central Council, December 21, 1978, and January 25, 1979, in ZA, B.1/7.387.

82. A later letter provides evidence that the Central Council at some point over the course of the year again transferred money to the Rabbinical Conference: letter from Grünewald to the members of the Rabbinical Conference, November 6, 1979, in ZA, B.1/7.387.

83. For a Liberal perspective, see the undated report "Germany: A Time to Build?," in AJA, MS16 G1/11.

84. Letter from Heinz Galinski to Lily Montagu, July 2, 1962, in AJA, MS16, G1/11.

85. Letter from Irene Militscher to Rabbi W. van der Zyl, September 18, 1967, in AJA, MS16 D5/5.

86. Letter from Albert H. Friedlander to Bertram Jacobs, October 24, 1967; letter from Irene Militscher to Bertram Jacobs, November 13, 1967; letter from Albert H. Friedländer to Irene Militscher, November 15, 1967, all in AJA, MS16, D5/5.

87. Letter from Bertram Jacobs to Irene Militscher, September 25, 1968, and November 7, 1969, as well as H. G. Brandt to D. Shepherd, January 30, 1970, and D. Shepherd to Irene Militscher, February 4, 1970, all in AJA, MS16 D5/5.

88. Letter from H. I. Grünewald to Emil Davidovic, April 17, 1980, in ZA, B.1/7.387. As early as the 1960s, Grünewald had fought with Liberal members of the Rabbinical Conference over the question of conversions. At that time, he was able to force them to recognize the *Schulchan Aruch* as the basic legal code. See L. Barner (2008), pp. 48–50.

89. Letter from H. I. Grünewald to the members of the Rabbinical Conference, November 6, 1979. Grünewald congratulated the new chair, Emil Davidovic, on his election but did not recognize him as his representative. Letter from H. I. Grünewald to Emil Davidovic, November 20, 1979. See also the letters from H. I. Grünewald to Emil Davidovic, November 6, 1979, to Hans Jakob Ginsburg, February 5, 1980, and to Werner Nachmann, February 14, 1980, all in ZA, B.1/7.387.

90. Letter from H. I. Grünewald to Pnina Navè Levinson, November 28, 1979, in ZA, B.1/7.387.

91. Letter from H. I. Grünewald to Werner Nachmann, November 25, 1980, in ZA, B.1/7.387.

92. Pnina Navè Levinson, "Standesamtliche Eheschließungen von Juden 1973–1981 nach den statistischen Jahrbüchern der Bundesrepublik 1975–1983," in ZA, B.1/7.332.

93. Hans Jakob Ginsburg, "Die Jugendtagung in Hannover: Forum jüdischer Aussprache; Probleme der Juden in Deutschland," *AJW*, October 12, 1979, p. 2.

94. "Im Mittelpunkt Religion und Familie: Die 6. Jugend- und Kulturtagung des Zentralrats in Stuttgart," *AJW*, December 2, 1983, pp. 1–2.

95. Flyer "Neue Jüdische Liste," September 1986, in ZA, B.1/7.263. Brumlik's statements were consistently pessimistic. See, for example, Stefan Wolf, "Junge Juden in Deutschland," *Jüdische Zeitung* (Munich), July 29, 1988, p. 6.

96. It was also sometimes hoped that the youth and cultural congresses might lead to relationships between the participants, thereby somewhat improving the "mixed marriage" statistics. Memo about the meeting of the board on September 8, 1985, in Frankfurt, in ZA, B.1/7.836.

97. Memo about the meeting of the preparatory committee for the youth and cultural congress on May 1, 1983, in Stuttgart, in ZA, B.1/7.339.

98. A. Quast (2001), p. 194.

99. Letter from Issy W. to the Jewish community of Frankfurt am Main, January 10, 1966, in ZA, B.1/13.580. The sources give no indication whether the recommendation was accepted.

100. Memo about the meeting of the preparatory committee for the youth and cultural congress on May 1, 1983, in Stuttgart, in ZA, B.1/7.339; and speech before a state association and planning for the future. The council meeting of the Central Council of Jews in Germany in Hannover, *AJW*, September 19, 1986, pp. 1–2, in ZA, B.1/7.256.

101. Minutes of the meeting of the Central Council on October 21, 1984, in Frankfurt, p. 3, in ZA, B.1/7.836.

102. Franklin Oberlaender, "Umgang mit der 'Mischehe': Ausgrenzen oder Integrieren?," *Frankfurter Jüdisches Gemeindeblatt*, no. 3 (June–August 1985), p. 8.

103. Heinz Galinski in the meeting of the board of the Central Council on August 31, 1980, in Frankfurt, in ZA, B.1/7.907.

104. Minutes of the meeting of the board of the Central Council on September 20, 1975, in Stuttgart, in ZA, B.1/7.904.

105. Letter from Herbert Dressel to Werner Nachmann, October 25, 1977, in ZA, B.1/7.106.

106. Meeting of the board of the Central Council on November 19, 1975, in Cologne, in ZA, B.1/7.904.

107. Meeting of the board of the Central Council on August 21, 1977, in Frankfurt, in ZA, B.1/7.904.

108. Letter from Heinz Galinski to Günter Singer, November 4, 1977, in ZA, B.1/7.106. See also letter from Heinz Galinski to Hans Rosenthal, December 15, 1977, in which Galinski complains about discriminatory behavior on the part of Werner Nachmann and Alexander Ginsburg, in ZA, B.1/7.904.

109. Minutes of the board meeting of the Central Council on December 18, 1977, in Düsseldorf, and minutes of the administrative council meeting of the Central Council on March 15, 1978, in Frankfurt, both in ZA, B.1/7.904.

110. Minutes of the board meeting of the Central Council on September 3, 1978, in Düsseldorf, in ZA, B.1/7.904. On the criticism of Nachmann by the State Association of North Rhine, see also the board meeting of the Central Council on May 28, 1980, in Frankfurt, in ZA, B.1/7.907.

111. Examination of various witnesses in 1988, in GLA, 309/217.

112. A. Kauders (2007), pp. 109–116.

113. Position paper "Thesen zur geistigen und politischen Situation der Juden in der Bundesrepublik," undated, in ZA, B.1/7.330.

114. Hans Jakob Ginsburg, "Die Jugendtagung in Hannover," *AJW*, October 12, 1979, pp. 1–2.

115. For more on the group, see S. Khasani (2006), and S. Khasani (2005).

116. Heinz Galinski stated that young Jews could only "align themselves with the Left." Minutes of the council meeting of the Central Council on May 23, 1968, in ZA, B.1/7.259. For natural similarities between Jews and universalist ideology, see D. Diner (2000), p. 236.

117. Micha Brumlik, "Krise der jüdischen Identität?," *Cheschbon*, Spring 1980, pp. 7–11.

118. Hersch Freudig, "Die 'Gefahr' der Selbstkritik," *Cheschbon*, Fall 1980, p. 7.

119. Minutes of the meeting of the board of the Central Council on June 28, 1981, in ZA, B.1/7.834. See also Schalom Ben-Chorin, "Fremd im eigenen Land? Die Lage der Juden in der Bundesrepublik, gesehen von einem Israeli," *AJW*, September 5, 1980, p. 18. Ben-Chorin believed that the "Jews in the Diaspora, too, cannot identify with the course taken by an Israeli government that does not always comport with their understanding of democracy and liberality."

120. Menachem Begin had claimed that as an *Oberleutnant* (senior lieutenant), Helmut Schmidt had never retracted his oath to Hitler and during World War II had attended a trial in the Volksgerichtshof (People's Court) presided over by Roland Freisler. Heinz Galinski believed that the controversy between Begin and Schmidt had harmed the Jewish community. Minutes of the meeting of the board of the Central Council of June 28, 1981, in Frankfurt, in ZA, B.1/7.834. See also N., "Die überflüssige Kontroverse," *AJW*, March 5, 1982, pp. 1–2.

121. See the various explanations in *Yad Tabenkin*, 15–135/4/5.

122. S. Khasani, "Eine Minderheit in der Minderheit," *Trumah* 14 (special issue, "Juden in der Bundesrepublik: Dokumentationen und Analysen") (2005), p. 63.

123. H. I. Grünewald, "Rückblick," *Cheschbon*, Fall 1980, p. 46.

124. Pamphlet, *Delegiertentagung der Zionistischen Organisation in Deutschland in Berlin*, October 23–24, 1982, pp. 22–23, in ZA, B.1/7.581.

125. Minutes of the meeting of the board of the Central Council, May 28, 1980, in ZA, B.1/7.834.

126. Georg Heuberger, "Ahawat Israel—oder macht Liebe blind?," *AJW*, December 4, 1981, pp. 3, 5.

127. See also A. Kauders (2007), pp. 79–88.

128. Dan Diner, "Sehnsucht nach Normalität: Israel-Reise der Grünen," *links*, no. 180 (March 1985), pp. 6–7.

129. Micha Brumlik, "Arnoldshain oder: Der Versuch, den Nationalismus zu verflüssigen," *links*, no. 181 (April 1985), pp. 9–10.

130. "Antisemitismus, Internationalismus, Nahostkonflikt: Ein Streitgespräch," *links*, no. 181 (April 1985), pp. 25–33.

131. Micha Brumlik, "Warum ich mit Ignatz Bubis solidarisch bin," *links*, no. 189 (December 1985), pp. 8–10. See also Dan Diner, "Rückkehr zur Normalität? These zum Streit um das Fassbinder-Stück," *links*, no. 189 (December 1985), p. 6.

132. Henryk Broder, "Warum ich gehe," *Die Zeit*, no. 10, February 27, 1981.

133. "Für Juden gibt es hier keine Normalität," *Der Spiegel*, April 20, 1981, p. 46.

134. L. Fleischmann (1980), p. 48.

11 THE JEWS IN GERMAN SOCIETY

THE BATTLE OVER RESTITUTION

The issue of restitution was central to how Jews related to the German political system after 1945.[1] In the West, the Jewish Conference on Material Claims against Germany (known as the Claims Conference), which was headquartered in New York, became the primary advocate for restitution. In the East, on the other hand, restitution was treated as a side issue by the former anti-Fascist resistance fighters who were closely allied with the Socialist Unity Party of Germany (Sozialistische Einheitspartei Deutschlands, SED), the ruling communist party in the Soviet zone. Predictably, the outcomes were very different in the two Germanys. Whereas the few Jews remaining in the German Democratic Republic were subject to a paternalistic system that was primarily tailored to the needs of the former resistance fighters, a comprehensive system of compensation and restitution was created in the Federal Republic that was designed to serve the needs of former German Jews and of Eastern European Jews who had found their way to the Federal Republic as DPs within a particular time period and had remained there. Both in the West and the East, restitution became a significant element in the "exchange of gifts" between Jews and non-Jews, since it served as proof that the Germans were distancing themselves from their National Socialist past.[2] By the early 1970s, however, these issues seemed to have been laid to rest. In any case, since the 1950s the GDR had categorically rejected any Jewish claims, especially from abroad, that went beyond the existing support system that the GDR had established. But even in the Federal Republic, the postwar era appeared to have come to an end.

The central element of West German restitution, the Federal Restitution Law (Bundesentschädigungsgesetz, BEG), allowed for no further claims after 1969. As a result, routine administration became the order of the day. But as tensions between the United States and the Soviet Union began to relax, it became increasingly possible for Jews in the Eastern Bloc countries to travel. In 1965 the Claims Conference had given assurances that, in exchange for relaxed eligibility for cases brought after 1953, it would make no claims in the name of Jews who might emigrate from the Soviet sphere of influence in the future. Since the situation had now changed, the Claims Conference backed away from these assurances. It now demanded a solution for the Jews who had emigrated from the Eastern Bloc after 1965.[3]

As a result, in the early 1970s the Claims Conference, to which twenty-three organizations, including the Central Council of Jews in Germany, belonged, began to petition the German federal government to grant a so-called *Abschlussgeste* (concluding gesture). The conference's main goal was to have the post-1965 cases included in the Federal Restitution Law. Initially, the federal government rejected the conference's request, primarily because the government was struggling to balance the national budget after the postwar boom. But at the same time, the government feared that relenting in this instance would prejudice the Eastern European restitution claims that had to date been rejected, as well as the claims made by groups of German soldiers who had been injured in the war. Finally, there was Germany's relationship with the Arab states, especially after the oil embargo of 1973 had for the first time made clear the direct connection between the economic well-being of the Federal Republic and German support for Israel.

Negotiations were initially conducted by Nahum Goldmann, the president of the Claims Conference, and as he had when Konrad Adenauer was chancellor, he first sought to engage the political leadership in direct and discreet discussion. On August 30, 1973, he met with Chancellor Willy Brandt, who accepted Goldmann's proposal for setting up a committee of all the factions in the Bundestag to discuss the proposed *Abschlussgeste*. However, the German government wished to prevent any amendments to the Federal Restitution Law, and so it proposed setting up a separate foundation for the purpose.[4] Such a foundation under international law would be designed to help persecuted Jews who had fallen through the cracks of the restitution laws. At the same time, this solution would have approached the issue from a humanitarian rather than a legalistic standpoint, which was also in Germany's interest.[5]

As finance minister, Helmut Schmidt had initially rejected the notion. But when he succeeded Willy Brandt as chancellor, he decided to make good on his predecessor's promise of a "concluding gesture of restitution" that would be supported by all parties in the Bundestag. Throughout 1974 the Claims Conference and the federal government discussed possible models for such a foundation, which was to be endowed with 600 million DM.[6] In exchange, the Claims Conference and Israel would each sign a disclaimer stating that they would renounce all future claims to restitution.[7] Goldmann was resistant to the idea of a foundation because he wanted a solution modeled after the Second Protocol to the Hague Convention, which would have given the Claims Conference sole discretion in the distribution of funds.[8] Of course, this was contrary to the interests of the German government, which was set on a political solution to the Jewish claims that had not yet been settled. But in addition, Israeli organizations of Jewish survivors viewed this model as a misappropriation of funds that would deny the rights of individual Holocaust victims.

The notion of a foundation ran into increasing trouble for a number of reasons. After the oil crisis of 1973–1974, which had a drastic effect on the German federal budget, the government would have preferred a postponement, especially because it was awaiting the results of parallel negotiations conducted by a delegation from the Claims Conference, led by Benjamin B. Ferencz, and the Committee of the Anti-Fascist Resistance Fighters in the GDR.[9] The United States had made such negotiations a precondition for establishing diplomatic relations with the GDR. In 1951 Israel and the Claims Conference demanded that the GDR pay $100 million, that is, the "missing third" demanded in restitution from Germany overall. Instead, the GDR agreed only to a token gesture, and in November 1976 the Committee of the Anti-Fascist Resistance Fighters transferred the sum of $1 million to the Claims Conference "to support the citizens of the Jewish faith in the United States who had been persecuted by the Nazi regime."[10] This transfer was accompanied by a declaration that the GDR accepted no legal or moral responsibility for those persecuted by the Nazis living outside of its territory. The Claims Conference immediately returned this "donation," which it considered wholly incommensurate with the dimensions of the problem.

Over the following years, the Claims Conference attempted in vain to induce the GDR to make a substantial restitution payment by dangling before it the prospect of most favored trading partner status with the United States. But for a time, negotiations with the Federal Republic also threatened to founder. Indiscretions committed by the usually prudent Goldmann were at least in part to blame, as he allowed details of secret negotiations to leak to the public.[11] At the same time, Werner Nachmann began to question the previous rules of the game. He criticized the "fix" between the Claims Conference and the federal government that in effect sidelined the Central Council, and his demands for inclusion in the negotiations became increasingly strident. He also demanded a greater role for German Jews in distributing the money, and in the end he threatened to reject any agreement concluded without the Central Council.[12] By doing this, he was attempting to overturn the distribution of roles that had become ingrained over decades by which the Central Council always took a back seat to the Claims Conference in restitution negotiations with the German government.[13]

Nachmann's misgivings, which he expressed in discussions with numerous German politicians, contributed to the failure of a meeting of the German chancellor and the party chairmen in the Bundestag that had been set for January 16,

1975.[14] The CDU-CSU faction refused to take part in Schmidt's all-party initiative. Although the faction agreed in principle, its members objected that, among other things, the interests of the German Jews were not being taken sufficiently into account—one of Nachmann's talking points.[15] For his part, Goldmann proclaimed the success of negotiations in various newspaper and radio interviews in Germany and Israel.[16] This tactic proved counterproductive, however, because other groups of Nazi victims immediately came forward with their own demands. In addition, the PLO joined Libya, Syria, and Kuwait in threatening the Federal Republic with "measures" if it paid further restitution to the Jews.[17] Given the mounting obstacles piling up in its path, the federal government tabled the project.

At the same time, differences among the Jews continued to sharpen. Some of the Jewish associations of survivors, especially those living in Israel, questioned the right of the Claims Conference to conclude such an agreement with the Federal Republic.[18] In addition, the Israeli government made claims regarding the use of the funds that would be transferred to it.[19] Finally, Nachmann continued to agitate for a greater role for the Central Council in any agreement that might be concluded. His main concern was the support of the Jewish communities, whose financial future looked dismal. According to him, these communities had had a guilty conscience about their existence in Germany after 1945. As a result, German Jews had failed to mount an adequate defense of the prewar assets belonging to their communities—which were then transferred to the Jewish successor organizations. And because of that they had "received practically no return flow of restitution."[20] (This issue is dealt with in detail in chapter 1 by Dan Diner.) Ernst Katzenstein, the representative of the Claims Conference in Germany, summarized the situation as follows in early 1978: "Even as the bear freely roams the woods, the internal Jewish battle over the division of his pelt is already under way, in public, under the noses of the Germans."[21]

Goldmann continued to press for a memorial foundation in Israel that would receive 400 of the hoped-for 540 million DM, with the remaining 140 million going into a hardship fund for Jewish victims of persecution throughout the world. The Israeli government, however, advocated for 600 million DM, of which 140 million would go to Jewish institutions within Israel, 400 million to victims of persecution in Israel, and a mere 60 million to victims of persecution outside of Israel.[22] Only under great pressure, including from within the Claims Conference, was Goldmann prepared to earmark a larger share for individual claims, especially claims brought by Soviet Jews. What mattered most to him was to strengthen Jewish institutions in Israel and the Diaspora (but not in Germany) and the museums and other commemorative institutions associated with them.[23] Goldmann also wanted the foundation to be a permanent memorial to himself.

The consent of the CDU-CSU faction was necessary, however, because an agreement would be possible only if all three factions in the Bundestag were in support. On April 26, 1978, Helmut Kohl announced his faction's "principled willingness" to agree to such a "concluding gesture of restitution," however, under "the condition that the Jewish community living in the Federal Republic of Germany be appropriately considered."[24] This step had been preceded by vigorous efforts on the part of the Central Council chair. From then on, Goldmann and Nachmann negotiated together with the German government, although expectations for a "concluding settlement" differed greatly. In essence, Goldmann favored cultural institutions in Israel, while Nachmann wished to direct the financial resources to the Jewish communities in Germany and wanted to have the German government set up an emergency fund for victims who had not yet been adequately compensated. Hardship cases could be referred to this fund in the future.

The bases for an agreement were finally reached in early 1979: 400 million DM were set aside for Jewish hardship cases. This sum was to be administered by the Claims Conference, which would have sole discretion over its distribution. Another 40 million DM were allocated to the Central Council.[25] The German government was nervous that news of this project would be leaked to the public, fearing that it would not only encourage competing groups of victims but also draw protests by the Arabs, who had gained considerable political leverage by using the "oil weapon" during the 1970s.[26] Possibly motivated by the latter concern, Nachmann was able to convince the government to route all monies earmarked for the Claims Conference via the Central Council. Heinz Galinski, among others, had protested in vain against this arrangement, but Nachmann was supported by Foreign Minister Hans-Dietrich Genscher, who saw it as a way to deflect Arab indignation.[27]

The 40 million DM for the Central Council were allocated solely for the purpose of assisting the Jewish communities in the Federal Republic and not for individual hardship cases. Nachmann justified this by saying that there were probably no more than ten Jews who had been persecuted by the Nazis and were still living in penury in the Federal Republic.[28] Goldmann, on the other hand, felt that his goal was now even more distant, which was why he again insisted on the Second Protocol to the Hague Convention during discussions conducted in Bonn in June 1980 with Genscher, Schmidt, and Finance Minister Matthöfer. He still held out hope of "using a considerable portion of the money for cultural purposes" in Israel.[29] Matthöfer, however, explained to Goldmann the political reasoning behind Germany's approach: "The difficulties did not lie with the 400 million DM for the Jews, but with the billions that the CDU was demanding for non-Jews."[30] By this he meant other groups of persons persecuted by the Nazis, as well as persons forced into exile and other German war victims. In the end, Goldmann resigned himself to the inevitable and as a compromise proposed joint negotiations for the precise formulation of the implementing provisions. The final allocation guidelines for the "concluding gesture" of up to 400 million DM (plus 40 million DM for the Central Council) established that a maximum of 5 percent of the funds could be spent to aid reconstruction of Jewish institutions in the Diaspora.[31] At the same time, several provisions placed stringent limitations on the number of potential beneficiaries: only persecuted persons who lived in poverty, had not already received compensation, and had suffered serious demonstrable health damage as a result of persecution or been deprived of liberty for at least two years could apply for a one-time award of 5,000 DM. This stipulation did not, however, apply to women over sixty or men over sixty-five. Finally, the funds were to be transferred, initially in trust, to the Central Council in several installments. The Central Council, in turn, could transfer the monies to the Claims Conference only in accordance with these guidelines.[32]

This resulted in an unusual financial arrangement that reflected several interests. For one thing, Nachmann wanted to elevate the Central Council in relation to the Claims Conference. The German government was also intent on finding a way to privilege Jewish claims over non-Jewish ones without drawing protests from other groups of victims or from the Arabs. And it wished to ensure that conflicts arising from day-to-day administration of restitution would not swamp the German government. Over the following years, monies that went directly to the Jewish communities in Germany and the funds used to pay restitution flowed through the Central Council to the Claims Conference. By July 30, 1986, approximately 124,000 applications had been submitted, of which the Claims Conference decided approximately 90,400 and approved assistance in about 64,000 cases (65 percent).[33]

THE NACHMANN CASE

After Werner Nachmann's death on January 21, 1988, it was disclosed that the former chair of the Central Council had abused his position as trustee, siphoning off the considerable interest income from the restitution funds parked in Central Council accounts to, among other things, modernize his dilapidated private companies. This embezzlement created a shortfall of approximately 30 million DM. No sooner had his memory been solemnly honored by the assembled German politicians at his funeral than the Jewish community was seized by the fear that these revelations could trigger another wave of antisemitism. Curiously, the German media proved exceedingly circumspect and treated the incident as an individual weakness, an approach very different from the scandalmongering that characterized their reporting on Philipp Auerbach's embezzlement trial and suicide in 1952, which had ramped up antisemitism. For example, in the *Süddeutsche Zeitung* Hermann Rudolph expressed the concern that "many may not accept it for what in fact it is: the failings of an individual, at most aided by the organizational policies of the leadership committee of a council that lacks the necessary oversight."[34] In effect, public airing of the "Nachmann case" all but put the possibility of German democracy on trial, and thus the media avoided anything that might have been used to whip up antisemitism. In part this was because the scandal surrounding CSU delegate Hermann Fellner was a mere two years in the past. In that notorious case, after Deutsche Bank had acquired large portions of the Flick industrial conglomerate and was challenged to make long-overdue restitution to Jewish forced laborers who had slaved for Flick during the war, Fellner had commented, "Jews are quick to pipe up whenever money jingles in German tills."[35] Although the whereabouts of the funds that Nachmann embezzled were never satisfactorily clarified, a year later, the new chair of the Central Council, Heinz Galinski, and the minister of the interior, Wolfgang Schäuble, declared: "With satisfaction we note in this connection the responsible behavior of the media and of the public overall."[36] In the end, Nachmann's corruption came to be viewed as a human weakness and not as the act of a typical Jew, as had been the case with Auerbach, and the media treated this man who had fallen so low as something of a criminal variant on Nathan the Wise.

The revelations had caused the Central Council, now under the leadership of Heinz Galinski, serious difficulties, especially as it was accused of a lack of oversight. Galinski characterized the affair as the "greatest shock since 1945" for the Jewish community in Germany.[37] While accepting a degree of "moral complicity" on the part of the Central Council, he also attempted to dissipate the potential for lasting damage by hiring an accounting firm and industrial investigators to determine how it could have happened and discover where the money went.[38] The public prosecutor's office in Karlsruhe initiated an investigation as well. Despite exhaustive efforts, the case was never completely solved, although the mechanism of Nachmann's embezzlement was satisfactorily explained.

Nachmann had routed restitution funds from the Central Council account at the Bank für Gemeinwirtschaft to a separate account in the name of the Central Council at his personal bank, the Karlsruhe branch of the Société Générale Alsacienne. From there, he transferred the rather considerable interest to other accounts, mainly in Germany and France, as he saw fit. Another 9.5 million DM were routed to the account of the State Association of Jews in Baden, to which Nachmann had complete access. However, the whereabouts of large sums that in all probability went to his private companies remain in doubt, although about 1 million DM turned up in a Swiss account, earmarked for ransom money in case he was ever kidnapped.[39] This financial scam had been possible only because Nachmann had been viewed as an authority beyond reproach by both the Central Council and the State Association in Baden. As a result, no one took it amiss that he and Alexander Ginsburg, the general secretary of the Central Council, had arranged for joint sole signature rights for the accounts in question. Naturally, the affair also forced Ginsburg to resign. Ginsburg, who may have been suffering from the early signs of dementia and was somewhat impaired in his judgment, later justified this action, saying that he was attempting to accommodate Nachmann, who wished to improve his chances as a candidate for the German Chamber of Industry and Commerce "because he would then be seen as 'a bigshot' with access to many millions."[40]

Much like Ignatz Bubis, who at the time was still a member of the Central Council board, many in those circles claimed that they had had "unlimited trust in Herr Nachmann": "It was viewed as Nachmann's achievement that this 'concluding gesture' came into being in the first place."[41] This attitude also makes Nachmann's autocratic practices more understandable; because of his excellent relations with German policymakers and his powers of persuasion, he had insisted that he alone could procure the necessary funding for Jewish institutions. And from that position of power, he came to believe that it was only natural for him to exercise unsupervised control over the use of the monies he had procured. And he was not shy about stating as much: "I acquire the money and therefore I decide."[42] As a result, he was able to prevent any attempt at examining his fiscal conduct. In fact, even the thought of conducting an audit was viewed as a sacrilege by the members of the Jewish institutions that he led. Nachmann justified this by saying, "We [Jews] are not an 'association' but a religious community to which special rules apply."[43]

Other factors presumably played a not inconsiderable role as well. The position of chair of the Central Council is a classic example of an office based on the elevation of notables or prominent personages that is completely at odds with the careful selection of paid professionals. In the former model, the economic independence of the officeholder is seen as critical. Accordingly, those in Nachmann's circle simply assumed that because he appeared to be a wealthy businessman, he could afford to take the position on an honorary basis.[44] But in fact, his businesses were doing poorly, which he was loath to admit in public, as it would have damaged his aura. And so Nachmann's economic circumstances, coupled with the available political power, caused him to blur the line between private and public monies, although the fear of exposure seems to have haunted him throughout the latter part of his life.[45]

Although he took his motives with him to the grave, it is possible to delineate some of the structural factors that made them possible. First, the unusual financial provisions associated with fulfillment of the "concluding gesture" gave him, as trustee, extensive control over financial transactions. Second, the unshakable faith of his followers and opponents in the Jewish institutions in his unusual qualities, as evidenced by his talent for obtaining financing, meant that he would go unchallenged. Finally, the staff in his office in Karlsruhe was too overworked with business details and other tasks to ask the necessary questions. What is of interest here is less the legal aspects of the case but rather his characterological makeup, in which authoritarian tendencies and a larger-than-life ego conspired to release the brakes on caution. In the end, we see in Werner Nachmann, the "failed bigshot," a combination of situational temptations and structural defects. Behind the personal tragedy, we may also glimpse the personal and political strains placed on the small Jewish community in Germany since the 1980s, and this may have been one of the prices paid for the German public's growing awareness of that community.

THE SEARCH FOR SECURITY

The relationship of the Jews in West and East Germany to politics and the public was largely determined by the need for security, with antisemitic propaganda and violence the most immediate perils. However, their insecurity was not simply a reflexive response to immediate concrete or abstract dangers. Rather, the perception of relative security resulted first and foremost from individual and collective perceptions of reality, which were influenced by past experiences and expectations of the future in the two Germanys.[46] This section will consider less the causes or forms of antisemitic violence but more the manner in which the Jews in Germany in the 1970s and 1980s perceived violence and responded to it—and hence defined their relationship to their immediate surroundings.

Antisemitic violence in Germany changed both qualitatively and quantitatively in the early 1970s. While the desecration of cemeteries, synagogues, and community buildings continued, bombings, arson, threats of assassination and kidnapping, and other violent acts became more common. This phenomenon was new and could not be attributed to the aftereffects of the Nazi era that might die down spontaneously once that generation had passed on. Rather, these perpetrators were with increasing frequency members of the postwar generation. In addition, the attacks were no longer exclusively from the Right but from the Left as well, usually bearing the label of anti-Zionism and anti-imperialism. Eventually, antisemitic violence became transnational, and the terrorism often characteristic of the conflict in the Middle East began to be felt in Germany as well.

The transformation in the form and intensity of antisemitic violence also affected the sense of security felt by Jews in Germany in both the East and the West. In the Federal Republic, the Central Council summarized the change that took place between the 1960s and 1970s as mixed. On the one hand, the most recent Bundestag elections seemed to have dampened the threat posed in the 1960s by the rise of right-wing radical parties like the National Democratic Party (N). However, the setting of a time bomb in the Jewish community building in Berlin on November 9, 1969, by the left-wing radical Tupamaros West-Berlin and the arson of a Jewish old-age home in Munich on February 13, 1970, committed by unknown persons, which claimed seven lives, led to the recognition that the Jewish community was faced with a new form of antisemitism.[47]

Meanwhile, the Jewish community continued to face the old, familiar forms of violence and symbols of incitement, such as cemetery and synagogue desecrations; antisemitic statements and songs uttered by more or less drunk politicians, Bundeswehr officers, and others; and the spectacle of former National Socialists once again achieving high political office.[48] Such incidents became commonplace over the following years. They included threatening letters and bomb threats against prominent Jewish figures and institutions, including threats to Jewish daycare centers. The low point occurred during the 1972 Munich Olympics, when Israeli athletes were murdered—followed by the German government's failed attempt to free the hostages at Fürstenfeldbruck Airport.

All of these incidents increased the sense of unease, which in turn forced the introduction of security precautions around Jewish facilities that continue to the present day: cameras, alarm systems, police protection, and the like.[49] In 1986, when the new community center in Frankfurt was dedicated, 10 percent of the building costs went to security installations such as bulletproof glass and security barriers.[50] Salomon Korn's oft-cited words, "Who builds a house intends to stay," required amendment: ". . . and to protect it."[51] Of course, the effect of all of these measures was paradoxical: although they provided protection and therefore "security," they also made the threat constantly visible, thereby increasing insecurity.

In addition, doubts about effective protection by the German state periodically led to proposals for "armed self-defense," especially when the threat was perceived to be high. This issue was repeatedly discussed in the Central Council, although Nachmann and Galinski, who trusted in the state's police powers and promises of protection, repeatedly rejected such proposals.[52] We can only speculate as to how people outside the Jewish institutions perceived security. However, there is evidence that Jewish perceptions of antisemitic violence in the 1970s and 1980s were colored partly by personal experience and partly by

Dedication of the Jewish community center in Frankfurt am Main on September 14, 1986. Photo by Klaus Meier-Ude; ©Institut für Stadtgeschichte Frankfurt am Main.

media reporting—but in addition by the uncomfortable realization that almost any non-Jewish German of a certain age whom one might encounter could have been a Nazi.[53]

Protecting the Jews who faced increased terrorist threats during the 1970s also became a matter of internal security for the federal government.[54] As a result, Jewish institutions cooperated closely with the Federal Ministry of the Interior, as well as with the state ministries of the interior and the police, who treated the protection of Jewish facilities and events as a top priority.[55] At the same time, representatives of the community regularly briefed high-ranking politicians on antisemitism and anti-Jewish violence. Over time, a sort of double strategy emerged that may be viewed as an element of the "exchange of gifts" between Jews and non-Jews in the Federal Republic. While Jewish officials, in particular the Central Council, repeatedly warned of the increase in antisemitic violence, making both politicians and the police aware of such incidents, until well into the 1980s, they often objected to the image of growing antisemitism that was mainly being propagated by foreign media. This latter tendency was, however, criticized as opportunistic, especially by Jews outside the Central Council.[56] In this dynamic, we see the germs of a quid pro quo.

The terms of the exchange came into fuller view in the aftermath of research funded by the German Research Foundation and conducted by the sociologist Alphons Silbermann, who had returned to Germany from Australia. Silbermann was trying to measure the types and extent of antisemitic prejudice prevalent in West German society. The results of the first part of the study, which dealt with the latency of antisemitic prejudice in the Federal Republic, were published in 1976 and caused an immediate furor. This was because a survey conducted by the polling firm Emnid had concluded that "in addition to a tolerant group of approximately 30 percent and a strongly antisemitic group of approximately 20 percent, half of the population of the Federal Republic exhibits at least the latent remnants of antisemitic attitudes."[57]

Apart from questions concerning the basic robustness of these figures, of particular interest here is how the debate over them was conducted.[58] Not only were the results exhaustively discussed in public, but they also elicited heated reactions within the Central Council, which contested the validity of these high figures. Among other things, the study came under withering criticism in an article in the *Allgemeine Jüdische Wochenzeitung* by Hans Lamm, the chair of the Munich Jewish community.[59] As Nachmann explained to Manfred Schüler, the head of the Office of the Federal Chancellor, the Silbermann study made it more difficult for the Central Council to "correct the image of Germans abroad." The extreme left wing, he pointed out, was looking for any expression of right-wing radicalism in the Federal Republic to paint "a negative image of Germans. The Jews are making efforts to assist with the necessary correction. This, however, to an increased extent requires clarifying and distanced opinions."[60]

In its public utterances, the Central Council attempted to downplay the significance of antisemitism during this decade. Behind the scenes, however, it reported every instance of it to the federal government and demanded effective countermeasures. For example, representatives of the Central Council repeatedly demanded that the government respond more forcefully to the right-wing radical attorney Manfred Roeder, who not only wrote the foreword to Thies Christophersen's screed *Die Auschwitz-Lüge* (The Auschwitz lie) but also repeatedly baited the federal government and its members, not to mention Simon Wiesenthal, with antisemitic slurs and tirades.[61] And so in 1976 Nachmann demanded that Chancellor Schmidt take sharper action and a public position against Roeder. The chancellor's office, however, wished to continue as it had, avoiding legal action in order not to give Roeder, whom it considered a "crank," the benefit of additional publicity. While it cited academic freedom during the controversy over the Silbermann study, here the government stressed the independence of the judiciary.[62] Once again, demands for state intervention by Jewish institutions clashed with government appeals to the moderating influence of democratic institutions and a liberal public sphere. Attempts by the Central Council to be treated as a privileged junior partner of the federal government continually collided against clear limits. Paradoxically, increasing insecurity in the face of antisemitic threats came up against a more liberal understanding of the state and society.

In the debate over "internal security," the representatives of the Central Council took a position against totalitarian tendencies of all stripes.[63] In May 1977, for example, Nachmann sent a letter to Minister of the Interior Maihofer, warning him against using the election results that favored the democratic parties as a basis for judgment and urging him to look at other activities as well: "What left-wing extremism is attempting to achieve by pressure, right-wing extremism does by moral corruption and propagandist lies."[64] Again, he demanded an official declaration from the government acknowledging its concern over this new and extreme right-wing phenomenon: "Our fellow Jewish citizens are alarmed, and it is understandable that these incidents are being highlighted abroad. We ourselves are constantly called upon at all international meetings to discuss these matters with the delegates from other countries."[65]

If the late 1970s were permeated with a sense of threat from both the Right and the Left, right-wing violence came to dominate in the early 1980s. Among other things, in 1980 the publisher Shlomo Levin, a former chair of the Jewish community of Nuremberg, was murdered in Erlangen. The perpetrator(s) presumably had connections with the neo-Nazi Hoffmann Military Sports Group (Wehrsportgruppe Hoffmann) in Franconia. Attacks on Jewish institutions in Antwerp and Paris, not to mention the terrorist attack during Oktoberfest in Munich in 1980, added to the sense of peril. Jews attending religious services and those in old-age homes felt especially vulnerable, and voices advocating self-defense were repeatedly heard in discussions in Jewish communities. The Federal Republic responded by tightening security, which primarily involved an augmented police presence at Jewish institutions.[66]

But none of the countermeasures could provide a real sense of security. Thus, for example, Heinz Galinski, who was generally very satisfied with his relations with the Berlin police and with the protections provided there, declared in 1981 at a meeting of the board of the Central Council that complete protection was impossible: "The security measures should, however, be optimal. If we believe that the state can no longer guarantee our safety, then we must draw the conclusions."[67] But increased protection was not the end-all and be-all. The Central Council advised the federal government along with the ministries and the political parties about the increasing threat of right-wing extremism and demanded a public informational and educational campaign along with planned police countermeasures.[68] The Central Council also intensified its efforts in this direction with publication of the SINUS Study on right-wing extremism, which had been commissioned by Chancellor Schmidt. According to this study, 13 percent of the electorate harbored an extreme right-wing worldview that was antisemitic to the core.[69] Nachmann again took this opportunity to try to speak with the chancellor, who sent ambivalent signals. While he was grateful that the question of right-wing extremism was not being trivialized, he was extremely wary about overemphasizing this problem in public.[70] What Schmidt found especially alarming was the possibility that this was a phenomenon of youth, and he suspected it was caused by a lack of education about the nature of National Socialism and the murder of the Jews, along with unfavorable economic trends and rising unemployment. The SINUS Study, which linked right-wing extremism and antisemitism with a rejection of parliamentary democracy,[71] by implication also linked the presence of Jews in the Federal Republic with the stability of its postwar democracy.

As a result of repeated intervention by Jewish institutions and officials, the government instituted a number of measures to counter right-wing extremism and antisemitism, especially in the areas of public education and criminal justice. In terms of the first category, the Central Council began to work more closely with the Education and Science Workers' Union (Gewerkschaft Erziehung und Wissenschaft, GEW) to create guidelines for "National Socialism in the classroom," which were distributed to the schools by the state education ministries in 1981.[72] The Center for Antisemitism Research at the Technical University of Berlin, which was founded in 1982 at Galinski's suggestion, also belongs in this category. In terms of criminal prosecution, an amendment to the defamation law (§ 194 StGB) was passed on April 25, 1985, over the objection of the SPD and the Greens. This tool, which was an initiative of the Schmidt administration, was meant to facilitate prosecution of those who spread radical right-wing propaganda and especially the denial of the Holocaust; however, it proved to be a largely blunt instrument and was widely criticized.[73]

A feature common to all of these measures was their emphasis on battling the problem "from above." This approach was consistent with the tradition of the Central Council as put forward by Nachmann and then Galinski, by which security was to be achieved by recourse to the powers of the state. The public protests by the Jewish community in 1985 against the performance of Fassbinder's *Der Müll, die Stadt und der Tod* (*Garbage, the City, and Death*), which has often been described as a "turning point," seem all the more significant in this light. The protagonist of the play is a rich Jewish real estate speculator who seeks vengeance for the murder of his parents in the Holocaust. With emotions ranging from "defiant to fearful,"[74] members of the Frankfurt Jewish community blocked the stage with homemade banners and prevented the play's premiere.[75] By doing so, they wrested from social scientists and lawyers the right to define what was and what was not antisemitic. They themselves would decide.[76] The shift from calling for state protection to identity politics and what in German is called *Zivilcourage* (civic courage) also caused a fundamental reorientation in some Jewish institutions, a process that may be viewed as consistent with the overall liberalization taking place in the Federal Republic as a whole.[77]

Security was also a subject of concern in the German Democratic Republic, although with different coordinates. The state controlled by the SED viewed itself as the guarantor of Jewish security, thereby drawing a clear line between it and the Federal Republic, which was demonized as a haven for former Nazis and neo-Nazis. In exchange for protection, the Jewish community was asked to perform "*ideological work*, especially as it lent substance to the antifascist self-image of the GDR."[78] Nonetheless, Jews in the GDR were also subject to antisemitic violence and especially to antisemitic propaganda during the 1970s and especially the late 1980s—but in the form of anti-Zionist and anti-Israeli slogans sanctioned by the government.[79] Given the lack of visible, living Jews, antisemitic violence in the GDR was mainly aimed at the remaining evidence of dead Jews, which meant that Jewish cemeteries were continually desecrated during those years. As in the Federal Republic, state officials went out of their way to trivialize these incidents as the apolitical acts of children.[80] In October 1976, however, two bombings at the office of the Jewish community in Halle demonstrated that the potential for outright violence existed in the GDR as well.[81]

East German officials were extremely worried about any form of publicity, fearing that such reports would reach the West. For example, in 1983 twenty-three gravestones in the Jewish cemetery in Erfurt were smeared with Nazi symbols, two others were knocked over, and one was completely destroyed. As it happened, a member of the Jewish community documented the incident on film, but, rather than take action, the Volkspolizei, the East German police force, immediately confiscated the film.[82] Such fear of publicity was also in evidence in several other incidents, as in the quashing of a suit against a border guard officer who, after a drinking spree, attempted to break into the Leipzig synagogue in 1983.[83] In the case of the cemetery desecrations that took place in the GDR at the end of the 1980s—in 1980, for example, the Jewish cemetery in Mühlhausen and the Berlin cemetery in the Schönhauser Allee were both attacked—suppressing the news proved impossible.[84] The five young people who were responsible for the incident in Berlin were charged in court, and their trial was fully reported in

East German media. But even here, the favored explanations were exculpatory: aside from family difficulties, they had also been seduced "by Fascist and neo-Nazi models transmitted by Western media." As the official SED party newspaper *Neues Deutschland* noted, the sentences and their reasoning made clear that "in the GDR such outrages have no following, are condemned categorically, and will be consistently prosecuted in accordance with the legal system of our country."[85] In order to avoid damage to the GDR's anti-Fascist reputation, a collaborative effort was brokered between the Free German Youth (Freie Deutsche Jugend, FDJ) and the Berlin Jewish community, whereby the youth association would tend the Jewish cemetery in Berlin-Weissensee. In the run-up to festivities commemorating the fiftieth anniversary of Kristallnacht, which was designed to showcase to the world the positive treatment of Jews in the GDR, the Ministry for State Security finally ordered increased monitoring of "Jewish objects" to prevent the desired image from being marred by antisemitic incidents.[86]

While the GDR used its police apparatus to combat such incidents (although not always successfully), thereby clearly distancing itself from the actions of right-wing extremists, in other arenas its behavior sometimes bordered on approval of or even support for such violence. As early as 1973 Heinz Galinski had sent a letter of protest to Erich Honecker regarding an agreement with the Palestinian Liberation Organization (PLO) that contained provisions for opening an office in East Berlin and promises of support. As far as Galinski was concerned, this agreement supported terrorist attacks on Jews in the West.[87] Five years later, Galinski deplored the symptoms of neo-Nazism and antisemitism among young people in the GDR in the *Allgemeine Jüdische Wochenzeitung*, blaming the externalizing of the Nazi past in official anti-Fascist state doctrine and the continuing anti-Israel propaganda.[88] After years of denunciations of antisemitism and neo-Nazism in the Federal Republic by representatives of East German Jews, the finger was now being pointed in the opposite direction.[89]

Precisely because the GDR believed itself immune to neo-Nazism and antisemitism, it felt uninhibited in propagating anti-Zionist ideas and supporting anti-Israel actions, to which it attempted to enlist the chairpersons of the small Jewish communities. The longtime chairperson of the Association of Jewish Communities in the GDR, Helmut Aris, who played a leading role in developing the official image of a country in which "antisemitism has been rooted out and all racist agitation is punishable,"[90] had few qualms about condemning the Federal Republic as a paradise for Nazis, both old and new. Matters were somewhat different in the face of demands that Jewish community leaders condemn Israel's policies as "imperialist" and "Zionist." Here, some were more reluctant,[91] and on occasion we even find evidence of courageous objections to antisemitic statements in the GDR media. For example, in 1985 the chair of the Jewish community of East Berlin, Peter Kirchner, protested against a parable published in the children's *ABC-Zeitung* about the land-stealing "fire dragon Zion" and against a caricature of an Israeli officer in the *Berliner Zeitung* that was all too reminiscent of similar caricatures in Julius Streicher's Weimar and Nazi-era *Der Stürmer*.[92] The editor of the *ABC-Zeitung* was taken aback and tried to thread the needle between the ideologically required condemnation of Israel and the mandatory rejection of antisemitism: "Naturally, it was not and is not our intention to equate the Jewish people and the imperialist state of Israel and its Zionist policies. Distinguishing in a manner consistent with this would have worked in the fairy tale as well." The author, too, supposedly saw the light as a result of the criticism, and the editor promised a follow-up to the fairy tale with a fable "in which the story concerns the friendship between Palestinian and Jewish children."[93] Questioning the extent to which anti-Zionism and anti-imperialism were permeated with antisemitic stereotypes would not have been possible given the intellectual horizon on display.

Given the tiny membership in the eight independent Jewish communities in the GDR, they could not possibly have retained more than exceedingly limited autonomy. Although formally independent bodies, the interests of the SED played a major role in the selection of community leaders.[94] In addition, a number of leading Jewish officials were themselves SED members and had ties to the Ministry for State Security (the Stasi). This arrangement may be viewed as an element of the "participatory dictatorship" that characterized the GDR, because by their collaboration with the party and the Stasi, many believed that they could in some way influence the actions of the state and the machinery of political power.[95] As a result, many defined their collaboration not as informing but as a kind of power sharing.

The case of Hans-Joachim Levy sheds light on the mechanisms of collaboration and the ambivalences that such collaboration engendered. In 1979 Levy had been elected chairperson of the Jewish community in Magdeburg, and in late 1989 he was invited, as the sole representative of the Jewish community, to take part in the "roundtable" discussions that led to the eventual dissolution of the GDR.[96] After having briefly acted as an informant of the Stasi in the early 1960s, he again attracted the attention of the security apparatus because of his function as head of the community. The Stasi viewed him as potentially useful because in his new office he had official relations with Christian churches and with Jews in foreign countries.[97] On April 15, 1980, Levy signed a formal letter of commitment and then began filing regular reports with the Stasi under the code name "Ludwig."[98] But even before that he had provided evidence of his determination to expose antistate forces. For example, in January 1980 he reported to the Stasi on the visit of a student, a "member of a denomination," who questioned Levy in his capacity as community chair about his opinion of the American and British boycott of the Moscow Olympic Games. Although he had forgotten the student's name, he nonetheless described him ("wearing glasses"), and then he offered to "establish" his identity the next time he attended a service of the Jewish community.[99] One question about this incident that cannot be answered is whether Levy denounced the student out of conviction or because he feared being trapped by an agent provocateur.

But the other side of this coin was that Levy used his loyalty to the system and contacts within the security apparatus to denounce antisemitic incidents. For example, in 1982 he complained directly to the Stasi about an incident that had occurred at a New Year's Eve celebration at a company in Magdeburg, to which a Jewish coworker had brought a handmade sign that the janitor had found inappropriate. The janitor then proceeded to dispense antisemitic insults in defense of the socialist nature of the business under his care. However, the Stasi refused to follow up, because the complainant (Levy) was supposedly a "psychopath."[100]

Although Levy supplied his client over many years with reports that hewed to the party line, in 1986 he observed something that caused him to become "unreliable." In the fall of 1985 he had traveled to Israel and several months later gave a slide presentation before the Free German Trade Union Federation (Freier Deutscher Gewerkschaftsbund, FDGB). In his commentary, Levy, who now came under observation himself, allegedly described, among other things, "how 2 PLO people ('Arafat people') had stopped an Israeli school bus and threatened the driver with submachine guns and set 2 limpet mines. The GDR press, according to P. Levi [sic], would never write about this, but if the Israelis had punished the guilty, the GDR press would be quick to condemn Israel. P. Levi sided openly with Israel and accused the PLO of a merciless and murderous terrorist attack on innocents."[101]

In response to this report, a Stasi operative had a good talk with the insubordinate Levy, during which he was accused of "taking no position on the aggressive character of the Israeli government and glorifying life in Israel" in his comments on his trip to representatives of the churches and to party members. Levy initially defended his eyewitness descriptions, but in the end he was reduced to justifying his presentation on the grounds that he had completely depoliticized it and removed anything that could have been interpreted as "pro-Israeli." But even this did not satisfy the operative—he demanded an unambiguous position consistent with the official line of the GDR government.[102] A short time after this unpleasant encounter, however, Levy once again routed incriminating information to his handlers. This time he prevented a janitorial position in his synagogue community from being filled by an unreliable applicant on the grounds that he had been active in "peace work" organized by a local Protestant pastor and could have used the rooms of the Jewish community for unauthorized meetings by this group.[103]

The detailed description of this collaboration, which is fully documented in the Stasi files, could be interpreted as a form of security pact. In exchange for providing information on activities that could threaten the security of the GDR, Levy used his direct contacts with the Stasi to protect his minuscule Jewish community from antisemitic incidents. But even here, any sign of dual loyalty to the GDR and to Israel became a sticking point. A retreat into political neutrality was not enough; what was required was adherence to the party line. This example underscores the fundamental dilemma that Jews faced in dealing with the East German state, which, on the one hand, guaranteed freedom from antisemitic violence but, on the other, itself became a source of anti-Jewish propaganda and violence under the pretext of anti-Zionism.

On November 22, 1989, a few days after the fall of the Berlin Wall, another long-planned discussion between the executive board of the Federation of Jewish Communities in the GDR and an operative of the former Ministry for State Security, which five days earlier had been renamed the Office for National Security (Amt für Nationale Sicherheit, AfNS). The main agenda item was right-wing, neo-Nazi, and antisemitic incidents and tendencies in the GDR. During the meeting, the AfNS operative presented a final review of the achievements of his agency in fighting these tendencies and their effects. He described the comprehensive measures taken on the occasion of the fiftieth anniversary of Kristallnacht, stressing the "security measures for the personal protection of prominent Jewish guests." After an overview of the prosecution of Nazis and war criminals, he presented the actual figures proving how involved his agency had been in the battle against the right-wing radicals; since the beginning of 1988 alone, 303 preliminary proceedings have been initiated against skinheads. At the same time, he openly admitted that the GDR had been remiss in terms of educating German youth. But, true to the old pattern, he focused on the dangers from the West given that the border between the two Germanys was now open. Among other things, he cited leaflets from the Republicans, an extreme right-wing German party. But in answer, the AfNS operative bandied about the usual militaristic wording, "smashing of groupings and the reestablishment of order and security," to which he added a tried-and-true formula: "by working closely and cooperatively with the citizenry to protect the basic positions of anti-Fascism in the GDR with all due consistency."[104] The draft press release by the executive board of the Federation of Jewish Communities in the GDR gave no hint that the Jewish officials who took part in the discussion had anything to say. Apparently, they listened to the security operative in complete silence but in the process witnessed the astonishing speed with which a member of the newly re-named state security apparatus was learning the language of civil society. Nonetheless, history quickly made superfluous this final attempt to use the Jews to stabilize the GDR's political structure. A few weeks later, the former Stasi offices were for the first time occupied by demonstrators, and the process of disintegration accelerated rapidly.[105] Antisemitic violence took new forms, merging with an epidemic of xenophobia that endangered Jews in both parts of Germany. In any case, the East German Jews now ceased to identify their hopes for the future with the GDR.

THE EXCHANGE OF GIFTS

Restitution, security, Germany's reputation in the world: these concerns were on the minds of Jewish and non-Jewish officials. But that was not all. Because both groups were now pursuing similar goals—though not always for the same reasons—their relationship changed fundamentally. Over time, this collaboration involved a kind of exchange of gifts that was not merely a feature of specific cooperative ventures; the relationship between Jewish and non-Jewish Germans began to coevolve as a result.

On August 25, 1972, the Jewish community of Munich, the Central Council, the Lutheran and Catholic Churches, and the International Dachau Committee organized a commemorative ceremony for the victims of National Socialism at the site of the former concentration camp. The ceremony was attended by five hundred guests. Official representatives from the Olympic Games were not included; the National Olympic Committee had not participated in the organization of the ceremony in order to distinguish these Munich games from the ones staged in Berlin in 1936 in the public mind. The committee attempted to portray the games as neutral and democratic. Surveys had shown that light blue on placards, pictograms, and uniforms was generally viewed as "apolitical"; the roof of the stadium, which had been designed by Behnisch & Partners, conveyed "openness, transparency, and clarity"; and the security staff for the games were to avoid anything that might draw comparisons with the Nazi police state. But then in the early morning of September 5 the unimaginable happened. Militants from the Black September PLO faction forced their way into the bedrooms of the Israeli athletes, shot two of them, and took nine others hostage. In the late evening, an attempt to free the hostages ended in catastrophe: all nine remaining athletes died at the military airport at Fürstenfeldbruck.[106]

The immediate reactions to the murder of the Israelis were anger and sorrow. Speakers at the Olympic stadium condemned the murders and professed solidarity with Israel, and German president Gustav Heinemann repeatedly blamed the Arab states for the crime. In the weeks that followed, Jewish communities in West Germany received dozens of condolence letters and telegrams, including from Lufthansa, the boards of various banks, and the Christian churches. People throughout Germany expressed their sympathy by submitting proposals for commemorating the victims. Among other things, it was suggested that the stadium be named after Moshe Weinberg, the first victim; another suggestion was to mint commemorative coins, with the proceeds going to family members; a medium-sized company in Reutlingen was prepared to bear the costs so that ten of its employees could volunteer to work in Israel for two to four weeks.[107] The reactions from politicians revealed another concern: the desire on the part of both Jewish and non-Jewish officials to ensure that the crime would not drive a wedge into the German-Israeli relationship.

When a memorial plaque was dedicated to the murdered athletes, Hans Lamm, president of the Jewish community of Munich, spoke before German and Israeli dignitaries, among them the prime minister of Bavaria and the Israeli ambassador. Lamm said that the attack was an attempt "to deal a death blow to the relationship between Jerusalem and Bonn," because spontaneous riots had already broken out on the streets of Israel, which, according to Lamm, showed that at least some had "lost the capacity to distinguish between murderers and the citizens of Munich." These demonstrations, he said, had already come to an end. Munich and the citizens of Munich were not being held to blame, and "despite the bitterness and the deep pain, understanding and reason had prevailed." This was certainly an overstatement, an attempt to maintain the communication ritual of mutual assurance and encouragement. Lamm's concluding words made this quite clear: "The blood of the Israeli athletes combines with the blood of the German police. Collectively, their blood cries out; not for revenge does it cry out, it cries out for a better world."[108]

What lay behind this wording? Over the course of the 1950s and 1960s, Jewish dignitaries had come up with a number of functions to justify their role in the Federal Republic. For example, as mediators they strengthened relations between Germans and Jews and between West Germany and Israel; or they claimed that their presence in Germany was necessary to ensure the democratization of the country.[109] Over time, what has been termed an exchange of gifts crystallized out of these various declarations. In effect, when Galinski, van Dam, and Nachmann spoke, their language conveyed the notion that the Jews were to be seen as a "gift" to the Germans: in the these men's eyes, the Jews' presence conferred democratic legitimacy on Germany, along with international recognition; in exchange, they expected acknowledgment of their engagement along with the right to participate in the political life of the land. This exchange of gifts need not be seen in a negative light. In contrast to many critics who reject such gifts as "hidden self-interest" or interpret them as "remnants of a Golden Age,"[110] anthropologists and sociologists generally view them as symbols of interpersonal relations.[111] People give gifts, but gifts, in turn, have a profound effect on people. Exchange recognizes social attachments, confirms them, and creates them. This was precisely what was happening in the 1970s and 1980s in the relationship between the Jewish elites and West German politicians.

The aftereffects of Munich are a good example. As early as September 6, the Central Council, meeting in special session, resolved to defend the Federal Republic from attacks by outsiders. Van Dam sent Chancellor Willy Brandt a letter to this effect: "The Central Council will resolutely resist all attempts to use the catastrophe at Fürstenfeldbruck to vent anti-German antipathies."[112] The chancellor replied nine days later. "I am very pleased," wrote Brandt, "that the Central Council will resist all attempts to use the tragic events at Munich to vent anti-German antipathies."[113] By using the Central Council's wording, there was no need for him to comment further. By acknowledging the efforts of the Jewish officials, he in effect recognized the exchange of gifts. During the time period under consideration here, occasions for exchange were frequent. At the same time, some Jewish officials increasingly came to view their mission in terms of publicizing this exchange of gifts widely, thereby demonstrating to the world the importance of their work.

Trips abroad were a favorite means of boosting their image. At a meeting of the Central Council in Berlin in June 1973, Nachmann presented a detailed report about Willy Brandt's visit to Israel. Nachmann, who had accompanied Brandt, told his colleagues that the trip had inaugurated "a new epoch in the work" of their organization. It has been a breakthrough, he claimed, "not only for Willy Brandt personally" but for the Jewish community as a whole. This was so because attempts to enlist "the federal government in helping the Central Council with problems that affect the Jews at the international level had also been successful."[114]

Whether this was actually the case cannot be fully determined at this point because of the paucity of sources. But a number of statements give a good indication of how Nachmann and other representatives of the community highlighted their role and that of the Central Council. Nachmann in particular hoped to convince both the Israelis and the Germans of the practical implications of having a Jewish community in the Federal Republic. The Central Council, so he believed, could mediate between Germans and Israelis and between Jews and Germans. Nonetheless, it is striking that these statements were often purely declamatory and had little basis in political realities. A certain one-sidedness is unmistakable when one examines the Central Council's declarations, especially those from Werner Nachmann. Thus, for example, he thanked Chancellor Brandt for allowing him to come along on his recent trip to Israel. And then for no discernible reason, Nachmann added that the Central Council would continue to "represent and safeguard" the interests of the Federal Republic "wherever that may be its task."[115] And in his retrospective account of Hans-Dietrich Genscher's trip to Israel in the winter of 1975, Nachmann spoke of the undoubtedly important role, even "attractiveness," of the West German–Jewish community—by which, of course, he meant that of the Central Council. Together, he claimed, they had proved that "the Federal Republic today is one of the most democratic countries in the world."[116]

Before his trip to Washington on the occasion of the annual meeting of the World Jewish Congress in October 1977, Nachmann again proclaimed his intention to defend the Federal Republic and its good name. In a letter to the head of the Chancellery Hans-Jürgen Wischnewski, he gave assurances that because the conference would take up antisemitic incidents in West Germany, he would do everything in his power to curb "the current trend regarding events in Germany."[117] Even more concretely, in his letter to Brandt, sent shortly before his departure for the United States, Nachmann made clear that he would "personally explain the reaction of the democratic parties and the population of the Federal Republic of Germany" regarding antisemitic tendencies "in order to correct the image of the 'bad Germans'" that was circulating once again. He requested that Brandt send him a written memo detailing Brandt's plans, which Nachmann received in short order.[118] As earlier, Brandt acknowledged the role of the Central Council and welcomed Nachmann's intention "to correct the image of the political realities in Germany, which have, unfortunately, recently been somewhat distorted"—especially given the fact that those "individual incidents" were "less frequent and important" than one would think, given the reactions abroad.[119]

The exchange of gifts continued after his meeting in Washington. In his report, Nachmann claimed to have prevented resolutions against the Federal Republic that had been brought forward by South American delegates by persuading them of a "true picture" of the country.[120] If we examine Nachmann's speech more closely, the extent to which he had adopted the rhetoric of West German politicians at a number of levels becomes clear. He warned his audience in Washington that their worries about right-wing radicalism in Germany should not blind them to the dangers of Soviet totalitarianism. Like the politicians whom he mentioned positively including Willy Brandt, Helmut Kohl, Hans-Dietrich Genscher, Franz-Josef Strauss, and Karl Carstens, he spoke repeatedly of the need to fight right-wing *and* left-wing extremism. Nachmann also noted how poorly the extremist parties had fared in various local, regional, and federal elections. In conclusion, he urged the delegates "to forge similar close collaborations with political representatives in their own countries," because both left-wing and right-wing extremism and antisemitism "are not just a German concern but a danger to Western democracy as a whole."[121] The head of the chancellery thanked Nachmann in Brandt's name for his efforts in clarifying the political situation in the Federal Republic.[122]

The exchange of gifts did not take place behind closed doors alone. At the event commemorating Kristallnacht at the Cologne synagogue in 1978, Nachmann told the assembled dignitaries, among them Foreign Minister Hans-Dietrich Genscher, Chancellor Helmut Schmidt, President Walter Scheel, and Gerhart Baum, about the "risk" that the Jews in Germany had accepted when they returned to the country and assisted in establishing democracy. "With satisfaction and not without pride," Nachmann averred, "we state that our presence and our cooperation in Germany and our activities abroad as ambassadors without portfolio have—also—contributed to reducing distrust of Germany and the young German democracy, and to transforming the fear, based on experience, into trust."[123] Similar statements were made in subsequent years as well.[124]

Werner Nachmann died in early 1988. The exchange of gifts that he had promoted was cited again in his obituaries and condolence messages. The Israeli ambassador, Yitzhak Ben-Ari, acknowledged at the memorial service in Karlsruhe that Nachmann sought not only to legitimize the Jews living in Germany but to champion "this country abroad" as well.[125] The German coordinating committee of the associations for Christian-Jewish cooperation viewed his contribution in much the same light. In a letter to Ginsburg, the committee thanked the Central Council for its work, without which democracy in the Federal Republic would not have developed as successfully.[126] The Confederation of German Employers' Associations (Bundesvereinigung der Deutschen Arbeitgeberverbände) also praised Nachmann's unstinting efforts. Their statement cited his immense contributions to the recognition of his "German fatherland among the community of nations."[127] Even Hans Filbinger, the retired prime minister and villain of the Jewish Left and others, concurred. Nachmann and his father, Filbinger agreed, had "performed labors for their fellow Jewish citizens that at the same time benefited the state of Baden-Württemberg and the Federal Republic."[128]

The policies advanced by Nachmann, Ginsburg, and Galinski have, however, been severely criticized by historians because they may have done more harm than good to the Jews in the Federal Republic. Micha Brumlik has claimed that the Central Council reintroduced the "fatal tradition" of the protected Jews, in that most Jewish officials did whatever they could to avoid conflicts with those wielding power.[129] No less critically, Y. Michal Bodemann has called the work of the Central Council bureaucratic patronage. In his view, it was characterized by "lines of vertical dependencies upward and downward" and by the "cultivation of good relations with influential politicians."[130] Erica Burgauer has taken this judgment a step further and demanded that Jews "overcome their role as ambassador for the democratization of Germany and as an ever-available partner in dialogue."[131]

But if power is understood as something that creates values, habits, and modes of perception, this aspect of post-1945 German-Jewish history can also be interpreted differently.[132] One way or another, the relations between Jewish and non-Jewish elites in the Federal Republic have created a set of shared values—and in particular an understanding of antisemitism as an attack on liberal democracy. Even if some appeals and commemorations have become ossified rituals, many people have over the years concluded that democracy and antisemitism are incompatible. Among other things, the exchange of gifts increased sensitivity to Jewish concerns, even though the Jewish community was small and their political power limited. The representatives of the Central Council may pride themselves on having made the public aware of the community's interests and needs. In the long run, the democratic system has in fact profited from the relationships between the Central Council and the various West German elites.

JEWISH NORMALCY AND NON-JEWISH NORMALIZATION

The first test case having the potential to undermine the political identity that the Jews had cultivated occurred in 1978. Shortly after a visit by Baden-Württemberg prime minister Hans Filbinger to the Stuttgart Jewish community, during which Jewish schoolchildren were excused from class,[133] the playwright Rolf Hochhuth exposed Filbinger's actions as a naval judge during the Nazi era. In February 1978 Hochhuth published a documentary tale titled *Eine Liebe in Deutschland* (A love in Germany) in the weekly newspaper *Die Zeit*. The story disclosed that Filbinger had been actively involved in numerous death sentences carried out shortly before the end of the war, and the public scandal quickly escalated. Attempts by Filbinger to force Hochhuth to cease and desist in these characterizations and to paint himself as a victim and committed anti-Nazi backfired badly—Hochhuth's description of Filbinger as a "terrible jurist" stuck like tar. As more and more details about his activities as a judge became known, his avowals and credibility were completely undermined, and public pressure forced him to resign that same year.[134]

The public scandal surrounding Filbinger's role and his stubborn refusal to admit to wrongdoing had a counterpart in a conflict that played out within the Jewish community. At issue was a letter of support written by Nachmann to Filbinger in May 1978 in Nachmann's capacity as chair of the State Association of Jews in Baden. In it, he expressly avoided any judgment of Filbinger's actions during the war and thanked him for his gracious support in rebuilding the Jewish communities in Baden-Württemberg. In particular, Nachmann expressly included Filbinger among the democratic forces and turned his personal defense into a defense of liberal democracy per se. He compared the attacks on Filbinger with the "disgraceful attacks during the Weimar era against outstanding men like Friedrich Ebert, Matthias Erzberger, Walther Rathenau, and Gustav Noske," which "had contributed to destroying the governmental structure of the time, thereby paving the way for Nazism and its disastrous consequences."[135] In effect, Filbinger's defense became a touchstone of "well-fortified democracy" against the totalitarian challenge, and Nachmann enlisted the Jews on the front lines in defense of the accused prime minister. In so doing, he had once again demonstrated the familiar reflex of cooperation by Jewish institutions in the political culture of the Federal Republic, but without recognizing that the political, cultural, and generational landscape had changed.

Nachmann's letter to Filbinger ignited a conflict that was already smoldering within the Central Council, especially in the state associations of Berlin and North Rhine, which were already considering seceding. The state associations attacked Nachmann, with his opponent Heinz Galinski characterizing the letter as a "free pass from Herr Nachmann to Herr Filbinger."[136] Many Jews outside the Central Council were also shocked, and the repercussions from this letter became the seed for Henryk Broder and Michel Lang's *Fremd im eigenen Land: Juden in der Bundesrepublik* (Alien in my own country: The Jews in the Federal Republic), which was published in 1979. A collection of thirty-seven personal accounts, the book's title itself soon became emblematic of the feelings of many Jews about life in Germany. In their introduction, the authors described their reaction to Nachmann's letter: "We asked ourselves, How representative were the statements of the Central Council? For whom does this committee actually speak—other than for itself? In conversations with Jewish friends it became clear to us that basically no one feels represented by the Central Council. And our non-Jewish friends already speak of 'professional Jews' whenever talk turns to the Central Council."[137] Sharp criticism of Nachmann's letter is a leitmotif of the book, and it galvanized people's fundamental dissatisfaction with the Central Council, which stood accused of alienating precisely those whom it claimed to represent while ingratiating itself to the German political establishment.

Generational change in the Jewish community coupled with the fundamental change in Germany's political culture were largely responsible for this change in attitude. Because the stability of West German democracy was of prime concern in the 1970s, not least because of the threat of left-wing terrorism, the postwar constellation continued, but under changed circumstances. But since the 1980s, the Federal Republic had increasingly made a claim to "normalcy," by which was meant the right to a conventional, positive conception of national identity. How, or even whether, the history of National Socialism and especially of the Holocaust could be integrated into a positive national identity remained a bone of contention.

The conflict over "normalizing" Germany's relationship with its history formed the backdrop of the numerous controversies surrounding the past that raged during the 1980s.[138] Although the arguments were often posed in terms of Right and Left, what underlay the various controversies was much larger, at least from the perspective of the Jews in Germany. The verbal skirmishes between Chancellor Helmut Schmidt (a Social Democrat who was a former lieutenant in the Wehrmacht) and Israeli prime minister Menachem Begin at the beginning of the decade, which revolved around Israel's concern that West Germany's loyalty to Israel was wavering, involved two members of the World War II generation. By contrast, Helmut Kohl (Schmidt's Christian Democratic successor and a former antiaircraft helper) claimed the "blessing of late birth" when he visited Israel in January 1984, thereby downplaying the formative role that the Hitler Youth played in the education of his generation. At the end of the war, the Nazis had enlisted adolescents and even children in their last-ditch effort to stave off defeat.

The Jewish community increasingly reacted to these developments in the political culture of the country by breaking with the roles that they had previously expected to play. Public protests against so-called meetings of old comrades, that is, former members of the Waffen-SS, became more frequent, such as those held in Bad Hersfeld and Nesselwang, at which Jewish demonstrators wore concentration camp uniforms.[139] However, the greatest challenge was posed by the appearance of Chancellor Kohl and President Ronald Reagan at the military cemetery at Bitburg on May 5, 1985. The political symbolism of this visit, the high point of which was a ceremony commemorating the fortieth anniversary of the end of World War II, had sparked controversy from the moment it was announced. Kohl planned to present the Federal Republic as a loyal ally of the West and not as the defeated enemy of the victorious Allies, and, as he had at his meeting with French president François Mitterrand on the battlefield of Verdun, he wished to stage this act of reconciliation at the graves of the fallen. The military cemetery at Bitburg was selected because both German and American soldiers were supposedly buried there side-by-side, and at Germany's request, the originally anticipated visit to the former concentration camp at Dachau was dropped. Peter Boenisch, the spokesman for the German government, was quoted as saying, "That's all we need, to have to traipse through concentration camps forty years after the end of the war."[140] But not long thereafter, it was discovered that Waffen-SS soldiers were buried there who had taken part in massacres of French civilians. For many observers, this fact tipped the scales. Protests broke out on

Protests occasioned by the visit to the Bitburg military cemetery by President Reagan and Chancellor Kohl, 1985. SZ-Photo / ddp images / AP.

both sides of the Atlantic that could not be quelled even by the announcement that President Reagan and Chancellor Kohl would visit the former concentration camp at Bergen-Belsen before proceeding to Bitburg.[141]

From the Jewish perspective, the incidents described—from Helmut Kohl's and the Greens' visits to Israel, to Bitburg—formed a chain of scandals on which, for once, both Daniel Cohn-Bendit and Ignatz Bubis could agree: what they all had in common was "insensitivity and self-righteousness."[142] In effect, the controversy united two prominent Jewish voices who had previously embodied different universes. In the early 1970s Cohn-Bendit had been one of the left-wing leaders in the fight against real estate speculation, especially in the West End of Frankfurt.[143] Violent protests broke out, some of them erupting into full-fledged street battles, against the tearing down of a neighborhood of old homes and villas, some of them from the 1870s in an Art Nouveau style, to make way for a banking quarter replete with skyscrapers. Students and others squatted in the threatened buildings. Jewish investors, among them Ignatz Bubis, became a favorite target of protesters, with the old stereotype of rich capitalist Jews freely bandied about. Bubis, who was accused of being a "speculator" and "enemy of the people," later remarked sarcastically, "The revolutionary Left discovered the beauties of bourgeois life, and the office tower became the object of aggression."[144]

In 1974 the police cleared the buildings owned by Bubis in which Cohn-Bendit and his comrades had lived illegally. The evictions led to violent street battles, which some quarters of the press blamed on the Jewish investor. In his memoir, Bubis saw a kind of antisemitic double standard at work: thirty years earlier, when the Jewish inhabitants of these neighborhoods were rousted out of their homes by the police, there had been no protests and no street battles. Now that a Jewish businessman was involved, who "at no time had violated current law," matters were very different.[145]

The planned premiere of Fassbinder's play *Der Müll, die Stadt und der Tod* in Frankfurt in 1984 also met with stiff resistance, led by the city's Jewish community. Ignatz Bubis, it should be noted, was at the time frequently identified with the "rich Jew," the central figure in the 1973 novel *Die Erde ist unbewohnbar wie der Mond* (The earth is as uninhabitable as the moon) by Gerhard Zwerenz. In the novel, Zwerenz transformed the Frankfurt housing battles into a parable about the capitalist Federal Republic. The "rich Jew," in avenging himself for the Holocaust by becoming a ruthless real estate speculator, himself becomes the agent of larger forces intent on "redeveloping" the city, using the guilt felt by West German society about the destruction of the Jews as a tool in their enterprise.

When Bubis learned about the contents of Fassbinder's play from Michel Friedman, head of the cultural department of the local Jewish community, he and the community organized protests against the Alte Oper and its general manager, Ulrich Schwab, because the play's performance there would sanctify an odious form of antisemitism in a publicly funded cultural venue.[146] Although Schwab stepped down as a result of the protests, this did not completely end the conflict, because the very next year Günther Rühle, the new artistic director of the Frankfurter Schauspielhaus, put the play on its program. In justification, he stated that Frankfurt must not succumb to censorship, and he denied the antisemitism of the play itself. Previously a sharp critic of the play, he now saw its message as "clear anti-Fascism." In this reading, the destructive hate-filled anti-Jewish fantasias were actually "bits of real life" that Fassbinder had gathered together but that "certainly did not express his opinion." In other words, while Rühle read Fassbinder's text "as an elegy to the impossibility of love in the world,"[147] the local Jewish community and many sympathizers feared publicly subsidized and staged antisemitism.[148] The debate quickly spread beyond Frankfurt and became a dispute over the "end of the honeymoon" for the Jews living in the Federal Republic, which, as Rühle noted, would finally be followed by a return to "normalcy."[149]

The so-called Historikerstreit (Historians' Dispute), which was widely reported in the German media between about 1986 and 1989, was part of this movement to create a "normalized" national identity in Germany that would no longer be weighted down by the Holocaust. This dispute concerned the relation between German and Jewish memory of World War II and the attempt by some German historians to "relativize" the Holocaust as part of German postwar national identity. Bubis later summarized his feelings about this development, stating, "I could not and would not accept back then that 'normalcy' among Jews and non-Jews living together means that Jews can again be insulted and abused simply for being Jews."[150] However, the sides were switched in the Frankfurt theater dispute in comparison to the Bitburg debate. Now, the CDU and the *Frankfurter Allgemeine Zeitung* came out against the "rising tide of 'antisemitism without antisemites' within the left-wing liberal spectrum (*Frankfurter Rundschau, Die Zeit, Süddeutsche Zeitung*, and segments of the Greens)."[151] For example, Erika Steinbach (a very conservative politician and member of the CDU) spoke against the Frankfurt premiere of Fassbinder's play, while Jutta Ditfurth (a sociologist and cofounder of the German Green Party) spoke in favor.

Because Rühle refused to cancel the performance, Bubis and the Frankfurt Jewish community announced that they would consider civil disobedience,[152] while Nachmann continued to appeal to responsible politicians in the name of the Central Council to put a stop to the threatening "demon."[153] About twenty-five members of the community occupied the stage on October 31, 1985, the day of the planned premiere. This act of civil disobedience, of which they had informed the authorities, led to a fierce and polarizing discussion, with Bubis and Cohn-Bendit once again finding themselves on opposite sides. The former squatter demanded that community members call off their occupation, while the current occupier (of the stage) refused just as vehemently.[154] Cohn-Bendit later accused Bubis, ironically, of having placed himself on the same level as the squatters by this act of trespass. In response, Bubis claimed that his group would immediately have obeyed police instructions to leave but that he had been assured in advance that the police would not intervene,[155] which meant that the occupiers knew, more or less, what the risks were. After much back and forth, Frankfurt mayor Walter Wallmann, though not wanting to stand accused of censorship, nonetheless convinced Rühle to drop the play.

These protests by the Frankfurt Jewish community marked an important turning point in the relationship of Jews to politics and the wider public in the Federal Republic.[156] During the Filbinger scandal, debates had taken place almost entirely within the Jewish community; now they were carried out in public. While Nachmann and the Central Council continued to pursue their traditional policy of "silent diplomacy" based on easy relationships with members of the

Ignatz Bubis (*center*), chair of the Central Council of Jews in Germany, and other demonstrators occupied the stage at the Frankfurt premiere of Rainer Werner Fassbinder's play *Der Müll, die Stadt und der Tod*, October 31, 1985. The banner reads, "Subsidized antisemitism." Deutsches Theatermuseum München / photograph by Abisag Tüllmann.

political establishment, public forms of intervention took on greater significance both for "dissidents" outside the Jewish institutions and, as the example of Frankfurt shows, for the individual Jewish communities.

But Jewish officials could quickly get themselves cornered, as the Börneplatz conflict, which broke out in Frankfurt shortly after the theater scandal, demonstrated. This conflict concerned excavations under the Börneplatz, during which the foundations of several Jewish houses from the former Jewish ghetto were discovered. In this instance, Bubis was caught between the negotiated assurances that he had made to city officials and the increasingly radical demands of the Jewish protesters, who for a time occupied the building site.[157] Micha Brumlik, who was one of the protesters at the time, later noted that Jewish community officials purportedly defended the building decisions that had been negotiated in public while privately sending their children to the protests and demonstrations.[158] Ultimately, the real problem facing Jewish institutions arose from an inherent contradiction: civil disobedience threatened to undermine precisely the state authority upon which the Jews counted for their sense of security. As a result, "Jewish normalcy" and the "normalization" of the Federal

Republic continually clashed, a state of affairs also conditioned by Germany's past and its present.[159]

This dynamic was also in evidence in a series of scandals about the political past that shook the West German political system.[160] On November 10, 1988, Philipp Jenninger, the president of the Bundestag, spoke there on the occasion of the fiftieth anniversary of the Nazi pogroms that have come to be known as Kristallnacht. He gave his speech at the end of a series of debates about the "normalization" of the Federal Republic and at the conclusion of a chain of events commemorating the violence that had occurred during the night of November 9, 1938. The Greens and the SPD, along with FDP delegate Wolfgang Lüder, had strongly advocated for having Heinz Galinski, who had only recently become chair of the Central Council, speak before the Bundestag on this occasion. Jenninger, however, opposed this plan, countering that he should give this speech and Galinski should listen. This led to fierce controversy as early as during the planning stage, which was aired in public.[161]

Aside from the Bundestag delegates and president, the Israeli ambassador and representatives from the Central Council and Christian churches were invited to attend the commemoration at the old waterworks in Bonn on November 10, 1988. The Bonn Bach Society provided the musical setting, consisting of Yiddish songs from the ghetto from the time of the Shoah. The Jewish actress, director, and head of the Hamburger Kammerspiele, Ida Ehre, recited Paul Celan's poem "Todesfuge" (published in English as "Death Fugue") to prepare the audience for Jenninger's speech. But then Jenninger broke with the conventional ritual of commemoration.[162] Rather than place the experiences of the victims at the center, he chose to speak from the perspective of the perpetrators, an approach that Werner Nachmann had allegedly urged upon him and that also derived from conversations he had had with young people. Jenninger attempted to explain how German society could have perpetrated violence against Jews.[163] Rather than providing a ritualized memorialization of the victims that attempted to bridge Jewish and Christian interpretations of history, he tried to explain the fascination with evil from the perspective of a descendant of the perpetrators.

Jenninger's delivery was generally monotone and rose in emphasis only as he portrayed for the audience the thought processes of the actors of the time, such as when he raised his voice in rhetorical questioning when reviewing Hitler's attempts to revise the provisions of the Versailles Treaty during the interwar years: "And as far as the Jews were concerned, hadn't they in the past arrogated to themselves a role—so the reasoning back then—that was not theirs to take? Shouldn't they finally have had to accept limitations? Hadn't they perhaps even earned being put back in their places? And especially, with the exception of wild

FDP delegates leave the plenary hall during the speech by Bundestag president
Philipp Jenninger on the occasion of the fiftieth anniversary of Kristallnacht,
November 10, 1988. ullstein bild / AP.

exaggerations that were not to be taken seriously, did not the propaganda largely
correspond to one's own suppositions and convictions?"[164]

The rhetorical clumsiness with which he switched from the perspective of the
victim to that of the perpetrator upset his audience in a manner that Jenninger
had never considered. Embarrassment and discomfort not only spread through
the ranks of the opposition delegates but also were felt by members of the governing coalition. About forty parliamentarians protested by leaving the room. From
the very beginning, negative domestic and foreign media commentaries called
for Jenninger's resignation because his speech was both tactless and embarrassing and was unworthy of a Bundestag president.[165] An argument broke out in the
Central Council about how to deal with this incident, in the process revealing
something of the internal power struggles taking place within the council. Galinski publicly disciplined his deputy, Michael Fürst (a rival in the Central Council
who represented the next generation), who had defended Jenninger's speech and
opposed the demand that he resign.[166]

After the shock of the media coverage of the Bitburg affair, which had occurred only three years earlier, Chancellor Kohl presumably did not wish to expose an open flank, and so when Jenninger announced his resignation the next day, the media attributed the decision to Kohl's firm hand.[167] But because Jenninger had already threatened to resign over the dispute around Galinski's invitation, the way had been paved for taking the final step.[168] He had rubbed people the wrong way by abandoning the sheath of ritual commemoration that provided cover for West German politicians.[169] He had failed in his attempt to educate the people, in his efforts to explain the behavior of a large portion of the population under National Socialism, and in the very purpose of a commemorative speech: the creation of a sense of complete inclusiveness. The "we" posited by this speech also created another problem: the symbolic revival of the separation between Jews and Germans.[170]

However, when the written transcript of his speech became public, the memory of his actual performance faded into the background, and soon voices were heard in his defense. Advocacy for the now former Bundestag president almost took on the semblance of a campaign.[171] These efforts were, however, far surpassed by newspaper reports in 1995 to the effect that Ignatz Bubis had—as a sort of experiment—read Jenninger's text at a commemoration of the Holocaust on November 9 without its eventuating in protests of any sort. These reports were understood as absolving Jenninger and his speech, which had become controversial only because of the context in which it had been given.[172] Bubis, for his part, denied the reports, stating that he had merely quoted excerpts from Jenninger's speech but none of his most criticized formulations.[173]

At the same time, the Jenninger scandal became a foil for the official self-presentation of the GDR, because whereas Galinski had gotten nowhere when he proposed a political ceremony in the Bundestag with a representative of the Jews as speaker, Erich Honecker, the head of state and general secretary of the SED, took the opportunity to send a political message. He embraced Galinski's proposal for a ceremony on the occasion of the fiftieth anniversary of Kristallnacht to be held on November 9, 1988, in the People's Chamber in East Germany. Galinski, as guest of honor, sat between Honecker and Egon Krenz, Honecker's deputy, while the president of the People's Chamber, Horst Sindermann, and the chair of the Federation of Jewish Communities in the GDR, Siegmund Rotstein, gave the ceremonial addresses.[174] In the headlines of its November 11, 1988, edition, *Neues Deutschland* contrasted the "scandal in the Bundestag of the FRG resulting from the Jenninger speech on Kristallnacht" with the "symbolic laying of the cornerstone for the New Synagogue Berlin."[175] This had been preceded, on November 9, by a front-page lead story about the "moving meeting between Erich Honecker and Jewish personages in the State Council."[176]

Aside from the golden opportunity to score points in the inter-German competition of political systems, this response was grounded in the special value that the GDR leadership placed on Jewish officials and organizations abroad at the end of the 1980s. The tendency of the East German leadership to magnify the influence wielded by Jewish officialdom was notorious, and beneath it, of course, lay barely concealed traditional notions of the "power of world Jewry." In any event, good relations with these officials were seen as a prerequisite to more favorable trade relations with the United States, which was deemed crucial to the survival of the economically backward country. Thus, from the East German perspective, "normalization" referred to its own role in the world economy and not to how it related to German history, because in any case East German anti-Fascism absolved the country of all guilt. Improvements in relations with the few Jews living in the GDR always served the country's international interests.

As a result, the politics of memorialization in the GDR were completely subject to the prerogatives of the state and party, which at least domestically permitted no critical public opinion or independent media. In this regard, the sociologist Y. Michal Bodemann has spoken aptly of "nationalized memory" and "friendly indifference."[177] Officially, relations between the Jewish communities and the East German state were predicated on conflict-free harmony, as demonstrated by the long-established ritualistic handling of Kristallnacht. Typical was an interview with Helmut Aris, the chair of the Federation of Jewish Communities in the GDR, conducted by ADN, the East German news agency, which was published in *Neues Deutschland* on November 8, 1978. First, the interview placed the historical event within the standard official narrative, after which the anti-Jewish policies of the National Socialists were viewed as collateral damage in the battle waged by imperialist monopoly capital against the forces of the proletariat. "Antisemitism and racism," according to Aris, "were largely the expression of the antihuman ideology of German fascism. They were a direct preparation for an imperialist war of predation and were designed to divert attention from class contradictions." This was followed by the usual incantation about the GDR having been a model in rooting out all remnants of Fascism and racial hate and having allowed the Jewish communities to thrive with generous support. Such progressive policies ensured a peaceful life for all Jews in the Socialist state. As a result, Aris noted, his federation stood firmly on the side of the Socialist states in the fight for peace. This was in contrast to the Federal Republic, where Fascist criminals were protected from prosecution, and neo-Nazi ideology was again rampant.[178] The declarations of the chairperson of the Jewish communities in the GDR and the official line of the state were congruent down to the last detail.

The Jewish communities were, however, experiencing different trends at ground level. For example, there was renewed interest in Jewish culture and religion among the children of high Communist officials, most of whom had no relationship with Judaism, as well as among young people of mixed marriages. Especially in Berlin, these younger people, who were often interested in the more secular manifestations of Jewishness, met in formal groups such as We for Ourselves—Jews for Jews, which in 1990 developed into the Jewish Cultural Association. The writer Jurek Becker, who had been living in the West since 1977, described the experiences of a Jewish Holocaust survivor in the GDR in his 1986 novel *Bronsteins Kinder* (published in English as *Bronstein's Children*). During the 1980s, a number of voices were heard in the Jewish community with respect to the culture of selective memory in the GDR. However, until 1984, the study by the Dresden historian Helmut Eschwege titled *Selbstbehauptung und Widerstand: Deutsche Juden im Kampf um Existenz und Menschenwürde 1933–1945* (Self-assertion and resistance: German Jews in the battle for existence and human dignity, 1933–1945) could be published only in the Federal Republic.

In 1985 the freelance interpreter Salomea Genin, who lived in East Berlin, complained directly to Erich Honecker about the bureaucratic harassment aimed at commemorative events that had not been officially sanctioned. Genin was born in Berlin in 1932 and had fled with her parents to Australia to avoid persecution in 1939, but she had returned to the GDR as a committed Communist in 1963. As such, she had agreed to collaborate with the Ministry for State Security and for a long time submitted reports to her handlers about the East German–Jewish community, of which she had become a member. In 1984, however, the Stasi stopped working with her, partly because of alleged personal problems and partly because she told the targets of her spying what she was doing, thereby negating her value to the authorities. Nonetheless, she had continued to view herself as a loyal citizen of the GDR and as a Communist; she was, however, dissatisfied with the realities of Socialism in her country.[179] And so she had reported to Honecker numerous instances in which private commemorations that had not been officially approved were either obstructed or suppressed by the police. Significantly, all of the incidents that she listed had been initiated by non-Jews; Jews appeared in her complaint, if at all, only in official capacities, as collaborators with state authorities.

The first instance described by Genin involved a young man who, with several others (all of whom she presumed to be members of a Christian church), laid flowers on November 9 at the Potsdam synagogue, which had been destroyed in 1938 and burned down during an air-raid in 1945. For this act of commemoration he had been picked up by the police at his home and interrogated; he was subsequently fined 300 East German marks for organizing an unapproved event. A similar incident occurred in Rostock, where members of a Catholic church who belonged to the local Schalomgesellschaft (Shalom Society) had tried to hold an unapproved ceremony on November 9 at the Jewish cemetery despite official warnings. The police intervened to suppress this commemoration as well, apparently at the behest of the chair of the Jewish community. It should be noted that they were spared the rough treatment meted out by the so-called *Bereitschaftspolizei* (riot police; literally "readiness police") to a group of eleven lesbians in April of the same year who had attempted to place a memorial wreath to the lesbians murdered at Ravensbrück on the occasion of the fortieth anniversary of the liberation of the concentration camp.[180] Genin's letters of complaint followed a typical rhetorical pattern in that they portrayed Honecker as the guarantor of Socialist norms who must, all too often, have been unaware of the abuses committed by his subordinates.[181]

In any event, the processing of this complaint followed the course that was routine for such cases in the GDR. The Stasi, rather than examining the incidents detailed in the complaints, placed the complainant under the microscope and asked whether she was not in fact a potential security risk. Stasi operatives, who visited her using false identities, reported that she evinced signs of "bourgeois ideology," although they were satisfied with her assurances that she intended no harm to the GDR and would do nothing to undermine the state.[182] In other words, Genin's criticisms of the suppression of a nonofficial culture of memorialization had been redefined as a security risk that required intervention by the secret police.

The solemn commemoration of the fiftieth anniversary of Kristallnacht, for which no detail was to be left to chance, was wholly consistent with the state's need to control the public culture of memorialization.[183] The high point was to be the dedication of the New Synagogue Berlin—Centrum Judaicum Foundation. Among the ninety-three journalists who attended the press conference organized for the occasion, twenty-two had come from the "capitalist countries," among them thirteen from the Federal Republic and West Berlin.[184] In contrast to the Federal Republic, the German Democratic Republic retained to the end the division between the fearful and cautious political leadership of the Jewish communities, which sided with the state and party to ensure its security, and the small groupings within, at the fringe of, or outside the Jewish communities that sometimes succumbed to collaboration with the Stasi but since the 1980s were attempting to establish a Jewish identity within a Socialist context.

Debates around the "normalization" of the country's relationship to German history, which in the West became a factor in helping Jews to clarify their role in German society, had no counterpart in East Germany. The overarching paradigm of anti-Fascism had from the outset provided both non-Jews and Jews a comforting identity, but one that was prone to the "anti-Fascism trap," which rendered the GDR impervious to criticism. Conversely, the debates and arguments taking place in the Federal Republic strengthened the clichés about neo-Nazi and nationalistic activities in the West. Because of the way these incidents were reported in East Germany, the small communities of Jews who now lived there were unwilling to contravene official policies. As a result, they remained passive in the conflict that was brewing between the state culture of memorialization "from above" and the tentative attempts at an alternate culture "from below." The examples described here, which were probably only the tip of the iceberg, indicate that *non-Jews* were more likely to initiate actions that had the potential for scandal than were the Jews themselves, who sometimes took part in them.

DISCOVERY AND APPROPRIATION

The 1970s and 1980s saw an increasing interest among non-Jewish Germans in Jewish life and culture, although the line between discovery and appropriation was frequently blurred. It seems as if the topic of national identity in Germany that was emerging at the time existed in dialectical relation to the hole that had been created by the expulsion and destruction of Jews and was therefore felt all the more strongly. This in turn led to increased fascination with the phenomenon of absence. As a result, the intensified interest in everything Jewish was directed less at the Jews who now actually lived in Germany than at an *imagined* Jewry. Jews became a preferred object of nostalgia—along with windmills and water towers.[185] It was argued in the 1970s that nostalgia is a reaction to the consequences of modernity and the loss of belonging. However, this particular preoccupation with the past was viewed less as compensation for the consequences of progress than for the loss of the Jews in the Holocaust (a term that came into wide usage only toward the end of the decade with the broadcast of the television series of that title).

This nostalgic preoccupation with all things Jewish was fed in the 1970s by the musical *Anatevka*, which had been a major success on Broadway in 1964 as *Fiddler on the Roof*.[186] The play depicts the pogroms taking place in prerevolutionary Russia in a style that may be fairly characterized as Eastern Jewish shtetl romanticism. The story centers on Tevye, a Jewish dairyman from the Ukrainian village of Anatevka who bickers with God because his marriageable daughters insist on choosing husbands of their own. After Tevye expresses all manner of complaints about disintegrating traditions, the world he knows suddenly collapses, and in the end he and the other Jews are forced to leave their village and go to America. The play was first performed in the Netherlands and Great Britain, with the first German adaptation staged in Hamburg in 1968 at the Operettenhaus and then in Düsseldorf and in West Berlin in 1969 at the Theater des Westens. Tevye was played in Germany by the Lithuanian-born Israeli actor Shmuel Rodensky and then by Ivan Rebroff, who became very popular as a result. Rebroff had premiered the role brilliantly in France before becoming famous in Germany with his rendition of "Wenn ich einmal reich wär" ("If I Were a Rich Man").

But the most successful staging in Germany was undoubtedly that of the Austrian Walter Felsenstein, who brought the play to the Komische Oper in East Berlin in 1971 under the title *Der Fiedler auf dem Dach*, where it was seen by half a million playgoers and where by 1988 it had gone through 506 performances. At times people had to wait for several years to get the coveted tickets. However, the libretto underwent some cleaning up in order not to offend the country's Russian patrons. Among other things, "Kiev" was changed to the Yiddish "Jegputz," while "pogrom" became "unofficial harassment"; "America" was dropped completely in an act of self-censorship.[187] The staging of this musical in East Berlin, although it was also aimed at a Western audience, helped pave the way for the officially sanctioned promotion of Jewish cultural identity in the GDR, which was primarily motivated by foreign policy considerations.[188]

While *Anatevka* and *Fiedler auf dem Dach* and the subsequent filmed version of 1971 conveyed a painstakingly reconstructed image of Eastern Jewish life in both parts of Germany, Ephraim Kishon, who had enjoyed phenomenal success since the 1960s, especially in West Germany, with best sellers like *Der seekranke Walfisch oder Ein Israeli auf Reisen* (published in English as *The Seasick Whale*) and *Der Blaumilchkanal* (also made into a film and released internationally as *The Big Dig*), gave the German public a picture of life in present-day Israel. The first book by Kishon to be published in the GDR was . . . *und die beste Ehefrau von allen* (*He & She*), and *Der Blaumilchkanal* was published in 1986 in a limited edition. Of the forty-one million copies of his books sold worldwide, about thirty-one million were bought in Germany, although his books found more favor among the general public than reviewers, who, among other things, noted that his West German publisher, Herbert Fleissner, also published works by rightist nationalist authors.[189] But as Josef Joffe, the publisher of *Die Zeit*, wrote in an obituary, "Kishon inscribed himself in the guilty consciences of the Germans, not to bring them pain, but to get them to laugh. He had become, as he himself noted, the favorite author of the descendants of his executioners."[190] While Kishon purveyed a satirically exonerating image of Israeli life to German readers, thousands of young West Germans made what became something of a mandatory pilgrimage in the 1970s to work on a kibbutz in Israel, where they picked oranges and quenched their enthusiasm for Israeli-style Socialism.[191]

Not long after Germans discovered the lost world of Eastern European Jewry and the present world of Israeli Jews, the 1979 television series *Holocaust* (aired in

Germany as *Holocaust—die Geschichte der Familie Weiss*) undertook to detail the persecution and murder of the German Jews. The increased interest in this topic was followed in the 1980s and 1990s by reunions in Germany with Jews who had fled or emigrated, who were invited to visit their old hometowns, often as part of officially sponsored programs.[192] In addition, non-Jewish civic groups began to encourage the reconstruction and building of synagogues and temples. But this interest on the part of German society in reconstructing its Jewish heritage did not always meet with unalloyed enthusiasm. For example, in 1980 Werner Nachmann warned the Central Council that "Jewish communities should take a cautious wait-and-see approach whenever proposals are presented to them, because in many cases the intentions that lie behind these efforts are not unambiguously discernible." Alfred Weichselbaum added that it would have to be determined "whether a particular reconstruction was to be turned into a business or whether such buildings were, for example, to be used for cultural purposes, such as a museum, etc."[193]

But such museumization of the Jews risked becoming a medium for nostalgia and even for commercialization. As a result, we may discern here the beginnings of a development that led to the creation of "Jewish spaces" that did not necessarily require the presence of actual Jews but primarily purveyed a "Jewish atmosphere."[194] This was not solely a West German phenomenon but reached its high point in the late 1980s in East Berlin, when the former *Scheunenviertel* (Jewish quarter) was redeveloped in the Oranienburger Strasse, although before 1945 it had in fact been located elsewhere in Berlin.

The gaps that the destruction of the Jews left in German society were also filled symbolically. For example, Jewish first names became increasingly popular during the 1970s. While the name David was only the 124th most common name in the 1960s, and Esther, Judith, and Ruth were similarly unpopular, the name Sarah, which previously had been one of the least popular girls' names, began a sharp ascent in the 1970s, and it was the fifth most favored name among West German parents in 1985. It has retained its popularity ever since. Sarah, of course, was the name that the Nazis had forced upon Jewish women. And by 2004 David was among the ten most popular boys' names.[195]

The blurred line between discovery and the appropriation of things Jewish may also be seen in the area of biography. Two prominent examples, one from East Germany and the other from West Germany, exemplify the phenomenon of "virtual Jews."[196] Karin Mylius had served as the elected chairperson of the Jewish community of Halle since 1968. Mylius, who was born in Münster in 1934, was the daughter of the police official Paul Loebel, who was later transferred to Halle. Neither of her parents was Jewish. Because she was protected by the state, she was able to retain her chair until 1986, despite persistent complaints.[197] This transformation from baptized Protestant to Jewish official took place shielded from the public sphere. By contrast, the metamorphosis of Edith Rosh, the Protestant-born daughter of a Wehrmacht soldier who died in Poland in 1944, into the television journalist Lea Rosh, who since about 1988 had begun to push for the erection in Berlin of a central memorial to the murdered Jews—and became an icon of self-identification with Judaism—took place under the glaring lights of the media.[198] Such confusing oddities within the evolving German society complicated the process of self-definition and of coming to terms with what it meant to be a Jew in Germany. To some extent this process came to be influenced by developments within Germany, and as a result, in the 1970s and 1980s the Jews more than ever began to show evidence of this intertwining of both German societies.

CONSTANTIN GOSCHLER is Professor of contemporary history at the University of Bochum. He has been a visiting scholar at, among other places, Harvard University and the University of Prague. Goschler's publications include "Keine neue Gestapo: Das Bundesamt für Verfassungsschutz und die NS-Vergangenheit" (co-author); *Die Entschädigung von NS-Zwangsarbeit am Anfang des 21. Jahrhunderts* (editor, four volumes); *Europäische Zeitgeschichte nach 1945* (with Rüdiger Graf); *Schuld und Schulden: Die Politik der Wiedergutmachung für NS-Verfolgte seit 1945*; and *Wiedergutmachung: Westdeutschland und die Verfolgten des Nationalsozialismus 1945–1954*.

ANTHONY KAUDERS is reader in modern European history at Keele University in England. He is currently researching the history of hypnosis in Germany in the twentieth century. His publications include *Der Freud-Komplex: Eine Geschichte der Psychoanalyse in Deutschland, Unmögliche Heimat: Eine deutsch-jüdische Geschichte der Bundesrepublik, Democratization and the Jews: Munich 1945–1965*, and *German Politics and the Jews: Düsseldorf and Nuremberg 1910–1933*.

NOTES

Technically, the term "restitution" (*Wiedergutmachung*) refers to repayment for seized or expropriated property and other material losses, while "compensation" (*Entschädigung*) covers personal damages. However, to minimize confusion here, we will use the term "restitution" for both.

    1. See also C. Goschler (2007); H. Hockerts (2001).

    2. For more on the exchange of gifts as a model, see chapter 7.

    3. See BArch, B 126/109455 and B 126/109456.

    4. Letter from Ernst Katzenstein to Saul Kagan, September 15, 1973, 2–3, in USHMM, BBFC RG-12.007.02, 2 of 3; see also letter from Gerhard Kraus (BMF) to Karl Schiller, September 28, 1973, in BArch, B 126/109457.

5. Cited from "Zur abschließenden Härteregelung über die Claims Conference," Saul Kagan's draft for the unpublished volume 7 of Walter Schwarz, *Die Wiedergutmachung nationalsozialistischen Unrechts durch die Bundesrepublik Deutschland*, in USHMM, BBFC RG-12.009.03, 3 of 5.

6. Letter from Ernst Katzenstein to Saul Kagan, May 3, 1974, in USHMM, BBFC RG-12.007.02*03, 5 of 7.

7. See, for example, the draft of a letter from the State of Israel to the German minister of finance, in USHMM, BBFC RG-12.007.02*03, 6 of 7.

8. Memorandum from Nahum Goldmann, enclosure to the letter from Goldmann to Alex Möller, April 26, 1974; letter from Ernst Katzenstein to Saul Kagan, April 29, 1974, both in USHMM, BBFC, RG-12.007.02*03, 5 of 7; notes about a conversation between Minister of Finance Helmut Schmidt and Nahum Goldmann on May 2, 1974, in AdsD, 1/HSAA 6968.

9. Letter from Minister of Finance Hans Apel to Chancellor Helmut Schmidt, September 12, 1974, in AdsD, 1/HSAA 6968.

10. Letter from Otto Funke to Benjamin B. Ferencz, November 22, 1976, cited from A. Timm (1997b), p. 207. See also S. Meining (2008); S. Meining (2002), pp. 392–395.

11. See, for example, "Bonn zahlt 600 Millionen Mark für NS-Verfolgte," *Quick*, October 24, 1974. See also the letter from Ernst Katzenstein to Saul Kagan, November 13, 1974, in USHMM, BBFC RG-12.007.02*03, 3 of 7.

12. Note by Leister (Office of the Chancellery A) about a telephone conversation with Werner Nachmann on October 7, 1974, in AdsD, 1/HSAA 6968; letter from Per Fischer (Office of the Chancellery A) to Chancellor Helmut Schmidt, December 12, 1974, both in AdsD, 1/HSAA 6968.

13. Letter from Werner Nachmann to Chancellor Helmut Schmidt, October 28, 1974, in BArch, B 106/70785.

14. See letter from Ernst Katzenstein to Saul Kagan, December 30, 1974; letter from Katzenstein to Nahum Goldmann, December 19, 1974; letter from Werner Nachmann to Goldmann, November 26, 1974; letter from Katzenstein to Goldmann, December 30, 1974, all in USHMM, BBFC RG-12.007.02*03, 1 of 7.

15. Note (signed Oldenkott) about a conversation between the chancellor and the chairpersons of the three factions of the German Bundestag regarding a financial "concluding gesture" to benefit the destitute victims of National Socialist violence, January 16, 1975, in AdsD, 1/HSAA 7005.

16. "Goldmann erreichte Wiedergutmachung," *Braunschweiger Zeitung*, February 12, 1975; "Goldmann verhandelt in Bonn über die Wiedergutmachung," *Die Welt* March 18, 1975; interview with Dr. Nahum Goldmann, president of the World Jewish Congress, broadcast on Deutschlandfunk on March 22, 1975, in USHMM, BBFC RG-12.007.02*04, 2 of 5.

17. Nahum Goldmann, "Weitere Entschädigungen," *Frankfurter Allgemeine Zeitung*, February 13, 1975; "Die PLO droht der Bundesrepublik," *Die Welt*, February 15, 1975; also "Syrien droht Bonn," *Bremer Nachrichten*, February 18, 1975; "Araber fordern: Bonn darf NS-Opfern nichts mehr zahlen," *Schwäbisches Tageblatt*, February 13, 1975.

18. See, for example, Sarah Honig, "Billions in Reparations Went to Wrong Places," *Jerusalem Post*, January 11, 1977; "Nazi Victims Protest at 'Final Reparations Act,'" *Jerusalem Post*, April 12, 1977.

19. Letter from Ernst Katzenstein to Saul Kagan, January 9, 1978, in USHMM, BBFC RG-12.007.02*05, 4 of 6.

20. Note (signed Loeck) about a conversation between Manfred Schüler (head of the Office of the Chancellery A) and Werner Nachmann and Alexander Ginsburg on October 20, 1975, in BArch, B 136/24655.

21. Letter from Ernst Katzenstein to Saul Kagan, January 11, 1978, in USHMM, BBFC RG 12 007.02*05, 4 of 6.

22. Synopsis of Ernst Katzenstein, "December 1977 proposals submitted in Bonn to the German Government," enclosure to a letter from Ernst Katzenstein to Saul Kagan, January 11, 1978, in USHMM, BBFC RG-12.007.02*05, 4 of 6.

23. Letter from Nahum Goldmann to Saul Kagan, undated (approximately early 1978); and letter from Nahum Goldmann to Herbert Wehner, April 25, 1978, both in USHMM, BBFC RG-12.007.02*05, 4 of 6.

24. Letter from Helmut Kohl to Helmut Schmidt, April 26, 1978, in BArch, B 136/24655.

25. Letter from Nahum Goldmann to Hans-Jürgen Wischnewski, January 13, 1979; and letter from Ernst Katzenstein to Saul Kagan, January 16, 1979, both in USHMM, BBFC RG-12.007.02*05, 3 of 6.

26. Letter from Ernst Katzenstein to Saul Kagan, May 29, 1979, in USHMM, BBFC RG-12.007.02*05, 3 of 6; letter from Ernst Katzenstein to Saul Kagan, January 21, 1980, in USHMM, BBFC RG-12.007.02*05, 1 of 6.

27. Letter from Ernst Katzenstein to Saul Kagan, January 21, 1980; letter from Ernst Katzenstein to Saul Kagan, March 5, 1980, both in USHMM, BBFC RG-12.007.02*05, 1 of 6.

28. Letter from Ernst Katzenstein to Saul Kagan, January 21, 1980, in USHMM, BBFC RG-12.007.02*05, 1 of 6.

29. Letter from Kurt May (URO) to Ernst Katzenstein, December 11, 1979, in USHMM, BBFC RG-12.007.02*05, 2 of 6.

30. Letter from Ernst Katzenstein to Saul Kagan, June 25, 1980, in USHMM, BBFC RG-12.007.02*06, 3 of 4.

31. "Richtlinien für die Vergabe von Mitteln an jüdische Verfolgte zur Abgeltung von weiteren Härten in Einzelfällen im Rahmen der Wiedergutmachung vom 3. Dezember 1980," *Bundesanzeiger,* no. 192, October 14, 1980; see also H.-J. Brodesser et al. (2000), pp. 122–123.

32. Letter from Hans Matthöfer to Werner Nachmann, September 17, 1980, in USHMM, BBFC RG-12.007.02*06, 2 of 6.

33. Bundestag printed material, tenth voting period, no. 6287, October 31, 1986, p. 21.

34. Hermann Rudolph, "Der Fall Nachmann und die Deutschen," *Süddeutsche Zeitung,* May 19, 1988.

35. Joachim Riedl, "Herrenloses Geld: Das Millionenkarussell des Werner Nachmann," *Die Zeit,* May 27, 1988.

36. Declaration of the BPA on December 14, 1989, in BPA, Zentrales Dokumentationssystem.

37. The editors, "Vertrauen wiedergewinnen," *AJW,* October 28, 1988.

38. "Moral complicity" is from "Fragen auch an Prüfer," *Frankfurter Rundschau,* May 27, 1988.

39. ". . . konnte nicht vollständig aufgearbeitet werden: Aus dem Bericht der 'Treuarbeit,' Frankfurt, über die Affäre Nachmann," *AJW,* October 28, 1988.

40. Examination of witness Alexander Ginsburg on July 5, 1988, in GLA, 309/217. On the relationship between Alexander Ginsburg and Werner Nachmann, see also H. J. Ginsburg, "Der Lebensretter," *Trumah* 14 (2004), here especially pp. 28–29.

41. Examination of witness Ignatz Bubis on November 18, 1988, in GLA, 309/215.

42. Cited from examination of witness Sigmund Nissenbaum on October 5, 1988, in GLA, 309/215; similarly, examination of witness Georges Stern on June 29, 1988, examination of witness Michael Fürst on September 29, 1988, examination of witness Max Willner on October 21, 1988, all in GLA, 309/216. Examination of witness Leo Rubinstein on October 12, 1988, in GLA, 309/217.

43. Examination of witness Leo Rubinstein on October 12, 1988, in GLA, 309/217.

44. See, for example, examination of witness Gerrard S. M. Breitbart on December 19, 1988, in GLA, 309/215.

45. Examination of witness Alexander Ginsburg on July 5, 1988, in GLA, 309/217.

46. On the general meaning of "security" as a sociocultural interpretive model, see also E. Conze, "'Sicherheit' als Kultur," *Vierteljahrshefte für Zeitgeschichte* 53 (2005), p. 363.

47. Annual report of the Central Council for 1969–1970, in ZA, B.1/7.250. See also W. Bergmann (1997), p. 314.

48. For example, the Central Council did not pursue a criminal complaint against CSU delegate Herbert Prochazka, who had sung an antisemitic song, "because the police had not reported a criminal complaint for resisting arrest and slander, citing the state of complete inebriation in which the politician had found himself." Given the loss of responsibility, the Central Council considered the outcome of a criminal complaint hopeless. Concretely, the Central Council also complained that "the former mayor of Litzmannstadt (Łódź), who had a high Nazi position, is also active as a senior government official in the ministry of expellees." See annual report of the Central Council for 1969–1970, in ZA, B.1/7.250.

49. See also E. Burgauer (1993), p. 85.

50. I. Bubis (1996), p. 132.

51. See Ulrich Knufinke, "Spiegel einer ambivalenten Geschichte: Die Architektur der Synagogen in Deutschland," *Jüdische Zeitung*, November 11, 2008.

52. Minutes of the meeting of the board of the Central Council on October 22, 1972, in Munich, in ZA, B.1/7.868; as well as the meetings of the board of the Central Council on October 26, 1980, in Frankfurt, in ZA, B.1/7.907. The discussion culminated in 1992 in an open letter from Jewish journalistRalph Giordano to Chancellor Kohl in which Giordano called for armed self-defense in response to attacks on foreigners and asylum seekers. See R. Giordano (1993). See also R.-B. Essig (2000), pp. 318–320.

53. For more, see also the interviews in H. Broder and R. Lang (1979a); M. Brumlik (2000).

54. See also E. Conze (2009), pp. 472–486; S. Scheiper (2010), pp. 353–396.

55. See, for example, the reports in StAM, LRA 16465; letter from Werner Nachmann to Minister of the Interior Werner Maihofer, May 20, 1977, in BArch, B 106/51649.

56. For more, see A. Plack (1985), pp. 188–189.

57. A. Silbermann (1982), p. 63.

58. On the sociological classification of this and other studies of antisemitism, see W. Bergmann (1991), p. 14.

59. Hans Lamm, "Mit untauglichen Methoden: Zu Prof. Silbermanns Studie über den Antisemitismus," *AJW*, July 9, 1976, p. 3; see also E. Burgauer (1993), pp. 90–92.

60. Note on the conversation between the head of the Office of the Chancellery, Secretary of State Dr. Schüler, and the chair of the board of the Central Council, Werner Nachmann, and Alexander Ginsburg, June 11, 1976, enclosure to the letter from Dr. Busse to the head of the Office of the Chancellery, June 16, 1976, in BArch, B 136/24655.

61. Letter from Dr. Melzer (Office of the Chancellery) to Rosen, October 17, 1975, in BArch, B 136/24655.

62. Letter from Werner Nachmann to Chancellor Helmut Schmidt, February 24, 1976; letter from Dr. Melzer (Office of the Chancellery) to the chancellor, March 12, 1976, both in BArch, B 136/24655.

63. See, for example, the speech by Heinz Galinski on November 9, 1978, "Informationsdienst Jüdische Gemeinde zu Berlin 9. November 1938: Fakten und Folgerungen," in BArch, B 136/24655.

64. Letter from Werner Nachmann to Minister of the Interior Werner Maihofer, May 20, 1977, in BArch, B 106/51649.

65. Letter from Werner Nachmann to Minister of the Interior Werner Maihofer, May 20, 1977, in BArch, B 106/51649.

66. Letter from Werner Nachmann to Minister of the Interior Werner Maihofer, May 20, 1977, in BArch, B 106/51649.

67. Minutes of the meeting of the board of the Central Council on September 6, 1981, in Frankfurt. See also Alexander Ginsburg and Alfred Weichselbaum in minutes of the meeting of the board of the Central Council on October 26, 1980, in Frankfurt, both in ZA, B.1/7.907.

68. Minutes of the meeting of the board of the Central Council on September 6, 1981, in Frankfurt, in ZA, B.1/7.907; letter from Milleker to the head of the Office of the Chancellery, April 30, 1981, in AdsD, 1/HSAA 6870; letters from Werner Nachmann to Hans-Dietrich Genscher, March 29, 1982, and May 7, 1982, in ADL, N52/303.

69. The study was published in 1981 under the title *5 Millionen Deutsche: "Wir sollten wieder einen Führer haben. . ." Die SINUS-Studie über rechtsextremistische Einstellungen bei den Deutschen*, with a foreword by Martin Greiffenhagen (Reinbek bei Hamburg, 1981).

70. Letter from Milleker to the head of the Office of the Chancellery, April 30, 1981, in AdsD, 1/HSAA 6870.

71. Letter from Werner Nachmann to Hans-Dietrich Genscher, March 29, 1982, in ADL, N52/303.

72. Minutes of the meeting of the board of the Central Council on October 26, 1980, in Frankfurt; minutes of the meeting of the board of the Central Council on March 10, 1981, in Berlin, both in ZA, B.1/7.907.

73. See S. Cobler, "Das Gesetz gegen die 'Auschwitz-Lüge,'" *Kritische Justiz* 18 (1985); T. Fischer and M. Lorenz (eds.) (2007), p. 90.

74. M. Brumlik (2000), pp. 172–173.

75. See M. Brumlik (2000), pp. 364 ff.

76. W. Bergmann (2002), pp. 37–38.

77. U. Herbert (ed.) (2002).

78. Y. Bodemann (1996), p. 107.

79. On the debate regarding the extent of antisemitism in the GDR, see especially T. Haury (2002); A. Timm (1997a); M. Kessler (1995); along with the hugely apologetic description by D. Joseph (2010).

80. Letter from Helmut Aris to the State Secretary for Church Questions, June 20, 1968, in BArch, D 04/1548; letter from Arnold Munter to Horst Ende, chief of police of the Berlin Volkspolizei, February 4, 1975, in BArch, D 04/1369.

81. Memorandum from the State Secretary for Church Questions (signed Janott) of November 1, 1976, in BArch, D 04/1548.

82. Memo from the counsel of the district of Erfurt, deputy chair of the interior, July 13, 1983, in BArch, D 04/1548.

83. Memorandum from the State Secretary for Church Questions (signed Jakel), September 6, 1983, in BArch, D 04/1548.

84. Concerning the Jewish cemetery in Mühlhausen, see the letter from Raphael Scharf-Katz, chairperson of the Jewish community of Thüringen, to the State Secretary for Church Questions, Klaus Gysi, June 3, 1988, in BArch, D 04/1548.

85. "Hohe Strafen für Schänder des jüdischen Friedhofs," *Neues Deutschland*, July 7, 1988. See also "'Ich wollte Chef sein . . .': Ein Prozeß offenbart Hintergründe abscheulicher Taten," *Neue Berliner Illustrierte*, no. 29 (1988); "Gründlich Ursachen der Untaten untersucht," *Junge Welt*, July 7, 1988.

86. Letter from Wiegand (Hauptabt. XX/4, MfS), District Administration for State Security, Sec. XX, Karl-Marx-Stadt, May 26, 1988, in BStU, MfS, Außenstelle Chemnitz, Sec. XX, no. 1245; letter from Wallner, District Administration for State Security, Sec. XX, Leipzig, to the Ministry for State Security, Main Sec. XX/4, Berlin, June 29, 1988, in BStU, MfS, BVfS Leipzig, Sec. XX, no. 2165.

87. Letter from Galinski to Honecker about the PLO office in East Berlin, *Der Tagesspiegel*, September 22, 1973.

88. Heinz Galinski, "Bedenkliche Symptome: DDR-Jugend gegen Neonazismus nicht völlig immun," *AJW*, October 6, 1978, pp. 1–2.

89. U. Offenberg (1998), pp. 184–189.

90. Interview with Helmut Aris, "Unsere Republik ist allen Bürgern eine gute Heimat," *Neues Deutschland*, November 8, 1978.

91. See also L. Mertens (1997), pp. 102–104.

92. Letter from Peter Kirchner to the editor of the *ABC-Zeitung*, Karl Heinz Semmelmann, January 15, 1985, in BArch, D 04/1342; letter from Peter Kirchner to the editor of the *Berliner Zeitung*, Dieter Kerschek, December 11, 1985, in BArch, D 04/1342.

93. Letter from Karl Heinz Semmelmann and Rainer Paetzold to N.N., January 26, 1985, in BArch, D 04/1342.

94. L. Mertens (1997); U. Offenberg (1998). For more on how the Stasi dealt with the Jewish communities, see also K. Hartewig (2000), pp. 603–609.

95. "Participatory dictatorship" is from M. Fulbrook (2008).

96. Hans-Joachim Levy was invited as the sole community chair to participate in the "roundtable" between members of the government and representatives of the opposition. E. Burgauer (1993), p. 244.

97. MfS, KD Magdeburg, Ref. III, Vorschlag zur Gewinnung als GMS, Magdeburg, March 15, 1980 (signatures illegible), in BStU, MfS, Ast. Magdeburg, no. 2680/89 C.

98. MfS, KD Magdeburg, Ref. III, letter of commitment from Hans-Joachim Levy, April 15, 1980, in report on the hiring of security agent (GMS) "Ludwig," April 15, 1980 (signatures illegible), in BStU, MfS, Ast. Magdeburg, no. 2680/89 C.

99. MfS, KD Magdeburg, Ref. III, report on the second conversation with H. Levy on January 30, 1980, in BStU, MfS, Ast. Magdeburg, no. 2680/89 C.

100. MfS, KD Magdeburg, Ref. III, information of January 6, 1982 (signature illegible); memorandum from Federmann of January 14, 1982, both in BStU, MfS, Ast. Magdeburg, no. 2680/89 C.

101. MfS, KD Magdeburg, Abt. XV, information on the appearance of the chair of the Magdeburg Jewish community, Paul Levi [*sic*], in BStU, MfS, Ast. Magdeburg, no. 2680/89 C.

102. MfS, KD Magdeburg, information from security agent "Robert" on a conversation with Hans Joachim Levy on March 13, 1986, in BStU, MfS, Ast. Magdeburg, no. 2680/89 C.

103. MfS, KD Magdeburg, Referat III, information from Major Hinze on August 12, 1986, in BStU, MfS, Ast. Magdeburg, no. 2680/89 C.

104. Draft press release by the board of the Federation of Jewish Communities in the GDR, undated, in BStU, MfS, HA IX, no. 4288.

105. E. Burgauer (1993), pp. 239–244.

106. K. Schiller (2008).

107. K. Schiller (2008), p. 142.

108. Speech by Hans Lamm at the unveiling of the memorial plaque in front of the house at Connolly-Strasse 31 on December 10, 1972, in ZA, B.1/7.115. In 1976 Heinz Galinski also complained that the president of the German National Olympic Committee, Willi Daume, had not urged that the murdered Olympic athletes be honored at the opening of the winter games in Innsbruck: "Both as a member of the Jewish community, against which the crimes of the terrorists were primarily directed, and as a German citizen to whom the international reputation of this country is important, I deeply regret that this initiative was not taken." Letter from Galinski to Daume, February 13, 1976, in ZA, B.1/7.115.

109. See also A. Kauders (2007), pp. 98–99, 131–147.

110. See, for example, M. Osteen, introduction in M. Osteen (ed.) (2002), p. 16.

111. M. Douglas, foreword in M. Mauss (ed.) (1990), p. ix; D. Cheal (1988), p. 15; J. Godbout (1998), p. 18; H. Böhme (2006), p. 285.

112. Letter from H. G. van Dam to Willy Brandt, September 11, 1972, in BArch, B 136/24655.

113. Letter from Willy Brandt to Hendrik G. van Dam, September 20, 1972, in BArch, B 136/24655.

114. Minutes of the meeting of the board of the Central Council on June 24, 1973, in Berlin, in ZA, B.1/7.176.

115. Letter from Werner Nachmann to Willy Brandt, June 19, 1973, in BArch, B 136/24655.

116. Werner Nachmann, "Die jüdische Gemeinschaft der Bundesrepublik wirkt an der Friedenspolitik der Bundesrepublik mit," *AJW*, December 12, 1975, p. 2. See also Friedo Sachser, "Unveränderte Grundsätze und Aufgaben," *AJW*, February 13, 1976, pp. 1–2.

117. Letter from Werner Nachmann to Staatsminister Hans-Jürgen Wischnewski, October 11, 1977, in BArch, B 136/24655.

118. Letter from Werner Nachmann to Willy Brandt, October 11, 1977, in BArch, B 136/24655.

119. Letter from Willy Brandt to Werner Nachmann, October 27, 1977, in BArch, B 136/24655.

120. Letter from Werner Nachmann to Willy Brandt, November 7, 1977, in BArch, B 136/24655.

121. The equation of left-wing and right-wing extremism is found elsewhere as well. See, for example, the letter from Werner Nachmann to Willy Brandt, October 20, 1977, in BArch, B 136/24655.

122. Letter from Dr. Schüler to Werner Nachmann, November 1977 (no exact date), in BArch, B 136/24655.

123. Hermann Levy, "Bekenntnis zum Miteinander: Die zentrale Veranstaltung zum 9. November," *AJW*, November 17, 1978, pp. 1, 3, 4, 5.

124. Werner Nachmann and Alexander Ginsburg, "Das Erreichte absichern und ausbauen: Botschaft des Zentralrats der Juden in Deutschland zum Jahre 5740," *AJW*, September 21, 1979, p. 1; Werner Nachmann, "Hitlers langer Schatten: Drei Thesen zu 1933," *AJW*, January 14, 1983, pp. 1–2; Werner Nachmann, "Jüdische Verantwortung," *AJW*, September 30, 1983, pp. 1–2; Werner Nachmann, "Juden—Bürger der Bundesrepublik," *AJW*, February 10, 1984, pp. 1–2; and Werner Nachmann, "Das jüdische Erbe in Deutschland," *AJW*, March 23, 1984, pp. 1–2.

125. Yitzhak Ben-Ari, "Sehr geehrte Trauergemeinde," in ZA, B.1/7.456.

126. Letter from the German coordinating committee of the associations for Christian-Jewish cooperation to Alexander Ginsburg, January 27, 1988, in ZA, B.1/7.456.

127. Letter from Dr. Murmann and Dr. Erdmann to the Central Council, January 28, 1988. Simon Bank responded similarly on January 22, 1988; Helmut Lohr, member of the board of Standard Elektrik Lorenz, on January 22, 1988; Waltraud Schoppe, chairperson of the Greens faction in the Bundestag, on January 22, 1988; and Wolfgang Brück, lord mayor of Frankfurt am Main, on January 27, 1988, all in ZA, B.1/7.456.

128. Letter from Hans Filbinger to the administrative council and board of the Central Council, January 29, 1988, in ZA, B.1/7.456.

129. M. Brumlik (1996), p. 2. See also M. Brumlik (2000), p. 178.

130. Y. Bodemann (1986), p. 65. See also Y. Bodemann (2002), p. 168.

131. E. Burgauer (1993), pp. 135–136.

132. T. Lemke (2005), p. 329.

133. Letter from State Rabbi Fritz Bloch (Württemberg) to the rector's office, January 14, 1977, in StadtAS, IRGW 1026/415.

134. T. Fischer and M. Lorenz (eds.) (2007), pp. 202–204; W. Wette (ed.) (2006), pp. 21–22.

135. Letter from Werner Nachmann to Hans Filbinger, May 29, 1978, in H. Filbinger (1994), p. 272.

136. Letter from Heinz Galinski to Alexander Ginsburg, July 21, 1978, in ZA, B.1/7.106. See also Hans Rosenthal at the meeting of the board of the Central Council on September 3, 1978, in ZA, B.1/7.904; Kurt Israel at the meeting of the board of the Central Council on August 31, 1980, in Frankfurt, in ZA, B.1/7.907.

137. H. Broder and M. Lang (1979), p. 11.

138. For an overview, see T. Fischer and M. Lorenz (eds.) (2007), pp. 224–242.

139. Hellmuth Karasek and Ulrich Manz in a *Spiegel* debate, "Wir haben eine Leiche im Keller: Ignatz Bubis und Daniel Cohn-Bendit über Juden in Frankfurt und den Fassbinder-Streit," *Der Spiegel*, November 11, 1985.

140. "Auf Kohls Rat hören wir nicht wieder: Das deutsch-amerikanische Trauerspiel um das Gedenken an den 8. Mai 1945," *Der Spiegel*, April 29, 1985.

141. See also T. Fischer and M. Lorenz (eds.) (2007), pp. 227–229; S. Derix (2009), pp. 165–175.

142. Karasek and Manz, "Wir haben eine Leiche."

143. For more detail, see M. Lenarz (2007).

144. I. Bubis (1996), pp. 97–111, quotation on p. 100.

145. I. Bubis (1996), p. 107.

146. S. Schönborn, "Ein reinigendes Gewitter," *Trumah* 14 (2004), p. 113; I. Bubis (1996), pp. 145–149.

147. Letter from Günther Rühle to Hilmar Hoffmann, June 4, 1985, in ISG Frankfurt, Kulturdezernat 68.

148. I. Bubis (1996), pp. 153–154.

149. H. Broder (1986), p. 7. The quotation can be found only in the first edition, because Günther Rühle was able to suppress this passage in court.

150. I. Bubis (1996), p. 142.

151. J. Bodek (1991), p. 232.

152. I. Bubis (1996), p. 153.

153. Letter from Werner Nachmann to Günther Rühle, October 21, 1985, in ISG Frankfurt, Kulturdezernat 68.

154. Reports in I. Bubis (1996), pp. 153–159; M. Brumlik (2000), pp. 172–173; M. Reich-Ranicki (1999), pp. 382–390; B. Korn (2007), pp. 67–77; and J. Bodek (1991), pp. 314–317.

155. For Bubis's claim, see Karasek and Manz, "Wir haben eine Leiche." For the assurance that the police would not intervene, see I. Bubis (1996), p. 153.

156. S. Schönborn, "Ein reinigendes Gewitter," *Trumah* 14 (2004), pp. 127–128; J. Bodek (1991), p. 232; A. Kauders (2007), pp. 120, 196–197.

157. For greater detail, see I. Bubis (1996), pp. 164–175; M. Brumlik (2000), pp. 176–184.

158. M. Brumlik (2000), p. 178.

159. For "Jewish normalcy," see I. Bubis (1996), p. 129.

160. For more, see especially Y. Bodemann (1996), pp. 87–89; H. Schmid (2001), pp. 429–449; J. Herf, "Philipp Jenninger," *Partisan Review* 56 (1989); L. Niethammer, "Jenninger," *Babylon* 5 (1989).

161. W. Bergmann (1997), pp. 455–456; H. Schmid (2001), pp. 432–433.

162. Copy of the spoken text in A. Laschet and H. Malangré (eds.) (1989), pp. 13–26.

163. J. König, "Wenn du einmal im Sarg liegst, kommst du nicht mehr raus," *Monatshefte für deutschsprachige Literatur und Kultur* 100/2 (2008), pp. 180–181.

164. König, "Wenn du einmal," pp. 17–18.

165. See also the comprehensive collection in BPA, Jenninger, Ph. 021-4/0-1.

166. "Kontroverse im Zentralrat der Juden um Jenninger-Rede," *Der Tagesspiegel*, November 12, 1988; I. Bubis (1996), pp. 196–197.

167. See, for example, "Erst nach einer Stunde war es soweit: Zähes Ringen um Jenningers Rücktritt im Gespräch mit Bundeskanzler Kohl," *Der Tagesspiegel*, November 12, 1988.

168. "Tragik liegt im Versagen des Philipp Jenninger," *Stuttgarter Nachrichten*, November 11, 1988.

169. For more on this in the following, see L. Niethammer, "Jenninger," *Babylon* 5 (1989), pp. 4–46.

170. E. Domansky, "Kristallnacht," *History & Memory* 4 (1992), pp. 66–67.

171. See, for example, A. Laschet and H. Malangré (eds.) (1989).

172. See, for example, "Das Experiment: Zweierlei Rede; Ignatz Bubis sprach 1989 Jenningers Text," *Frankfurter Allgemeine Zeitung*, December 1, 1995; Stephan-Andreas Casdorff, "Viele müßten jetzt Abbitte leisten: Philipp Jenningers Rede und Rücktritt in neuem Licht," *Stuttgarter Zeitung*, December 2, 1995.

173. I. Bubis (1996), pp. 198–200.

174. U. Offenberg (1998), p. 234; L. Mertens (1997), p. 284.

175. "Skandal im Bundestag der BRD wegen Jenninger-Rede zur Reichspogromnacht," *Neues Deutschland*, November 11, 1988.

176. "Symbolische(n) Grundsteinlegung für die Neue Synagoge Berlin," *Neues Deutschland*, November 9, 1988.

177. Bodemann (1996), table of contents and pp. 110–111.

178. "Unsere Republik ist allen Bürgern eine gute Heimat," *Neues Deutschland*, November 8, 1978.

179. Brief message from the MfS, HA XX/4 (signed Hauptmann Sprotte) to Salomea Genin, December 27, 1985, in BStU, MfS, HA XX/4, no. 3655.

180. Letter from Salomea Genin to Erich Honecker, December 2, 1985, in BStU, MfS, HA XX/4, no. 3655.

181. M. Fulbrook (2008), p. 301.

182. Note by the MfS, HA XX/4 about a conversation with Salomea Genin on January 21, 1986; note by the MfS, HA XX/4 (signed Major Sprotte) about a conversation with Salomea Genin on November 7, 1986, both in BStU, MfS, HA XX/4, no. 3655.

183. L. Mertens (1997), pp. 188–195; U. Offenberg (1998), pp. 234–241.

184. Information no. 2789/88 of the MfS, HA XX/4 of July 7, 1988, "Internationale Pressekonferenz des Verbandes der Jüdischen Gemeinden in der DDR," in BStU, MfS, HA XX/4, no. 2183.

185. H. Lübbe (1982).

186. "Gott und das Geld," *Der Spiegel*, January 29, 1968.

187. Lothar Weber, "Der fünfte Berliner Sektor: Eine lange Nacht über die Traditionen des Milchmanns Tewje," broadcast on Deutschlandfunk on May 16, 2009, http://www.deutschlandfunk.de/der-fuenfte-berliner-sektor.704.de.html?dram:article_id=85823.

188. C. Granata, "The Cold War Politics of Cultural Minorities," *German History* 27 (2009).

189. "Irrsinn in Kimmelquell," *Der Spiegel*, November 24, 1969; interview by Cornelia Geissler with Ephraim Kishon, *Berliner Zeitung*, August 22–23, 1992; Martin Doerry, "Adolfs süßer Traum," *Der Spiegel*, September 27, 1993.

190. Josef Joffe, "Trostspender: Zum Tod von Ephraim Kishon," *Die Zeit*, February 3, 2005.

191. See, for example, the report by Dietrich Reiß, "Kibbuz 71: Eindrücke eines deutschen 'Gastarbeiters,'" *Lübecker Nachrichten*, May 1, 1971.

192. W. Benz, "Rückkehr auf Zeit," in W. Benz (ed.) (1991a), pp. 410–419; L. Nikou (2011).

193. Minutes of the meeting of the board of the Central Council on August 31, 1980, in Frankfurt, in ZA, B.1/7.907.

194. A. Kauders (2007), p. 217. For a discussion of "Jewish Spaces," see D. Pinto (2006); S. Lustig and I. Levenson (eds.) (2006), pp. 187–204; R. Gruber (2002).

195. Sources: http://www.beliebte-vornamen.de/4819-sarah.htm; http://www.beliebte-vornamen.de/4914-david.htm. See also M. Wolffsohn and T. Brechenmacher (1995).

196. R. Gruber (2002), pp. 43–50.

197. L. Mertens (1997), pp. 137–142.

198. Rafael Seligmann, "Das Markenzeichen der Lea Rosh ist der erhobene Zeigefinger," *Die Welt*, June 23, 1999; Klaus Harpprecht, "Ein Hauch von Demut," *Süddeutsche Zeitung*, August 7, 2001; Petra Steinberger, "Lea Rosh: Publizistin und Mit-Initiatorin des Holocaust-Mahnmals," *Süddeutsche Zeitung*, October 28, 2003.

PART FOUR: 1990–2012
NEW DIRECTIONS

12 THE RUSSIAN-JEWISH IMMIGRATION

YFAAT WEISS AND LENA GORELIK

THE GDR OPENS ITS GATES

Despite its minuscule Jewish minority (there were only eight small Jewish communities in East Germany in the 1980s totaling barely four hundred members), astonishingly, the most important historical turning point in German-Jewish life after the Holocaust originated in the German Democratic Republic (GDR). From the GDR's beginnings through the first half of the 1980s, the East German–Jewish communities were almost entirely dependent on funding from the state; at the same time, the rigid anti-imperialist and anticapitalist state ideology meant that a more nuanced historical interpretation of the destruction of the Jewish community as a whole under National Socialism was almost impossible. However, the GDR's inflexible institutional structures began to lose some of their rigidity during the 1980s as well.

Alongside the "memorial epidemic" that spread through the GDR in 1988 with numerous commemorations of the fiftieth anniversary of Kristallnacht, the country began to entertain new initiatives and contacts.[1] In early 1988 Erich Honecker, the East German head of state, met with Siegmund Rotstein, the newly elected president of the Association of Jewish Communities in the GDR, and Heinz Galinski, the chair of the Central Council of Jews in Germany. The American rabbi Isaac Neuman was invited to assume the rabbinate in East Berlin, which he did between September 1987 and May 1988.

Previously scorned international personalities were invited to East Berlin. Thus, for example, in October 1988 Edgar Bronfman, the president of the World Jewish Congress, made an official visit to the GDR, which his hosts hoped to exploit to improve trade relations between the GDR and the United States and to open up the American market to East German exports. This visit had been preceded in 1987 by a meeting between Honecker and rabbis Israel Miller (Nahum Goldmann's successor as president of the Jewish Claims Conference) and his deputy, Saul Kagan. Despite signaling a willingness to pay compensation in principle, the political leadership of the GDR was unable to shake off the doctrinal and ideological shackles that had for decades stood in the way of restitution. "For hours, [Honecker] advised his guests—who had come to the GDR in the hope of a belated commitment to compensate the Jews who had been persecuted under National Socialism—that the anti-Fascists had been on one side and the Nazis on the other and that the GDR was paying pensions and benefits to the anti-Fascists living here and supported the small Jewish religious community."[2]

The GDR leadership was simply unable to break loose from these iron-clad principles because they were integral to the narrative by which the East German state legitimized its existence.[3] Rainer Lepsius analyzed this tactic of legitimation in an essay in which he contrasted the basic patterns employed to deal with guilt for the Nazi crimes. The three successor states to the Greater German Reich proceeded along different tacks: internalization in the Federal Republic; externalization in Austria; and universalization in the GDR.[4]

At his meeting with Galinski and Bronfman, Honecker stated this principled readiness to consider Jewish demands for compensation, which his country had stubbornly refused to do for forty years. The figure under discussion involved a symbolic payment of $100 million, which would be delivered as humanitarian aid to Holocaust survivors living outside the GDR. These pledges were never actually made good, with the exception of a few million DM, which the government of Prime Minister Hans Modrow transferred to the Amcha organization in Israel in early 1990. Official contacts between Israel and officials in the GDR had been initiated in 1988, when Josef Burg, the then Israeli minister of the interior and religion, who originally came from Dresden, and Yitzhak Arad, the chair of Yad Vashem, arrived in the GDR to commemorate the fiftieth anniversary of Kristallnacht. Cooperative agreements between the GDR archives and Yad Vashem were even worked out at a meeting with Kurt Löffler, the new state secretary for religious affairs. Yet as far as improvements in relations with Israel were concerned, the GDR lagged behind the other Eastern Bloc states, which had already begun to build bilateral relations in the mid-1980s. The citizens of the GDR, who had been prepared neither for a change in attitude toward Israel nor a correction to the image of Jewish history propagated by their state, reacted cautiously. Just how ambivalent this reversal remained is evident from Löffler's visit to Israel in February 1989, when, in the best GDR tradition, he announced that his country bore no responsibility for the crimes committed against the Jews and had itself been an indirect victim of National Socialism. To the very end, the GDR attempted to draw a firm line between actions it took to improve trade relations with the United States and recognition of its responsibility for the crimes of the Third Reich.

Erich Honecker receives Edgar Bronfman (*third from left*), the president of the World Jewish Congress, October 17, 1988. Bundesarchiv / ADN / photograph by Peter Zimmermann.

As a result, relations between the GDR and its Jewish citizens remained ambivalent, and real changes occurred only when Hans Modrow came into office. On February 9, 1990, Modrow officially conceded the GDR's responsibility for the persecution of Jews under National Socialism in a statement to the Israeli government and to Bronfman. He announced that his country was prepared to offer Jewish survivors material support and solidarity, which he referred to as a "humanitarian duty." As was the case with Honecker, the Modrow government's gesture also contained a fundamentally self-serving aspect based on recognition by Israel: the hope that Israel would stand up for the GDR for fear of a unified Germany. The government of Modrow's successor Lothar de Maizière hewed to this line after its election when, on April 14, 1990, it entered into negotiations based on the Reparations Agreement between Israel and West Germany (the Luxembourg Agreement). However, these efforts came to naught with the currency union of July 1, 1990. In the end, a unified Germany, which officially came into being on October 3, 1990, belatedly assumed these obligations.[5]

Imprisoned by its own self-legitimizing ideology, the GDR was unable to recognize its historical responsibility even after 1989 or effectively negotiate questions of restitution. At the same time, and without arousing substantial opposition, extraordinary measures with regard to Jewish immigration were introduced during the brief period of post-Communist independence. These were the fruits of efforts by civil rights organizations that had convened at a roundtable conference.[6] During the first phase, these extraparliamentary organizations conveyed their position to the Modrow government; by January 1990 representatives of the government had joined the roundtable discussions. First steps with regard to Soviet Jews were then initiated, which proved to have major consequences. Given media reports about antisemitic attacks in the Soviet Union, the East German government signaled its readiness to open the borders of the GDR to Soviet Jews. In a move that was unprecedented—the GDR had not signed the 1951 Convention Relating to the Status of Refugees—the East German Council of Ministers approved the admission of persecuted Jews from the Soviet Union. This action was also in line with the efforts of the de Maizière government to legitimize the existence of a separate East German state—legitimation that was consistent with the GDR's understanding of itself as an anti-Fascist state, the state of the victims, and the state of those persecuted by National Socialism.

On the strength of this decision, in April 1990 a small number of Soviet Jews traveled to East Berlin on tourist visas—a total of 2,650 persons by October of that year.[7] They were handed residence permits for a period of five years and received support from various institutions, among them the Lutheran Church, the Jewish community, and the Office for Foreigners' Affairs in the Council of Ministers of the GDR, and from the group of Jewish intellectuals who had spearheaded the initiative. The Contact and Counseling Office for Foreign Jewish Citizens (Kontakt- und Beratungsstelle für ausländische jüdische Bürger) was established in East Berlin for the purpose of coordination and organization. Ironically, its office was located in the building that had once housed Goebbels's Ministry of Propaganda.[8] The significance of this fact was undoubtedly more symbolic than material; the international press, however, drew public attention to this initiative.

In the Federal Republic, on the other hand, the conditions for admitting Jewish immigrants from the Soviet Union were less accommodating at the time. Initially, they received no official status as refugees, which meant that they were dependent on volunteer initiatives.[9] On the eve of reunification, Wolfgang Schäuble, the West German minister of the interior, looked askance at these efforts, even demanding a halt to the processing of immigration applications at West German consulates in the Soviet Union until official policies could be worked out. In effect, the Federal Republic closed its borders to Soviet Jews wishing to immigrate and demanded that the German Democratic Republic do the same. As a result, from then until the end of the year, Soviet Jews could enter the GDR only by illegal or semilegal means. Galinski, who in early 1990 still viewed mass Jewish migration from the Soviet Union with displeasure, changed his position as a result of what he observed in the GDR and began to urge the West German government to admit these immigrants over and above the regular quota.[10] It is doubtful whether he appreciated at the time the full significance of this step for the future of the Jewish community in Berlin and in Germany as a whole.

THE FOURTH WAVE

The 2,650 Soviet Jews who reached East Berlin during the final days of the German Democratic Republic's existence as a sovereign nation marked the beginning of a massive wave of emigration from the Soviet Union. Just as this emigration would have been impossible had the Communist German state not been on the verge of collapse, this wave also signaled the imminent collapse of the Soviet Union. Jewish immigration to Germany over the past two decades constituted a link in a long chain of emigration from the Soviet Union, and many of the characteristics of this particular emigration should be viewed within this more general context. In historiography, this wave of emigration, which began with the disintegration of the Soviet Union in the late 1980s, is often termed the "fourth wave."[11] It was preceded by the first wave of Eastern European Jews moving westward after the Bolshevik Revolution, the second wave during and after World War II and the Nazi occupation, and finally the third wave during the 1970s. From its founding until the end of the 1980s, some 4.7 million people left the Soviet Union, even though no legislation regulating emigration was on the books in the Soviet Union, and citizens were barred from moving freely both within the country and abroad.[12] Most emigrations were ethnically motivated: almost 1.5 million of those who left the Soviet Union between 1950 and 1991 belonged to ethnic or religious minorities. Almost half of these were Jews, approximately a third (37 percent) were Germans, 7 percent Armenians, and 2 percent Greeks.[13] The emigration of minorities was generally supported by the countries in which they formed a majority. This also held true for the Jews, whose emigration, as with other ethnic groups, was based on the principle of family reunification. The extent of ethnic migration depended on the current state of relations between the Soviet Union and the absorbing country. Thus, for example, improved bilateral relations between the Soviet Union and the Federal Republic during the 1970s resulted in an increased exodus of German Russians, ethnic Germans who had settled in Russia since the 1500s. It is noteworthy that between 1950 and 1991, the majority of individuals who migrated from Eastern to Western Europe—68 percent—were taken in by Germany.[14]

The fourth wave, which was to transform Jewish life in Germany from the ground up, began approximately two years after Mikhail Gorbachev assumed office and was part of a general transformation in the traditionally restrictive Soviet policies toward emigration. As early as 1988, even before the legal situation had officially changed, the Soviet Union had begun to permit Jews, Russian Germans, Greeks, and other Soviet citizens who had received a personal invitation from the West to emigrate virtually unhindered. As a result, the number of emigrants rose sharply from 39,000 in 1988 to 108,000 in the following year. In 1990 this figure doubled from that of the previous year. During this period, most of the emigrants came from the larger cities and urban centers, especially in Russia, Ukraine, and Kazakhstan, but also from Belarus and Moldavia. Most of the emigrants in this wave also belonged to ethnic minorities.

An early sign of the impending legislative changes was the drafting of an emigration law submitted to the Supreme Soviet in October 1989. The new law also covered emigration for reasons other than family reunification. At the same time, Soviet authorities began to discuss the possibility of labor migration. The modest outcome of this chain of events was a 1993 agreement between Russia and the Federal Republic regarding work permits for two thousand foreign workers in Germany. The Supreme Soviet had already approved amendments to the emigration law in May 1991, but with the disintegration of the Soviet state in December 1991, the successor states now became the competent authorities. In Russia, for example, the emigration law came into effect in January 1993. Since then, all Russian citizens have been permitted to emigrate, thus putting them on an equal footing with the few ethnic minorities that had already enjoyed this right.[15]

In order to understand the process of Jewish emigration—leaving one's old homeland and making a new life in another country—one must understand the significance and peculiarities of Jewish ethnicity in the Soviet Union.

In contrast to other ethnic minorities, such as the Russian Germans, the Jewish minority did not possess what in the sociological and anthropological literature is referred to as a "thick culture"—a common language, culinary tradition, clothing, and/or religious practices.[16] Essentially, the only expression of Jewish ethnic belonging was registration as such in the population register, a seemingly purely technical and administrative act, but one whose far-reaching consequences are felt to this day. Entry in the register was introduced in 1931–1932 for the entire urban population of the Soviet Union and is emblematic of one of the numerous paradoxes of Soviet politics. Whereas ethnic identity was considered ideologically irrelevant, in practice the register became an instrument of population politics. At the age of sixteen, all citizens were legally required to declare their national identity; that is, they had to specify either their father's or mother's national identity from a list of 160 nationalities and indicate the family name of one or the other. This meant, of course, that if both of one's parents were Jewish, a person had no choice but to specify his or her nationality as Jewish. However, in the case of mixed marriages there were no legal provisions regarding patrilineal or matrilineal identification, so that many chose to specify their non-Jewish parent.[17] Given that even in the 1970s about half of the Jews in the Soviet Union were married to non-Jews,[18] an enormous gap had formed between the number of Jews registered in the population register and the number of those who were considered Jewish according to religious law, which recognizes descent from a Jewish mother alone.

For many Soviet citizens, national identity, which was noted on identity cards in the infamous "column 5," determined how their lives would develop and what opportunities would become available to them.[19] The identity card had to be produced in a variety of situations, such as when enrolling at a university, mailing a package, or buying an airline ticket. As a result, a person's ethnic identity was constantly on display. The notation "Yevrey" on Jews' identity cards could stand in the way of getting a job or entering university, or it could restrict the types of positions they could hold in the army, the secret police, or the foreign ministry, as well as in the sciences, political institutions, and the press. An unofficial ethnic quota system, well known to all, operated for many years, and it limited Jewish access to many professions and jobs.[20]

This "passportization" of Jewish identity was of a piece with the Russification that had characterized Soviet nationality policies since the early 1930s and that greatly favored Russian nationals above all other Soviet nationalities.[21] The origins of the fragile, internally contradictory adherence to Jewish identity in the Soviet Union may be found in the tension and disjunctions between acculturation, "passportization," and Russification. As a result of Soviet policies, the Jews lost their specific cultural, linguistic, and religious characteristics over the course of several decades and began to acculturate to their surroundings. This acculturation was very successful, and their contributions to Russian cultural life have been impressive by any standard. However, whether forced or voluntary, this acculturation did not lead to the hoped-for assimilation. Against the backdrop of the trauma of the Holocaust and the virulence of official Soviet antisemitism, the *dissimilation* of the Soviet Jews, which had begun in the 1940s, gathered pace—as a result of which many Jews readopted their ethnic identity.[22]

Benjamin Pinkus has termed this persistent Soviet-Jewish identity "negative nationalism,"[23] while John Klier has found that "perhaps the most striking accomplishment of the Communist experiment has been to replace the religious culture of Judaism with a Soviet-style ethnic identity for Jews, which has persisted even in the face of the disappearance of many ethnic markers."[24] The ethnic identity of the Jews in the Soviet Union thus developed along very different lines from that of other ethnic identities; it was based neither on a community of interest nor on organizational connections or culture in a higher sense. The sociologist Stephen Cornell locates the ethnic identity of the Soviet Jews in their identification with a symbolic community: "What group members share, in such cases, is an attachment to a particular set of identity symbols, derivative perhaps of historical events, of contemporary circumstances which sustain occasional intragroup interactions, or simply of assignment by non-members, but unattached to any set of substantial and distinctive interests, exclusive institutions, or more elaborate cultural constructions."[25]

Which factors, then, nourished the Soviet Jews' symbolic group identification, their "latent ethnicity"?[26] Clearly, more than one factor was involved. According to the historian Zvi Gitelman, there were four different sources: socialization in childhood; the experience of antisemitism; the sense of Jewish outsiderness emanating from the non-Jewish population; and forms of behavior that were typical of an ethnic identity.[27] The historian Ya'acov Ro'i has similarly described an ethnic Jewish identity that is difficult to pin down:

> Jewish culture was not reinstated, except for a few gestures made to assuage foreign critics. Not that Soviet Jews for the most part took a direct interest in Yiddish or other features of Jewish culture. Nor were they attracted to the Jewish religion. Their culture remained Soviet and Russian, but their identity was not. In other words, they were what one scholar has called acculturated rather than assimilated, assimilation having been manifestly demonstrated to be a non-viable option. . . . The single characteristic that the majority would probably have agreed was "Jewish" was their high level of education, which remained far higher than that of any other ethnic group.[28]

The elaboration of this ethnic Jewish identity, which did not emerge from a religious culture and does not include Judaism as a source of identity, is the reason for the current tension between the Soviet-Jewish immigrants and the established Jewish communities in Germany, whose self-definition and identity are based on religious values.

Their ethnic Jewish identity, or, more precisely, their official classification as a Jewish ethnic minority, was the formal precondition for the Jews' emigration from the disintegrating Soviet Union. Apart from specific factors that motivated Jews to leave, there were also circumstances and developments in the country that impacted the population as a whole.[29] The motives of Soviet-Jewish emigrants have changed considerably over the past fifty years.[30] During the early post-Stalin era, most Jews emigrated to be reunited with their families; Zionist or religious convictions played a role for some. In the early 1970s many Jews left the Soviet Union in response to discriminatory policies in education and employment, which also affected other ethnic groups whose majority populations lived outside the Soviet Union. Over time, other motives such as a sense of physical insecurity and the economic situation became more salient. The fourth wave of emigration was thus the result of a combination of motives both general and specific. The political and economic crises that beset the Soviet Union, environmental catastrophes, ethnic conflicts, and religious tensions affected Jews in the same way they affected all Soviet citizens. The transition to a market economy in the Soviet Union and later in Russia exacerbated economic insecurity. Falling wages and rising unemployment in the successor states of the Soviet Union, alongside a rate of inflation approaching 1,000 percent, severely impaired the standard of living. As the Soviet Union broke up into individual states, this process of disintegration led to ethnic, political, and social tensions among the minority groups that lived in the new states. Although the Jews were not directly affected, they felt threatened by these conflicts. And these cultural, linguistic, and religious differences would only deepen. As members of an ethnic minority without a territory of their own in the Soviet Union, the Jews regarded themselves as potential casualties of the struggles raging around them.[31]

The late 1980s and early 1990s saw the formation of antisemitic groups such as Pamyat and Otkazniki that reawakened fears of the sorts of pogroms that generally accompany revolutions—fears that were fed by the historical memory of the Russian Jews, especially by the memory of anti-Jewish rioting that occurred during the revolution of 1905. This fear was all the stronger because intellectuals equated the Soviet Union with Fascism and antisemitism. Many Jews became aware of the violent incidents that were occurring only through reports in the mass media. Live reporting generated a new type of apprehension that served to stoke subjective concerns. As the political scientist Mischa Gabowitsch has noted: "Because it was traditionally assumed that only a fraction of the truth was ever reported in the newspapers, it was understood that each report, such as about an antisemitic demonstration, was to be interpreted as a sign of a much larger phenomenon."[32] The fear of pogroms grew with expectations of rioting in the large cities, although in the end this proved overblown. No antisemitic pogroms took place, and, as it turned out, African students, East Asians, and families from the Asiatic republics were considerably more likely to be victimized. Nevertheless, one cannot appreciate merely from the actual incidents that occurred the extent of fear and threat felt by Jews during the late 1980s. Paradoxically, the negative sense of threat outweighed the positive effects of perestroika.[33]

An array of factors, some of them interconnected, others independent, underlay the emigration of Jews to Germany from the former Soviet Union. This movement began with the growing efforts in the GDR to achieve international recognition and to improve its trade balance and continued with the disintegration of the Soviet Union and the destabilization in the region. At the same time, this development led to an immediate change in American policy in the fall of 1989. Jews who now left the Soviet Union were no longer automatically recognized as refugees. A transit camp that had been in operation in Rome since the

Caricature from the antisemitic pamphlet *Narodnoye Dyelo* (The cause of the people). The caption at the top reads, "We will stamp out the vermin!" The spider at the center of the web represents the "businessman in the porn business." From Dmitrij Belkin, ed., *Ausgerechnet Deutschland! Jüdisch-russische Einwanderung in die Bundesrepublik*, catalogue for the exhibition at the Jewish Museum, Frankfurt am Main, from March 12 to July 25, 2010, p. 35.

1970s was dissolved.[34] In the period before the United States introduced stricter immigration policies, Germany had not been a favored destination for Soviet-Jewish refugees. The number of immigrants to Germany remained low from 1987 to 1989, and most of those who arrived settled in West Berlin.[35] After 1989 only the State of Israel remained a viable destination. Yet once the "German option" became a real alternative to the "American dream," Germany became a destination of choice for Jewish migrants who for whatever reason did not wish to settle in Israel.

THE "QUOTA REFUGEES"

In the early 1990s both Russia and Germany opened their doors at the same time, albeit in opposite directions. In contrast to the former Soviet Union, Russia now permitted emigration, while Germany accepted immigrants, although cautiously at first. During the early period of German reunification, the Federal Republic did not support Soviet-Jewish immigration from the East and even attempted to block it. For example, despite the urging of the East German delegation to the negotiations on reunification, the agreement reached on October 3, 1990, made no mention of Jewish immigration.[36] But under pressure from the press and the public, the Bundestag was forced to debate the issue, and Germany soon reversed its immigration policies altogether. This reversal mirrored the transformation of identity that was occurring among Germans as well as the changing official stances developing at the political, ideological, and administrative levels. At the same time, the new policies engendered fundamental changes in Jewish life in Germany.

Differences in the attitudes of the political class in Germany became evident during the first Bundestag debates to take up the question of Soviet-Jewish immigrants in late October and mid-November 1990. While the left-wing opposition parties argued for the inauguration of a generous, preferably "nonbureaucratic" process for Soviet Jews wishing to integrate, the coalition parties were far less forthcoming. They stressed the risks and potential abuse along with the need for an "orderly," that is, regulated, immigration process.[37] But all Bundestag factions agreed that Germany could not close its borders to the Jews. They also agreed that the parties should avoid discord in public and excessive publicity overall. This last point undoubtedly arose from the fear that a public debate could devolve into arguments about tightening the approval process for asylum seekers and arouse public anxiety about how migration from Eastern Europe might swamp Germany. Not least, the politicians feared stirring up antisemitism in German society.

The morally loaded speeches of the Bundestag delegates demonstrated clearly that these politicians viewed the impending decision about the future of refugees as a touchstone of sorts for the reunited Germany.[38] The weight of international public opinion undoubtedly played a role here as well. The Greens politician Dietrich Wetzel, for example, articulated what was probably on the minds of many: "This response will also be understood internationally as indicating the extent to which reservations about and fears of the new Germany are justified."[39] Other important arguments in the debate were infused with a sense of historical responsibility and memories of Jewish life in Germany prior to National Socialism.[40]

At the end of the 1990s, a broad political consensus probably kept media responses in check as well. Given all of the questions and issues facing Germany in the immediate aftermath of reunification, the subject of immigration was probably not paramount in many people's minds. Upon the conclusion of the debate in the Bundestag, the question was transferred to the committee on internal affairs and the interior ministers of the states. At its meeting on December 14, 1990, the conference of German interior ministers formulated its recommendations, which were then presented to the chancellor, the foreign minister, the minister of the interior, and Heinz Galinski.[41] On January 6, 1991, the chancellor and prime ministers of the states met in joint session and set out the application procedure and conditions of admission for Jewish immigrants from the Soviet Union.[42] In 1997 these decisions, which established the guidelines for Jewish immigration to Germany until 2005, became the directives sent from the foreign office to Germany's diplomatic representatives abroad.[43]

Initially, the policies of the German authorities were based on decisions made by the executive branch, essentially without a formal legal basis.[44] But the magic formula that would resolve this issue was found in January 1991. It was agreed that the 1980 Act Concerning Measures for Refugees Accepted as Part of Humanitarian Campaigns, the so-called Refugees Quota Law, could be applied to immigrants from the former Soviet Union. This law had originally been passed as a humanitarian gesture in response to the plight of refugees from Indochina, the so-called boat people.[45] "By definition, the Federal Republic is not a country of immigration," the former minister of the interior Wolfgang Schäuble later asserted before concluding that "a legal mechanism had to be found for the few thousand people who wanted to come from the Soviet Union: they weren't German Russians, nor really expellees, nor asylum seekers in the narrower sense."[46] The formula of quota refugees (a certain quota was allocated to Jewish refugees from the former Soviet Union) made it possible to reconcile "between a special generosity and magnanimity toward the Jews and a limiting position toward immigration processes in general."[47]

The legal formulation "quota refugees," which was intended to simplify bureaucratic procedures and avoid public discussion, lay at the core of the considerable ambivalence sensed by the German public with regard to Jewish migrants. It was difficult to divorce the legal formula from the conventional images adhering to the status of a refugee, and when these failed to match the character and the status of the actual Russian-Jewish immigrants, the disparity between image and reality eroded the stature of the immigrants.[48] But while other asylum seekers had to relinquish their papers and received a refugee identity card in accordance with the Geneva Convention (and Jewish quota refugees were required to give up their papers at the beginning), the Russian Jews were handed German travel documents instead.

This approach was adopted to head off diplomatic tensions, lest the impression be given that Germany was implicitly accusing the Commonwealth of Independent States (CIS), the loose federation of post-Soviet states, of persecuting its Jews. In this respect, it was reminiscent of the approach taken by the GDR government in July 1990, which mentioned neither refugees nor the Soviet Union.[49] The immigrants were subsequently permitted to retain their former citizenship so that they could travel freely between Germany and their countries of origin; furthermore, in early July 1991 the Soviet Union ceased to link the granting of emigration visas to renunciation of Soviet citizenship.[50] In any event, the retention of Soviet citizenship posed no legal problem for the German government, since it was operating under the Refugees Quota Law. However, in the eyes of the German public, the freedom granted the immigrants to travel between nations was inconsistent with their status as persecuted persons.[51] From the perspective of the immigrants, their freedom to travel helped to mitigate the trauma that is always associated with migration.[52] When some of the Jewish quota refugees began to travel to revive business connections in their former homelands, the public began to view the immigrants' motives more critically, and it did not take long for the image of the immigrants to change. Allegations began to be voiced to the effect that they had come to take advantage of economic opportunity and not because of antisemitism, as had been claimed at the outset. Some of the immigrants were even accused of having been members of the ruling elite in their homelands, which again stood in glaring contrast to the image of the refugee. The legal formulation that had been employed to avoid enacting a special law, which would have entailed public discussion, had now given rise to an image filled with contradictions that was damaging to the immigrants. The former status of the refugees led to tensions, because the public had come to expect a relationship of dependency between a powerful grantor of asylum and a relatively powerless asylum seeker.[53] For many, the Jewish immigrants from the states of the former Soviet Union did not meet these expectations; the German public wished to view these migrants as a community of victims—a description that was simply not apt.[54]

To understand the tension between the immigrants' legal status, public opinion, and reality as they experienced it, it is important to examine more closely the process that was put into place, because many of the contradictions and disparities in expectations were inherent to that process. According to the legal provisions in force up to 2005, potential emigrants received initial counseling and were asked to fill out certain forms at the German diplomatic missions in the states that comprised the CIS. They were required to present their Soviet passport and birth certificate to prove their Jewish identity. It should be noted that the guidelines contained no definition of any sort of "Jewish ancestry," which meant that this was left entirely to the discretion of the diplomatic mission in question.[55] Who was to be viewed as a Jew was defined in the principles and guidelines issued by the German foreign ministry only in 1997: only persons with at least one Jewish parent who did not belong to any non-Jewish religious community could enter Germany as quota refugees.[56] Falsifications and forgeries were rife under this system, as were legal ambiguities.[57] Once the forms had been filled out and had undergone preliminary review by the consulate—especially regarding Jewish ancestry—the file was sent to Bonn. There, the German Federal Administration Office assigned the individual immigration applicants to the various German states according to a previously established formula, which determined the allocation of immigrants based on tax revenues and the population of the individual states. This formula was applied not just to Jews specifically but to refugees generally. Applicants who had proved they were the children of a Jewish father or mother would receive an entry visa, along with their spouse, juvenile children, and adult children, provided they were single and lived with their parents. It should be noted that the German provisions placed stricter limitations on the immigration of Jews, both quantitatively and qualitatively, than does the Israeli Law of Return, since the latter also extends to grandchildren. In addition, Israeli law grants citizenship to *olim* (immigrants) immediately, whereas Germany stipulated a six- to eight-year waiting period for naturalization to take effect. Ethnic German migrants (*Aussiedler*), on the other hand, are naturalized immediately.[58]

The assignment of some immigrants to regions that had limited resources and few opportunities for employment or that for decades had had no Jewish population was the result of a top-down approach. "In the end, this state-imposed welfare principle contributed to further fueling the distrust of Russian-speaking Jews," Karen Körber concluded in an ethnographic study conducted in the late 1990s on relations between the immigrants from the CIS, the Jewish establishment, and the local population of a small town in the state of Saxony-Anhalt.[59] The fact that no Jews had lived in this town since Kristallnacht in 1938 and the subsequent murder or expulsion of all remaining Jews may give the impression that this was an extreme case. Yet a great many Jewish immigrants were assigned in accordance with the above-mentioned formula to similar small towns that had no Jewish community. Körber's conclusions—though based on only one selected ethnographic case—are thus significant, especially in terms of the inevitable disconnect between the ruling from above and the nature of the absorbing communities and of the immigrants themselves. The high levels of

Transitional housing in Stuttgart, Viehwasen 22, August 1992. Anatoli Uschomirski.

unemployment and the restricted economic possibilities in the regions to which the Jewish refugees were assigned led many of them, especially those who were more mobile, to resettle in larger cities. This development, in turn, fueled and intensified preexisting antisemitic stereotypes.[60] In her study, Körber detailed the unsubstantiated, idealized notions of the Soviet-Jewish immigrants that local officials and educated classes in these eastern German towns entertained. Their hopes that these newcomers would revive the German-Jewish tradition were inevitably disappointed.

As long as the Russian-speaking immigrants conformed to the expectation that they would revive the tradition of the German-Jewish Enlightenment that had distinguished a town or city in its heyday, Germans were prepared to welcome them. During a brief transitional period, the Jews, their traditions, and their religious and cultural institutions were understood as part of the Enlightenment tradition. But this expectation was based on the assumption that there was a direct, continuous link between the German-Jewish community that had existed in the pre-Nazi period and the Jewish immigrants from the Commonwealth of Independent States. With their help, Germans might travel back in time into a German-Jewish past, or, rather, into their notion of an imagined earlier local Jewish community.[61] But whatever called this identity into question diminished the image of the immigrants in the eyes of the local population—whether this was because some of them were not recognized as Jewish in accordance with religious law and were therefore ineligible for membership in the Jewish community; or because their own ethnic identity was inconsistent with the religious definition of the Jewish community in Germany; or because they had no interest whatsoever in questions of identity, and certainly not in German-Jewish identity. These circumstances continue to weigh heavily on the relationship between the immigrants and the old, established German-Jewish communities.

FIGURES AND THEIR INTERPRETATION

The interplay of relations between the Jewish quota refugees and the Jewish communities, the place of the immigrants within the German-Jewish and inter-Jewish discourses of memory, and their particularities in comparison to other migrants, such as the German Russians, are of special interest. But to understand these issues, it is necessary to examine the demographics of this last wave of immigration. Estimates of the total number of immigrants and their other demographic characteristics vary greatly. Because of the discrepancy between the total number of persons entitled to immigrate and the number considered Jewish under Jewish religious law, official German statistics and those of the Jewish communities differ considerably.[62] But even setting aside these understandable differences, estimates of the total number of quota refugees vary greatly. The data pertaining to the first two decades of immigration range from 170,000 to 300,000 persons, including their non-Jewish family members.[63] Despite the differences between the various estimates, there is no doubt that at the turn of the twenty-first century, Germany was the only European country that experienced an increase in its Jewish population.[64]

The number of emigrants from the successor states of the Soviet Union who actually became members of the Jewish communities can be established more precisely: between 1990 and 2010, they numbered 103,200 persons. Of the 104,000 community members registered in 2010, approximately 80 percent came from this population.[65] In Bavaria, for example, membership in the Jewish communities between 1989 and 2010 increased from 199 to 1,492 in Augsburg, from 179 to 1,044 in Würzburg, from 117 to 1,001 in Regensburg, from 106 to 928 in Bamberg, from 39 to 507 in Bayreuth, and from 36 to 409 in Hof.[66] The trend was similar or even more pronounced outside Bavaria. New Jewish communities were founded from Emmendingen and Lörrach in the southwest to Rostock and Schwerin in the northeast. North Rhine–Westphalia absorbed an especially large proportion of immigrants, and Düsseldorf became the fastest growing of the larger communities; in 2010, with more than 7,000 members, it was the third largest Jewish community in Germany after Berlin and Munich. In Wuppertal, the number of members rose from 82 to 2,266 between 1989 and 2010, and in Dortmund from 337 to 3,200.[67]

Figures are never neutral in such contexts, just as the selection of quantification criteria is based on value systems and is therefore colored by them. Of course, these figures represent institutions and individuals who, consciously or unconsciously, are the bearers of political, cultural, or social understandings or viewpoints. Demographic analysis of the last wave of immigration is thus not necessarily a more objective tool than other ways of achieving understanding, and no claim can be made that such an analysis achieves a higher degree of scientific reliability than does textual or ethnographic analysis, the evaluation of press releases, discourse analysis, the assessment of interviews, or other forms of research. Their decided advantage, however, lies in their potential for predicting future developments and in their usefulness to decision-makers. The conclusions reached through demographic research are not verifiable or realizable simply because they are correct a priori but because they influence decision-makers whose decisions impact the real world.

What, then, are the fundamental findings of the demographic analysis of the last wave of immigration? In the first place, the analysis delineates the geographic origins of the immigrants and their gender and age distribution within Germany. In addition, demographic research is aimed primarily at assessing whether immigration was successful, that is, whether it met the expectations of those who initiated, promoted, supported, and participated in it, namely, the expectations of the immigrants themselves, as well as those of the states that took them in and of the Jewish communities. Of course, success is a normative, fluid, and subjective concept that may perhaps be approached through interviews and questionnaires and that may correlate with the subjective experience of the immigrants, which is difficult to capture by means of data. Nonetheless, the statistics do allow us to make a series of assessments that are of considerable importance both to the immigrants and to the absorbing society. Statistically, success is measured by the integration of the immigrants into the economy and labor market of the receiving country, taking into account their original level of education and their standard of living in their new homeland. This entails a comparison between the Russian-Jewish refugees and other groups of immigrants in Germany, or between Soviet-Jewish immigrants in the United States or Israel over the same time period. The data on age distribution and births is of special interest, since one of the goals associated with this immigration was to strengthen and revitalize Jewish life in Germany; this was also an argument advanced to justify preferential treatment for the quota refugees above other migrant groups.

The majority of the Jewish refugees from the former Soviet Union were of European descent: of the 166,300 immigrants who arrived in Germany between

1989 and 2001, 92,700 came from Ukraine, 45,000 from the Russian Federation, and 7,200 from other successor states of the Soviet Union.[68] Since 1998 the proportion of immigrants from Ukraine has exceeded that from the Russian Federation. Over the same time period, the proportion of immigrants entering the United States from Ukraine was lower than that from the Russian Federation.[69] This finding becomes all the more significant when we consider other criteria, especially the level of education in the Soviet Union in general and among Jews in particular. Of the Jews arriving from the Russian Federation, 61.1 percent were university educated; for the cities of Moscow and St. Petersburg, the figures were 66.8 percent and 63.3 percent, respectively. By comparison, "only" 49.2 percent of the Jews from Ukraine possessed that level of education.[70] In other words, statistically speaking, the Jews from the Russian Federation were better educated than those from Ukraine. The true extent of this gap is actually greater because of the overall higher quality of the educational institutions in the Russian Federation.

The education index provides additional data that may shed indirect light on the last wave of immigration. Since the end of the 1990s, there has been a general decrease in the relative proportion of highly educated Jewish immigrants to all destinations. From this one may conclude that those with a higher level of education began emigrating in the early 1990s as soon as this became possible.[71] In the late 1990s, the number of those who immigrated to Germany overtook the number of those who migrated to the United States. From then on Germany became the second most popular destination, after Israel, for Jewish emigrants from the former Soviet Union.[72] This trend continued after 2000, with the beginning of the second *intifada* and the economic slump that occurred in Israel. Between 2000 and 2004, more emigrants from the former Soviet Union were admitted to Germany than entered Israel.[73]

The available statistics do not paint a precise picture of the migrants' educational level, since they only relate to those who acquired a first university degree—which is generally viewed as crucial to obtaining a good job in countries with a highly developed economy. The data for the late 1990s indicate that among the Jewish emigrants from the CIS states to the United States, 60.3 percent of the men were academics, to Israel 43.3 percent, and to Germany 35.7 percent. The proportions for the women are similar: 58.4 percent, 44.2 percent, and 37.4 percent, respectively.[74] The proportion of university graduates among the immigrants is markedly higher than the average for the respective populations (Germany, 14.5 percent; Israel, 22.5 percent).[75] The demographers Yinon Cohen, Yitzhak Haberfeld, and Irena Kogan employ the so-called self-selection model to explain the divide in the educational profile of the CIS migrants, specifically, the especially high educational level of those who immigrated to the United States. According to this model, migrants who possess strong professional qualifications tend to immigrate to countries where social inequality is especially high and the social safety net is weak. These migrants assume that with their qualifications they will be able to integrate into the labor market relatively quickly and achieve professional and economic success. Consequently, they are less concerned about the weak system of social supports, because they believe that they will not need them. And indeed, more migrants with a higher level of education prefer to immigrate to the United States, with its relatively weak safety net; conversely, a higher proportion of less educated migrants prefer Germany, which offers elaborate social supports. Furthermore, Cohen, Haberfeld, and Kogan find no significant difference between the level of education of those immigrating to Israel and those who immigrated to Germany; in their opinion, the significant difference is that between these two countries and the United States. Of course, both Germany and Israel provide levels of support payments, cash assistance, and other benefits that are not available in the United States.[76]

According to calculations made by the Jewish Agency in 2003, there is no substantial difference between Germany and Israel in terms of financial outlay on immigrants during their first year in the country. Over time, however, Germany's financial outlay significantly outstrips that of Israel. It spends three times as much as Israel on immigrants who have been in the country for five years, and after a decade its expenditure is 6.8 times higher than Israel's.[77] At this point, it should be made clear that generalizations and statistics cannot adequately explain individual motives for migration. Given the significant economic benefits on offer, one would have expected that the migrants who chose to come to Germany, whose prospects for integration into the labor market were relatively slim, would tend to be older. However, this was not the case: the older migrants tended to select Israel as their destination.[78] This suggests that considerations other than economic factors were at play.[79] A study conducted by Cohen and Kogan suggests that a large proportion of quota immigrants to Germany (50 percent!) are not considered Jewish according to Jewish religious law. This figure compares to 30 percent among immigrants to Israel. In other words, the Jewish character of the State of Israel appears to be an important factor in attracting or deterring individual migrants, influencing their decision in a manner consistent with their religious and cultural identity. In their responses to the questions put by this study, most of the immigrants to Germany tended to cite their cultural identity with Europe as a deciding factor rather than the financial benefits.[80] Interviews conducted in the early 1990s with Jewish immigrants in Germany indicated that they were less influenced by an expectation that they should immigrate to Israel, while at the same time Germany's past history—and the notion that no Jews should live there—had exerted less normative pressure on them.[81] Given the multiplicity of considerations, it is clear that the individual migrant's motives are complex and that generalizations based on statistical data or interviews can neither quantify nor adequately describe them.

Education is the resource that the migrants take with them. Based on these original data, researchers have studied integration into the labor market as a major indicator of integration overall. This perspective, however, distorts the reality of quota refugees in Germany. Whereas in Israel in 2003 the unemployment rate among male immigrants from the former Soviet Union was 12.3 percent, approximately 5 percentage points above the average unemployment rate of 7.5 percent, in Germany, with an average of 8.6 percent unemployment, 50.3 percent of male immigrants had not found work. Approximately two-thirds of the female quota refugees in Germany had not entered the labor force.[82] There are many reasons for this discrepancy. Among other factors, the low unemployment benefits in Israel drove immigrants to take a job quickly, even if it was below their qualifications. Furthermore, some of these migrants had already experienced a similar disconnect between their qualifications and the jobs they found themselves doing because discrimination in the former Soviet Union had rendered employment in their chosen profession all but impossible. This pattern was frequently repeated in the destination country.[83] However, during the first year of immigration to Israel, only some 15 percent of those with high professional or technical qualifications had found a job commensurate with their education, while this figure was far higher in Germany.[84] The employment situation for immigrants exposes many contradictions of the German welfare state: because the benefits that they received in the beginning meant that they did not have to accept the first job offer that came their way, the welfare state tended to inhibit their integration into the labor market.[85] Integration has also tended to proceed slowly because the German labor market is inflexible. In stark contrast to the German Russians, the professional education of the quota refugees is not automatically credited, and the years that they have already worked in their country of origin are taken into account neither in hiring nor in calculating pensions. In addition, because German citizenship is a precondition for various civil service positions, these have remained closed to the immigrants for the first six to eight years, that is, until they become naturalized.[86] This is another key difference between the quota immigrants and the ethnic Germans, who were granted German citizenship automatically upon arrival. If we examine the treatment of quota refugees over the past decade in terms of Germany's stated policy of attracting specialists and academics to the country, the prospects for success are not especially good.[87]

Even two decades after immigration began, integration of the quota immigrants into the labor market remains slow: although the percentage of those employed among immigrants rises steadily over the years after their arrival, the proportion of those unemployed six to ten years after immigration continues to hover at around 24 percent for men and 41 percent for women. The rate of unemployment among Russian-Jewish immigrants in Israel is even higher than the average in the Israeli economy.[88] Of course, integration into the labor market has numerous social, psychological, and economic consequences. As far as income is concerned, immigrants to Israel receive around 87 percent of the average wage, and in Germany only 62 percent. However, in absolute terms the purchasing power of these wages is higher in Germany than in Israel.

The fact that quota refugees are unable to fully exploit their experiences and academic training in their new country leads to numerous emotional problems. As Mark Izkovitsch has written, "The sense of insecurity and even self-pity that results from the impossibility of using one's knowledge and capabilities leads to depressive states in many migrants, which in turn increases nostalgia for the past."[89]

THE IMMIGRANTS AND THE COMMUNITIES

The integration of quota refugees was facilitated by an extraordinary political act intended to revive Jewish life in Germany after the Holocaust. From the very beginning, this goal has been the cause of the tense relationship between the Jewish communities and the immigrants—a consequence of the discrepancy between the profile of the immigrants and the expectations kindled by their arrival. An employee of the Berlin Jewish community's welfare office characterized the immigrants as follows: "The typical Soviet-Jewish immigrant of the 1990s is apolitical, secular, and Western in outlook; he has also been molded by the Soviet system, and a large proportion of his family members is non-Jewish."[90] This was how a social worker with ten years of experience in the Berlin community characterized both the typical profile of the post-Soviet immigrants and the disappointment felt about them in the Jewish communities. From the very beginning the immigrants were assigned to existing Jewish communities by German policy-makers and the Jewish establishment and given no choice in the matter. In a fascinating comparison between the legal status and administrative treatment of the ethnic Germans, on the one hand, and the quota refugees, on the other, Jannis Panagiotidis has demonstrated how the identity of the new refugees was molded by administrative definitions.[91]

According to Panagiotidis, the identity of the Eastern European immigrants had for decades remained unclear, and the two categories—German and Jewish—had not been viewed as mutually exclusive. The "German cultural circle," that vague and multilayered category, had provided an umbrella definition that included both the German Russians and the Jewish immigrants. A strict division between them was put into place only after the Eastern Bloc had disintegrated and the principle of the quota refugees applied. From the moment they were classified either as Germans or as Jews, very different expectations were projected onto these migrant groups, and their administrative treatment differed accordingly. It was expected that the ethnic Germans who had immigrated from Russia would integrate into German society as Germans, while the quota refugees would retain their separate identity. One glaring example cited by Panagiotidis was the policy on name changes, which encouraged the ethnic Germans to trade their Slavic names for German ones. This was meant to solidify their inclusion in German society and blur their foreign origins. No similar approach was attempted with regard to the Jewish refugees. As Panagiotidis noted, "As a result, the ethnic Germans were dissolved, at least on paper, as a separate group identifiable by their Russian origins. For the quota refugees, who from an administrative perspective are not Germans, no such special provision is envisaged. As a group, they remain recognizable as foreigners, either as Jews or as Russians. In contrast to the past, a Jewish immigrant can no longer become a German, not even by name. This is the paradoxical outcome of ethnically legitimized immigration in a supposedly postnational age."[92]

Panagiotidis's thesis is validated upon examining the a priori assignment of quota refugees to Jewish communities and its consequences. The legitimization of their migration was based on a simplification of their essential identity—which has always been problematic and beset by serious internal contradictions. The expectation that an essential spiritual and religious affinity would emerge between the immigrants and the local communities soon proved illusory and was followed by disappointment upon realizing that the immigrants wanted little more than social assistance from the existing communities. Their dependence on aid from the Jewish communities was itself a consequence of the special status of the Jewish refugees, because as noncitizens they were not entitled to the same level of assistance as the ethnic Germans. And in any case, this arrangement encouraged the emergence of a largely paternalistic relationship between the migrants and the established communities.[93] Because they were dependent on assistance, the immigrants felt obliged to adapt to the religious mindset of the communities—a situation that reminded them of the Soviet indoctrination that they had sought to leave behind. One of the immigrants expressed this bind as follows: "In order to get help in resolving the many problems, people who have no notion of religion or any desire to adopt one, are forced to become members of religious Jewish communities."[94] In any case, the linkage between support and such cultural content is very different from the assistance offered by the state on a universal basis, which is aimed at encouraging the immigrants to become independent.[95] Franziska Becker has aptly described the paradox inherent in this cultural collision: "The particular dilemma of Jews in Germany is made more than clear by the process of immigration: on the one hand, the 'newcomers' rescue the Jewish communities quantitatively, on the other hand, they strengthen its transformation away from a religious identity to one of representing the interests of [secular] Jewish people."[96]

THE IMMIGRANTS' SELF-PERCEPTION

How the immigrants viewed their own situation is evident from the articles that appeared in the Russian-language Jewish press in Germany. Although an analysis of these texts cannot replace an empirical study of their self-perception, we may assume that they reflect a mood prevalent among a large number of Jewish refugees. *Krug* (Circle), which began to appear in 1996, was the first newspaper of this type. It was later joined by *Nasha gazeta* (Our newspaper), which ceased publication in 1999. By then, *Yevreyskaya gazeta* (The Jewish newspaper), founded in 2002, had come to monopolize that market. Because the newspapers were written in Russian, the Jewish refugees were able to discuss their plight among themselves, "unobserved." The word *discussion* is very apt here, because the articles and commentaries were written by readers for readers. Furthermore, an especially large proportion of each edition was given over to letters, and some of the discussion threads would continue for months. In addition, editorial commentary was not always written by the same established journalists but often by readers who contributed commentaries and essays. Little effort was made to provide "objective" journalism; most of the texts consisted of opinion pieces. Unsurprisingly, most of these expressed complaints and disappointments. Because the immigrant readers, most of whom had for one reason or another not joined the Jewish communities, played such an important role in the development of these newspapers, these sources provide us with unusually free access to the internal discussions that were taking place.

These discussions show that many of the newcomers viewed the old established community members as aloof and uninterested in their welfare. The following description is typical of the Russian-Jewish press: "We usually meet with unsympathetic indifference, arrogant condescension, mistrustful tension, and now and then open rejection."[97] This behavior was largely attributed to the fact that the established members were dealing with completely different problems and concerns: "German Jews—they're usually pretty well fixed financially. Many of them are pious Jews, or they at least observe the outward religious practices. They place great emphasis on the problems confronting Israel and world Jewry. They have extensive contacts with their German neighbors and are not locked into the inner circle of their communities. It is not easy for them to understand many of our problems."[98]

Many of the discussions invoked the image of a wall, which the old community members had supposedly built up with the help of the Central Council and were unwilling to tear down.[99] The immigrants proceeded from the assumption that the Central Council of Jews in Germany represented the interests of its most prominent members. They attributed its behavior to fear for its own security and a desire to maintain the roles that had become second nature to its representatives. As a result, it was unreceptive to anything new. It should be noted, however, that this negative image of the old established community members was not formed from the outset. Between about 1990 and 1992, when this wave of immigration was just beginning, the newcomers generally penned grateful and emotional reports that spoke of the "open arms that received us like unfortunate brothers."[100] However, this euphoria over the hospitality they met evaporated as ever more immigrants arrived. For example, Russian-speaking members of the Jewish community of Hannover related how they were systematically excluded from elections and how the community leaders had refused to teach the quota refugees something about the traditions of Judaism.[101] Many of the refugees rejected parallels drawn between their own experiences and those of the Eastern European Jews who had arrived in Germany after the war: "And the response of the German, or rather the local Polish-Romanian Jews whose help we await, is not arbitrary: integrate into the German reality just as we did when we arrived, and then you, too, will get your rights and citizenship and work."[102]

On the other hand, the initial enthusiasm felt by many established community members, who hoped that the newcomers would replenish their numbers, soon turned to frustration as they found themselves transformed into a minority within their communities, as Russian increasingly came to be the common language spoken at community events. The small and elderly communities were often simply swamped by the arrival of so many immigrants and proved unable to integrate them. And for the Russians, May 9, Victory Day, the day the Nazis capitulated to the Soviet Union, had more resonance than November 9, the day on which Kristallnacht was commemorated.

Although almost all of the Jewish communities had greatly expanded their social service departments during the 1990s, the quota refugees often found the assistance on offer to be inadequate. They had hoped for more discussions, counseling, and receptiveness, and in their written accounts they spoke about their intention to repay what they had received.[103] If community members, for example, would communicate with them through interpreters in their language—Russian—about Jewish religious life, they, in turn, might be more accepting: "That is what 'progressive' Jews do. Not wait for the 'newcomers' to learn German or Hebrew. Some of them won't be able to do that. The [community members] have to approach them rather than sit back and wait. Or as some of them are trying to do, 'shut the doors against the newcomers,' because 'they don't speak our language.' I wrote recently that I had attended a Hanukkah celebration in Israel that was conducted in Russian for Russians. That's how it has to be done."[104]

A sense of resignation about the incompatibility of the two camps increasingly crept into the writings of the Russian immigrants, often tinged by regret and sorrow but seldom admitted any shortcomings of their own. For example, in an article titled "No One Can Force You to Be Nice," the chair of the Association of Russian-Speaking Jews in North Rhine–Westphalia opined, "We have tried to come to terms with the old-established Jews, and what has come of it?" He related how little interest they had shown in dialogue, how indifferent they were to the problems of the immigrants, and how the latter had been systematically excluded from political participation.[105] For many years the recent immigrants accused the communities of denying Russian-speaking members participation in their elected boards, thereby thwarting the interests of this majority.[106] The way in which the established members sought to "control" the communities reminded them of the old detested Soviet mechanisms of power.[107]

Over several decades, the initial language and cultural barriers that had stood in the immigrants' way began to dissolve. Numerous Jewish communities now have chairpersons drawn from the ranks of the immigrants; they are even represented on the six-member board of the Central Council, one of whom is Küf Kaufmann, the cabaret artist and chair of the Jewish community of Leipzig. In 2008 the lawyer and publicist Sergey Lagodinsky, who was born in Astrakhan in 1975 and cofounded the Working Group of Jewish Social Democrats in 2007, was elected to the board of the Jewish community of Berlin. He has consistently and robustly spoken on behalf of the immigrants in the media.

Russian-speaking community members have often been rebuked for allowing previously religious Jewish communities to degenerate into cultural venues.[108] Their response has been that a community is a Jewish center, and those who wish to pray there should be given the opportunity to do so, but that those who simply want to meet other Jews should be able to do that as well. In other words, the quota refugees seek not only political participation but also acceptance of the fact that, in the wake of the emigration of Jews from the former Soviet Union, the Jewish communities in Germany can no longer be based solely on the principle of religion.[109]

The Russian newcomers have found it difficult to understand that in Germany people are not classified by nationality. There is no such thing as "Jew" stamped in a German passport; a person is Jewish by religious affiliation. This has meant that they not only have lost their country, their friends and relatives, their language, and the lives that they led—that is, a part of their Russian identity—but also have been robbed of their national identity as Jews. That this has been disorienting for many is evident from Russian-language debates in which they declare that they came to Germany "as Jews" and had hoped that they would be able to relate to this part of their identity in their adopted country. This expectation was especially prevalent among the quota refugees who emigrated in later years and whose primary reasons for emigrating were no longer economic and political. Their emigration was in part driven by the hope of living out in Germany the Jewish culture that had recently been revitalized in the countries of the former Soviet Union, where new community centers had been created, Jewish schools opened, and Jewish culture celebrated once again more openly.

The widespread conviction that was nurtured in the Soviet Union, that Jewishness was a function of nationality rather than religion, or perhaps at most of culture or tradition, explains many of the misunderstandings and ambivalences that came to the fore in the Jewish communities in Germany. This explains why more than a few immigrants imagined that they could be Christians or atheists—but still retain their Jewish identity in the German context. For example, according to one account, a quota refugee failed to check the box "religious affiliation" when filling out an official form because he viewed himself as an atheist. When a government official pointed out to him that he was living in Germany as a Jew, which conferred permanent residence status (i.e., that the box had to be checked), he responded with complete incomprehension. This incident also raises the question whether the official's behavior had not been motivated by antisemitism.[110] Numerous studies have confirmed that this type of self-identification is common among the quota refugees. For example, when asked in a survey conducted in 1996 by the Moses Mendelssohn Center, "What does it mean to you to be Jewish?" 36.3 percent of the quota refugees responded, "Descent from a Jewish family," 19.6 percent "The presence of certain characteristics and behaviors," and 15.7 percent "A sense of belonging to Jewish history." Only 2.2 percent of those surveyed checked "Religious affiliation."[111] Some of the quota refugees, never religious to begin with, even appear to have developed an aversion to religion over time. This is evident from articles and letters published in the Russian-language newspapers. One writer let it be known that "we will not be forced," meaning that no one can impose a religion on others. And this, too, was based on the understanding that although a person could not choose to be born a Jew, religion was a different matter entirely.

A further major issue concerned a prosaic matter that, however, is more problematic at the symbolic level, namely, the Holy Days. Understandably, Jewish communities celebrate the Jewish Holy Days; the immigrants from the former Soviet Union, however, brought their own modes of celebration along with them, such as New Year's Day, which in the context of antireligious socialist realism had replaced Christmas and was celebrated as a family holiday with costumes and gifts, along with a so-called New Year's tree. Another was May 9, the day the Nazis surrendered to the Red Army—the day on which war veterans were traditionally honored for their sacrifices. As a result, while the established members were appalled at the possible specter of former veterans of the Soviet Army celebrating May 9 in Jewish communities in Germany, the quota refugees were faced with the question whether they could or should celebrate Purim and other Jewish holidays.[112]

At the same time, the quota refugees were very conscious of how others perceived them. The fact that the established members of the Jewish communities often accused them of ignorance about religion and tradition, not to mention a lack of interest in them, and therefore of being insufficiently Jewish, was a recurring topic in Russian-Jewish newspapers. As one contributor noted, "The leaders of the communities were disappointed in the 'quality' of the newly arrived contingent: they don't believe in God, they don't keep the traditions, they expect assistance from the communities of an integrative, material, and cultural sort—real parasites, that's what they are!"[113] A particular sentiment that has since become a dictum appeared in numerous variations whenever identity was discussed: "I used to be a Jew, now I'm a Russian." In other words, the quota refugees viewed their Jewish identity through the lens of Soviet antisemitism, which for so long had turned them into "second-class citizens"—a perspective shared neither by German Jews nor by Germans more generally after the Second World War.[114] To the quota refugees, their previous circumstances could explain and justify their lack of knowledge about religion and unfamiliarity with Hebrew. This outlook also brings home the extent to which their sense of being outsiders, which was part of their identity in the Soviet Union, had solidified in Germany. In the Soviet Union they were Jewish; in Germany they were not Jewish enough. A polemically formulated article by a German-Jewish woman in the Düsseldorf Jewish community bulletin entitled "Can We Still Be Saved?" had posed the question whether German Jews actually wished to cede their own identity to the "Russians," who allegedly sought to take over the communities and to compromise their fundamental purpose—the observance of Judaism.[115] In response to this article a Russian-Jewish immigrant noted, "We have gotten used to it. In Russia we were 'the damned Jews'; for Frau Klüger [the author of the original article] we're 'the damned Russians.'"[116] If we add to this the general sense among many quota refugees that everything Russian was negatively tinged, the feeling of alienation is complete: "When I arrived in Cologne, I was often asked, 'Where do you come from?' and answered, 'From Russia,' and what I heard in response was, 'Oh, Russian mafia!'"[117]

In addition, writers often noted that in the Soviet Union, Jews had lived "as well as was possible," even if this usually meant trying to conceal their Jewishness.

A letter to the Central Council from the Jewish community in Hannover that was signed by ninety-seven members declared: "In that country, we felt our Jewishness because of the enmity of those around us. We have become united as a result of difficulties in finding work, strict quotas at the universities and in teaching and the sciences, and a ban on taking an array of administrative and select jobs and even on entire professions. That is precisely why we are here in Germany."[118] In other words, the quota refugees had expected greater understanding of their origins, education, and life histories in the Soviet Union from the established members of the Jewish community and German society generally.

And with regard to their own identity, poised between the Soviet past, the German present, and the individual's Jewish self, the question "Who are we?" led to a fundamental and broad debate that evidently concerned many. Hardly anyone concluded that he or she felt exclusively Jewish; many found the characterization "Russian Jew" to be an apt term because it encompassed Soviet education, which had been so formative, their past, and Russian as a mother tongue. Because their homeland, the Soviet Union, had ceased to exist in the form that most quota refugees had known, the Russian language had assumed even greater importance, binding people together and granting them identity. Furthermore, even many educated immigrants had only a minimal command of German, and this was another factor that tended to isolate them in their adoptive country. The supposed adherence to Russian culture, so often discussed in the relevant literature, was frequently more an adherence to the Russian language, which allowed the quota refugees to feel that they were still "people who are taken seriously"— an expression often heard in this regard.[119] The refugees frequently complained that the process of recognition of professional degrees was unnecessarily complicated and that their residence status as quota refugees without a German passport made their lives difficult.[120] It was this mode of processing the immigrants that engendered incomprehension and a sense of resignation: "In Germany, even our status as 'quota refugees' remains legally ambiguous, socially inferior, economically uncertain, and psychologically uncomfortable."[121]

Only seldom does one encounter self-critical voices among the refugees that mention that they had been invited to Germany to revitalize Jewish culture and traditions and Jewish life within the communities. As one writer noted, "It is certainly no secret that many newcomers say, shamelessly, 'If you want to be a Jew, go to Israel!' or 'We are people of the Russian culture!' or 'We are atheists!' And many who talk like this have no problem with achieving power in the communities (it should be noted, the religious communities)."[122]

Those who were considered non-Jewish according to Jewish religious law were confronted with an especially thorny problem of identification. Distressed and bitter accounts such as the following are not uncommon: "Last name Rabi-

Jewish veterans of the Great Patriotic War in front of the Neue Wache memorial in Berlin, 2005. Florian Willnauer, Berlin.

novich. Have a Jewish face. In the Soviet Union all esteemed universities were taboo as a result. And here, here I'm suddenly not a Jew." To which the writer added, "It would be funny if it weren't so sad."[123]

One might assume that the quota refugees and the established "German" Jews had at least one thing in common: a close relationship with Israel. While this was frequently mentioned in the Russian-Jewish press, it also became the source of a further problem of identification because the newcomers all too often felt the need to explain why they had immigrated to Germany instead of going to Israel.[124] They wrote numerous essays and letters on topics such as "Israel is nonetheless a Jewish homeland" and "Living in Germany, loving Israel."[125] In his autobiographical novel *Moi nemetski dom: Emigrantskie dnevniki* (My German house: Diaries of an emigrant), Mikhail Vershchovskii wrote: "I live here, but I wish the State of Israel all the best. I love it. May my tongue fall from my mouth if I ever deny it, if I ever betray it. But I can't live there. It is too late for that. There are objective reasons for this, which I will not list, and unfortunately, financial reasons as well. Furthermore, what would the State of Israel get from me? And nonetheless, do I feel guilty? I do. Feel ashamed? I do."[126]

The culture of memory of World War II presents yet another reason why Soviet-Jewish immigrants have had difficulty establishing an identity. Everyone in the Soviet Union grew up with the understanding that they were the victors in the Great Patriotic War, and almost all members of the older generation are former war veterans who proudly brought their many medals with them. Each year on May 9 they are again celebrated and honored as heroes both officially and in private.[127] The early editions of Russian-Jewish newspapers carried numerous articles in which the veterans of the Soviet Army spoke about their service on the front. And their heroism in World War II was painstakingly depicted and honored. But over the years, there developed in parallel a growing sense that in Germany they were also regarded as victims of the Holocaust. Articles began to emphasize that the present-day quota refugees had feared being persecuted as Jews during World War II. However, their suffering was overshadowed by that of the concentration camp survivors, who came to define themselves by this experience. The quota refugees increasingly pointed to the concentration camps that were built on Soviet soil to emphasize their own suffering. The stories of individual survivors of these concentration camps who now lived in Germany were related repeatedly.[128] For example, the Russian-Jewish press has almost every year devoted a page or even a special insert to Babi Yar, where in September 1941 more than thirty-three thousand Jews from Kiev were shot over a two-day period, an atrocity that plays a central role in Jewish collective memory of the Holocaust in the Soviet Union.[129] Contributors recalled that it was the Soviet army that had liberated Europe from National Socialist domination and that many Jews had served in this army. These former soldiers now expected to be honored in their adopted country. In January 1999 World War II veterans from the Jewish community in Koblenz penned an open letter to Ignatz Bubis, who at the time served as president of the Central Council: "It is symbolic and fateful that I, a soldier and a Jew from the Ukrainian shtetl of Kryzhopil, whose mother and two brothers were tortured to death in the ghetto there, took part in the liberation of the Majdanek concentration camp. I was wounded twice. I ended the war in Berlin, at the Reichstag and the Reich Chancellery, where, according to the official version, Adolf Hitler, who had raised antisemitism to the level of state policy, was burned, and punished for this by God."[130] Such reminiscences were invariably followed by the complaint that the signatories were not considered victims of National Socialism, along with a request that a committee of veterans of World War II be established by the Central Council.

Surprisingly, many quota refugees—in contrast to the established community members—were not especially concerned by the fact that they were now living in the land of the perpetrators. The predominant feelings for their adoptive country are admiration, warmth, and gratitude, although its history has been

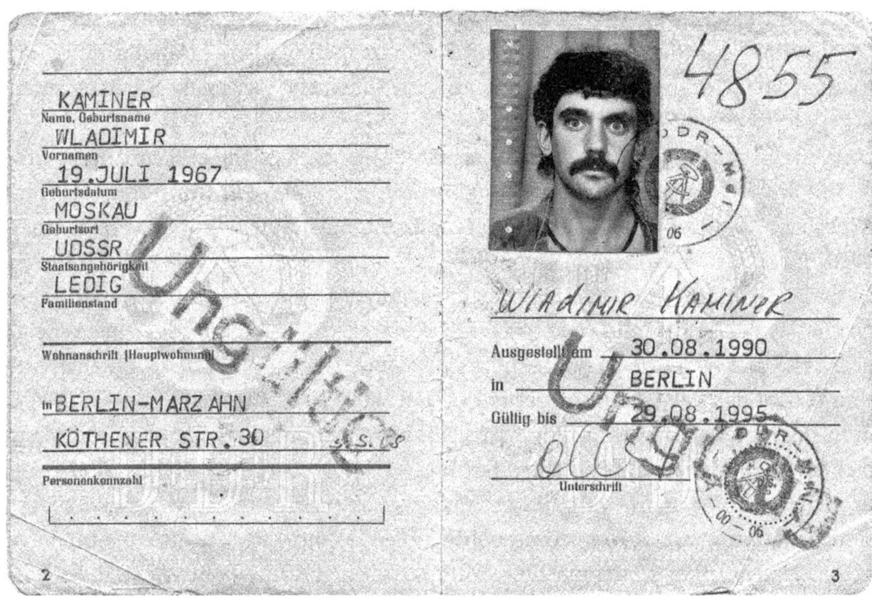

The writer Wladimir Kaminer's 1990 residency permit issued by the GDR, which still existed at the time. From Dmitrij Belkin, ed., *Ausgerechnet Deutschland! Jüdisch-russische Einwanderung in die Bundesrepublik*, catalogue for the exhibition at the Jewish Museum, Frankfurt am Main, from March 12 to July 25, 2010, p. 51 / photograph by Wladimir Kaminer.

neither forgotten nor revised: "Jews and Germans. Our ancestors lived together for centuries. And if we want our grandchildren and great-grandchildren to continue living here (why else would we have immigrated?), we must overcome the sense of alienation. Take one step forward. Enter into this culture to which the Jews have contributed much. Not at the price of giving up our own culture and our own faith (for those who have one)."[131]

After about the year 2000, a group was formed by a number of more adaptable new migrants who sought to distinguish themselves from their "Soviet" co-migrants, whom they reproached for failing to adapt and for a lack of interest in religion. One such reproach read: "Our emigrants continue to feel that they are not Jews, but Soviets, and it seems that they miss the departments and organizations of the Communist Party of the Soviet Union, like the Soviet trade union, which secretly sponsor trips, lunches, cultural events, and other amenities here."[132] A marked division began to emerge between "Soviet" and "German" quota refugees, with the former holding fast to their original patterns of identification and the latter beginning to take an active interest in the Jewish communities in Germany by, among other things, attending religious services. Often, adaptation to German life and German society also entailed a return to Judaism: very rarely did people come to view themselves as solely German; most lay claim to being German Jews.

All of the problems described here were the result of the extraordinary historical and cultural circumstances surrounding this wave of immigration. They were, however, problems that manifested during the first few years and have since been outgrown. Members of the older generation found ways to build a life in Germany, even though the lives they have led have perhaps not lived up to their original expectations and were to a large extent based on Russian-language social networks that were "existentially necessary" for this group.[133] The second generation of Russian-Jewish immigrants exhibits, at least at the professional level, a high degree of integration. For many younger immigrants, the great value attached to education among their families has helped them quickly to acquire proficiency in German, which has in many cases enabled them to pursue professions in academia and to become politically and culturally engaged. Some have achieved prominent positions. One example is Marina Weisband. Born in Kiev in 1987, she views herself as an observant Jew and in 2011 became the most familiar face of the newly founded German Pirate Party. Another example is the writer and columnist Wladimir Kaminer, who immigrated in 1990. Since then he has become one of the most prominent contemporary authors, garnering attention with his work *Russendisko* (published in English as *Russian Disco*) and the novel *Militärmusik* (Military music), about the life of his Jewish family in Moscow and his flight to Germany.

When Germany opened its doors to Jewish immigrants from the East, the principle guiding its politicians was an abstract one: the renewal of Jewish life. It did not take into account the concrete problems that arise in all immigrations. Given the trade-offs available at the time, in comparison to the approximately three million members of the ethnic German minority who streamed into Germany from the territories of the former Soviet Union, the two hundred thousand Jews who immigrated at about the same time barely seem worthy of mention. In addition, the professional potential of the quota refugees—primarily immigrants from the cities in the European portion of the Soviet Union, about half of whom possessed a university education—seemed greater than that of other migrants. In any event, the symbolic value attributed to a renewal of Jewish life in Germany outweighed all practical concerns. Given the difficulties that emerged, however, by 2005 the federal government had decided to rescind the old immigration provisions for quota refugees and to enact new criteria.

Since that year, potential immigrants must demonstrate proficiency in the German language before receiving a visa for Germany. In addition, they must show that they are eligible to be accepted into a Jewish community in Germany and that they are able to make a living. These amendments have indirectly turned Jewish religious law into the basis for accepting potential immigrants and have drastically reduced the number of candidates who have few prospects for successful integration into the German labor market and society generally. In fact, these new provisions marked the end of mass migration from the successor states of the Soviet Union to Germany. With the exception of 2007, the number of immigrants has stabilized at approximately one thousand persons per year.[134] Consequently, the mass post-Soviet emigration to Germany may be considered a matter of history as of 2005.

YFAAT WEISS is Professor of Jewish history at Hebrew University Jerusalem and is director of the Simon Dubnow Institute for Jewish History and Culture at Leipzig University. Her research focuses primarily on citizenship, cultural heritage, and memory. Her publications include *A Confiscated Memory: Wadi Salib and Haifa's Lost Heritage, Lea Goldberg: Lehrjahre in Deutschland 1930–1933, Staatsbürgerschaft und Ethnizität: Deutsche und polnische Juden am Vorabend des Holocaust*, and *Schicksalsgemeinschaft im Wandel: Jüdische Erziehung im nationalsozialistischen Deutschland 1933–1938*.

LENA GORELIK immigrated to Germany from Russia in 1992. She graduated from journalism school in 2004 and studied Eastern and Southeastern European history, politics, and economics at the University of Munich. Her master's thesis is titled "Jews—Russians—Germans: The Transformation in the Perception of Russian Jews in the German Media (1989–2006) against the Backdrop of German-Jewish Relations." Gorelik is a novelist and journalist in Munich and is finishing her dissertation, titled "Russians—Jews—Germans: The Integration of Russian-Jewish Contingent Refugees into German and German-Jewish Society; A Media Study of Russian-Language Sources."

NOTES

1. For "memorial epidemic," see S. Schreiner (1992), p. 190.
2. C. Goschler (1993), pp. 93–94, 110–112, quotation on p. 93. The topic is addressed in M. Wolffsohn (1995).
3. C. Goschler (1993), p. 110.
4. M. R. Lepsius (1989), pp. 247–264.
5. O. Groehler (1992a); O. Groehler (1994); O. Groehler (1992b); A. Timm (1994).
6. R. Ostow (2003), pp. 1–3; P. Harris (1998).
7. For the decision, see A. Berger (2010).
8. A. Berger (2010), p. 57.
9. P. Harris (1998), p. 122; E. Weizsäcker (2004), p. 97.

10. F. Becker (2001), pp. 45–50.

11. A. Vishnevsky and Z. Zayonchkovskaya (1994), pp. 239–243; B. Dietz and K. Segbers (1997), pp. 147–150.

12. S. Heitman (1987).

13. H. Fassmann and R. Münz (1994), p. 526.

14. H. Fassmann and R. Münz (1994), pp. 532–533.

15. L. Shevtsova (1992), p. 242.

16. Z. Gitelman (2003), p. 108.

17. M. Tolts (2005), p. 56; F. Becker (2001), p. 286.

18. Z. Gitelman (2003), p. 110.

19. I. Runge (1995), pp. 9–10.

20. Z. Gitelman (2003), p. 108.

21. Y. Ro'i (2003), p. 184. See also D. Shumsky (2002), pp. 156–160; D. Shumsky (2007), pp. 466–468.

22. Y. Ro'i (2003), p. 186; Y. Slezkine (2004), p. 286.

23. B. Pinkus (1984), p. 16.

24. J. D. Klier (2003), p. 156.

25. S. Cornell (1996), p. 271.

26. Z. Gitelman (2003), p. 108.

27. Z. Gitelman (2003), p. 106.

28. Y. Ro'i (2003), pp. 189–191.

29. M. Brenner (2002), p. 53; S. Haug and M. Wolf (2006), pp. 65–66.

30. T. H. Friedgut (2010).

31. D. Aptekman (1993), pp. 20–23.

32. M. Gabowitsch (2010), p. 43.

33. M. Gabowitsch (2010), p. 42.

34. P. Harris (1998), pp. 113–116; Y. Cohen et al. (2008), p. 186.

35. B. Dietz et al. (2001), p. 34; P. Harris (1998), pp. 116–117.

36. F. Becker (2001), pp. 45–46; M. Tress (1997), pp. 24–25.

37. P. Harris (1998), pp. 105–109.

38. See Deutscher Bundestag, 11th legislative period, 231st session, October 25, 1990, p. 18360.

39. Deutscher Bundestag, October 25, 1990, p. 18360. He further stated that if Germany merely provided a stopover for Soviet Jews, this would create the impression that it wished to create a state that was "free of Jews."

40. This was also emphasized by Dietrich Wetzel of the Greens, Peter Glotz of the SPD, Burkhard Hirsch of the FDP, Ingrid Bittner of the PDS, and Johannes Gerster of the CDU-CSU.

41. P. Harris (1998), p. 138.

42. P. Harris (1998), p. 140; E. Weizsäcker (2004), p. 97.

43. Grundsatzerlass des Auswärtigen Amtes an alle Auslandsvertretungen in den GUS-Staaten und im Baltikum, March 25, 1997, AZ 514-516-20/7, cited, for example, in *Migrationsbericht der Ausländerbeauftragten im Auftrag der Bundesregierung*, p. 33, http://www.zuwanderung.de/SharedDocs/Downloads/DE/Broschueren/2001/migrationsbericht_2001. pdf?__blob=publicationFile; A. Hochreuter (2000), pp. 1376–1381; S. Haug and M. Wolf (2006), p. 68.

44. G. Biehler (2000), pp. 265–283; J. Raabe (2004).

45. Gesetz über Maßnahmen für im Rahmen humanitärer Hilfsaktionen aufgenommene Flüchtlinge, July 22, 1980 (HumHAG), *BGBl.* 1, p. 1057; P. Harris (1998), p. 140; G. Biehler (2000), p. 271.

46. Interview with Wolfgang Schäuble, July 8, 2009, Berlin, in D. Belkin and R. Gross (eds.) (2010), p. 53.

47. F. Becker (2001), p. 50.

48. F. Becker (2001), pp. 59–66.

49. A. Berger (2010), p. 57.

50. S. Haug and M. Wolf (2006), p. 66.

51. F. Becker (2001), pp. 60–61.

52. Y. M. Bodemann and O. Bagno (2008), p. 160.

53. F. Becker (2001), p. 63.

54. F. Becker (2001), pp. 46–47; K. Körber (2009), pp. 233–254.

55. E. Weizsäcker (2004), p. 97.

56. For further details on the Grundsatzerlass (n. 43), see A. Hochreuter (2000), pp. 1377–1378; J. Raabe (2004), p. 410.

57. A. Hochreuter (2000), pp. 1378–1380.

58. Y. Cohen and I. Kogan (2005).

59. K. Körber (2010), p. 64.

60. K. Körber (2010), p. 90.

61. K. Körber (2005), p. 118.

62. B. Dietz et al. (2001), p. 37.

63. In a 2009 essay, Körber estimated the total number of Russian-Jewish immigrants between 1989 and 2005 to be 190,000, of whom approximately half joined the Jewish communities. This brought the total number of members of the Jewish communities to approximately 105,000. See K. Körber (2009), p. 233. In a 2009 paper, Mark Tolts estimated the number of Russian-speaking Jewish immigrants between 1989 and 2006 at 219,000. In 2006, after the changes to the immigration law, Haug und Wolf provided a somewhat higher figure, 225,572 (S. Haug and M. Wolf [2006], p. 71). In 2004 the Zentralwohlfahrtsstelle der Juden in Deutschland estimated the total number of quota refugees at 200,000 and the new community members at 83,000 (J. Kessler [2008], p. 135). In the spring of 2010 the catalog for an exhibition titled *Ausgerechnet Deutschland!* at the Jewish Museum in Frankfurt estimated the number of Soviet Jewish immigrants, including their non-Jewish family members over the past two decades, at between 170,000 and 300,000. According to the authors, the correct number should be 212,000, and the number of immigrants who joined the Jewish communities 90,000. See D. Belkin and R. Gross (eds.) (2010), p. 15.

64. B. Dietz et al. (2001), p. 30.

65. ZWST (ed.) (2011), p. 6.

66. ZWST (ed.) (2011), p. 10.

67. ZWST (ed.) (2011), pp. 39, 58.

68. M. Tolts (2009), table 2.

69. M. Tolts (2005), p. 28.

70. M. Tolts (2008), p. 205.

71. Y. Cohen et al. (2008), p. 196.

72. M. Tolts (2005), p. 27.

73. Y. Cohen and I. Kogan (2005), p. 250; Y. Cohen and I. Kogan (2007), 157.

74. Y. Cohen and I. Kogan (2005), p. 250; Y. Cohen and I. Kogan (2007), 157.

75. Y. Cohen and I. Kogan (2007), p. 161. For more on the high educational and vocational level of the quota refugees in Bavaria, in their countries of origin, and in comparison to the general population, see S. Haug (2007), pp. 25–30, 33.

76. Y. Cohen et al. (2008), pp. 189–190; M. Tress (1997), pp. 31–35.

77. Y. Cohen et al. (2008), p. 190.

78. Y. Cohen and I. Kogan (2005), p. 259.

79. Y. Cohen and I. Kogan (2005), p. 194.

80. Y. Cohen and I. Kogan (2005), p. 255.

81. Y. Schütze (1997).

82. Y. Cohen and I. Kogan (2005), p. 262.

83. S. Haug (2007), p. 33.

84. Y. Cohen and I. Kogan (2005), p. 262.

85. J. Kessler (2008), p. 133.

86. Y. Cohen et al. (2008), p. 192; Y. Cohen and I. Kogan (2007), p. 254.

87. S. Haug (2007), p. 43.

88. Y. Cohen and I. Kogan (2005), pp. 249–265.

89. Mark S. Izkovitsch, "Prozhit' zhizn' dal'che: Razruschit li emigrazija lichnost'?" (Continue to live: Will emigration destroy the personality?), *Yevreyskaya gazeta* 1/41 (January 2006), p. 14.

90. J. Kessler (2008), p. 133.

91. J. Panagiotidis (2010).

92. J. Panagiotidis (2010), p. 81.

93. J. Kessler (2008), p. 134; Y. M. Bodemann and O. Bagno (2008), pp. 163–166.

94. Jelena S. Gubenko, "Evreiskoe soobshchestvo Germanii: Poisk puti; Kritika, analiz, i vzglyad v budushchee" (The Jewish community in Germany: The search for a path; Criticism, analysis, prospects), *Yevreyskaya gazeta* 8/84 (August 2009), p. 9.

95. M. Tress (1997), p. 49.

96. F. Becker (2001), p. 74.

97. David S. Schimanovskii, "'Chzhiie' sredi 'svoikh'?" (Living among "our own people"?), *Krug* 3 (July/August 1996), p. 6.

98. O. Brusilovskii, "Ne nado ryby—daite udochku" (We don't need fish—give us a fishing rod), *Nasha gazeta* 1/5 (January 1997), p. 4.

99. See, among others, Tsatskes, "O nekotorykh problemakh 'russkikh evreiev'" (Regarding a few problems of the "Russian Jews"), *Nasha gazeta* 1/18 (February 1998), p. 8.

100. Brusilovskii, "Ne nado ryby—daite udochku," p. 4; Ella Guseynova, "Vot tak my i zhivem" (This is how we live), *Nasha gazeta* 7/11 (July 1997), p. 6.

101. See the letter to the Central Council of Jews from members of the Hannover Jewish community, published in *Nasha gazeta* 10/14 (October 1997), p. 11.

102. See Mikhail Rumer, "Starye voprosy i trudnye otvety" (Old questions and difficult answers), *Nasha gazeta* 8/24 (August 1998), p. 9.

103. See, among others, "Helft uns doch, Brüder! Und selbst wenn Eure Hilfe für uns mehr wert sein sollte, als das, was wir zurückgeben können, wir sind doch schließlich eine Familie! Sobald wir auf eigenen Beinen stehen, werden wir nicht in Eurer Schuld stehen bleiben!," in Brusilovskii, "Ne nado ryby—daite udochku," p. 4. The words "brothers" and "family" appear frequently, such as, for example, in Lev Madorskii, "My-odna sem'ya" (We are a family), *Nasha gazeta* 9/25 (September 1998), p. 9.

104. See David Garbar, "Starye problemy s 'novoi' immigratsiei" (Old problems of the "new" migration), *Krug* 23 (September 1998), p. 6.

105. See David Shimanovskii, "Nasil'no mil ne budesh" (You can't be forced to be nice), *Nasha gazeta* 8/36 (August 1999), p. 8.

106. David S. Shimanovskii, "Chego my eshche zhdem? Nado deistvovat'!" (What are we waiting for? We must act!), *Nasha gazeta* 1/17 (January 1998), p. 6.

107. See Yu. Zeytlin, "Evreiskaia obshchina eto mif" (The Jewish community is a myth), *Yevreyskaya gazeta*, January 2004, p. 18.

108. See, among others, Vladimir Stal'skii, "Gospodin Shpigel ne mozhet vozglavliat' TS E G" (Herr Spiegel may not be chairman of the Central Council of the Jews in Germany), *Yevreyskaya gazeta*, February 2004, p. 16.

109. See, among others, Tatiana Tselikson, "O religioznom i svetskom" (On the religious and the social), *Yevreyskaya gazeta*, June 2004, p. 16.

110. See, among others, Svetlana Schunkhoff, "Uzly neponimaniia" (The knots of incomprehension), *Yevreyskaya gazeta*, September 2002, p. 13.

111. See J. H. Schoeps et al. (1996), p. 149.

112. See Aleksandr Tsun, "Prazdnovat' li 'russkim' Purim v Germanii?" (Should "Russians" celebrate Purim in Germany?), *Krug* 2/17 (February 1998), p. 4.

113. Tselikson, "O religioznom i svetskom," p. 16.

114. "Second-class citizens" is from Konstantin S. Gutsant, "Kleimo" (The stigma), *Nasha gazeta* 1/17 (January 1998), p. 7; and "Stalin i podgotovka genozida evreev" (Stalin and preparations for the genocide of the Jews), *Krug* 1 (May 1996), p. 1.

115. "Can We Still Be Saved?" is cited in Dr. Ernest S. Korobchinskii, "Zhit' i davat' zhit' drugim" (Live and let live), *Nasha gazeta* 9/25 (September 1998), p. 8.

116. Korobchinskii, "Zhit' i davat' zhit' drugim," p. 8.

117. See Aleksandr Bronfman, "Prestupniki, prostitutki, nedoumki ili. . ." (Criminals, prostitutes, dumbbells, or . . .), *Krug*, April 1997, p. 7.

118. See the letter to the Central Council of Jews from members of the Hannover Jewish community, published in *Nasha gazeta* 10/14 (October 1997), p. 11.

119. Just how far from the mark this was may be seen from the titles of essays such as "Wir sind kein Staub im Wind" (We are not dust in the wind); see, among others, Aleksandr Kopelevich, "My ne pyl' na vetru," *Nasha gazeta* 1/17 (January 1998), pp. 8–9.

120. See, among others, Kolonka redaktora (editor's column), *Nasha gazeta* 5/9 (May 1997), p. 1.

121. David S. Schimanovskij, "Wer ist schuld?" (Who is to blame?), *Nasha gazetu* 5/9 (May 1997), p. 6. The author is a former scholar of Marxism-Leninism who was born in Kiev in 1929. In Germany he writes for *Yevreyskaya gazeta* and for the Russian-language newspaper *Evropa Express*.

122. F. S. Blotnikov, "O tekh li problemakh my govorim vse vremia?" (Are we actually talking about the real problems?), *Nasha gazeta* 11/39 (November 1999), p. 13.

123. See Boris Bederak, "Iz odnogo doma v drugoi" (From one house and into the other), *Nasha gazeta* 8/48 (August 2000), p. 9.

124. See, among others, L. Madorskii, "Warum?" (Why?), *Nasha gazeta* 12/16 (December 1997), p. 5, in which the author discusses the question, "Why not Israel?" He offers prosaic reasons such as "heat, war, financial security in Germany," for which he expresses shame.

125. See, among others, Lazar Gorodinskii, "Pochemu ia zdes'" (Why I am here), *Nasha gazeta* 11/27 (November 1998), p. 9.

126. See Verschvovskij (1997), p. 34.

127. S. Roberman (2005).

128. See Rafail Barkan, "Spasennye i spasiteli" (The rescued and the rescuers), *Nasha gazeta* 2/30 (February 1999), p. 5; and Viktor Kuznetsov, "Poslednaia avtobiografiia" (The last autobiography), *Nasha gazeta* 12/40 (December 1999), p. 17.

129. Especially the commemoration of this tragedy by Yevgeny Yevtushenko in the 1961 poem of the same name, which was set to music by Dmitri Shostakovich and which played a major role in the discourse of memory. See, among others, Mikhail L'vov, "Babyi Jar" (Babi Yar), *Nasha gazeta* 1 (September 1996), p. 6; E. R. Wiehn (2011); F. Grüner (2006).

130. See Leonid Glejzer, Asja Glejzer, and Maja Fajnberg, among others: "Otkrytoje pis'mo Presidentu Zentral'nogo Soveta evrejjev v Germanii Ignazu Bibisu, Kopiju: Presidentu FRG Rmanu Gerzogu" (Open letter to Ignatz Bubis, the chairman of the Central Council of Jews in Germany, copy to Roman Herzog, president of the Federal Republic of Germany), *Nasha gazeta* 1/29 (January 1999), p. 8.

131. David S. Garbar, "Yevrei i nemzy" (Jews and Germans), *Krug* 4/19 (April 1998), p. 10.

132. S.B.V., "O chöm spor, gospoda?" (What are we fighting about, gentlemen?), *Yevreyskaya gazeta*, January 2004, p. 17.

133. See J. Bernstein (2005).

134. Bundesministerium des Innern (ed.) (2011), p. 92.

13 A NEW GERMAN JEWRY?

MICHAEL BRENNER

THE IMMIGRATION FROM the countries of the former Soviet Union fundamentally transformed Jewish life in Germany. Without this growth, membership in the Jewish communities would likely have fallen below twenty thousand by now, and viable communities would exist in only a few large cities. But in fact, in 2015 there were 108 Jewish communities with a total membership of just over one hundred thousand. By some estimates, the total number of Jews living in Germany may be twice as high, although the actual figures are difficult to ascertain. One reason is that a growing number of Jews simply do not become members of a community. For example, about twenty thousand Israelis live in Berlin alone; they are developing their own culture and only rarely belong to the official Jewish community. In addition, the definition of who qualifies as a Jew in the twenty-first century is contested: while Orthodox criteria require birth to a Jewish mother or conversion by an Orthodox rabbi, others call for the recognition of a Jewish father in the absence of a Jewish mother and non-Orthodox conversion. Furthermore, the documentation brought by many immigrants from the former Soviet Union may be unclear. But however they are counted, even after the end of the immigration in about 2005, Jews comprised less than 0.3 percent of the total population in the united Germany.

German chancellor Gerhard Schröder recognized the new situation when he and Paul Spiegel, the president of the Central Council of Jews, signed an agreement in January 2003 that would guarantee annual funding from the German government to ensure that Jewish life in the country would continue to flourish. It was an official recognition that the wave of immigration had changed the overall situation, and it sealed the "ongoing cooperation in partnership." The document further stated that "the Federal government will contribute to the preservation and protection of the German-Jewish cultural heritage, to building a Jewish community, and to the integrative and social tasks of the Central Council in Germany."[1]

What the agreement stated in official language was expressed in more emotion-laden words by Charlotte Knobloch, the then president of the Jewish community in Munich—and later successor to Spiegel as the head of the Central Council—at the groundbreaking ceremony for the Jewish community center in Munich in November 2003: "Today I feel that I have come home—and can finally unpack my bags."[2] Three years later, on the occasion of the dedication of the new synagogue in Munich, she added, "We have built, and we will stay because we belong here."[3]

REAL AND SYMBOLIC EXISTENCE

The new Munich Jewish community center, the largest built in Western Europe since World War II, symbolized both the desire of the Jews to remain in Germany and the desire among non-Jews for a visible Jewish presence. Until then, the synagogue in Munich remained hidden in a rear courtyard, well out of sight of the non-Jewish population. The new complex, which includes a synagogue, community center, nursery school, elementary school, and museum, in the historical center of the city, only a few minutes from city hall, has become a much admired landmark in Munich, along with its beer cellars, churches, and museums. The Jewish community, which had swelled with Russian immigrants, undoubtedly needed a new home, but the city of Munich also wanted a new architectural structure to represent the Jewish presence, as the city's impressive main synagogue had been torn down during the summer of 1938. On the day it was opened to the public for the first time after the dedication, thousands of Munich's citizens stood in line to view one of the few significant examples of modern architecture in the city. Since then, more than a hundred thousand visitors have gone on guided tours.

The Dresden synagogue is modern in much the same way as the one in Munich, both having been designed by the same architectural firm. The synagogues in Duisburg (1999) and in Mainz (2010) are similarly modernist structures.[4] In contrast to most of the synagogues built in countries like the United States, England, and France, they not only serve the needs of the Jewish communities but also have symbolic meaning for the non-Jewish population. They recall the Wailing Wall, an open book for the people of the book, and Hebrew letters. The new synagogues have been awarded numerous architectural prizes and are viewed as outstanding examples of sacred architecture. These modern buildings mirror the discourse on Judaism in the larger non-Jewish public—though not necessarily the spirit of the communities that use them, which tend to be more conservative in their taste.

The continued symbolism of the existence of the Jews in Germany at the beginning of the twenty-first century is exemplified by two institutions in Berlin and their buildings: the Centrum Judaicum, located in the Oranienburger

German chancellor Angela Merkel, Munich lord mayor Christian Ude, and Charlotte Knobloch, president of the Central Council, at the Munich synagogue, February 28, 2008. Bundesarchiv / photograph by Guido Bergmann.

Strasse, and the Jewish Museum in Kreuzberg. Reconstruction of the golden dome of the synagogue in the Oranienburger Strasse, which had been destroyed during the war, was primarily politically motivated and began even before the collapse of the GDR. It was completed in unified Berlin and exemplifies the extent to which the broader public perception can differ from the purpose of a building. Most Germans believe that the renovated building again houses the synagogue that used to seat thousands of worshippers before its destruction during the Nazi era. However, beneath the dome, which is visible from afar, there are today only offices, a museum, an archive (the Centrum Judaicum), and a small prayer room. Only a plaque outside the building testifies to the former synagogue. As with this synagogue, Jewish life in Germany frequently takes place behind magnificent façades. But the everyday reality—even after the end of the wave of immigration—is much more modest than it looks.

Daniel Libeskind's spectacular Jewish Museum Berlin has become one of the main tourist attractions in a city that is surely not lacking in them. To some extent, the museum, which opened in September 2001, stands in stark contrast to the Centrum Judaicum. While the latter conjures up an architectural continuity, at least from the outside, Libeskind's design symbolizes a break with the past and with the void created by the Shoah. The three intersecting axes of exile

The restored façade of the Berlin synagogue in the Oranienburger Strasse. akg-images / L. M. Peter.

from Germany, the Holocaust, and continuity in German history are as symbol-laden as the museum's Garden of Exile, the Holocaust Tower, and the concave "voided" spaces. The forty-nine concrete columns in the Garden of Exile refer to 1948, the year of Israel's founding, with the forty-ninth column symbolizing Berlin.

Memorials, along with synagogues and museums, have also become centers of the Jewish presence. None has drawn more attention than the Memorial to the Murdered Jews of Europe, also known as the Holocaust Memorial, which is centrally located next to the city's main landmark, the Brandenburg Gate. The initiative for this memorial came from non-Jewish Germans, namely, from the historian Eberhard Jäckel and the journalist Lea Rosh, who on their own drafted plans for a memorial to the victims from the descendants of the perpetrators. Both the Central Council and Jewish organizations abroad made a conscious decision not to become embroiled in the heated debates around this memorial. Nonetheless, the German public came to view it as a German-Jewish initiative, at

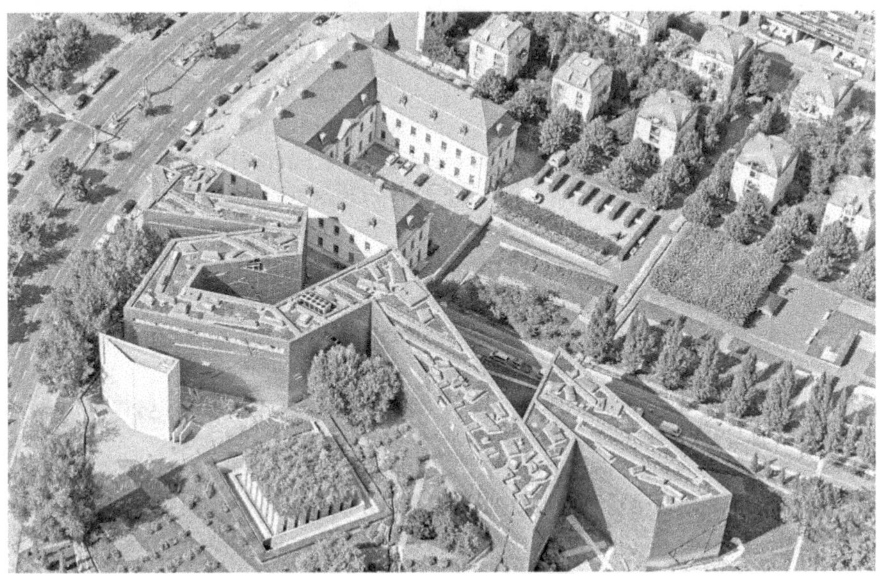

Bird's-eye view of the Jewish Museum Berlin, designed by Daniel Libeskind, opened in 1999. akg-images / Reimer Wulf.

least in part because Rosh was falsely identified as Jewish, or as an American Jewish initiative, because the architect Peter Eisenman was an American Jew. Rudolf Augstein, the publisher of *Der Spiegel*, for example, called the planned memorial, in a barely hidden reference to American Jews, a "stigma on the capital" and conjured up fear of the "New York press and the sharks in lawyers' clothing" who dictated from abroad "how we shape our new capital in memorializing the past."[5]

Finally, in 1995 the Cologne artist Gunter Demnig came up with the idea of embedding small raised blocks in the pavement in front of the homes of deported Jews, which he called "stumbling blocks" (*Stolpersteine*). This initiative was also extremely controversial in some places. While some Jewish communities welcomed such individual memorials, the community in Munich and the mayor of the city felt that because people might "trample on" the names of the victims, the blocks actually did a disservice to the memory of the dead.[6]

DEBATES AND CONTROVERSIES

The debates surrounding the memory of the Shoah are not limited to architecture. A number of fierce controversies erupted over how to commemorate that darkest chapter in German history. The touring exhibit on the crimes of the Wehrmacht

(1995–1999), which highlighted the crimes committed by the German army during the war along the Eastern Front and was produced by the Hamburg Institute for Social Research; publication of Daniel Goldhagen's best-selling *Hitler's Willing Executioners* (1996), which sought to portray "eliminationist antisemitism" as a project of the German people as a whole; and the controversy ignited by Martin Walser on the occasion of his acceptance speech of the 1998 Peace Prize of the German Book Trade were landmark events. The latter incident, which led to a sharp clash between Walser and Central Council president Ignatz Bubis, signaled a more critical tone and made it clear that the Jews of Germany could no longer rely on the discourse of memory to which they had become accustomed.

In his acceptance speech, Walser had remonstrated "against the perpetual presentation of our shame. Instead of being grateful for the incessant presentation of our shame, I am beginning to look away." Auschwitz, he went on, should not become "a means of intimidation or a moral cudgel."[7] Walser presented himself in his speech as an outsider in a discourse that, according to him, was controlled by the media but did not reflect the voice of the people. Much like conservative historian Ernst Nolte, who a decade earlier during the so-called Historians' Dispute had taken it upon himself to represent the *pays réel*, the people's voice, against the *pays légal*, the officially sanctioned, that is, "politically correct," position of the government and the press, Walser, too, felt buoyed by the thousands of letters that applauded his words.[8] In a speech given in Duisburg on November 28, 1998, he defended the letter writers as a representative sampling of popular opinion: "Each letter speaks from a different personal history; every sort of education and training and professional experience is represented, and yet all have in common that they agree with a speech that publicly stated what everyone had previously only thought or felt. My speech, and this is obvious, was perceived as liberating."[9]

It was certainly felt as liberating by a Protestant pastor from the Rhineland ("a revolt against forced political correctness and against the manipulation of the conscience") and other voices "from among the people" who found it about time that "a man of stature and renown such as yourself speaks out publicly against the incessant demagoguery and defamation against us Germans. It is simply unconscionable, in fact, it repulses one in the end that the same responsible persons and representatives of the Jews in Germany repeatedly and incessantly polemicize against us." Walser's speech was also welcomed by the right-wing extremists in the country. The editor-in-chief of *Neue Freiheit* (New freedom) wrote, "We are experiencing the beginning of a new era in Germany," and Franz Schönhuber, the founder of a short-lived right-wing party (Die Republikaner), seemed almost insulted, virtually insisting on ownership of Walser's arguments: "Martin Walser expressed hardly anything about coming to terms with the past that I have not

Ignatz Bubis speaking out against xenophobia and violence at the Berlin Lustgarten, November 8, 1992. ullstein bild / Thomas Böhme.

written in my books and stated in my speeches."[10] And Horst Mahler, the former attorney for the left-wing terrorist group Red Army Fraction (or Faction, RAF) and later Holocaust denier, joined the chorus in praise of Walser.[11]

After some hesitation, Walser agreed to a public discussion with Bubis, his principal critic and opponent. When they met, Walser rebutted Bubis, a Holocaust survivor no less, saying, "I was involved in this field at a time when you were involved with very different things. You came to these problems later than I did." Bubis, who had refused to applaud Walser when he gave his acceptance speech at the Paulskirche and accused him of "intellectual arson," was left momentarily speechless.[12]

The political backdrop to these debates was the increasing anxiety about a new and virulent form of right-wing extremism that was beginning to show its face, manifesting in arson attacks against foreigners in places like Rostock, Hoyerswerda, and Solingen. The political advances made by right-wing parties, especially in the eastern part of Germany, which included electoral dominance in some small towns, contributed to the general apprehensiveness among Jewish officials. Bubis, who in 1992 succeeded Heinz Galinski, the perpetual voice of caution, as chairperson of the Central Council, consistently put himself on the line in protests against the threat from the Right. He also spoke tirelessly at schools and on television talk shows. In 1993 the newspaper *Die Woche* (The week) proposed that Bubis run for the federal presidency. Although he rejected the idea, Jutta Limbach, a former constitutional judge, called him "a sort of unofficial federal president."[13] This was quite a turnaround for someone who, a half century earlier, had been imprisoned in a concentration camp and who for many years had been a target of the Left as a speculator and real estate wheeler-dealer. Under Bubis, the office of the chairperson of the Central Council, which was now renamed the presidency, increased its public profile considerably. Without slighting Auschwitz or neglecting Israel, Bubis positioned himself at the center of German public discourse, although his initial optimism soon gave way to increasing skepticism. In his final interview with *Stern* magazine in July 1999, Bubis, who was nearing death, expressed doubts about having accomplished anything and about the possibility of Jewish life in Germany. In his view, he had effected "nothing or almost nothing"; Germans and Jews remained estranged. In the end, he arrived at much the same point as Galinski: "He had Auschwitz in his heart, and he was fixated on the past, that has to be understood. I wanted to get past this phase, I tried to connect the past and the future. Today I am closer to Galinski, even in terms of bitterness."[14] Bubis's final request, that he be buried in Israel, may have grown from the knowledge that Galinski's gravestone in a Jewish cemetery in Berlin had twice been desecrated and nearly been destroyed by explosives.

A NEW PLURALISM

Paul Spiegel was elected president of the Central Council after Bubis's death in 1999. He generally followed the path charted by Bubis and proved to be both combative and engaged, a person for whom internal and external integration was a priority. For example, he tried to integrate the newly formed Liberal communities (which combined Reform and Conservative approaches) into the Central Council in order to solidify the council's position as sole representative of the Jews in Germany.[15] Given the growing religious pluralism in the Jewish community, maintaining this primacy was among the greatest challenges faced by Bubis and Spiegel and by their successors, Charlotte Knobloch, the first woman to lead the Central Council (2006–2010), Dieter Graumann (2010–2014), and Josef Schuster (since 2014). Some of the Liberal communities have been integrated into unified communities, as in Berlin; others have formed separate ones, as in Munich; and some have even created their own state associations, as in Lower Saxony. Since 1995 female rabbis have for the first time led communities, initially smaller ones, such as in Oldenburg and Weiden, but then in Berlin as well.

Paul Spiegel, president of the Central Council in front of the Holocaust Memorial in Berlin, May 10, 2005. ddp images / photograph by Robert Pfeil.

The founding of two different rabbinical associations and two new rabbinical seminaries, the Liberal Abraham Geiger Kolleg in Potsdam and the Orthodox Hildesheimer Rabbinerseminar in Berlin, are further expressions of this pluralism. While rabbis had to be imported to Germany during the 1990s, Graumann in his capacity as president of the Central Council spoke in November 2011 on the occasion of the ordination of four rabbis from the Geiger Kolleg, even voicing the hope that in the future "Rabbis Made in Germany" might become a "trademark" and "hot export item."[16] It speaks for the increasing integration of the immigrants from the former Soviet Union that they now make up the majority of rabbinical students.

The umbrella organization of Liberal Judaism in Germany, the Union of Progressive Jews in Germany, is made up of more than twenty Liberal communities with about five thousand members; the Ultra-Orthodox community, on the other side of the religious spectrum, is gathered under the Chabad-Lubavitch organization. This Hasidic movement, headquartered in New York, has messianic tendencies because of its veneration of the Rebbe Menachem Mendel Schneerson, who died in 1994. It seeks to recruit secular Jews in order to introduce them to a religious life. By 2015 Germany was home to seventeen Chabad communities, just over twenty years after their first rabbi settled in Munich. The Chabad movement founded its own yeshiva in Berlin as part of a new community center.

The diversification of Jewish life has also led to the founding of synagogues and communities based on ethnic origin. Unlike the earlier groups of Iranian Jews in Hamburg and Bukharian Jews in Pforzheim, which joined existing Jewish organizations, in 2006 the immigrants from the Caucasus established their own Sephardic synagogue, Tiferet Israel, in Berlin and founded a Jewish Bukharian community in Hannover, which received its own building in 2011.[17]

This new religious diversity is by no means limited to Jewish life in Germany. Whereas before 1933 the Jews were the only significant non-Christian minority in Germany, they are today part of an increasingly pluralistic society: more Buddhists now live in Germany than Jews, and the number of Hindus is growing rapidly. But it is the approximately four million Muslims who are setting the new religious tone. Relations between Jews and Muslims are often influenced by developments in the Middle East. In contrast to France and Great Britain, however, organized acts of anti-Jewish violence by radical Muslims in response to the conflict between the Israelis and the Palestinians have to date been relatively few. Those that have occurred have been isolated, such as an attempted attack on the synagogue in Düsseldorf on October 2, 2000. Studies have shown that younger male Muslims in Germany in particular harbor more anti-Jewish prejudices than the overall population and that these are frequently stirred up by conspiracy theories propagated in the media, particularly on the Internet.[18] On the other hand, there are also attempts, especially by members of the Turkish community, to pattern their own integration on that of the German Jews in the nineteenth century.[19] With the influx of hundreds of thousands of immigrants from Syria and other Arab states in 2015, the Jewish community has voiced strong concerns and demanded that as part of their integration into German society they should be taught about the Jewish community and Germany's special relationship with the State of Israel.

There is a broad spectrum of opinions among Jews living in Germany regarding their relationship to the Muslim population. On one side of the spectrum, the journalist and author Ralph Giordano vehemently opposed the building of the central mosque in Cologne.[20] On the other side, Lala Süsskind, the former chairwoman of the Jewish community in Berlin, spoke for many community members when she proclaimed, "If minarets are going to be banned, then I, too, feel affected."[21] Many Jews have resisted their inclusion in the currently fashionable framing of a "Judeo-Christian West," which in the final analysis amounts to nothing more than the rhetorical exclusion of Islam from the European community of values.

Jews and Muslims understand that both are potential victims of the right-wing extremism that has grown visibly since German reunification. Even though the Jews are less conspicuous targets for neo-Nazi violence than some other mi-

Dieter Graumann, president of the Central Council, at the ordination of Rabbi Antje Yael Deusel at the Bamberg synagogue, November 23, 2011. picture alliance / dpa / photograph by Daniel Karmann.

norities, prejudices against them remain considerable, as a study sponsored by the Ministry of the Interior in 2012 made clear. While antisemitism may be observed outside right-wing and Islamist circles, there now exists "a habituation to everyday anti-Jewish tirades and practices that extends well into the broad mass of society."[22] Furthermore, physical threats have by no means disappeared, as was demonstrated by a bombing that was prevented a few weeks before the groundbreaking ceremony for the new synagogue in Munich.

Among the most prevalent antisemitic stereotypes is that of the overblown influence of the Jews. Several right-wing bloggers have been spreading the "news" that there are more than a hundred Jewish delegates to the Bundestag. But in fact, ever since the three Social Democrats Jeanette Wolff, Jakob Altmaier, and Peter Blachstein had left the Bundestag by the late 1960s, there have been no Jewish members at all. The few politicians with a Jewish background who are known throughout the country are spread across the political spectrum: Ignatz Bubis was a member of the executive board of the liberal FDP, and Michel Friedman that of the conservative CDU. Daniel Cohn-Bendit first represented the German and then the French Greens in the European parliament, Gregor Gysi was chair of the Left faction in the Bundestag, while Marina Weisband became political director of the German Pirate Party. Peter Feldmann became mayor of Frankfurt am Main in 2012; he had been the spokesman for the Working Group of Jewish Social Democrats. As with the Jewish politicians, no single political orientation is discernible in the Jewish community as a whole either.

The public perception of the Jewish community has mostly been shaped by the few Jews working in the media and not by politicians. Marcel Reich-Ranicki's Jewishness was on full display in his *Literarische Quartett* (Literary quartet), which was among the most successful programs ever on German television. His autobiographical account of surviving in the Warsaw Ghetto, which was later filmed, was a major contribution to German-Jewish history. Michel Friedman's talk show *Vorsicht Friedman!* (Beware, Friedman!) was one of the most discussed programs on German television. Friedman served as vice president of the Central Council, although this involvement came to an abrupt end in 2003, when he was implicated in a prostitution and narcotics scandal. In the area of print media, Josef Joffe, the publisher of *Die Zeit*, and Rachel Salamander, the publisher of *Literarische Welt* and founder of Jewish bookstores in Munich and Berlin, are among the few successors to a once rich and diverse German-Jewish publishing scene. Henryk M. Broder, who was awarded the prestigious Börne Prize in 2007, remains one of the most provocative journalists in Germany.

"A COMPLETELY NORMAL CASE"?

The last two decades of the twentieth century saw the emergence of a new generation of German-Jewish writers.[23] Barbara Honigmann, Maxim Biller, and Esther Dischereit are probably the best-known representatives of this new literature, which often examines Jewish subjects. These writers are well aware that, in contrast to those writing in England and France, it is still considered somewhat exotic to be a Jewish writer in Germany. The result has been a self-conscious display for a non-Jewish audience; as Dischereit once explained, it is "a sort of prostitution—Jewish prostitution—I know, but the alternative would be silence."[24]

With growing distance from the Shoah, some writers began poking an ironic and provocative finger at the ways in which things Jewish are dealt with in German society. The comedian Oliver Polak, for example, became known for his show *Ich darf das, ich bin Jude* (I can do that, I'm a Jew); Michael Wuliger, an editor of the Jewish weekly *Jüdische Allgemeine*, wrote a book of "kosher etiquette" that promised to help his non-Jewish readers avoid embarrassing themselves in interactions with Jews. As the Russian-Jewish writer Wladimir Kaminer likes to put it, his well-known *Russendisko* (Russian Disco) was born out of the rumor that "Honecker is accepting Jews from the Soviet Union as a sort of compensation for the fact that the GDR never shared in the German payments to Israel."[25] Even the title of Lena Gorelik's 2011 novel, *Lieber Mischa: . . . der Du fast Schlomo Adolf Grinblum geheißen hättest, es tut mir so leid, dass ich Dir das nicht ersparen konnte: Du bist ein Jude* (Dear Mischa . . . who was almost called Schlomo Adolf Grinblum, I'm sorry to have to break it to you, but you're a Jew), is an ironic play on how the word *Jew* is handled in Germany. The movie *Alles auf Zucker!* (Go for Zucker!) by Dani Levy, a Swiss-born director living in Berlin, became a huge box-office success. All of these efforts have in common a kind of looseness with Jewish subjects that is welcomed by both Jewish and non-Jewish Germans. Along these lines, the lead story in the February 4, 2010, edition of *Die Zeit* on young Jews in Germany was titled "Time for a Change: A Young Generation Wants Finally to Live Here Unencumbered."[26]

But if we examine more closely the Web pages and other materials that this emerging Jewish culture produces, it quickly becomes evident that it is anything but unencumbered by the past. Unlike in England or France, every performance on Jewish topics in Germany is accompanied by the drive to educate the audience about Jewish matters. For example, Bimah, the Jewish theater in Berlin, advertises that it performs plays by Jewish authors for the following reason: "The theatrical programs presented by the Jewish theater Bimah are intended to make Jewish culture accessible to a non-Jewish public in an unforced manner, and by so doing promote tolerance and mutual respect between the cultures."[27] The booklet produced for *Alles auf Zucker!* by the Federal Center for Political Education advances the notion that the movie can help to "dismantle fear of contact" because "what Levy proposes here is nothing less than a universal model of tolerance for secular and religious Jews, for Jews and non-Jews, for people in the East and West."[28] The booklet urges educators to use the movie to ask their students, "What do we know about klezmer music?" and "Did you know that the words 'mishpoche' and 'mazel' were originally from Yiddish?" It also suggests: "Create a guide—'Jewish life for beginners.' In it, explain all of the objects, commandments, and traditions shown in the film that relate to Judaism. Supplement the guide with information from your own research, such as from conversations with Jewish fellow citizens or from a visit to a synagogue."[29]

The necessity of such education was evidenced by the heated debate in the summer of 2012 surrounding the ritual circumcision of Jewish and Muslim male children that resulted from a court judgment in Cologne banning the circumcision of minors without a medical indication or without their consent. What most astonished Jews involved in the debate was not the legal and medical arguments but that the emotionalism all too often used to advance those arguments was usually based on ignorance of Jewish ritual. Representatives of the Central Council and of the European Rabbinical Conference made clear that a ban on circumcision was without precedence in a democratic country and that such a ban would make the free exercise of religion impossible for Jews. For a moment, it appeared as if the decades spent on educating the German public about Jewish life might have been in vain. In the end, the Bundestag voted with a sound majority for a solution that would guarantee the future practice of the Jewish circumcision ritual. But the normalcy of Jewish life in Germany had once again come into question.

When in November 2011 a television crime series presented an episode about a fictional murder at the new synagogue in Munich, the episode, which contained numerous attempts to explain the Jewish Holy Days, Jews' relationship to the State of Israel, and of course the sensitivities surrounding Jewish life in Germany, was titled "A Completely Normal Case." But even seven decades after the Holocaust, the history of Jews in Germany seems anything but normal.

MICHAEL BRENNER is Professor of Jewish history and culture at the University of Munich and Seymour and Lillian Abensohn Chair in Israel Studies at American University in Washington, DC. He is a member of the Bavarian Academy of Sciences and international president of the Leo Baeck Institute. Brenner's publications include *A Short History of the Jews*, *Prophets of the Past: Interpreters of Jewish History*, *Zionism: A Short History*, and as coauthor, the four-volume *German-Jewish History in Modern Times*.

NOTES

1. http://www.zentralratdjuden.de/de/article/1.html.

2. http://www.emma.de/artikel/charlotte-knobloch-knobloch-ist-gewaehlt-264050.

3. http://alt.ikg-m.de/fileadmin/downloads/Eroeffnungsrede_Knobloch.pdf.

4. A profusely illustrated overview of newly built synagogues in Germany can be found in Stiftung Baukultur Rheinland-Pfalz (ed.) (2010).

5. Rudolf Augstein, "Wir sind alle verletzbar," *Der Spiegel*, November 30, 1998, pp. 32–33.

6. Anne Goebel, "Neue Diskussion über die 'Stolpersteine,'" *Süddeutsche Zeitung*, June 14, 2004, p. 42.

7. M. Walser (1998), pp. 11–12.

8. http://www.hdg.de/lemo/html/dokumente/NeueHerausforderungen_rede-Nolte 1986/index.html.

9. F. Schirrmacher (ed.) (1999), p. 259.

10. Previous quotes in F. Schirrmacher (ed.) (1999), pp. 33, 41, 46.

11. For more on the extreme right-wing reception of the Walser speech, see M. Dietzsch et al. (eds.) (1999).

12. S. Schönborn (2010), pp. 195–196. See also Rachel Salamander, "Man kann nicht Wurzeln im Nichts schlagen: Rede zur Verleihung des kulturellen Ehrenpreises der Stadt München," *Frankfurter Allgemeine Zeitung*, January 27, 1999, p. 42, as well as H.-J. Hahn (2007).

13. Jutta Limbach in conversation with Christian Böhme and Judith Hart, "Ignatz Bubis als Bundespräsident, das wäre mein Traum gewesen," *Jüdische Allgemeine*, December 11, 2003, p. 3.

14. "'Herr Bubis, was haben Sie bewirkt?' 'Nichts, fast nichts.'" The interview was conducted by Michael Stoessinger and Rafael Seligmann, *Stern*, July 29, 1999.

15. See, for example, the remarks in his New Year's message for the year 5761 with regard to the past and future claim of sole representation by the Central Council. Paul Spiegel, "Mit Besorgnis und Hoffnung," *AJW*, September 28, 2000, p. 1.

16. Ursula Quass, "Jubeltag für Juden," *Süddeutsche Zeitung*, November 24, 2011, p. R21.

17. Regarding Berlin, see https://web.archive.org/web/20140207095451/http://www .berlin-juedisch.de/info_tifered-israel.html; regarding Hannover, see Beate Rossbach, "Der Turm kommt weg," *Jüdische Allgemeine*, July 28, 2011, p. 10.

18. For more on this, see V. Georgi (2003); A. Stiftung (ed.) (2009).

19. For one of many examples, see the essays by Zafer Senocak, as well as his novel *Gefährliche Verwandtschaft*.

20. "Stoppt den Bau dieser Moschee" (May 16, 2007), http://www.ksta.de/html/artikel /1176113436263.shtml. The writer Ralph Giordano, who opposed the project, and Bekir Alboga, the spokesman for the builder, Ditib, met at the offices of the *Kölner Stadtanzeiger* for the broadcast of "Streit im Turm." The debate with Giordano over building the central mosque in Cologne was led by Franz Sommerfeld and transcribed by Helmut Frangenberg.

21. Jörg Lau, "Leben statt Mahnen," *Die Zeit*, February 4, 2010, p. 9.

22. Bundesministerium des Innern (ed.) (2011), p. 178.

23. See, for example, S. Gilman (1995); S. Gilman and K. Remmler (eds.) (1994).

24. Cited from Y. M. Bodemann, "Öffentliche Körperschaft," in Y. M. Bodemann (2002), p. 152.

25. W. Kaminer (2009), p. 9.

26. Jörg Lau, "Leben statt Mahnen," *Die Zeit*, February 4, 2010, pp. 1, 8–9.

27. https://web.archive.org/web/20120510203225/http://www.juedischestheaterberlin .de/Theater.php?Bereich=DanLahav.

28. P. Bühler (2004), p. 10.

29. P. Bühler (2004), p. 10.

APPENDIX

ACKNOWLEDGMENTS

When the Leo Baeck Institute published its four-volume *German-Jewish History in Modern Times* in 1996 and 1997, the final volume ended in 1945. A brief epilogue examined only the history of German Jews in exile. But with the onset of Jewish emigration from the former Soviet Union in the 1990s, it became clear that the history of the Jews in Germany after 1945 was more than just an epilogue. As a result, the British historian John Grenville urged the institute to publish a fifth volume, an overview of Jewish life in Germany from 1945 to the present. Unfortunately, Grenville, who died in 2011, did not live to see the publication of this work. This undertaking also represents a new emphasis in the Leo Baeck Institute's mission. The institute, which had been founded by émigrés in Jerusalem, London, and New York to preserve the German-Jewish legacy, initially intended to focus only on the history of German Jewry from the Enlightenment to its destruction under National Socialism. The international president of the Leo Baeck Institute at the time, Michael A. Meyer, supported this initiative from the outset. We owe him and the institute an enormous debt of gratitude.

This study, the culmination of many years of archival research, was made possible by the generous support of the Volkswagen Foundation. We wish to thank the following archives and archivists, institutions, and individual persons: Frank Ahland, American Jewish Archives, American Jewish Joint Distribution Committee, Arbeitskreis jüdischer Sozialdemokraten (Peter Feldmann), Archiv Centrum Judaicum (Barbara Welker), Archiv der Akademie der Künste, Archiv für Christlich-Demokratische Politik (Angela Keller-Kühne), Archiv des Liberalismus (Monika Wittmann), Archiv der sozialen Demokratie (Petra Gierz), Bayerisches Hauptstaatsarchiv (Gerhard Fürmetz), John W. Brinsfield, Bundesarchiv (Kerstin Schenke), Der Bundesbeauftragte für die Stasiunterlagen (Manuela Gehrke), Bundesministerium für Migration und Flüchtlinge (Rita Rampelt), Bundespresseamt (Wolfgang Koßmann), The Central Archives for the History of the Jewish People Jerusalem, Citavi (Peter Meurer), Fachstelle für Internationale Jugendarbeit der Bundesrepublik Deutschland e. V. (Dirk Haenisch), Gemeindearchiv Bad Wörishofen, Gemeindearchiv Pocking, Generallandesarchiv

Karlsruhe, Gesamtverband Textil + Mode e. V. (Alka Raak), Gesellschaft für Geschichte des Brauwesens e. V. (Michaela Knör), Haus der Stadtgeschichte Offenbach, Hoover Institution, Institut für Stadtgeschichte Frankfurt am Main, Institut für Zeitgeschichte, Internationaler Suchdienst Bad Arolsen (Udo Jost), Israelitische Religionsgemeinschaft Württembergs, Jabotinsky Institute, JDV Jerusalem (Sara Kadosh), Jüdische Gemeinde in Hamburg, Jüdisches Museum Berlin, Landesarchiv Berlin, Landesverband der Israelitischen Kultusgemeinden in Bayern, Leo Baeck Institute New York, Monia Mahling (LMU), National Archives and Records Administration in Washington, D.C., Benjamin Ortmeyer, Jürgen Sielemann, Staatsarchiv Amberg, Staatsarchiv Darmstadt, Staatsarchiv Hamburg, Staatsarchiv München, Stadtarchiv München (Andreas Heusler), Stadtarchiv Starnberg, Stadtarchiv Stuttgart (Roland Müller), UN Archives, United States Holocaust Memorial Museum, Yad Vashem Jerusalem, YIVO Institute for Jewish Research, WIZO Frankfurt (Frau Hirsch), Zentralarchiv zur Erforschung der Geschichte der Juden in Deutschland (Peter Honigmann), Zentralwohlfahrtsstelle der Juden in Deutschland e. V., Referat Öffentlichkeitsarbeit (Ellen Rubinstein, Heike von Bassewitz), Zentralrat der Juden in Deutschland (Stephan Kramer), Zentrum für Antisemitismusforschung Berlin (Regina Schulz).

The authors had available to them a competent team of coworkers in sifting through and evaluating the archival material. These included Lida Barner, Ehud Brosh, Kierra Crago-Schneider, Marco Esseling, Fabian Gottwald, Monika Halbinger, Daniel Mahla, Hendrik Niether, Ann-Kathrin Pollmann, Christian Riepl, Oren Roman, Andrea Sinn, and Maximilian Strnad. I wish to thank Elisabeth Rees-Dessauer, Hans-Jakob Ginsburg, and Michael A. Meyer for reading parts of the manuscript. We gratefully acknowledge the United States Holocaust Memorial Museum for its generous invitation to conduct research.

This volume could not have been published without the coordination provided by Tamar Lewinsky with the able support of Monika Halbinger and Maximilian Strnad. The same may be said of the editorial support provided by Andrea Sinn. Special thanks go out to them all.

I wish to thank the project's advisory committee, consisting of Steven Ascheim, Micha Brumlik, Raphael Gross, Hans Günter Hockerts, Peter Honigmann, Jürgen Kocka, and Anson Rabinbach, for their thought-provoking ideas as well as for their comments on different versions of the text.

It was my pleasure to work again with Indiana University Press. Its editorial director, Dee Mortensen, has shown great enthusiasm and support for this project from the very first stage until its completion. Our copyeditor, Mary M. Hill, was crucial to transforming the manuscript into a book. My special thanks go to our translator, Ken Kronenberg, for turning the very different styles of our authors in the original German into one coherent English edition.

TIMELINE

July 22, 1945	Conference of the Jewish DPs from both the British and the American zones of occupation in St. Ottilien
August 3, 1945	Earl G. Harrison submits his report on the status of Jewish survivors to President Truman
January 26–27, 1946	First Congress of the Liberated Jews in the American zone in Munich
July 4, 1946	The pogrom in the Polish city of Kielce triggers the mass flight of Polish Jews to the American zone in Germany
September 1947	After the British intercept the refugee ship Exodus 1947 outside the port of Haifa, the Jewish refugees are returned to an internment camp in Germany
May 14, 1948	The founding of the State of Israel is the beginning of the end of the presence of Jewish DPs in Germany
June 25, 1948	The United States Immigration Act opens the doors to more Jewish immigrants into the United States
June 27–July 6, 1948	The World Jewish Congress urges the Jews to leave Germany's "bloodstained soil"
July 9, 1948	Founding of the first German Society for Christian-Jewish Cooperation in Munich
April 1949	Street protests after the first acquittal of Veit Harlan, the director of the film Jud Süss
July 31, 1949	The advisor of the American military administration convenes a conference in Heidelberg on the future of the Jews in Germany
June 18, 1950	Dedication of the first new synagogue in postwar Germany in Dresden after its conversion from a former mourning chapel
July 19, 1950	Founding of the Central Council of Jews in Germany
1950	Arnold Zweig is elected president of the German Academy of the Arts in the GDR
July 20, 1951	The right-wing radical Bundestag delegate Wolfgang Hedler is sentenced to nine months' imprisonment for insulting the victims of the Nazis
August 20, 1951	Founding of the Central Welfare Office for Jews in Germany
September 27, 1951	Official declaration by Konrad Adenauer titled "Attitude of the Federal Republic of Germany toward the Jews" before the German Bundestag
March 1952	The first Week of Brotherhood takes place in Germany

May 25, 1952	Anna Seghers returns from exile in Mexico and becomes president of the East German Writers' Association
August 16, 1952	Philipp Auerbach, the former Bavarian state commissioner for racial, religious, and political victims and cofounder of the Central Council, commits suicide after the verdict against him
September 10, 1952	Signing of the Restitution Agreement between Israel and West Germany and the Claims Conference
End of 1952–beginning of 1953	Flight of numerous Jews from the GDR in reaction to anti-semitic campaigns in the Soviet Union and Czechoslovakia
September 18, 1953	First draft of the German Federal Restitution Law for victims of Nazi persecution
June 9, 1955	Leonhard Schlüter, the culture minister of Lower Saxony, forced to resign because of radical right-wing statements
1955	The Diary of Anne Frank, which was initially published in 1950, is brought out in paperback and becomes a best seller
February 1957	Dissolution of the last DP camp in Föhrenwald
March 1957	Founding of the Rabbinical Conference in West Germany
January 15, 1958	The Federal Constitutional Court sides with Erich Lüth in his freedom of speech case against Veit Harlan
November 24, 1958	Right-wing teacher Ludwig Zind absconds to Egypt four days before the appeal of his verdict for having publicly approved of Nazi crimes
December 24, 1959	Antisemitic synagogue desecration in Cologne
April 11, 1961	Start of the Eichmann trial in Israel
January 13, 1963	Herbert Lewin, a gynecologist from Offenbach, is elected chairperson of the Central Council
December 20, 1963	Start of the first Auschwitz trial in Frankfurt
May 12, 1965	Diplomatic relations between the Federal Republic of Germany and Israel are established
March 1968	Founding of the Federal Association of Jewish Students in Germany
1968	Emigration of Jews from Czechoslovakia and Poland after anti-Jewish propaganda in their homelands
February 1, 1968	Premiere of Anatevka, the German adaptation of Fiddler on the Roof, at the Operettenhaus in Hamburg
November 9, 1969	Failed bomb attack on the Jewish community center in Berlin
February 13, 1970	Attack on the Jewish old-age home in Munich claims seven lives

September 5, 1972	Eleven Israeli athletes are killed during an attack at the Olympic Games in Munich
1973	First wave of Russian-Jewish emigration begins as part of the political thaw between East and West
February 1978	The playwright Rolf Hochhuth exposes the Nazi past of Hans Filbinger, the governor of Baden-Württemberg, forcing him to resign
January 22–26, 1979	Broadcast of the American TV series Holocaust
1979	Founding of the College of Jewish Studies in Heidelberg
1979	Henryk M. Broder and Michel R. Lang publish Fremd im eigenen Land (Alien in my own country), a collection of thirty-seven stories written mainly by German Jews
1980	Critical young Jews found the Jewish Group in Frankfurt
April 25, 1985	Holocaust denial is criminalized
May 5, 1985	Controversy surrounding the visit to the military cemetery at Bitburg by German chancellor Kohl and US president Reagan
October 31, 1985	Members of the Jewish community prevent the performance of Rainer Werner Fassbinder's controversial play Der Müll, die Stadt und der Tod in Frankfurt am Main
September 1987	The Jewish community of East Berlin gets a rabbi after a long vacancy, the American Isaac Neuman
January 21, 1988	Werner Nachmann's embezzlement of restitution funds becomes known after his death; his successor as chairperson of the Central Council, Heinz Galinski, initiates an immediate investigation
October 17, 1988	Edgar Bronfman, the president of the World Jewish Congress, pays an official visit to the GDR
November 9, 1988	The Volkskammer (parliament) of the GDR commemorates Kristallnacht for the first time, on the occasion of its fiftieth anniversary
September 10, 1988	Groundbreaking for the synagogue in the Oranienburger Strasse in Berlin
November 11, 1988	Resignation of Bundestag president Philipp Jenninger after his controversial speech in the Bundestag on the occasion of the fiftieth anniversary of Kristallnacht
February 9, 1990	Hans Modrow, the chairperson of the ministerial council of the GDR, for the first time recognizes officially the responsibility of the GDR for the persecution of the Jews under National Socialism

April 1990	The first group of Soviet Jews travels to Germany as a result of an agreement between the Soviet Union and the GDR
January 6, 1991	The details for accepting Jewish emigrants from the Soviet Union are worked out during a meeting between the German chancellor and the governors of the German states
January 4, 1995	Start of Cologne artist Gunter Demnig's "stumbling blocks" (Stolpersteine) project, which placed memorial stones in front of the former homes of murdered Jews
1997	Discussion on the occasion of the publication of Daniel Goldhagen's German edition of Hitler's Willing Executioners
October 11, 1998	Martin Walser's speech at the Paulskirche in Frankfurt triggers the Bubis-Walser debate
November 12, 2000	Opening of the Abraham Geiger College at the University of Potsdam, the first rabbinical seminary in Germany since the war
September 9, 2001	Opening of the Jewish Museum Berlin
January 28, 2003	Signing of the agreement between the federal government of Germany and the Central Council of Jews in Germany
2005	The federal government decides on more restrictive immigration criteria for Jewish refugees from the former Soviet Union
2005	Dani Levy's comedy Alles auf Zucker! (Go for Zucker!) is awarded the German Film Prize
May 10, 2005	Opening of the memorial to Europe's murdered Jews in Berlin

CHAIRPERSONS AND (SINCE 1992) PRESIDENTS OF THE CENTRAL COUNCIL OF JEWS IN GERMANY

1953–1954	Carl Katz (Bremen)
1954–1963	Heinz Galinski (Berlin)
1963–1969	Herbert Lewin (Offenbach)
1969–1988	Werner Nachmann (Karlsruhe)
1988–1992	Heinz Galinski (Berlin)
1992–1999	Ignatz Bubis (Frankfurt)
2000–2006	Paul Spiegel (Düsseldorf)
2006–2010	Charlotte Knobloch (Munich)
2010–2014	Dieter Graumann (Frankfurt)
2014–	Josef Schuster (Würzburg)

MEMBERS IN GERMANY'S TEN LARGEST JEWISH COMMUNITIES

	1925	1955	1989	2014
Berlin	172,676	4,354 (West)	6,411 (West)	10,009
		1,100 (East)	203 (East)	
Munich	10,687	1,847	4,050	9,471
Düsseldorf	5,130	491	1,510	6,851
Frankfurt	29,385	1,308	4,842	6,667
Hannover	5,521	368	379	4,375
Cologne	16,093	869	1,358	4,126
Dortmund	3,820	285	337	2,946
Stuttgart[2]	4,017	540	677	2,908
Hamburg	19,904	1,102	1,344	2,452
Wuppertal[3]	3,056	116	82	2,211

ABBREVIATIONS

AdK	Archiv der Akademie der Künste, Berlin
ADL	Anti-Defamation League
ADL	Archiv des Liberalismus, Gummersbach
ADN	Allgemeiner Deutscher Nachrichtendienst (General German News Service of the GDR)
AdsD	Archiv der sozialen Demokratie, Bonn
AFN	American Forces Network
AfNS	Amt für Nationale Sicherheit (Office for National Security of the GDR)
AJA	American Jewish Archives, Cincinnati, USA
AJDC	American Jewish Joint Distribution Committee (also referred to as the "Joint")
AJW	*Allgemeine Jüdische Wochenzeitung*
ARMS	United Nations Archives and Records Management Section, New York
Ast.	Außenstelle (branch office)
AWJD	*Allgemeine Wochenzeitung der Juden in Deutschland*
BArch	Bundesarchiv, Koblenz
BEG	Bundesentschädigungsgesetz (German Federal Restitution Law)
BErG	Bundesergänzungsgesetz (Federal Supplementary Law)
BFSS	British Field Secret Service
BGBl	Bundesgesetzblatt (Federal Law Gazette)
BGH	Bundesgerichtshof (Federal Supreme Court)

BHE   Bund der Heimatvertriebenen und Entrechteten
BJSD   Bundesverband Jüdischer Studenten in Deutschland
BK   Bundeskanzleramt (Federal Chancellery)
BKA   Bundeskriminalamt (Federal Criminal Police Office)
BMF   Bundesministerium der Finanzen (Federal Ministry of Finance)
BMI   Bundesministerium des Innern (Federal Ministry of the Interior)
BPA   Presse- und Informationsamt der Bundesregierung / Bundespresseamt
           (Federal Press Office)
BRD   Bundesrepublik Deutschland (Federal Republic of Germany)
BStU   Der Bundesbeauftragte für die Stasi-Unterlagen (Federal commissioner
           for the STASI files)
BT   Bundestag
BVerfG   Bundesverfassungsgericht (Federal Constitutional Court)
BvR   Verfassungsbeschwerde (constitutional complaint)
CDU   Christlich Demokratische Union (Christian Democratic Union)
CJA   Archiv der Stiftung Neue Synagoge Berlin – Centrum Judaicum
CORA   Court of Restitution Appeals, Nuremberg
ČSSR   Tschechoslowakei (Czechoslovakia)
CSU   Christlich-Soziale Union (Christian Social Union)
CZA   Central Zionist Archives, Jerusalem, Israel
DDR   Deutsche Demokratische Republik
DEFA   Deutsche Film AG, Potsdam-Babelsberg, DDR
DGB   Deutscher Gewerkschaftsbund
DIVO   Deutsches Institut für Volksumfragen; today, Institut für
           Wirtschafts forschung, Sozialforschung und angewandte Mathematik
DM   Deutsche Mark
DP   Displaced person
EMNID   Erforschung der öffentlichen Meinung, Marktforschung, Nachrichten,
           Informationen, Dienstleistung
FDJ   Freie Deutsche Jugend, DDR
FDP   Freie Demokratische Partei (Free Democratic Party)
GEW   Gewerkschaft für Erziehung und Wissenschaft
GLA   Generallandesarchiv Karlsruhe
GMS   Gesellschaftlicher Mitarbeiter für Sicherheit (Informant to State
           Security in the GDR)
GUS   Gemeinschaft Unabhängiger Staaten (Commonwealth of Independent
           States, CIS)
HIAS   Hebrew Immigrant Aid Society
HICOG   High Commission for Occupied Germany
HJ   Hitlerjugend (Hitler Youth)

IGJZ	Initiativgruppe für Jugendfragen beim Zentralrat (Initiative group for youth questions of the Central Council)
IKG	Israelitische Kultusgemeinde (Jewish religious community)
IRGW	Israelitische Religionsgemeinschaft Württembergs
IRO	International Refugee Organization
IRSO	Jewish Restitution Successor Organization (also JRSO)
ISG	Institut für Stadtgeschichte Frankfurt am Main
ITS	Internationaler Suchdienst Bad Arolsen (International Tracing Service)
JCR	Jewish Cultural Reconstruction, Inc.
JDCA	(American Jewish) Joint Distribution Committee Archive
JDC	See AJDC
JMB	Jüdisches Museum Berlin
Joint	See AJDC
JRC	Jewish Restitution Commission
JRU	(British) Jewish Relief Unit
JSU	Jewish Student Union
KD	Kreisdienststelle (district office)
KPD	Kommunistische Partei Deutschland (Communist Party of Germany)
KZ	Konzentrationslager (concentration camp)
LAB	Landesarchiv Berlin
LBI	Leo Baeck Institute, New York
LMU	Ludwig-Maximilians-Universität München
LVB	Landesverband der Israelitischen Kultusgemeinden in Bayern (State Association of Israelite Religious Communities in Bavaria)
MfS	Ministerium für Staatssicherheit (Ministry for Security of the GDR)
NDR	Norddeutscher Rundfunk
NKVD	Innenministerium der UdSSR, also NKWD (Ministry of the Interior of the USSR)
NL	Nachlass (Estate)
NPD	Nationaldemokratische Partei Deutschlands (National Democratic Party of Germany)
NSDAP	Nationalsozialistische Deutsche Arbeiterpartei (National Socialist German Workers Party)
OMGUS	Office of Military Government for Germany
ORT	Organization for Rehabilitation through Training
PDS	Partei des Demokratischen Sozialismus (Party of Democratic Socialism)
PLO	Palestine Liberation Organization
RAF	Rote Armee Fraktion (Red Army Fraction)
SA	Sturmabteilung (Paramilitary wing of the NSDAP)
SAP	Sozialistische Arbeiterpartei (Socialist Workers Party)

SDS	Sozialistischer Deutscher Studentenbund
SED	Sozialistische Einheitspartei Deutschlands (Socialist Unity Party of Germany)
SHAEF	Supreme Headquarters, Allied Expeditionary Forces
SINUS	SINUS Markt- und Sozialforschung GmbH
SPD	Sozialdemokratische Partei Deutschlands (Social Democratic Party of Germany)
SS	Schutzstaffel (paramilitary organization of the NSDAP)
StadtAM	Stadtarchiv München
StadtAS	Stadtarchiv Stuttgart
StAHH	Staatsarchiv Hamburg
StAM	Staatsarchiv München
UdSSR	Union of Soviet Socialist Republics
UN	United Nations
UNRRA	United Nations Relief and Rehabilitation Administration
UNSCOP	United Nations Special Committee on Palestine
URO	United Restitution Organization
USHMM	United States Holocaust Memorial Museum, Washington, D.C.
VVN	Vereinigung der Verfolgten des Naziregimes (Association of Persecutees of the Nazi Regime / Federation of Antifascists in the GDR)
WB	West Berlin
WIZO	Women's International Zionist Organization
WJC	World Jewish Congress
WP	Wahlperiode (electoral term)
WUJS	World Union of Jewish Students
YIVO DPG	YIVO-Bestand, Displaced Persons Camps in Germany, 1945–1952
YIVO LWSP	YIVO holdings, Leo W. Schwarz Papers
YIVO	Yiddish Scientific Institute, New York
ZA	Zentralarchiv zur Erforschung der Geschichte der Juden in Deutschland, Heidelberg
ZK	Zentralkomitee (Central Committee)
ZWST	Zentralwohlfahrtsstelle der Juden in Deutschland e. V.

ARCHIVES

Archiv der Akademie der Künste (AdK), Berlin Archiv des Liberalismus (ADL), Gummersbach

Archiv der sozialen Demokratie (AdsD), Bonn

American Jewish Archive (AJA), Cincinnati

(American Jewish) Joint Distribution Committee Archives (JDC A), New York

Archiv des Landesverbandes der Israelitischen Kultusgemeinden in Bayern (Archiv LVB), Munich

Bundesarchiv (BArch), Koblenz

Presse- und Informationsamt der Bundesregierung / Bundespresseamt (BPA), Berlin

Der Bundesbeauftrage für die Stasi-Unterlagen (BStU), Berlin

Archiv der Stiftung Neue Synagoge Berlin—Centrum Judaicum (CJA), Berlin Central Zionist Archives (CZA), Jerusalem, Israel

Generallandesarchiv Karlsruhe (GLA), Karlsruhe

Institut für Stadtgeschichte Frankfurt am Main (ISG), Frankfurt am Main

Internationaler Suchdienst Bad Arolsen (ITS), Bad Arolsen Jüdisches Museum Berlin (JMB), Berlin

Landesarchiv Berlin (LAB), Berlin Leo Baeck Institute (LBI), New York

Stadtarchiv Stuttgart (StadtAS), Stuttgart

Staatsarchiv Hamburg (StAHH), Hamburg Staatsarchiv München (StAM), Munich

United Nations Archives and Records Management Section (ARMS), New York

United States Holocaust Memorial Museum (USHMM), Washington, D.C.

Yad Tabenkin—The Research and Documentation Center of the Kibbutz Movement, Ramat Efala, Israel

YIVO—Institute for Jewish Research (YIVO), New York

Zentralarchiv zur Erforschung der Geschichte der Juden in Deutschland (ZA), Heidelberg

REFERENCES

Abelshauser, Werner. 2011. *Deutsche Wirtschaftsgeschichte von 1945 bis zur Gegenwart.* Munich: C. H. Beck Verlag.

Aden-Grossmann, Wilma. 2007. *Berthold Simonsohn: Biographie des jüdischen Sozialpädagogen und Juristen (1912–1978).* Frankfurt am Main: Campus Verlag.

Adler, Eliyana. 2014. "Hrubieszów at the Crossroads: Polish Jews Navigate the German and Soviet Occupations." *Holocaust and Genocide Studies* 28/1, pp. 1–30.

Adorno, Theodor W. 1998a. "Education after Auschwitz." In T. W. Adorno, *Critical Models: Interventions and Catchwords*, p. 204. New York: Columbia University Press.

———. 1998b. "The Meaning of Working Through the Past." In T. W. Adorno, *Critical Models: Interventions and Catchwords*, pp. 89–102. New York: Columbia University Press.

Ahonen, Pertti. 2003. *After the Expulsion: West Germany and Eastern Europe 1945–1990.* London: Oxford University Press.

Amadeo, Antonio Stiftung, ed. 2009. *"Die Juden sind schuld": Antisemitismus in der Einwanderungsgesellschaft am Beispiel muslimisch sozialisierter Milieus.* Berlin: Amadeo Antonio Stiftung.

Andreas-Friedrich, Ruth. 1947. *Berlin Underground 1938–1945.* New York: Paragon House.

Andresen, Knud. 2007. *Widerspruch als Lebensprinzip: Der undogmatische Sozialist Heinz Brandt (1909–1986).* Bonn: Dietz Verlag.

Angermair, Elisabeth, et al., eds. 1999. *Beth Ha-Knesseth—Ort der Zusammenkunft: Zur Geschichte der Münchner Synagogen, ihrer Rabbiner und Kantoren.* Munich: Stadtarchiv München.

Angersdorfer, Andreas. 2009. "Jüdische Displaced Persons in Regensburg und im Großraum Regensburg 1945–1952: Eine noch zu schreibende Geschichte." In Sabine Koller, ed., *Ein Tag im Jüdischen Regensburg mit Joseph Opatoshu und Marc Chagall*, pp. 87–101. Regensburg: Stutz Verlag.

Anthony, Tamara. 2004. *Ins Land der Väter oder der Täter? Israel und die Juden in Deutschland nach der Schoah.* Berlin: Metropol.

Aptekman, David. 1993. "Jewish Emigration from the USSR, 1990–1992: Trends and Motivations." *Jews in Eastern Europe* 20/1, pp. 15–33.

Arendt, Hannah. 1950. "The Aftermath of Nazi Rule: Report from Germany." *Commentary* 10/4, p. 342.

Arendt, Hannah, and Blücher, Heinrich. 1999. *Briefe 1936–1968.* Ed. Lotte Köhler. Munich: Piper.

Arnold-Forster, W. 1946. "U.N.R.R.A.'s Work for Displaced Persons in Germany." *International Affairs* 22, pp. 1–13.

Arnsberg, Paul. 1983. "Die Geschichte der Frankfurter Juden seit der Französischen Revolution." In Hans-Otto Schembs, ed., *Biographisches Lexikon der Juden in den Bereichen*, vol. 3: *Wissenschaft, Kultur, Bildung, Öffentlichkeitsarbeit in Frankfurt am Main*, pp. 74–75. Kuratorium für Jüdische Geschichte e. V., Frankfurt am Main. Darmstadt: E. Rother.

Asaria, Zvi. 1959a. *Die Juden in Köln: Von den ältesten Zeiten bis zur Gegenwart*. Cologne: Bachem.

———. 1959b. "Über die Juden in Köln." In Wilhelm Unger, ed., Zur Weihe der wieder-hergestellten Synagoge Roonstraße und des jüdischen Kulturzentrums in Köln, 20. September 1959 (17. Elul 5719), pp. 24–28. Cologne: Synagogen-Gemeinde Köln.

———. 1970. *Samson Raphael Hirsch: Seine rechtliche Stellung als Landesrabbiner und sein segensreiches Wirken im Lande Niedersachsen*. Hameln: Adolf Sponholtz Verlag.

———. 1975. *Wir sind Zeugen*. Hannover: Landeszentrale für politische Bildung.

———. 1979. *Die Juden in Niedersachsen: Von den ältesten Zeiten bis zur Gegenwart*. Leer, East Friesland: Gerhard Rautenberg Verlag.

Aviner, Shlomo Haim Ha-Cohen. 2000. *On the Shoah* (in Hebrew). Jerusalem.

Backhaus, Fritz, et al., eds. 2007. *Ignatz Bubis: Ein jüdisches Leben in Deutschland*. Frankfurt am Main: Jüdischer Verlag im Suhrkamp Verlag.

Bade, Klaus. 2002. *Europa in Bewegung: Migration vom späten 18. Jahrhundert bis zur Gegenwart*. Munich: C. H. Beck.

Balabkins, Nicholas. 1971. *West German Reparations to Israel*. New Brunswick, N.J.: Rutgers University Press.

Bankier, David, ed. 2005. *The Jews Are Coming Back: The Return of the Jews to Their Countries of Origin after WW II*. New York: Berghahn Books.

Barkai, Avraham. 1991. "Zur Wirtschaftsgeschichte der Juden in Deutschland: Historiographische Quellen und Tendenzen vor und nach 1945." *Tel Aviver Jahrbuch für deutsche Geschichte* 20, pp. 195–214.

———. 1997. "Das letzte Kapitel." In Michael A. Meyer, ed., *Deutsch-jüdische Geschichte in der Neuzeit*, vol. 4: *Aufbau und Zerstörung 1918–1945*, pp. 343–368. Munich: C. H. Beck.

Barker, Rodney. 1990. *Political Legitimacy and the State*. Oxford: Oxford University Press.

Barner, Lida. 2008. "Von Irmgard zu Irith: Konversionen zum Judentum im Deutschland der 1950er und 1960er Jahre." Master's thesis, LMU Munich.

Bartov, Omer, et al., eds. 2002. *Crimes of War: Guilt and Denial in the Twentieth Century*. New York: New Press.

Baruch, Rony. 1994. "The German Union of Jewish Students (BJSD)." In Uri R. Kaufmann, ed., *Jewish Life in Germany Today*, pp. 99–102. Bonn: Inter Nationes.

Barzel, Neima. 1994. "The Attitude of Jews of German Origin in Israel to Germany and Germans after the Holocaust, 1945–1952." *Leo Baeck Institute Yearbook* 39, pp. 271–301.

———. 1996. "The 'No Forgiveness—No Atonement' Attitude of the Israeli Government and Society toward Germany, 1945–1957." In Israel Gutman, ed., *Major Changes within the Jewish People in the Wake of the Holocaust*. Proceedings of the Ninth Yad Vashem International Historical Conference, Jerusalem, June 1993, pp. 567–585. Jerusalem: Yad Vashem.

Bauer, Richard, and Michael Brenner, eds. 2006. *Jüdisches München: Vom Mittelalter bis zur Gegenwart*, pp. 185–208. Munich: C. H. Beck.

Bauer, Yehuda. 1970a. *Flight and Rescue: Brichah*. New York: Random House.

———. 1970b. "The Initial Organization of the Holocaust Survivors in Bavaria." *Yad Vashem Studies* 8, pp. 127–157.

———. 1989. *Out of the Ashes: The Impact of American Jews on Post-Holocaust European Jewry.* Oxford: Oxford University Press.

———. 1990. "The Bricha." In Israel Gutman and Avital Saf, eds., *She'erit Hapletah, 1944–1948: Rehabilitation and Political Struggle.* Proceedings of the Sixth Yad Vashem International Historical Conference, Jerusalem, October 1985, pp. 51–116. Jerusalem: Yad Vashem.

Baumel, Yehuda T. 1997. *Kibbutz Buchenwald: Survivors and Pioneers.* New Brunswick, N.J.: Rutgers University Press.

Beck, Gad. 1999. *An Underground Life: The Memoirs of a Gay Jew in Nazi Berlin.* Madison: University of Wisconsin Press.

Becker, Franziska. 2001. *Ankommen in Deutschland: Einwanderungspolitik als biographische Erfahrung im Migrationsprozeß russischer Juden.* Berlin: Dietrich Reimer Verlag.

Becker, Jurek. 1969. *Jacob the Liar.* Translated by Leila Vennewitz. New York: Arcade Publishing.

———. 1988. *Bronstein's Children.* Translated by Leila Vennewitz. New York: Harcourt Brace Jovanovich.

Bein, Reinhard, and Schmidt-Czaia, Bettina, eds. 2005. *Wenn man ein Haus baut, will man bleiben.* Braunschweig: Stadtarchiv Braunschweig.

Belkin, Dmitrij, and Gross, Raphael. 2010. *Ausgerechnet Deutschland! Jüdisch-russische Einwanderung in die Bundesrepublik.* Publication accompanying the exhibition at the Jewish Museum Frankfurt, March 12–July 25, 2010. Berlin: Nikolaische Verlagsbuchhandlung.

Belsky, Natalie. 2015. "Encounters in the East: Evacuees in the Soviet Hinterland during the Second World War." Ph.D. diss., University of Chicago.

Ben, Abraham. 2004. "Leben wie im Schtetl: Alltag in Föhrenwald." In Roman Haller, ed., *. . . und bleiben wollte keiner: Jüdische Lebensgeschichten im Nachkriegsbayern,* pp. 136–145. Hamburg: Dölling und Galitz.

Bendix, Werner. 2002. *Die Hauptstadt des Wirtschaftswunders: Frankfurt am Main 1945–1956.* Frankfurt am Main: Verlag Waldemar Kramer.

Benz, Wolfgang, ed. 1991a. *Das Exil der kleinen Leute: Alltagserfahrungen deutscher Juden in der Emigration.* Munich: C. H. Beck.

———, ed. 1991b. *Zwischen Antisemitismus und Philosemitismus: Juden in der Bundesrepublik.* Berlin: Metropol Verlag.

———, ed. 1995. *Die Vertreibung der Deutschen aus dem Osten: Ursachen, Ereignisse, Folgen.* Frankfurt am Main: Fischer Verlag.

———, ed. 2003. *Überleben im Dritten Reich: Juden im Untergrund und ihre Helfer.* Munich: C. H. Beck

Berg, Nicolas. 2003. *Der Holocaust und die westdeutschen Historiker: Erforschung und Erinnerung.* Göttingen: Wallstein Verlag.

Berger, Almuth. 2010. "Ein Tabu der Nachkriegsgeschichte wird gebrochen: Aufnahme russischjüdischer Emigranten in der DDR. Ein Zeitzeugenbericht." In *Ausgerechnet Deutschland! Jüdisch-russische Einwanderung in die Bundesrepublik.* Publication accompanying the exhibition at the Jewish Museum Frankfurt, March 12–July 25, 2010, pp. 55–59. Berlin: Nikolaische Verlagsbuchhandlung.

Berger, Joseph A. 1947. "Displaced Persons: A Human Tragedy of World War II." *Social Research* 14 (March), pp. 45–58.

Bergmann, Werner. 1990a. "Antisemitismus als politisches Ereignis: Die antisemitische Schmierwelle im Winter 1959/60." In Werner Bergmann and Rainer Erb, eds., *Antisemitismus in der politischen Kultur nach 1945*, pp. 253–276. Opladen: Westdeutscher Verlag.

———. 1990b. "Sind die Deutschen antisemitisch?" In Werner Bergmann and Rainer Erb, eds., *Antisemitismus in der politischen Kultur nach 1945*, pp. 122–123. Opladen: Westdeutscher Verlag.

———. 1994. "Medienöffentlichkeit und extremistisches Meinungsspektrum: Die Süddeutsche Zeitung und der Fall Adolf Bleibtreu." *Jahrbuch für Antisemitismusforschung* 3, pp. 51–67.

———. 1997. *Antisemitismus in öffentlichen Konflikten: Kollektives Lernen in der politischen Kultur der Bundesrepublik 1949–1989.* Frankfurt am Main: Campus Verlag.

———. 1999. "Philipp Auerbach—Wiedergutmachung war 'nicht mit normalen Mitteln' durchzusetzen." In Claudia Fröhlich and Michael Kohlstruck, eds., *Engagierte Demokraten: Vergangenheitspolitik in kritischer Absicht*, pp. 57–70. Münster: Westfälisches Dampfboot.

———. 2001. "'Der Antisemitismus in Deutschland braucht gar nicht übertrieben zu werden...': Die Jahre 1945 bis 1953." In Julius H. Schoeps, ed., *Leben im Land der Täter: Juden im Nachkriegsdeutschland (1945–1952)*, pp. 191–207. Berlin: Jüdische Verlagsanstalt.

———. 2002. "Die Beobachter beobachten: Zur Einschätzung des Antisemitismus in der Bundesrepublik Deutschland." In Wolfgang Benz and Angelika Königseder, eds., *Judenfeindschaft als Paradigma: Studien zur Vorurteilsforschung*, pp. 31–39. Berlin: Metropol.

Bergmann, Werner, and Erb, Rainer, eds. 1990. *Antisemitismus in der politischen Kultur nach 1945.* Opladen: Westdeutscher Verlag.

———, eds. 1991. *Antisemitismus in der Bundesrepublik Deutschland: Ergebnisse der empirischen Forschung von 1946–1989.* Opladen: Westdeutscher Verlag.

Berkowitz, Michael, and Brown-Fleming, Suzanne. 2010. "Perceptions of Jewish Displaced Persons as Criminals in Early Postwar Germany: Lingering Stereotypes and Self-Fulfilling Prophecies." In Michael Berkowitz and Avinoam Patt, eds., *We Are Here: New Approaches to Jewish Displaced Persons in Postwar Germany*, pp. 167–193. Detroit: Wayne State University Press.

Berkowitz, Michael, and Patt, Avinoam, eds. 2010. *We Are Here: New Approaches to Jewish Displaced Persons in Postwar Germany.* Detroit: Wayne State University Press.

Bernstein, Julia. 2005. "Transmigration und Kapitalismus: Migranten und Migrantinnen aus der ehemaligen Sowjetunion und ihre Erfahrungen in Deutschland." *PROKLA: Zeitschrift für kritische Sozialwissenschaften* 35/140, no. 3, pp. 407–422.

Berthold-Hilpert, Monika. 1998. "Die frühe Nachkriegsgeschichte der jüdischen Gemeinde Fürth." *Menora* 9, pp. 361–380.

———. 2002. "Jüdisches Leben in Franken nach 1945 am Beispiel der Gemeinde Fürth." In Gunnar Ochs and Hartmut Bobzin, eds., *Jüdisches Leben in Franken*, pp. 197–212. Würzburg: Ergon Verlag.

Bertram, Jürgen. 2008. *Wer baut, der bleibt: Neues jüdisches Leben in Deutschland.* Frankfurt am Main: Fischer Taschenbuch Verlag.

Best, Michael, ed. 1988. *Der Frankfurter Börneplatz: Zur Archäologie eines politischen Konflikts.* Frankfurt am Main: Fischer Taschenbuch Verlag.

Biehler, Gernot. 2000. "Ausländerrecht und jüdische Emigration aus der früheren Sowjetunion." In Dietrich Murswiek et al., eds., *Staat—Souveränität—Verfassung: Festschrift für Helmut Quaritsch zum 70. Geburtstag,* pp. 265–283. Berlin: Duncker & Humblot.

Bleich, J. David. 1983. *Contemporary Halakhic Problems.* New York: KTAV Publishing House.

Bodek, Janusz. 1991. *Die Fassbinder-Kontroversen: Entstehung und Wirkung eines literarischen Textes; Zu Kontinuität und Wandel einiger Erscheinungsformen des Alltagsantisemitismus in Deutschland nach 1945, seinen künstlerischen Weihen und seiner öffentlichen Inszenierung.* Frankfurt am Main: Peter Lang Verlag.

Bodemann, Y. Michal. 1986. "Staat und Ethnizität: Der Aufbau der jüdischen Gemeinden im Kalten Krieg." In Micha Brumlik et al., eds., *Jüdisches Leben in Deutschland seit 1945,* pp. 49–69. Frankfurt am Main: Judischer Verlag bei Athenaum.

———. 1995. "'Ich verlasse dieses Land in Verbitterung, doch vor keinem Volke darf man die Fensterläden zuschlagen. . .': Zur Abschiedspredigt von Rabbiner Dr. Wilhelm Weinberg (1901–1976) in Frankfurt am Main am 11. November 1951." *Menora* 6, pp. 345–357.

———. 1996a. *Gedächtnistheater: Die jüdische Gemeinschaft und ihre deutsche Erfindung.* Berlin: Rotbuch Verlag.

———, ed. 1996b. *Jews, Germans, Memory: Reconstruction of Jewish Life in Germany.* Ann Arbor: University of Michigan Press.

———. 2002. *In den Wogen der Erinnerung: Jüdische Existenz in Deutschland.* Munich: Deutscher Taschenbuch Verlag.

———. 2005. *A Jewish Family in Germany Today: An Intimate Portrait.* Durham, N.C.: Duke University Press.

———, ed. 2008. *The New German Jewry and the European Context: The Return of the European Jewish Diaspora.* New York: Palgrave Macmillan.

Bodemann, Y. Michal, and Bagno, Olena. 2008. "In the Ethnic Twilight: The Paths of Russian Jews in Germany." In Y. Michal Bodemann, ed., *The New German Jewry and the European Context: The Return of the European Jewish Diaspora,* pp. 158–176. New York: Palgrave Macmillan.

Bodemann, Y. Michal, and Brumlik, Micha, eds. 2010. *Juden in Deutschland—Deutschland in den Juden: Neue Perspektiven.* Göttingen: Wallstein Verlag.

Boehm, Eric H., ed. 1985. *We Survived: Fourteen Histories of the Hidden and Hunted of Nazi Germany.* Santa Barbara: ABC-Clio.

Böhme, Hartmut. 2006. *Fetischismus und Kultur: Eine andere Theorie der Moderne.* Reinbek bei Hamburg: Rowohlt Taschenbuch Verlag.

Böll, Heinrich. 1965. *The Clown.* New York: HarperCollins.

Boll, Monika, and Gross, Raphael, eds. 2009. *Die Frankfurter Schule und Frankfurt: Eine Rückkehr nach Deutschland.* Göttingen: Wallstein Verlag.

———, eds. 2013. *"Ich staune, dass Sie in dieser Luft atmen können": Jüdische Intellektuelle in Deutschland nach 1945.* Schriftenreihe des Fritz Bauer Instituts, vol. 28. Frankfurt am Main: S. Fischer Verlag.

Boveri, Margret. 2004. *Tage des Überlebens: Berlin 1945.* Berlin: Piper Verlag.

Braemer, A. 2006. "Die Gründung der 'Rabbinerkonferenz in der Bundesrepublik.'" In S. Schönborn, ed., *Zwischen Erinnerung und Neubeginn: Zur deutsch-jüdischen Geschichte nach 1945,* pp. 84–89. Munich: Martin Meidenbauer.

Braese, Stephan. 2001. *Die andere Erinnerung: Jüdische Autoren in der westdeutschen Nachkriegsliteratur.* Berlin: Philo Verlag.

Brämer, Andreas. 2006. "Die Gründung der 'Rabbinerkonferenz in der Bundesrepublik.'" In Susanne Schönborn, ed., *Zwischen Erinnerung und Neubeginn: Zur deutsch-jüdischen Geschichte nach 1945*, pp. 76–91. Munich: Peter Lang Gmbh, Internationaler Verlag der Wissenschaften.

Brandt, Leon. 1984. *Menschen ohne Schatten: Juden zwischen Untergang und Untergrund 1938 bis 1945.* Berlin: Oberbaum.

Breitsprecher, Ulrike. 2010. "Die Bedeutung des Judentums und des Holocaust in der Identitätskonstruktion dreier jüdischer Kommunisten in der frühen DDR: Alexander Abusch, Helmut Eschwege und Leo Zuckerman." *Jahrbuch für historische Kommunismusforschung*, pp. 193–208.

Brenner, Michael. 1997. *After the Holocaust: Rebuilding Jewish Lives in Postwar Germany.* Princeton, N.J.: Princeton University Press.

———. 2001a. "Displaced Persons." In Walter Laqueur, ed., *The Holocaust Encyclopaedia*, pp. 150–159. New Haven, Conn.: Yale University Press.

———. 2001b. "Religion, Nation oder Stamm: Zum Wandel der Selbstdefinition unter deutschen Juden." In Heinz-Gerhard Haupt, ed., *Nation und Religion in der deutschen Geschichte*, pp. 587–601. Frankfurt am Main: Campus Verlag.

———. 2002. "The Transformation of the German Jewish Community." In Leslie Morris and Jack Zipes, eds., *Unlikely History: The Changing German-Jewish Symbiosis, 1945–2000*, pp. 49–61. New York: Palgrave Macmillan.

———. 2006. *Propheten des Vergangenen: Jüdische Geschichtsschreibung im 19. und 20. Jahrhundert.* Munich: C. H. Beck.

———. 2007. "Von den Hintertüren der Diplomatie auf die Bühne der Öffentlichkeit: Der Wandel in der Repräsentation des Zentralrats der Juden in Deutschland." In Fritz Backhaus, ed., *Ignatz Bubis: Ein jüdisches Leben in Deutschland*, pp. 124–133. Frankfurt am Main: Jüdischer Verlag im Suhrkamp Verlag.

———. 2008a. *Kleine Jüdische Geschichte.* Munich: C. H. Beck.

———. 2008b. "Vergessene Historiker: Ein Kapitel deutsch-jüdischer Geschichtsschreibung der fünfziger und sechziger Jahre." In Irmela von der Lühe et al., eds., *"Auch in Deutschland waren wir nicht wirklich zu Hause": Jüdische Remigration nach 1945*, pp. 207–223. Göttingen: Wallstein Verlag.

———. 2010. *In the Shadow of the Holocaust: The Changing Image of German Jewry after 1945.* Washington, D.C.: United States Holocaust Memorial Museum.

———. 2012. "Jüdische Geistesgeschichte zwischen Exil und Heimkehr: Hans-Joachim Schoeps im Kontext der Wissenschaft des Judentums." In Monika Boll and Raphael Gross, eds., *"Ich staune, dass Sie in dieser Luft atmen können": Jüdische Intellektuelle in Deutschland nach 1945.* Frankfurt am Main: Fischer Taschenbuch Verlag.

Brenner, Michael, and Höpfinger, Renate, eds. 2008. *Die Juden in der Oberpfalz.* Munich: R. Oldenbourg Verlag.

Brenner, Michael, and Reuveni, Gideon, eds. 2006. *Emanzipation durch Muskelkraft: Juden und Sport in Europa.* Göttingen: Vandenhoeck & Ruprecht.

Brink, Cornelia. 2000. *"Auschwitz in der Paulskirche": Erinnerungspolitik in Fotoausstellungen der sechziger Jahre.* Marburg: Jonas Verlag.

Brocke, Michael, and Carlebach, Julius, eds. 2009. *Biographisches Handbuch der Rabbiner*, vol. 2: *Die Rabbiner im Deutschen Reich.* Munich: K. G. Saur Verlag.

Broder, Henryk M. 1986. *Der ewige Antisemit: Über Sinn und Funktion eines beständigen Gefühls*. Frankfurt am Main: Fischer Taschenbuch Verlag.

Broder, Henryk M., and Lang, Michel R., eds. 1979a. *Fremd im eigenen Land: Juden in der Bundesrepublik*. Frankfurt am Main: Fischer Taschenbuch Verlag.

———. 1979b. "Vorneweg." In Henryk M. Broder and Michel R. Lang, eds., *Fremd im eigenen Land: Juden in der Bundesrepublik*, pp. 11–12. Frankfurt am Main: Fischer Taschenbuch Verlag.

Brodesser, Hermann-Josef, et al. 2000. *Wiedergutmachung und Kriegsfolgenliquidation: Geschichte—Regelungen—Zahlungen*. Munich: C. H. Beck.

Brodzki, Bella, and Varon, Jeremy. 2005. "The Munich Years: The Jewish Students of Postwar Germany." In Johannes-Dieter Steinert and Inge Weber-Newth, eds., *Beyond Camps and Forced Labour: Current International Research on Survivors of Nazi Persecution; Proceedings of the First International Multidisciplinary Conference at the Imperial War Museum. London, 29.–31. January 2003*, pp. 154–163. Osnabrück: Secolo Verlag.

Brumlik, Micha. 1996. "The Situation of the Jews in Today's Germany." In Y. Michal Bodemann, ed., *Jews, Germans, Memory: Reconstruction of Jewish Life in Germany*, pp. 1–16. Ann Arbor: University of Michigan Press.

———. 2000. *Kein Weg als Deutscher und Jude: Eine bundesrepublikanische Erfahrung*. Munich: Ullstein Verlag.

Brumlik, Micha, et al., eds. 1986. *Jüdisches Leben in Deutschland seit 1945*. Frankfurt am Main: Athenaeum.

Brunner, José, and Nachum, Iris. 2009. "'Vor dem Gesetz steht ein Türhüter': Wie und warum israelische Antragsteller ihre Zugehörigkeit zum deutschen Sprach- und Kulturkreis beweisen mussten." In Norbert Frei et al., eds., *Die Praxis der Wiedergutmachung: Geschichte, Erfahrung und Wirkung in Deutschland und Israel*, pp. 387–424. Göttingen: Wallstein Verlag.

Bubis, Ignatz, with Peter Sichrovsky. 1996. *"Damit bin ich noch längst nicht fertig": Die Autobiographie*. Frankfurt am Main: Campus Verlag.

Bühler, Philipp. 2004. *Filmheft: Alles auf Zucker*. Bonn: Bundeszentrale für politische Bildung.

Bundesministerium des Innern, ed. 2011. *Antisemitismus in Deutschland: Erscheinungsformen, Bedingungen, Präventionsansätze*. Berlin: Publikationsversand der Bundesregierung.

Burgauer, Erica. 1993. *Zwischen Erinnerung und Verdrängung: Juden in Deutschland nach 1945*. Reinbek bei Hamburg: Rowohlt Verlag.

Büttner, Ursula. 1986. "Not nach der Befreiung: Die Situation der deutschen Juden in der britischen Besatzungszone, 1945 bis 1948." In Ursula Büttner, ed., *Das Unrechtsregime: Internationale Forschung über den Nationalsozialismus*, vol. 2: *Verfolgung, Exil, belasteter Neubeginn*, pp. 373–406. Hamburg: Christians Verlag.

———. 1997. "Die ersten jüdischen Organisationen in Hamburg nach der Schoah: Ein vergleichender Kommentar zur hannoverschen Entwicklung." In Herbert Obenaus, ed., *Im Schatten des Holocaust: Jüdisches Leben in Niedersachsen nach 1945*, pp. 75–82. Hannover: Verlag Hahnsche Buchhandlung.

———. 2008. "Schwierige Rückwanderung nach Hamburg: Wie Briten und Deutsche den jüdischen Flüchtlingen im Wege standen." In Irmela von der Lühe et al., eds., *"Auch in Deutschland waren wir nicht wirklich zu Hause": Jüdische Remigration nach 1945*, pp. 40–68. Göttingen: Wallstein Verlag.

Carlebach, Emil. 1988. *Am Anfang stand ein Doppelmord: Autobiography*, vol. 1. Cologne: Röderberg-Programm bei Pahl-Rugenstein.

———. 1995. *Tote auf Urlaub: Autobiography*, vol. 2. Bonn: Pahl-Rugenstein Nachf.

Carlebach, Julius, and Brämer, Andreas. 1997. "Continuity or New Beginning: Issac Emil Lichtigfeld, Rabbi in Frankfurt am Main and Hessen, 1954–1967." *Leo Baeck Institute Yearbook* 42, pp. 275–302.

Cheal, David. 1988. *The Gift Economy*. New York: Routledge.

Chin, Rita, et al. 2009. *After the Nazi Racial State: Difference and Democracy in Germany and Europe*. Ann Arbor: University of Michigan Press.

Claussen, Detlev. 2005. *Theodor W. Adorno: Ein letztes Genie*. Frankfurt am Main: Fischer Verlag.

Cobler, Sebastian. 1985. "Das Gesetz gegen die 'Auschwitz-Lüge': Anmerkungen zu einem rechtspolitischen Ablaßhandel." *Kritische Justiz* 18, pp. 159–170.

Cohen, Yinon, Haberfeld, Yitzhak, and Kogan, Irena. 2008. "Jüdische Immigration aus der ehemaligen Sowjetunion: Ein natürliches Experiment zur Migrationsentscheidung." In Frank Kalter, ed., *Migration und Integration: Kölner Zeitschrift für Soziologie und Sozialpsychologie*, Sonderheft 48, pp. 185–201.

Cohen, Yinon, and Kogan, Irena. 2005. "Jewish Immigrants from the Former Soviet Union in Germany and Israel." *Leo Baeck Institute Yearbook* 50, pp. 249–265.

———. 2007. "Next Year in Jerusalem . . . or in Cologne? Labour Market Integration of Jewish Immigrants from the Former Soviet Union in Israel and Germany in the 1990s." *European Sociological Review* 23/2, pp. 155–168.

Conze, Eckart. 2005. "'Sicherheit' als Kultur: Überlegungen zu einer modernen Politikgeschichte der Bundesrepublik." *Vierteljahrshefte für Zeitgeschichte* 53, pp. 357–381.

———. 2009. *Die Suche nach Sicherheit: Eine Geschichte der Bundesrepublik Deutschland von 1945 bis in die Gegenwart*. Munich: Siedler Verlag.

Conze, Eckart, et al. 2010. *Das Amt und die Vergangenheit: Deutsche Diplomaten im Dritten Reich und in der Bundesrepublik*. Munich: Verlagsgruppe Random House.

Cornell, Stephen. 1996. "The Various Ties That Bind: Content and Circumstances in Ethnic Processes." *Ethnic and Racial Studies* 19/2, pp. 265–289.

Crago-Schneider, Kierra. 2010. "Antisemitism or Competing Interests? An Examination of German and American Perceptions of Jewish Displaced Persons Active on the Black Market in Munich's Möhlstrasse." *Yad Vashem Studies* 38/1, pp. 167–194.

Davies, Norman, and Polonsky, Antony, eds. 1991. *Jews in Eastern Poland and the USSR, 1939–1946*. London: Macmillan.

Deligdisch, Jekutiel. 1974. *Die Einstellung der Bundesrepublik Deutschland zum Staate Israel: Eine Zusammenfassung der Entwicklung seit 1949*. Bonn: Verlag Neue Gesellschaft.

Derix, Simone. 2009. *Bebilderte Politik: Staatsbesuche in der Bundesrepublik Deutschland, 1949–1990*. Göttingen: Vandenhoeck & Ruprecht.

Dietrich, Susanne, and Schulze-Wessel, Julia. 1998. *Zwischen Selbstorganisation und Stigmatisierung: Die Lebenswirklichkeit jüdischer Displaced Persons und die neue Gestalt des Antisemitismus in der deutschen Nachkriegsgesellschaft*. Stuttgart: Klett-Cotta Verlag.

Dietz, Barbara, and Segbers, Klaus. 1997. "German Policies toward Russia and Other Successor States." In Rainer Münz and Myron Weiner, eds., *Migrants, Refugees, and Foreign Policy: U.S. and German Policies toward Countries of Origin*, pp. 141–164. Providence: Berghahn Books.

Dietz, Barbara, et al. 2001. "The Jewish Emigration from the Former Soviet Union to Germany." *International Migration* 40/2, pp. 29–47.

Dietzsch, Martin, et al., eds. 1999. *Endlich ein normales Volk? Vom rechten Verständnis der Friedenspreis-Rede Martin Walsers: Eine Dokumentation.* Duisburg: Duisburger Institut für Sprach- und Sozialforschung.

Diner, Dan. 1997. "Elemente der Subjektwerdung: Jüdische DPs in historischem Kontext." In Fritz Bauer Institut, ed., *Überlebt und unterwegs: Jüdische Displaced Persons im Nachkriegsdeutschland*, pp. 229–248. Frankfurt am Main: Campus Verlag.

———. 1999. *Das Jahrhundert verstehen: Eine universalgeschichtliche Deutung.* Munich: Luchterhand Verlag.

———. 2000. "'Man hat mit der Sache eigentlich nichts mehr zu tun.'" In Richard Chaim Schneider, ed., *Wir sind da! Die Geschichte der Juden in Deutschland von 1945 bis heute*, pp. 233–252. Berlin: Ullstein Verlag.

———. 2007. *Gegenläufige Gedächtnisse über Geltung und Wirkung des Holocaust.* Göttingen: Vandenhoeck & Ruprecht.

———. 2008a. "Ambiguous Semantics: Reflections on Jewish Political Concepts." *Jewish Quarterly Review* 98/1 (Winter), pp. 89–102.

———. 2008b. "Residues of Empire: The Paradigmatic Meaning of Jewish Trans-territorial Experience for an Integrated European History." In Y. Michal Bodemann, ed., *The New German Jewry and the European Context: The Return of the European Jewish Diaspora*, pp. 33–49. New York: Palgrave Macmillan.

———. 2010. "Skizze zu einer jüdischen Geschichte der Juden in Deutschland nach '45." In *Münchner Beiträge zur Jüdischen Geschichte und Kultur* 4/1, pp. 8–16.

Dinnerstein, Leonhard. 1982. *America and the Survivors of the Holocaust.* New York: Columbia University Press.

Domansky, Elisabeth. 1992. "'Kristallnacht,' the Holocaust and German Unity: The Meaning of November 9 as an Anniversary in Germany." *History & Memory* 4, pp. 60–94.

Döring-Manteuffel, Anselm. 2007. "Nach dem Boom: Brüche und Kontinuitäten der Industriemoderne seit 1970." *Vierteljahrshefte für Zeitgeschichte* 55, pp. 559–581.

Dörner, Dieter. 2009. "Die neuzeitlichen Judengemeinden in Amberg." In Michael Brenner and Renate Höpfinger, eds., *Die Juden in der Oberpfalz*, pp. 119–137. Munich: Oldenbourg Verlag.

Douglas, Mary. 1990. Foreword. In Marcel Mauss, ed., *The Gift: The Form and Reason for Exchange in Archaic Societies*, pp. vii–xviii. London: Routledge.

Douma, Eva. 1994. "Ausgegrenzt und verdrängt im 'Dritten Reich'—Ungeliebt in der Bundesrepublik: Die jüdischen Rechtsanwälte." In Arno Herzig et al., eds., *Verdrängung und Vernichtung der Juden in Westfalen*, pp. 215–223. Münster: Ardrey Verlag.

Dreesen, Renate, and Dror-Batalion, Lea, eds. 2011. *Die Jüdische Berufsfachschule in Masada Darmstadt.* Exhibition catalog. Darmstadt: Renate Dreesen.

Drummer, Heike, and Zwilling, Jutta. 2007. "Von der Grüneburg zum Campus Westend: Die Geschichte des IG Farben-Hauses." Exhibition catalog published by der Johann Wolfgang Goethe Universität, Frankfurt am Main.

Eichener, Volker. 2000. *Die unternehmerische Wohnungswirtschaft: Emanzipation einer Branche, der Strukturwandel der deutschen Wohnungswirtschaft seit dem ausgehenden 19. Jahrhundert.* Frankfurt am Main: F. Knapp.

Elkan, Hugo. 1959. *Festschrift zu Weihe der Neuen Essener Synagoge am 19. Tischri 5720, dem 21. Oktober 1959, bürgerliche Zeitrechnung.* Düsseldorf-Benrath.

Engel, David. 1998. "Patterns of Anti-Jewish Violence in Poland, 1944–1946." *Yad Vashem Studies* 26, pp. 43–85.

———. 2008. "Poland since 1939." In Gershon Hundert, ed., *The YIVO Encyclopedia of Jews in Eastern Europe*, vol. 2, p. 1404. New Haven, Conn.: Yale University Press.

Erhard, Ludwig. 2002. "Regierungserklärung vom 10. November 1965." In Klaus Stüwe, ed., *Die großen Regierungserklärungen der deutschen Bundeskanzler von Adenauer bis Schröder*, pp. 121–145. Opladen: Westdeutscher Verlag.

Erker, Paul, ed. 2004. *Rechnung für Hitlers Krieg: Aspekte und Probleme des Lastenausgleichs.* Heidelberg: Regionalkultur Verlag.

Eschwege, Helmut. 1991. *Fremd unter meinesgleichen: Erinnerungen eines Dresdner Juden.* Berlin: Cristoph Links Verlag.

Essig, Rolf-Bernhard. 2000. *Der offene Brief: Geschichte und Funktion einer publizistischen Form von Isokrates bis Günter Grass.* Würzburg: Königshausen & Neumann.

Faber, Richard. 2009. "'Theokratie von oben versus Theokratie von unten': Die Antipoden Hans-Joachim Schoeps und Jacob Taubes." In Gideon Botsch et al., eds., *Wider den Zeitgeist: Studien zum Leben und Werk von Hans-Joachim Schoeps (1909–1980)*, pp. 63–92. Hildesheim: Olms Vrlag.

Fabian, Roberto. 1999. "Ein Erbe als Herausforderung: Die jüdische Gemeinde Frankfurt am Main von 1945 bis heute." *Tribüne* 38/149, pp. 186–200.

Fassl, Peter, et al., eds. 2011. *Nach der Shoa: Jüdische Displaced Persons in Bayerisch-Schwaben 1945–1951.* Munich: UVK Verlagsgesellschaft.

Fassmann, Heinz, and Münz, Rainer. 1994. "European East–West Migration, 1945–1992." *International Migration Review* 28/3 (Fall), pp. 520–538.

Faulenbach, Bernd. 2004. "Die Siebzigerjahre—ein sozialdemokratisches Jahrzehnt?" *Archiv für Sozialgeschichte* 44, pp. 1–37.

Fehrenbach, Heide. 2005. *Race after Hitler: Black Occupation Children in Postwar Germany and America.* Princeton, N.J.: Princeton University Press.

Feinberg, Anat. 1988. *Wiedergutmachung im Programm: Jüdisches Schicksal im deutschen Nachkriegsdrama.* Cologne: Prometh Verlag.

Feldman, Lily Gardner. 2003. "Annäherung, Widerstreben und Ablehnung: Das Dreiecksverhältnis zwischen Deutschland, Israel und dem amerikanischen Judentum." In Frank Stern and Maria Gierlinger, eds., *Die deutsch-jüdische Erfahrung: Beiträge zum kulturellen Dialog*, pp. 309–330. Berlin: Aufbau Verlag.

Ferencz, Benjamin B. 1979. *Less Than Slaves: Jewish Forced Labor and the Quest for Compensation.* Cambridge, Mass.: Harvard University Press.

Filbinger, Hans. 1994. *Die geschmähte Generation: Politische Erinnerungen.* 3rd expanded ed. Esslingen: Bechtle.

Finder, Gabriel N. 2008. "'Boxing for Everyone': Jewish DPs, Sports, and Boxing." *Studies in Contemporary Jewry: Jews and the Sporting Life; an Annual* 23, pp. 36–53.

Finder, Gabriel N., and Jockusch, Laura, eds. 2015. *Jewish Honor Courts: Revenge, Retribution and Reconciliation in Europe and Israel after the Holocaust.* Detroit: Wayne State University Press.

Fischer, Erika. 1995. *Aimée & Jaguar: A Love Story.* Translated by Edna McCown. New York: HarperCollins.

Fischer, Torben, and Lorenz, Matthias N., eds. 2007. *Lexikon der "Vergangenheitsbewältigung" in Deutschland. Debatten- und Diskursgeschichte des Nationalsozialismus nach 1945.* Bielefeld: transcript Verlag.

Fleischmann, Lea. 1980. *Dies ist nicht mein Land: Eine Jüdin verläßt die Bundesrepublik.* Munich: Hoffmann und Campe.

Fleyer, Eduard. 2010. "Kontingentflüchtlinge: Eine Statusbeschreibung." In Dmitrij Belkin and Raphael Gross, eds., *Ausgerechnet Deutschland! Jüdisch-russische Einwanderung in die Bundesrepublik.* Publication accompanying the exhibition at the Jewish Museum Frankfurt, March 12–July 25, 2010, pp. 76–78. Berlin: Nikolaische Verlagsbuchhandlung.

Foschepoth, Josef. 1991. "'Helfen Sie uns, und Sie helfen Deutschland . . .': Die Anfänge der Gesellschaften für christlich-jüdische Zusammenarbeit." In Wolfgang Benz, ed., *Zwischen Antisemitismus und Philosemitismus: Juden in der Bundesrepublik,* pp. 63–70. Berlin: Metropol Verlag.

———. 2001. "Die Gründung der Gesellschaften für christlich-jüdische Zusammenarbeit." In Julius H. Schoeps, ed., *Leben im Land der Täter: Juden im Nachkriegsdeutschland (1945–1952),* pp. 254–264. Berlin: Jüdische Verlagsanstalt.

Foschepoth, Josef, and Jochmann, Werner. 1993. *Im Schatten der Vergangenheit: Die Anfänge der Gesellschaften für christlich-jüdische Zusammenarbeit.* Göttingen: Vandenhoeck & Ruprecht.

Frei, Norbert. 2002. *Adenauer's Germany and the Nazi Past: The Politics of Amnesty and Integration.* Foreword by Fritz Stern. Translated by Joel Golb. New York: Columbia University Press.

———. 2008. *1968: Jugendrevolte und globaler Protest.* 3rd ed. Munich: C. H. Beck.

———. 2009. *1945 und wir: Das Dritte Reich im Bewußtsein der Deutschen.* Munich: C. H. Beck.

Frei, Norbert, et al., eds. 2009. *Die Praxis der Wiedergutmachung: Geschichte, Erfahrung und Wirkung in Deutschland und Israel.* Göttingen: Wallstein Verlag.

Freimark, Peter. 1989. "Vom Hamburger Umgang mit der Geschichte einer Minderheit: Vorgeschichte und Gründung des Instituts für die Geschichte der deutschen Juden." *Zeitschrift des Vereins für Hamburgische Geschichte* 74/75, pp. 100–106.

Freimüller, Tobias. 2009. "Max Horkheimer und die Jüdische Gemeinde Frankfurt am Main nach 1945." In Monika Boll and Raphael Gross, eds., *Die Frankfurter Schule und Frankfurt: Eine Rückkehr nach Deutschland,* pp. 150–158. Göttingen: Wallstein Verlag.

———. 2010a. "Frankfurt am Main—intellektuelles Zentrum jüdischen Lebens in der Bundesrepublik." *Münchner Beiträge zur Jüdischen Geschichte und Kultur* 4/1, pp. 78–90.

———. 2010b. "Mehr als eine Religionsgemeinschaft: Jüdisches Leben in Frankfurt am Main nach 1945." In *Zeithistorische Forschungen / Studies in Contemporary History* 7/3, pp. 386–407.

Friedgut, Theodore H. 2010. "Warum sie gingen: Gründe für die jüdische Emigration aus der Sowjetunion, 1973–2000." In Dmitrij Belkin and Raphael Gross, eds., *Ausgerechnet Deutschland! Jüdisch-russische Einwanderung in die Bundesrepublik.* Publication accompanying the exhibition at the Jewish Museum Frankfurt, March 12–July 25, 2010, pp. 38–41. Berlin: Nikolaische Verlagsbuchhandlung.

Friedla, Katarina. 2010. "Von Breslau nach Erfurt." *Münchner Beiträge zur Jüdischen Geschichte und Kultur* 4/1, pp. 42–56.

Friedman, Maurice S. 1988. *Martin Buber's Life and Work: The Later Years, 1945–1965.* Detroit: Wayne State University Press.

Fritz Bauer Institut, ed. 1997. *Überlebt und unterwegs: Jüdische Displaced Persons im Nachkriegsdeutschland*. Frankfurt am Main: Campus Verlag.

Fröhlich, Elke. 1988. "Philipp Auerbach (1906–1952): 'Generalanwalt für Wiedergutmachung.'" In Manfred Treml and Wolf Weigand, eds., *Geschichte und Kultur der Juden in Bayern: Lebensläufe*, pp. 315–320. Munich: K. G. Saur.

Fuchs, Abraham. 1995. *The Shoah in Rabbinical Sources* (in Hebrew). Jerusalem.

Fulbrook, Mary. 2005. *The People's State: East German Society from Hitler to Honecker*. New Haven, Conn.: Yale University Press.

Gabowitsch, Mischa. 2010. "Pogromgerüchte in der UdSSR der Perestroika-Zeit." In Dmitrij Belkin and Raphael Gross, eds., *Ausgerechnet Deutschland! Jüdisch-russische Einwanderung in die Bundesrepublik*. Publication accompanying the exhibition at the Jewish Museum Frankfurt, March 12–July 25, 2010, pp. 42–45. Berlin: Nikolaische Verlagsbuchhandlung.

Galinski, Heinz. 1997. "New Beginning of Jewish Life in Berlin." In Michael Brenner, *After the Holocaust: Rebuilding Jewish Lives in Postwar Germany*, pp. 100–102. Princeton, N.J.: Princeton University Press.

Gallas, Elisabeth. 2010. "Bewahren und Erneuern: Zur Restitution jüdischer Kulturgüter nach 1945." In Birgit Hofmann et al., eds., *Diktaturüberwindung in Europa: Neue nationale und transnationale Perspektiven*, pp. 21–35. Heidelberg: Universitätsverlag Winter.

———. 2011. "Das Retten der Bücher: Vom Offenbacher Depot zum jüdischen Geschichtsdenken nach dem Holocaust." Ph.D. diss., University of Leipzig.

———. 2012. *"Das Leichenhaus der Bücher": Kulturrestitution und jüdisches Geschichtsdenken nach 1945*. Göttingen: Vandenhoeck & Ruprecht.

Ganther, Heinz, ed. 1959. *Die Juden in Deutschland, 1951/52, 1958/59: Ein Almanach*. Hamburg: Gala Verlag.

Gar, Yosef. 1957. "Bafrayte yidn." *Fun noentn over* 3, pp. 77–188. New York.

———. 1959. "Bafrayte yidn: Tsu der geshikhte fun der sheyres-hapleyte in der amerikaner zone in Daytshland (hemshekh fun band III)." *Fun noentn over* 4, pp. 235–299. New York.

Gay, Ruth. 2002. *Safe among the Germans: Liberated Jews after World War II*. New Haven, Conn.: Yale University Press.

Geis, Jael. 1999. *Übrig sein Leben "danach": Juden deutscher Herkunft in der britischen und amerikanischen Zone Deutschlands, 1945–1949*. Berlin: Philo & Philo Fine Arts.

———. 2010. "Baruch Graubard: 'Ein für das Gemeinwohl tätiger Mensch, Erzieher, Schriftsteller, dem Massaker Entkommener, Erneuerer der Kultur.'" *Nurinst: Beiträge zur deutschen und jüdischen Geschichte*, pp. 63–79.

Gelber, Yoav. 1983. *Jewish-Palestinian Volunteers in the British Army during World War Two. Volume 3: Mission of Rescue for the Jewish People* (in Hebrew). Jerusalem: Yad Izhak Ben-Zvi.

Gelber, Yoav. 2005. "The Meeting between the Jewish Soldiers from Eretz Israel and the Surviving Remnant." In I. Gutman and A. Saf, eds., *She'erit Hapletah, 1944–1948: Rehabilitation and Political Struggle*, pp. 60–79. Proceedings of the Yad Vashem sixth international conference, Jerusalem, 1985.

Geller, Jay H. 2005. *Jews in Post-Holocaust Germany, 1945–1953*. Cambridge: Cambridge University Press.

———. 2006. "Theodor Heuss and German-Jewish Reconciliation after 1945." *German Politics and Society* 24/2 (Summer), pp. 1–22.

Gemeinhardt, Anne. 2008. "Der Wiederaufbau jüdischen Lebens im Saarland nach 1945." Master's thesis, LMU Munich.

———. 2010. "Der Saarländische Sonderweg: Die Synagogengemeinde Saar 1947–1955." *Münchner Beiträge zur jüdischen Geschichte und Kultur* 4/1, pp. 26–41.

Georgi, Viola. 2003. *Entliehene Erinnerung: Geschichtsbilder junger Migranten in Deutschland*. Hamburg: Hamburger Edition.

Gesellschaft für christlich-jüdische Zusammenarbeit Celle e. V., ed. 2005. *Jüdisches Leben in Celle nach 1945*. Bielefeld: Verlag für Regionalgeschichte.

Giere, Jacqueline. 1997. "Einleitung." In Fritz Bauer Institut, ed., *Überlebt und unterwegs: Jüdische Displaced Persons im Nachkriegsdeutschland*, pp. 13–26. Frankfurt am Main: Campus Verlag.

Gillis, Fritz, and Knopf, H. 1944. *The Reparation Claim of the Jewish People*. Tel Aviv: Edition Olympia.

Gilman, Sander L. 1995. *Jews in Today's German Culture*. Bloomington: Indiana University Press.

Gilman, Sander L., and Remmler, Karen, eds. 1994. Re-emerging Jewish Culture in Germany: Life and Literature since 1989. New York: New York University Press.

Ginsburg, Hans Jakob. 2004. "Der Lebensretter." *Trumah* 14, pp. 15–36.

Ginzel, Günther B. 1996. *Der Anfang nach dem Ende: Jüdisches Leben in Deutschland 1945 bis heute*. Düsseldorf: Droste Verlag.

Giordano, Ralph. 1990. *Die zweite Schuld oder Von der Last, ein Deutscher zu sein*. Munich: Knaur.

———. 1993. *Wird Deutschland wieder gefährlich? Mein Brief an Kanzler Kohl—Ursachen und Folgen*. Cologne: Kiepenheuer & Witsch.

———. 2007. "Erinnerungen eines Davongekommenen." In *Die Autobiographie*. Cologne: Kiepenheuer & Witsch.

Gitelmann, Zvi, ed. 1997. *Bitter Legacy: Confronting the Holocaust in the USSR*. Bloomington: Indiana University Press.

———. 2003. "Becoming Jewish in Russia and Ukraine." In Zvi Gitelmann et al., eds., *New Jewish Identities: Contemporary Europe and Beyond*, pp. 105–138. Budapest: Central European University Press.

Godbout, Jacques T. 1998. *The World of the Gift*. Montreal: McGill-Queen's University Press.

Goldberg, Jacob. 1991. "Die jüdischen Gutspächter in Polen-Litauen und die Bauern im 17. und 18. Jahrhundert." In Manfred Alexander et al., eds., *Kleine Völker in der Geschichte Osteuropas: Festschrift für Günther Stöckl zum 75. Geburtstag*, pp. 13–21. Stuttgart: Franz Steiner Verlag.

———. 2008. "Tavernkeeping." In *The YIVO Encyclopedia of Jews in Eastern Europe*, vol. 2, pp. 1849–1852. New Haven, Conn.: Yale University Press.

Goldberg, Jakob. 1979. ". . . ist ein Mittel zur Ablenkung geblieben." In Henryk M. Broder and Michel R. Lang, *Fremd im eigenen Land: Juden in der Bundesrepublik*, pp. 190–249. Frankfurt am Main: Fischer Taschenbuch Verlag.

Goldlust, John. 2012. "A Different Silence: The Survival of More Than 200,000 Polish Jews in the Soviet Union during World War II as a Case Study in Cultural Amnesia." *Australian Jewish Historical Journal* 21/1, pp. 13–60.

Goldmann, Nahum. 1980. *Mein Leben als deutscher Jude*. Munich: Langen Müller.

Goldschmidt, Helmut. 1959. "Zum Aufbau der Synagoge Roonstraße." In Wilhelm Unger, ed., *Zur Weihe der wiederhergestellten Synagoge Roonstraße und des jüdischen Kulturzentrums in Köln*, pp. 29–32. Cologne: Synagogen-Gemeinde Köln.

Goldstein-Lackó, Georgette. 1961. *Die Geschichte des Rabbi Goldstein in Berlin: Eine Dokumentation aus den Jahren 1957 bis 1961*. Tübingen: Heos Verlag.

Gorelik, Lena. 2010. "Russen statt Einsteins: Wie die Zuwanderung der osteuropäischen Juden das jüdische Leben in Deutschland veränderte." In Y. Michal Bodemann and Micha Brumlik, eds., *Juden in Deutschland—Deutschland in den Juden: Neue Perspektiven*, pp. 167–171. Göttingen: Wallstein Verlag.

Goschler, Constantin. 1989. "Der Fall Philipp Auerbach: Wiedergutmachung in Bayern." In Ludolf Herbst and Constantin Goschler, eds., *Wiedergutmachung in der Bundesrepublik Deutschland*, pp. 77–98. Munich: Oldenbourg Verlag.

———. 1992. *Wiedergutmachung: Westdeutschland und die Verfolgten des Nationalsozialismus 1945–1954*. Munich: Oldenbourg Verlag.

———. 1993. "Paternalismus und Verweigerung: Die DDR und die Wiedergutmachung für jüdische Verfolgte des Nationalsozialismus." *Jahrbuch für Antisemitismusforschung* 2, pp. 93–117.

———. 2002. "Die Politik der Rückerstattung in Westdeutschland." In Constantin Goschler and Jürgen Lillteicher, eds., *"Arisierung" und Restitution: Die Rückerstattung jüdischen Eigentums in Deutschland und Österreich nach 1945 und 1989*, pp. 99–125. Göttingen: Wallstein Verlag.

———. 2007. *Schuld und Schulden: Die Politik der Wiedergutmachung für NS-Verfolgte seit 1945*. 2nd ed. Göttingen: Wallstein Verlag.

———, ed. 2012. *Die Entschädigung von NS-Zwangsarbeit am Anfang des 21. Jahrhunderts*. 4 vols. Göttingen: Wallstein Verlag.

Goschler, Constantin, and Graf, Rüdiger. 2010. *Europäische Zeitgeschichte seit 1945*. Berlin: Akademie Verlag.

Goschler, Constantin, and Lillteicher, Jürgen, eds. 2002. *"Arisierung" und Restitution: Die Rückerstattung jüdischen Eigentums in Deutschland und Österreich nach 1945 und 1989*. Göttingen: Wallstein Verlag.

Gosewinkel, Dieter. 1991. *Adolf Arndt: Die Wiederbegründung des Rechtsstaats aus dem Geist der Sozialdemokratie (1945–1961)*. Bonn: Verlag J. H. W. Dietz Nachf.

Gottwald, Astrid. 1997. "Jews in Germany: Israeli Perceptions in the 1950s." *Tel Aviver Jahrbuch für deutsche Geschichte* 26, pp. 455–477.

Gotzmann, Andreas. 1994. "Rabbiner und Bann: Zur Problematik der Analyse und Bewertung zweier Topoi des aufklärerischen Diskurses." *Aschkenas: Zeitschrift für Geschichte und Kultur der Juden* 4/1, pp. 99–127.

Government of the Federal Republic of Germany, ed. 1960. *The Anti-Semitic and Nazi Incidents from 25 December 1959 until 28 January 1960*. Bonn: Government of the Federal Republic of Germany.

Grabitz, Helge, et al., eds. 1994. *Die Normalität des Verbrechens: Bilanz und Perspektiven der Forschung zu den nationalsozialistischen Gewaltverbrechen; Festschrift für Wolfgang Scheffler zum 65. Geburtstag*. Berlin: Hentrich Verlag.

Graml, Hermann. 1953. *Der 9. November 1938: Reichskristallnacht*. Bonn: Bundeszentrale für Heimatdienst.

Grammes, Philipp. 2006. "Ichud Landsberg gegen Makabi München: Der Sport im DP-Lager, 1945–1948." In Michael Brenner and Gideon Reuveni, eds., *Emanzipation durch Muskelkraft: Juden und Sport in Europa*, pp. 190–215. Göttingen: Vandenhoeck & Ruprecht.

Granata, Cora. 2009. "The Cold War Politics of Cultural Minorities: Jews and Sorbs in the German Democratic Republic, 1976–1989." *German History* 27, pp. 60–83.

Greenberg, Moshe, and Cohn, Haim Hermann. 2007. "Herem." In *Encyclopaedia Judaica*, vol. 9, 2nd ed., pp. 10–16. Detroit: Macmillan Reference.

Gringauz, Samuel. 1948. "Our New German Policy and the DPs: Why Immediate Resettlement Is Imperative." *Commentary* 5, pp. 508–514.

Grobman, Alex. 2004. *Battling for Souls: The Vaad Hatzala Rescue Committee in Post-Holocaust Europe*. Jersey City: KTAV Publishing House.

Grodzinsky, Yosef. 2004. *In the Shadow of the Holocaust: The Struggle between Jews and Zionists in the Aftermath of World War II*. Monro: Common Courage Press.

Groehler, Olaf. 1992a. "Der Holocaust in der Geschichtsschreibung der DDR." In Ulrich Herbert and Olaf Groehler, *Zweierlei Bewältigung: Vier Beiträge über den Umgang mit der NS Vergangenheit in den beiden deutschen Staaten*, pp. 41–66. Hamburg: Ergebnisse Verlag.

———. 1992b. "Erblasten: Der Umgang mit dem Holocaust in der DDR." In Hanno Loewy, ed., *Holocaust: Die Grenzen des Verstehens; Eine Debatte über die Besetzung der Geschichte*, pp. 110–127. Reinbek bei Hamburg: Rowohlt Verlag.

———. 1994. "Der Umgang mit dem Holocaust in der DDR." In Rolf Steininger, ed., *Der Umgang mit dem Holocaust: Europa–USA–Israel*, pp. 233–245. Vienna: Böhlau Verlag.

Gross, Jan T. 1991. "The Sovietization of Western Ukraine and Western Byelorussia." In Norman Davies and Antony Polonsky, eds., *Jews in Eastern Poland and the USSR, 1939–1946*, pp. 60–76. New York: St. Martin's Press.

———. 2006. *Fear: Anti-Semitism in Poland after Auschwitz*. New York: Random House.

Gross, Leonard. 1982. *The Last Jews in Berlin*. New York: Simon and Schuster.

Gross, Nachum, ed. 1975. *Economic History of the Jews*. Jerusalem: Keter Publishing House.

Grossmann, Atina. 1995. *Reforming Sex: The German Movement for Birth Control and Abortion Reform, 1920–1950*. New York: Oxford University Press.

———. 2005. "Versions of Home: German Jewish Refugee Papers out of the Closet and into the Archives." *New German Critique*, Fall, pp. 95–122.

———. 2007. *Jews, Germans, and Allies: Close Encounters in Occupied Germany*. Princeton, N.J.: Princeton University Press.

———. 2009a. "From Victims to 'Homeless Foreigners': Jewish Survivors in Postwar Germany." In Rita Chin et al., *After the Nazi Racial State: Difference and Democracy in Germany and Europe*, pp. 55–79. Ann Arbor: University of Michigan Press.

———. 2009b. "Living On: Remembering Feldafing." In Jürgen Matthäus, ed., *Approaching an Auschwitz Survivor: Holocaust Testimony and Its Transformations*, pp. 79–85. New York: Oxford University Press.

———. 2012a. "Remapping Relief and Rescue: Flight, Displacement, and International Aid for Jewish Refugees during World War II." *New German Critique* 39/3, pp. 61–79.

———. 2012b. *Wege in der Fremde: Deutsch-jüdische Begegnungsgeschichte zwischen Feldafing, New York und Teheran*. Göttingen: Wallstein Verlag.

———. 2015. *Remapping Survival: Jewish Refugees and Lost Memories of Displacement, Trauma, and Rescue in Soviet Central Asia, Iran, and India*. Princeton, N.J.: Princeton University Press, 2015.

Grossmann, Kurt R. 1951. *The Jewish DP Problem*. New York: Institute of Jewish Affairs, World Jewish Congress.

Grove-Pollak, Fay, ed. 1970. *The Saga of a Movement: WIZO 1920–1970*. Tel Aviv: Department of Organisation & Education of Wizo.

Gruber, Ruth Ellen. 2002. *Virtually Jewish: Reinventing Jewish Culture in Europe*. Berkeley: University of California Press.

Gruber, Ruth. 2007. *Exodus 1947: The Ship That Launched a Nation*. New York: Union Square Press.

Grüner, Frank. 2006. "Die Tragödie von Babij Jar im sowjetischen Gedächtnis: Künstlerische Erinnerung versus offizielles Schweigen." In Frank Grüner et al., eds., *"Zerstörer des Schweigens": Formen künstlerischer Erinnerung an die nationalsozialistische Rassen- und Vernichtungspolitik in Osteuropa*, pp. 57–96. Cologne: Böhlau Verlag.

Gutman, Israel, and Saf, Avital, eds. 1990. *She'erit Hapletah, 1944–1948: Rehabilitation and Political Struggle*. Proceedings of the Sixth Yad Vashem International Historical Conference, Jerusalem, October 1985. Jerusalem: Yad Vashem.

Hahn, Hans-Joachim. 2007. "Die Rolle von Ignatz Bubis in der Walser-Bubis-Debatte." In Fritz Backhaus et al., eds., *Ignatz Bubis: Ein jüdisches Leben in Deutschland*, pp. 149–155. Frankfurt am Main: Jüdischer Verlag im Suhrkamp Verlag.

Halamish, Aviva. 1998. *The Exodus Affair: Holocaust Survivors and the Struggle for Palestine*. Syracuse, N.Y.: Syracuse University Press.

Haller, Roman. 2001. *Davidstern und Lederhose: Eine Kindheit in der Nachkriegszeit*. Zürich: Pendo Verlag.

———, ed. 2004. *. . . und bleiben wollte keiner: Jüdische Lebensgeschichten im Nachkriegsbayern*. Hamburg: Dölling und Galitz.

Hansen, Niels. 2002. *Aus dem Schatten der Katastrophe: Die deutsch-israelischen Beziehungen in der Ära Konrad Adenauer und David Ben Gurion*. Düsseldorf: Droste Verlag.

Harris, Paul. 1998. "Jewish Immigration to the New Germany: The Policy Making Process Leading to the Adoption of the 1991 Quota Refugee Law." In Dietrich Thränhardt, ed., *Einwanderung und Einbürgerung in Deutschland: Jahrbuch Migration 1997/1998*, pp. 105–147. Münster: LIT Verlag.

———. 2007. "Russischsprachige Juden in Deutschland." In Klaus J. Bade et al., eds., *Enzyklopädie Migration in Europa: Vom 17. Jahrhundert bis zur Gegenwart*, pp. 37–38. Paderborn: Schöningh Verlag.

Hartewig, Karin. 1993. "Eine dritte *Identität*? Jüdische Kommunisten in der Gründergeneration der DDR." In Elke Scherstjanoi, ed., *"Provisorium für längstens ein Jahr": Die Gründung der DDR*, pp. 292–302. Berlin: Akademie Verlag.

———. 2000. *Zurückgekehrt: Die Geschichte der jüdischen Kommunisten in der DDR*. Cologne: Böhlau Verlag.

Haug, Sonja. 2007. *Sozialdemographische Merkmale, Berufsstruktur und Verwandtschaftsnetzwerke jüdischer Zuwanderer*. Working Paper 8. Nuremberg: Bundesamt für Migration und Flüchtlinge.

Haug, Sonja, and Wolf, Michael. 2006. "Jüdische Zuwanderung nach Deutschland." In Sonja Haug and Frank Swiaczny, eds., *Neue Zuwanderergruppen in Deutschland: Materialien zur Bevölkerungswissenschaft*, pp. 65–82. Wiesbaden: Bundesinstitut für Bevölkerung.

Haunfelder, Bernd. 2006. *Nordrhein-Westfalen: Land und Leute, 1946–2006; Ein biographisches Handbuch*. Münster: Aschendorff Verlag.

Haury, Thomas. 2002. *Antisemitismus von links, Kommunistische Ideologie, Nationalismus und Antizionismus in der frühen DDR*. Hamburg: Hamburger Edition.

Heiber, Helmut. 1966. *Walter Frank und sein Reichsinstitut für Geschichte des Neuen Deutschlands*. Stuttgart: Deutsche Verlags-Anstalt.

Heikaus, Ulrike, ed. 2011. *Das war spitze! Jüdisches in der deutschen Fernsehunterhaltung*. Jüdisches Museum München. Essen: Klartext Verlag.

Heilmann, Kristina. 1989. "Die Israelitische Kultusgemeinde Nürnberg nach 1945." Master's thesis, University of Erlangen.

Heitman, Sidney. 1987. "The Third Soviet Emigration: Jewish, German and Armenian Emigration from the USSR since World War II." *Berichte des Bundesinstituts für ostwissenschaftliche und internationale Studien* 21, pp. ii, 12–19.

Held, Steffen. 1995. *Zwischen Tradition und Vermächtnis: Die israelitische Religionsgemeinde zu Leipzig nach 1945*. Hamburg: Dölling und Galitz.

Henne, Thomas, and Riedlinger, Arne, eds. 2005. *Das Lüth-Urteil aus (rechts-)historischer Sicht: Die Konflikte um Veit Harlan und die Grundrechtsjudikatur des Bundesverfassungsgerichts*. Berlin: Berliner Wissenschafts-Verlag.

Herbert, Ulrich, ed. 2002. *Wandlungsprozesse in Westdeutschland: Belastung, Integration, Liberalisierung, 1945–1980*. Göttingen: Wallstein Verlag.

Herbst, Ludolf, and Goschler, Constantin, eds. 1989. *Wiedergutmachung in der Bundesrepublik Deutschland*. Munich: Oldenbourg Verlag.

Heredia, David. 2010. "Zur Geschichte von Jewish Cultural Reconstruction, Inc." In Marie Luise Knott and David Heredia, eds., *Hannah Arendt–Gershom Scholem: Der Briefwechsel, 1939–1964*, pp. 534–552. Frankfurt am Main: Suhrkamp Verlag.

Herf, Jeffrey. 1989. "Philipp Jenninger and the Dangers of Speaking Clearly." *Partisan Review* 56, pp. 225–236.

———. 1994. "Antisemitismus in der SED: Geheime Dokumente zum Fall Paul Merker aus SED- und MfS-Archiven." *Vierteljahrshefte für Zeitgeschichte* 42, pp. 635–667.

———. 1998. *Zweierlei Erinnerung: Die NS-Vergangenheit im geteilten Deutschland*. Berlin: Propyläen Verlag.

Herman, Dana. 2008. "Hashavat Avedah: A History of Jewish Cultural Reconstruction, Inc." Ph.D. diss., Department of History, McGill University, Montreal.

Hesse, Jan O., and Kühne-Büning, Lidwina. 2005. "Wirtschaftliche Entwicklung und die Bedeutung der Wohnungs- und Immobilienwirtschaft." In Lidwina Kühne-Büning, ed., *Grundlagen der Wohnungs- und Immobilienwirtschaft*, pp. 191–211. Hamburg: Knapp Verlag.

Heuberger, Georg, ed. 1992a. *Jüdische Sozialarbeit im Wandel der Zeit: 75 Jahre Zentralwohlfahrtsstelle der Juden in Deutschland 1917–1992*. Frankfurt am Main: Jüdisches Museum.

———. 1992b. *Stationen des Vergessens: Der Börneplatzkonflikt; Begleitbuch zur Eröffnungsausstellung Museum Judengasse Frankfurt am Main*. Frankfurt am Main: Jüdisches Museum.

Heuberger, Georg, et al., eds. 1998. *Wer ein Haus baut, will bleiben: 50 Jahre Jüdische Gemeinde Frankfurt am Main; Anfänge und Gegenwart*. Frankfurt am Main: Jüdisches Museum.

Heuberger, Rachel. 1999. "Jüdische Jugend in Deutschland: Zwischen Isolation und Integration." *Tribüne* 149, pp. 114–126.

Heusler, Andreas, ed. 2007. *Biographisches Gedenkbuch der Münchner Juden 1933–1945*. 2 vols. Munich: Stadtarchiv München.

Heuss, Theodor. 1964a. "Glückwünsche zum jüdischen Neujahrsfest." In Theodor Heuss and Hans Lamm, eds., *An und über Juden: Aus Schriften und Reden (1906–1963)*, pp. 113–120. Düsseldorf: Econ-Verlag.

———. 1964b. "Mut zur Liebe." In Theodor Heuss and Hans Lamm, eds., *An und über Juden: Aus Schriften und Reden (1906–1963)*, pp. 121–127. Düsseldorf: Econ-Verlag.

———. 1964c. "Vor einer schweren Aufgabe." In Theodor Heuss and Hans Lamm, eds., *An und über Juden: Aus Schriften und Reden (1906–1963)*, pp. 161–165. Düsseldorf: Econ-Verlag.

Heymont, Irving. 1982. *Among the Survivors of the Holocaust, 1945: The Landsberg DP Camp Letters of Major Irving Heymont, United States Army*. Cincinnati: American Jewish Archives.

Hochhut, Rolf. 1964. *The Deputy*. Translated by Richard and Clara Winston. New York: Grove Press.

Hochreuter, Anna. 2000. "Zuwanderung als Wiedergutmachung? Das Verfahren der jüdischen Zuwanderung aus den Staaten auf dem Gebiet der ehemaligen Sowjetunion." *Neue Zeitschrift für Verwaltungsrecht* 19, pp. 1376–1381.

Hockerts, Hans Günter. 1989. "Anwälte der Verfolgten: Die United Restitution Organization." In Ludolf Herbst and Constantin Goschler, eds., *Wiedergutmachung in der Bundesrepublik Deutschland*, pp. 249–271. Munich: Oldenbourg Verlag.

———. 2001. "Wiedergutmachung in Deutschland: Eine historische Bilanz 1945– 2000." *Vierteljahrshefte für Zeitgeschichte* 49, pp. 167–214.

Höhn, Maria. 2002. *GIs and Fräuleins: The German-American Encounter in 1950s West Germany*. Chapel Hill: University of North Carolina Press.

———. 2008. *Amis, Cadillacs und "Negerliebchen": GIs im Nachkriegsdeutschland*. Berlin: Verlag für Berlin-Brandenburg.

Holian, Anna. 2008. "Displacement and the Postwar Reconstruction of Education: Displaced Persons at the UNRRA University of Munich, 1945–1948." *Contemporary European History* 17/2 (May), pp. 167–195.

———. 2011. *Between National Socialism and Soviet Communism: Displaced Persons in Postwar Germany*. Ann Arbor: University of Michigan Press.

———. 2012. "The Ambivalent Exception: American Occupation Policy in Postwar Germany and the Formation of Jewish Refugee Spaces." *Journal of Refugee Studies*, June, 452–473.

Honigmann, Peter. 1994. "Die Gründung der 'Vereinigung für Toratreues Judentum' 1954 in Fürth." *Nachrichten für den Jüdischen Bürger Fürths*, pp. 38–41.

———. 1997. "Talmuddrucke im Nachkriegsdeutschland." In Fritz Bauer Institut, ed., *Überlebt und unterwegs: Jüdische Displaced Persons im Nachkriegsdeutschland*, pp. 249–266. Frankfurt am Main: Campus Verlag.

———. 2004. "Das Projekt von Rabbiner Dr. Bernhard Brilling zur Errichtung eines jüdischen Zentralarchivs im Nachkriegsdeutschland." In Klaus Hödl, ed., *Historisches Bewußtsein im jüdischen Kontext*, pp. 223–241. Innsbruck: Studien Verlag.

Hughes, Michael L. 1999. *Shouldering the Burdens of Defeat: West Germany and the Reconstruction of Social Justice*. Chapel Hill: University of North Carolina Press.

Hundert, Gershon, ed. 2008. *The YIVO Encyclopedia of Jews in Eastern Europe*, vol. 2. New Haven, Conn.: Yale University Press.

Hyman, Abraham S. 1950. "Displaced Persons." *American Jewish Year Book* 51, pp. 315–324.

———. 1993. *The Undefeated.* Jerusalem: Gefen Publishing House.

Illichmann, Jutta. 1997. *Die DDR und die Juden: Die deutschlandpolitische Instrumentalisierung von Juden und Judentum durch die Partei- und Staatsführung der SBZ/DDR von 1945 bis 1990.* Frankfurt am Main: Peter Lang.

"Interview with Wolfgang Schäuble, Berlin, July 8, 2009." In Dmitrij Belkin and Raphael Gross, eds., *Ausgerechnet Deutschland! Jüdisch-russische Einwanderung in die Bundesrepublik.* Publication accompanying the exhibition at the Jewish Museum Frankfurt, March 12–July 25, 2010, p. 53. Berlin: Nikolaische Verlagsbuchhandlung.

Jablokoff, Herman. 1969. *Arum der velt mit yidish teater,* vol. 2. New York: Hebrew Actors Union.

Jacobmeyer, Wolfgang. 1983. "Jüdische Überlebende als 'Displaced Persons': Untersuchungen zur Besatzungspolitik in den deutschen Westzonen und zur Zuwanderung osteuropäischer Juden 1945–1947." *Geschichte und Gesellschaft* 9/3, pp. 421–452.

———. 1985. *Vom Zwangsarbeiter zum Heimatlosen Ausländer: Die Displaced Persons in Westdeutschland, 1945–1951.* Göttingen: Vandenhoeck & Ruprecht.

Jelinek, Yeshayahu A. 1988. "Like an Oasis in the Desert: The Israel Consulate in Munich, 1948– 1953." *Studies in Zionism* 9/1, pp. 81–98.

———. 1997. "Implementing the Luxembourg Agreement: The Purchasing Mission and the Israeli Economy." *Journal of Israeli History* 18/2, pp. 191–210.

———. 2004. *Deutschland und Israel 1945–1965: Ein neurotisches Verhältnis.* Munich: Oldenbourg Verlag.

Jelinek, Yeshayahu A., and Blasius, Rainer. 1997. "Ben Gurion und Adenauer im Waldorf Astoria: Gesprächsaufzeichnungen vom israelisch-deutschen Gipfeltreffen in New York am 14. März 1960." *Vierteljahrshefte für Zeitgeschichte* 45/2, pp. 309–344.

Jochims, Sigrun. 1998. "Juden in Schleswig-Holstein nach 1945." In Ole Harck, ed., *Jüdische Vergangenheit—Jüdische Zukunft,* pp. 91–100. Kiel: Landeszentrale für Politische Bildung Schleswig-Holstein.

Jochims-Bozic, Sigrun. 2004. *"Lübeck ist nur eine kurze Station auf dem jüdischen Wanderweg": Jüdisches Leben in Schleswig-Holstein 1945–1950.* Berlin: Metropol.

Jockusch, Laura. 2006. "Jüdische Geschichtsforschung im Lande Amaleks: Jüdische historische Kommissionen in Deutschland 1945–1949." In Susanne Schönborn, ed., *Zwischen Erinnerung und Neubeginn: Zur deutsch-jüdischen Geschichte nach 1945,* pp. 20–41. Munich: Peter Lang.

———. 2007. "'Khurbn Forshung': Jewish Historical Commissions in Europe, 1943–1949." *Jahrbuch des Simon-Dubnow-Instituts* 6, pp. 441–473.

———. 2012. *"Collect and Record!": Jewish Holocaust Documentation in Postwar Europe.* New York: Oxford University Press.

Jockusch, Laura, and Lewinsky, Tamar. 2010. "Paradise Lost? Postwar Memory of Polish Jewish Survival in the Soviet Union." *Holocaust and Genocide Studies* 24/3, pp. 373–399.

Jonas, Hans. 2008. *Memoirs.* Ed. Christian Wiese, trans. Krishna Winston. Hanover, N.H.: University Press of New England.

Joseph, Detlev. 2010. *Die DDR und die Juden: Eine kritische Untersuchung.* Berlin: Das Neue Berlin.

Kaczerginski, Shmerke. 1955. "Bitokhn, amkho!" *Shmerke Katsherginski ondenk-bukh,* pp. 424–427. Buenos Aires.

Kaganovitch, Albert. 2010. "Jewish Refugees and Soviet Authorities during World War II." *Yad Vashem Studies* 38/2, pp. 85–121.

———. 2012. "Stalin's Great Power Politics, the Return of Jewish Refugees to Poland, and Continued Migration to Palestine, 1944–1946." *Holocaust and Genocide Studies* 26 (Spring), pp. 59–94.

Kahane, Charlotte. 1999. *Rescue and Abandonment: The Complex Fate of Jews in Nazi Germany*. Melbourne: Scribe.

Kalman, Matthew. 1987. *The Kids Are Alright: Chapters in the History of the World Union of Jewish Students*. Jerusalem: Union of Jewish Students.

Kaminer, Wladimir. 2002. *Russian Disco*. Translated by Michael Hulse. London: Ebury.

Käpernick, Thomas. 2008. "Berthold Simonsohn." *Tribüne* 187, pp. 175–182.

Kaplan, Israel. 1947. *In der togteglekher historisher arbet: Fortrag gehaltn af dem tsuzamenfor fun di historishe komisyes, Minkhen, dem 12tn may 1947*. Munich.

Kaplan, Marion A. 1998. *Between Dignity and Despair: Jewish Life in Nazi Germany*. New York: Oxford University Press.

Kaplan, Yosef. 2008. "Amsterdam, the Forbidden Lands, and the Dynamics of the Sephardi Diaspora." In Yosef Kaplan, ed., *The Dutch Intersection: The Jews and the Netherlands in Modern History*. pp. 33–62. Leiden: Brill.

Kapralik, Charles I. 1962. *Reclaiming the Nazi Loot*. London: Sidnew Press.

Karbach, Oscar. 1962. "The Evolution of Jewish Political Thought." In *The Institute Anniversary Volume (1941–1961)*, pp. 23–48. New York: Institute for Jewish Affairs.

Kardorff, Ursula von. 1962. *Berliner Aufzeichnungen aus den Jahren 1942 bis 1945*. Munich: Biederstein Verlag.

Karger-Karin, Mendel, ed. 1966. *Israel und Wir: Keren Hajessod-Jahrbuch der jüdischen Gemeinschaft in Deutschland 1955–1965*. Frankfurt am Main: Verlag des Keren Hajessod.

———. 1970. *Israel und Wir: Keren Hayessod-Jahrbuch 1967–1970*. Frankfurt am Main: Verlag des Keren Hajessod.

Kasel, Walter. 1960. "Die jüdische Gemeinde." In *Saarbrücken 1909–1959: 50 Jahre Großstadt*, pp. 226–231. Saarbrücken: Kulturdezernat der Stadt Saarbrücken.

Kashi, Uriel. 2005. "Religiöse und kulturelle Identität jüdischer Studenten in West-Deutschland zwischen 1968 und 1989: Eine Untersuchung am Beispiel der Geschichte des Bundesverbandes jüdischer Studenten in Deutschland." Master's thesis, Free University of Berlin.

Katcher, Leo. 1968. *Post Mortem: The Jews in Germany Today*. London: Hamilton.

Katsherginski, Shmerke. 1955. "Yidishe lager-institutsyes in Daytshland." *Shmerke-Katsherginski ondenk-bukh*, pp. 432–435. Buenos Aires.

Kauders, Anthony D. 2004. *Democratization and the Jews, Munich, 1945–1965*. Lincoln: University of Nebraska Press.

———. 2007. *Unmögliche Heimat: Eine deutsch-jüdische Geschichte der Bundesrepubli*. Munich: Deutsche Verlags-Anstalt.

———. 2008. "Heimat ausgeschlossen: Von Schuldgefühlen im falschen Land." In Irmela von der Lühe et al., eds., *"Auch in Deutschland waren wir nicht wirklich zu Hause": Jüdische Remigration nach 1945*, pp. 86–100. Göttingen: Wallstein Verlag.

Kauders, Anthony D., and Lewinsky, Tamar. 2006. "Neuanfang mit Zweifeln (1945–1970)." In Richard Bauer and Michael Brenner, eds., *Jüdisches München: Vom Mittelalter bis zur Gegenwart*, pp. 185–208. Munich: C. H. Beck.

Kaufmann, Uri R., ed. 1994. *Jewish Life in Germany Today*. Bonn: Inter Nationes.

Kavanaugh, Sarah. 2008. *ORT, the Second World War and the Rehabilitation of Holocaust Survivors.* London: Vallentine Mitchell.

Keilson-Lauritz, Marita. 2009. "Hans-Joachim Schoeps, Hans Blüher und der Männerbund: Überlegungen zu Hans-Joachim Schoeps und dem Thema Homosexualität." In Gideon Botsch et al., eds., *Wider den Zeitgeist: Studien zum Leben und Werk von Hans-Joachim Schoeps (1909–1980)*, pp. 199–212. Hildesheim: Olms Verlag.

Kellenbenz, Hermann. 1958. *Sephardim an der unteren Elbe: Ihre wirtschaftliche und politische Bedeutung vom Ende des 16. bis zum Beginn des 18. Jahrhunderts.* Wiesbaden: Steiner Verlag.

Kemp, Paul. 1997. "The British Army and the Liberation of Bergen-Belsen, April 1945." In Joanne Reilly et al., eds., *Belsen in History and Memory*, pp. 134–148. London: Frank Cass.

Kempner, Robert M. W. 1983. *Ankläger einer Epoche: Lebenserinnerungen.* Frankfurt am Main: Ullstein Taschenbuchverlag.

Kessler, Judith. 2008. "Homo Sovieticus in Disneyland: The Jewish Communities in Germany Today." In Y. Michal Bodemann, ed., *The New German Jewry and the European Context: The Return of the European Jewish Diaspora*, pp. 131–143. New York: Palgrave Macmillan.

Kessler, Mario. 1995. *Die SED und die Juden: Zwischen Repression und Toleranz; Politische Entwicklungen bis 1967.* Berlin: Akademischer Verlag.

Keynan, Irit. 1996. *Lo nirga ha-ra'aw: Nitsule hascho'a we-schliche Eretz Isra'el; Germanija, 1945–1948* (Hunger has not been eased: The survivors of the Holocaust and the emissaries from prestate Israel; Germany, 1945–1948). Tel Aviv.

Khasani, Shila. 2005. "Eine Minderheit in der Minderheit: Das politische Engagement der linksorientierten Juden in der Frankfurter Jüdischen Gruppe." In *Trumah: Juden in der Bundesrepublik—Dokumentationen und Analysen*, vol. 14, pp. 55–74.

———. 2006. "Oppositionelle Bewegung oder Selbsterfahrungsgruppe? Entstehung und Engagement der Frankfurter Jüdischen Gruppe." In Susanne Schönborn, ed., *Zwischen Erinnerung und Neubeginn: Zur deutsch-jüdischen Geschichte nach 1945*, pp. 160–177. Munich: Peter Lang.

Kingreen, Monica. 2008. "Zurück nach Frankfurt: Rückkehr aus dem Exil in die Stadt am Main." In Irmela von der Lühe et al., eds., *"Auch in Deutschland waren wir nicht wirklich zu Hause": Jüdische Remigration nach 1945*, pp. 121–143. Göttingen: Wallstein Verlag.

Kirschnick, Sylke. 2009. *Anne Frank und die DDR: Politische Deutungen und persönliche Lesarten des berühmten Tagebuchs.* Berlin: Ch. Links Verlag.

Kishon, Ephraim. 1960. *Look Back Mrs. Lot.* Translated by Yohanon Goldman. Tel Aviv: Tversky Publishing.

Klausner, Abraham J. 2002. A *Letter to My Children from the Edge of the Holocaust.* San Francisco: Holocaust Center of Northern California.

Klein, Gerda Weismann, and Klein, Kurt. 2000. *The Hours After: Letters of Love and Longing in War's Aftermath.* New York: St. Martin's Press.

Kleinjung, Tilmann. 1998. *Aus der Not geboren: Überlebende des Holocaust im Kloster St. Ottilien.* Munich: Bayerischer Rundfunk.

Klier, John D. 2003. "The Jewish Press and Jewish Identity: Leningrad / St. Petersburg, 1989–1992." In Zvi Y. Gitelman et al., eds., *New Jewish Identities: Contemporary Europe and Beyond*, pp. 139–157. Budapest: Central European University Press.

Klingebiel, Harald. 2009. "Jüdische Sportler bei Werder Bremen." In Arnd Krüger and Bernd Wedemeyer-Kolwe, eds., *Vergessen, verdrängt, abgelehnt: Zur Geschichte der Ausgrenzung im Sport*, pp. 60–62. Berlin: LIT Verlag.

Klüger, Ruth. 2001. *Still Alive: A Holocaust Girlhood Remembered*. New York: Feminist Press at the City University of New York.

Knef, Hildegard. 1971. *The Gift Horse: Report of a Life*. New York: McGraw-Hill.

Knufinke, Ulrich. 2008. "Neue Synagogen in Deutschland nach 1945." In Aliza Cohen-Mushlin and Harmen H. Thies, eds., *Synagogenarchitektur in Deutschland: Dokumentation zur Ausstellung; ".. . und ich wurde ihnen zu einem kleinen Heiligtum. . .*"; *Synagogen in Deutschland*, pp. 97–108. Petersberg: Michael Imhof Verlag.

Kochavi, Arieh J. 1990. "Anglo-American Discord: Jewish Refugees and United Nations Relief and Rehabilitation Administration Policy, 1945–1947." *Diplomatic History* 14, pp. 529–551.

———. 2001. *Post-Holocaust Politics: Britain, the United States and Jewish Refugees, 1945–1948*. Chapel Hill: University of North Carolina Press.

Kolinsky, Eva. 2004. *After the Holocaust: Jewish Survivors in Germany after 1945*. London: Pimlico.

König, Jan C. L. 2008. "'Wenn du einmal im Sarg liegst, kommst du nicht mehr raus': Nach Vorlage genehmigte Niederschrift des Gesprächs mit dem Bundestagspräsidenten a. D., Dr. Philipp Jenninger, am Dienstag, 16. Mai 2006." *Monatshefte für deutschsprachige Literatur und Kultur* 100/2, pp. 179–190.

Königseder, Angelika. 1997. "Durchgangsstation Berlin: Jüdische DPs 1945–1948." In Fritz Bauer Institut, ed., *Überlebt und Unterwegs: Jüdische Displaced Persons im Nachkriegsdeutschland*, pp. 189–206. Frankfurt am Main: Campus Verlag.

———. 1998. *Flucht nach Berlin: Jüdische Displaced Persons 1945–1948*. Berlin: Metropol.

Königseder, Angelika, and Wetzel, Juliane. 1994. *Waiting for Hope: Jewish Displaced Persons in Post–World War II Germany*. Evanston: Northwestern University Press.

Könke, Günter. 1988. "Wiedergutmachung und Modernisierung: Der Beitrag des Luxemburger Abkommens von 1952 zur wirtschaftlichen Entwicklung Israels." *Vierteljahrschrift für Sozial- und Wirtschaftsgeschichte* 75, pp. 503–548.

Körber, Karen. 2005. *Juden, Russen, Emigranten: Identitätskonflikte jüdischer Einwanderer in einer ostdeutschen Stadt*. Frankfurt am Main: Campus Verlag.

———. 2009. "Puschkin oder Thora? Der Wandel der jüdischen Gemeinden in Deutschland." *Tel Aviver Jahrbuch für deutsche Geschichte* 37, pp. 233–254.

———. 2010. "Von Samarkand nach Schortewitz: Die Einwanderung russischsprachiger Juden nach Ostdeutschland." In Dmitrij Belkin and Raphael Gross, eds., *Ausgerechnet Deutschland! Jüdisch-russische Einwanderung in die Bundesrepublik*. Publication accompanying the exhibition at the Jewish Museum Frankfurt, March 12–July 25, 2010, pp. 62–64. Berlin: Nikolaische Verlagsbuchhandlung.

Korman, Gerd. 1983. "Survivors, Talmud and the U.S. Army." *American Jewish History* 73/1, pp. 252–285.

Korn, Benjamin. 2007. "Der Schock ist fruchtbar noch: Ein Skandal, mit dem wir nicht fertig sind: Frankfurt und die Fassbinder Affäre 1985." In Fritz Backhaus et al., eds., *Ignatz Bubis: Ein jüdisches Leben in Deutschland*, pp. 67–77. Frankfurt am Main: Jüdischer Verlag im Suhrkamp Verlag.

Korn, Salomon. 1991. "Die 4. jüdische Gemeinde in Frankfurt am Main: Zukunft oder Zwischenspiel?" In Karl E. Grözinger, ed., *Judentum im deutschen Sprachraum*, pp. 409–433. Frankfurt am Main: Suhrkamp Verlag.

———. 1992. "Zur Geschichte der Synagogal-Architektur in der Nachkriegszeit." In Andreas Nachama, ed., *Aufbau nach dem Untergang: Deutsch-jüdische Geschichte nach 1945*, pp. 187–214. Berlin: Argon.

———. 2001. *Beiträge zur "deutsch-jüdischen" Gegenwart*. Berlin: Philo Verlag.

Kortner, Fritz. 1986. *Aller Tage Abend: Autobiographie*. Munich: Drömer Knaur.

Kossert, Andreas. 2008. *Kalte Heimat: Die Geschichte der deutschen Vertriebenen nach 1945*. Munich: Siedler Verlag.

Kratz, Philipp. 2016. "Der Umgang mit der nationalsozialistischen Vergangenheit: Eine Fallstudie zu Wiesbaden 1945–2005." Ph.D. diss., University of Jena.

Kraushaar, Wolfgang. 1995. "Der Kampf gegen den 'Jud-Süß'-Regisseur Veit Harlan: 'Ein Meilenstein in der Grundrechtsprechung des Bundesverfassungsgerichts.'" *Mittelweg 36*, 4/6, pp. 4–33.

———. 1996a. *Die Protest-Chronik 1949–1959: Eine illustrierte Geschichte von Bewegung, Widerstand und Utopie*. Hamburg: Rogner & Bernhard.

———. 1996b. *Die Protest-Chronik 1949–1952*. Hamburg: Rogner & Bernhard.

———. 1996c. *Die Protest-Chronik 1953 bis 1956*. Hamburg: Rogner & Bernhard.

———. 2005. *Die Bombe im jüdischen Gemeindehaus*. Hamburg: Hamburger Edition.

Krauss, Marita. 2001. *Heimkehr in ein fremdes Land: Geschichte der Remigration nach 1945*. Munich: C. H. Beck.

Krohn, Helga. 2006. *Deutschland—trotz alledem? Jüdische Sozialarbeit nach 1945*. Frankfurt am Main: Fachhochschulverlag.

Kroll, Frank-Lothar. 2001. *Das geistige Preußen: Zur Ideengeschichte eines Staates*. Paderborn: Schöningh Verlag.

Kufeke, Kay. 2002. "Der Umgang mit dem Holocaust in Deutschland nach 1945." In Burkhard Asmuss, ed., *Holocaust: Der nationalsozialistische Völkermord und die Motive seiner Erinnerung*, pp. 239–304. Wolfratshausen: Deutsches Historisches Museum.

Kuhlbrodt, Dietrich. 1997. "'Jud Süß' und der Fall Harlan/Lüth: Zur Entnazifizierung des NSFilms." In Peter Reichel, ed., *Das Gedächtnis der Stadt: Hamburg im Umgang mit seiner nationalsozialistischen Vergangenheit*, pp. 101–112. Hamburg: Dölling und Galitz Verlag.

Kühne-Büning, Lidwina, ed. 2005. *Grundlagen der Wohnungs- und Immobilienwirtschaft*. Hamburg: Knapp Verlag.

Kulischer, Eugene. 1948. *Europe on the Move: War and Population Changes 1917–1947*. New York: Columbia University Press.

Kulka, Otto Dov. 1986. "The Reichsvereinigung and the Fate of the German Jews, 1938/1939–1942." In Arnold Pauker, ed., *Die Juden im nationalsozialistischen Deutschland 1933–1943*, pp. 353–363. Tübingen: Mohr Siebeck.

———. 1998. *Deutsches Judentum unter dem Nationalsozialismus*. Tübingen: Mohr Verlag.

Lagrou, Pieter. 2005. "Return to a Vanished World: European Societies and the Remnants of Their Jewish Communities, 1945–1947." In David Bankier, ed., *The Jews Are Coming Back: The Return of the Jews to Their Countries of Origin after World War II*, pp. 1–24. New York: Berghahn Books.

Landauer, Georg. 1951. "Urgency of Jewish Property Restitution." *Zion* 2/3, pp. 11–14.

———. 1957. *Der Zionismus im Wandel dreier Jahrzehnte*. Tel Aviv: Bitaon Verlag.

Laschet, Armin, and Malangré, Heinz, eds. 1989. *Philipp Jenninger: Rede und Reaktion*. Aachen: Einhard Verlag.

Lavsky, Hagit. 1995. "British Jewry and the Jews in Post-Holocaust Germany: The Jewish Relief Unit, 1945–50." *Journal of Holocaust Education* 4/1, pp. 29–40.

———. 2002. *New Beginnings: Holocaust Survivors in Bergen-Belsen and the British Zone in Germany*. Detroit: Wayne State University Press.

———. 2010. "The Experience of the Displaced Persons in Bergen-Belsen: Unique or Typical Case?" In Avinoam J. Patt and Michael Berkowitz, eds., *"We Are Here": New Approaches to Jewish Displaced Persons in Postwar Germany*, pp. 227–256. Detroit: Wayne State University Press.

Legerer, Anton. 2011. *Tatort: Versöhnung; Aktion Sühnezeichen in der BRD und in der DDR und Gedenkdienst in Österreich*. Leipzig: Evangelische Verlagsanstalt.

Lemke, Michael. 1990. "Umstrittene Wiedergutmachung: Das Luxemburger Abkommen 1952." In Martin Robbe, ed., *Palästina: Sehnsucht und Machtpolitik; Geschichte, Strukturen und Perspektiven eines Konfliktes*, pp. 132–140. Berlin: Edition Neue Wege.

Lemke, Thomas. 2005. "Nachwort: Geschichte und Erfahrung; Michel Foucault und die Spuren der Macht." In Michel Foucault, *Analytik der Macht*, ed. Daniel Defert and François Ewald, pp. 317–347. Frankfurt am Main: Suhrkamp Verlag.

Lenarz, Michael. 2007. "Ignatz Bubis und die Auseinandersetzungen um das Frankfurter Westend." In Raphael Gross and Michael Lenarz, eds., *Ignatz Bubis: Ein jüdisches Leben in Deutschland*, pp. 52–66. Frankfurt am Main: Jüdischer Verlag im Suhrkamp Verlag.

Lepsius, M. Rainer. 1989. "Das Erbe des Nationalsozialismus und die politische Kultur der Nachfolgestaaten des 'Großdeutschen Reiches.'" In *Kultur und Gesellschaft: Verhandlungen des 24. Deutschen Soziologentags, des 11. Österreichischen Soziologentags und des 8. Kongresses der Schweizerischen Gesellschaft für Soziologie in Zürich 1988*, pp. 247–264. Frankfurt am Main: Campus Verlag.

Levinson, Julian. 2004. "Die jüdische Wanderschaft des Harry Maor." In Wolfdietrich Schmied-Kowarzik, ed., *Auseinandersetzungen mit dem zerstörten jüdischen Erbe*, pp. 211–216. Kassel: Kassel University Press.

Levinson, Nathan Peter. 1997. "The Functions of a Rabbi in Postwar Germany." In Michael Brenner, *After the Holocaust: Rebuilding Jewish Lives in Postwar Germany*, pp. 107–110. Princeton, N.J.: Princeton University Press.

Lewinsky, Tamar. 2008. *Displaced Poets: Jiddische Schriftsteller im Nachkriegsdeutschland, 1945–1951*. Göttingen: Vandenhoeck & Ruprecht.

———. 2010. "Jüdische Displaced Persons im Nachkriegsmünchen." *Münchner Beiträge zur jüdischen Geschichte und Kultur* 4/1, pp. 17–25.

———, ed. 2011. *Unterbrochenes Gedicht: Jiddische Literatur in Deutschland 1944– 1950*. Munich: Oldenbourg Verlag.

Liebert, Frank. 2005. "Vom Karrierestreben zum 'Nötigungsnotstand': 'Jud Süß,' Veit Harlan und die westdeutsche Nachkriegsgesellschaft (1945–50)." In Thomas Henne and Arne Riedlinger, eds., *Das Lüth-Urteil aus (rechts-)historischer Sicht: Die Konflikte um Veit Harlan und die Grundrechtsjudikatur des Bundesverfassungsgerichts*, pp. 111–146. Berlin: Berliner Wissenschafts-Verlag.

Lillteicher, Jürgen. 2007. *Raub, Recht und Restitution: Die Rückerstattung jüdischen Eigentums in der frühen Bundesrepublik*. Göttingen: Wallstein Verlag.

Litvak, Joseph. 1983. "Plitim yehudim mipolin be-brit ha-moatsot, 1939–1946" (Jewish refugees from Poland in the Soviet Union). Ph.D. diss., Hebrew University, Jerusalem.

———. 1997. "Jewish Refugees from Poland in the USSR." In Zvi Gitelman, ed., *Bitter Legacy: Confronting the Holocaust in the USSR*, pp. 123–150. Bloomington: Indiana University Press.

Loewy, Hanno. 1998. "Das gerettete Kind: Die 'Universalisierung' der Anne Frank." In Stephan Braese et al., eds., *Deutsche Nachkriegsliteratur und der Holocaust*, pp. 19–41. Frankfurt am Main: Campus Verlag.

Loewy, Hanno, and Loewy, Peter. 2001. *Das IG-Farben-Haus*. Munich: Keyahoff Verlag.

London, Ephraim. 1957. "Religious Life in Belsen." In Irgun Sheerit Hapleita Me'haezor Habriti, ed., *Belsen*, pp. 182–185. Tel Aviv.

Lörcher, Andreas. 2008. "Antisemitismus in der öffentlichen Debatte der späten fünfziger Jahre: Mikrohistorische Studie und Diskursanalyse des Falls Zind." Ph.D. diss., University of Freiburg.

Lübbe, Hermann. 1982. *Der Fortschritt und das Museum: Über den Grund unseres Vergnügens an historischen Gegenständen*. London: Institute of Germanic Studies.

Ludwig, Esther. 1994. "Die Auswirkungen des Prager Slánsky-Prozesses auf die Leipziger Juden." In Ephraim Carlebach Stiftung, ed., *Judaica Lipsiensis*, pp. 228–244. Leipzig: Ephraim Carlebach Stiftung.

Ludyga, Hannes. 2005. *Philipp Auerbach (1906–1952): Staatskommissar für rassisch, religiös und politisch Verfolgte*. Berlin: Berliner Wissenschafts-Verlag.

———. 2006. "'Als Kamerad für Kameraden': Philipp Auerbach (1906–1952)." In Sabine Hering, ed., *Jüdische Wohlfahrt im Spiegel von Biographien*, pp. 46–55. Frankfurt am Main: Fachhochschulverlag.

———. 2007. "Eine antisemitische Affäre im Nachkriegsdeutschland: Der 'Staatskommissar für politisch, religiös und rassisch Verfolgte' Philipp Auerbach (1906–1952)." *Kritische Justiz* 40/4, pp. 410–428.

Lühe, Irmela von der, et al., eds. 2008. *"Auch in Deutschland waren wir nicht wirklich zu Hause": Jüdische Remigration nach 1945*. Göttingen: Wallstein Verlag.

Lustig, Sandra, and Levensohn, Ian. 2006. "Caught between Civil Society and the Cultural Market: Jewry and the Jewish Space in Europe; A Response to Diana Pinto." In Sandra Lustig and Ian Levensohn, eds., *Turning the Caleidoscope: Perspectives on European Jewry*, pp. 187–204. New York: Oxford University Press.

Maginnis, John J. 1971. *Military Government Journal: Normandy to Berlin*. Amherst: University of Massachusetts Press.

Mandl, Simon. 1898. *Der Bann: Ein Beitrag zum mosaisch-rabbinischen Strafrecht*. Brünn: Bernhard Epstein.

Mankowitz, Zeev W. 1990. "The Formation of the She'erit Hapleita, November 1944–July 1945." *Yad Vashem Studies* 20, pp. 337–370.

———. 2002. *Life between Memory and Hope: The Survivors of the Holocaust in Occupied Germany*. Cambridge: Cambridge University Press.

Manley, Rebecca. 2009. *To the Taskhent Station: Evacuation and Survival in the Soviet Union at War*. Ithaca, N.Y.: Cornell University Press.

Maor, Harry. 1961. "Über den Wiederaufbau der jüdischen Gemeinden in Deutschland seit 1945." Ph.D. diss., University of Mainz.

Marrus, Michael. 1985. *The Unwanted*. New York: Oxford University Press.

Marten, Heinz-Georg. 1987. *Der niedersächsische Ministersturz: Protest und Widerstand der Georg-August-Universität Göttingen gegen den Kultusminister Schlüter im Jahre 1955*. Göttingen: Vandenhoeck & Ruprecht.

Marx, Karl, and Adenauer, Konrad. 1996. "Bekenntnis zur Verpflichtung." *Allgemeine Wochenzeitung der Juden in Deutschland*, November 25, 1949, p. 1. In *Dokumente zur Deutschlandpolitik* II/2: *Die Konstituierung der Bundesrepublik Deutschland und der Deutschen Demokratischen Republik, 7. September bis 31. Dezember 1949*, ed. Hanns Jürgen Küsters, pp. 293–296. Munich: A. Metzner Verlag.

Marx, Lilli. 1997. "The Renewal of the German-Jewish Press." In Michael Brenner, *After the Holocaust: Rebuilding Jewish Lives in Postwar Germany*, pp. 125–129. Princeton, N.J.: Princeton University Press.

Meining, Stefan. 2001. "Mit der Geschichtswaffe in die Geschichtsfalle: Der ostdeutsch-jüdischamerikanische Wiedergutmachungspoker (1970–1976)." In Michael Wolffsohn and Thomas Brechenmacher, eds., *Geschichte als Falle: Deutschland und die jüdische Welt*, pp. 259–292. Neuried: Ars Una.

———. 2002. *Kommunistische Judenpolitik: Die DDR, Israel und die Juden*. Hamburg: LIT Verlag.

———. 2008. "Geschichtswaffe." In M. Wolffsohn and T. Brechenmacher, eds., *Deutschland, jüdisch Heimatland: Die Geschichte der deutschen Juden vom Kaiserreich bis heute*, pp. 277–279. Munich: Piper Verlag.

Meißner, Werner, et al., eds. 1999. *Der Poelzig-Bau: Vom IG Farben-Haus zur Goethe-Universität*. Frankfurt am Main: Fischer Verlag.

Mendel, Meron. 2004. "The Policy for the Past in West Germany and Israel: The Case of Jewish Remigration." *Leo Baeck Institute Yearbook* 49, pp. 121–136.

Mensing, Hans Peter, ed. 1987. *Adenauer: Briefe 1951–1953*. Berlin: Siedler Verlag.

Mertens, Lothar. 1997. *Davidstern unter Hammer und Zirkel: Die jüdischen Gemeinden in der SBZ/DDR und ihre Behandlung durch Partei und Staat, 1945–1990*. Hildesheim: Olms Verlag.

———. 2001. "Schwieriger Neubeginn." In Julius H. Schoeps, ed., *Leben im Land der Täter: Juden in Nachkriegsdeutschland (1945–1952)*, pp. 171–188. Berlin: Jüdische Verlagsanstalt.

———. 2002. "Eine Christin als 'Rabbinerin': Karin Mylius." In Irene Diekmann and Julius H. Schoeps, eds., *Das Wilkomirski-Syndrom: Eingebildete Erinnerungen oder von der Sehnsucht, Opfer zu sein*, pp. 262–272. Zürich: Pendo Verlag.

Metzler, Gabriele. 2002. "Am Ende aller Krisen? Politisches Denken und Handeln in der Bundesrepublik der sechziger Jahre." *Historische Zeitschrift* 275, pp. 57–103.

Meyer, Beate. 2011. *Tödliche Gratwanderung: Die Reichsvereinigung der Juden in Deutschland zwischen Hoffnung, Zwang, Selbstbehauptung und Verstrickung (1939–1945)*. Göttingen: Wallstein Verlag.

Meyer, Michael A. 1996–1997. *Deutsch-jüdische Geschichte in der Neuzeit*. 4 vols. Munich: C. H. Beck.

Michalski, Raoul W. 1991. "Die Jüdische Gemeinde in Hamburg seit den 50er Jahren." In Arno Herzig, ed., *Die Juden in Hamburg 1590 bis 1990: Wissenschaftliche Beiträge der Universität Hamburg zur Ausstellung "Vierhundert Jahre Juden in Hamburg,"* pp. 383–392. Hamburg: Dölling & Galitz.

Mohr, Anna J. 2011. "Wiedergutmachung: Der Fall Dr. Aaron Ohrenstein im Auerbach Prozess." Teacher's exam thesis, University of Munich.

Moneta, Jakob. 1991. *Mehr Macht für die Ohnmächtigen: Reden und Aufsätze*. Frankfurt am Main: ISP-Verlag.

Morris, Leslie, and Zipes, Jack, eds. *Unlikely History: The Changing German-Jewish Symbiosis, 1945–2000*. New York: Palgrave Macmillan.

Moses, Siegfried. 1944. *Die jüdischen Nachkriegsforderungen*. Tel Aviv: Irgun olej merkas Europa.

Moß, Christoph. 2003. *Jakob Altmeier: Ein jüdischer Sozialdemokrat in Deutschland (1889–1963)*. Cologne: Böhlau Verlag.

———. 2006. "Jakob Altmaier, MdB: Ein jüdischer Politiker in der Bundesrepublik der 1950er und 1960er Jahre." In Susanne Schönborn, ed., *Zwischen Erinnerung und Neubeginn: Zur deutsch-jüdischen Geschichte nach 1945*, pp. 111–134. Munich: Peter Lang.

Mroczka, Ludwik. 1999. "Die Berufs- und Sozialstruktur der wichtigsten ethnischen Gruppen in Lódz und ihre Entwicklung in den Jahren 1918–1939." In Jürgen Hensel, ed., *Polen, Deutsche und Juden in Lódz 1820–1939*, pp. 45–66. Osnabrück: Fibre Verlag.

Mühlen, Norbert. 1993. *The Return of Germany: A Tale of Two Countries*. Chicago: Henry Regnery.

Müller, Arnd. 1968. *Geschichte der Juden in Nürnberg 1146–1945*. Nuremberg: Stadtsbibliothek Nürnberg.

Müller, Ingo. 1997. "Robert M. W. Kempner (1899–1993)." In Hans Erler et al., eds., *"Meinetwegen ist die Welt erschaffen": Das intellektuelle Vermächtnis des deutschsprachigen Judentums*, pp. 362–368. Frankfurt am Main: Campus Verlag.

Muller, Jerry Z. 2013. "Reisender in Ideen: Jacob Taubes zwischen New York, Jerusalem, Berlin und Paris." In Monika Boll and Raphael Gross, eds., *"Ich staune, dass Sie in dieser Luft atmen können": Jüdische Intellektuelle in Deutschland nach 1945*, Schriftenreihe des Fritz Bauer Instituts, vol. 28, pp. 40–61. Frankfurt am Main: Fischer Verlag.

Müller, Ulrich. 1990. *Fremde in der Nachkriegszeit: Displaced Persons—zwangsverschleppte Personen—in Stuttgart und Württemberg-Baden 1945–1951*. Stuttgart: Klett-Cotta Verlag.

Müller, Wolfgang. 1994. "Die Jüdische Gemeinde Detmold in der Nachkriegszeit." In Wolfgang Müller et al., eds., *Detmold in der Nachkriegszeit: Dokumentation eines stadtgeschichtlichen Projekts*, pp. 161–192. Bielefeld: Aisthesis Verlag.

Münch, Peter L. 1997. "Zwischen 'Liquidation' und Wiederaufbau: Die deutschen Juden, der Staat Israel und die internationalen jüdischen Organisationen in der Phase der Wiedergutmachungsverhandlungen." *Historische Mitteilungen* 10/1, pp. 81–111.

Myers Feinstein, Margarete. 2010. *Holocaust Survivors in Postwar Germany, 1945–1957*. Cambridge: Cambridge University Press.

Nachama, Andreas. 1995. "Nach der Befreiung: Jüdisches Leben in Berlin 1945–1953." In Reinhard Rürup, ed., *Jüdische Geschichte in Berlin: Essays und Studien*, pp. 267–288. Berlin: Edition Hentrich.

——— 1999. "Heinz Galinski: Wir wollten, dass die Geschichte des Judentums in Deutschland nicht zu Ende ist." In Claudia Fröhlich, ed., *Engagierte Demokraten: Vergangenheitspolitik in kritischer Absicht*, pp. 95–105. Münster: Westfälisches Dampfboot.

Nachama, Andreas, and Schoeps, Julius H., eds. 1992. *Aufbau nach dem Untergang: Deutsch-jüdische Geschichte nach 1945*. Berlin: Argon Verlag.

Neumann, Moritz, ed. 1991. *Max Willner: Würdigung eines verdienten Mannes*. Alsbach: Landesverband der Jüdischen Gemeinden in Hessen.

———. 1994. "'Ein Mann der leisen Töne': Erinnerungen an Max Willner." In Werner Klaus, ed., *Zur Geschichte der Juden in Offenbach am Main: Werden und Vergehen – Aufstieg, Buchdruck, Friedhöfe, Erinnerungen*, vol. 3, pp. 159–166. Offenbach am Main: Magistrat der Stadt Offenbach.

Niemann, Sabine. 1995. *Die Carlebachs: Eine jüdische Rabbinerfamilie aus Deutschland*. Hamburg: Dölling & Galitz.

Niethammer, Lutz. 1989. "Jenninger: Vorzeitiges Exposé zur Erforschung eines ungewöhnlich schnellen Rücktritts." *Babylon* 5, pp. 40–46.

Niether, Hendrik. 2015. *Leipziger Juden und die DDR: Eine Existenzerfahrung im Kalten Krieg.* Göttingen: Vandenhoeck & Ruprecht.

Niewyk, Donald. 1998. *Fresh Wounds: Early Narratives of Holocaust Survival.* Chapel Hill: University of North Carolina Press.

Nikou, Lina. 2011. *Zwischen Imagepflege, moralischer Verpflichtung und Erinnerung: Das Besuchsprogramm für jüdische ehemalige Hamburger Bürgerinnen und Bürger.* Munich: Dölling & Galitz.

Noelle, Elisabeth, and Neumann, Erich-Peter, eds. 1974. *Jahrbuch der Öffentlichen Meinung 1968–1973.* Allensbach: Verlag für Demoskopie.

Nothmann, Hugo. 1953. "Die religiöse Situation im Nachkriegsdeutschland." In Heinz Ganther, ed., *Die Juden in Deutschland: Ein Almanach, 1951/52–5712,* pp. 185–187. Frankfurt am Main: Neuzeit Verlag.

Obenaus, Herbert, ed. 1997. *Im Schatten des Holocaust: Jüdisches Leben in Niedersachsen nach 1945.* Hannover: Verlag Hahnsche Buchhandlung.

Ofer, Dalia. 1995. "Emigration and Aliyah: A Reassessment of Israeli and Jewish Policies." In Robert S. Wistrich, ed., *Terms of Survival: The Jewish World since 1945,* pp. 59–85. New York: Routledge.

Offenberg, Ulrike. 1998. *"Seid vorsichtig gegen die Machthaber": Die jüdischen Gemeinden in der SBZ und der DDR 1945–1990.* Berlin: Aufbau Verlag.

———. 2001. "Die Jüdische Gemeinde zu Berlin 1945–1953." In Julius H. Schoeps, ed., *Leben im Land der Täter: Jüdisches Leben im Nachkriegsdeutschland (1945–1952),* pp. 133–156. Berlin: Jüdische Verlagsbuchhandlung.

Opalski, Magdalena. 1986. *The Jewish Tavern-Keeper and His Tavern in Nineteenth-Century Polish Literature.* Jerusalem: Zalman Shazar Center.

Oppelland, Torsten. 2002. *Gerhard Schröder (1910–1989): Politik zwischen Staat, Partei und Konfession.* Düsseldorf: Droste Verlag.

Oppenheimer, Walter W. Jacob. 1967. *Jüdische Jugend in Deutschland.* Munich: Juventa Verlag.

Osteen, Mark, ed. 2002. *The Question of the Gift: Essays across Disciplines.* New York: Routledge.

Ostow, Robin. 2003. "From Objects of Administration to Agents of Change: Fourteen Years of Post-Soviet Jewish Immigration to Germany." *East European Jewish Affairs* 33/2, pp. 1–6.

Panagiotidis, Jannis. 2010. "Deutsche und jüdische Zuwanderer in die Bundesrepublik Deutschland: Eine Beziehungsgeschichte." In Dmitrij Belkin and Raphael Gross, eds., *Ausgerechnet Deutschland! Jüdisch-russische Einwanderung in die Bundesrepublik.* Publication accompanying the exhibition at the Jewish Museum Frankfurt, March 12–July 25, 2010, pp. 79–81. Berlin: Nikolaische Verlagsbuchhandlung.

Patt, Avinoam. 2009. *Finding Home and Homeland: Jewish Youth and Zionism in the Aftermath of the Holocaust.* Detroit: Wayne State University Press.

Peck, Jeffrey. 1990. "Jewish Survivors of the Holocaust in Germany. Revolutionary Vanguard or Remnants of a Destroyed People?" *Tel Aviver Jahrbuch für deutsche Geschichte* 19, pp. 33–45.

———. 2006. *Being Jewish in the New Germany.* New Brunswick, N.J.: Rutgers University Press.

Pettiss, Susan T., and Taylor, Lynne. 2004. *After the Shooting Stopped: The Story of a UNRRA Welfare Worker in Germany 1945–1947.* Victoria, B.C.: Trafford.

Picht, Barbara, ed. 1997. *Ich handle mit Vernunft: Ein Almanach zum fünfzehnjährigen Bestehen der Literaturhandlung.* Munich: C. H. Beck.

Pinkus, Benjamin. 1984. *The Soviet Government and the Jews 1948–1967: A Documented Study.* Cambridge: Cambridge University Press.

Pinson, Koppel S. 1947. "Jewish Life in Liberated Germany." *Jewish Social Studies* 9/1, pp. 101–126.

Pinto, Diana. 2006. "The Jewish Space in Europe." In Sara Lustig and Ian Leveson, eds., *Turning the Kaleidoscope: Perspectives on European Jewry,* pp. 179–186. New York: Berghahn Books.

Plack, Arno. 1982. *Wie oft wird Hitler noch besiegt? Neonazismus und Vergangenheitsbewältigung.* Frankfurt am Main: Erb Verlag.

Pollock, Friedrich, ed. 1955. *Gruppenexperiment: Ein Studienbericht; Mit einem Geleitwort von Franz Böhm.* Frankfurt am Main: Europäische Verlags-Anstalt.

Posener, Julius. 2001. *In Deutschland, 1945 bis 1946: Kommentierte Ausgabe.* Berlin: Siedler Verlag.

Presser, Ellen. 1992. "Auerbach-Affäre." In Julius H. Schoeps, ed., *Neues Lexikon des Judentums,* p. 82. Gütersloh: Bertelsmann Lexikon Verlag.

———. "Jüdisches Leben in Deutschland heute: 'Wer ein Haus baut, will bleiben.'" *Das Parlament,* no. 15, April 11, 2005.

Proudfoot, Malcolm J. 1956. *European Refugees 1939–1952: A Study in Forced Population Movement.* Evanston: Faber & Faber.

Quast, Anke. 1996. "Vom Provisorium zum Gemeindezentrum: Die jüdische Gemeinde in Hannover 1955–1963." In Marlis Bucholz et al., eds., *Nationalsozialismus und Region: Festschrift für Herbert Obenaus zum 65. Geburtstag,* pp. 117–130. Bielefeld: Verlag für Regionalgeschichte.

———. 1997. "Jewish Committee und Jüdische Gemeinde Hannover: Der schwierige Anfang einer Gemeinschaft." In Herbert Obenaus, ed. *Im Schatten des Holocaust: Jüdisches Leben in Niedersachsen nach 1945,* pp. 55–77. Hannover: Verlag Hahnsche Buchhandlung.

———. 2001. *Nach der Befreiung: Jüdische Gemeinden in Niedersachsen seit 1945; Das Beispiel Hannover.* Göttingen: Wallstein Verlag.

Raabe, Jörg. 2004. "Rechtswidrige Verwaltungspraxis bei der Zuwanderung jüdischer Emigranten aus der ehemaligen Sowjetunion?" *Zeitschrift für Ausländerrecht und Ausländerpolitik* 24, pp. 410–415.

Rahe, Thomas. 2005. "Die jüdische DP-Gemeinde in Celle 1945–1951." In Gesellschaft für christlich-jüdische Zusammenarbeit Celle e. V., ed., *Jüdisches Leben in Celle nach 1945,* pp. 9–42. Bielefeld: Verlag für Regionalgeschichte.

Rath, Alfred. 1999. "Berliner Caféhäuser 1890–1933." In Michael Rössner, ed., *Literarische Kaffeehäuser, Kaffeehausliteraten,* pp. 108–125. Vienna: Böhlau Verlag.

Rauschenberger, Katharina. 2008. "The Restitution of Jewish Cultural Objects and the Activities of Jewish Cultural Reconstruction, Inc." *Leo Baeck Institute Yearbook* 53, pp. 193–211.

Rees-Dessauer, Elisabeth. "'Wer ein Haus baut, will bleiben': Synagogen und Selbstverständnis der jüdischen Gemeinden seit 1945." Ph.D. diss., Ludwig Maximilian University Munich, 2017.

Reichel, Peter. 2001. *Vergangenheitsbewältigung in Deutschland: Die Auseinandersetzung mit der NS-Diktatur von 1945 bis heute*. Munich: C. H. Beck.

Reichel, Peter, and Schmid, Harald. 2005. *Von der Katastrophe zum Stolperstein: Hamburg und der Nationalsozialismus nach 1945*. Hamburg: Dölling & Galitz.

Reich-Ranicki, Marcel. 2001. *The Author of Himself: The Life of Marcel Reich-Ranicki*. Princeton, N.J.: Princeton University Press.

Reilly, Joanne. *Belsen 1998: The Liberation of a Concentration Camp*. London: Routledge.

Reilly, Joanne, et al., eds. *Belsen in History and Memory*. London: Frank Cass.

Rheins, Carl J. 1981. "Deutscher Vortrupp, Gefolgschaft deutscher Juden 1933–1935." *Leo Baeck Institute Yearbook* 26, pp. 207–229.

Richarz, Monika. 1998. "Heinz Mosche Graupe (Nachruf)." *uni hh* 29/1, p. 64.

———. 2006. "Zwischen Berlin und New York: Adolf Leschnitzer—der erste Professor für jüdische Geschichte in der Bundesrepublik." In Jürgen Matthäus and Klaus-Michael Mallmann, eds., *Deutsche—Juden—Völkermord: Der Holocaust als Geschichte und Gegenwart*, pp. 73–86. Darmstadt: Wissenschaftliche Buchgesellschaft.

———. 2007. "Leben in einem gezeichneten Land: Juden in Deutschland seit 1945." In Arno Herzig and Cay Rademacher, eds., *Die Geschichte der Juden in Deutschland*, pp. 238–249. Hamburg: Ellert & Richter.

Richtering, Helmut. 1988. "Bernhard Brilling zum Gedenken." In Peter Freimark and Helmut Richtering, eds., *Gedenkschrift für Bernhard Brilling*, pp. 9–13. Hamburg: H. Christians.

Riedlinger, Arne. 2005. "Vom Boykottaufruf zur Verfassungsbeschwerde: Erich Lüth und die Kontroverse um Harlans Nachkriegsfilme (1950–1958)." In Thomas Henne and Arne Riedlinger, eds., *Das Lüth-Urteil aus (rechts-)historischer Sicht: Die Konflikte um Veit Harlan und die Grundrechtsjudikatur des Bundesverfassungsgerichts*, pp. 147–186. Berlin: Berliner Wissenschafts-Verlag.

Riemer, Jehuda. 1992. *Fritz Perez Naphtali: Sozialdemokrat und Zionist*. Gerlingen: Bleicher Verlag.

Ries, Rotraud. 2010. "Erinnerungen an David Schuster (1910–1999) in Zeitzeugengesprächen: Herkunft und Heimat." In Rotraud Ries and Roland Flade, eds., *David Schuster: Blicke auf ein fränkisch-jüdisches Leben im 20. Jahrhundert*, pp. 29–33. Würzburg: Schöningh Verlag.

Ro'i, Ya'acov. 2003. "Soviet Jewry from Identification to Identity." In Eliezer Ben-Rafael et al., eds., *Contemporary Jewries: Convergence and Divergence*, pp. 183–193. Leiden: Brill.

Roberman, Sveta. 2005. *Memory in Migration: Red Army Soldiers in Israel*. Jerusalem: Magnes Press.

Robinson, Nehemiah. 1944. *Indemnification and Reparations: Jewish Aspects*. New York: Institute of Jewish Affairs of the American Jewish Congress and World Jewish Congress.

———. 1964. *Ten Years of German Indemnification*. New York: Conference on Jewish Material Claims against Germany.

Röder, Werner, and Strauss, Herbert A., eds. 1980. *Biographisches Handbuch der deutschsprachigen Emigration nach 1933*. Munich: K. G. Saur Verlag.

Roesler, Jörg. 2006. "Łódź: Die Industriestadt als Schmelztiegel der Ethnien? Probleme des Zusammenlebens von Polen, Juden und Deutschen im 'polnischen Manchester' (1865–1945)." *Jahrbuch für Forschungen zur Geschichte der Arbeiterbewegung* 2, pp. 121–129.

Rohrbacher, Stefan. 2000. "Jüdische Geschichte." In Michael Brenner and Stefan Rohrbacher, eds., *Wissenschaft vom Judentum: Annäherungen nach dem Holocaust*, pp. 164–176. Göttingen: Vandenhoeck & Ruprecht.

Rosenberg, Leibl. 2004. "Wie ein Raumschiff auf einem fremden Planeten: Geschichten aus Föhrenwald." In Roman Haller, ed., . . . *und bleiben wollte keiner: Jüdische Lebensgeschichten im Nachkriegsbayern*, pp. 90–106. Munich: Dölling & Galitz.

Rosengold, Juan. 1966. "Der Magbit: Eine Pflicht." In Mendel Karger-Karin, ed., *Israel und Wir: Keren Hajessod-Jahrbuch der jüdischen Gemeinschaft in Deutschland 1955–1965*, pp. 111. Frankfurt am Main: Verlag des *Keren Hajessod*.

Rosensaft, Josef. 1957. "Our Belsen." In Irgun She'erit Hapleita Me'ha-ezor Habriti, ed., *Belsen*, pp. 24–51. Tel Aviv: Irgun Sheerit Hapleita Me'haezor Habriti.

Rosenthal, Hans. 1987. *Zwei Leben in Deutschland*. Bergisch-Gladbach: Lübbe Verlag.

Rössner, Michael, ed. 1999. *Literarische Kaffeehäuser, Kaffeehausliteraten*. Vienna: Böhlau Verlag.

Roth, Cecil. 1944. "The Restoration of Jewish Libraries, Archives and Museums." *Contemporary Jewish Record* 7/3, pp. 253–257.

———. 1957. "Was There a Herem against the Return of the Jews to Spain?" *Le Judaisme Sephardi* 15, pp. 675–677.

Rumpf, Joachim Robert. 2010. *Der Fall Wollheim gegen die IG Farbenindustrie AG in Liquidation*. Frankfurt am Main: Peter Lang.

Runge, Irene. 1995. *"Ich bin kein Russe": Jüdische Zuwanderung zwischen 1989 und 1994*. Berlin: Dietz Verlag.

Sagi, Nana. 1981. *German Reparations: A History of the Negotiations*. Jerusalem: Magnes Press.

———. 1989. "Jüdische Organisationen in den USA und die Claims Conference." In Ludolf Herbst and Constantin Goschler, eds., *Wiedergutmachung in der Bundesrepublik Deutschland*, pp. 99–118. Munich: Oldenbourg Verlag.

Salamander, Beno. 2011. *Kinderjahre im Displaced-Persons-Lager Föhrenwald*. Munich: Bayerische Landeszentrale für politische Bildungsarbeit.

Sander, Ronald. 1988. *Shores of Refuge: A Hundred Years of Jewish Immigration*. New York: Henry Holt.

Sauer, Thomas. 1988. "Geschichte der Würzburger Jüdischen Gemeinde nach Zeitungsberichten 1945–1970." Teacher's exam thesis, University of Würzburg.

Schäfer-Lichtenberger, Christa. 1994. "Bedeutung und Funktion von Herem in biblisch-hebräischen Texten." *Biblische Zeitschrift* 38, pp. 270–275.

Scheffler, Wolfgang. 1960. *Judenverfolgung im Dritten Reich*. Berlin: Colloquium-Verlag. Revised new edition, Berlin, 1990.

Scheiper, Stephan. 2010. *Innere Sicherheit: Politische Anti-Terror-Konzepte in der Bundesrepublik Deutschland während der 1970er Jahre*. Paderborn: Schöningh Verlag.

Scheller, Berthold. 1992. "Zedaka in neuem Gewand: Neugründung und Neuorientierung der 'Zentralwohlfahrtstelle der Juden in Deutschland' nach 1945." In Georg Heuberger, ed., *Zedaka: Jüdische Sozialarbeit im Wandel der Zeit; 75 Jahre Zentralwohlfahrtstelle der Juden in Deutschland 1917–1992*, pp. 142–157. Frankfurt am Main: Jüdisches Museum.

Schildt, Axel. 2007. *Die Sozialgeschichte der Bundesrepublik Deutschland bis 1989/90*. Munich: Oldenbourg Verlag.

Schiller, Kay. 2008. "Death at the Munich Olympics." In Alon Confino et al., eds., *Between Mass Death and Individual Loss: The Place of the Death in 20th-Century Germany*. Oxford: Oxford University Press.

Schirrmacher, Frank, ed. 1999. *Die Walser-Bubis-Debatte: Eine Dokumentation.* Frankfurt am Main: Suhrkamp Verlag.

Schlee, Emil. 1964. *Begegnung mit Israel: Eindrücke und Erlebnisse einer Offenbacher Jugendgruppe.* Offenbach: Stadt Offenbach am Main, Schuldezernat.

Schmalhausen, Bernd. 2002. Josef Neuberger (1902–1977). *Ein Leben für eine menschliche Justiz.* Baden-Baden: Nomos Verlag.

Schmid, Harald. 2001. *Erinnern an den "Tag der Schuld": Das Novemberpogrom von 1938 in der deutschen Geschichtspolitik.* Hamburg: Ergebnisse Verlag.

Schnee, Heinrich. 1953–1967. *Die Hoffinanz und der moderne Staat.* 6 vols. Berlin: Duncker & Humblot.

Schneider, Richard Chaim. 2000. *Wir sind da! Die Geschichte der Juden in Deutschland von 1945 bis heute.* Berlin: Ullstein Verlag.

Schneider, Ulrich. 1997. *Zukunftsentwurf Antifaschismus: 50 Jahre Wirken der VVN für "eine neue Welt des Friedens und der Freiheit."* Bonn: Pahl-Rugenstein Verlag.

Schochet, Simon. 1983. *Feldafing.* Vancouver, B.C.: November House.

Schoeps, Hans-Joachim. 1934. *Wir deutschen Juden.* Berlin: Vortrupp Verlag.

———. 1953. "Jüdischer Glaube und jüdisches Gesetz heute." In Heinz Ganther, ed., *Die Juden in Deutschland: Ein Almanach, 1951/52–5712,* pp. 212–213. Frankfurt am Main: Neuzeit Verlag.

———. 1963. *Rückblicke: Die letzten dreißig Jahre (1925–1955) und danach.* 2nd expanded ed. Berlin: Olms Verlag.

Schoeps, Julius H., ed. 1985. *Im Streit um Kafka und das Judentum: Max Brod–Hans-Joachim Schoeps: Briefwechsel.* Königstein im Taunus: Jüdischer Verlag bei Athenäum.

———. 1992. *Neues Lexikon des Judentums.* Munich: Bertelsmann Lexikon Verlag.

———. 2000. "'Nil inultum remanebit': Die Erlanger Universität und ihr Umgang mit dem deutsch-jüdischen Remigranten Hans-Joachim Schoeps (1909–1980)." *Zeitschrift für Religions- und Geistesgeschichte* 52, pp. 266–278.

———. 2001, ed. *Leben im Land der Täter: Juden im Nachkriegsdeutschland (1945–1952).* Berlin: Jüdische Verlagsantalt.

Schoeps, Julius H., et al., eds. 1996. *Russische Juden in Deutschland: Integration und Selbstbehauptung in einem fremden Land.* Weinheim: Beltz Athenäum.

Scholem, Gershom. 1995. *Briefe II: 1948–1970.* Ed. Thomas Sparr. Munich: C. H. Beck.

Schönborn, Susanne. 2004. "'Ein reinigendes Gewitter': Die Fassbinder-Debatte 1984/85 als Markstein deutsch-jüdischer Nachkriegsgeschichte." *Trumah* 14, pp. 109–128.

———, ed. 2006. *Zwischen Erinnerung und Neubeginn: Zur deutsch-jüdischen Geschichte nach 1945.* Munich: Peter Lang.

———. 2010. *Im Wandel: Entwürfe jüdischer Identität in den 1980er und 1990er Jahren.* Munich: Peter Lang.

Schott, Sebastian. 2009. "Die Geschichte der jüdischen Gemeinde Weiden bis zur Mitte des 20. Jahrhunderts." In Michael Brenner and Renate Höpfinger, eds., *Die Juden in der Oberpfalz,* pp. 105–118. Munich: Oldenbourg Verlag.

Schreiber, Ruth. 1997. "New Jewish Communities in Germany after World War II and the Successor Organizations in the Western Zones." *Journal of Israeli History* 18/2–3, pp. 167–190.

Schreiner, Stefan. 1992. "Zwischen Hoffnung und Furcht: Die jüdischen Gemeinden in der DDR nach der Wende." In Dieter Voigt and Lothar Mertens, eds., *Minderheiten und Übersiedler aus der DDR,* pp. 189–202. Berlin: Duncker & Humblot.

Schuster, David. 1987. "Die jüdischen Kultusgemeinden in Bayern nach 1945." In Rudolf Endres, ed., *Jüdische Gemeinden in Franken 1100 bis 1975*, pp. 31–37. Würzburg: Verlag Frankenbund.

Schütze, Yvonne. 1997. "Warum Deutschland und nicht Israel: Begründungen russischer Juden für die Migration nach Deutschland." *Bios* 10/2, pp. 186–208.

Schwarz, Leo W., ed. 1949. *The Root and the Bough: The Epic of an Enduring People*. New York: Reinhart.

———. 1953. *The Redeemers: A Saga of the Years 1945–1952*. New York: Farrar, Straus and Young.

Segel, Harold B. 1993. *The Vienna Coffeehouse Wits, 1890–1938*. West Lafayette: Purdue University Press.

Seligmann, Avraham. 1992. "An Illegal Way of Life in Nazi Germany." *Leo Baeck Institute Yearbook* 37, pp. 327–361.

Senocak, Zafer. 1998. *Gefährliche Verwandtschaft: Roman*. Munich: Babel Verlag.

Shafir, Shlomo. 1999. *Ambiguous Relations: The American Jewish Community and Germany since 1945*. Detroit: Wayne State University Press.

Shapiro, Leon. 1980. *The History of ORT: A Jewish Movement for Social Change*. New York: Schocken Books.

Shapiro, Marc. 1989. "The Herem on Spain: History and Halakâ." *Sefarad* 49/2, pp. 381–394.

Shephard, Ben. 2005. *After Daybreak: The Liberation of Bergen-Belsen 1945*. New York: Schocken Books.

Shevtsova, Lilia. 1992. "Post-Soviet Emigration Today and Tomorrow." *International Migration Review*, special issue, "The New Europe and International Migration," 26/2 (Summer), pp. 241–257.

Shinnar, Felix E. 1966. *Under the Burden of Necessity and Emotions*. Tel Aviv.

Shumsky, Dimitry. 2002. "Ethnicity and Citizenship in the Perception of Russian Israelis." In Daniel Levy and Yfaat Weiss, eds., *Challenging Ethnic Citizenship: German and Israeli Perspectives on Immigration*, pp. 154–178. New York: Berghahn Books.

———. 2007. "The Historiography on the Jews of the Soviet Union as a Blind Spot of Modern Jewish History Writing: Reflections on the 'Jewish Century'" (in Hebrew). *Zion* 72/4, pp. 457–470.

Silbermann, Alphons. 1982. *Sind wir Antisemiten? Ausmaß und Wirkung eines sozialen Vorurteils in der Bundesrepublik Deutschland*. Cologne: Wissenschaft und Politik.

Simon, Hermann. 2003. "Martin Mosche ben Chajim Riesenburger (1896–1965)." In Andreas Nachama and Hermann Simon, eds., *Martin Riesenburger: Das Licht verlösche nicht; Ein Zeugnis aus der Nacht des Faschismus*, pp. 7–33. Berlin: Die Jüdische Gemeinde Nordwest.

Sinn, Andrea. 2008. *"Und ich lebe wieder an der Isar": Exil und Rückkehr des Münchner Juden Hans Lamm*. Munich: Oldenbourg Verlag.

———. 2010a. "'Aber ich blieb trotzdem hier': Karl Marx und die Anfänge jüdischen Lebens im Nachkriegsdeutschland." *Nurinst: Beiträge zur deutschen und jüdischen Geschichte*, pp. 80–97.

———. 2010b. "Warum Düsseldorf? Zur Diskussion um die Verlegung des Hauptsitzes des Zentralrates der Juden in Deutschland." *Münchner Beiträge zur jüdischen Geschichte und Kultur* 4/1, pp. 57–65.

———. 2011. "Die Anfänge des Zentralrats der Juden und der Jüdischen Allgemeinen: Hendrik G. van Dam und Karl Marx als Repräsentanten jüdischen Lebens in Deutschland nach 1945." Ph.D. diss., University of Munich.

Skriebeleit, Jörg. 2009. "Aus den Vernichtungslagern in die Oberpfalz: Eine Bestandsaufnahme zu den jüdischen Häftlingen im KZ Flossenbürg." In Michael Brenner and Renate Höpfinger, eds., *Die Juden in der Oberpfalz*, pp. 213–229. Munich: Oldenbourg Verlag.

Skriver, Ansgar. 1962. *Aktion Sühnezeichen: Brücken über Blut und Asche*. Stuttgart: Kreuz-Verlag.

Slezkine, Yuri. 2004. *The Jewish Century*. Princeton, N.J.: Princeton University Press.

Smolorz, Roman P. 2009. *Displaced Persons (DPs): Autoritäten und Anführer im angehenden Kalten Krieg im östlichen Bayern*. Regensburg: Stadtarchiv Regensburg.

Snyder, Timothy. 2010. *Bloodlands: Europe between Hitler and Stalin*. New York: Basic Books.

Spannuth, Jan Philipp. 2007. *Rückerstattung Ost: Der Umgang der DDR mit dem "arisierten" Eigentum der Juden und die Rückerstattung im wiedervereinigten Deutschland*. Essen: Klartext.

Spiegel, Paul. 1961. "Wiederaufbau und Entwicklung (1945 bis 1960)." In Paul Spiegel, ed., *Festschrift zur Weihe der neuen Synagoge in Münster/Westf., 12. März 1961/24, Adar 5721*, pp. 33–39. Düsseldorf-Benrath: Jüdische Kultusgemeinde Münster.

———. 2003. *Wieder zu Hause? Erinnerungen*. Berlin: Ullstein Verlag.

———. 2006. *Gespräch über Deutschland: Ein Interview mit Wilfried Köpke*. Freiburg: Herder Verlag.

Stadt Nürnberg. 1993. *Juden in Nürnberg: Geschichte der jüdischen Mitbürger vom Mittelalter bis zur Gegenwart*. Nuremberg: Tümmels.

Stadtarchiv München, ed. 2000. *".. . verzogen, unbekannt wohin": Die erste Deportation von Münchner Juden im November 1941*. Zürich.

Stern, Frank. 1990. "Entstehung, Bedeutung und Funktion des Philosemitismus in Westdeutschland nach 1945." In Werner Bergmann and Rainer Erb, eds., *Antisemitismus in der politischen Kultur nach 1945*, pp. 180–196. Opladen: Westdeutscher Verlag.

———. 1991. *Im Anfang war Auschwitz: Antisemitismus und Philosemitismus im deutschen Nachkrieg*. Gerlingen: Bleicher Verlag.

———. 1992a. "Antagonistic Memories: The Post-war Survival and Alienation of Jews and Germans." In Luisa Passerini, ed., *International Yearbook of Oral History and Life Stories*, vol. 1, *Memory and Totalitarianism*, pp. 21–43. New York: Oxford University Press.

———. 1992b. "Wider Antisemitismus für christlich-jüdische Zusammenarbeit: Aus der Entstehungszeit der Gesellschaften und des Koordinierungsrats." *Menora* 3, pp. 182–209.

Stern, Philip D. 1991. *The Biblical Herem: A Window on Israel's Religious Experience*. Atlanta: Scholars Press.

Stiftung Baukultur Rheinland-Pfalz, ed. 2010. *Gebauter Aufbruch: Neue Synagogen in Deutschland*. Regensburg: Schnell & Steiner.

Stopnitzer, David. 2004. "Geh zum Mörder Semmeln holen." In Roman Haller, ed., *. . . und bleiben wollte keiner: Jüdische Lebensgeschichten im Nachkriegsbayern*, pp. 152–167. Munich: Dölling & Galitz.

Strathmann, Donate. 2003. *Auswandern oder Hierbleiben? Jüdisches Leben in Düsseldorf und Nordrhein 1945–1960*. Essen: Klartext.

Strnad, Maximilian. 2011. *Zwischenstation "Judensiedlung": Verfolgung und Deportation der jüdischen Münchner 1941–1945*. Munich: Oldenbourg Verlag.

Strobel, Georg W. 2006. "Das multinationale Łódź, die Textilmetropole Polens, als Produkt von Migration und Kapitalwanderung." In Hans W. Rautenberg, ed., *Wanderungen und Kulturaustausch im östlichen Mitteleuropa: Forschungen zum ausgehenden Mittelalter und zur jüngeren Neuzeit*, pp. 163–223. Munich: Oldenbourg Verlag.

Südbeck, Thomas. 1994. *Motorisierung, Verkehrsentwicklung und Verkehrspolitik in der Bundesrepublik Deutschland*. Hamburg: Steiner Verlag.

Sutzkever, Avrom. 1963. *Poetishe verk*, vol. 1. Tel Aviv: Yovel.

Sword, Keith. 1991. "The Welfare of Polish Jewish Refugees in the USSR, 1941–1943: Relief Supplies and Their Distribution." In Norman Davies and Antony Polonsky, eds., *Jews in Eastern Poland and the USSR, 1939–46*, pp. 145–160. New York: St. Martin's Press.

Synagogengemeinde Düsseldorf. 1958. *Die neue Synagoge in Düsseldorf: Zur Einweihung am 7. September 1958*. Düsseldorf: Kalima-Druck.

Syrkin, Marie. 1980. *State of the Jews*. Washington, D.C.: New Republic Books.

Sznaider, Natan. 2009. "Die Rettung der Bücher: Hannah Arendt in München (1949/50)." *Mittelweg 36*/2, pp. 61–76.

Takei, Ayka. 2002. "The 'Gemeinde Problem': The Jewish Restitution Successor Organization and the Postwar Jewish Communities in Germany, 1947–1954." *Holocaust and Genocide Studies* 16/2 (Fall), pp. 266–288.

———. 2004. "The Jewish People as the Heir: The Jewish Successor Organizations (JRSO, JTC, French Branch) and the Postwar Jewish Communities in Germany." Ph.D. diss., University of Tokyo.

Tamari, Ittai J. 2009. "Vater und Sohn, oder über die Anfänge der Jüdischen Studien an der Ludwig-Maximilians-Universität München." *Münchner Beiträge zur Jüdischen Geschichte und Kultur* 2, pp. 107–118.

Tauber, Alon. 2008. *Zwischen Kontinuität und Neuanfang: Die Entstehung der jüdischen Nachkriegsgemeinde in Frankfurt am Main 1945–1949*. Wiesbaden: Kommission für die Geschichte der Juden in Hessen.

Tauchert, Stephanie. 2007. *Jüdische Identitäten in Deutschland: Das Selbstverständnis von Juden in der Bundesrepublik und der DDR 1950 bis 2000*. Berlin: Metropol.

Tenorth, Heinz-Elmar. 2010. *Geschichte der Erziehung: Einführung in die Grundzüge ihrer neuzeitlichen Entwicklung*. 5th ed. Weinheim: Juventa Verlag.

Thompson, Jerry E. 1978. "Jews, Zionism, and Israel: The Story of the Jews in the German Democratic Republic since 1945." Ph.D. diss., Washington State University.

Timm, Angelika. 1994. "Der 9. November 1938 in der politischen Kultur der DDR." In Rolf Steininger, ed., *Der Umgang mit dem Holocaust: Europa–USA–Israel*, pp. 246–262. Vienna: Böhlau Verlag.

———. 1997a. *Hammer, Zirkel, Davidstern: Das gestörte Verhältnis der DDR zu Zionismus und Staat Israel*. Bonn: Bouvier Verlag.

———. 1997b. *Jewish Claims against East Germany: Moral Obligations and Pragmatic Policy*. Budapest: Central European University Press.

———. 2002. "Ein ambivalentes Verhältnis: Juden in der DDR und der Staat Israel." In Moshe Zuckermann, ed., *Zwischen Politik und Juden in der DDR*, pp. 17–33. Göttingen: Wallstein Verlag.

Timme, Eva-Maria. 1992. "Bibliographie zur Nachkriegsgeschichte der Juden in Deutschland." In Andreas Nachama and Hans-Joachim Schoeps, eds., *Aufbau nach dem Untergang: Deutsch-jüdische Geschichte nach 1945*, pp. 427–436. Berlin: Argon Verlag.

Tobias, Jim G. 2006. "Arojs mitn bal cu di tojznter wartnde cuszojer. Die Fußballvereine und -ligen der jüdischen Displaced Persons, 1946–1948." *Nurinst: Beiträge zur deutschen und jüdischen Geschichte*, pp. 105–120.

Tolts, Mark. 2005. "Demographische Trends unter den Juden der ehemaligen Sowjetunion." *Menora* 15, pp. 15–44.

———. 2008. "The Jews in the Three Post-Soviet Slavic Countries: Selected Population Trends." In Wolf Moskovich and Leonid Finberg, eds., *Jews, Ukrainians and Russians: Essays on Intercultural Relations*, pp. 187–196. Jerusalem: Hebrew University of Jerusalem.

———. 2009. "Post-Soviet Aliyah and Jewish Demographic Transformation." Paper presented at the 15th World Congress of Jewish Studies, Jerusalem, August 2–6, 2009.

Tomaszewski, Jerzy. 1991. "Jews in Łódź in 1931 According to Statistics." *Polin* 6, pp. 178–184.

Tress, Madeleine. 1997. "Foreigners or Jews? The Soviet Jewish Refugee Populations in Germany and the United States." *East European Jewish Affairs* 27/2, pp. 21–38.

Treue, Wilhelm. 1951. "Rezension zu *The Court Jew: A Contribution to the History of the Period of Absolutism in Central Europe*. By Selma Stern. Philadelphia, 1950." *Historische Zeitschrift* 171, pp. 571–577.

Varon, Jeremy. 2014. *The New Life: The Jewish Students of Postwar Germany*. Detroit: Wayne State University Press.

Verschvovskij, Mihail. 1997. *Moj nemezkij dom: Emigrantskije dnevniki* (My German house: Diaries of an emigrant). Saint Petersburg.

Vida, George. 1977. *From Doom to Dawn: A Jewish Chaplain's Story of Displaced Persons*. New York: Jonathan David Publishers.

Vishnevsky, Anatoli, and Zayonchkovskaya, Zhanna. 1994. "Emigration from the Former Soviet Union: The Fourth Wave." In Heinz Fassmann and Rainer Münz, eds., *European Migration in the Late Twentieth Century: Historical Patterns, Actual Trends, and Social Implications*, pp. 239–259. Aldershot: Edward Elgar.

Vogel, Rolf, ed. 1969. *The German Path to Israel: A Documentation*. Stuttgart: Wolff.

Volkov, Shulamit. 2006. "Jewish History: The Nationalism of Transnationalism." In Gunilla Budde et al., eds., *Transnationale Geschichte: Themen, Tendenzen und Theorien*, pp. 191–201. Göttingen: Vanderhoeck & Ruprecht.

Wahrhaftig, Zorach. 1946. *Uprooted: Jewish Refugees and Displaced Persons after Liberation*. New York: Institute of Jewish Affairs of the American Jewish Congress and World Jewish Congress.

Walk, Joseph. 1988. "Karl Marx." In *Kurzbiographien zur Geschichte der Juden 1918–1945*, p. 257. Munich: K. G. Saur.

Walser, Martin. 1965. "Unser Auschwitz." *Kursbuch* 1, pp. 189–200.

———. 1998. "Erfahrungen beim Verfassen einer Sonntagsrede." In Börsenverein des Deutschen Buchhandels, ed., *Friedenspreis des deutschen Buchhandels 1998: Martin Walser; Ansprachen aus Anlaß der Verleihung*, pp. 9–14. Frankfurt am Main: Börsenverein des Deutschen Buchhandels.

Warscher, Josef. 1997. "From Buchenwald to Stuttgart." In Michael Brenner, *After the Holocaust: Rebuilding Jewish Lives in Postwar Germany*, pp. 111–113. Princeton, N.J.: Princeton University Press.

Webster, Ronald. 1993. "American Relief and Jews in Germany, 1945–1960." *Leo Baeck Institute Yearbook* 38, pp. 293–321.

Weger, T. 1999. "Die ehemalige orthodoxe Synagoge." In Elisabeth Angermair et al., eds., *Beth Ha-Knesseth—Ort der Zusammenkunft: Zur Geschichte der Münchner Synagogen, ihrer Rabbiner und Kantoren*, pp. 204–205. Munich: Stadtarchiv München.

Weingardt, Markus. 2005. "Deutsche Israel-Politik: Etappen und Kontinuitäten." *Aus Politik und Zeitgeschichte* 15, pp. 22–31.

Weiß, Christoph. 2000. *Auschwitz in der geteilten Welt: Peter Weiss und die "Ermittlung" im Kalten Krieg*. 2 vols. St. Ingbert: Röhrig Verlag.

Weiss, Peter. 1966. *The Investigation*. Translated by Alexander Gross. London: Calder & Boyars.

Weizsäcker, Esther. 2004. "Jüdische Migranten im geltenden deutschen Staatsangehörigkeits- und Ausländerrecht." *Zeitschrift für Ausländerrecht und Ausländerpolitik* 24, pp. 93–101.

Wenig, Larry. 2002. *From Nazi Inferno to Soviet Hell*. Hoboken: KTAV Publishing House.

Wette, Wolfram, ed. 2006. *Filbinger: Eine deutsche Karriere*. Springe: zu Klampe.

Wetzel, Juliane. 1987. *Jüdisches Leben in München 1945–1951: Durchgangsstation oder Wiederaufbau?* Munich: Kommissionsverlag Uni-Druck.

———. 1995. "Trauma und Tabu: Jüdisches Leben in Deutschland nach dem Holocaust." In Hans-Erich Volkmann, ed., *Ende des Dritten Reiches, Ende des Zweiten Weltkriegs*, pp. 433–444, 454. Munich: Piper Verlag.

Wiegand, Lutz. 1992. *Der Lastenausgleich in der Bundesrepublik Deutschland 1949 bis 1985*. Frankfurt am Main: Peter Lang.

Wiehn, Erhard Roy. 2011. *Kiew Babij Jar: Ein fast vergessenes Verbrechen*. Constance: Hartung-Gorre Verlag.

Wiggershaus, Rolf. 1987. *Die Frankfurter Schule: Geschichte, Theoretische Entwicklung, Politische Bedeutung*. 2nd ed. Munich: Hanser Verlag.

Willingham, Rob. 2004. "New Beginnings in Saxony: Reviving Jewish Life in Leipzig after the Second World War." *Leipziger Beiträge zur jüdischen Geschichte und Kultur* 2, pp. 331–345.

Wiltmann, Ingrid, ed. 1999. *Jüdisches Leben in Deutschland: Siebzehn Gespräche*. Frankfurt am Main: Suhrkamp Verlag.

Winstel, Tobias. 2006. *Verhandelte Gerechtigkeit: Rückerstattung und Entschädigung für jüdische NS-Opfer in Bayern und Westdeutschland*. Munich: Oldenbourg Verlag.

———. 2010. "Die Testamentsvollstrecker: Zur Rolle von Anwälten und Rechtshilfeorganisationen." In Norbert Frei et al., eds., *Die Praxis der Wiedergutmachung: Geschichte, Erfahrung und Wirkung in Deutschland und Israel*, pp. 533–553. Bonn: Wallstein Verlag.

Wirsching, Andreas. 2002. "Jüdische Friedhöfe in Deutschland 1933–1957." *Vierteljahrshefte für Zeitgeschichte* 50, pp. 1–40.

Wojak, Irmtrud, ed. 2001. *"Gerichtstag halten über uns selbst. . .": Geschichte und Wirkung des ersten Frankfurter Auschwitz-Prozesses*. Frankfurt am Main: Campus Verlag.

———. 2009. *Fritz Bauer 1903–1968: Eine Biographie*. Munich: C. H. Beck.

Wolffsohn, Michael. 1988. "Das deutsch-israelische Wiedergutmachungsabkommen von 1952 im internationalen Zusammenhang." *Vierteljahrshefte für Zeitgeschichte* 36/4, pp. 691–731.

———. 1995. *Die Deutschland-Akte: Juden und Deutsche in Ost und West; Tatsachen und Legenden*. Munich: Edition Ferenczy bei Bruckman.

Wolffsohn, Michael, and Brechenmacher, Thomas, eds. 2008. *Deutschland, jüdisch Heimatland: Die Geschichte der deutschen Juden vom Kaiserreich bis heute*. Munich: Piper Verlag.

Wyden, Peter. 1992. *Stella: One Woman's True Tale of Evil, Betrayal, and Survival in the Holocaust*. New York: Anchor Books.

Wyman, Mark. 1998. *DPs: Europe's Displaced Persons, 1945–1951*. Ithaca, N.Y.: Cornell University Press.

Yahil, Chaim. 1980. "The Activities of the Delegation Sent from Eretz Israel to the Displaced Persons" (in Hebrew). *Yalkut Moreshet*, part A (November), pp. 7–39.

———. 1981. "The Activities of the Delegation Sent from Eretz Israel to the Displaced Persons" (in Hebrew). *Yalkut Moreshet*, part B (April), pp. 133–176.

Zahra, Tara. 2011. *The Lost Children: Reconstructing Europe's Families after World War II*. Cambridge, Mass.: Harvard University Press.

Zalashik, Rakefet. 2009. "Zwischen Orient und Okzident: Die Entschädigung der Palästina- und Israel-Emigranten." In Norbert Frei et al., eds., *Die Praxis der Wiedergutmachung: Geschichte, Erfahrung und Wirkung in Deutschland und Israel*, pp. 470–493. Göttingen: Wallstein Verlag.

Zertal, Idith. 1999. *From Catastrophe to Power: Holocaust Survivors and the Emergence of Israel*. Berkeley: University of California Press.

Zieher, Jürgen. 2005. *Im Schatten von Antisemitismus und Wiedergutmachung: Kommunen und jüdische Gemeinden in Dortmund, Düsseldorf und Köln 1945–1960*. Berlin: Metropol Verlag.

Zweig, Ronald W. 2001. *German Reparations and the Jewish World: A History of the Claims Conference*. London: Routledge.

ZWST, ed. 2011. *Mitgliederstatistik der jüdischen Gemeinden und Landesverbände in Deutschland für das Jahr 2010*. Frankfurt am Main: Zentralwohlfahrtsstelle der Juden in *Deutschland*.

American Jewish organizations, 167. *See also* Jewish organizations; *and specific organizations*

American occupied zone, 9, 16, 20–21, 24, 34–35, 41, 57–59, 62–69, 72–80, 90, 94–95, 137; American departure from, 165; Central Committee of Liberated Jews in, 92; Central Committees of Liberated Jews in, 135; DP camps in, 97; DPs in, 58, 75–76, 84n75, 85–86, 97; Eastern European Jewish transit society under Allied protection in, 80; Eastern European Jews fleeing to, 73–80; "free livers" in, 70; German Jews in, 114–115, 120; Germany, 135; Jewish communities in, 114; Jewish refugees in, 75, 76; *kibbutzim* in, 78; Polish Jews in, 57, 120; the press in, 89–90; Rabbinical Council (Vaad Harabanim) for, 93; religious schools in, 92; as safe haven for Holocaust survivors, 62–67; She'erit Hapletah (Surviving Remnant, or the Remainder of Israel) in, 95; societies for Christian-Jewish cooperation in, 248–252; theater groups performing in, 90

am Yisrael (the Jewish people), 18–19

Anglo-American Committee of Inquiry, 66–67, 80

Ankermüller, Willi, 22

Anti-Defamation League (ADL), 210–211, 270

anti-Fascism, 167, 241, 325, 327, 340, 359, 361–362, 382

anti-Fascist resistance fighters, 325, 327

anti-imperialism, 297, 313, 333, 340–341

anti-Israel propaganda, 340–341, 343. *See also* anti-Zionism

antimilitarism, 313

antisemitic violence, 333, 337, 339–344, 427; double strategy of "exchange of gifts" against, 335–336; by Muslims, 426; perceptions of, 334–335; transformation of, 333–334

antisemitism, 11, 44–46, 149, 167, 197, 203, 217, 228–229, 241–248, 266–271, 331, 359, 422, 427–428; Adenauer and, 284n34; Adorno on, 272; antisemitic boycotts, 122; antisemitic institutes, 187; antisemitic propaganda, 427–428, 333; antisemitic rioting, 387; anti-Zionism and, 314–316; black marketeering and, 294; Central Council of Jews of Germany and, 368n48; democracy and, 338, 349; double strategy of "exchange of gifts" against, 335–336; in DP camps, 61; in East German media, 340–341; educational programs to overcome, 248, 249; emergency legislation in response to, 284n34; experience of, 386; faced by Jewish actors and writers, 125–126; in Federal Republic of Germany, 333–339; in GDR, 339–344; German public opinion about, 241–242, 242t, 250; government measures against, 338–339; Jewish immigration and, 389; Jewish institutions and, 339; Jewish settlement in Palestine and, 316; Kielce pogrom, 57, 59, 72, 76; left-wing anticapitalism and, 317; monitoring of, 208; Nachmann and, 347–348; nationalism and, 229–230; old and new, 257–261; open postwar, 266–271; in Poland, 73, 74–75; in postwar Eastern Europe, 75; in postwar Europe, 94–95; in postwar Germany, 107, 121, 140–141, 142n18; prosecution of, 236; protests against, 247; reactions in international press, 284n35; Soviet-Jewish immigrants and, 393–394, 405; in Soviet Union, 385, 386, 387, 388; in Soviet zone of occupied Germany, 84n75; strength and quality of, 241; studies of, 336, 337; in *Süddeutsche Zeitung*, 137–139, 143n25; suppression of, 107; in the tavern, 261–266; in theater, 353–354; theatrical portrayals of, 196; upsurge in, 261. *See also* antisemitic violence; *and specific types of incidents*

anti-Zionism, 280, 281, 314–316, 333, 340–341, 343

Antwerp, antisemitic attacks in, 337

apprenticeship training, 106

appropriation, 362–365